NEW GOLF GUIDE
THE DIRECTORY FOR PUBLIC PLAY™

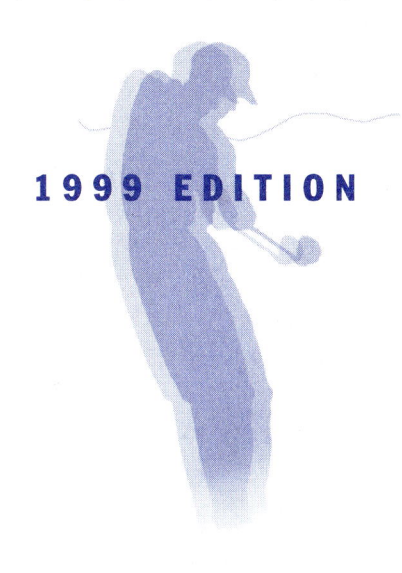

1999 EDITION

366 River Road
Carlisle, MA 01741
phone: (800) 833-6387
fax: (978) 287-0125
e-mail: GOLFGUID@ix.netcom.com
www.newenglandgolfguide.com

Publishers:	Leona Curhan
	Irwin Garfinkle
Editor:	John DiCocco
Designer:	Diane Novetsky/Nova Graphics
Cover Photographer:	John R. Johnson
Consultant:	Rick Walsh
Contributor:	Alan Pollard
Data Input:	Ana Russ

*Cover Photograph of the 6th hole at
Green Mountain National Golf Course, Sherburne, Vermont
by Photographer John R. Johnson, courtesy of
Johnson Design Golf Photographics, Seattle, Washington.*

©1998, NEW ENGLAND GOLFGUIDE®

All rights reserved.

ISBN 0-9624717-5-5

Printed in Canada

Reproduction in whole or in part, in any form, and by any means, without the expressed written permission of NEW ENGLAND GOLFGUIDE® is strictly prohibited.

NEW ENGLAND GOLFGUIDE®, and THE DIRECTORY FOR PUBLIC PLAY"™ are trademarks of the NEW ENGLAND GOLFGUIDE®.

NEW ENGLAND GOLFGUIDE®, its advertisers and contributors do not assume liability for any inadvertent error appearing in the book. Every effort has been made to provide the most up-to-date information as of press time, but data does change, and errors do occur. We appreciate receiving corrections for inclusion in the 2000 Edition.

We're Celebrating Our 10TH Anniversary!

We recently heard from a golfer who had the original 1990 NEW ENGLAND GOLFGUIDE®. He wondered "if we have a later edition?" As our faithful readers know, and we have about 15,000 of them per year, we publish a new edition of the NEW ENGLAND GOLFGUIDE® every year. This is our 10th Edition.

Among the more noticeable changes from the First Edition in 1990 is the unprecedented increase in the number of public access golf courses throughout New England. In 1990 there were 458 courses. In this 1999 edition, there are 604. In the 1990 GOLFGUIDE® there were 70 discount coupons "Worth $1000s." There are now 247 discount coupons for greens fees, bucket of balls at driving ranges, and for merchandise at golf shops. The 1999 NEW ENGLAND GOLFGUIDE® more than pays for itself. In 1990, we published the scorecard from the middle tees. Now we publish the yardage, par, rating, and slope from the front, middle, and back tees.

What's New in this 1999 Edition?

- 21 new regulation golf courses
- 6 new par 3 golf courses
- More course ratings
- Improved maps
- Golf Websites
- Junior programs
- Day camps
- Course architects
- Women's golf
- Trainers
- Updated info
- The Past 10 Years of Golf in New England
- The Ryder Cup, New England's main event in 1999!
- New and more coupons

Much of our information is supplied by our readers. So keep in touch, by phone, e-mail, fax, U. S. Mail or on the web. We want to hear from you. The numbers are on the cover page.

Leona Curhan & Irwin Garfinkle

The Publishers

Contents:
Features, Indexes, Directories and Coupons

Features
    NE Public Golf – The Past Ten Years.................................6
    The Ryder Cup Comes to New England..........................9
    Women's Golf Continues to Rise.....................................10
    Junior Golf is Cool for Kids..12
    Golf Websites Worth a Look..17
    Getting Ready for the Game..18
    Ratings..20
    Handicap & Slope Defined...21
    New England: An Architect's Delight...........................22
    New Listings...25

Indexes – Courses by State..339-344

FYI – Course Categories
    Open Year Round..346
    Walkable...347
    Designer Courses..348
    Websites..349
    Junior Day Camps..350-351
    Par 27 to 33/Executive Courses...................................352

Discount Coupons and Directories
    Merchandise & Service Directory.........................354-356
    Merchandise & Service Coupons..........................357-367
    GolfGuide Gift Coupon..367
    Driving Range Directory......................................370-371
    Driving Range Coupons.......................................373-395
    Golf Course Coupon Listings...............................398-399
    Golf Course Coupons...401-487

Contents: The Golf Courses

Greater Boston/South Shore/Cape Cod 39-81

Boston's North Shore & Central Massachusetts 82-115

Western Massachusetts 116-140

Southeastern Massachusetts & Rhode Island 141-167

New Hampshire 168-212

Southern Maine 213-238

Northern Maine 239-263

Vermont 264-291

Northern & Eastern Connecticut 292-313

Southern & Western Connecticut 314-338

GB CC/ MA

NE/ CTRL MA

W MA

SE MA /RI

NH

S ME

N ME

VT

NE CT

SW CT

New England Public Golf
The Past Ten Years

The first issue of the New England GolfGuide in 1990 coincided with the biggest boom seen in the golf industry since the late 50s and early 60s when Arnie, Jack, and television ignited the sport's popularity. What's happened in the past ten years of public golf?

An Improving Economy. More disposable income has allowed more people access to this relatively expensive sport and the baby boomers are are now choosing less strenuous sports.

New Public Courses. In New England, new public golf courses far outnumbered new private courses. Since our first issue, we've added 150 golf course listings. Long waiting lists and prohibitive initiation fees have driven many players to rediscover the joys of public golf. Younger players prefer course variety. And more public courses are marketing themselves and their "golf experience" to appeal to those seeking an upscale experience.

A Squeeze on the Tee. On the downside, the 90s have witnessed an unprecedented crunch of tee times in New England, and things are not improving—even with the number of new courses. Even the driving ranges are crowded. But at many golf courses, you now can phone ahead and reserve tee-times by credit card. As a partial solution to the tee time struggle, traveling tournament clubs emerged. Such clubs book blocks of teetimes and run tournaments for their members.

Editor John DiCocco

New Magic in Your Bag. In the past decade, we've seen a surge in new manufacturing ideas and marketing ploys. Odyssey putters became the flatstick of choice with their "stronomic" faces. We saw the rise of big, great big, and the biggest club heads from Callaway, followed by bigger shafts. Now the Adams Tight Lies is leading a boom in smaller clubhead designs. Big or small, they have all become lighter. Titanium shafts were the answer for seniors and wornen needing lighter clubs. And in just two years, metal spikes are becoming history. Does high tech translate to lower scores? Mid-to-low handicappers seem to think so, (depending on the day's score). Higher handicappers are still fiddling with their grips, swings, ball choices, and divot tools.

The Web. Also in the technology vein, there are scores of golf websites. See page 17 for the ones you don't want to miss including the NEW ENGLAND GOLFGUIDE® site. Over 50 courses (see page 349) reported their www.s in this issue.

Looking Good, Feeling Good. Golf fashion emerged from the lime green and shocking plaid camp to become mainstream sportswear. You'll see as many golfwear displays in departments stores as you do in pro shops. In retailing, off-course shops really boomed as well, offering brand name equipment to urban and suburban shoppers, often at prices lower than country club pro shops. There is a directory of leading shops on page 354.

Getting in Shape. The advent of personal trainers in general has led to a specialization in golf. We now have golf conditioning. (See related story on page 18.) Again, the baby boomers are increasingly attentive to their aches and pains, and a whole industry is springing up to help them out.

Lessons. Golf schools aren't new, but they were on the rise in New England this decade. They're increasingly tailored as well. You can now find special sessions for women, juniors, the short game. Some pros will even hold a clinic at your work site.

Electronic and Interactive. For spectators, there's more golf than ever before on weekend network TV: the PGA, LPGA, and Senior PGA. But if you're truly a junkie, there's always the Golf Channel, offering 24 hours of live and taped tournaments from around the world, short lessons, and classic matches replayed. Other cable channels also pick up the early rounds of major tournaments, too. And dozens of CD-ROM games are on store shelves.

Driving and Driving Don't Mix. Carts equal profits and therefore we have seen more courses trying to force them upon us. But carts equal slower play. When you carry a bag or have a pull cart, you can move quickly from tee to fairway to green. A golf cart requires parking in designated areas, walking from the cart path over to your ball (often on the opposite side of the fairway) and back to your cart for every shot. We at the New England GolfGuide fully support the USGA Walking Program, initiated in 1998 to encourage players to return to the game as it was meant to be played.

The Next Decade? We'll See:

1. More tee boxes at more courses to accommodate a greater range of players.
2. More target-style courses as environmental constraints force architects to minimize earth-moving and tree removal.
3. More new and bizarre technology (maybe balls that beep when you lose them).
4. We may see hybrids of golf with bigger holes and shorter courses. Aside from bringing in more players, it might just speed up play.
5. The USGA will still be fiddling with its handicap system.
6. The miniature golf pro tour will get its own cable channel.
7. Slow golfers will be required to wear electronic implants so that marshals can jolt them every few holes.
8. **And, dear Reader, sometime this coming decade, you will break 80. We said it here *first*.**

Editor John DiCocco recalls the past and predicts the future of New England Golf.

The Ryder Cup Comes to New England in 1999

The Ryder Cup, September 24, 25, and 26, 1999 at the Counry Club in Brookline, MA.

The Ryder Cup, one of the world's greatest sporting events, pits twelve professional golfers from the United States against the best twelve professionals from Europe. What used to be a US walkover is now a hotly contested event, a gentlemanly, but intense three days of the best match play on earth. Held every two years, and alternating between a US and European site, the Ryder Cup is being held this time at the venerable Country Club in Brookline, MA. The pros compete for country, honor, competitiveness and fun. Not a dime goes to winners or losers.

If you do not yet have tickets by the time you read this, you will have to watch the event on TV, since all the tickets will have gone out to applicants who were randomly selected by computer in September, 1998.

The competitions have three formats, all variations of match play. The first two days, the morning play is usually four matches of foursomes, where two partners play one ball, each hitting alternate shots. The afternoon is four teams of fourball, where two men on each team each play a ball, and score the better ball of the team. The last day is twelve match play singles, where each hole can have a dramatic bearing on the overall outcome. Each match is worth one point, for a total of 28. The Europeans currently hold the '98 Cup, by virtue of trampling the US the first two days to build an incredible 10 1/2 to 5 1/2 lead at Valderaama CC in Spain. The final score of 14 1/2 to 13 1/2 didn't tell the story.

Europe has won the last two meetings, and four of the last seven (with one tie). Here on U.S. soil, U.S. Captain Ben Crenshaw hopes to take The Cup away. In the event of a tie, Europe keeps it.

For additional events in New England, visit our website at www.newenglandgolfguide.com

Women's Golf Continues to Rise

Mary Porter (Center) Publisher of *Tee Times Magazine* and friends from SWING.

Not so long ago, Mary Porter would determine course attitudes toward females with a simple test. She'd call and ask for an early weekend teetime and be told that the first available time was noon. Had she called too late? Moments later, she'd have her teenage son call, and sometimes he'd get a prime slot—8:30, for instance. "It was infuriating. They just felt that women would slow the place down," she says.

"Quite a few courses have changed and become much more woman-friendly in the past few years, though," says Porter, organizer of a women's traveling tournament club called SWING (Sporting Women's Invitational Golf). "Bay Pointe, Onset, MA, for example, goes out of their way when we play a tournament there. Poquoy Brooks, Lakeville, MA, new management is very welcoming as well."

Porter founded SWING to fill a missing niche—someone who cared about women's issues in golf. SWING runs non-competitive outings for women only. Many don't even keep score, she says. She also publishes *TeeTime Magazine*, about women's golf in New England. Similar women's associations in all six states have reported increasing activity over the past five years.

Unlike men, who like to try out new courses, women tend to stick to familiar places, Porter says. But her group brings them to a different destination every week.

Jan Porkola, the Director of Women's Golf for The Tour, a traveling tournament club that welcomes both men and women, says she's seen a great improvement in course attitudes toward women. She has also found that men are more accepting of women players when they get paired together on the first tee. "Once they see you know what you're doing, it's usually fine.

> "It's too bad women have had the slow play rap hung on them," says Porkola. "Some courses say they prefer women because they feel we play faster."

"It's too bad women have had the slow play rap hung on them," says Porkola. "Some courses say they prefer women because they feel we play faster. Not only that, women are better about repairing divots and ball marks, and they never take three views to line up a three-foot putt."

Women's golf is getting new respect for another reason. The younger stars of women's professional golf tour are beginning to make inroads into the national consciousness the same way Tiger Woods did for kids. The 1998 Women's U.S. Open finish is a case in point, where the playoff duel between Jenny Chuasiriporn of Maryland and Se Ri Pak of Korea rivaled the greatest drama of any Master's championship.

Be forewarned, there will be more and more women on the course, and we at THE NEW ENGLAND GOLFGUIDE® are glad to see it. Unlike any other sport, because of handicaps and multiple tee boxes, people of different ages, sexes, and abilities can all compete together on the same course—at the same time—and everyone has an equal chance of winning and having an enjoyable day. Just one more reason why ours is the best sport.

Golf is COOL for Kids

As more and more youngsters are getting into golf, more courses and golf schools are catering to their particular needs. Golf pros all around New England are providing opportunities for junior players to learn the game alongside their peers. More than half of our region's courses offer some kind of junior program, as do over 35 driving ranges. According to our *GolfGuide* statistics, 209 courses and 41 driving ranges offer junior discounts. Twelve courses also offer junior memberships, 73 host junior schools, and 62 have day camps. (See page 350-351.)

Kids tee off at the Wayland Country Club during the *Clubs for Kids* program sponsored by Ed, Bob and Tom Quirk.

"Clubs for Kids." In 1998, the Quirk brothers Ed, Bob, and Tom of Wayland Golf, ran a very successful "Clubs for Kids" program, which they plan to repeat and grow in 1999. Wayland Golf has been collecting "previously loved" golf equipment which it refurbishes and gives to kids in need. For the Club's inaugural in July 1998, the Quirks closed the Wayland Country Club for a day and got 25 pros to volunteer for about 100 kid's from area Boys and Girls Clubs. The kids got everything they needed to play the game, including full sets of golf clubs, shirts, balls, hats, lessons, and the opportunity to play free at 12 area golf courses, by presenting a membership ID which is valid to age 18. "Tiger Woods", says Ed Quirk, "tells the kids to dream big. It's great to want to be like Tiger, but it can be expensive, and even impossible, for parents. So somebody has to get those dreams out of the starting blocks." We say, "Thank you Ed, Bob, and Tom".

The Country Club of Billerica, MA runs an impressive program, the Barrie Bruce Golf School, for six-year-olds right up through high school age players. They even have a particular program for girls "designed to promote and sustain female golfers throughout high school," taught by women instructors. The Little Tykes Golf Course at the club, a six-hole junior course with greens fees of just $5, is open 11am-3pm Monday through Friday. Staffed by golf school personnel, it's a mini-course set up on the driving range. Parents are invited to play with their children if they like. The club even provides balls and equipment for novices. The emphasis is on playing in a safe and responsible manner.

The Barrie Bruce Invitational Junior Workshop is offered at The Country Club of Billerica, MA.

At Larry Gannon Municipal in Lynn, MA, head professional Mike Foster runs a program during six or seven Mondays every summer consisting of an 8am clinic, followed by a 9-hole shotgun tournament at 10am. Each is free to residents of Lynn. They close down the front nine all morning, just for the youngsters. "You really have to credit the town," he says, "They're giving away several mornings' revenue, but it's a great commitment to junior

Jim Callahan, teaching pro at Kimball Farms Golf Center, Westford, MA, gives expert instruction to a young golfer, his daughter Nicole.

golf. For the clinics, we might have as many as 150 boys and girls out here. Then for the tournaments afterward, maybe 80-100 kids will stay." Several inner club members volunteer as marshals for the tournaments, helping kids learn about speed of play, and divot repairing. "I think some of our older members enjoy the morning as much as the youngsters do," Foster says. "We've even had some families donate clubs as awards. What we try to emphasize is having fun, not competition. For some of the younger ones, it's just fun to haul off at the ball. As the kids get older, the competitive aspect gets a little more serious."

It's a Family Game. Jim Callahan is a teaching pro at Kimball Farms Golf Center in Westford, MA. Like most people working with young players, he emphasizes the enjoyment over the competition. Jim teaches children at Kimball Farms as well as conducting clinics at Acton Indoor Sports and Nashoba Valley Summer Camp. He comes from a golfing family and started playing at age 8, tagging along with family members. "Moms and dads can't usually go out and play in a soccer game or a gymnastics meet with the kids. But the whole family can go out in a golf foursome. When I talk to parents about lessons for their kids, it's not about making Jimmy the next Tiger Woods; I'm always emphasizing the family aspect of golf." For the younger ones, Callahan concentrates on the pitch and putt aspects of the game. "They can see the green — and reach it — which is important, and besides, 70% of golf is played inside 90 yards, so learning the short game versus emphasizing the big drives is better in the long run.

Golf in Schools. The Golf in Schools program was developed by the PGA of America to introduce more juniors to the game. While golf is offered to high school students in many physical education classes, this program seeks to introduce the game to students in grades four through six. The program is comprised of four sections: safety, five building blocks of a golf swing, teaching the swing through exercise, and supervised hitting of balls. The PGA invites interested schools to contact them.

High School Teams. Rick Wash, our consultant and coach of the girls golf team at Braintree High School Braintree, MA, points out that participation on a golf team is another way to give the young golfer the opportunity to learn the mechanics, the rules, the etiquette, and the love of the sport. He even learned that sometimes the coach needs to become the student. Rick said, "I've watched Bob Beach the head professional at Braintree Municipal G C, giving instruction to the girls I coach. This spring after much frustration with diminishing distance in my own swing, I finally scheduled a lesson with Bob and I became the student. One lesson gave me a tremendous amount of help which I then was able to pass on to the girls on the team. Multiplicity in action."

NEPGA Clinics. The New England PGA runs more than ten junior clinics for boys and girls between the ages of 7 and 17. The June and July clinics provide introductory instruction and are an opportunity to receive group lessons, at no cost, from PGA professionals.

Junior Club Champions Championship. The New England PGA also conducts the John Boda Memorial Junior Club Championship at Andover (MA) Country Club, sponsored by the club and Maxfli. This tournament is open to boys and girls who are junior champions at courses employing a PGA pro. Contact your local pro for an entry to this event.

Connecticut has several venues for junior golfers. The Mountain Dew Junior Golf Tour is open to all members of the Connecticut PGA Junior Golf Association ages 13-17 and is run in conjunction with existing tournaments. There's a Junior Tournament of Champions and player of the year standings. The Greater Hartford Open Junior Golf Series is for boys and girls ages 10 to 17. Each event is preceded by a instructional clinic. See www.ctgolfer.com for more information.

Top Flite Tour. The Top-Flite Tour is sponsored by Top-Flite Professional Golf, and supported by Pepsi Cola. The purpose of the tour is to provide boys and girls the opportunity to play in professionally-run golf tournaments (approximately 25 per year) throughout the New England section. Each is a separate stroke play event, and the entry fee includes golf, tee gift, and lunch. The point leaders in each category participate in a season-ending tour championship in late August, with prizes for the winners in each of the following divisions: Boys 13 and under, 14 & 15, and 16 & 17; and Girls 15 and under, and 16 & 17. August 31 is the age cutoff date and it is recommended that juniors be at least ten and have handicaps no higher than 18.

If your youngsters are interested in playing the game, there are plenty of ways to get them involved. Ask the professional at your local club or driving range how to get started.

Golf Websites Worth a Look

ctgolfer.com is a terrific Connecticut site, linked to many other related sites as well Good articles and lots of information for CT juniors.

ghin.com You have to bookmark this one. Just type in your USGA GHIN number and your most recently updated handicap appears with the ten scores used to figure it.

golfdesign.org (American Society of Golf Course Architects) Get the architects' views from the inside.

golfthetour.com TheTour of Greater Boston, a traveling tournament club for amateurs in eastern New England. Tee times, tournaments, bulletin board, and more.

golfweb.com Links all over the place and has pages devoted to travel, a pro shop, "Club Tiger" (where your kids can get bilked for all kinds of Tiger junk), a fun poll, a Players' Club, links to Fantasy Golf (CBS Sportsline), and more.

igolf.com has games you can play (once you join) and is a service of Golf magazine.

lpga.com has everything you wanted to know about the women's tour, including stories, profiles, and standings.

mgalinks.org Massachusetts Golf Association. Both beautiful and helpful, this site lists all the clubs in the state, all the state tournaments and entry requirements, and great links.

newenglandgolfguide.com See what we're up to. Help us update our information and rate the courses of New England.

pga.com New and old stories of PGA events and the 1999 Ryder Cup, a PGA bookstore, a kids section, Rules section, a fitness center, and a section for PGA Members.

usga.org gives you all kinds of info about the USGA, its various tournaments, membership in the USGA, and a whole section on the Rules and Decisions on the Rules.

yahoo.com/recreationlsportslgolflchat is where you can meet other golfers online and talk up the game.

See page 349 for listing of courses with websites.

Get Ready for the Game

Susan DiRocco, physical therapist at Health South/Braintree Rehab Hospital, Hanover, MA says that "Many golfers don't realize they can do as much or more for their game off the golf course. Everyone likes to go to the driving range, but sometimes you can do more, especially in building more length off the tee—just by adding strength or increasing flexibility in the right muscle groups." In February, 1999, DiRocco will run an eight-week clinic in Hanover for golfers of all abilities who want to get ready for the season. Using various apparatus and stretches and exercises with no equipment, she'll help people get ready before they take that first swing of the season.

Along with Tom Cavicchi, teaching pro at Wollaston Golf Club in Milton, MA, DiRocco's physical therapy department, runs some golf-specific activities. "We're here to serve patients who have either been injured and want to return to golf, or those who want to develop some muscles and skills to take up the game." For those recovering from injury or illness, the clinic takes on patients with a physician's referral. Others can come by signing up and paying their own way. DiRocco con-

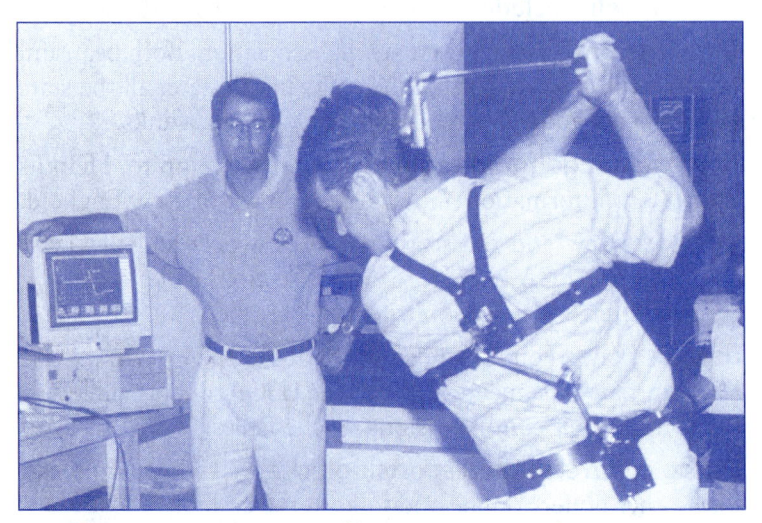

A golfer receives a diagnosis of his swing as part of Braintree Rehab's golf-specific activities program.

tinues, "Clients can work with Tom, who diagnoses swing faults or inefficiencies in the swing. I focus on muscle development, stretches, conditioning. People can work with either of us or both. Over the past few years, we've worked with about 300 people so far."

Cavicchi videotapes a client's swing and then breaks it down and shows the person where he or she can improve. "When you watch the pros swing, they rotate maybe 90 degrees and swing relatively easily. But most amateurs swing out of their shoes and rotate upwards of 120 degrees. A golf swing is not a baseball swing—you have a vertical plane rather than a horizontal plane—your body should not be moving the same way. People can be very inefficient, and much more out of alignment than they think. We can help them."

DiRocco teams up with professional, Bob Beach of Braintree Municipal, to work with physically challenged golfers, such as handicapped and amputees. Beach can modify equipment while DiRocco develops a physical regimen to help people maximize their swings and improve distance and accuracy. "It feels great to bring the game to people who might not otherwise have much access to it," says Beach. "If we can help them get the ball 40 yards farther down the fairway, or just help them to build a stable stance for their swing, we've given them their game back, and nothing pleases us more." You can reach Susan DiRocco at 781-826-0281.

Are you getting "golfer's elbow?"

The New England. Baptist Bone & Joint Institute in Boston informs us that the.elbow is most at risk during the impact and follow-through phases of sports, such as swinging a golf club. Gripping too hard, using awkward wrist postures, or over-bending the elbow can increase the risk of injury. Here are few exercises they suggest to minimize "golfer's elbow."

1. Drop arm to your side.
2. Rotate arm outward so palm is face up.
3. Lift entire arm away from body.
4. Bend wrist backward, straightening and stretching fingers. Stretch should be felt along the inside of the arm.
5. Hold for 10 to 15 seconds; repeat 5 to 10 times on each side. If you are already experiencing serious pain, see a physician or therapist familiar with athletic injuries.

The Ratings

The Ratings take into account three main factors:

1. **Course layout.** Is it interesting and varied? Will you remember several holes a few days later? Is it challenging but also fair?
2. **Course condition.** Is there grass on the tees or is it worn off? Is the rough cleaned out? Are the fairways green? Are the greens conducive to putting true? Are the greens in good shape?
3. **Staff and ownership service attitude.** Are carts required? (If so, this is a negative point.) Are the prices fair for greens fees and pro shop merchandise? Is the signage on the course helpful? Is there enough drinking water on the course?
   Are the clubhouse personnel friendly and helpful? (A poor rating on the service attitude hurt many courses.)

✪✪✪✪ Four Stars means the course competes with any course, public or private in the nation.

✪✪✪ Three Stars are awarded for excellent courses our consultants and readers have enjoyed and highly recommend.

✪✪ Two Stars are earned by offering a great golfing experiences in nearly every category.

Our ratings are 100% subjective. No two golfers will ever agree on every golf course. Remember it is impossible to visit every course every year. So a course may (or may not) be listed based on its past reputation.

We were delighted by the response to the ratings. We hope that you will continue to register your opinions. E-mail your comments to us at: **golfguid@ix.netcom.com**. Or you can comment on our web site at **www.newenglandgolfguide.com**, or send a fax, 978-287-0125, or send us an old fashioned letter in the U.S. Mail.

Handicap & Slope Defined

A handicap is a golfer's personal rating. It is a number which "levels" the ability of golfers, thus allowing any golfer to play any other golfer on a competitive basis. Most public golf courses can help you obtain a handicap if you join their "inner club" which usually includes the ability to get preferred tee times and to play in club tournaments. The USGA has a patented handicap formula which is pretty much the standard around the country. It's based on the lowest ten of your most recent twenty scores.

To calculate your own handicap use the following steps:
1. Subtract the course rating from your score
2. Multiply that difference by 113.
3. To compute a differential:
   Divide the answer in step 2 by the course slope rating
4. Repeat steps 1 to 3 for the 10 lowest scores of your last 20 rounds
5. Add the 10 lowest differentials of your last 20 rounds.
6. Divide the total of step 5 by 10 to get the average.
7. Then multiply the average by .96.
8. Your handicap is the number you get in step 7, to the last tenth.

Slope

"Slope" is a registered trademark of the USGA and is a term which refers to the difficulty of a course. It's based on a number of factors including length of the holes; number and placement of traps, water, and hazards; size and design of the greens, width of fairways and height of rough; hilliness; required carries; and the presence or lack of visual cues to help the golfer get around the course. The highest sloped public courses in New England from the back tees are Sugarloaf Golf Club in Maine at 151, the Shattuck in New Hampshire at 145, and Crumpin Fox in Massachusetts at 141.

New England:
An Architect's Delight

by John DiCocco

Golfers in New England are a privileged group. We have a wondrous variety of fabulous courses in our region: seaside, lakeside, links-style, wood-lined, and mountainside courses, sometimes with two or three of these thrown together. For this we can' thank nature and outstanding golf architects. In New England, we can particularly thank Donald Ross, who created at least 30 public courses in New England during the 1900s to the 1920s. And we can thank Geoffrey Cornish, who designed 37 courses in the 1960s and 1970s and then, joining with Brian Silva and Mark Mungeam, dozens more. Many other excellent designers have also left their mark on New England courses. Rees Jones has completed Blackstone National in Sutton, MA, and Al Zikorus has given us Topstone and Rolling Meadows in Connecticut. Current PGA Senior star and multiple US Open winner Hale Irwin redesigned the great New England Country Club layout.

The best architects take the land as they see it, and reveal the course that lays hidden there. This is, of course, a little easier in New England, where the terrain has character, as opposed to Florida, where it doesn't. They retain the hills, water, open stretches, and trees, and they guide us around as if we were on a natural trail. Along the way, we have only to keep track of a small white pebble, and occasionally knock it into a hole.

Increasing environmental restrictions have actually brought architects back from the earth-moving school to more natural layouts. Designers today have developed more courses with "landing areas," rather than continuous fairways, where the player has more forced carries over marshes and wetlands. Silva, today one of the area's most prolific designers, has created many such "target" style courses, such as The Shattuck, Ocean Edge, and the brand new Waverly Oaks, where accuracy is more important than length. His design partner Mungeam has also favored this target style at many courses,

Cyprian Keyes in Boylston, MA, was designed in 1997 by Mark Mungeam.

as evidenced by such gems as Cyprian Keyes.

What is good architecture? For me, there are four main factors. **First,** the course must have variety, and that translates to beauty and memorability. A few days after a round, can you remember the best six or seven holes on the course? **Second,** the layout should have a rhythm, varying the length, direction, elevation, and par of the holes, as well as following the natural lay of the land.

Third, it has to be fair, which is to say, playable. A good course should allow the average player to "stay in it," while challenging him or her to do something courageous from time to time. It should reward smart shot selection and punish bad decisions. But it should also provide a few easier holes as breathers, even if only once a nine.

To their credit, course architects today are doing more to make courses fair, without taking away the challenge for those who really want an all-out test. Today, they are designing in multiple tees to accommodate all levels of play from juniors on up to professionals.

Fourth, good courses offer both a mental as well as a physical challenge for you. To that end, architects will often introduce visual tricks into their design. Sometimes the appearance of a par 3 green will seem tiny from the tee, but the angle of view may obscure the fact that is it much longer (and therefore an easier target) than you thought. Architects often provide subtle clues, too, if you're paying attention. Ross, who incorporated numerous blind shots into his courses, often used the tallest tree behind the green.

Length is overrated. Every golf magazine will tell you the key to scoring isn't length off the tee— it's position off the tee. Smart course management, playing each shot as a preparation for the next shot, is what gives you a chance to score. I've met many players who think that unless they're "playing the whole course," that is, hitting off the back or "pro" tees, they aren't truly experiencing the course. Nonsense. What they're probably experiencing is more rough, more woods, certainly more length, but not necessarily a better golf experience.

No course reveals all its secrets the first time you play it. Remember, an architect designs a golf course so that par is the goal of the scratch golfer, not the average golfer.

Ben Crenshaw writes in the introduction to Tom Doak's superb book on golf architecture, *The Anatomy of a Golf Course* (Lyons & Buford Publishers, 1992) "I think every course worth playing retains some small element or spirit of the Old Course at St. Andrews. She is the original—the course that has survived and defended the spirit of the game against the advancement of technology and the efforts of a few cocky know-it-alls who are unwilling to learn her many fascinations. St. Andrews is a living testament to the canny Scots, who have always had the good sense to leave well enough alone and walk hand-in-hand with Nature."

In the end, you have to decide for yourself why you like or dislike a course, why one course allows you to score well and another beats the daylights out of you. But no matter where you play or whatever your handicap, just remember to look around once in awhile, and enjoy the architect's handiwork. He did it for you.

New Listings

We were amazed to find 27 more courses this year, 19 built as 18 hole courses. There are 9 new listings alone in the Greater Boston area, 7 in Maine, 3 in New Hampshire, 1 in Rhode Island, and 4 in Vermont, and 4 Par 3's in Connecticut. There are several brand new upscale courses: Acushnet River Valley, Blackstone National, Waverly Oaks in Massachusetts; Vermont National in South Burlington (a Jack Nicklaus course). In Maine, Dunegrass in Old Orchard Beach is a "golf community" and Belgrade Lakes is completely sodded! New courses, Okemo and Ragged Mountain are built into the mountains of Vermont and New Hampshire, respectively. Owl's Nest and Stonebridge in New Hampshire have already achieved golfers' acclaim. Many of the courses carry a "designer" label. Look them all over, and enjoy!

At press time, two new courses were reported: Riverbend in W. Bridgwater, MA, (508-583-5764) and Tewksbury CC, in Tewksbury, MA, (978-640-0033).

The White Mountains and the Pemigewasset River provide the natural setting for the clubhouse and greens of Owl's Nest Golf Club in Campton, New Hampshire.

Acushnet River Valley Golf Course

Acushnet, MA (508) 998-7777

Club Pro:
Pro Shop: Full inventory
Payment: Most major
Tee Times: 1 week adv.
Fee 9 Holes: Weekday: $18.00
Fee 18 Holes: Weekday: $27.00
Cart Rental: $24pp/18 $12pp/9
Lessons: Yes **School:** Yes
Driving Range: $5/lg $3/sm.
Other: Snack bar/ Clubhouse/ Bar lounge

Tees	Holes	Yards	Par	USGA	Slope
BACK	18	6168	72		
MIDDLE	18	5735	72		
FRONT	18	5099	72		

Weekend: $23.00
Weekend: $32.00
Discounts: Senior & Junior
Junior Golf: Yes **Membership:** Yes
Non-Metal Spikes: Required

Massachusetts newest upscale public facility opened August, 1998. Discounts given to residents.

	1	2	3	4	5	6	7	8	9
PAR	4	4	4	5	4	3	4	3	5
YARDS	375	289	275	436	336	119	382	141	501
HDCP	N/A								
	10	11	12	13	14	15	16	17	18
PAR	4	3	5	4	5	4	4	3	4
YARDS	315	113	470	388	529	257	328	145	336
HDCP									

Directions: Route 128 to Route 24 South to Route 140 South. Take Exit 6 to Route 18 South. Stay on Route 18 South for 2 miles. At lights, take Tarkin Hill Rd. which becomes Main St. in Acushnet. Course will be on left about 2 miles after Acushnet Town Hall.

Allendale Country Club

No. Dartmouth, MA (508) 992-8682

Club Pro: Steven Brown, PGA
Pro Shop: Full inventory
Payment: Most major
Tee Times: Yes
Fee 9 Holes: Weekday: $18.00 after 3:30pm
Fee 18 Holes: Weekday: $30.00
Cart Rental: $12pp/18, $7pp/9
Lessons: No **School:** No
Driving Range: No
Other: Clubhhouse/ Full Restaurant/ Bar-Lounge/ Snack Bar

Tees	Holes	Yards	Par	USGA	Slope
BACK	18	6583	72	71.6	126
MIDDLE	18	6322	72	70.4	124
FRONT	18	5615	74	72.2	121

Weekend: $18.00 after 3:30pm
Weekend: $35.00
Discounts: None
Junior Golf: Yes **Membership:** No
Non-Metal Spikes: Required

A walkable 18 hole course that offers a variety of holes with a challenging back 9. Call for directions from Providence and Cape Cod.

	1	2	3	4	5	6	7	8	9
PAR	4	5	3	4	3	5	4	4	5
YARDS	356	480	162	349	152	514	394	429	481
HDCP	13	5	15	11	17	3	9	1	7
	10	11	12	13	14	15	16	17	18
PAR	4	4	3	4	3	5	4	4	4
YARDS	387	406	151	386	141	466	343	334	391
HDCP	10	2	16	4	18	8	14	12	6

Directions: Route 24 South to Exit 12 (140 South). Follow 140S to end. (Rte 6). Right on Rte.6 to first set of lights. Turn left onto Slocum Rd. Go left to first set of lights. Turn right onto Allen St. Course is 1/2 mile on right.

Blackstone National Golf Club

Sutton, MA (508) 865-2111

Club Pro: James Bombard, PGA
Pro Shop: Full inventory
Payment: Visa, MC, Amex, Disc.
Tee Times: 5 days adv.
Fee 9 Holes: Weekday: No
Fee 18 Holes: Weekday: $39.00
Cart Rental: N/R
Lessons: Yes **School:** No
Driving Range: $5/lg. $4/med.
Other: Full Restaurant / Clubhouse / Lockers / Showers / Bar-Lounge

Tees	Holes	Yards	Par	USGA	Slope
BACK	18	7010	72		
MIDDLE	18	6500	72		
FRONT	18	6100	72		

Weekend: No
Weekend: $49.00
Discounts: N/R
Junior Golf: Yes **Membership:** Yes
Non-Metal Spikes: Required

Rees Jones Signature Design- "...Property is ideal for a golf course because of it's interesting topography." Bent grass tees, fairways, and greens. www.blackstonegolfclub.com

	1	2	3	4	5	6	7	8	9
PAR	4	5	3	4	4	4	3	5	4
YARDS	390	590	180	400	380	450	220	490	380
HDCP									
	10	11	12	13	14	15	16	17	18
PAR	4	3	4	3	4	4	5	4	5
YARDS	420	170	380	210	390	460	600	410	490
HDCP									

Directions: From Worcester take Route 146 South to Central Turnpike Exit. Make a right on to Central Turnpike (west). Follow for 3 miles to 4 way stop sign. Make left onto Putnam Hill Road 1/4 mile on left.

Northampton CC

Leeds, MA (413) 586-1898

Club Pro: Tim Walko
Pro Shop: Full inventory
Payment: Cash only
Tee Times: No
Fee 9 Holes: Weekday: $10.00
Fee 18 Holes: Weekday: $16.00
Cart Rental: $22/18, $12/9: for 2
Lessons: $25.00 for 30 min **School:** Jr.
Driving Range: No
Other: Bar-Lounge

Tees	Holes	Yards	Par	USGA	Slope
BACK	9	3041	35	69.0	119
MIDDLE	9	2948	35	68.0	116
FRONT	9	2502	36	67.8	112

Weekend: $12.00
Weekend: $18.00
Discounts: None
Junior Golf: Yes **Membership:** Yes
Non-Metal Spikes: Required

COUPON

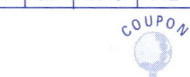

Short, but tricky. Small greens prove challenging for most players. Hit to centers of greens for a successful day. Open all year.

	1	2	3	4	5	6	7	8	9
PAR	5	4	4	4	4	4	3	3	4
YARDS	503	343	374	339	327	256	222	162	422
HDCP	13	9	7	5	3	15	11	17	1
	10	11	12	13	14	15	16	17	18
PAR									
YARDS									
HDCP									

Directions: From I 90, take 2nd Northampton Exit (Northampton/Amherst). Go through 4 sets of lights to crossing of Route 9. Take right on Route 9, 2 miles turn left on Florence St., 1st left on Arch St. follow until fork, bear left, go over bridge.

4 =Excellent **3** =Very Good **2** =Good

The Brookside Club

Bourne, MA (508) 743-4653

Club Pro: Dwight Bartlett Jr., PGA
Pro Shop: Full inventory
Payment: Visa, MC, Amex, Dis. and checks
Tee Times: 7 days adv.
Fee 9 Holes: Weekday: $25.00 M-Th
Fee 18 Holes: Weekday: $25.00 M-Th
Cart Rental: $15pp/18 7.50pp/9
Lessons: $35/30 min **School:** Junior
Driving Range: $5.00
Other: New Clubhouse in Spring/ Bar

Tees	Holes	Yards	Par	USGA	Slope
BACK	18	6300	70	71.1	126
MIDDLE	18	5814	70	68.1	124
FRONT	18	5130	70	69.6	118

Weekend: $35.00F/S/S/H
Weekend: $35.00F/S/S/H
Discounts: Senior & Junior
Junior Golf: No **Membership:** No
Non-Metal Spikes: Required

Rolling terrain, breathtaking views of Buzzards Bay, Cape Cod Canal and famous Railroad Bridge make Brookside was redesigned by John Sanford in 1996. www.golfcapecod.com/brookside.htm

	1	2	3	4	5	6	7	8	9
PAR	4	3	4	4	5	3	4	4	4
YARDS	379	156	359	365	503	96	361	421	332
HDCP	9	15	13	5	3	17	7	1	11
	10	11	12	13	14	15	16	17	18
PAR	5	4	4	3	4	4	4	3	4
YARDS	576	336	330	155	354	306	313	130	142
HDCP	2	10	6	16	4	12	14	18	8

Directions: Routes 495/25 over Bourne Bridge to Route 28 South. Golf Course is 1.4 miles on right.

The Woods of Westminster CC

Westminster, MA (978) 874-0500

Club Pro: Rod Van Gilder, PGA
Pro Shop: Limited inventory
Payment: Visa, MC, Disc., Checks
Tee Times: 3 days adv.
Fee 9 Holes: Weekday: $11.00
Fee 18 Holes: Weekday: $22.00
Cart Rental: $11.00pp/18 $7.00pp/9
Lessons: $25/30 min. **School:** Jr.
Driving Range: $5.00/ lg. $3.50/ sm.
Other: Full Restaurant / Clubhouse / Bar

Tees	Holes	Yards	Par	USGA	Slope
BACK	18	5810	72		
MIDDLE	18	5505	72	N/A	N/A
FRONT	18	4765	72		

Weekend: $14.00
Weekend: $28.00
Discounts: Senior & Junior
Junior Golf: Yes **Membership:** No
Non-Metal Spikes: Required

Typical N.E. rolling terrain with large greens. Scenic with mountain views. 2 driving ranges. Open year round. "Apropos name. Plans to widen fairways and move blue tee boxes." R.W.

	1	2	3	4	5	6	7	8	9
PAR	5	4	5	4	4	3	4	3	4
YARDS	460	275	525	295	345	175	405	145	320
HDCP									
	10	11	12	13	14	15	16	17	18
PAR	5	4	4	5	3	4	3	4	4
YARDS	345	220	330	435	145	315	130	300	340
HDCP									

Directions: Take Exit 27 off of Route 2 onto Depot Road. Route 2 merges with Route 2A. Take South Ashburnham Road. Take right onto Bean Porridge Hill Road.

Waverly Oaks Golf Club

Plymouth, MA (508) 224-6016

Club Pro: Lonnie McGowan
Pro Shop: Limited inventory
Payment: Visa, MC, Amex
Tee Times: 7 days adv.
Fee 9 Holes: Weekday: N/A
Fee 18 Holes: Weekday: $65.00
Cart Rental: $10.00pp/18 $5.00pp/9
Lessons: $30.00/half hour **School:** Jr.
Driving Range: $5.00/lg. bucket
Other: Full Restaurant / Clubhouse / Bar-Lounge

Tees	Holes	Yards	Par	USGA	Slope
BACK	18	7114	72	73.5	126
MIDDLE	18	6182	72	70.5	121
FRONT	18	5587	72	68.5	119

Weekend: N/A
Weekend: $65.00
Discounts: None
Junior Golf: No **Membership:** No
Non-Metal Spikes: Yes

New upscale daily fee. No memberships. Course features 5 sets of tees, with forgiving fairways, total bent grass playing surfaces. Additional 9 (Par 34) to open. "The gem of the new courses. Kudos." R.W.

	1	2	3	4	5	6	7	8	9
PAR	4	4	3	5	5	4	4	3	4
YARDS	301	377	152	490	495	391	378	169	316
HDCP	7	3	17	11	13	1	5	15	9
	10	11	12	13	14	15	16	17	18
PAR	4	4	4	5	3	4	5	3	4
YARDS	358	336	294	502	139	413	577	161	333
HDCP	2	6	16	4	18	14	8	12	10

Directions: Route 3 South to Exit 3. Right off ramp, 300 yards to stop sign. Go right for 2 miles. Club is on right. Course has 4000 feet of frontage on Route 3.

Belgrade Lakes CC

Belgrade Lakes, ME (207) 495-GOLF

Club Pro: No
Pro Shop: Limited inventory
Payment: Visa, MC, Amex
Tee Times: Recommended
Fee 9 Holes: Weekday: TBA
Fee 18 Holes: Weekday: $50.00
Cart Rental: $32.00/18
Lessons: No **School:** TBA
Driving Range: Planned
Other: Snack Bar/ Temporary Clubhouse

Tees	Holes	Yards	Par	USGA	Slope
BACK	18	6800	71	68.4	133
MIDDLE	18	6100	71	66.4	123
FRONT	18	5200	71	64.1	126

Weekend: TBA
Weekend: $50.00
Discounts: None
Junior Golf: Yes **Membership:** No
Non-Metal Spikes: Required

Opened September of 1998. Traditional layout. Walkable! Caddies available. Bent grass from tees to fairways to greens. Completely sodded course. "Majestic first tee to a downhill par 4." R.W.

	1	2	3	4	5	6	7	8	9
PAR	4	3	5	4	3	5	4	3	4
YARDS	370	150	453	400	157	477	363	170	417
HDCP	N/A								
	10	11	12	13	14	15	16	17	18
PAR	4	4	5	3	4	4	5	3	4
YARDS	343	350	496	170	360	333	540	140	383
HDCP									

Directions: 95 North. Take Exit 31B. Turn left on to Route 27. Go for 12 miles into the town of Belgrade Lakes. Turn left at the Sunset Grille onto West Road. Course is 1/4 mile on left.

4✪ =Excellent 3✪ =Very Good 2✪ =Good

Dunegrass Golf Club

Old Orchard Beach, ME (207) 934-4513

Club Pro: Gene McNabb, PGA
Pro Shop: Full inventory
Payment: Visa, MC, Amex
Tee Times: 7 days adv.
Fee 9 Holes: Weekday: $25 cart incl.
Fee 18 Holes: Weekday: $55 cart incl.
Cart Rental: included
Lessons: $18/30 min **School:** Jr.
Driving Range: $3.75
Other: Clubhouse / Full restaurant / Lockers/ Showers/ Bar-Lounge / Hotel / Inn

Tees	Holes	Yards	Par	USGA	Slope
BACK	18	6515	71		
MIDDLE	18	6111	71	N/A	N/A
FRONT	18	5479	71		

Weekend: $25.00 cart included
Weekend: $55.00 cart included
Discounts: None
Junior Golf: Yes **Membership:** Yes
Non-Metal Spikes: Required

Challenging, yet fair beautiful championship course with four sets of tees. Bentgrass from tee to green. "Expertise needed. Greens look fairly flat, but no putt is straight." R.W. www.dunegrass.com

	1	2	3	4	5	6	7	8	9
PAR	5	3	4	4	4	4	5	3	4
YARDS	539	151	359	301	368	346	530	136	333
HDCP	3	17	9	11	7	1	5	15	13
	10	11	12	13	14	15	16	17	18
PAR	4	3	4	3	4	5	4	3	5
YARDS	357	125	417	189	404	443	410	179	524
HDCP	12	18	8	16	10	4	6	14	2

Directions: From I-95 take Exit 5 to Exit 2 B (Route 1 North). Travel about .1 mile on Route 1 to Ross Road on right. Take Ross Rd. for about 2 miles. See Wild Dunes Way and golf course on right.

Sebasco Harbor Resort Golf Club

Sebasco Estates, ME (800) 225-3819

Club Pro: Lewis A. Kingsbury
Pro Shop: Limited inventory
Payment: Visa, MC, Amex, Disc.
Tee Times: No
Fee 9 Holes: Weekday: $19.00
Fee 18 Holes: Weekday: $19.00
Cart Rental: N/R
Lessons: $25/30 min. **School:** Clinics
Driving Range: No
Other: Full Restaurant / Clubhouse / Hotel / Inn / Lockers / Showers /Bar-Lounge

Tees	Holes	Yards	Par	USGA	Slope
BACK					
MIDDLE	9	3824	64		
FRONT					

Weekend: $19.00
Weekend: $19.00
Discounts: None
Junior Golf: No **Membership:** N/R
Non-Metal Spikes: Not Required

The course is now a "short, challenging course with a lot of character in its greens," with soft, lush bent grass in top notch condition. Seasonal rates. www.sebasco.com

	1	2	3	4	5	6	7	8	9
PAR	4	3	4	4	4	3	4	3	4
YARDS	370	113	294	250	205	134	270	193	280
HDCP									
	10	11	12	13	14	15	16	17	18
PAR	4	3	4	3	3	3	4	3	4
YARDS	292	87	237	160	182	117	228	162	250
HDCP									

Directions: South of Bath on Route 209 to Phippsburg. Stay on Route 209 until Route 217. 1/2 mile to Sebasco Harbor Resort Golf Club.

Squaw Mt. Village CC

Greenville Junction, ME (207) 695-3609

Club Pro:
Pro Shop: No
Payment: Cash only
Tee Times: No
Fee 9 Holes: Weekday: $12.00
Fee 18 Holes: Weekday: $18.00
Cart Rental: $15.00/18 $10.00/9
Lessons: School: No
Driving Range: No
Other:

Tees	Holes	Yards	Par	USGA	Slope
BACK	N/A				
MIDDLE	9	2463	34	N/A	N/A
FRONT	N/A				

Weekend: N/R
Weekend: N/R
Discounts: None
Junior Golf: N/R **Membership:** Yes
Non-Metal Spikes: Not Required

Discount on membership for juniors, seniors, and families.

	1	2	3	4	5	6	7	8	9
PAR	4	3	5	4	4	3	4	3	4
YARDS	310	126	455	295	330	120	360	117	350
HDCP	9	15	1	11	7	13	3	17	5
	10	11	12	13	14	15	16	17	18
PAR									
YARDS									
HDCP									

Directions:

St. Croix Country Club

Calais, ME (207) 454-8875

Club Pro: Duane Ellis, PGA
Pro Shop: Full inventory
Payment: Visa, MC
Tee Times: No
Fee 9 Holes: Weekday: $12.00
Fee 18 Holes: Weekday: $20.00
Cart Rental: $17.00/18 $11.00/9
Lessons: $20.00/half hour **School:** No
Driving Range: No
Other: Clubhouse / Showers / Bar-Lounge

Tees	Holes	Yards	Par	USGA	Slope
BACK	N/A				
MIDDLE	9	2735	35	64.8	102
FRONT	N/A				

Weekend: $12.00
Weekend: $20.00
Discounts: None
Junior Golf: Yes **Membership:** Yes
Non-Metal Spikes: Required

The easternmost golf course in the U.S. Challenging course - scenic - with nice variety of holes. Call ahead for league or tournament times. Reduced cart rate for members. Open May 1 - Oct. 31.

	1	2	3	4	5	6	7	8	9
PAR	3	5	4	4	5	3	4	3	4
YARDS	165	500	315	400	435	125	290	190	315
HDCP	15	1	7	3	5	17	11	13	9
	10	11	12	13	14	15	16	17	18
PAR									
YARDS									
HDCP									

Directions: Head east on Route 1. 2 miles outside of Calais.

4✪ = Excellent 3✪ = Very Good 2✪ = Good

The Ledges Golf Club

York, ME (207) 351-3000

Club Pro: Chris Kasheta, PGA
Pro Shop: Full inventory
Payment: Visa, MC
Tee Times: 4 days adv.
Fee 9 Holes: Weekday:
Fee 18 Holes: Weekday: $60.00
Cart Rental: N/R
Lessons: $35/35 min. **School:** No
Driving Range: $5.00/lg. $3.00/sm.
Other: Bar-Lounge

Tees	Holes	Yards	Par	USGA	Slope
BACK	9	3495	36	N/A	N/A
MIDDLE	9	2934	36	N/A	N/A
FRONT	9	2476	36	N/A	N/A

Weekend:
Weekend: $60.00 with cart
Discounts: None
Junior Golf: N/R **Membership:** No
Non-Metal Spikes: Yes

9 holes open in 1998. Full 18 will open late spring 1999. Takes full advantage of natural terrain. Can play 7000 yards from black tees. Scorecard below is for 9 holes.

	1	2	3	4	5	6	7	8	9
PAR	4	4	4	5	3	4	5	3	4
YARDS	374	284	316	510	137	358	461	173	321
HDCP	3	15	13	1	17	5	9	7	11
	10	11	12	13	14	15	16	17	18
PAR									
YARDS									
HDCP									

Directions: From Route 95 take Exit 4 to Route 236. Take a right onto Route 91. Course is 5.5 miles on right.

Owl's Nest Golf Club

Campton, NH (603) 726-3076

Club Pro: Dale H. Ezyk, PGA., Joe Clark Sr.,
Pro Shop: Full inventory
Payment: Visa, MC, Amex, Disc.
Tee Times: 5 days adv.
Fee 9 Holes: Weekday: $29.00
Fee 18 Holes: Weekday: $39.00
Cart Rental: M-F: $26/18 $16/9
Lessons: $50.00/half hour **School:** Jr. & Sr.
Driving Range: $6/lg. $5/md. $4/sm.
Other: Full Restaurant / Clubhouse / Bar-Lounge

Tees	Holes	Yards	Par	USGA	Slope
BACK	18	7012	72	74.0	133
MIDDLE	18	6045	72	69.7	124
FRONT	18	5296	72	67.8	117

Weekend: $35.00
Weekend: $45.00
Discounts: Jr PGA camp experience
Junior Golf: Yes **Membership:** Yes
Non-Metal Spikes: Required

Sculpted around the natural topography of the Pemigewasset River and the White Mountains. Committed to unparalleled N.E. golf. "Dramatic variety of holes." R.W. www.owlnestgolf.com

	1	2	3	4	5	6	7	8	9
PAR	4	4	4	5	3	4	3	4	5
YARDS	345	350	385	509	150	325	173	326	488
HDCP	9	7	5	1	17	13	15	11	3
	10	11	12	13	14	15	16	17	18
PAR	3	4	4	5	3	4	4	5	4
YARDS	130	315	376	460	165	273	440	490	345
HDCP	18	10	8	2	16	14	4	6	12

Directions: I 93, Exit 28, west on Route 49. North on Owl Street.

Ragged Mountain

Danbury, NH (603) 768-3600

Club Pro:
Pro Shop:
Payment: Visa, MC
Tee Times:
Fee 9 Holes: Weekday: $28
Fee 18 Holes: Weekday: $38
Cart Rental: $13
Lessons: School:
Driving Range:
Other: Full Restaurant / Clubhouse / Lockers / Showers / Bar Lounge

Tees	Holes	Yards	Par	USGA	Slope
BACK	18	7059			
MIDDLE	18	6482	72		
FRONT	18	5063			

Weekend: $32
Weekend: $42
Discounts:
Junior Golf: Membership:
Non-Metal Spikes: Yes

A true mountain course with spectacular views. Under two hurs from Boston to open Spring '99. Four sets of tees provides playability for all levels.

	1	2	3	4	5	6	7	8	9
PAR	4	5	4	4	3	4	3	5	4
YARDS	395	484	407	341	171	345	139	496	335
HDCP									
	10	11	12	13	14	15	16	17	18
PAR	4	5	4	3	4	3	4	5	4
YARDS	378	499	729	123	420	209	434	520	407
HDCP									

Directions: Call.

Stonebridge Country Club

Goffstown, NH (603) 497-T-OFF (8633)

Club Pro: John Jelley, PGA
Pro Shop: Full inventory
Payment: Visa, MC, Amex, Disc.
Tee Times: 3 days adv.
Fee 9 Holes: Weekday: $17.00
Fee 18 Holes: Weekday: $30.00
Cart Rental: $12 pp/18 $8 pp/9
Lessons: $40.00/half hour **School:** No
Driving Range: $6/ lg. $4/md. $2/sm.
Other: Full Restaurant / Clubhouse / Lockers / Showers / Bar-Lounge

Tees	Holes	Yards	Par	USGA	Slope
BACK	18	6808	72	73.0	138
MIDDLE	18	6408	72	70.8	134
FRONT	18	5629	72	68.1	127

Weekend: No
Weekend: $37.00
Discounts: Junior Wkdays bef. 3 pm
Junior Golf: Yes **Membership:** Yes
Non-Metal Spikes: Required

Front 9 are more open, back nine are longer and tighter. Four sets of tees challenge all levels. Large greens." The final six holes alone are worth the greens fee." R.W.

	1	2	3	4	5	6	7	8	9
PAR	5	4	4	3	4	3	4	4	4
YARDS	480	398	370	152	366	156	332	408	417
HDCP	9	7	13	17	11	15	3	1	5
	10	11	12	13	14	15	16	17	18
PAR	5	4	4	3	5	4	3	5	4
YARDS	496	325	349	193	526	369	150	521	400
HDCP	8	16	14	12	6	10	18	2	4

Directions: Route 93 to Route 114. Stay on 114 for 9 miles, go through center of Goffstown. Take Parker Station Road on right, go for about 100 yards. First right is Gorham Pond Road. Course is 3/4 mile on left.

4✪ =Excellent 3✪ =Very Good 2✪ =Good

Weekapaug Golf Club

Westerly, RI (401) 322-7870

Club Pro: Chris and Susan Bond
Pro Shop: Full inventory
Payment: Visa, MC, Disc, Check
Tee Times: 1 day adv.
Fee 9 Holes: Weekday: $15.00
Fee 18 Holes: Weekday: $22.00
Cart Rental: $12.00pp/18 $7.00pp/9
Lessons: $35.00/half hour **School:** Jr. & Sr.
Driving Range: $9/lg $6/med $3/sm
Other: Full Restaurant / Clubhouse / Bar-Lounge

Tees	Holes	Yards	Par	USGA	Slope
BACK	9	3253	36	69.9	114
MIDDLE	9	3181	36	67.6	109
FRONT	9	2674	36	66.0	107

Weekend: $18.00
Weekend: $25.00
Discounts: None
Junior Golf: Yes **Membership:** Yes
Non-Metal Spikes: Required

COUPON

A nice test of golf with holes bordering a salt pond, a constant wind off the water adds to the links feel. Receive private club service at a public facility. Open year round.

	1	2	3	4	5	6	7	8	9
PAR	4	4	3	4	5	4	4	3	5
YARDS	410	336	176	342	466	417	371	151	512
HDCP	3	15	9	5	13	1	11	17	7
	10	11	12	13	14	15	16	17	18
PAR									
YARDS									
HDCP									

Directions: Take Exit 1 from I-95. Bear right off ramp to Route 3 for 3-4 miles to Route 78 East. Take Route 1, turn left. Go 2 miles to light, turn right. At Route 1A turn right. Course is 1/2 mile on left.

Bradford Golf Course

Bradford, VT (802) 222-5207

Club Pro:
Pro Shop: Limited inventory
Payment: Cash only
Tee Times: No
Fee 9 Holes: Weekday: $16.00
Fee 18 Holes: Weekday: $16.00
Cart Rental: $12pp/18 $9pp/9
Lessons: No **School:** No
Driving Range: N/R
Other: Snacks

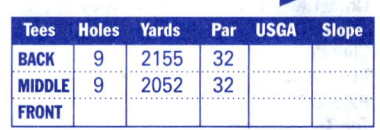

Tees	Holes	Yards	Par	USGA	Slope
BACK	9	2155	32		
MIDDLE	9	2052	32		
FRONT					

Weekend: $19.00
Weekend: $19.00
Discounts: Junior
Junior Golf: No **Membership:** Yes
Non-Metal Spikes: Required

Par 32, 18 sets of tees.

	1	2	3	4	5	6	7	8	9
PAR	3	4	3	3	4	3	5	4	3
YARDS	174	239	160	115	304	185	431	294	150
HDCP									
	10	11	12	13	14	15	16	17	18
PAR									
YARDS									
HDCP									

Directions: From I 91, take Exit 16, turn right and go 3/4 of a mile. Turn left, go 1 mile north. Turn right, go by Bradford Academy to bottom of hill.

Okemo Valley Golf Club

Ludlow, VT (802) 228-8871

Club Pro: James Remy, PGA
Pro Shop: Full inventory
Payment: Visa, MC, Amex
Tee Times: Yes
Fee 9 Holes: Weekday: TBD
Fee 18 Holes: Weekday: TBD
Cart Rental: TBD
Lessons: Yes **School:** Jr. & Sr.
Driving Range: Yes
Other: Full Restaurant / Clubhouse / Hotel / Inn / Lockers / Showers / Bar

Tees	Holes	Yards	Par	USGA	Slope
BACK					
MIDDLE	18		72		
FRONT					

Weekend:
Weekend:
Discounts: N/R
Junior Golf: Yes **Membership:** Yes
Non-Metal Spikes: Required

New 18 hole course, opens midsummer of 1999. Course is under construction. Open April 25 - October 31.

	1	2	3	4	5	6	7	8	9
PAR	TBA								
YARDS									
HDCP									
	10	11	12	13	14	15	16	17	18
PAR	TBA								
YARDS									
HDCP									

Directions: Just North of Ludlow about 2 miles on Route 103. Right on Fox Lane (signs on highway).

Vermont National CC

S. Burlington, VT. (802) 864-7770

Club Pro: Troy Sprister
Pro Shop:
Payment: Most major
Tee Times: 3 days in adv.
Fee 9 Holes: Weekday: $35.00
Fee 18 Holes: Weekday: $50.00
Cart Rental: $15/18, $9/9
Lessons: $35/45 min. **School:** N/R
Driving Range: $6.00, $3.00
Other: Clubhouse / Bar Lounge

Tees	Holes	Yards	Par	USGA	Slope
BACK	18	7035	72	74.0	130
MIDDLE	18	6211	72	69.4	123
FRONT	18	5156	72	70.6	116

Weekend: $40.00
Weekend: $60.00
Discounts: Junior
Junior Golf: No **Membership:** Yes
Non-Metal Spikes: Required

Tour caliber course designed by Jack Nicklaus and son has large dep bunkers and undulating greens. 5 sets of tees featured to accomodate all levels. Dress code. Front 9 opened in July '98.

	1	2	3	4	5	6	7	8	9
PAR	4	5	4	3	5	4	4	3	4
YARDS	293	489	321	151	524	397	403	153	343
HDCP	9	7	6	8	2	1	3	5	4
	10	11	12	13	14	15	16	17	18
PAR	4	5	4	3	4	3	5	3	5
YARDS	396	543	349	151	381	165	465	167	520
HDCP	4	1	7	9	6	8	5	3	2

Directions: I-89 Exit 14 East to Dorset Street. South 2 miles to club on right.

4 ✪ =Excellent 3 ✪ =Very Good 2 ✪ =Good

New Courses 35

The Orchards Golf Course

Milford, CT. (203) 877-8200

Club Pro: No
Pro Shop: Yes
Payment: Cash
Tee Times: 7days advance
Fee 9 Holes: Weekday: $11.00
Fee 18 Holes: Weekday: $21.00
Cart Rental: Pull carts
Lessons: No **School:** N/R
Driving Range: Putting green
Other: Snacks

Tees	Holes	Yards	Par	USGA	Slope
BACK					
MIDDLE	9	1625	32		
FRONT	9	1433	32		

Weekend: $12.00
Weekend: $23.00
Discounts: Senior & Junior
Junior Golf: Membership:
Non-Metal Spikes: Required

Executive. Built in 1997 and well maintained. Second round of nine receives $1.00 discount. Resident discounts.

	1	2	3	4	5	6	7	8	9
PAR	4	3	4	4	4	3	3	3	4
YARDS	242	93	222	207	217	120	167	91	266
HDCP									
	10	11	12	13	14	15	16	17	18
PAR									
YARDS									
HDCP									

Directions: I 95, take Exit 39. Go South on Route 1 to Route 121 North (North Street). Turn right onto Kozlowski Rd.

A view of hole #1 at Dunegrass CC in Old Orchard Beach, Maine.

Par 3 Courses

Cyprian Keyes Golf Club, Par 3

Boylston, MA (508) 869-9900

Club Pro:
Pro Shop:
Payment:
Tee Times: No
Fee 9 Holes: Weekday: $12.00 M-Th
Fee 18 Holes: Weekday:
Cart Rental: Pull, $3.00
Lessons: Yes **School:** TBA
Driving Range: $5.00 bucket
Other: Clubhouse/ Restaurant/ Function facilities

Tees	Yards	Par
MIDDLE	1260	27
FRON		

Weekend: $15.00 F-Sun
Weekend:
Discounts: $9 (under 18) M-Sun
Junior Golf: Yes **Membership:**
Non-Metal Spikes: Required

COUPON

Truly a par 3 course. Good for beginners, while allowing the experienced golfer quick play.
Directions: Route 290 to Exit 23B (Route 140 North). Go 1 mile and take third right onto East Temple Street.

Loons Cove Golf Course

Skowhegan, ME (207) 474-9550

Club Pro:
Pro Shop:
Payment:
Tee Times:
Fee 9 Holes: Weekday: $5.00
Fee 18 Holes: Weekday: $8.00/18 $10 all day
Cart Rental:
Lessons: School: No
Driving Range: No
Other: Snacks/ Beverages

Tees	Yards	Par
MIDDLE	1115	27
FRONT		

Weekend: $5.00
Weekend: $8.00/18 $10 all day
Discounts: For members
Junior Golf: Yes **Membership:** Yes
Non-Metal Spikes: Not Required

Host for Central Maine Junior Program
Directions: 6 miles from I 95 on Route 201 in Skowhegan

Barcomb Hill at Apple Tree Bay Resort

South Hero, VT (802) 372-4135

Club Pro: No
Pro Shop: Limited inventory
Payment: Cash, Checks
Tee Times: No
Fee 9 Holes: Weekday: $9.00
Fee 18 Holes: Weekday: $9.00
Cart Rental: N/R
Lessons: No **School:** No
Driving Range: No
Other:

Tees	Yards	Par
MIDDLE	1108	27
FRONT		

Weekend: $10.00
Weekend: $10.00
Discounts: None
Junior Golf: No **Membership:** Yes
Non-Metal Spikes: Required

No one under 5 years allowed. Open May 1 - October 20.
Directions: Exit 17 off I 89. 6 miles on left. Must drive through campground to reach.

4✪=Excellent 3✪=Very Good 2✪=Good

Gainfield Farms GC

Southbury, CT (203) 262-1100

Club Pro: Bert Boyce
Pro Shop: Yes
Payment:
Tee Times: Yes
Fee 9 Holes: Weekday: $12.00
Fee 18 Holes: Weekday: $20.00
Cart Rental:
Lessons: School:
Driving Range: Yes, mt. and net
Other: Snacks

Tees	Yards	Par
MIDDLE	1384	27
FRONT	1203	27

Weekend: $13.00
Weekend: $22.00
Discounts: Senior / Junior
Junior Golf: Membership:
Non-Metal Spikes:

Executive style, resident discounts

Directions: I-84 to Exit 15. Go north on Route 67. Turn left on Main Street. Turn right on Poverty Road. Then left on Old Field Road.

South Pine Creek Par 3 GC

Fairfield, CT (203) 256-3173

Club Pro:
Pro Shop:
Payment:
Tee Times: Yes
Fee 9 Holes: Weekday: $9.00
Fee 18 Holes: Weekday:
Cart Rental:
Lessons: School:
Driving Range: Putting green
Other: Snacks

Tees	Yards	Par
MIDDLE	1240	27
FRONT	1073	27

Weekend: $10.00
Weekend:
Discounts: Senior & Junior
Junior Golf: Membership:
Non-Metal Spikes:

Residents half price! Great place to learn the game. Busy.

Directions: From I-95, take Exit 21 (Mill Plain Rd.) Turn right on Route 1 West. Turn left on South Pine Creek Road. Turn left on Old Dam Road.

Villa Hills Golf Course

Storrs,CT. 860-429-6344

Club Pro:
Pro Shop:
Payment:
Tee Times: No
Fee 9 Holes: Weekday: $6.50
Fee 18 Holes: Weekday: $12.00
Cart Rental:
Lessons: School:
Driving Range: No
Other: Restaurant / Snack Bar / Bar- lounge

Tees	Yards	Par
MIDDLE	1158	27
FRONT		

Weekend: $6.50
Weekend: $12.00
Discounts: Senior & Junior
Junior Golf: Membership:
Non-Metal Spikes:

Built in 1995. Women friendly.

Directions: Take I 384 East to Route 44. Course is on left.

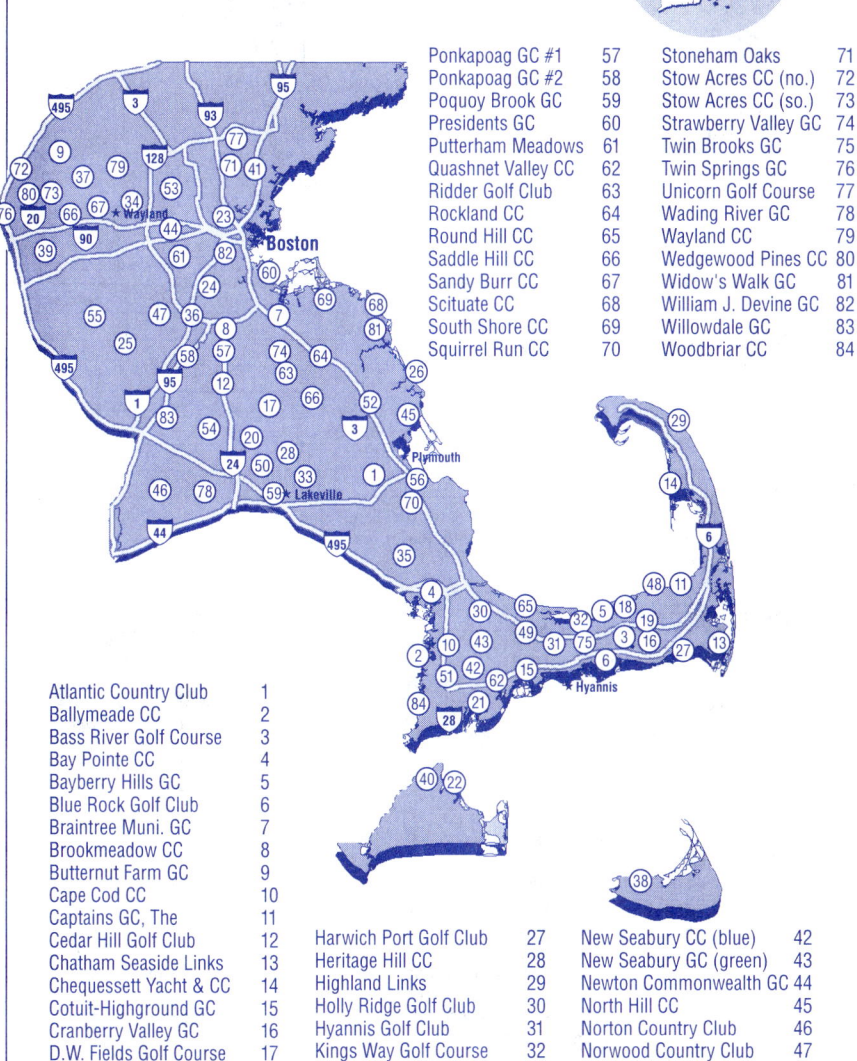

CHAPTER 1
Boston & South Shore

Ponkapoag GC #1	57	Stoneham Oaks	71
Ponkapoag GC #2	58	Stow Acres CC (no.)	72
Poquoy Brook GC	59	Stow Acres CC (so.)	73
Presidents GC	60	Strawberry Valley GC	74
Putterham Meadows	61	Twin Brooks GC	75
Quashnet Valley CC	62	Twin Springs GC	76
Ridder Golf Club	63	Unicorn Golf Course	77
Rockland CC	64	Wading River GC	78
Round Hill CC	65	Wayland CC	79
Saddle Hill CC	66	Wedgewood Pines CC	80
Sandy Burr CC	67	Widow's Walk GC	81
Scituate CC	68	William J. Devine GC	82
South Shore CC	69	Willowdale GC	83
Squirrel Run CC	70	Woodbriar CC	84

Atlantic Country Club	1	Harwich Port Golf Club	27	New Seabury CC (blue)	42
Ballymeade CC	2	Heritage Hill CC	28	New Seabury GC (green)	43
Bass River Golf Course	3	Highland Links	29	Newton Commonwealth GC	44
Bay Pointe CC	4	Holly Ridge Golf Club	30	North Hill CC	45
Bayberry Hills GC	5	Hyannis Golf Club	31	Norton Country Club	46
Blue Rock Golf Club	6	Kings Way Golf Course	32	Norwood Country Club	47
Braintree Muni. GC	7	Lakeville Country Club	33	Ocean Edge GC	48
Brookmeadow CC	8	Leo J. Martin GC	34	Olde Barnstable Fair. GC	49
Butternut Farm GC	9	Little Harbor CC	35	Olde Scotland Links	50
Cape Cod CC	10	Lost Brook Golf Club	36	Paul Harney GC	51
Captains GC, The	11	Maynard Country Club	37	Pembroke Country Club	52
Cedar Hill Golf Club	12	Miacomet Golf Club	38	Pine Meadows GC	53
Chatham Seaside Links	13	Millwood Farm Golf Course	39	Pine Oaks GC	54
Chequessett Yacht & CC	14	Mink Meadows GC	40	Pinecrest GC	55
Cotuit-Highground GC	15	Mt. Hood Golf Course	41	Plymouth CC	56
Cranberry Valley GC	16
D.W. Fields Golf Course	17
Dennis Highlands	18
Dennis Pines GC	19
Easton Country Club	20
Falmouth Country Club	21
Farm Neck Golf Club	22
Fresh Pond Golf Club	23
George Wright GC	24
Glen Ellen CC	25
Green Harbor Golf Club	26

NEW ENGLAND GOLFGUIDE   Greater Boston/South Shore/Cape Cod

Atlantic Country Club ★★ ▶ 1

Plymouth, MA (508) 759-6644

Club Pro: Don Daley, PGA
Pro Shop: Full inventory
Payment: Cash, MC, Visa
Tee Times: 2 days in advance
Fee 9 Holes: Weekday: $20.00
Fee 18 Holes: Weekday: $35.00
Cart Rental: $13.00 pp/18 $7 pp/9
Lessons: $30.00/half hour **Schools:** No
Driving Range: Yes
Other: Soft drinks/ Snack Bar / Banquet Facilities

Tees	Holes	Yards	Par	USGA	Slope
BACK	18	6262	72	70.8	127
MIDDLE	18	5840	72	69.0	119
FRONT	18	4918	72	68.3	116

Weekend: $35, $25 after 4 pm
Weekend: $40, $25 after 3 pm
Discounts: None
Junior Golf: No **Membership:** Wait. List
Non-Metal Spikes: Preferred

COUPON

Championship, up scale public course on 200 acres designed by Mark Mungeam of Cornish and Silva. Rolling terrain. Cape style. Bent fairways, greens, and tees. Twilight rates. www.negolf.com

	1	2	3	4	5	6	7	8	9
PAR	4	3	4	5	4	5	3	4	4
YARDS	302	144	410	475	343	467	134	387	345
HDCP	11	17	3	7	13	9	15	1	5
	10	11	12	13	14	15	16	17	18
PAR	4	3	4	4	5	4	5	3	4
YARDS	336	156	310	281	460	330	491	105	364
HDCP	8	12	4	18	6	14	10	16	2

Directions: Take Route 3 to Exit 2. Right onto Long Pond Road. Left onto Carter's Bridge Road. Right onto Upland Road to Little Sandy Pond Road. Course is 1 mile on left.

Ballymeade CC ★★ ▶ 2

N. Falmouth, MA (508) 540-4005

Club Pro: Jody Shaw
Pro Shop: Full inventory
Payment: Cash and credit cards
Tee Times: 1 week adv.
Fee 9 Holes: Weekday: N/A
Fee 18 Holes: Weekday: $40.00-$68.00
Cart Rental: see 'fees'
Lessons: $30.00/half hour **Schools:** No
Driving Range: $6.00/lg. bucket
Other: Restaurant / Clubhouse / Bar-lounge / Lockers / Snack Bar / Showers

Tees	Holes	Yards	Par	USGA	Slope
BACK	18	6928	72	74.3	139
MIDDLE	18	6358	72	71.7	134
FRONT	18	5001	72	69.9	119

Weekend: N/A
Weekend: $50.00-$90.00(F,S,S)
Discounts: None
Junior Golf: Yes **Membership:** No
Non-Metal Spikes: Yes

COUPON

18 holes of championship golf from the highest point on the cape. Rolling terrain with spectacular ocean views. Open all year. Winter rates. www.ballymeade.com

	1	2	3	4	5	6	7	8	9
PAR	4	3	5	4	3	4	4	5	4
YARDS	355	183	464	333	164	419	367	464	390
HDCP	17	11	9	7	13	1	5	15	3
	10	11	12	13	14	15	16	17	18
PAR	5	3	4	4	3	4	4	4	5
YARDS	500	164	403	415	380	331	156	367	503
HDCP	8	6	2	10	14	16	18	12	4

Directions: Over Bourne Bridge to Route 28 South. Take the North Falmouth Route 151 exit, 9 miles from the bridge. Turn right off the exit ramp. Course is less than 1 mile on right.

Bass River Golf Course

3

GB CC/ MA

So. Yarmouth, MA (508) 398-9079

Club Pro: Al Lupis
Pro Shop: Full inventory
Payment: Visa, MC
Tee Times: 4 days adv.

Tees	Holes	Yards	Par	USGA	Slope
BACK	18	6129	72	69.3	122
MIDDLE	18	5734	72	67.7	117
FRONT	18	5343	72	69.9	115

Fee 9 Holes: Weekday: No   **Weekend:** $40.00
Fee 18 Holes: Weekday: $40.00   **Weekend:** $40.00
Cart Rental: $23.00/18 $12.00/9   **Discounts:** None
Lessons: Yes **Schools:** No   **Junior Golf:** Yes **Membership:** No
Driving Range: No   **Non-Metal Spikes:** No
Other: Clubhouse / Snack bar / Bar-lounge

Generous fairway landing area, small greens, ocean breezes. Donald Ross designed.
www.sunsol.com/bassrivergolf

	1	2	3	4	5	6	7	8	9
PAR	4	4	4	3	5	3	3	4	4
YARDS	329	348	282	105	464	139	190	282	391
HDCP	8	9	17	18	5	13	7	14	2
	10	11	12	13	14	15	16	17	18
PAR	4	4	5	5	3	4	5	4	4
YARDS	247	386	450	500	140	333	474	319	339
HDCP	16	1	4	3	15	6	11	12	10

Directions: Take Exit 8 off of Route 6 East. Take left onto Regional Ave. Turn right at second stop sign to entrance.

Bay Pointe CC

4

Onset, MA (508) 759-8802, 1-800-24T-TIME

Club Pro: Rusty Gunnarson
Pro Shop: Full inventory
Payment: Amex
Tee Times: 3 days adv.

Tees	Holes	Yards	Par	USGA	Slope
BACK	NA				
MIDDLE	18	6201	70	71.6	125
FRONT	18	5380	72	71.3	125

Fee 9 Holes: Weekday: $20.00 M-Th   **Weekend:** $25.00
Fee 18 Holes: Weekday: $33.00, M-Th   **Weekend:** $35.00. F/S/S/Hol.
Cart Rental: $14.00/rider   **Discounts:** None
Lessons: $30.00/half hour **Schools:** N/R   **Junior Golf:** No **Membership:** Yes
Driving Range: Members only   **Non-Metal Spikes:** Preferred
Other: Clubhouse / Lockers / Showers / Snack bar / Restaurant / Bar-lounge /Pool / Tennis

COUPON

Visit the new clubhouse. Perfect for corporate outings and functions. Typical Cape course, superbly manicured, excellent greens and fairways. Twi-light rate. Open year round.

	1	2	3	4	5	6	7	8	9
PAR	3	4	3	4	3	5	4	5	4
YARDS	195	391	203	360	208	526	337	492	390
HDCP	10	2	12	14	16	6	18	8	4
	10	11	12	13	14	15	16	17	18
PAR	5	4	4	3	4	4	3	3	5
YARDS	481	465	384	189	452	283	101	227	517
HDCP	5	1	7	15	3	13	17	11	9

Directions: I-495 turns into Route 25. Take Exit 1 from Route 25. At 7th light go right, course 2/3 mile on right. From Route 3 South take Route 6 at Sagamore Rotary toward Wareham. Cross Buttermilk Bay into Wareham and go left a first light. Course 2/3 mile on right.

4✪ =Excellent **3**✪ =Very Good **2**✪ =Good   Greater Boston/South Shore/Cape Cod **41**

Bayberry Hills GC

5

S. Yarmouth, MA (508) 394-5597

Club Pro: Al Lupis
Pro Shop: Full inventory
Payment: MC, Visa, Cash
Tee Times: 4 days adv.
Fee 9 Holes: Weekday: N/A
Fee 18 Holes: Weekday: $40.00
Cart Rental: $23.00/18 $12.00/9
Lessons: $35.00/half hour **Schools:** No
Driving Range: $8/lg. $6/md. $4/sm.
Other: Clubhouse/Bar-lounge

Tees	Holes	Yards	Par	USGA	Slope
BACK	18	6523	72	71.7	125
MIDDLE	18	6067	72	69.6	119
FRONT	18	5323	72	69.4	111

Weekend: $40.00
Weekend: $40.00
Discounts: None
Junior Golf: No **Membership:** No
Non-Metal Spikes: Yes

COUPON

Opened in 1988 and designed by Brian Silva. Offers 5 sets of tees to challenge all levels.
www.sunsol.com/bayberryhills/index.html

	1	2	3	4	5	6	7	8	9
PAR	4	5	3	4	4	4	5	3	4
YARDS	375	485	140	336	335	350	505	146	350
HDCP	3	9	17	7	15	13	1	11	5
	10	11	12	13	14	15	16	17	18
PAR	4	4	3	4	4	5	4	3	5
YARDS	372	384	130	320	352	503	349	160	475
HDCP	4	2	18	16	8	10	6	14	12

Directions: Take Exit 8 off Route 6 East. Right onto Old Townhouse Rd. at second set of lights. Old Townhouse Rd. ends in Bayberry Hills' parking lot.

Blue Rock Golf Club

⭐⭐⭐ 6

S. Yarmouth, MA (508) 398-9295

Club Pro: Robert V. Miller
Pro Shop: Full inventory
Payment: Visa, MC, Cash, Check
Tee Times: 7 days adv.
Fee 9 Holes: Weekday: Breakfast Club
Fee 18 Holes: Weekday: $29.00
Cart Rental: Pull carts $3.00 daily
Lessons: 35.00/45 minutes **Schools:** Yes
Driving Range: Members only
Other: Clubhouse / Snack bar / Restaurant / Bar-lounge / Hotel / Tennis / Pool / Golf School /Clinic

Tees	Holes	Yards	Par	USGA	Slope
BACK	18	2890	54	56.4	83
MIDDLE	18	2563	54	56.4	83
FRONT	18	2170	54	56.4	83

Weekend: Breakfast Club
Weekend: $31.00
Discounts: None
Junior Golf: Yes **Membership:** Yes
Non-Metal Spikes: No

Rated by New England GolfGuide's Reader's Response Survey as favorite par 3 course. "Absolute gem.", Golf World. Challenging. www.bluerockgolfcourse.com

	1	2	3	4	5	6	7	8	9
PAR	3	3	3	3	3	3	3	3	3
YARDS	103	127	118	125	247	145	170	165	165
HDCP	17	15	13	11	1	9	5	7	3
	10	11	12	13	14	15	16	17	18
PAR	3	3	3	3	3	3	3	3	3
YARDS	150	117	190	147	185	185	144	129	173
HDCP	10	18	2	12	6	8	14	16	4

Directions: Take Mid Cape Highway East to Exit 8. Turn right off the ramp. First left White's Path, right to intersection, turn left Great Western Road. Course is 1/4 mile on right.

Braintree Muni. GC

Braintree, MA (781) 843-6513

Club Pro: Robert Beach
Pro Shop: Full inventory
Payment: Visa, MC
Tee Times: 3 days adv.
Fee 9 Holes: Weekday: No
Fee 18 Holes: Weekday: $23.00
Cart Rental: $24.00/18 $13.00/9
Lessons: $35.00/40 minutes **Schools:** N/R
Driving Range: No
Other: Restaurant / Clubhouse / Snack Bar

Tees	Holes	Yards	Par	USGA	Slope
BACK	18	6489	72	75.1	128
MIDDLE	18	6423	72	70.1	126
FRONT	18	5471	72	67.3	118

Weekend: No
Weekend: $28.00
Discounts: Senior & Junior Wkdy
Junior Golf: Yes **Membership:** Residents only
Non-Metal Spikes: Yes

Busy course. Water comes into play on several holes. Active junior golf programs. Open April - November.

	1	2	3	4	5	6	7	8	9
PAR	4	4	3	4	3	5	4	5	4
YARDS	329	347	196	320	189	526	387	507	370
HDCP	18	14	4	16	12	6	2	10	8
	10	11	12	13	14	15	16	17	18
PAR	5	4	3	5	4	4	3	4	4
YARDS	497	421	183	468	427	401	181	351	323
HDCP	9	1	15	17	3	5	13	7	11

Directions: Take Route 3 to Union Street Exit, Braintree. Follow Union Street toward South Braintree. Go under "T" overpass. Take left at lights, take next right at lights. Left at the end. Follow Route 37 to right on Jefferson Street. Course is on the right.

Brookmeadow CC

Canton, MA (781) 828-4444

Club Pro: Joe Videtta
Pro Shop: Full inventory @ discount
Payment: Cash , Visa, MC, Disc
Tee Times: Everyday
Fee 9 Holes: Weekday: $16.00
Fee 18 Holes: Weekday: $25.00
Cart Rental: $28.00/18
Lessons: $35.00/half hour **Schools:** No
Driving Range: $5.00/med. bucket
Other: Clubhouse / Lockers / Showers / Snack bar / Bar-lounge / Function Room

Tees	Holes	Yards	Par	USGA	Slope
BACK	18	6659	72	71.6	123
MIDDLE	18	6309	72	69.2	118
FRONT	18	5606	72	N/A	114

Weekend: $18.00
Weekend: $30.00
Discounts: Sr & Jr. M- Th before 10:30.
Junior Golf: Yes **Membership:** No
Non-Metal Spikes: No

Well conditioned course. Easy to walk, yet challenging to all levels of skill. Open March - December. Inventory discounted at Pro Shop.

	1	2	3	4	5	6	7	8	9
PAR	4	4	4	3	4	3	4	5	5
YARDS	376	387	308	181	346	151	385	475	522
HDCP	11	1	13	15	7	17	9	5	3
	10	11	12	13	14	15	16	17	18
PAR	4	3	5	4	4	3	5	4	4
YARDS	348	179	458	349	358	210	528	344	404
HDCP	10	18	8	12	14	6	2	16	4

Directions: Exit 11A (Neponset St.-Canton) off Route 95. Go 1 mile and take a right before Viaduct (Stone bridge) onto Walpole St. Club is 1 mile on right.

4✪ =Excellent 3✪ =Very Good 2✪ =Good **Greater Boston/South Shore/Cape Cod**

Butternut Farm GC 🚩 9

115 Wheeler Rd., Stow, MA (978) 897-3400

Club Pro: No
Pro Shop: Full inventory
Payment: Cash only
Tee Times: 5 days
Fee 9 Holes: Weekday: $18.00
Fee 18 Holes: Weekday: $27.00
Cart Rental: $24.00
Lessons: No **Schools:** No
Driving Range: No
Other: Clubhouse / Bar-Lounge / Snack Bar

Tees	Holes	Yards	Par	USGA	Slope
BACK	18	6205	70	69.9	125
MIDDLE	18	5755	70	69.9	125
FRONT	18	4778	70	67.0	115

Weekend: $19.00 Twi-light rate
Weekend: $34.00
Discounts: Senior
Junior Golf: N/R **Membership:** Inner Club
Non-Metal Spikes: Yes

Carolina type fairways real tight, bent grass on fairways and tees, tall trees. Signature hole is 8th; stone wall from tee to green. Challenging course. Open April - November.

	1	2	3	4	5	6	7	8	9
PAR	4	3	4	3	4	4	5	4	5
YARDS	314	155	375	150	403	383	434	268	452
HDCP	16	18	2	14	6	4	12	8	10

	10	11	12	13	14	15	16	17	18
PAR	5	3	4	3	4	4	3	4	4
YARDS	600	128	351	190	364	325	173	340	350
HDCP	1	17	5	13	3	9	15	7	11

Directions: Take 495 to Exit 27. Take Route 117 East for approx. 4 mi. Take right onto Wheeler Rd. (or) Route 2 West to Route 62 West. Follow through Stow center to 1st set of lights. Take left. 2nd right is Wheeler Rd.

Cape Cod CC ✪✪ 🚩 10

N. Falmouth, MA (508) 563-9842

Club Pro: Chuck Holmes
Pro Shop: Full inventory
Payment: Cash, MC, Visa
Tee Times: Fri., for following Fri-Sun
Fee 9 Holes: Weekday: $18.00
Fee 18 Holes: Weekday: $32.00
Cart Rental: $26.00/18
Lessons: $25.00/half hour **Schools:** No
Driving Range: No
Other: Clubhouse / Snack bar / Bar-lounge

Tees	Holes	Yards	Par	USGA	Slope
BACK	18	6404	71	70.6	120
MIDDLE	18	6018	71	68.8	116
FRONT	18	5348	72	70.6	119

Weekend: N/A
Weekend: $40.00
Discounts: Senior & Junior
Junior Golf: N/R **Membership:** No
Non-Metal Spikes: Not Required

COUPON

A marvelous Emmet & Tull 1928 classic. It plays longer than indicated by the scorecard statistics. The course sports impeccable fairways lined with pine trees. A Friel Golf Company.

	1	2	3	4	5	6	7	8	9
PAR	4	3	5	4	4	5	4	4	3
YARDS	307	175	460	419	360	509	300	407	156
HDCP	11	13	17	1	7	5	15	3	9

	10	11	12	13	14	15	16	17	18
PAR	4	5	3	5	4	3	3	4	4
YARDS	405	515	220	461	351	180	183	300	310
HDCP	4	6	8	12	2	14	10	18	16

Directions: Take Route 28 South of Bourne Bridge, take right onto Route 151. Course is approximately 3 miles on right.

Captains GC, The ◎◎ 11

Brewster, MA (508) 896-5100

Club Pro: Michael Robichaud, PGA
Pro Shop: Full inventory
Payment: Visa, MC
Tee Times: 2 days adv.
Fee 9 Holes: Weekday: No
Fee 18 Holes: Weekday: $45.00
Cart Rental: $24.00/18 $13.00/9
Lessons: $50.00/ 45 minutes **Schools:** No
Driving Range: $3.00/bucket
Other: Clubhouse / Snack bar

Tees	Holes	Yards	Par	USGA	Slope
BACK	18	6794	72	72.7	130
MIDDLE	18	6176	72	69.8	123
FRONT	18	5388	72	70.6	116

Weekend: No
Weekend: $45.00
Discounts: None
Junior Golf: Yes **Membership:** No
Non-Metal Spikes: Yes

Cornish Silva design. Ranked by *Golf Digest* in top 50 public courses in U.S. Expanding to 27 holes. Tight, tree-lined . Well trapped with contoured fairways. Juniors' Summer camp.

	1	2	3	4	5	6	7	8	9
PAR	4	4	3	5	4	5	4	3	4
YARDS	350	378	157	478	323	501	344	182	317
HDCP	13	5	17	7	11	3	1	15	9
	10	11	12	13	14	15	16	17	18
PAR	4	3	4	4	5	4	4	3	5
YARDS	321	127	370	426	531	331	354	171	575
HDCP	12	18	6	10	2	14	8	16	4

Directions: Take Route 6 to Exit 11. Take right off the ramp and go 1.6 miles. Take right onto Freemans Way. Go 2 miles, course on right.

Cedar Hill Golf Club 12

1137 Park St., Route 27. Stoughton, MA (781) 344-8913

Club Pro: Ronald Dobosz
Pro Shop: Limited inventory
Payment: Cash only
Tee Times: No
Fee 9 Holes: Weekday: No
Fee 18 Holes: Weekday: $13.00
Cart Rental: $20.00/18 $10.00/9
Lessons: $20/30 min. **Schools:** Yes
Driving Range: No
Other: Snack bar / Bar-lounge / Clubhouse

Tees	Holes	Yards	Par	USGA	Slope
BACK	N/A				
MIDDLE	9	4310	66	60.4	92
FRONT	N/A				

Weekend: $20.00
Weekend: $20.00
Discounts: Senior & Junior M-F
Junior Golf: No **Membership:** Yes
Non-Metal Spikes: Yes

New clubhouse with restaurant. Owned by the town of Stoughton, "nice place to come to."

	1	2	3	4	5	6	7	8	9
PAR	4	4	4	4	3	4	3	3	4
YARDS	258	302	286	268	120	324	140	176	281
HDCP	5	9	11	17	15	1	13	3	7
	10	11	12	13	14	15	16	17	18
PAR	4	4	4	4	3	4	3	3	4
YARDS	258	302	286	268	120	324	140	176	281
HDCP	6	10	12	18	16	2	14	4	8

Directions: Route 24, Exit 18B, turn onto Route 27. Course is on left.

4◎ =Excellent 3◎ =Very Good 2◎ =Good **Greater Boston/South Shore/Cape Cod**

Chatham Seaside Links 13

Chatham, MA, (508) 945-4774

Club Pro: John Giardino & Bill Cotter
Pro Shop: Limited inventory
Payment: Cash, MC, Visa
Tee Times: No
Fee 9 Holes: Weekday: $15.00
Fee 18 Holes: Weekday: $24.00
Cart Rental: $21.00/18 $12.60/9
Lessons: $30.00/half hour **Schools:** No
Driving Range: No
Other: Snacks

Tees	Holes	Yards	Par	USGA	Slope
BACK	N/A				
MIDDLE	9	4930	68	65.6	107
FRONT	9	4800	68	65.6	109

Weekend: $15.00
Weekend: $24.00
Discounts: None
Junior Golf: No **Membership:** Yes
Non-Metal Spikes: No

Links style golf course with ocean views. Open April 1 - October 31.

	1	2	3	4	5	6	7	8	9
PAR	4	4	3	3	4	4	4	4	4
YARDS	295	285	150	140	350	305	325	295	320
HDCP	3	11	17	7	1	13	5	15	9
	10	11	12	13	14	15	16	17	18
PAR	4	4	3	3	4	4	4	4	4
YARDS	295	285	150	140	350	305	325	295	320
HDCP	3	11	17	7	1	13	5	15	9

Directions: Route 6 to Exit 11 (Route 137.) Go left to Route 28 and left again to Main Street Chatham. Take Seaview off Main Street to course.

Chequessett Yacht & CC 14

Wellfleet, MA (508) 349-3704

Club Pro: Dick Sjogren
Pro Shop: Full inventory
Payment: Visa, MC
Tee Times: Yes
Fee 9 Holes: Weekday: $27.00
Fee 18 Holes: Weekday: $40.00
Cart Rental: $18.00/18 $12.00/9
Lessons: $25.00/half hour **Schools:** No
Driving Range: No
Other: Snack Bar (seasonal)

Tees	Holes	Yards	Par	USGA	Slope
BACK	N/A				
MIDDLE	9	5169	70	65.1	110
FRONT	9	4608	70	66.2	113

Weekend: $27.00
Weekend: $40.00
Discounts: None
Junior Golf: Yes **Membership:** No
Non-Metal Spikes: No

Limited availability for public play. Call ahead. Scenic nine hole overlooking Wellfleet Harbor. Open May 25 - September 8.

	1	2	3	4	5	6	7	8	9
PAR	4	3	4	5	3	4	4	4	4
YARDS	235	132	365	431	109	299	363	369	278
HDCP	13	15	3	7	17	9	1	5	11
	10	11	12	13	14	15	16	17	18
PAR	4	3	4	5	3	4	4	4	4
YARDS	235	153	342	444	168	243	363	377	263
HDCP	14	16	4	8	18	10	2	6	8

Directions: Turn left at red light on Route 6 toward center, take first left toward Town Harbor - follow road approx. 2 miles.

Cotuit-Highground GC   15

Cotuit, MA   (508) 428-9863

GB CC/ MA

Club Pro: Steve Heher
Pro Shop: Limited inventory
Payment: Cash only
Tee Times: No
Fee 9 Holes: Weekday: N/A
Fee 18 Holes: Weekday: $12.00
Cart Rental: Some available
Lessons: Yes **Schools:** N/R
Driving Range: No
Other: Bar-Lounge / Snack Bar

Tees	Holes	Yards	Par	USGA	Slope
BACK	N/A				
MIDDLE	9	1360	28	N/A	N/A
FRONT	9	1215	28	N/A	N/A

Weekend: N/A
Weekend: $12.00
Discounts: Senior & Junior after 4pm
Junior Golf: Yes **Membership:** Yes
Non-Metal Spikes: Yes

This is a links-style course with very tight greens. Accuracy is very important.

	1	2	3	4	5	6	7	8	9
PAR	3	3	4	3	3	3	3	3	3
YARDS	115	180	290	130	140	110	100	180	115
HDCP	N/A	N/A	N/A	N/A	N/A	N/A	N/A	N/A	N/A
	10	11	12	13	14	15	16	17	18
PAR									
YARDS									
HDCP									

Directions: Take Route 6 to Exit 2 (Route 130 South), left onto Route 28, right onto Main Street in Cotuit Center. Take right onto School Street then second left onto Crocker Neck Road.

Cranberry Valley GC   ✪✪✪   16

Oak St., Harwich, MA   (508) 430-7560

Club Pro: Jim Knowles
Pro Shop: Full inventory
Payment: Cash only
Tee Times: 2 days adv.: 432-4653/mem.
Fee 9 Holes: Weekday: No
Fee 18 Holes: Weekday: $45.00
Cart Rental: $20.00/18 $12.00/9
Lessons: $30.00/halfhour **Schools:** N/R
Driving Range: $3.00-$5.00
Other: Snack bar

Tees	Holes	Yards	Par	USGA	Slope
BACK	NA				
MIDDLE	18	6296	72	70.4	125
FRONT	18	5518	72	71.5	115

Weekend: No
Weekend: $45.00
Discounts: None
Junior Golf: Yes **Membership:** Yes, residents
Non-Metal Spikes: N/R

Tree-lined gently rolling fairways. Bent grass greens. Very large teeing areas. 53 sand bunkers. Open March - December. Seasonal rates, inquire.

	1	2	3	4	5	6	7	8	9
PAR	4	5	4	3	4	4	3	5	4
YARDS	357	473	382	188	424	323	164	502	378
HDCP	9	11	3	15	1	13	17	7	5
	10	11	12	13	14	15	16	17	18
PAR	4	4	4	3	5	4	4	3	5
YARDS	350	345	361	165	439	303	438	211	493
HDCP	6	14	8	18	12	16	2	10	4

Directions: Take Exit 10 off Route 6. Take a right off the ramp and take first left at the flashing yellow light (Queen Anne Road). Take third right (Oak Street). 1/2 mile on left.

4✪ =Excellent 3✪ = Very Good 2✪ = Good **Greater Boston/South Shore/Cape Cod**

D.W. Fields Golf Course   17

Brockton, MA (508) 580-7855

Club Pro: Gerry Mackedon, Brian Mattos
Pro Shop: Full inventory
Payment: Visa, MC
Tee Times: No

Tees	Holes	Yards	Par	USGA	Slope
BACK	18	5972	70	68.4	120
MIDDLE	18	5630	70	66.9	116
FRONT	18	5370	70	70.1	111

Fee 9 Holes: Weekday: No **Weekend:** No
Fee 18 Holes: Weekday: $18.00 **Weekend:** $22.00
Cart Rental: $22.00/18 $11.00/9 **Discounts:** None
Lessons: $30.00/half hour **Schools:** No **Junior Golf:** Yes **Membership:** Yes
Driving Range: No **Non-Metal Spikes:** No
Other: Snack bar

The course is flat with no water holes. Considered an easy walker. Open year round. Greens fee $12.00 after 5 pm. Dress code.

	1	2	3	4	5	6	7	8	9
PAR	4	5	5	4	3	4	4	3	4
YARDS	305	485	485	300	165	340	335	135	355
HDCP	18	4	6	2	10	12	14	16	8

	10	11	12	13	14	15	16	17	18
PAR	4	4	4	4	3	4	4	3	4
YARDS	315	340	360	405	125	300	345	175	360
HDCP	15	9	3	1	17	13	5	11	7

Directions: Take Route 24 to Brockton/Stoughton Exit, go toward Stoughton, take right at first light (Oak Street).

Dennis Highlands   18

Dennis, MA (508) 385-8347

Club Pro: Jay Haberl
Pro Shop: Full inventory
Payment: MC, Visa, Cash
Tee Times: 4 days adv.

Tees	Holes	Yards	Par	USGA	Slope
BACK	18	6400	71	70.4	118
MIDDLE	18	6076	71	68.7	115
FRONT	18	4927	71	67.4	112

Fee 9 Holes: Weekday: $22.00 **Weekend:** $22.00
Fee 18 Holes: Weekday: $40.00 **Weekend:** $40.00
Cart Rental: $24.00/18 $13.75/9 **Discounts:** None
Lessons: $25.00/half hour **Schools:** Yes **Junior Golf:** Yes **Membership:** Yes
Driving Range: $5.00/lg., $3.00/sm. **Non-Metal Spikes:** Yes
Other: Clubhouse / Restaurant / Bar-lounge

Opened in 1984, architect Mike Hurdsdan made full use of the hilly terrain. Putting is the key to a good round since several of the greens are multi-tiered or have intimidating swales.

	1	2	3	4	5	6	7	8	9
PAR	4	5	3	4	4	4	3	5	3
YARDS	304	502	152	334	352	398	161	467	140
HDCP	16	4	15	14	9	1	12	7	18

	10	11	12	13	14	15	16	17	18
PAR	4	3	4	4	4	5	3	4	5
YARDS	374	159	366	392	381	535	168	377	514
HDCP	9	17	10	7	11	3	13	5	2

Directions: Take Route 6 to Exit 9. Take left off ramp, follow 1/2 mile. Take left onto Access Road, at end take right onto Old Bass River Road, course is 2 miles up on left.

Dennis Pines GC

✪✪ 19 ▶

Rt. 134, S. Dennis, MA (508) 385-8347

Club Pro: Jay Haberl
Pro Shop: Full inventory
Payment: MC, Visa, Cash
Tee Times: 4 days adv.

Tees	Holes	Yards	Par	USGA	Slope
BACK	18	7029	72	71.9	127
MIDDLE	18	6525	72	71	122
FRONT	18	5798	72	73.1	122

Fee 9 Holes: Weekday: $22.00 **Weekend:** $22.00
Fee 18 Holes: Weekday: $40.00 **Weekend:** $40.00
Cart Rental: $24.00/18 $13.75/9 **Discounts:** None
Lessons: $25.00/half hour **Schools:** Yes **Junior Golf:** Yes **Membership:** Yes
Driving Range: $5.00/lg., $3.00/sm. **Non-Metal Spikes:** Yes
Other: Snack bar / Restaurant / Bar-lounge

Course requires accuracy off the tees with plenty of trouble off the fairways. Water comes into play on four holes. One of the busiest courses on the Cape.

	1	2	3	4	5	6	7	8	9
PAR	4	4	5	3	5	4	3	4	4
YARDS	373	369	471	188	476	423	187	442	389
HDCP	9	7	11	17	13	5	15	1	3

	10	11	12	13	14	15	16	17	18
PAR	4	4	5	3	4	5	4	3	4
YARDS	351	357	518	172	405	472	344	183	405
HDCP	8	10	2	16	4	14	12	18	6

Directions: Take Route 6 to Exit 9, take left off ramp, follow Route 134 for 2 miles, course is on right.

Easton Country Club

20 ▶

S. Easton, MA (508) 238-2500

Club Pro: Chandler Phinney
Pro Shop: Full inventory
Payment: MC, Visa, Cash
Tee Times: 2 days adv.

Tees	Holes	Yards	Par	USGA	Slope
BACK	18	6328	71	68.9	119
MIDDLE	18	6050	71	67.5	114
FRONT	18	5271	71	70.2	112

Fee 9 Holes: Weekday: No **Weekend:** No
Fee 18 Holes: Weekday: $27.00 M-Th **Weekend:** $30.00
Cart Rental: $22.00/18 **Discounts:** None
Lessons: $30.00/half hour **Schools:** No **Junior Golf:** No **Membership:** Junior
Driving Range: $4.00/bucket **Non-Metal Spikes:** Yes
Other: Clubhouse / Lockers / Showers / Snack bar / Bar-lounge / Function room

A par 4 over water, a par 3 over a creek, and two long par 4s have taken the wheels off of many a good round. Twilight rates.

	1	2	3	4	5	6	7	8	9
PAR	4	5	4	3	4	3	4	4	5
YARDS	390	486	269	136	382	159	411	304	488
HDCP	2	10	12	16	6	8	4	18	14

	10	11	12	13	14	15	16	17	18
PAR	4	4	4	5	3	4	3	4	4
YARDS	331	353	330	519	140	361	162	410	419
HDCP	13	11	17	9	15	3	7	1	5

Directions: Take Route 24 South to Exit 17B. Take Route 123 West to Route 138 South to Purchase Street on right (approx. 2 miles). Take a right onto Purchase Street, course is 7/10 mile on left.

4✪=Excellent 3✪=Very Good 2✪=Good **Greater Boston/South Shore/Cape Cod**

Falmouth Country Club

Falmouth, MA (508) 548-3211

Club Pro: Lenny Beford
Pro Shop: Full inventory
Payment: All major cards
Tee Times: 1 week adv.
Fee 9 Holes: Weekday: No **Weekend:** No
Fee 18 Holes: Weekday: $30.00 **Weekend:** $40/$45 F/S/S/H
Cart Rental: $24.00/18 $12.00/9 **Discounts:** Junior,after 5 M-TH.
Lessons: No **Schools:** No **Junior Golf:** No **Membership:** No
Driving Range: $5.00/bucket **Non-Metal Spikes:** No
Other: Restaurant / Clubhouse / Hotel / Snack bar / Bar-lounge

Tees	Holes	Yards	Par	USGA	Slope
BACK	18	6535	72	70.0	118
MIDDLE	18	6227	72	68.8	114
FRONT	18	5754	72	74	125

Course redesigned for 1999. A straight course; you get what you see. Most interesting shot is the down hill 125-yard par 3 fourth hole. Water comes into play on front nine. Open year round.

	1	2	3	4	5	6	7	8	9
PAR	4	3	4	3	5	5	4	3	4
YARDS	380	155	365	125	535	495	370	165	370
HDCP	5	15	11	17	1	3	7	13	9
	10	11	12	13	14	15	16	17	18
PAR	5	3	4	4	4	4	5	4	4
YARDS	465	152	385	280	420	340	530	330	365
HDCP	12	16	6	18	4	10	2	14	8

Directions: Take Route 28 South into Falmouth. Take right onto Route 151 East, follow 3.5 miles to Sandwich Road on right. Look for signs, left onto Carriage Shop Road.

Farm Neck Golf Club

Oak Bluffs, MA (508) 693-3057

Club Pro: Mike Zoll
Pro Shop: Full inventory
Payment: Visa, MC, Amex, Cash
Tee Times: 2 days adv.
Fee 9 Holes: Weekday: $50.00 (In Season) **Weekend:** $50.00 (In Season)
Fee 18 Holes: Weekday: $80.00 (In Season) **Weekend:** $80.00 (In Season)
Cart Rental: $26.00/18 $13.20/9 **Discounts:** None
Lessons: $30.00/half hour **Schools:** No **Junior Golf:** Yes **Membership:** Waiting List
Driving Range: $6/lg. $4/med. $2/sm **Non-Metal Spikes:** Yes
Other: Restaurant / Bar-Lounge / Snack bar / Lockers / Showers

Tees	Holes	Yards	Par	USGA	Slope
BACK	18	6807	72	72.1	129
MIDDLE	18	6155	72	68.9	126
FRONT	18	5034	72	68.3	120

Scenic and challenging, 65-70 traps in total. Overlooks Nantucket Sound. Front 9 are easier than back. Great course for match play. Off season fee- $36/18, $24/9. Interim season fee- $50/18, $33/9.

	1	2	3	4	5	6	7	8	9
PAR	4	5	4	3	4	3	4	5	3
YARDS	360	476	322	151	325	182	357	457	164
HDCP	2	6	16	18	12	10	8	4	14
	10	11	12	13	14	15	16	17	18
PAR	4	5	4	4	4	3	4	4	5
YARDS	375	519	381	330	320	165	382	365	524
HDCP	7	11	1	17	15	13	9	3	5

Directions: On Country Road in Oak Bluffs, Martha's Vineyard.

Fresh Pond Golf Club

Cambridge, MA (617) 349-6282

Club Pro: Robert Carey
Pro Shop: Full inventory
Payment: Cash, Check
Tee Times: No
Fee 9 Holes: Weekday: $16.00
Fee 18 Holes: Weekday: $23.00
Cart Rental: $11 pp/18 $6 pp/9
Lessons: $30-$35/half hour **Schools:** No
Driving Range: No
Other: Snack bar

Tees	Holes	Yards	Par	USGA	Slope
BACK	9	6322	70	70.2	120
MIDDLE	9	6000	70	68.9	114
FRONT	9	5420	70	70.0	113

Weekend: $19.00
Weekend: $29.00
Discounts: Senior & Junior
Junior Golf: Yes **Membership:** Yes
Non-Metal Spikes: Yes

Great course for intermediates and beginners that is located on the edge of Fresh Pond. Season tickets available. Open April - December.

	1	2	3	4	5	6	7	8	9
PAR	4	4	3	4	5	3	4	3	5
YARDS	417	312	169	401	476	221	370	146	465
HDCP	1	13	17	5	3	11	9	15	7
	10	11	12	13	14	15	16	17	18
PAR	4	4	3	4	5	3	4	3	5
YARDS	417	312	169	401	476	221	370	146	465
HDCP	2	14	18	6	4	12	10	16	8

Directions: Take Route 2 to Huron Avenue to course.

George Wright GC

Hyde Park, MA (617) 361-8313

Club Pro: Donald Lyons
Pro Shop: Full inventory
Payment: Visa, MC
Tee Times: Weekends, 11 am on Th.
Fee 9 Holes: Weekday: $13.50
Fee 18 Holes: Weekday: $24.00
Cart Rental: $23.00/18 $12.00/9
Lessons: $50/hour **Schools:** No
Driving Range: No
Other: Snack bar / Bar-lounge

Tees	Holes	Yards	Par	USGA	Slope
BACK	18	6367	70	69.5	126
MIDDLE	18	6166	70	68.6	123
FRONT	18	5054	70	70.3	115

Weekend: $14.50 after 4 pm
Weekend: $27.00
Discounts: Junior
Junior Golf: Yes **Membership:** Yes
Non-Metal Spikes: No

Restored by Bill Flynn, it was built by Donald Ross during the Depression. The front nine are challenging; the back nine are varied. Reduced resident rates.

	1	2	3	4	5	6	7	8	9
PAR	4	4	5	3	4	4	4	3	4
YARDS	367	313	480	150	400	380	387	162	440
HDCP	11	13	5	17	3	7	9	15	1
	10	11	12	13	14	15	16	17	18
PAR	4	4	4	4	3	5	4	3	4
YARDS	449	347	399	369	182	493	318	158	372
HDCP	2	10	6	8	16	4	14	18	12

Directions: Take Route 1 to Washington Street (left) in Hyde Park. Take a right onto Beach Street. Follow signs to course.

4✪ = Excellent 3✪ = Very Good 2✪ = Good **Greater Boston/South Shore/Cape Cod**

Glen Ellen CC 25

Rt.115, Millis, MA (508) 376-2775

Club Pro: Harry E. Parker III
Pro Shop: Full inventory
Payment: Visa, MC, Amex
Tee Times: 7 days adv.
Fee 9 Holes: Weekday: $16.00 M-Th.
Fee 18 Holes: Weekday: $22.00 M-Th.
Cart Rental: $26.00/18
Lessons: $25-$30/half hour **Schools:** No
Driving Range: $4.00/ bucket
Other: Snack bar/ Showers/ Bar-Lounge

Tees	Holes	Yards	Par	USGA	Slope
BACK	18	6552	72	71.6	123
MIDDLE	18	6073	72	69.2	118
FRONT	18	5123	72	69.2	121

Weekend: N/A
Weekend: $45 until 1, cart inc.
Discounts: Senior(50+),M-Th/$16
Junior Golf: N/R **Membership:** Yes
Non-Metal Spikes: Yes

COUPON

Many unique situations for all levels, including par 3 island hole. Twilight rates F-Sun. Open year round depending on weather.

	1	2	3	4	5	6	7	8	9
PAR	4	4	4	5	3	5	4	3	5
YARDS	428	332	363	428	145	506	335	119	445
HDCP	1	13	5	7	15	3	9	17	11
	10	11	12	13	14	15	16	17	18
PAR	5	4	3	4	4	3	4	4	4
YARDS	500	368	178	382	353	155	375	315	346
HDCP	2	14	16	4	12	10	6	18	8

Directions: Take I-495 to Route 109 East (Exit 19). Left at 3rd light (4 miles) onto Holliston. Right after 2 miles onto Goulding Street. Course is 1 mile on left.

Green Harbor Golf Club 26

Marshfield, MA (781)834-7303

Club Pro: Erik Nelson, PGA
Pro Shop: Full inventory
Payment: Cash only
Tee Times: 2 days/18, same day/9
Fee 9 Holes: Weekday: $17.00
Fee 18 Holes: Weekday: $28.00
Cart Rental: Pull carts $3.50
Lessons: Yes **Schools:** No
Driving Range: No
Other: Clubhouse / Snack bar / Lounge

Tees	Holes	Yards	Par	USGA	Slope
BACK	18	6211	71	69.1	115
MIDDLE	18	5808	71	67.3	111
FRONT	18	5355	71	69.3	109

Weekend: $19.00
Weekend: $32.00
Discounts: None
Junior Golf: Yes **Membership:** No
Non-Metal Spikes: No

Flat, open course. Water on five holes. Features velvet bent grass. Open March 15 - December 15.

	1	2	3	4	5	6	7	8	9
PAR	4	4	4	4	3	4	5	3	4
YARDS	404	357	401	307	175	333	544	176	333
HDCP	3	9	5	13	17	11	1	15	9
	10	11	12	13	14	15	16	17	18
PAR	4	5	3	4	5	4	4	3	4
YARDS	381	523	199	292	484	375	402	173	352
HDCP	4	2	14	16	10	6	8	18	12

Directions: Take Route 3 to Exit 12 (Route 139). 139 East 4.5 miles. Right on Webster Street, 1 mile on left.

Harwich Port Golf Club

27

GB CC/ MA

Harwich Port, MA (508) 432-0250

Club Pro: No
Pro Shop: Limited inventory
Payment: Cash only
Tee Times: No
Fee 9 Holes: Weekday: $14.00
Fee 18 Holes: Weekday: $23.00
Cart Rental: Pull carts
Lessons: No **Schools:** No
Driving Range: No
Other: Snack bar

Tees	Holes	Yards	Par	USGA	Slope
BACK	N/A				
MIDDLE	9	5076	68	N/A	N/A
FRONT	N/A				

Weekend: $14.00
Weekend: $23.00
Discounts: None
Junior Golf: No **Membership:** Yes
Non-Metal Spikes: No

The course is considered an easy walker. Recommended for beginners and senior citizens. Members only after 5:30.

	1	2	3	4	5	6	7	8	9
PAR	4	3	4	4	4	4	3	4	4
YARDS	358	170	340	330	325	255	155	295	310
HDCP	1	9	7	11	3	15	17	5	13
	10	11	12	13	14	15	16	17	18
PAR	4	3	4	4	4	4	3	4	4
YARDS	358	170	340	330	325	255	155	295	310
HDCP	2	10	8	12	4	16	18	6	14

Directions: Take Route 6 to Exit 9 or 10. Take Route 28 to South Street. Course 200 yards.

Heritage Hill CC

28

Lakeville, MA (508) 947-7743

Club Pro: Bill Raynor
Pro Shop: Full inventory
Payment: Visa, MC, Amex, Disc
Tee Times: Yes
Fee 9 Holes: Weekday: N/A
Fee 18 Holes: Weekday: $21.00
Cart Rental: $19.00/18
Lessons: $15.00 **Schools:** No
Driving Range: No
Other: Bar-Lounge / Snack Bar / Showers

Tees	Holes	Yards	Par	USGA	Slope
BACK	18	3012	54	54.7	84
MIDDLE	18	2575	54	54.7	84
FRONT	18	2155	54	54.7	84

Weekend: N/A
Weekend: $24.00
Discounts: Senior & Junior
Junior Golf: No **Membership:** Yes
Non-Metal Spikes: Yes

A very well-maintained executive par 3 course. Narrow fairways. Water is a factor on seven holes. Open year round.

	1	2	3	4	5	6	7	8	9
PAR	3	3	3	3	3	3	3	3	3
YARDS	155	190	160	140	145	155	115	170	145
HDCP	3	1	11	16	13	5	17	9	7
	10	11	12	13	14	15	16	17	18
PAR	3	3	3	3	3	3	3	3	3
YARDS	140	130	125	110	145	120	145	160	125
HDCP	8	4	15	18	12	14	2	6	10

Directions: I-495 to Route 18 to Lakeville. Continue through two traffic lights. Take Highland Rd. on the right, followed by an immediate right to Heritage Hill Rd. Course is 1 mile on left.

Highland Links

29

N. Truro, MA (508) 487-9201

Club Pro: Manuel Macara
Pro Shop: Full inventory
Payment: Cash only
Tee Times: 2 days adv.
Fee 9 Holes: Weekday: $16.00
Fee 18 Holes: Weekday: $30.00
Cart Rental: $21.00/18 $13.65/9
Lessons: $25.00/half hour **Schools:** No
Driving Range: No
Other: Club house / Snack bar

Tees	Holes	Yards	Par	USGA	Slope
BACK	N/A				
MIDDLE	9	5299	70	65.0	103
FRONT	9	4587	72	66.6	109

Weekend: $16.00
Weekend: $30.00
Discounts: None
Junior Golf: Yes **Membership:** Seasonal
Non-Metal Spikes: N/R

Cape Cod's oldest golf course (1892). A true Scottish links course. Tee placements on back nine. Open April 7 - November 1. Dress code. Seasonal Pass available.

	1	2	3	4	5	6	7	8	9
PAR	4	5	3	4	4	5	3	4	3
YARDS	250	460	160	346	380	464	171	353	136
HDCP	11	7	15	5	1	3	13	9	17
	10	11	12	13	14	15	16	17	18
PAR	4	4	3	5	4	5	3	4	3
YARDS	242	377	118	415	361	453	159	349	105
HDCP	12	6	16	4	2	10	14	8	18

Directions: Take Route 6 to Truro. Course is just past the Truro elementary school. (Look for signs on Route 6.)o

Holly Ridge Golf Club

✪✪✪ **30**

S. Sandwich, MA (508) 428-5577

Club Pro: J. Frost, J. Enright, & D. Pascal
Pro Shop: Full inventory
Payment: Visa, MC, Amex
Tee Times: 7 days in adv.
Fee 9 Holes: Weekday: $15.00
Fee 18 Holes: Weekday: $23.00
Cart Rental: $18.00/18
Lessons: $40/half hour **Schools:** Jr. & Sr.
Driving Range: $8.50/Jumbo bucket
Other: Restaurant / Bar-lounge.

Tees	Holes	Yards	Par	USGA	Slope
BACK	18	2952	54	N/A	N/A
MIDDLE	18	2715	54	N/A	N/A
FRONT	18	2194	54	N/A	N/A

Weekend: $23.00
Weekend: $23.00
Discounts: Jr., M&Th. 1/2 price, Sr.
Junior Golf: Yes **Membership:** No
Non-Metal Spikes: No

Par 3 designed by Geoffrey Cornish. Voted one of the country's top 75 women friendly courses two years running. Open year round. Twilight fee in season. www.hollyridgegolf.com

	1	2	3	4	5	6	7	8	9
PAR	3	3	3	3	3	3	3	3	3
YARDS	163	183	142	158	120	184	187	130	202
HDCP	9	5	13	11	17	7	3	15	1
	10	11	12	13	14	15	16	17	18
PAR	3	3	3	3	3	3	3	3	3
YARDS	124	167	183	128	189	188	211	138	155
HDCP	16	10	6	18	8	4	2	14	12

Directions: Take Route 3 South over Sagamore Bridge, follow Route 6 to Exit 2. Go South on Route 130 for 1.6 miles, take left onto Cotuit Road for 1.4 miles, and left onto Farmersville Road for 1.6 miles. Follow signs for HRGC.

Hyannis Golf Club

Hyannis, MA (508) 362-2606

Club Pro: Mick Herron, PGA
Pro Shop: Full inventory
Payment: Visa, MC, Amex, Disc.
Tee Times: 12 months!
Fee 9 Holes: Weekday: $25.00
Fee 18 Holes: Weekday: $40.00
Cart Rental: $28
Lessons: $35.00/half hour **Schools:** Jr. & Sr.
Driving Range: $5.00/bucket
Other: 3 practice greens/ dining room/ bar & lounge/ snack bar/ lockers/ outings accepted

Tees	Holes	Yards	Par	USGA	Slope
BACK	18	6711	71	69.4	121
MIDDLE	18	6002	71	68.2	115
FRONT	18	5149	71	69.7	125

Weekend: $30.00
Weekend: $50.00
Discounts: Senior
Junior Golf: Yes **Membership:** Yes
Non-Metal Spikes: Preferred

Noted for the best greens of any public course on Cape Cod. Home of the Cape Cod Open- NEPGA Oldmobile Scramble- Southeastern Mass. Amateur. Outings accepted. **www.golfcapecod.com**

	1	2	3	4	5	6	7	8	9
PAR	4	4	4	4	5	4	3	3	4
YARDS	370	420	380	417	554	405	160	211	440
HDCP	13	1	9	3	5	15	17	11	7
	10	11	12	13	14	15	16	17	18
PAR	4	4	4	4	5	3	4	4	4
YARDS	487	230	387	327	575	149	370	400	429
HDCP	8	16	4	12	6	18	14	10	2

Directions: Take Route 6 (Mid-Cape Highway) to Exit 6 (Route 132). Go south on Route 132 for 1/4 mile and golf course is on left.

Kings Way Golf Course

Yarmouthport, MA (508) 362-8820

Club Pro: Trevor Bateman, Michael Surette
Pro Shop: Full inventory
Payment: MC, Visa, Cash
Tee Times: 5 days adv.
Fee 9 Holes: Weekday: $45.00
Fee 18 Holes: Weekday: $45.00
Cart Rental: Included
Lessons: $30.00/half hour **Schools:** No
Driving Range: No
Other: Restaurant / Clubhouse / Bar-lounge / Snack Bar / Lockers / Showers

Tees	Holes	Yards	Par	USGA	Slope
BACK	18	3953	59	60.5	95
MIDDLE	18	3629	59	58.8	94
FRONT	18	2937	59	55.8	85

Weekend: $45.00
Weekend: $45.00
Discounts: None
Junior Golf: No **Membership:** No
Non-Metal Spikes: Yes

The course has varied terrain and narrow fairways. Golf carts are required before 2:00 pm. Pull carts not permitted. Open March 15 - December 15.

	1	2	3	4	5	6	7	8	9
PAR	4	3	3	4	3	3	3	3	4
YARDS	346	198	155	375	207	181	140	147	409
HDCP	5	7	15	1	5	9	13	11	3
	10	11	12	13	14	15	16	17	18
PAR	3	3	4	3	3	3	3	3	4
YARDS	215	193	297	167	167	138	181	211	354
HDCP	14	12	4	18	8	10	16	6	2

Directions: From Route 6, take Exit 8. Go north to Route 6A. Turn right at flashing yellow light. Course is on the left.

4✪ =Excellent 3✪ =Very Good 2✪ =Good **Greater Boston/South Shore/Cape Cod**

Lakeville Country Club 33

Lakeville, MA (508) 947-6630

Club Pro: No
Pro Shop: Full inventory
Payment: Visa, MC, Disc, Cash
Tee Times: 1 week adv.
Fee 9 Holes: Weekday: $18.00
Fee 18 Holes: Weekday: $27.00
Cart Rental: $22.00/18
Lessons: No **Schools:** No
Driving Range: No
Other: Restaurant / Clubhouse / Snack bar / Bar-lounge

Tees	Holes	Yards	Par	USGA	Slope
BACK	18	6274	72	70.1	123
MIDDLE	18	5853	72	68.5	118
FRONT	18	5297	72	70.0	113

Weekend: $21.00
Weekend: $32.00
Discounts: None
Junior Golf: No **Membership:** No
Non-Metal Spikes: Yes

New owner and superintendent have lengthened and created a challenging layout. Large fast greens. Open year round.

	1	2	3	4	5	6	7	8	9
PAR	4	4	4	4	5	5	3	5	3
YARDS	300	295	310	390	510	500	175	495	150
HDCP	10	14	12	1	8	4	16	6	15
	10	11	12	13	14	15	16	17	18
PAR	4	4	4	4	5	4	3	3	4
YARDS	305	350	410	300	440	310	130	138	345
HDCP	5	11	2	13	7	9	18	17	3

Directions: Take I-495 to Exit 5. Go south on Route 18. Take left at first light to Route 79, then first right on to Clear Pond. Entrance is 1/4 mile on right.

Leo J. Martin GC 34

Weston, MA (781) 894-4903

Club Pro: Mike Wortis, PGA
Pro Shop: Full inventory
Payment: Cash only
Tee Times: 2 days adv
Fee 9 Holes: Weekday: $12.00
Fee 18 Holes: Weekday: $17.00
Cart Rental: $23.00/18, $12.60/9
Lessons: $35.00/half hour **Schools:** Jr.
Driving Range: $5.00/bucket
Other: Snack bar

Tees	Holes	Yards	Par	USGA	Slope
BACK	18	6320	72	68.6	120
MIDDLE	18	6140	72	68.8	115
FRONT	18	6140	75	67.9	115

Weekend: $12.00
Weekend: $20.00
Discounts: Senior & Junior
Junior Golf: Yes **Membership:** No
Non-Metal Spikes: Not Required

All summer, golf academy. Considered an easy walker. Excellent course for beginners and seniors.

	1	2	3	4	5	6	7	8	9
PAR	4	5	3	5	3	4	4	4	4
YARDS	315	500	155	525	140	360	325	355	265
HDCP	9	7	13	1	15	3	11	5	17
	10	11	12	13	14	15	16	17	18
PAR	3	4	3	4	4	4	5	4	5
YARDS	140	290	240	400	420	360	530	260	560
HDCP	16	14	10	8	4	12	6	18	2

Directions: Take Mass Pike to Weston Exit (Route 30), take first left onto Park Road to course on left.

Little Harbor CC

Wareham, MA (508) 295-2617

Club Pro: Shawn Lapworth
Pro Shop: Full inventory
Payment: Visa, MC, Cash
Tee Times: 3 days adv.
Fee 9 Holes: Weekday: $14.00
Fee 18 Holes: Weekday: $20.00
Cart Rental: $18.00/18 $9.00/9
Lessons: $35.00/40 minutes **Schools:** No
Driving Range: No
Other: Clubhouse / Snack bar

Tees	Holes	Yards	Par	USGA	Slope
BACK	N/A				
MIDDLE	18	3038	56	54.4	79
FRONT	18	2692	56	51.9	72

Weekend: $14.00
Weekend: $20.00
Discounts: Senior & Junior
Junior Golf: N/R **Membership:** No
Non-Metal Spikes: No

COUPON

35 — GB CC/MA

Best greens in New England. Holes range from 110 yards to 315 yards. Great condition. Open year round.

	1	2	3	4	5	6	7	8	9
PAR	3	3	3	3	3	4	4	3	3
YARDS	100	135	142	138	225	291	275	162	189
HDCP	17	15	13	7	1	5	9	11	3
	10	**11**	**12**	**13**	**14**	**15**	**16**	**17**	**18**
PAR	3	3	3	3	3	3	3	3	3
YARDS	205	125	140	132	183	100	156	132	208
HDCP	4	10	14	12	6	18	8	16	2

Directions: Take Route 6 to Minot Forest road to Great Neck Road.

Lost Brook Golf Club

Norwood, MA (781) 769-2550

Club Pro: No
Pro Shop: Limited inventory
Payment: Cash only
Tee Times: Weekends
Fee 9 Holes: Weekday: $13.00
Fee 18 Holes: Weekday: $19.00
Cart Rental: Yes (Pull carts) $2.00
Lessons: No **Schools:** No
Driving Range: No
Other: Clubhouse / Snack Bar

Tees	Holes	Yards	Par	USGA	Slope
BACK	N/A				
MIDDLE	18	3002	54	N/A	N/A
FRONT	18	2468	58	N/A	N/A

Weekend: No
Weekend: $22.00
Discounts: Senior & Junior
Junior Golf: No **Membership:** No
Non-Metal Spikes: Yes

36

Expertly maintained Par 3 golf course. Tree lined fairways surround the elevated greens.

	1	2	3	4	5	6	7	8	9
PAR	3	3	3	3	3	3	3	3	3
YARDS	90	208	212	210	141	158	170	190	102
HDCP	15	5	3	1	13	11	9	7	17
	10	**11**	**12**	**13**	**14**	**15**	**16**	**17**	**18**
PAR	3	3	3	3	3	3	3	3	3
YARDS	162	171	168	167	126	148	202	190	187
HDCP	8	14	12	10	18	16	2	4	6

Directions: Take Route 128 to Exit 13. Follow signs for 1.5 miles to course.

4✪ =Excellent 3✪ =Very Good 2✪ =Good   **Greater Boston/South Shore/Cape Cod**

Maynard Country Club   37

Maynard, MA (508) 897-9885

Club Pro: Jim Duggan, Golf Dir.
Pro Shop: Limited inventory
Payment: Visa, MC
Tee Times: Wknds after 2
Fee 9 Holes: Weekday: $20.00
Fee 18 Holes: Weekday: $35.00
Cart Rental: $18.00/18 $10.00/9
Lessons: No **Schools:** No
Driving Range: No
Weekend: $20.00
Weekend: $35.00
Discounts: None
Junior Golf: N/R **Membership:** Yes
Non-Metal Spikes: Yes
Other: Clubhouse / Lockers / Showers / Snack bar / Bar-lounge

Tees	Holes	Yards	Par	USGA	Slope
BACK					
MIDDLE	9	5379	68	66.1	121
FRONT	9	5024	69	69.5	121

The course has narrow fairways with two significant water hazards. Some holes are very close together.

	1	2	3	4	5	6	7	8	9
PAR	4	4	3	4	4	3	4	4	4
YARDS	375	358	143	311	353	204	342	328	290
HDCP	6	10	17	15	2	7	4	12	14
	10	11	12	13	14	15	16	17	18
PAR	4	4	3	4	4	3	4	4	4
YARDS	375	358	143	345	353	141	342	328	290
HDCP	5	9	16	8	1	18	3	11	13

Directions: Take Route 2 East or West to Route 27 South. 3 miles on left.

Miacomet Golf Club   38

Nantucket, MA (508) 325-0333

Club Pro: Jim LeBlanc
Pro Shop: Full inventory
Payment: Visa, MC, Amex, Disc
Tee Times: 1 week adv.
Fee 9 Holes: Weekday: $24.00
Fee 18 Holes: Weekday: $45.00
Cart Rental: $30.00/half 16.00/9
Lessons: $35.00/half hour **Schools:** Yes
Driving Range: $4.00/lg. bucket
Weekend: $24.00
Weekend: $45.00
Discounts: None
Junior Golf: Yes **Membership:** No
Non-Metal Spikes: Yes
Other: Restaurant / Clubhouse / Snack bar / Bar-lounge

Tees	Holes	Yards	Par	USGA	Slope
BACK					
MIDDLE	9	6674	74	72.1	118
FRONT	9	3002	38	73.5	118

A links-style sea side course. Definite Scottish links look. Resident, non-resident fee schedules. Fees subject to change.

	1	2	3	4	5	6	7	8	9
PAR	4	4	4	4	3	4	5	4	5
YARDS	374	332	384	367	163	407	463	378	469
HDCP	9	15	13	3	17	5	11	1	7
	10	11	12	13	14	15	16	17	18
PAR	4	4	4	4	3	4	5	4	5
YARDS	374	332	384	367	163	407	463	378	469
HDCP	10	16	14	4	18	6	12	2	8

Directions: Nantucket is an island 25 miles off the coast of Cape Cod. Airport and ferry boat dock are in Hyannis.

Millwood Farm Golf Course   39

Framingham, MA (508)877-1221

Club Pro: No
Pro Shop: Limited inventory
Payment: Visa, MC
Tee Times: 5 days advance
Fee 9 Holes: Weekday: N/A
Fee 18 Holes: Weekday: $18.00 (14 holes)
Cart Rental: $16.75
Lessons: No **Schools:** No
Driving Range: No
Other: Snack bar

Tees	Holes	Yards	Par	USGA	Slope
BACK					
MIDDLE	14	3798	53	63.1	102
FRONT					

Weekend: N/A
Weekend: $21.00 (14 holes)
Discounts: N/R
Junior Golf: No **Membership:** N/R
Non-Metal Spikes: Yes

A friendly family owned course, with 14 holes. Open April to November.

	1	2	3	4	5	6	7	8	9
PAR	4	3	4	4	4	3	4	4	5
YARDS	338	112	306	230	363	156	281	312	438
HDCP	3	14	10	11	1	8	6	9	5
	10	11	12	13	14	15	16	17	18
PAR	4	3	4	3	4				
YARDS	362	160	295	138	307				
HDCP	2	12	4	13	7				

Directions: Route 9 west from route 128 to route 30 exit (Edgell Road). At light, make right onto Edgell Road for 1 mile. Turn left onto Belknap Road, then third right onto Millwood Street.

Mink Meadows GC   40

Vineyard Haven, MA (508) 693-0600

Club Pro: Allan Menne
Pro Shop: Full inventory
Payment: Visa, MC, checks, cash
Tee Times: 2 days adv.
Fee 9 Holes: Weekday: $30.00
Fee 18 Holes: Weekday: $50.00
Cart Rental: $25.00/18 $17.00/9
Lessons: $30/30 min. **Schools:** Jr. clinics Wed.
Driving Range: $4/lg. $3/sm.
Other: Snack Bar

Tees	Holes	Yards	Par	USGA	Slope
BACK	9	6045	71	69.1	124
MIDDLE	9	6004	70	68.6	118
FRONT	9	5521	71	69.5	118

Weekend: $27.00
Weekend: $45.00
Discounts: Junior- membership discount only
Junior Golf: Yes **Membership:** Yes
Non-Metal Spikes: Yes

Excellent layout designed by Wayne Stiles in the 1930's. Ongoing improvements under a master plan by Ron Prichard to restore it's character and update the course.

	1	2	3	4	5	6	7	8	9
PAR	4	4	4	4	3	4	3	5	4
YARDS	339	314	354	410	165	401	156	497	373
HDCP	11	13	5	1	15	3	17	9	7
	10	11	12	13	14	15	16	17	18
PAR	4	4	4	4	3	4	3	5	4
YARDS	339	314	354	410	185	401	156	497	373
HDCP	12	14	6	2	16	4	18	10	8

Directions: From ferry, proceed to Main St. in Vineyard Haven. Take 2nd left and proceed to 2nd right (Franklin St.). Go 1.25 miles down Franklin St. to club entrance on left.

Mt. Hood Golf Course   41

Melrose, MA (781) 665-8139

Club Pro: Carl Marchio
Pro Shop: Full inventory
Payment: Visa, MC
Tee Times: Weekends, 2 days adv.
Fee 9 Holes: Weekday: $15.00
Fee 18 Holes: Weekday: $25.00
Cart Rental: $22.00/18 $11.00/9
Lessons: $35.00/half hour **Schools:**
Driving Range: No

Tees	Holes	Yards	Par	USGA	Slope
BACK	N/A				
MIDDLE	18	5553	69	65.7	107
FRONT	18	5318	74	NA	NA

Weekend: $17.00
Weekend: $28.00
Discounts: Senior
Junior Golf: Yes **Membership:** For residents
Non-Metal Spikes: No

Other: Clubhouse / Lockers / Showers / Snack bar / Restaurant / Bar-lounge

Many new improvements. 1st, 4th, and 7th holes redone.

	1	2	3	4	5	6	7	8	9
PAR	5	4	3	5	4	4	3	4	3
YARDS	477	340	202	532	303	338	215	362	183
HDCP	15	11	17	1	13	9	3	7	5
	10	11	12	13	14	15	16	17	18
PAR	3	4	4	4	5	3	4	4	3
YARDS	140	282	396	332	450	210	321	304	166
HDCP	18	12	4	10	2	6	8	14	16

Directions: Route 1 North. Take left onto Essex Street then left onto Waverly Avenue. Take left onto Slayton Road.

New Seabury CC (blue)   ✪✪✪✪   42

Mashpee, MA (508) 477-9110

Club Pro: Mike Pryo
Pro Shop: Yes
Payment: Visa, MC, Amex
Tee Times: 1 day adv.
Fee 9 Holes: Weekday: N/A
Fee 18 Holes: Weekday: $85.00
Cart Rental: $30.00
Lessons: $55.00/50 minutes **Schools:** No
Driving Range: $5.00/bucket

Tees	Holes	Yards	Par	USGA	Slope
BACK	18	6900	72		
MIDDLE	18	6508	72	71.7	124
FRONT	18	5764	72		

Weekend: N/A
Weekend: $85.00
Discounts: None
Junior Golf: Yes **Membership:** Yes
Non-Metal Spikes: Yes

Other: Restaurant / Clubhouse / Hotel / Bar-lounge / Snack Bar / Lockers / Showers

The blue course is championship caliber with spectacular ocean views. For open play dates and seasonal rates it is best to call.

	1	2	3	4	5	6	7	8	9
PAR	5	4	4	3	5	4	4	3	4
YARDS	487	390	393	172	480	365	386	195	410
HDCP	9	7	1	15	5	11	13	17	3
	10	11	12	13	14	15	16	17	18
PAR	5	3	4	4	3	5	4	4	4
YARDS	480	163	358	383	167	526	377	397	379
HDCP	8	18	14	4	16	2	6	10	12

Directions: Route 3 to Route 6 East over Sagamore Bridge. Take Exit 2, follow signs to New Seabury.

New Seabury GC (green)   43

Mashpee, MA (508) 477-9110

Club Pro: Mike Pry
Pro Shop: Yes
Payment: Visa, MC, Amex
Tee Times: 1 day adv.
Fee 9 Holes: Weekday: N/A
Fee 18 Holes: Weekday: $55.00
Cart Rental: $30.00
Lessons: $55.00/50 minutes **Schools:** No
Driving Range: $5.00/bucket
Other: Restaurant / Clubhouse / Hotel / Bar-lounge / Snack Bar / Lockers / Showers

Tees	Holes	Yards	Par	USGA	Slope
BACK	18	5900	70		
MIDDLE	18	5105	70	61.6	110
FRONT	18	5105	68		

Weekend: N/A
Weekend: $55.00
Discounts: None
Junior Golf: Yes **Membership:** Yes
Non-Metal Spikes: Yes

The green course is relatively narrow with tree-lined fairways and no water holes. Rates vary seasonally. Call for play availability.

	1	2	3	4	5	6	7	8	9
PAR	4	3	4	4	4	4	4	3	5
YARDS	397	191	266	311	198	282	309	167	387
HDCP	1	15	13	5	9	11	7	17	3
	10	11	12	13	14	15	16	17	18
PAR	3	5	4	4	4	5	3	3	4
YARDS	408	166	380	216	323	430	162	160	352
HDCP	4	18	6	12	10	2	16	14	8

Directions: Route 3 to Route 6 East over Sagamore Bridge. Take Exit 2, follow signs to New Seabury.

Newton Commonwealth GC   44

Chestnut Hill, MA (617) 630-1971

Club Pro: Bob Travers, PGA
Pro Shop: Full inventory discounted
Payment: Cash, MC, Visa
Tee Times: 4 days adv.
Fee 9 Holes: Weekday: N/A
Fee 18 Holes: Weekday: $23.00
Cart Rental: $24.00/18 $14.00/9
Lessons: $35.00/half hour **Schools:** Jr. & Sr.
Driving Range: No
Other: Snack bar

Tees	Holes	Yards	Par	USGA	Slope
BACK	18	5336	70	67.0	125
MIDDLE	18	5009	70	66.0	122
FRONT	18	4349	70	69.4	118

Weekend: N/A
Weekend: $29.00
Discounts: Sr & Jr. Weekdays only.
Junior Golf: Yes **Membership:** Yes
Non-Metal Spikes: Yes

COUPON

Narrow fairways and small greens, Built in 1897 by Donald Ross. Well conditioned. Outings welcome. Managed by Kevin Osgood of Sterling Golf Mgt. Open year round. www.newtongolf.com

	1	2	3	4	5	6	7	8	9
PAR	4	5	3	3	5	4	3	5	3
YARDS	252	476	179	110	435	255	162	473	197
HDCP	15	1	5	17	3	9	11	7	13
	10	11	12	13	14	15	16	17	18
PAR	4	5	3	4	4	4	4	3	4
YARDS	231	422	130	367	355	259	295	148	263
HDCP	10	6	18	4	2	14	8	12	16

Directions: From Route 128, take exit 12, Route 30 East. Follow 4.8 mi. to Grant Ave. Go left and follow the Golfer Logo signs.

4✪ =Excellent 3✪ =Very Good 2✪ =Good   **Greater Boston/South Shore/Cape Cod**

North Hill CC

45

Duxbury, MA (781) 934-3249

Club Pro: Jeff Stewart, Head Pro
Pro Shop: Yes
Payment: Visa, MC
Tee Times: 3 days adv.
Fee 9 Holes: Weekday: $13.00
Fee 18 Holes: Weekday: $21.00
Cart Rental: $24.00/18 $12.00/9
Lessons: Private and Group **Schools:** No
Driving Range: Limited
Other: Snack bar / Bar-lounge

Tees	Holes	Yards	Par	USGA	Slope
BACK	9	7002	71	71.6	121
MIDDLE	9	6610	72	70.5	115
FRONT	9	4984	74	N/A	N/A

Weekend: $15.00
Weekend: $24.00
Discounts: Yes, 10-Round coupons
Junior Golf: Yes **Membership:** Yes
Non-Metal Spikes: Yes

COUPON

The hilly terrain of the course makes it play long. Several blind shots keep you on your toes.

	1	2	3	4	5	6	7	8	9
PAR	5	4	4	3	4	5	4	3	4
YARDS	540	465	445	165	440	495	410	235	440
HDCP	3	5	1	17	15	9	13	11	7
	10	11	12	13	14	15	16	17	18
PAR	5	4	4	3	4	5	4	3	4
YARDS	540	465	445	165	440	495	410	235	440
HDCP	4	6	2	16	14	10	12	18	8

Directions: Route 3 to Exit 11, get on to Route 14 East, course is approximately 2 miles on right (Merry Avenue).

Norton Country Club

46

Norton, MA (508) 285-2400

Club Pro: John Del Bonis
Pro Shop: Full inventory
Payment: Visa, MC
Tee Times: 3 days advance
Fee 9 Holes: Weekday: $20.00
Fee 18 Holes: Weekday: $33.00 M-Th
Cart Rental: $12 per person
Lessons: $30/30 min **Schools:** No
Driving Range: No
Other: Clubhouse / Lockers / Showers / Snack bar / Bar-lounge

Tees	Holes	Yards	Par	USGA	Slope
BACK	18	6545	71	72.2	137
MIDDLE	18	6201	71	69.9	133
FRONT	18	5040	71	70.5	123

Weekend: N/A
Weekend: $52 F/S/S inc. cart
Discounts: Juniors & Seniors, Wkdays.
Junior Golf: Yes **Membership:** Yes
Non-Metal Spikes: Preferred

Completely redone by Cornish & Silva. A course for serious golfers with tree-lined fairways and 58 pot bunkers. Open April-Oct.

	1	2	3	4	5	6	7	8	9
PAR	4	4	3	5	5	4	3	4	4
YARDS	346	426	143	500	492	419	105	383	313
HDCP	15	1	17	5	9	3	13	7	11
	10	11	12	13	14	15	16	17	18
PAR	4	4	3	4	5	4	3	4	4
YARDS	328	344	138	298	489	414	120	358	389
HDCP	14	10	6	12	4	2	18	16	8

Directions: Take Route 123 (Exit 10) off 495. Take 123 W toward Norton Center to Oak Street. Club is 1 mile on the left.

Norwood Country Club 47

Norwood, MA (781) 769-5880

Tees	Holes	Yards	Par	USGA	Slope
BACK	18	6292	71	67.1	112
MIDDLE	18	6092	71	65.9	108
FRONT	18	5950	71	68.7	108

Club Pro: Mike McGoldrick
Pro Shop: Full inventory
Payment: Cash only
Tee Times: 1 week adv.
Fee 9 Holes: Weekday: $14.00   **Weekend:** $18.00 after 4 pm
Fee 18 Holes: Weekday: $20.00 M-Th   **Weekend:** $25.00 F/S/S
Cart Rental: $24.00/18 $12.00/9   **Discounts:** Senior
Lessons: $35.00/half hour **Schools:** No   **Junior Golf:** No **Membership:** Yes
Driving Range: $6.00/lg. bucket   **Non-Metal Spikes:** Preferred
Other: Clubhouse / Lockers / Showers / Bar-lounge

It is basically a straightaway tract. Excellent course for seniors and beginners.

	1	2	3	4	5	6	7	8	9
PAR	4	4	4	4	5	4	3	3	5
YARDS	360	280	320	395	435	320	156	130	450
HDCP	5	13	9	1	7	11	15	17	3

	10	11	12	13	14	15	16	17	18
PAR	4	4	5	3	4	3	4	4	4
YARDS	300	305	480	150	347	130	390	330	367
HDCP	12	10	4	16	8	18	2	14	6

Directions: Route 128 to Route 1 South to Norwood. Note: course is on the northbound side of Route 1. To change direction, go to Norwood exit and then go around rotary toward Dedham.

Ocean Edge GC   ✪✪✪   48

Brewster, MA (508) 896-5911

Tees	Holes	Yards	Par	USGA	Slope
BACK	18	6665	72	71.9	129
MIDDLE	18	6127	72	68.7	125
FRONT	18	5168	72	70.6	123

Club Pro: Ron Hallett, PGA
Pro Shop: Full inventory
Payment: Visa, MC, Amex
Tee Times: M-Th 1 Wk, F-S/H 2 days
Fee 9 Holes: Weekday: $35.00   **Weekend:** $35.00
Fee 18 Holes: Weekday: $59.00   **Weekend:** $59.00
Cart Rental: $14.00pp/18 $7.00pp/9   **Discounts:** Junior
Lessons: $30.00/half hour **Schools:** Jr. & Sr. **Junior Golf:** Yes **Membership:** Limited
Driving Range: $4.00/lg. bucket   **Non-Metal Spikes:** Yes
Other: Hotel/Clubhouse / Lockers / Showers / Snack bar / Restaurant / Bar-lounge

Designed by Cornish and Silva, this par 72 beauty challenges play with superbly maintained fairways. A great stay-and-play resort. Off season greens fees. **www.oceanedge.com**

	1	2	3	4	5	6	7	8	9
PAR	4	4	4	4	4	4	3	5	4
YARDS	291	400	320	381	339	306	155	546	350
HDCP	11	3	17	5	9	13	15	1	7

	10	11	12	13	14	15	16	17	18
PAR	4	4	3	5	4	4	4	3	5
YARDS	301	345	131	521	342	293	398	174	534
HDCP	16	12	18	6	8	14	4	10	2

Directions: Route 6 East (Cape Cod), Exit 11, turn right on Route 137. Follow 2.6 miles, Ocean Edge is on right side.

4✪ = Excellent 3✪ = Very Good 2✪ = Good **Greater Boston/South Shore/Cape Cod**

Olde Barnstable Fairgrounds GC 49

Marstons Mills, MA (508) 420-1141

Club Pro: Gary Philbrick
Pro Shop: Full inventory
Payment: Cash , MC, Visa
Tee Times: Yes
Fee 9 Holes: Weekday: $39.00
Fee 18 Holes: Weekday: $45.00
Cart Rental: $24.00/18 $13.00/9
Lessons: $35.00/half hour **Schools:** Jr.
Driving Range: $5.00/lg., $3.00/sm. bucket
Other: Restaurant/Clubhouse/Bar-Lounge

Tees	Holes	Yards	Par	USGA	Slope
BACK	18	6479	71	70.7	123
MIDDLE	18	6113	71	69.1	120
FRONT	18	5122	71	69.2	118

Weekend: $45.00
Weekend: $45.00
Discounts: Jr.(18 or under) after 12 pm
Junior Golf: Membership: N/A
Non-Metal Spikes: Yes

"Very enjoyable" - *Golf Digest*; "One of the best public courses you will find. " - Boston Globe.

	1	2	3	4	5	6	7	8	9
PAR	5	3	5	3	4	4	4	4	4
YARDS	485	140	503	158	365	351	430	317	385
HDCP	9	17	5	13	3	15	1	11	7
	10	11	12	13	14	15	16	17	18
PAR	5	4	3	4	4	3	4	3	5
YARDS	510	335	157	340	380	172	395	155	535
HDCP	6	14	18	12	10	8	4	16	2

Directions: Sagamore Bridge Route 6, Exit 5, take right off ramp. Bear right on Route 149. Course is 1/2 mile on left.

Olde Scotland Links 50

Bridgewater, MA (508) 279-3344

Club Pro: Scott Hall, PGA
Pro Shop: Yes
Payment: Visa, MC, Amex
Tee Times: 7 days adv.
Fee 9 Holes: Weekday: $18.00
Fee 18 Holes: Weekday: $30.00
Cart Rental: $24.00/18 $12.00/9
Lessons: $30/30 min. **Schools:** Jr.
Driving Range: $3.00/lg.
Other: Snack Bar

Tees	Holes	Yards	Par	USGA	Slope
BACK	18	6790	72	N/A	N/A
MIDDLE	18	6015	72	N/A	N/A
FRONT	18	4949	72	N/A	N/A

Weekend: $22.00
Weekend: $35.00
Discounts: Senior & Junior M-Th
Junior Golf: Yes **Membership:** No
Non-Metal Spikes: Yes

COUPON

"Straight forward design with several challenging holes. The par 5s require the golfer to be a shotmaker". R. W. Dress code. Open April 1-Nov. 1.

	1	2	3	4	5	6	7	8	9
PAR	4	4	3	4	4	5	4	3	5
YARDS	392	363	144	292	359	489	348	154	440
HDCP	N/A								
	10	11	12	13	14	15	16	17	18
PAR	4	4	5	3	4	4	3	4	5
YARDS	423	339	490	189	340	349	112	314	478
HDCP	N/A								

Directions: Follow Route 24 to Exit 15. Follow Route 104 east for about 1/2 mile to Old Pleasant Road. Take right onto Old Pleasant Road and follow for 2 miles. Course is on the right.

Paul Harney GC

51

East Falmouth, MA (508) 563-3454

Club Pro: Mike Harney
Pro Shop: Limited inventory
Payment: Cash, Check
Tee Times: No
Fee 9 Holes: Weekday: No
Fee 18 Holes: Weekday: $25.00
Cart Rental: $10/9 $20/18
Lessons: $30/30 min. **Schools:** No
Driving Range: No
Other: Bar-Lounge / Snack bar

Weekend: No
Weekend: $30.00
Discounts: None
Junior Golf: Yes **Membership:** No
Non-Metal Spikes: No

Tees	Holes	Yards	Par	USGA	Slope
BACK					
MIDDLE	18	3725	59	59.8	90
FRONT	18	3200	61	61.0	89

An executive-style course. Good for beginners and those who want to improve their iron game. Renovations on going.

	1	2	3	4	5	6	7	8	9
PAR	4	3	3	3	3	3	4	3	3
YARDS	285	140	160	215	155	190	260	160	165
HDCP	15	17	5	1	13	2	11	9	6
	10	11	12	13	14	15	16	17	18
PAR	3	3	3	3	4	4	3	3	4
YARDS	175	225	140	100	275	270	160	170	255
HDCP	3	4	12	18	16	10	8	7	14

Directions: Take Route 28 into Falmouth Center, take Route 151 toward New Seabury, Hatchville, East Falmouth.

Pembroke Country Club

52

Pembroke, MA (781) 826-5191

Club Pro: Chris Masterton
Pro Shop: Full inventory
Payment: Visa, MC, Cash, Check
Tee Times: 2 days adv. for wkends
Fee 9 Holes: Weekday: No
Fee 18 Holes: Weekday: $27.00 until 2:00
Cart Rental: $26.00/18
Lessons: $30.00/half hour **Schools:** Jr
Driving Range: $5.00/bucket
Other: Clubhouse / Snack bar / Restaurant / Bar-lounge / Junior memberships

Weekend: No
Weekend: $50 w/cart, $40 walk
Discounts: None
Junior Golf: No **Membership:** Yes
Non-Metal Spikes: Yes

Tees	Holes	Yards	Par	USGA	Slope
BACK	N/A				
MIDDLE	18	6532	71	71.1	124
FRONT	18	5887	75	73.4	120

New tees and traps rebuilt for '99. A good test of golf and one of Phil Wogan's best creations. If you can par the third, fourth and fifth holes in succession, you deserve a pat on the back. Twilight rate available.

	1	2	3	4	5	6	7	8	9
PAR	5	4	3	4	4	4	3	4	4
YARDS	531	341	221	434	421	349	143	436	344
HDCP	11	13	7	3	1	15	17	5	9
	10	11	12	13	14	15	16	17	18
PAR	4	3	4	5	4	4	4	3	5
YARDS	415	168	431	564	341	370	345	188	490
HDCP	4	14	2	6	10	8	12	16	18

Directions: Take Route 3 to Exit 13, right onto Route 53 South, take right at 5th light onto Broadway, take left at island onto Elm Street, course is 2 miles on right.

Pine Meadows GC

53

Lexington, MA (781) 862-5516

Club Pro: No
Pro Shop: Yes
Payment: Cash, Check
Tee Times: 7 days adv.
Fee 9 Holes: Weekday: $15, $13 for res
Fee 18 Holes: Weekday: No
Cart Rental: $12.00
Lessons: No **Schools:** No
Driving Range: No
Other: Snack bar

Weekend: $17,$15 for residents
Weekend: No
Discounts: Senior. M-Th.
Junior Golf: N/R **Membership:** No
Non-Metal Spikes: Yes

Tees	Holes	Yards	Par	USGA	Slope
BACK	N/A				
MIDDLE	9	5518	70	64.5	110
FRONT	9	5048	70	69.2	117

The course has open fairways and is excellent for beginners and intermediate players.

	1	2	3	4	5	6	7	8	9
PAR	5	5	4	3	4	3	4	4	3
YARDS	484	481	241	225	336	201	324	301	166
HDCP	3	1	15	9	5	11	13	7	17

	10	11	12	13	14	15	16	17	18
PAR	5	5	4	3	4	3	4	4	3
YARDS	484	481	241	225	336	201	324	301	166
HDCP	4	2	16	10	6	12	14	8	18

Directions: Take Route 128 to Exit 31A, through 2 lights, right onto Hill Street, right onto Cedar Street.

Pine Oaks GC

54

S. Easton, MA (508) 238-2320

Club Pro: Leigh Bader
Pro Shop: Full inventory
Payment: Visa, MC, Dis, Cash, Check
Tee Times: No
Fee 9 Holes: Weekday: $17.75
Fee 18 Holes: Weekday: $23.75
Cart Rental: $22.00/18, $12.00/9
Lessons: $35.00/half hour **Schools:** No
Driving Range: No
Other: Clubhouse / Lockers / Snack bar / Bar-lounge / Discount Golf Shop

Weekend: $19.00
Weekend: $27.00
Discounts: Senior & Junior
Junior Golf: Yes **Membership:** Yes
Non-Metal Spikes: No

Tees	Holes	Yards	Par	USGA	Slope
BACK	9	5945	68	67.0	115
MIDDLE	9	5824	68	67	111
FRONT	9	5000	68	67.0	111

Plenty of water for a nine hole course. Pro shop is one of the best in the country.

	1	2	3	4	5	6	7	8	9
PAR	4	5	4	3	4	3	3	4	4
YARDS	326	558	407	175	378	245	149	302	372
HDCP	11	1	4	15	8	9	17	12	6

	10	11	12	13	14	15	16	17	18
PAR	4	5	4	3	4	3	3	4	4
YARDS	326	558	407	175	378	245	149	302	372
HDCP	10	3	2	18	7	14	16	13	5

Directions: Take Route 24 to Exit 16-B. Take Route 106 West approximately 3 miles. 200 yards on right hand side.

Pinecrest Golf Club

55

GB CC/ MA

Holliston, MA (508) 429-9871

Club Pro: Joe McKinney, Head Pro
Pro Shop: Limited inventory
Payment: Cash
Tee Times: Fri, Sat, Sun
Fee 9 Holes: Weekday: $13.00
Fee 18 Holes: Weekday: $19.00
Cart Rental: $22.00/18 $12.00/9
Lessons: $25.00/half hour **Schools:** No
Driving Range: $6.50/lg. $4.50/sm.
Other: Clubhouse / Snack bar / Bar-lounge

Tees	Holes	Yards	Par	USGA	Slope
BACK	N/A				
MIDDLE	18	5003	66	63	103
FRONT	18	4300	66	63.2	103

Weekend: $20.00 after 1 pm
Weekend: $25.00
Discounts: Senior & Junior Wkdays
Junior Golf: Yes **Membership:** Residents only
Non-Metal Spikes: Yes

The course is relatively level and easy to walk. Very tight greens that are a true test of one's iron shot accuracy. The par 3s are fairly long. Most golfers are able to play 18 holes in under 4 hours.

	1	2	3	4	5	6	7	8	9
PAR	4	3	5	4	4	4	3	3	3
YARDS	279	205	472	245	405	290	227	200	222
HDCP	15	17	3	9	1	11	5	13	7
	10	11	12	13	14	15	16	17	18
PAR	4	3	4	3	4	3	4	4	4
YARDS	398	165	275	153	340	190	317	325	295
HDCP	2	18	14	16	4	12	8	6	10

Directions: Take Route 495 to Route 85 Exit toward Holliston. Follow 3 miles to first flashing yellow light. Take right onto Chestnut Street, look for signs.

Plymouth Country Club ✪✪✪

56

Plymouth, MA (508) 746-0476

Club Pro: Tom Hanifan
Pro Shop: Full inventory
Payment: MC, Visa
Tee Times: Weekdays, 1 day adv.
Fee 9 Holes: Weekday: N/A
Fee 18 Holes: Weekday: $65.23
Cart Rental: Included
Lessons: $30.00/half hour **Schools:** No
Driving Range: No
Other: Clubhouse / Lockers / Showers / Snack bar / Restaurant / Bar-lounge

Tees	Holes	Yards	Par	USGA	Slope
BACK	18	6228	69	70.1	125
MIDDLE	18	6164	69	69.1	119
FRONT	18	5299	70	71.1	125

Weekend: N/A
Weekend: N/A
Discounts: None
Junior Golf: Yes **Membership:** Yes, waiting list
Non-Metal Spikes: Preferred

One of the nicest courses in Southern Massachusetts. The course has small, fast greens. Junior clinics for members.

	1	2	3	4	5	6	7	8	9
PAR	4	4	3	4	4	4	4	3	4
YARDS	345	406	215	400	390	290	345	140	411
HDCP	12	6	14	2	10	16	8	18	4
	10	11	12	13	14	15	16	17	18
PAR	3	4	4	4	4	3	5	4	4
YARDS	175	423	442	330	380	185	510	395	382
HDCP	15	3	1	13	7	17	11	5	9

Directions: Take Route 3 to Exit 4; go South 1 1/4 miles, turn right on Country Club Drive.

4✪ =Excellent 3✪ =Very Good 2✪ =Good **Greater Boston/South Shore/Cape Cod**

Ponkapoag GC #1

Canton, MA (781) 575-1001

Club Pro: Kenneth Campbell
Pro Shop: Full inventory
Payment: Visa, MC, Cash
Tee Times: Weekends
Fee 9 Holes: Weekday: $12.00
Fee 18 Holes: Weekday: $17.00
Cart Rental: $20.00/18 $12.00/9
Lessons: $35/30 min **Schools:** Jr.
Driving Range: $5.00/lg. bucket
Other: Restaurant / Clubhouse / Beer & wine/ Showers

Tees	Holes	Yards	Par	USGA	Slope
BACK	18	6728	72	72.0	126
MIDDLE	18	6256	72	69.8	120
FRONT	18	5523	74	70.8	115

Weekend: $12.00
Weekend: $20.00
Discounts: Senior & Junior
Junior Golf: Yes **Membership:** Limited, Juniors
Non-Metal Spikes: No

A Donald Ross designed course. Open April - December.

	1	2	3	4	5	6	7	8	9
PAR	4	3	5	4	4	4	4	3	5
YARDS	393	169	532	332	395	437	402	192	520
HDCP	11	17	1	13	9	5	7	15	3
	10	11	12	13	14	15	16	17	18
PAR	4	5	3	5	4	4	3	4	4
YARDS	406	480	182	489	375	402	221	386	413
HDCP	8	2	18	8	14	10	16	12	6

Directions: Course is 1 mile south of Route 128 on Route 138.

Ponkapoag GC #2

Canton, MA (781) 575-1001

Club Pro: Kenneth Campbell
Pro Shop: Full inventory
Payment: Visa, MC, Cash
Tee Times: Weekends
Fee 9 Holes: Weekday: $12.00
Fee 18 Holes: Weekday: $17.00
Cart Rental: $20.00/18 $12.00/9
Lessons: $35/30 min **Schools:** Jr.Yes
Driving Range: $5.00/lg.
Other: Restaurant / Clubhouse / Beer & Wine / Showers

Tees	Holes	Yards	Par	USGA	Slope
BACK	18	6332	71	70.3	116
MIDDLE	18	5769	71	67.5	112
FRONT	18	5114	72	68.5	113

Weekend: $12.00
Weekend: $20.00
Discounts: Senior & Junior
Junior Golf: Yes **Membership:** Juniors only
Non-Metal Spikes: No

Great Par 71, designed by Donald Ross.

	1	2	3	4	5	6	7	8	9
PAR	4	4	3	5	4	4	4	3	4
YARDS	385	434	202	473	266	412	341	188	416
HDCP	9	3	15	1	13	7	11	17	5
	10	11	12	13	14	15	16	17	18
PAR	5	3	4	5	4	3	4	4	4
YARDS	498	166	351	482	401	192	402	323	408
HDCP	2	18	12	4	10	16	6	14	8

Directions: Course is 1 mile south of Route 128 on Route 138.

Poquoy Brook GC

Lakeville, MA (508) 947-5261

Club Pro: Bob Stanghellini-Teaching Pro.
Pro Shop: Full inventory
Payment: Cash, all major credit cards
Tee Times: M-F, 7 days. adv., S/S, 2 days.
Fee 9 Holes: Weekday: $20.00
Fee 18 Holes: Weekday: $33.00
Cart Rental: $14.00 per person
Lessons: $35.00/half hour **Schools:** Yes
Driving Range: $3.00/sm. $5.00/lg.
Other: Clubhouse / Lockers / Showers / Snack bar / Restaurant / Bar-lounge

Tees	Holes	Yards	Par	USGA	Slope
BACK	18	6762	72	72.4	128
MIDDLE	18	6286	72	69.9	125
FRONT	18	5415	73	71.0	114

Weekend: $22.00
Weekend: $37.00
Discounts: Junior
Junior Golf: Yes **Membership:** No
Non-Metal Spikes: Yes

Nicely bunkered with several lateral water hazards. Undulating fairways, large greens, and picturesque terrain. One of the finest public courses in New England. Open year round. **www.poquoybrook.com**

	1	2	3	4	5	6	7	8	9
PAR	4	4	3	4	5	4	4	3	5
YARDS	351	385	176	307	518	326	381	180	485
HDCP	9	1	17	15	5	7	3	13	11
	10	11	12	13	14	15	16	17	18
PAR	4	4	3	4	5	3	4	4	5
YARDS	372	336	185	366	436	173	426	428	455
HDCP	6	12	14	8	18	16	4	2	10

Directions: I-495 South - take Exit 5, Route 18 South. Bear right off exit. Take first right at flashing yellow light (Taunton Street) and then first left onto Leonard Street. Course on right.

Presidents Golf Course

Quincy, MA (617) 328-3444

Club Pro: Arthur Cicconi
Pro Shop: Full inventory
Payment: Cash only
Tee Times: 2 days adv. for weekends
Fee 9 Holes: Weekday: No
Fee 18 Holes: Weekday: $20.00
Cart Rental: $24.00/18 $12.00/9
Lessons: $35.00/half hour **Schools:** No
Driving Range: No
Other: Clubhouse / Lockers / Showers / Snack bar / Restaurant/Putting green

Tees	Holes	Yards	Par	USGA	Slope
BACK	18	5645	70	66.8	114
MIDDLE	18	5055	70	66.4	108
FRONT	18	4425	70	65.0	107

Weekend: No
Weekend: $25.00
Discounts: Senior & Junior
Junior Golf: Yes **Membership:** Yes
Non-Metal Spikes: Yes

Bent greens, very hilly, undulated greens, water on two holes, overlooking Boston skyline. No tank tops or work boots. Open April - December.

	1	2	3	4	5	6	7	8	9
PAR	4	3	4	3	5	4	3	4	4
YARDS	300	90	270	150	440	355	120	350	285
HDCP	7	15	9	13	5	1	17	3	11
	10	11	12	13	14	15	16	17	18
PAR	3	4	5	3	4	5	5	4	3
YARDS	150	260	465	165	365	460	425	300	105
HDCP	16	12	6	14	4	2	8	10	18

Directions: From I-93 South, take Exit 11A. Take left at first light (Approx. 1 mile). Take left at next light. From I-93 North, take Exit 9. Go straight approx. 1 mile. Right 1 mile at lights. Left at next light.

Putterham Meadows   61

Brookline, MA (617) 730-2078

Club Pro: Jack Neville
Pro Shop: Full inventory
Payment: Visa, MC, Amex, Cash
Tee Times: 7 days adv.

Tees	Holes	Yards	Par	USGA	Slope
BACK	18	6307	71	70.2	123
MIDDLE	18	6003	71	68.3	118
FRONT	18	5680	72	72.1	121

Fee 9 Holes: Weekday: $16 M-Th 'til 7:30 am **Weekend:** No
Fee 18 Holes: Weekday: $27.00 M-Th   **Weekend:** $32.00
Cart Rental: $26.00/18 $14.00/9   **Discounts:** Senior & Junior
Lessons: $35.00/half hour **Schools:** Jr.Yes   **Junior Golf:** Yes **Membership:** No
Driving Range: No   **Non-Metal Spikes:** Yes
Other: Restaurant / Clubhouse / Bar-Lounge / Lockers / Showers

Stiles & Van Kleek course opened 1931. Tight fairways, elevated greens, low terrain, small hills, and lots of brooks. Many trees. Dress code: shirts with collars. Open April - December.

	1	2	3	4	5	6	7	8	9
PAR	5	4	3	4	3	5	4	4	4
YARDS	460	335	163	317	177	506	340	390	384
HDCP	12	10	18	16	14	8	4	2	6

	10	11	12	13	14	15	16	17	18
PAR	4	4	3	4	4	5	4	3	4
YARDS	330	290	109	380	400	520	330	160	412
HDCP	11	13	17	5	1	7	9	15	3

Directions: From I-95 N & S to Route 9 East 4 miles to Chestnut Hill Mall on left. Exit onto Hammond Pond Parkway South. Go to rotary; opposite rotary 100 yards on left. From Boston: Route 9 to Hammond Street. Turn left. 1 mile to rotary — all the way around rotary.

Quashnet Valley CC   ★★ 62

Mashpee, MA (508) 477-4412

Club Pro: Bob Chase
Pro Shop: Full inventory
Payment: Visa, MC
Tee Times: 1 wk, Prepay 6 mos.

Tees	Holes	Yards	Par	USGA	Slope
BACK	18	6601	72	71.7	132
MIDDLE	18	6093	72	69.1	126
FRONT	18	5094	72	70.3	119

Fee 9 Holes: Weekday: $16.00 M- Th.   **Weekend:** $19 F; $26 S/S/Hldy
Fee 18 Holes: Weekday: $32 M-Th; $37 Fri   **Weekend:** $52.00 Sat/Sun/Hldy
Cart Rental: $13.00 pp   **Discounts:** None
Lessons: $35.00/half hour **Schools:** Yes   **Junior Golf:** Yes **Membership:** Yes. Limited.
Driving Range: $3.15/bucket   **Non-Metal Spikes:** Yes
Other: Clubhouse /Showers/ Snack bar / Bar-lounge /Banquet facilities

COUPON

The name of the game is accuracy. Nicely designed layout adds to the scenery at this well maintained course. The experience begins and ends with challenging par 5s. Twi-light rate.

	1	2	3	4	5	6	7	8	9
PAR	5	3	4	4	3	4	5	3	4
YARDS	505	135	328	310	153	420	488	173	349
HDCP	1	17	13	9	15	3	5	11	7

	10	11	12	13	14	15	16	17	18
PAR	4	4	4	5	4	4	4	3	5
YARDS	302	390	322	530	354	360	339	155	480
HDCP	14	6	16	4	10	8	12	18	2

Directions: Take Route 6 East to Exit 2. Take right onto Route 130 South, follow 7.2 miles then take a right onto Great Neck Road. Follow 1.6 miles, take right onto Old Barnstable Road. Course is on left at the end.

Ridder Golf Club

Whitman, MA (781) 447-9003

Club Pro: Jeff Butler
Pro Shop: Full inventory
Payment: Cash only
Tee Times: 2 days adv.
Fee 9 Holes: Weekday: $16.00
Fee 18 Holes: Weekday: $28.00 M-TH
Cart Rental: $21.00/18 $10.50/9
Lessons: $30/30min **Schools:** No
Driving Range: Yes
Other: Restaurant / Snack bar / Bar-lounge

Tees	Holes	Yards	Par	USGA	Slope
BACK	18	5909	70	68.1	113
MIDDLE	18	5857	70	66.3	110
FRONT	18	4981	70	67.1	107

Weekend: $16.00
Weekend: $30.00 F,S,S
Discounts: Junior
Junior Golf: Yes **Membership:** Yes
Non-Metal Spikes: Preferred

Junior summer program. Marked improvements, more challenging. Open March - December.

	1	2	3	4	5	6	7	8	9
PAR	4	4	3	4	4	4	4	3	4
YARDS	334	368	154	289	384	299	257	197	387
HDCP	16	7	14	15	5	17	18	8	4
	10	11	12	13	14	15	16	17	18
PAR	4	5	4	3	4	3	4	5	4
YARDS	312	468	370	166	427	225	385	476	359
HDCP	12	10	6	13	1	3	2	11	9

Directions: Take Route 3 to Route 18 South to Route 14 East.

Rockland CC

Rockland, MA (781) 878-5836

Club Pro: Holly Taylor
Pro Shop: Full inventory
Payment: Visa, MC, Disc
Tee Times: 3 days adv.
Fee 9 Holes: Weekday: $12.00
Fee 18 Holes: Weekday: $22.00
Cart Rental: $21.00/18 $14.00/9
Lessons: $30.00/half hour **Schools:** Jr.
Driving Range: No
Other: Clubhouse / Snack bar / Restaurant / Bar-lounge

Tees	Holes	Yards	Par	USGA	Slope
BACK	18	3300	54	56.0	78
MIDDLE	18	3014	54	58.0	87
FRONT	18	3014	60	N/A	N/A

Weekend: $12.00
Weekend: $22.00 F/S/S
Discounts: Sr & Jr. Wkdys Only
Junior Golf: Yes **Membership:** Yes
Non-Metal Spikes: No

Longest par 3 course in the nation. Tees and greens are in fine shape, but rough areas can balloon your scores.

	1	2	3	4	5	6	7	8	9
PAR	3	3	3	3	3	3	3	3	3
YARDS	212	136	202	137	146	152	171	95	207
HDCP	2	14	4	16	8	12	10	18	6
	10	11	12	13	14	15	16	17	18
PAR	3	3	3	3	3	3	3	3	3
YARDS	227	202	137	145	162	228	152	132	171
HDCP	3	9	15	1	13	5	7	17	11

Directions: Take Route 3 to Exit 16B. Left onto Route 139 for 3 to 4 miles. Course is on right.

4✪ =Excellent 3✪ =Very Good 2✪ =Good

Round Hill CC   65

E. Sandwich, MA (508) 888-3384

Club Pro: Greg Martzolf
Pro Shop: Full inventory
Payment: MC, Visa, Check
Tee Times: 1 week adv.

Tees	Holes	Yards	Par	USGA	Slope
BACK					
MIDDLE	18	5920	71	68.6	120
FRONT					

Fee 9 Holes: Weekday: $10.00-$25.00   **Weekend:** $15.00-$30.00
Fee 18 Holes: Weekday: $15.00-$40.00   **Weekend:** $20.00-$50.00
Cart Rental: $28.00/18 $14.00/9   **Discounts:** Senior Mon
Lessons: Yes **Schools:** Adult Introductory   **Junior Golf:** Yes **Membership:** Full and seasonal
Driving Range: $5.00/lg. bucket   **Non-Metal Spikes:** No
Other: Clubhouse /Restaurant / Lounge/Function Facilities

The course is hilly and tight. Accurate shots are essential. Open year round. Regular tees and greens. Twilight rates available.

	1	2	3	4	5	6	7	8	9
PAR	5	4	3	4	4	5	3	4	4
YARDS	485	325	120	305	347	570	177	340	406
HDCP	9	11	17	15	3	7	5	13	1
	10	11	12	13	14	15	16	17	18
PAR	4	4	3	4	5	3	4	4	4
YARDS	300	380	175	285	520	160	340	355	330
HDCP	18	6	12	14	8	10	16	2	4

Directions: Take Route 6 to Exit 3. Take right off ramp. First left onto Service Rd. 1/2 mile on right.

Saddle Hill CC   66

Hopkinton, MA (508) 435-4630

Club Pro: Steve Gelineau
Pro Shop: Full inventory
Payment: MC, Visa
Tee Times: 1 week adv.

Tees	Holes	Yards	Par	USGA	Slope
BACK	18	6900	72	72.8	124
MIDDLE	18	6140	72	69.4	119
FRONT	18	5619	72	70.3	108

Fee 9 Holes: Weekday: $16 after 4:00   **Weekend:** $18.00 after 3 pm
Fee 18 Holes: Weekday: $25.00   **Weekend:** $28.00
Cart Rental: $24.00/18   **Discounts:** Senior & Junior
Lessons: $30.00/half hour **Schools:** No   **Junior Golf:** N/R **Membership:** No
Driving Range: $4.00/lg., $2.00/sm. bucket   **Non-Metal Spikes:** No
Other: Bar-Lounge / Snack bar

The course is moderately difficult. The front nine are level and the back nine are hilly. Open fairways allow you to crack a driver. Course open year round (weather permitting).

	1	2	3	4	5	6	7	8	9
PAR	5	4	3	4	5	3	4	4	4
YARDS	464	396	218	340	480	161	352	372	362
HDCP	9	1	3	13	5	17	15	11	7
	10	11	12	13	14	15	16	17	18
PAR	4	3	4	4	5	4	3	5	4
YARDS	361	160	292	365	504	302	153	458	400
HDCP	10	8	16	6	2	14	18	12	4

Directions: Take I-495 to Route 9 West; Take Computer Drive. Left off exit. Right onto Fruit Street. Turn left onto Saddle Hill Road to course.

Sandy Burr CC

Wayland, MA (508) 358-7211

Club Pro: Charles Estes
Pro Shop: Full inventory
Payment: Visa, MC, Amex
Tee Times: Fri, Sat & Sun

Tees	Holes	Yards	Par	USGA	Slope
BACK	18	6412	72	70.8	125
MIDDLE	18	6229	72	69.9	122
FRONT	18	4561	72	66.2	110

Fee 9 Holes: Weekday: $22 6-8am & 1-3pm **Weekend:** $25.00 after 3pm
Fee 18 Holes: Weekday: $34.00 **Weekend:** $38.00
Cart Rental: $28.00 **Discounts:** Senior & Junior: $22
Lessons: $30/30 min **Schools:** No **Junior Golf:** No **Membership:** No
Driving Range: No **Non-Metal Spikes:** Yes
Other: Clubhouse / Snack bar / Bar-lounge / Showers

Challenging eighteen holes. Plays long; contour fairways are tight. Early tee times are suggested. Outings can be scheduled. Discounts for seniors 62 and up and juniors 16 and under.

	1	2	3	4	5	6	7	8	9
PAR	5	5	3	4	3	4	4	4	4
YARDS	471	491	147	429	220	409	335	353	281
HDCP	15	5	17	3	13	1	7	9	11

	10	11	12	13	14	15	16	17	18
PAR	3	5	4	3	4	4	4	5	4
YARDS	193	450	384	185	369	352	409	521	406
HDCP	10	18	8	14	16	12	4	6	2

Directions: Take Route 128 to Route 20 West Exit, at Wayland Center take left onto Route 27 S. Course is 1/4 mile on right.

Scituate Country Club

Scituate, MA (781) 545-9768

Club Pro: John M. Kan
Pro Shop: Full inventory
Payment: Cash only
Tee Times: 2 days adv.

Tees	Holes	Yards	Par	USGA	Slope
BACK	N/A				
MIDDLE	9	6051	70	69.7	121
FRONT	9	5407	72	71.6	119

Fee 9 Holes: Weekday: $17 after 11am **Weekend:** N/A
Fee 18 Holes: Weekday: $25 after 11am **Weekend:** N/A
Cart Rental: $24.00/18 $14.00/9 **Discounts:** None
Lessons: $30.00/half hour **Schools:** No **Junior Golf:** No **Membership:** Yes
Driving Range: No **Non-Metal Spikes:** Preferred
Other: Restaurant / Clubhouse / Bar-Lounge / Showers / Lockers / Snack Bar

Open to the public on Mondays only after 11 am. Beautifully maintained seaside golf links with rolling terrain. Open April - November.

	1	2	3	4	5	6	7	8	9
PAR	4	3	5	4	4	4	4	3	4
YARDS	407	156	504	373	308	359	357	124	386
HDCP	2	6	12	8	16	4	10	18	14

	10	11	12	13	14	15	16	17	18
PAR	4	3	5	4	4	4	4	3	4
YARDS	422	165	525	385	320	370	365	130	395
HDCP	1	5	11	7	15	3	9	17	13

Directions: Take Route 3 to Exit 13. Go left off exit. Go to first set of lights, take right onto Route 123. Go to end, go straight across Route 3A. Go onto Driftway Road. Course is 1 mile on right.

4✪ = Excellent 3✪ = Very Good 2✪ = Good **Greater Boston/South Shore/Cape Cod**

South Shore CC

Hingham, MA (781) 749-8479

Club Pro: Joe Keefe
Pro Shop: Full inventory
Payment: Cash, Check, Credit
Tee Times: 24 hrs. adv.
Fee 9 Holes: Weekday: $18.00
Fee 18 Holes: Weekday: $29.00
Cart Rental: $21.00/18 $12.60/9
Lessons: $50.00/ 45 minutes **Schools:** Jr.Yes
Driving Range: Yes
Other: Snack bar / Restaurant / Bar-lounge / Clubhouse / Lockers / Showers

Tees	Holes	Yards	Par	USGA	Slope
BACK	18	6444	72	71.0	128
MIDDLE	18	6197	72	71	128
FRONT	18	5064	72	69.3	116

Weekend: N/A
Weekend: $33.00
Discounts: None
Junior Golf: Yes **Membership:** No, Waiting list
Non-Metal Spikes: Yes

Superb 18 hole championship golf course. www.jkgolfpro.com

	1	2	3	4	5	6	7	8	9
PAR	4	3	5	4	4	4	4	3	5
YARDS	277	156	521	319	371	410	360	197	502
HDCP	13	17	1	15	3	5	7	11	9
	10	11	12	13	14	15	16	17	18
PAR	4	3	4	4	4	5	4	3	5
YARDS	295	179	372	401	327	530	380	148	452
HDCP	14	16	6	4	12	2	8	18	10

Directions: Take Route 3 to Exit 14 onto Route 228 North; Continue 4 miles through flashing red light to flashing yellow light. Turn left, 1/2 mile to club on left hand side.

Squirrel Run CC

Plymouth, MA (508) 746-5001

Club Pro: David Moore
Pro Shop: Full inventory
Payment: Visa, MC, Cash
Tee Times: 7 days adv.
Fee 9 Holes: Weekday: No
Fee 18 Holes: Weekday: $22.00
Cart Rental: $20.00/18
Lessons: Yes **Schools:** No
Driving Range: No
Other: Restaurant / Clubhouse / Bar-Lounge / Snack Bar

Tees	Holes	Yards	Par	USGA	Slope
BACK	18	2859	57	55.4	85
MIDDLE	18	2338	57	53.7	82
FRONT	18	1990	57	56.0	83

Weekend: No
Weekend: $25.00
Discounts: Senior & Junior
Junior Golf: N/R **Membership:** No
Non-Metal Spikes: Yes

Tees and greens are immaculate. A challenge to anyone's short game. (Paul Harber — Boston Globe.)

	1	2	3	4	5	6	7	8	9
PAR	4	3	3	3	4	3	3	3	4
YARDS	286	105	125	90	263	98	131	123	206
HDCP	1	13	3	17	7	9	11	5	15
	10	11	12	13	14	15	16	17	18
PAR	3	3	3	3	3	3	3	3	3
YARDS	99	78	102	102	140	100	116	74	100
HDCP	14	18	12	8	2	10	6	16	4

Directions: From Route 3 take Exit 6 to Route 44 West. Go Approx. 2 miles to course on left. Look for Squirrel Run sign.

Stoneham Oaks

Stoneham, MA (781)-438-7888

Tees	Holes	Yards	Par	USGA	Slope
BACK	N/A				
MIDDLE	9	1125	27	N/A	N/A
FRONT	N/A				

Club Pro: Mike Munro
Pro Shop: Limited inventory
Payment: Cash only
Tee Times: No
Fee 9 Holes: Weekday: $10.00 **Weekend:** $12.00
Fee 18 Holes: Weekday: $17.00 **Weekend:** $19.00
Cart Rental: Pull carts, $2.00 **Discounts:** None
Lessons: No **Schools:** No **Junior Golf:** N/R **Membership:** No
Driving Range: No **Non-Metal Spikes:** No
Other:

COUPON

A par 3 course. Very hilly, Many trees. Very Scenic. Various reduced weekday rates between 7:00 am and 2:00 pm.

	1	2	3	4	5	6	7	8	9
PAR	3	3	3	3	3	3	3	3	3
YARDS	89	147	179	128	95	113	153	139	82
HDCP	17	7	1	11	9	15	5	3	13
	10	11	12	13	14	15	16	17	18
PAR									
YARDS									
HDCP									

Directions: From I-93, take exit 36, Stoneham, Montvale Ave., 1 block. Course is at rear of the Stoneham Ice Rink.

Stow Acres CC (north)

Randall Rd., Stow, MA (978) 568-1100

Tees	Holes	Yards	Par	USGA	Slope
BACK	18	6939	72	72.8	130
MIDDLE	18	6310	72	70.5	127
FRONT	18	6011	72	72.5	130

Club Pro: Mike Giles, PGA
Pro Shop: Full inventory
Payment: Visa, MC, Amex
Tee Times: 6 days adv.
Fee 9 Holes: Weekday: $21 after 3pm M-Th **Weekend:** $25 after 3 pm
Fee 18 Holes: Weekday: $34 M-Th **Weekend:** $43 F/S/S
Cart Rental: $26.00/18 $15.00/9 **Discounts:** Senior & Junior
Lessons: $35.00/half hour **Schools:** Yes **Junior Golf:** Yes **Membership:** Yes, waiting list
Driving Range: $7/lg. $5/med $4/sm. **Non-Metal Spikes:** Yes
Other: Clubhouse / Snack bar / Bar-lounge

75th U.S. Amateur Public Links Championship host. Private course conditions and championship layouts. Top 50 public — *Golf Digest*. Open mid March - mid Dec.

	1	2	3	4	5	6	7	8	9
PAR	5	4	4	4	5	3	4	3	4
YARDS	503	374	354	387	472	180	318	165	426
HDCP	5	11	13	3	7	9	15	17	1
	10	11	12	13	14	15	16	17	18
PAR	4	4	5	3	4	4	3	4	5
YARDS	359	392	424	169	340	369	166	376	536
HDCP	4	6	18	16	14	8	12	10	2

Directions: Take Route I-95/128 to Route 20/117 Exit. Go west on Route 117 approx. 15 miles; left in Stow Center onto 62 West, follow signs from Route 62.

Stow Acres CC (south)   73

Randall Rd., Stow, MA (978) 568-1100

Club Pro: Mike Giles, Head Pro.
Pro Shop: Full inventory
Payment: Visa, MC, Amex
Tee Times: 6 days adv.

Tees	Holes	Yards	Par	USGA	Slope
BACK	18	6520	72	71.8	120
MIDDLE	18	6105	72	70.5	118
FRONT	18	5642	72	72.5	120

Fee 9 Holes: Weekday: $21 after 3 pm M-Th **Weekend:** $25.00 after 3 pm
Fee 18 Holes: Weekday: $34 M-Th **Weekend:** $43.00 F/S/S
Cart Rental: $26/18 $15/9 **Discounts:** Senior & Junior
Lessons: $35.00/half hour **Schools:** Yes **Junior Golf:** Yes **Membership:** Yes, waiting list
Driving Range: $7/lg. $5/med $3/sm. **Non-Metal Spikes:** Yes
Other: Clubhouse / Snack bar / Bar-lounge

Rated in top 100 golf shops by Golf Shop Operations Magazine. Well known for variety of instructional packages: schools, clinics and lessons for juniors.

	1	2	3	4	5	6	7	8	9
PAR	4	4	3	4	5	5	3	4	4
YARDS	375	416	123	301	476	487	212	346	368
HDCP	13	1	17	9	5	7	3	15	11
	10	11	12	13	14	15	16	17	18
PAR	5	3	4	4	5	3	4	3	5
YARDS	543	127	366	292	441	151	407	167	507
HDCP	4	18	10	14	16	12	2	8	6

Directions: Take Route I-95/128 to Route 20/117 Exit. Go west on Route 117 approx. 15 miles; left in Stow Center onto 62 West, follow signs from Route 62.

Strawberry Valley GC   74

Abington, MA (781) 871-5566

Club Pro: John Oteri
Pro Shop: Full inventory
Payment: MC, Visa, Cash
Tee Times: No

Tees	Holes	Yards	Par	USGA	Slope
BACK					
MIDDLE	9	4638	69	66.9	99
FRONT					

Fee 9 Holes: Weekday: $15.00 **Weekend:** $15.00
Fee 18 Holes: Weekday: $20.00 **Weekend:** $20.00
Cart Rental: $21.00/18 $12.00/9 **Discounts:** Senior, Wkdays
Lessons: $50.00/ hour **Schools:** N/R **Junior Golf:** Yes **Membership:** Yes
Driving Range: No **Non-Metal Spikes:** No
Other: Snack bar

Great course for women and beginners. If you hit the ball for distance, be cautious of the blind shots. Sixth hole is a nifty par 3 over water. Open year round.

	1	2	3	4	5	6	7	8	9
PAR	4	4	4	4	4	3	3	4	4
YARDS	228	357	385	233	215	119	132	302	309
HDCP	17	3	1	9	11	15	13	7	5
	10	11	12	13	14	15	16	17	18
PAR	4	4	5	4	4	3	3	4	4
YARDS	223	336	475	233	243	103	148	288	309
HDCP	18	4	2	12	10	16	14	8	6

Directions: Take Route 3 to Route 18 South. Course is approximately 7 miles on right.

Twin Brooks GC At Sheraton ✪✪✪✪ 75

Hyannis, MA (508) 775-7775

Club Pro: No
Pro Shop: Full inventory
Payment: Visa, MC, Amex, Cash
Tee Times: 2 days adv.
Fee 9 Holes: Weekday: N/A
Fee 18 Holes: Weekday: $25.00
Cart Rental: $19.95/18
Lessons: No **Schools:** Jr.
Driving Range: No
Other: Restaurant / Hotel / Bar-lounge / Showers

Tees	Holes	Yards	Par	USGA	Slope
BACK	N/A				
MIDDLE	18	2621	54	N/A	N/A
FRONT	N/A				

Weekend: $30.00
Weekend: $30.00
Discounts: Senior
Junior Golf: N/R **Membership:** Yes
Non-Metal Spikes: Yes

GB CC/ MA

The course was rated the toughest Par 3 on Cape Cod by *Golf Digest*. Very challenging layout. Open year round. Formerly known as Tara Hyannis Golf Course.

	1	2	3	4	5	6	7	8	9
PAR	3	3	3	3	3	3	3	3	3
YARDS	135	90	165	144	110	102	175	140	135
HDCP	6	18	4	12	14	16	2	10	8
	10	11	12	13	14	15	16	17	18
PAR	3	3	3	3	3	3	3	3	3
YARDS	190	140	150	115	170	215	150	160	135
HDCP	3	13	7	15	5	1	9	11	17

Directions: Take Route 6 to Exit 6 (Hyannis), follow Route 132 to Hyannis, follow signs to West End Hyannis. At rotary, you will see the Sheraton.

Twin Springs Golf Club 76

Bolton, MA (978) 779-5020

Club Pro: Robert Keene
Pro Shop: Full inventory
Payment: MC, Visa, Amex
Tee Times: Weekends
Fee 9 Holes: Weekday: $11.50
Fee 18 Holes: Weekday: $16.00
Cart Rental: $2.00/pull carts
Lessons: $30.00/ hour **Schools:** Jr.
Driving Range: No
Other: Snack bar

Tees	Holes	Yards	Par	USGA	Slope
BACK					
MIDDLE	9	5224	68	64.8	113
FRONT					

Weekend: $13.50
Weekend: $19.50
Discounts: Senior & Junior
Junior Golf: Yes **Membership:** Yes
Non-Metal Spikes: No

The course has a good mix of terrain with small greens.

	1	2	3	4	5	6	7	8	9
PAR	4	4	4	3	3	4	4	4	4
YARDS	327	294	300	140	161	318	368	320	384
HDCP	7	9	13	15	11	3	1	17	5
	10	11	12	13	14	15	16	17	18
PAR	4	4	4	3	3	4	4	4	4
YARDS	327	294	300	140	161	318	368	320	384
HDCP	8	10	14	16	12	4	2	18	6

Directions: Take I-495 to Exit 27 to Route 117 West into center of Bolton. Go straight for .7 of a mile. Turn left up hill at Wilder Rd. Course is 2 miles on right.

4✪ =Excellent   3✪ =Very Good   2✪ =Good   **Greater Boston/South Shore/Cape Cod**

Unicorn Golf Course

Stoneham, MA (781) 438-9732

Club Pro: Paul Munro
Pro Shop: Yes
Payment: Cash only
Tee Times: No
Fee 9 Holes: Weekday: $13.00
Fee 18 Holes: Weekday: $26.00
Cart Rental: $12.00/9
Lessons: Yes **Schools:** N/R
Driving Range: No
Other: Snack bar

Tees	Holes	Yards	Par	USGA	Slope
BACK	N/A				
MIDDLE	9	6370	70	68.7	109
FRONT	9	5804	74	N/R	N/R

Weekend: $15.00
Weekend: $30.00
Discounts: Senior & Junior Wkdays
Junior Golf: Yes **Membership:** No
Non-Metal Spikes: No

The course is level with eight greens. Previously eighteen holes, it was converted to nine holes so it's relatively long. Reduced fees for residents.

	1	2	3	4	5	6	7	8	9
PAR	4	4	4	3	4	5	4	3	4
YARDS	389	326	335	168	395	499	448	178	447
HDCP	5	13	11	17	1	9	3	15	7

	10	11	12	13	14	15	16	17	18
PAR	4	4	4	3	4	5	4	3	4
YARDS	389	326	335	168	395	499	448	178	447
HDCP	6	14	12	18	2	10	4	16	8

Directions: Take I-93 to to Montevale Avenue. Follow to end. Left onto Route 28, left at next set of lights (Williams Street.). Course is 1/4 mile on left.

Wading River GC

Rt. 123, Norton, MA (508) 226-1788

Club Pro: No
Pro Shop: No
Payment: Cash only
Tee Times: No
Fee 9 Holes: Weekday: $8.00
Fee 18 Holes: Weekday: $12.00
Cart Rental: $12.00/18 $9.00/9
Lessons: No **Schools:** No
Driving Range: No
Other: Lounge

Tees	Holes	Yards	Par	USGA	Slope
BACK					
MIDDLE	18	2421	54		
FRONT	18	2321	56		

Weekend: $9.00
Weekend: $14.00
Discounts: Members
Junior Golf: No **Membership:** Yes
Non-Metal Spikes: No

This executive par-three is a good place to work on your irons and short game. Open year round.

	1	2	3	4	5	6	7	8	9
PAR	3	3	3	3	3	3	3	3	3
YARDS	117	135	82	140	93	91	115	136	108
HDCP	12	4	18	14	6	15	8	3	10

	10	11	12	13	14	15	16	17	18
PAR	3	3	3	3	3	3	3	3	3
YARDS	131	138	125	203	141	113	147	233	173
HDCP	17	5	13	11	9	16	7	1	2

Directions: Take I-495 to Exit 10 (Route 123 W). Go approximately 4 miles. Course is on left.

Wayland Country Club

79

Wayland, MA (508) 358-4775

Club Pro: Joe Potty
Pro Shop: Full inventory
Payment: Cash only
Tee Times: Call Mon. for wknd.dys in adv.

Tees	Holes	Yards	Par	USGA	Slope
BACK	18	5836	70	67.9	113
MIDDLE	18	5974	70	67.3	112
FRONT	18	4875	71	70.0	120

Fee 9 Holes: Weekday: No   **Weekend:** No
Fee 18 Holes: Weekday: $30, $18 after 1 pm   **Weekend:** $35, $25 after 3 pm
Cart Rental: $24/18   **Discounts:** Senior & Junior
Lessons: $35/30 min.   **Schools:** No   **Junior Golf:** Yes   **Membership:** No
Driving Range: No   **Non-Metal Spikes:** Yes
Other: Restaurant / Clubhouse / Snack bar / Bar-lounge

The course is fairly flat and wide open. Has an extensive pro shop that is open year round. Included in national ranking of best 100 golf shop operations. Greens fee is $15 after 6 pm every day.

	1	2	3	4	5	6	7	8	9
PAR	5	4	4	3	4	3	4	3	4
YARDS	443	412	384	139	353	188	260	153	405
HDCP	11	1	5	15	13	9	17	7	3

	10	11	12	13	14	15	16	17	18
PAR	4	4	5	4	3	4	4	3	5
YARDS	320	326	500	346	174	378	400	198	457
HDCP	16	12	8	10	18	4	2	6	14

Directions: Take Route 128/95; take Route 20 West; right onto Route 27 North; approximately 1 mile right.

Wedgewood Pines CC

80

Harvard Rd., Stow, MA (978)- 562-0066

Club Pro: Tom Wessner
Pro Shop: Yes
Payment: Visa, MC, Cash, Check
Tee Times: 1 week adv.

Tees	Holes	Yards	Par	USGA	Slope
BACK	18	6659	71	72.4	131
MIDDLE	18	6374	71	71.0	127
FRONT	18	4913	71	70.5	120

Fee 9 Holes: Weekday: $20.00   **Weekend:** $20.00
Fee 18 Holes: Weekday: $40.00   **Weekend:** $40.00
Cart Rental: $28.00/18 $15.00/9   **Discounts:** 25% if guest of member
Lessons: $40.00/half hour   **Schools:** No   **Junior Golf:** Yes   **Membership:** Yes
Driving Range: Yes   **Non-Metal Spikes:** Yes
Other: Temporary Clubhouse/ Snack bar

Built on rolling terrain and incoporates natural wetlands on many of the holes. Front nine is also characterized by tall pine-lined fairways. Natural wetland areas on every hole in back nine.

	1	2	3	4	5	6	7	8	9
PAR	4	3	5	4	5	3	4	4	4
YARDS	345	190	481	398	512	164	385	394	416
HDCP	15	11	13	6	10	16	8	4	1

	10	11	12	13	14	15	16	17	18
PAR	4	3	4	5	3	5	3	4	5
YARDS	425	167	344	506	147	453	149	374	522
HDCP	3	14	12	9	18	2	17	7	5

Directions: Take I-495 to Route 117 East (Exit 27). Go four miles and take a left onto Harvard Rd. Club is located at #215 Harvard Rd.

4✪ =Excellent 3✪ =Very Good 2✪ =Good **Greater Boston/South Shore/Cape Cod**

Widow's Walk Golf Course   81

Scituate, MA (781) 544-7777

Club Pro: Bob Sanderson, PGA
Pro Shop: Yes
Payment: Visa, MC, Amex, Cash
Tee Times: 6 days adv.
Fee 9 Holes: Weekday: $17.00
Fee 18 Holes: Weekday: $28.00
Cart Rental: $24.00/ 18 $12.00/ 9
Lessons: $45.00/ 45 minutes **Schools:** No.
Driving Range: $3.00/ bucket
Other: Restaurant / Bar

Tees	Holes	Yards	Par	USGA	Slope
BACK	18	6403	72	69.8	123
MIDDLE	18	6062	72	68.3	120
FRONT	18	4562	72	65.9	109

Weekend: $23.00
Weekend: $38.00
Discounts: Senior & Junior M-Th
Junior Golf: Yes **Membership:** No
Non-Metal Spikes: Yes

1997 winner of *Golf Digest's* "Environmental Leaders in Golf" award. Spectacular views from elevated tees. www.cjhgolf.com

	1	2	3	4	5	6	7	8	9
PAR	5	3	4	4	3	5	4	3	5
YARDS	504	126	313	412	183	486	312	191	520
HDCP	9	17	7	1	13	3	11	15	5
	10	11	12	13	14	15	16	17	18
PAR	4	3	4	4	4	5	3	4	5
YARDS	425	140	350	351	302	486	167	313	481
HDCP	2	18	12	6	14	4	16	10	8

Directions: Route 3 to Exit 13, Route 53 North to Route 123 East. Go straight through Route 3A intersection. Take first right after .1 mile and proceed to stop sign. Go straight. Course is 7/10 mile on left.

William J. Devine GC   82

Dorchester, MA (617) 265-4084

Club Pro: Bill Flynn, George Lyons
Pro Shop: Full inventory
Payment: Visa, MC
Tee Times: Weekends, 2 days adv.
Fee 9 Holes: Weekday: $12.50
Fee 18 Holes: Weekday: $22.00
Cart Rental: $20.00/18 $10.00/9
Lessons: $25.00/half hour **Schools:** No
Driving Range: No
Other: Clubhouse / Snack Bar

Tees	Holes	Yards	Par	USGA	Slope
BACK	18	6175	70	69.8	113
MIDDLE	18	6009	70	68.6	113
FRONT	18	5240	72	70.0	113

Weekend: $13.50
Weekend: $25.00
Discounts: Senior & Junior
Junior Golf: Yes **Membership:** Yes, waiting list
Non-Metal Spikes: No

Renovated in 1989. Quite possibly the oldest public course in the country. Golf played here December 12, 1890, making it the first attempt at golf in America. The layout is a wonderful park.

	1	2	3	4	5	6	7	8	9
PAR	4	4	4	3	4	4	4	3	4
YARDS	382	289	417	187	350	395	435	175	360
HDCP	7	13	3	15	11	5	1	17	9
	10	11	12	13	14	15	16	17	18
PAR	4	5	4	3	4	3	4	4	5
YARDS	365	525	415	165	375	195	330	305	510
HDCP	8	2	4	18	10	16	12	14	6

Directions: Follow signs to Franklin Park Zoo.

Willowdale Golf Course

83

Mansfield, MA (508) 339-3197

Club Pro: No
Pro Shop: Limited inventory
Payment: Cash only
Tee Times: No
Fee 9 Holes: Weekday: $10.00
Fee 18 Holes: Weekday: $13.00
Cart Rental: Pull cart, $2.00
Lessons: No **Schools:** No
Driving Range: No
Other: Snack bar / Bar-lounge / Clubhouse

Tees	Holes	Yards	Par	USGA	Slope
BACK					
MIDDLE	9	3870	60	N/A	N/A
FRONT					

Weekend: $12.00
Weekend: $15.00
Discounts: Senior
Junior Golf: Yes **Membership:** No
Non-Metal Spikes: Preferred

An executive-style par 60; considered an easy walker. Open April 1 - December 1.

	1	2	3	4	5	6	7	8	9
PAR	4	3	3	4	4	3	3	3	3
YARDS	265	180	190	320	285	180	100	210	205
HDCP	2	5	8	3	1	7	9	4	6
	10	11	12	13	14	15	16	17	18
PAR	4	3	3	4	4	3	3	3	3
YARDS	265	180	190	320	285	180	100	210	205
HDCP	2	5	8	3	1	7	9	4	6

Directions: Take I-95 to Mansfield exit. Route 140 to Mansfield Center, School Street exit. First right on Willow Street.

Woodbriar CC

84

Falmouth, MA (508) 495-5500

Club Pro: Ken Mcintyre
Pro Shop: No
Payment: Cash or credit card
Tee Times: No
Fee 9 Holes: Weekday:
Fee 18 Holes: Weekday: $20.00
Cart Rental: $2.00/pull cart
Lessons: Yes **Schools:** No
Driving Range: Net
Other: Snack bar

Tees	Holes	Yards	Par	USGA	Slope
BACK	N/A				
MIDDLE	9	1410	27	N/A	N/A
FRONT	N/A				

Weekend:
Weekend: $20.00
Discounts: None
Junior Golf: Yes **Membership:** Yes
Non-Metal Spikes: No

COUPON

An executive-style nine hole golf course. A good course to learn golf or improve short game. Open year round.

	1	2	3	4	5	6	7	8	9
PAR	3	3	3	3	3	3	3	3	3
YARDS	142	129	115	139	270	162	168	127	158
HDCP	5	9	6	7	1	3	4	8	2
	10	11	12	13	14	15	16	17	18
PAR									
YARDS									
HDCP									

Directions: Take Route 28 to Brick Kiln Road Exit, take left at end of off-ramp, take right at first red light onto Gifford Street, course is 2.5 miles on left.

4✪ =Excellent 3✪ =Very Good 2✪ =Good

CHAPTER 2
Central Massachusetts & Boston's North Shore

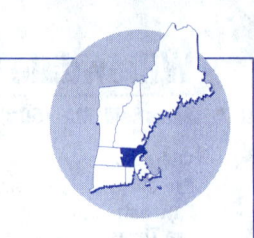

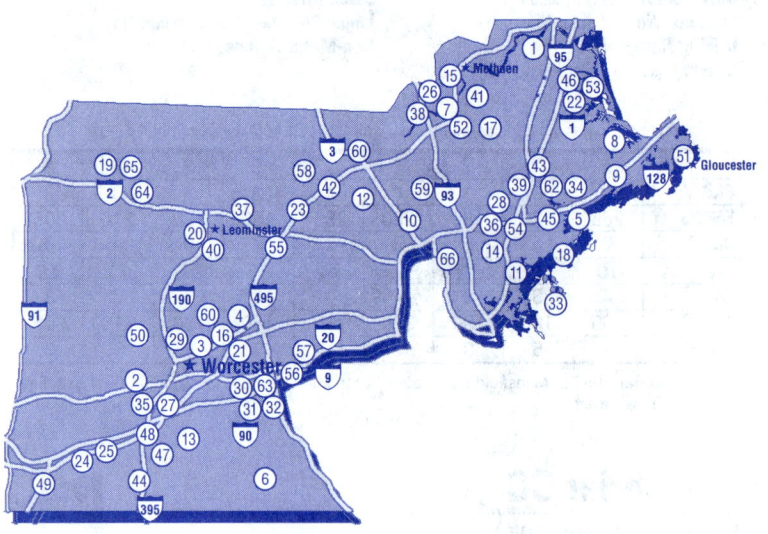

Amesbury Golf & CC	1	Hemlock Ridge GC	24
Bay Path Golf Course	2	Heritage CC	25
Bedrock Golf Club	3	Hickory Hill GC	26
Berlin Country Club	4	Hillcrest Country Club	27
Beverly Golf & Tennis	5	Hillview Golf Course	28
Blissful Meadows GC	6	Holden Hills CC	29
Bradford Country Club	7	Indian Meadows GC	30
Candlewood Golf Club	8	Juniper Hill GC (Lakeside)	31
Cape Ann Golf Club	9	Juniper Hill GC (Riverside)	32
CC of Billerica	10		
Cedar Glen Golf Club	11	Kelley Greens By The Sea	33
Chelmsford CC	12	Lakeview Golf Course	34
Clearview Golf Course	13	Leicester Country Club	35
Colonial Golf Club	14	Lynnfield Center GC	36
Crystal Springs CC	15	Maplewood Golf Course	37
Cyprian Keyes	16	Merrimack Valley GC	38
Far Corner Golf Course	17	Middleton Golf Course	39
Gannon Muni. GC	18	Monoosnock CC	40
Gardner Municipal GC	19	Murphy's Garrison Par 3 Golf Center	41
Grand View CC	20		
Green Hill Municipal GC	21	Nabnasset Lake CC	42
Green Valley GC	22	New Meadows GC	43
Groton Country Club	23		
Nichols College GC	44	Rowley Country Club	53
Olde Salem Greens	45	Sagamore Spring GC	54
Ould Newbury GC	46	Shaker Hills Golf Club	55
Pakachoag Golf Course	47	St. Mark's Golf Course	56
Pine Ridge Country Club	48	Stony Brook Golf Course	57
Quaboag Country Club	49	Townsend Ridge CC	58
Quail Hollow Golf & CC	50	Trull Brook Golf Course	59
Rockport Golf Course	51	Tyngsboro CC	60
Rolling Green GC	52	Wachusett CC	61
		Wenham Country Club	62
		Westboro CC	63
		Westminster CC	64
		Winchendon CC	65
		Woburn Country Club	66

Amesbury Golf & CC

1

Monroe St., Amesbury, MA (978) 388-5153

Club Pro: Butch Mellon
Pro Shop: Full inventory
Payment: Cash only
Tee Times: 5 days adv.

Tees	Holes	Yards	Par	USGA	Slope
BACK	N/A				
MIDDLE	9	6095	70	70.5	125
FRONT	9	5381	70	71.9	126

NE/ CTRL MA

Fee 9 Holes: Weekday: $12.00 **Weekend:** $14.00
Fee 18 Holes: Weekday: $23.00 **Weekend:** $25.00
Cart Rental: $24.00/18 $12.00/9 **Discounts:** None
Lessons: $25.00/half hour **Schools:** No **Junior Golf:** Yes **Membership:** Yes
Driving Range: No **Non-Metal Spikes:** Yes
Other: Clubhouse / Lockers / Showers / Snack bar / Bar-lounge

Rolling hills, picturesque, and challenging.

	1	2	3	4	5	6	7	8	9
PAR	4	3	4	4	5	4	4	3	4
YARDS	381	170	349	309	524	299	365	162	380
HDCP	7	17	11	13	3	9	1	15	5
	10	11	12	13	14	15	16	17	18
PAR	4	3	4	4	5	4	4	3	4
YARDS	387	230	354	324	530	335	414	181	395
HDCP	8	16	12	14	4	10	2	18	6

Directions: Take I-95 North to Route 110 West; then take right at lights near Burger King; take right onto Monroe Street. Course is 1/3 mile on left.

Bay Path Golf Course

2

East Brookfield, MA (508) 867-8161

Club Pro: No
Pro Shop: Full inventory
Payment: Cash or check
Tee Times: No

Tees	Holes	Yards	Par	USGA	Slope
BACK					
MIDDLE	9	3015	36	69.5	113
FRONT					

Fee 9 Holes: Weekday: $9.00 **Weekend:** $12.00
Fee 18 Holes: Weekday: $15.00 **Weekend:** $18.00
Cart Rental: $18.00/18, $10.00/9 **Discounts:** None
Lessons: No **Schools:** **Junior Golf:** No **Membership:** Yes Limited
Driving Range: No **Non-Metal Spikes:** Yes
Other: Clubhouse / Snack bar / Bar-lounge

Very flat and easy to walk for Central Mass. MGA handicapping available for an additional fee. School teams use facilities. Open April - until it snows.

	1	2	3	4	5	6	7	8	9
PAR	4	4	5	4	3	5	4	3	4
YARDS	325	300	525	395	165	495	285	185	340
HDCP	15	13	3	1	7	9	17	11	5
	10	11	12	13	14	15	16	17	18
PAR									
YARDS									
HDCP									

Directions: Mass. Pike to Route 20 East (Sturbridge exit). Then take Route 20 East to route 49 North to Route 9 West to Route 67 North (North Brookfield Road). Course is approximately 1/4 mile on left.

4✪ =Excellent 3✪ =Very Good 2✪ = Good

Bedrock Golf Club

Rutland, MA (508) 886-0202

Club Pro: Joe Carr
Pro Shop: Limited inventory
Payment: Cash only
Tee Times: Weekends
Fee 9 Holes: Weekday: $10.00
Fee 18 Holes: Weekday: $15.00
Cart Rental: $23.00/18 $11.50/9
Lessons: No **Schools:** No
Driving Range: No
Other: Clubhouse / Bar-Lounge / Snack Bar

Tees	Holes	Yards	Par	USGA	Slope
BACK					
MIDDLE	9	6013	72	69.8	127
FRONT					

Weekend: $15.00
Weekend: $25.00
Discounts: Junior, Wkdays
Junior Golf: No **Membership:** Yes
Non-Metal Spikes: No

COUPON

Opened in 1992. Gently rolling, narrow landing areas. Small, undulating greens, challenging. Collared shirts required. Open April - November.

	1	2	3	4	5	6	7	8	9
PAR	4	5	4	3	4	5	3	4	4
YARDS	340	460	380	184	355	487	166	348	411
HDCP	15	17	1	11	3	7	9	13	5
	10	11	12	13	14	15	16	17	18
PAR	4	5	4	3	4	5	3	4	4
YARDS	327	410	356	165	335	433	139	323	394
HDCP	14	18	2	8	6	10	12	16	4

Directions: The the Mass Pike to Auburn Exit (10). Then take Route 20 W to Route 56 N to Route 122. In Paxton. Course is 4 miles on left.

Berlin Country Club

25 Carr Rd., Berlin, MA (978) 838-2733

Club Pro: No
Pro Shop: Full inventory
Payment: Cash only
Tee Times: No
Fee 9 Holes: Weekday: $12.00
Fee 18 Holes: Weekday: $18.00
Cart Rental: $20.00/18 $12.00/9
Lessons: No **Schools:** No
Driving Range: No (Close-by)
Other: Clubhouse / Snack bar / Bar-lounge / Banquet Facility

Tees	Holes	Yards	Par	USGA	Slope
BACK					
MIDDLE	9	2233	33	62.9	108
FRONT	9	2072	37	N/A	N/A

Weekend: $12.00
Weekend: $18.00
Discounts: Senior & Junior
Junior Golf: No **Membership:** Yes
Non-Metal Spikes: No

Mildly sloping fairways with challenging greens. Golf shirts and golf shoes required. Golf school and driving range near-by. Open March - November.

	1	2	3	4	5	6	7	8	9
PAR	4	4	4	3	4	4	3	4	3
YARDS	312	326	332	127	264	349	108	282	133
HDCP	13	5	3	15	11	1	17	9	7
	10	11	12	13	14	15	16	17	18
PAR									
YARDS									
HDCP									

Directions: From I-495 take Route 62 to Berlin Center and follow signs. From I-290 take Solomon Pond Rd. to Berlin Center and follow signs.

Beverly Golf & Tennis

✪✪✪ 5

134 McKay Beverly, MA (978) 922-9072

Club Pro: Bill Tragakis
Pro Shop: Full inventory
Payment: Cash only
Tee Times: 1 week adv.

Tees	Holes	Yards	Par	USGA	Slope
BACK	18	6237	70	70.6	123
MIDDLE	18	5966	70	69.2	121
FRONT	18	5429	73	70.3	113

Fee 9 Holes: Weekday: $17.00
Fee 18 Holes: Weekday: $30.00
Cart Rental: $23.00/18 $13.00/9
Lessons: $50/hour **Schools:** No
Driving Range: No
Weekend: $20.00 twilight
Weekend: $36.00
Discounts: Senior. Carts only weekdays.
Junior Golf: Yes **Membership:** Yes. Wait list.
Non-Metal Spikes: No
Other: Clubhouse / Lockers / Showers / Snack bar / Restaurant / Bar-lounge

NE/
CTRL
MA

A Friel Golf Company course. Undulating fairways and medium sized greens. Members only until 1:30 on Weekends and 10 am - 2 pm on Wednesdays and Fridays. Discount for residents.

	1	2	3	4	5	6	7	8	9
PAR	4	4	3	4	4	3	4	5	4
YARDS	431	413	147	390	271	159	372	571	300
HDCP	3	5	13	9	17	11	7	1	15
	10	11	12	13	14	15	16	17	18
PAR	4	3	3	5	4	3	4	5	4
YARDS	266	235	193	462	347	143	382	500	384
HDCP	16	6	12	4	14	18	8	2	10

Directions: Take Route 128 to Exit 20 South onto Cabot St.; turn right onto McKay. Course is approximately 1/4 mile on right.

Blissful Meadows GC

6

Uxbridge, MA (508) 278-6113

Club Pro: Mike Marsh, Head Pro
Pro Shop: Full inventory
Payment: Visa, MC, Amex
Tee Times: 2 days adv.

Tees	Holes	Yards	Par	USGA	Slope
BACK	18	6588	72	71.3	128
MIDDLE	18	6156	72	68.7	124
FRONT	18	5065	72	69.1	122

Fee 9 Holes: Weekday: $16.00
Fee 18 Holes: Weekday: $25.00
Cart Rental: $22.00/18 $11.50 pp
Lessons: $30.00/half hour **Schools:** No
Driving Range: $6.00/lg. $4.00/sm.
Other: Restaurant / Clubhouse / Bar-lounge
Weekend: $20.00
Weekend: $35.00
Discounts: Senior
Junior Golf: Yes **Membership:** Yes
Non-Metal Spikes: Yes

COUPON

Rolling hills, fifty tree varieties, and scenic country setting. Back nine opened in 1996. Bent grass greens and tees. Proper golf attire required. Open April - November.

	1	2	3	4	5	6	7	8	9
PAR	4	3	5	4	3	4	4	5	4
YARDS	326	148	510	343	132	368	310	540	334
HDCP	11	15	3	9	17	5	13	1	7
	10	11	12	13	14	15	16	17	18
PAR	5	4	4	3	4	3	5	4	4
YARDS	488	335	345	139	306	150	493	370	398
HDCP	4	12	8	18	14	16	2	10	6

Directions: Take route 146 to Route 16 West. Take first left on to West Street. Follow signs 3 miles. Take right at dead end.

4✪ = Excellent 3✪ = Very Good 2✪ = Good   **Boston's North Shore & Central MA 85**

Bradford Country Club

Bradford, MA (978) 372-8587

Club Pro: Mike Shoueiry, PGA
Pro Shop: Full inventory
Payment: MC, Visa, Amex, Checks
Tee Times: 5 days adv.
Fee 9 Holes: Weekday: $16.00
Fee 18 Holes: Weekday: $28.00
Cart Rental: $12.60/18, $7.35/9
Lessons: $30/30 min $50/60 min **Schools:** No **Junior Golf:** No **Membership:** Yes
Driving Range: No
Other: Clubhouse / Bar-lounge / Restaurant / Lockers/ Outings / Leagues

Tees	Holes	Yards	Par	USGA	Slope
BACK	N/A				
MIDDLE	18	6469	70	70.3	134
FRONT	N/A				

Weekend: $17.00
Weekend: $34.00
Discounts: Senior & Junior
Non-Metal Spikes: Preferred

Cornish and Silva design. Beautifully manicured bent grass. Front nine built around protected wetlands and lakes. Panoramic views from hillier back nine. Open March - November.

	1	2	3	4	5	6	7	8	9
PAR	4	4	3	4	4	3	4	5	4
YARDS	368	346	156	375	382	146	353	491	479
HDCP	13	7	15	9	5	17	11	3	1
	10	11	12	13	14	15	16	17	18
PAR	4	3	5	4	4	4	4	3	4
YARDS	427	195	510	413	418	401	410	171	428
HDCP	10	16	2	4	8	14	12	18	6

Directions: Route 495 to Exit 48. North on Route 125 to Salem St. Turn right. Right onto Boxford Road (1st street after Bradford House Restaurant). Take first right on Chadwick Road to Clubhouse.

Candlewood Golf Club

Rt. 133, Ipswich, MA (978) 356-5377

Club Pro: Bob Robinson
Pro Shop: Yes
Payment: Cash only
Tee Times: No
Fee 9 Holes: Weekday: $11.00
Fee 18 Holes: Weekday: $16.00
Cart Rental: $9.00/9
Lessons: $25.00/hour **Schools:** N/R
Driving Range: No
Other: Snack Bar

Tees	Holes	Yards	Par	USGA	Slope
BACK	N/A				
MIDDLE	9	2108	32	N/A	N/A
FRONT	N/A				

Weekend: $12.00
Weekend: $17.00
Discounts: Senior M-F $2
Junior Golf: N/R **Membership:** Yes
Non-Metal Spikes: No

The course is easy to walk and is good for senior citizens and beginners. Twilight rate is $9.00 after 5pm.

	1	2	3	4	5	6	7	8	9
PAR	4	4	3	3	3	4	4	4	3
YARDS	350	350	120	140	135	253	290	280	190
HDCP	N/A	N/A	N/A	N/A	N/A	N/A	N/A	N/A	N/A
	10	11	12	13	14	15	16	17	18
PAR									
YARDS									
HDCP									

Directions: Take Route 128 to Route 1A North. Take Route 133 South towards Essex.

Cape Ann Golf Club 9

Rt. 133, Essex, MA (978) 768-7544

Club Pro: No
Pro Shop: Limited inventory
Payment: Cash or credit card
Tee Times: No
Fee 9 Holes: Weekday: $15.00
Fee 18 Holes: Weekday: $27.00
Cart Rental: $11.00/9
Lessons: Yes **Schools:** No
Driving Range: No
Other: Bar-lounge / Snack Bar

Tees	Holes	Yards	Par	USGA	Slope
BACK					
MIDDLE	9	5866	69	67.2	110
FRONT	9	4608	69	65.2	102

Weekend: $17.00
Weekend: $27.00
Discounts: Senior & Junior
Junior Golf: N/R **Membership:** No
Non-Metal Spikes: No

NE/CTRL MA

Pleasant and scenic course on the north shore of Boston. Junior discount 7 days a week. Tuesday is Ladies Day.

	1	2	3	4	5	6	7	8	9
PAR	4	4	3	4	4	4	3	4	4
YARDS	359	351	170	437	330	280	189	379	341
HDCP	7	5	15	1	9	11	13	3	17
	10	11	12	13	14	15	16	17	18
PAR	4	4	3	5	4	4	3	4	4
YARDS	367	389	181	463	348	289	234	410	349
HDCP	8	6	18	12	14	10	4	2	16

Directions: Take Route 128 North to Exit 15 (School Street), follow signs toward Essex.

CC of Billerica 10

Billerica, MA (978) 667-8061

Club Pro: Barrie Bruce, PGA
Pro Shop: Full inventory
Payment: Cash or credit card
Tee Times: No
Fee 9 Holes: Weekday: $13.00
Fee 18 Holes: Weekday: $23.00
Cart Rental: $22.00/18 $11.00/9
Lessons: $25.00/half hour **Schools:** Yes
Driving Range: $6 lg. / $4/sm.
Other: Restaurant / Bar-lounge / Clubhouse

Tees	Holes	Yards	Par	USGA	Slope
BACK	18	5368	66	65.9	112
MIDDLE	18	4965	66	63.9	107
FRONT	18	4185	66	63.0	99

Weekend: $15.00
Weekend: $25.00
Discounts: None
Junior Golf: Yes **Membership:** Yes
Non-Metal Spikes: No

COUPON

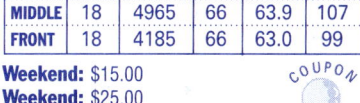

Recently expanded to 18 holes. "Fun, challenging course for beginners through accomplished players." JD. Strong junior program.

	1	2	3	4	5	6	7	8	9
PAR	4	3	4	4	5	3	4	4	4
YARDS	415	150	349	397	543	126	382	299	373
HDCP	5	15	11	1	3	17	7	13	9
	10	11	12	13	14	15	16	17	18
PAR	4	3	4	3	3	3	4	3	4
YARDS	279	189	327	137	125	141	312	149	272
HDCP	4	8	6	16	18	14	2	12	10

Directions: Take Route 128 to Route 3A North. Take Route 3A North into Billerica Center. Take right before Friendly's restaurant and at the end of the road, take a right and then the third left onto Baldwin Street. Course is on right.

4✪ =Excellent 3✪ =Very Good 2✪ =Good   **Boston's North Shore & Central MA 87**

Cedar Glen Golf Club

11

Saugus, MA (781) 233-3609

Club Pro: No
Pro Shop: Limited inventory
Payment: Cash only
Tee Times: No
Fee 9 Holes: Weekday: $14.00
Fee 18 Holes: Weekday: $20.00
Cart Rental: $20.00/18
Lessons: No **Schools:** N/R
Driving Range: No
Other: Clubhouse / Snack bar

Tees	Holes	Yards	Par	USGA	Slope
BACK	N/A				
MIDDLE	9	5890	70	66.7	107
FRONT	9	3000	35	67	107

Weekend: $15.00
Weekend: $23.00
Discounts: Senior, $10
Junior Golf: No **Membership:** No
Non-Metal Spikes: No

This course offers moderate challenge, a good course for beginners.

	1	2	3	4	5	6	7	8	9
PAR	4	5	3	4	4	3	4	4	4
YARDS	350	475	220	335	380	135	310	340	400
HDCP	3	2	4	7	1	9	8	6	5
	10	11	12	13	14	15	16	17	18
PAR	4	5	3	4	4	3	4	4	4
YARDS	350	475	220	335	380	135	310	340	400
HDCP	3	2	4	7	1	9	8	6	5

Directions: Take I-95 to Walnut Street. Follow Walnut Street east to Water Street. Take right, course is on left.

Chelmsford Country Club

12

66 Park Rd., Chelmsford, MA (978) 256-1818

Club Pro: Gerry Fitzgerald
Pro Shop: Yes
Payment: Visa, MC, Cash, Checks
Tee Times: Yes
Fee 9 Holes: Weekday: $12.00
Fee 18 Holes: Weekday: $16.00
Cart Rental: $20.00/18 $12.00/9
Lessons: Yes **Schools:** Jr. & Sr.
Driving Range: $5.00/bucket
Other: Snack bar / Bar-lounge / Function Hall

Tees	Holes	Yards	Par	USGA	Slope
BACK	N/A				
MIDDLE	9	5088	68	65.3	114
FRONT	9	5088	68	65.6	112

Weekend: $14.00
Weekend: $20.00
Discounts: Senior & Junior
Junior Golf: Yes **Membership:** Yes
Non-Metal Spikes: No

COUPON

Short course with improved conditions. 5 of 9 holes have water. Excellent greens. New hole opening this year! Managed by Sterling Golf Management, Inc. www.Boston:com

	1	2	3	4	5	6	7	8	9
PAR	4	3	3	5	4	3	4	5	3
YARDS	251	207	142	472	349	145	312	464	202
HDCP	17	1	15	9	7	15	5	11	3
	10	11	12	13	14	15	16	17	18
PAR	4	3	3	5	4	3	4	5	3
YARDS	251	207	142	472	349	145	312	464	202
HDCP	18	2	14	10	8	16	6	12	4

Directions: Take Route 3 or Route 495 to Route 110 to Chelmsford Center. Then take Route 27 S. Take left onto Park Road. Course is 200 yards on left.

Clearview Golf Course　　13

Millbury, MA   (508) 753-9201

Club Pro: Steve Gelineaux
Pro Shop: Full inventory
Payment: Visa, MC, cash
Tee Times: Every day
Fee 9 Holes: Weekday: $11.00
Fee 18 Holes: Weekday: $15.00
Cart Rental: $11.00/18 $6.00/9
Lessons: Yes **Schools:** No
Driving Range: No
Other: Snack bar / Bar-lounge

Tees	Holes	Yards	Par	USGA	Slope
BACK	N/A				
MIDDLE	9	5569	71	66.3	107
FRONT	9	5236	71	67.7	112

Weekend: $13.00
Weekend: $17.00
Discounts: Senior $1
Junior Golf: No **Membership:** Yes
Non-Metal Spikes: No

NE/CTRL MA

The course has hilly terrain and well conditioned greens.

	1	2	3	4	5	6	7	8	9
PAR	3	5	5	3	5	3	4	4	3
YARDS	147	472	484	192	477	135	348	290	179
HDCP	18	8	2	10	6	16	4	12	14
	10	11	12	13	14	15	16	17	18
PAR	3	5	5	3	5	4	4	4	3
YARDS	160	485	491	207	489	304	365	305	193
HDCP	17	7	1	9	5	15	3	11	13

Directions: I-90 (Mass Pike) to Route 122 to Route 20 West. Take left at third traffic light. Half mile on Park Hill Ave. on left.

Colonial Golf Club　　14

Wakefield, MA   (781) 245-0335

Club Pro: Tim Frazer, Head Pro
Pro Shop: Full inventory
Payment: Most major
Tee Times: 3 days in adv.
Fee 9 Holes: Weekday: $27.00
Fee 18 Holes: Weekday: $45.00
Cart Rental: Included
Lessons: $35.00/session **Schools:** No
Driving Range: Yes
Other: Restaurant / Clubhouse / Hotel / Bar-lounge / Lockers / Snack Bar / Showers

Tees	Holes	Yards	Par	USGA	Slope
BACK	18	6565	70	72.8	130
MIDDLE	18	6187	70	71.1	129
FRONT	18	5580	72	70.5	119

Weekend: $32.00
Weekend: $57.00
Discounts: None
Junior Golf: N/R **Membership:** No
Non-Metal Spikes: No

Golf course is nestled within the fresh water marshes of Lynnfield. Greens are fast. Open April 1 - December 15.

	1	2	3	4	5	6	7	8	9
PAR	4	4	3	4	3	5	4	5	4
YARDS	419	345	136	422	195	531	339	537	315
HDCP	3	13	17	1	9	5	11	7	15
	10	11	12	13	14	15	16	17	18
PAR	4	4	4	4	3	4	4	3	4
YARDS	398	333	356	390	169	411	330	171	390
HDCP	8	10	12	2	18	4	14	16	6

Directions: Course is located off I-95 at Exit 43, 12 miles north of Boston.

4✪ =Excellent 3✪ =Very Good 2✪ =Good   **Boston's North Shore & Central MA**

Crystal Springs CC   15

N. Broadway, Haverhill, MA (978) 374-9621

Club Pro: Ed Tompkins
Pro Shop: Full inventory
Payment: Cash only
Tee Times: 7 days adv.

Tees	Holes	Yards	Par	USGA	Slope
BACK	18	6706	72	70.8	116
MIDDLE	18	6436	72	70.8	114
FRONT	18	5596	72	70.8	116

Fee 9 Holes: Weekday: $10.00   **Weekend:** $12.00
Fee 18 Holes: Weekday: $18.00   **Weekend:** $20.00
Cart Rental: $20.00/18 $12.00/9   **Discounts:** None
Lessons: $30.00/half hour **Schools:** No   **Junior Golf:** No **Membership:** Yes
Driving Range: $5.00   **Non-Metal Spikes:** No
Other: Snack bar / Restaurant / Bar-lounge

Although the fairways are wide, the course is challenging. Golfers who hit for distance will enjoy Crystal Springs. Beautiful views of the lake.

	1	2	3	4	5	6	7	8	9
PAR	4	3	4	4	5	3	4	5	4
YARDS	367	213	351	395	472	207	387	475	415
HDCP	5	15	7	1	11	17	9	13	3
	10	11	12	13	14	15	16	17	18
PAR	4	5	4	3	4	4	3	4	5
YARDS	389	491	394	210	332	316	135	415	472
HDCP	6	8	4	16	10	12	18	2	14

Directions: Route 495 North to Exit 50 (Route 97). At end of ramp, go across Route 97 to monument. and turn left at the blinking red light. Course 2.5 miles on left.

Cyprian Keyes   16

Boylston, MA (508) 869-9900

Club Pro: Eric Kohberger, PGA
Pro Shop: Full inventory
Payment: Visa, MC, Amex, Disc
Tee Times: 3 days adv.

Tees	Holes	Yards	Par	USGA	Slope
BACK	18	6844	72	72.7	132
MIDDLE	18	6123	72	69.7	127
FRONT	18	5079	72	69.2	119

Fee 9 Holes: Weekday: N/A   **Weekend:** N/A
Fee 18 Holes: Weekday: $40.00 M-Th   **Weekend:** $50.00 F/S/S/H
Cart Rental: $15.00pp/18   **Discounts:** Junior
Lessons: Yes **Schools:** TBA   **Junior Golf:** Yes **Membership:** No
Driving Range: $5.00 /bucket   **Non-Metal Spikes:** Yes
Other: Restaurant/ Function facilities

COUPON

"Maybe the best new New England course built in the '90's. A thinking persons course. Highest caliber staff." (R.W.) Home to New England Section of the PGA.

	1	2	3	4	5	6	7	8	9
PAR	4	4	5	5	4	3	4	4	3
YARDS	332	367	510	476	376	180	357	369	155
HDCP	13	11	5	7	3	15	1	9	17
	10	11	12	13	14	15	16	17	18
PAR	5	3	4	4	4	4	3	4	5
YARDS	475	175	350	318	406	348	162	297	470
HDCP	10	8	14	4	2	6	18	16	12

Directions: Route 290 to Exit 23B (Route 140 North). Go 1 mile and take third right onto East Temple Street.

Far Corner Golf Course ◎◎ 17

W. Boxford, MA (978) 352-8300

Club Pro: John O'Connor and Bob Flynn
Pro Shop: Full inventory
Payment: Cash, MC, Visa
Tee Times: Fri.,Sat.,Sun.
Fee 9 Holes: Weekday: $15.00
Fee 18 Holes: Weekday: $30.00
Cart Rental: $12.60pp/18 $6.30pp/9
Lessons: $30/30 min. **Schools:** Jr.Yes
Driving Range: $4.00/med. All grass.
Other: Snack bar / Restaurant / Bar-lounge / Clubhouse / Showers

Tees	Holes	Yards	Par	USGA	Slope
BACK	18	6719	72	72.9	130
MIDDLE	18	6189	72	70.9	126
FRONT	18	5655	73	71.4	115

Weekend: $17.00
Weekend: $34.00
Discounts: Senior & Junior
Junior Golf: No **Membership:** No
Non-Metal Spikes: No

COUPON

NE/ CTRL MA

Third nine opened in 1996: Yardage:3092 , Par: 36 , Rating: 35.1 , Slope:131. Open year round.

	1	2	3	4	5	6	7	8	9
PAR	5	4	4	3	4	4	3	4	5
YARDS	510	350	310	190	460	330	170	390	450
HDCP	7	3	17	15	1	9	13	5	11
	10	11	12	13	14	15	16	17	18
PAR	4	5	4	5	4	3	4	3	4
YARDS	270	470	360	530	380	170	320	135	390
HDCP	14	10	12	2	4	14	18	16	6

Directions: From I-95 North, take Exit 53B to Route 97 Georgetown. Follow to Route 133 West to West Boxford Village. Go right onto Main Street. Course is 2 miles on left.

Gannon Muni. GC 18

Lynn, MA (781) 592-8238

Club Pro: Mike Foster
Pro Shop: Full inventory
Payment: Cash only
Tee Times: No
Fee 9 Holes: Weekday: $17.00
Fee 18 Holes: Weekday: $30.00
Cart Rental: $22.00/18 $11.50 /9
Lessons: No **Schools:** No
Driving Range: No
Other: Snack bar / Grille

Tees	Holes	Yards	Par	USGA	Slope
BACK	18	6106	70	67.9	113
MIDDLE	18	6036	70	67.9	113
FRONT	18	5215	71	68.8	115

Weekend: $19.00 after 3 pm
Weekend: N/A
Discounts: None
Junior Golf: Yes **Membership:** Residents only
Non-Metal Spikes: On Wknds

Many new improvements. Active junior golf program for residents. Monday free junior clinic from 8:00 to 9:30, unlimited play on front nine 10:00-2:00. Weekly clinics for juniors at local park.

	1	2	3	4	5	6	7	8	9
PAR	4	4	4	4	4	3	4	4	3
YARDS	346	309	357	404	333	187	318	414	216
HDCP	5	15	7	1	9	17	11	3	13
	10	11	12	13	14	15	16	17	18
PAR	4	4	4	4	3	5	3	4	5
YARDS	309	335	401	383	158	486	228	319	588
HDCP	12	16	4	6	18	8	10	14	2

Directions: Route 1 North. Take Route 129 East (towards Lynn). Stay on 129 E (Lynnfield St.) for 2 mi. Course is on the right.

4◎ =Excellent 3◎ =Very Good 2◎ = Good   **Boston's North Shore & Central MA**

Gardner Municipal GC 19

Gardner, MA (978) 632-9703

Club Pro: Mike Egan
Pro Shop: Full inventory
Payment: Cash only
Tee Times: Weekends, Holidays

Tees	Holes	Yards	Par	USGA	Slope
BACK	18	6106	71	68.9	124
MIDDLE	18	5857	71	67.6	120
FRONT	18	5557	75	71.7	122

Fee 9 Holes: Weekday: N/A **Weekend:** N/A
Fee 18 Holes: Weekday: $25.00 **Weekend:** $30.00
Cart Rental: $22.00/18 $12.00/9 **Discounts:** Junior
Lessons: $25.00/half hour **Schools:** N/A **Junior Golf:** Yes **Membership:** Yes
Driving Range: Yes **Non-Metal Spikes:** Yes
Other: Clubhouse / Snack bar / Restaurant / Bar-lounge

New driving range. New irrigation system operational since May '97. Hosted NEPGA Pro AM '97 and MA PubLinx Qualifier '97. Open April 15 – snow.

	1	2	3	4	5	6	7	8	9
PAR	4	4	3	4	5	3	5	3	4
YARDS	320	297	215	316	525	137	530	142	406
HDCP	11	13	7	9	5	17	1	15	3

	10	11	12	13	14	15	16	17	18
PAR	4	5	4	4	3	5	3	4	4
YARDS	300	450	323	370	136	478	207	352	353
HDCP	14	12	16	2	18	4	10	6	8

Directions: Route 2 West to Route 140 North, follow for 5 miles (cross Route 101) to Gardner District Court. Right onto Green Street. Course is across from Mt. Wachusett Community College.

Grand View Country Club 20

Leominster, MA (978) 537-0614

Club Pro: John Novak
Pro Shop: Full inventory
Payment: No
Tee Times: Weekends

Tees	Holes	Yards	Par	USGA	Slope
BACK	N/A				
MIDDLE	18	6746	72	68.8	113
FRONT	9	3161	37	68.8	113

Fee 9 Holes: Weekday: $12.00 after 4 pm **Weekend:** $16.00 after 4 pm
Fee 18 Holes: Weekday: $20.00 **Weekend:** $23.00
Cart Rental: $22.00/18 $11.00/9 **Discounts:** None
Lessons: $35/45 min. **Schools:** No **Junior Golf:** No **Membership:** Yes
Driving Range: No **Non-Metal Spikes:** No
Other: Restaurant / Clubhouse / Bar-Lounge / Snack Bar

Water comes into play on many of the front-nine holes and only one hole on the back.

	1	2	3	4	5	6	7	8	9
PAR	4	5	3	5	3	4	4	4	4
YARDS	418	482	148	540	156	386	396	450	413
HDCP	2	14	18	12	16	6	4	10	8

	10	11	12	13	14	15	16	17	18
PAR	4	4	3	4	3	4	5	4	5
YARDS	337	358	195	425	175	440	491	397	539
HDCP	7	5	15	1	17	9	13	11	3

Directions: Route 2 to Route 12 (Main Street.), Go through lights, by People's Bank, bear right at at fork onto Pleasant Street. Follow 3 miles to Wachusett Street. Course is on right.

Green Hill Municipal GC

21

Worcester, MA (508) 799-1352

Club Pro: Matt Moison
Pro Shop: Full inventory
Payment: Cash only
Tee Times: 2 days adv.
Fee 9 Holes: Weekday: $13.00
Fee 18 Holes: Weekday: $18.00
Cart Rental: $22/18 $11.00/9
Lessons: $40.00/hour **Schools:** Yes
Driving Range: No- Coming.
Other: Clubhouse / Lockers / Showers / Snack bar

Tees	Holes	Yards	Par	USGA	Slope
BACK	18	6487	72	68.4	112
MIDDLE	18	6110	72	67.4	106
FRONT	18	5547	71	69.9	116

Weekend: $13.00
Weekend: $22 before 2 , $20 aft.2
Discounts: None
Junior Golf: Yes **Membership:** Yes
Non-Metal Spikes: Preferred

NE/CTRL MA

This tract offers varied challenges. Short par fives let you make up strokes. Greens fees $13.00 before 8 am (for 9 holes only).

	1	2	3	4	5	6	7	8	9
PAR	4	4	5	4	4	3	4	3	5
YARDS	375	334	455	357	342	192	340	157	475
HDCP	1	17	4	3	13	7	11	15	5
	10	11	12	13	14	15	16	17	18
PAR	4	3	4	5	4	3	5	4	4
YARDS	358	196	328	482	380	131	458	371	379
HDCP	4	12	16	2	14	18	8	6	10

Directions: Take I-290 to Exit 20. Take left onto Lincoln Street, take right onto Marsh Avenue.

Green Valley GC

22

Newburyport, MA (978) 463-8600

Club Pro: Yes
Pro Shop: Limited inventory
Payment: Cash only
Tee Times: No
Fee 9 Holes: Weekday: $10.00
Fee 18 Holes: Weekday: $17.00
Cart Rental: $15.00/18 $10.00/9
Lessons: $12.00 **Schools:** No
Driving Range: No
Other: Snack Bar and deck

Tees	Holes	Yards	Par	USGA	Slope
BACK	N/A				
MIDDLE	9	5681	70	67.4	110
FRONT	N/A				

Weekend: $12.00
Weekend: $20.00
Discounts: Senior, M-Th.
Junior Golf: No **Membership:** Yes
Non-Metal Spikes: No

COUPON

Super plush greens of Penncross bent grass, beautiful tees. Good for beginners and for walking. Friendly atmosphere. Flock of herons is an added attraction. Open April - Nov.

	1	2	3	4	5	6	7	8	9
PAR	4	4	4	5	3	4	4	3	4
YARDS	370	300	420	460	155	390	305	165	215
HDCP	4	6	1	5	7	3	8	2	9
	10	11	12	13	14	15	16	17	18
PAR	4	4	4	5	3	4	4	3	4
YARDS	385	310	430	475	171	410	315	185	220
HDCP	5	7	2	6	8	4	9	3	10

Directions: I-95, Exit 57. Go east. Take left at Friendly's, then left at stop sign,. 300 ft. on left is entrance to club.

4✪ =Excellent 3✪ =Very Good 2✪ = Good

Groton Country Club 23

Groton, MA (978) 448-2564

Club Pro: Brad Durrin
Pro Shop: Full inventory
Payment: MC, Visa, Discover
Tee Times: 7 days adv.
Fee 9 Holes: Weekday: $11.00   **Weekend:** $16.00
Fee 18 Holes: Weekday: $16.00   **Weekend:** $21.00
Cart Rental: $20.00/18 $12.00/9   **Discounts:** Senior & Junior
Lessons: $25/30 min. & Clinics **Schools:** Yes **Junior Golf:** Yes **Membership:** Yes
Driving Range: $5.00/lg bucket   **Non-Metal Spikes:** No
Other: Full Restaurant / Clubhouse / Bar-Lounge / Snack Bar / Showers

COUPON

Tees	Holes	Yards	Par	USGA	Slope
BACK	N/R				
MIDDLE	9	5506	70	66.5	116
FRONT					

This uniquely laid out course offers beautiful views of surrounding Groton countryside. Collared shirts are required. Open April - November.

	1	2	3	4	5	6	7	8	9
PAR	4	4	4	3	3	4	4	5	4
YARDS	330	260	325	140	210	326	335	450	300
HDCP	7	17	1	15	3	11	5	9	13
	10	11	12	13	14	15	16	17	18
PAR	4	4	4	3	3	4	4	5	4
YARDS	330	260	325	140	210	326	335	450	300
HDCP	7	17	1	15	3	11	5	9	13

Directions: The course is located six miles from I-495 on Route 119 in Groton.

Hemlock Ridge GC 24

Fiskdale, MA (508) 347-9935

Club Pro: No
Pro Shop: No
Payment: Cash only
Tee Times: No
Fee 9 Holes: Weekday: $10.00   **Weekend:** $11.00
Fee 18 Holes: Weekday: $18.00   **Weekend:** $20.00
Cart Rental: $18.00/18 $9.00/9   **Discounts:** Senior. $1.00 off
Lessons: No **Schools:** No   **Junior Golf:** Yes **Membership:** Yes
Driving Range: No   **Non-Metal Spikes:** N/R
Other: Clubhouse / Snack bar / Showers

Tees	Holes	Yards	Par	USGA	Slope
BACK	N/A				
MIDDLE	9	6272	72	70.6	117
FRONT	9	5206	72	69.0	109

Hilly scenery. Conditions good for both fairways and greens. No dress code. Open April 1 - November 1.

	1	2	3	4	5	6	7	8	9
PAR	4	4	3	4	4	5	4	3	5
YARDS	308	382	154	449	370	471	317	170	515
HDCP	15	3	17	1	7	9	11	13	5
	10	11	12	13	14	15	16	17	18
PAR	4	4	3	4	4	5	4	3	5
YARDS	308	382	154	449	370	471	317	170	515
HDCP	16	4	18	2	8	10	12	14	6

Directions: Take Route 20 West through Sturbridge to Holland Road, turn left. Course is 1 mile up Holland Road.

Heritage Country Club   25

Charlton, MA (508) 248-51111

Club Pro: John Aldrich
Pro Shop: Full inventory
Payment: Visa, MC
Tee Times: Weekends only
Fee 9 Holes: Weekday: $15.00
Fee 18 Holes: Weekday: $22.00
Cart Rental: $22.00/18 $12.00/9
Lessons: $25.00/half hour **Schools:** No
Driving Range: $4.00/ bucket
Other: Clubhouse / Lockers / Showers / Snack bar / Bar-lounge

Weekend: $20.00
Weekend: $29.00
Discounts: Junior
Junior Golf: Yes **Membership:**
Non-Metal Spikes: No

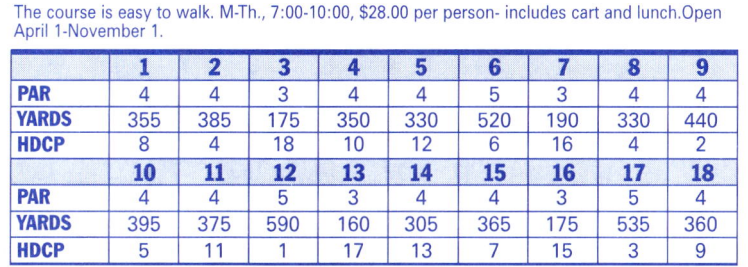

NE/ CTRL MA

Tees	Holes	Yards	Par	USGA	Slope
BACK	18	6400	71	69.3	118
MIDDLE	18	6335	71	69.7	113
FRONT	18	5415	72	70.6	114

The course is easy to walk. M-Th., 7:00-10:00, $28.00 per person- includes cart and lunch. Open April 1-November 1.

	1	2	3	4	5	6	7	8	9
PAR	4	4	3	4	4	5	3	4	4
YARDS	355	385	175	350	330	520	190	330	440
HDCP	8	4	18	10	12	6	16	4	2
	10	11	12	13	14	15	16	17	18
PAR	4	4	5	3	4	4	3	5	4
YARDS	395	375	590	160	305	365	175	535	360
HDCP	5	11	1	17	13	7	15	3	9

Directions: Located on Route 20 in Charlton. 3 miles east of Old Sturbridge Village.

Hickory Hill GC   26

Methuen, MA (978) 686-0822

Club Pro: Paul Rapazzo
Pro Shop: Limited inventory
Payment: Visa, MC
Tee Times: Fri, Sat, Sun. & holidays
Fee 9 Holes: Weekday: $18.00
Fee 18 Holes: Weekday: $32.00
Cart Rental: $22.00/18 $14.00/9
Lessons: $30/30 min. **Schools:** Sr. & Jr.
Driving Range: $5.00/sm.
Other: Clubhouse / Showers / Restaurant / Bar-lounge

Weekend: N/A
Weekend: $36.00
Discounts: None
Junior Golf: No **Membership:** No
Non-Metal Spikes: Yes

Tees	Holes	Yards	Par	USGA	Slope
BACK	18	6276	71	69.2	122
MIDDLE	18	6017	71	67.9	119
FRONT	18	5397	73	73.2	127

The front nine are open and flat with four ponds. The back nine are hilly and cut into the woods. Straight tee shots essential. Open March 15 - November 15.

	1	2	3	4	5	6	7	8	9
PAR	4	3	5	4	4	5	4	3	4
YARDS	349	173	511	382	379	513	367	155	348
HDCP	13	15	3	5	7	1	11	17	9
	10	11	12	13	14	15	16	17	18
PAR	5	4	4	3	4	4	4	3	4
YARDS	489	390	340	141	326	357	304	114	379
HDCP	2	6	8	16	12	10	14	18	4

Directions: Take Route 93 to Exit 46. Take Route 113 West, follow 1.5 miles, course is on left.

4✪ =Excellent **3✪** =Very Good **2✪** =Good

Hillcrest Country Club   27

Leicester, MA (508) 892-1855

Club Pro: Michael Lally
Pro Shop: Full inventory
Payment: Cash only
Tee Times: No
Fee 9 Holes: Weekday: $8.00
Fee 18 Holes: Weekday: $16.00
Cart Rental: $20/18 $10/9 wknds
Lessons: No **Schools:** No
Driving Range: No
Other: Clubhouse / Snack bar / Restaurant / Bar-lounge

Weekend: $10.00
Weekend: $20.00
Discounts: Junior
Junior Golf: No **Membership:** Yes
Non-Metal Spikes: No

Tees	Holes	Yards	Par	USGA	Slope
BACK	9	5977	70	67.1	103
MIDDLE	9	5546	70	67.1	103
FRONT	9	4775	72	67.2	113

COUPON

Call for offer for 2 persons with cart. Proper dress is required. Friendly congenial atmosphere. Open April 1 - November 1.

	1	2	3	4	5	6	7	8	9
PAR	5	4	3	5	4	4	3	4	3
YARDS	500	262	143	500	402	375	110	340	141
HDCP	7	15	13	11	1	3	17	9	5
	10	11	12	13	14	15	16	17	18
PAR	5	4	3	5	4	4	3	4	3
YARDS	500	262	143	500	402	375	110	340	141
HDCP	8	16	14	12	2	4	18	10	6

Directions: Take Mass Pike to Auburn Exit (Exit 10). Take right onto Route 12, follow 3 miles, take right onto Route 20, follow 3 miles take right onto Route 56, 4 miles.

Hillview Golf Course   28

No. Reading, MA (978) 664-4435

Club Pro: Chris Carter
Pro Shop: Full inventory
Payment: Cash only
Tee Times: Weekends
Fee 9 Holes: Weekday: $15.00
Fee 18 Holes: Weekday: $27.00
Cart Rental: $24.00/18 $12.00/9
Lessons: $35.00/half hour **Schools:** No
Driving Range: $5.00/lg., $2.50/sm.
Other: Snack bar / Restaurant / Bar-lounge / Clubhouse

Weekend: $17.00
Weekend: $29.00
Discounts: Senior & Junior
Junior Golf: N/R **Membership:** No
Non-Metal Spikes: Yes

Tees	Holes	Yards	Par	USGA	Slope
BACK	N/A				
MIDDLE	18	5754	69	66	106
FRONT	18	5184	70	68.7	108

COUPON

A popular course in a good location. The layout is interesting.

	1	2	3	4	5	6	7	8	9
PAR	5	3	4	4	4	4	4	5	3
YARDS	464	216	410	325	357	323	394	539	191
HDCP	11	7	5	15	17	13	3	1	9
	10	11	12	13	14	15	16	17	18
PAR	4	4	4	4	3	4	3	4	3
YARDS	372	310	346	355	180	324	236	239	173
HDCP	8	10	2	14	12	6	4	18	16

Directions: Take Exit 40 off I-93, and follow Route 62 East 1-1/2 miles. Turn left on North Street. Course is 1/2 mile up on left.

Holden Hills CC

29

Holden, MA (508) 829-3129

Club Pro: Tim Bishop
Pro Shop: Full inventory
Payment: MC, Visa
Tee Times: Weekends, 1 week adv.
Fee 9 Holes: Weekday: $14.00
Fee 18 Holes: Weekday: $22.00
Cart Rental: $26.00/18 $14.00/9
Lessons: $30.00/half hour **Schools:** No
Driving Range: No
Other: Clubhouse / Snack bar / Restaurant / Bar-lounge

Tees	Holes	Yards	Par	USGA	Slope
BACK	18	6973	71	71.9	125
MIDDLE	18	5826	71	71.9	125
FRONT	18	5241	74	70.6	115

Weekend: $17.00
Weekend: $27.00
Discounts: Senior, M-Th
Junior Golf: Yes **Membership:** Yes
Non-Metal Spikes: No

NE/CTRL MA

Picturesque course set among hills, ponds and streams. While not long, the holes demand good placement and are challenging. Well manicured with good greens. Open April-December.

	1	2	3	4	5	6	7	8	9
PAR	4	5	3	4	4	3	4	5	4
YARDS	354	592	163	309	312	147	340	478	348
HDCP	9	1	15	13	5	17	7	3	11
	10	11	12	13	14	15	16	17	18
PAR	3	4	4	5	4	4	4	4	3
YARDS	164	269	278	433	359	341	414	327	216
HDCP	14	16	18	6	12	4	2	10	8

Directions: Route 290 to Route 190 North. Take second Exit (Holden). Go straight through lights, then bear right. Bear left at next light, up hill. Right on Main Street to Route 122A North. Course is 5 miles on right.

Indian Meadows Golf Club

30

Westboro, MA (508) 836-5460

Club Pro: Art Billingham
Pro Shop: Full inventory
Payment: Cash and check
Tee Times: 3 days adv.
Fee 9 Holes: Weekday: $15.00
Fee 18 Holes: Weekday: $24.00
Cart Rental: $6.30/9
Lessons: $25.00/half hour **Schools:** No
Driving Range: No
Other: Restaurant / Clubhouse / Bar-lounge / Snack Bar

Tees	Holes	Yards	Par	USGA	Slope
BACK	9	6530	72	71.7	124
MIDDLE	9	6530	72	70.6	119
FRONT	9	4936	72	69.0	N/A

Weekend: $18.00
Weekend: $28.00
Discounts: Senior & Junior
Junior Golf: Yes **Membership:** Yes
Non-Metal Spikes: Yes

Nine hole course built in 1990. Water on every hole. Semi-private. Excellent condition. Shirts with collars required. Open April - December.

	1	2	3	4	5	6	7	8	9
PAR	5	4	4	4	3	5	4	3	4
YARDS	451	340	420	316	136	455	415	173	313
HDCP	5	15	1	13	17	7	3	11	9
	10	11	12	13	14	15	16	17	18
PAR	5	4	4	4	3	5	4	3	4
YARDS	451	340	420	316	136	455	415	173	313
HDCP	6	16	2	14	18	8	4	12	10

Directions: The course in on Route 9 (Turnpike Road) in Westboro, 3 miles west of 495.

4✪ =Excellent 3✪ =Very Good 2✪ =Good

Juniper Hill GC (Lakeside) ✪✪ 31

Northboro, MA (508) 393-2444

Club Pro: Ken Chzran
Pro Shop: Full inventory
Payment: Check
Tee Times: 7 days adv.

Tees	Holes	Yards	Par	USGA	Slope
BACK	N/A				
MIDDLE	18	6282	71	69.9	127
FRONT	18	4707	71	65.3	102

Fee 9 Holes: Weekday: $15.00   **Weekend:** $18.00
Fee 18 Holes: Weekday: $27.00   **Weekend:** $32.00
Cart Rental: $24.00/18 $16.00/9   **Discounts:** Senior & Junior M-Th am
Lessons: Yes **Schools:** Jr. & Sr.Yes   **Junior Golf:** Yes **Membership:** No
Driving Range: Practice green   **Non-Metal Spikes:** Yes
Other: Clubhouse / Lockers / Showers / Snack bar / Bar-lounge / Teaching facility

Eighteen holes of championship caliber with a lot of character. Collared shirts required. 1999 rates TBA.

	1	2	3	4	5	6	7	8	9
PAR	3	5	4	4	3	4	5	3	4
YARDS	187	524	313	392	169	314	522	146	307
HDCP	10	6	12	2	14	8	4	16	18
	10	11	12	13	14	15	16	17	18
PAR	4	4	4	4	3	5	4	5	3
YARDS	377	365	336	420	206	482	441	602	179
HDCP	9	15	17	7	1	11	5	3	13

Directions: Take Mass Pike to 495 North. Exit to Route 9 West and continue onto Route 135 West. Follow for 1.4 miles. Right onto Brigham Street. Follow for 1 mile to course.

Juniper Hill GC (Riverside) 32

Northboro, MA (508) 393-2444

Club Pro: Ken Chrzan
Pro Shop: Full inventory
Payment: Visa, MC, Cash, Check
Tee Times: 7 days adv.

Tees	Holes	Yards	Par	USGA	Slope
BACK	N/A				
MIDDLE	18	6306	71	70.4	123
FRONT	18	53 73	71	70.2	117

Fee 9 Holes: Weekday: $15.00   **Weekend:** $18.00
Fee 18 Holes: Weekday: $27.00   **Weekend:** $32.00
Cart Rental: $24.00/18, $16.00/9   **Discounts:** Senior & Junior M-Th AM
Lessons: Yes **Schools:** Jr. & Sr   **Junior Golf:** Yes **Membership:** No
Driving Range: Practice green   **Non-Metal Spikes:** Yes
Other: Clubhouse / Lockers / Showers / Snack bar / Bar-lounge / Teaching facility

Some open fairways let you let loose with the driver. 1999 rates TBA. Collared shirts required.

	1	2	3	4	5	6	7	8	9
PAR	4	4	5	4	3	4	3	4	4
YARDS	370	336	495	387	193	330	156	405	350
HDCP	4	6	2	8	12	16	18	10	14
	10	11	12	13	14	15	16	17	18
PAR	5	4	4	4	4	3	4	3	5
YARDS	529	391	367	381	371	157	391	220	476
HDCP	1	5	7	13	15	17	9	3	11

Directions: Take Mass Pike to 495 North. Exit to Route 9 West and continue onto Route 135 West. Follow for 1.4 miles. Right onto Brigham Street. Follow for 1 mile to course.

Kelley Greens By The Sea   33

Nahant, MA (781) 581-0840

Club Pro: Jack Delaney
Pro Shop: Yes
Payment: Cash & Credit cards
Tee Times: 3 day adv.
Fee 9 Holes: Weekday: $10.00
Fee 18 Holes: Weekday: $16.00
Cart Rental: $28.00/18 $14.00/9
Lessons: $35 /30 min **Schools:** No
Driving Range: No
Other: Snack bar / Restaurant / lounge

Tees	Holes	Yards	Par	USGA	Slope
BACK	9	3880	60	60.0	103
MIDDLE	9	3784	60	57	87
FRONT	9	3342	60	60.0	103

Weekend: $14.00
Weekend: $20.00
Discounts: None
Junior Golf: Yes **Membership:** Yes
Non-Metal Spikes: Yes

COUPON

NE/CTRL MA

	1	2	3	4	5	6	7	8	9
PAR	3	3	3	3	3	4	4	4	3
YARDS	137	179	186	142	213	325	260	249	174
HDCP	17	3	5	13	1	7	11	15	9
	10	11	12	13	14	15	16	17	18
PAR	3	3	3	3	3	4	4	4	3
YARDS	137	179	186	142	213	325	260	249	174
HDCP	18	4	6	14	2	8	12	16	10

Directions: Take Route 1A North to Lynn Center. Go toward Nahant over causeway (Nahant Road). Follow signs to course.

Lakeview Golf Club   34

Main St., Rt. 1A, Wenham, MA (978) 468-6676

Club Pro: Michael Flynn
Pro Shop: Yes
Payment: Cash,MC/Visa
Tee Times: Yes
Fee 9 Holes: Weekday: $12.50- TBA '99
Fee 18 Holes: Weekday: $18.00
Cart Rental: $15.00
Lessons: Private and Group **Schools:** No
Driving Range: No
Other: No

Tees	Holes	Yards	Par	USGA	Slope
BACK	N/A				
MIDDLE	9	4080	62	59.3	91
FRONT	9	3900	31		

Weekend: $13.50
Weekend: $19.00
Discounts: None
Junior Golf: Yes **Membership:** No
Non-Metal Spikes: No

COUPON

Newly renovated bunkers and traps. Executive-style golf course. Easy walking. Largest selection of women's sportswear on North Shore.

	1	2	3	4	5	6	7	8	9
PAR	4	3	3	4	3	4	3	3	4
YARDS	325	215	165	320	125	255	150	160	325
HDCP	1	9	11	3	17	7	15	13	5
	10	11	12	13	14	15	16	17	18
PAR	4	3	3	4	3	4	3	3	4
YARDS	325	215	165	320	125	255	150	160	325
HDCP	2	10	12	4	18	8	16	14	6

Directions: Take Route 128 North to Exit 20 North (Route 1A). The course is 2 miles on the right.

4✪ =Excellent 3✪ =Very Good 2✪ = Good   **Boston's North Shore & Central MA 99**

Leicester Country Club   35

Leicester, MA   (508) 892-1390

Club Pro: Ray Lajoie, PGA
Pro Shop: Limited inventory
Payment: Visa, MC
Tee Times: 5 days adv.
Fee 9 Holes: Weekday: $15.00
Fee 18 Holes: Weekday: $20.00
Cart Rental: $10pp/18 $5pp/9
Lessons: $30/30 min. **Schools:** No
Driving Range: No
Other: Snack bar / Bar-lounge / Banquet Facility / Handicap computer fee

Tees	Holes	Yards	Par	USGA	Slope
BACK	N/A				
MIDDLE	18	5732	70	68.4	118
FRONT	18	4820	70	72.0	113

Weekend: $18, $12 after 4:00
Weekend: $25, $18 after 2:00
Discounts: Senior
Junior Golf: No **Membership:** No
Non-Metal Spikes: No

Very rustic with covered bridge on one of holes. Narrow, tree-lined fairways. Walker's rates for 18 holes. Weekday special: $28 pp, w/ cart + lunch. Formerly Strawberry Hills CC.

	1	2	3	4	5	6	7	8	9
PAR	4	4	3	4	5	3	4	4	5
YARDS	300	325	165	420	510	185	345	440	490
HDCP	13	7	16	1	4	17	6	5	3
	10	11	12	13	14	15	16	17	18
PAR	3	4	4	4	4	4	3	4	4
YARDS	202	350	275	285	380	325	175	285	275
HDCP	18	8	11	15	2	12	9	10	14

Directions: Take Mass Pike to Route 9 West to Main Street in Leicester Center.

Lynnfield Center GC   36

Lynnfield, MA   (781) 334-9877

Club Pro: Bob Ryan
Pro Shop: Limited inventory
Payment: Cash only
Tee Times: No
Fee 9 Holes: Weekday: $13.00
Fee 18 Holes: Weekday: $23.00
Cart Rental: $19.00/18 $11.00/9
Lessons: $25/30 min. **Schools:** N/R
Driving Range: Yes
Other: Clubhouse/Bar-lounge/Snack Bar

Tees	Holes	Yards	Par	USGA	Slope
BACK	9	5120	68	63	NA
MIDDLE	9	4970	68	63	N/A
FRONT	9	4480	68	63	NA

Weekend: $14.00
Weekend: $24.00
Discounts: Senior
Junior Golf: No **Membership:** Sr. Memberships
Non-Metal Spikes: Yes

A good, popular nine-hole tract. Wide open fairways leading to large, well-maintained greens. A good place to practice. Dress code.

	1	2	3	4	5	6	7	8	9
PAR	4	4	3	4	5	3	4	4	3
YARDS	350	355	225	260	476	139	270	340	145
HDCP	5	2	1	8	4	7	3	6	9
	10	11	12	13	14	15	16	17	18
PAR	4	4	3	4	5	3	4	4	3
YARDS	350	355	225	260	476	139	270	340	145
HDCP	5	2	1	8	4	7	3	6	9

Directions: Take Route 128 to Exit 41, follow to Main Street in Lynnfield Center.

Maplewood Golf Course   37

Lunenburg, MA (978) 582-6694

Club Pro: Joe Benevento, Head Pro
Pro Shop: Full inventory
Payment: Visa, MC
Tee Times: Wkends only
Fee 9 Holes: Weekday: $11.00
Fee 18 Holes: Weekday: $17.00
Cart Rental: $12.00/18pp $6.00/9pp
Lessons: No **Schools:** No
Driving Range: No
Other: Clubhouse / Snack bar

Tees	Holes	Yards	Par	USGA	Slope
BACK	N/A				
MIDDLE	9	5370	70	63.9	106
FRONT	9	5040	70	66.5	105

Weekend: $13.00
Weekend: $22.00
Discounts: Senior
Junior Golf: No **Membership:** No
Non-Metal Spikes: Yes

NE/CTRL MA

Affordable and enjoyable golf. Proper golf attire required. Open April - November.

	1	2	3	4	5	6	7	8	9
PAR	4	4	4	4	3	4	5	4	3
YARDS	350	320	310	340	175	350	480	230	130
HDCP	1	7	11	9	15	3	5	13	17
	10	11	12	13	14	15	16	17	18
PAR	4	4	4	4	3	4	5	4	3
YARDS	350	320	320	340	175	350	480	230	130
HDCP	2	8	12	10	16	4	6	14	18

Directions: Route 2 to Route 13 North. Go past Whalom Park to stop sign. Take right, 1/8 mile to top of hill. Take left back on Route 13 North, go 2 miles to Northfield Road. Take left, go 1/2 mile. Clubhouse on right.

Merrimack Valley GC   38

Methuen, MA (978) 685-9717

Club Pro: No
Pro Shop: Limited inventory
Payment: Cash only
Tee Times: Fri, Wkends and hlydys
Fee 9 Holes: Weekday: $14.00
Fee 18 Holes: Weekday: $20.00
Cart Rental: $22.00/18 $12.00/9
Lessons: No **Schools:** Jr.
Driving Range: No
Other: Restaurant / Bar-lounge

Tees	Holes	Yards	Par	USGA	Slope
BACK	18	6220	71	69.3	120
MIDDLE	18	5871	71	67.7	117
FRONT	18	5151	72	72.3	116

Weekend: $15.00
Weekend: $25.00
Discounts: Senior & Junior: $10
Junior Golf: Yes **Membership:** Yes
Non-Metal Spikes: Yes

Early bird and twilight rates for 9 holes on weekends.

	1	2	3	4	5	6	7	8	9
PAR	5	4	4	3	4	4	3	4	4
YARDS	454	342	312	158	386	404	187	354	301
HDCP	9	5	15	13	3	1	7	11	17
	10	11	12	13	14	15	16	17	18
PAR	4	3	5	4	4	5	3	4	4
YARDS	356	158	441	418	310	482	138	405	265
HDCP	8	16	10	4	12	6	18	2	14

Directions: I-93 to Route 213 (Exit 48), follow to Pleasant Street Exit (Exit 3). Go left. Take left at first light onto Howe Street. Course is 1 mile on left.

4✪ =Excellent 3✪ =Very Good 2✪ = Good   **Boston's North Shore & Central MA 101**

Middleton Golf Course ✪✪✪ 39

Middleton, MA (978) 774-4075

Club Pro: George LaVoie
Pro Shop: Full inventory
Payment: Major cards, cash
Tee Times: Weekend AM

Tees	Holes	Yards	Par	USGA	Slope
BACK	18	3215	54	N/A	N/A
MIDDLE	18	3000	54	N/A	N/A
FRONT	18	2280	54	N/A	N/A

Fee 9 Holes: Weekday: $15.00   **Weekend:** $15.00
Fee 18 Holes: Weekday: $25.00   **Weekend:** $28.00 am/ $25 pm
Cart Rental: $18.00/18, $12.00/9; Reserve!   **Discounts:** Junior
Lessons: $40 Priv. Free Sat. clinic   **Schools:** Yes   **Junior Golf:** Yes   **Membership:** No
Driving Range: No   **Non-Metal Spikes:** No
Other: Clubhouse / Bar (beer & wine only) / Snack bar / Club Fitting Center

One of New England's finest par 3s. Holes range from 115 to 240 yds., with modern tees, large greens, and gently rolling fairways. Open year round. www.middletongolf.com

	1	2	3	4	5	6	7	8	9
PAR	3	3	3	3	3	3	3	3	3
YARDS	170	160	185	170	150	170	145	215	190
HDCP	13	9	5	11	15	7	17	1	3

	10	11	12	13	14	15	16	17	18
PAR	3	3	3	3	3	3	3	3	3
YARDS	135	110	195	160	155	240	215	225	225
HDCP	16	18	10	14	12	2	8	6	4

Directions: From Route 1 or Route 95 go approx. 2.5 miles west on Route 114. Parking lot entrance on left.

Monoosnock CC 40

Leominster, MA (978) 537-1872

Club Pro: Steve LeBlanc
Pro Shop: Full inventory
Payment: Visa, MC, Amex
Tee Times: No

Tees	Holes	Yards	Par	USGA	Slope
BACK	N/A				
MIDDLE	9	6102	70	69.8	120
FRONT	9	5645	72	69.8	120

Fee 9 Holes: Weekday: $12.00   **Weekend:** No
Fee 18 Holes: Weekday: $20.00   **Weekend:** No
Cart Rental: $16.00/18 $5.50pp/9   **Discounts:** N/R
Lessons: $25/30 min.   **Schools:** N/R   **Junior Golf:** Yes   **Membership:** N/R
Driving Range: $3.00/bucket   **Non-Metal Spikes:** Yes
Other: Clubhouse / Restaurant / Bar-lounge

The course is closed to the public on Saturday and Sundays. The fairways are narrow and brooks cross through 5 holes. Full practice area. Open April 1 - November 30.

	1	2	3	4	5	6	7	8	9
PAR	5	4	3	4	4	5	4	3	3
YARDS	335	515	378	158	235	450	387	214	379
HDCP	10	6	14	2	12	8	4	18	16

	10	11	12	13	14	15	16	17	18
PAR	5	4	3	4	4	5	4	3	3
YARDS	335	515	378	158	235	450	387	214	379
HDCP	9	5	13	1	11	7	3	17	5

Directions: Take Route 2 to Route 13, right off exit. Course is 1/2 mile on right.

Murphy's Garrison Par 3 GC   41

Haverhill, MA (978)374-9380

Club Pro: Ted Murphy
Pro Shop: Full inventory
Payment: Visa, MC
Tee Times: N/A
Fee 9 Holes: Weekday: $7.00
Fee 18 Holes: Weekday: $13.00
Cart Rental: $1.00/9
Lessons: $30/session **Schools:** No
Driving Range: Yes, $5.00
Other: Bar/Lounge/Snack Bar

Tees	Holes	Yards	Par	USGA	Slope
BACK					
MIDDLE	9	1005	27		
FRONT					

Weekend: $8.00
Weekend: 14.00
Discounts: Senior
Junior Golf: Yes **Membership:** N/R
Non-Metal Spikes: Yes

NE/CTRL MA

A short testing 9 hole par 3 with beautiful vesper velvet greens. Designed in 1966 by legendary Manuel Francis. Great course for women and juniors.

	1	2	3	4	5	6	7	8	9
PAR	3	3	3	3	3	3	3	3	3
YARDS	105	100	130	75	100	130	130	135	100
HDCP	N/A								
	10	11	12	13	14	15	16	17	18
PAR									
YARDS									
HDCP									

Directions: 495 N toward Haverhill at Exit 50. Straight across to stop sign. Straight across to next stop, take a left on Hill Dale Ave. Course is 1/2 mile on left.

Nabnasset Lake CC   42

Westford, MA (978) 692-2560

Club Pro: Tom Thibeault
Pro Shop: Yes
Payment: Cash only
Tee Times: N/R
Fee 9 Holes: Weekday: $20.00
Fee 18 Holes: Weekday: $30.00
Cart Rental: $22.05/18 $14.70/9
Lessons: Private **Schools:** No
Driving Range: No
Other: Snack bar / Bar-lounge

Tees	Holes	Yards	Par	USGA	Slope
BACK	NA				
MIDDLE	9	5408	70	67.4	118
FRONT	9	5005	71	69	119

Weekend: N/A
Weekend: N/A
Discounts: None
Junior Golf: Members **Membership:** Yes
Non-Metal Spikes: Yes

The course is relatively short but made challenging by the rough along the fairways. Available to the public on weekdays only. www.locomotiondj.com/nabnasset.html

	1	2	3	4	5	6	7	8	9
PAR	4	3	5	4	4	3	4	4	4
YARDS	226	137	456	346	383	214	292	328	322
HDCP	11	17	3	7	1	15	13	9	5
	10	11	12	13	14	15	16	17	18
PAR	4	3	5	4	4	3	4	4	4
YARDS	226	137	456	346	383	214	292	328	322
HDCP	12	18	4	8	2	16	14	10	6

Directions: Take Route 3 to Exit 33, go west to Oak Hill Road. Course is 1 mile up.

4✪ =Excellent 3✪ =Very Good 2✪ =Good

New Meadows GC   43

Topsfield, MA (978) 887-9307

Club Pro: No
Pro Shop: Limited inventory
Payment: Cash only
Tee Times: N/A
Fee 9 Holes: Weekday: $13.00
Fee 18 Holes: Weekday: $24.00
Cart Rental: $10.50/9
Lessons: No **Schools:** No
Driving Range: No
Other: Clubhouse / Snack Bar

Tees	Holes	Yards	Par	USGA	Slope
BACK	N/A				
MIDDLE	9	2883	35	N/A	117
FRONT	N/A				

Weekend: $15.00
Weekend: $28.00
Discounts: None
Junior Golf: N/R **Membership:** No
Non-Metal Spikes: No

Dress code - shirts with sleeves.

	1	2	3	4	5	6	7	8	9
PAR	4	4	3	4	4	4	5	3	4
YARDS	352	365	160	348	345	368	459	128	358
HDCP	13	3	15	11	5	7	1	17	9
	10	11	12	13	14	15	16	17	18
PAR									
YARDS									
HDCP									

Directions: Take I-95 to old Route 1 past Topsfield fairgrounds on right about 3 miles.

Nichols College GC   ✪✪   44

Dudley, MA (508) 943-9837

Club Pro: Mike Santa Maria
Pro Shop: Full inventory
Payment: Visa, MC
Tee Times: No
Fee 9 Holes: Weekday: $15.00
Fee 18 Holes: Weekday: $23.00
Cart Rental: $15.00/18 $9.00/9
Lessons: $30.00/half hour **Schools:** No
Driving Range: No
Other: Snack bar / bar lounge

Tees	Holes	Yards	Par	USGA	Slope
BACK	N/A				
MIDDLE	9	6482		71.4	123
FRONT	9	5696	72	71.3	115

Weekend: $15.00
Weekend: $23.00
Discounts: None
Junior Golf: No **Membership:** Residents only
Non-Metal Spikes: Yes

The course is relatively level, the rough cut deep, and the par 3's challenging. Open April - Nov.

	1	2	3	4	5	6	7	8	9
PAR	4	4	3	4	4	4	4	5	5
YARDS	367	384	170	399	232	323	423	509	472
HDCP	7	5	15	3	17	13	1	9	11
	10	11	12	13	14	15	16	17	18
PAR	4	4	3	4	4	4	4	5	5
YARDS	367	384	170	399	232	323	423	509	472
HDCP	8	6	16	4	18	14	2	10	12

Directions: Take I-395 to Exit 2 onto Route 12 West. Go through Webster. Road becomes Route 197, bear right at fork. Course is on Route 197 approximately 1 mile.

Olde Salem Greens   45

Salem, MA (978) 744-2149

Club Pro: No
Pro Shop: No
Payment: Cash only
Tee Times: Weekends, holidays
Fee 9 Holes: Weekday: $14.00
Fee 18 Holes: Weekday: $22.00
Cart Rental: $22.00/18 $11.00/9
Lessons: Residents only **Schools:** N/R
Driving Range: No
Other:

Tees	Holes	Yards	Par	USGA	Slope
BACK	9	7292	70	68.4	116
MIDDLE	9	6056	70	68.5	116
FRONT	9	4966	70	68.4	112

Weekend: $15.00
Weekend: N/A
Discounts: Sr., Jr., & Residents
Junior Golf: No **Membership:** Yes, residents
Non-Metal Spikes: No

NE/ CTRL MA

Small greens and fairways with many bumps and ridges. Accuracy is more important than distance. The par three second is a blind tee shot: aim at a target on a tree.

	1	2	3	4	5	6	7	8	9
PAR	4	3	4	5	4	4	4	3	4
YARDS	374	253	367	545	345	398	291	153	304
HDCP	7	5	9	1	11	3	13	15	17
	10	11	12	13	14	15	16	17	18
PAR	4	3	4	5	4	4	4	3	4
YARDS	374	253	367	545	345	398	291	153	304
HDCP	8	6	10	2	12	4	14	16	18

Directions: Route 128 to Route 114 toward Salem. Take Essex Street to Highland Avenue. Take a left on Wilson Street to course.

Ould Newbury GC   46

Newburyport, MA (978) 465-9888

Club Pro: James Hilton
Pro Shop: Full inventory
Payment: Cash, Disc, MC, Visa
Tee Times: No
Fee 9 Holes: Weekday: $15.00
Fee 18 Holes: Weekday: $25.00
Cart Rental: $22.00/18 $14.00/9
Lessons: $30.00/half hour **Schools:** No
Driving Range: No
Other: Clubhouse / Lockers / Showers / Snack bar

Tees	Holes	Yards	Par	USGA	Slope
BACK	N/A				
MIDDLE	9	6184	70	69	120
FRONT	9	5700	75	71.1	115

Weekend: N/A
Weekend: N/A
Discounts: None
Junior Golf: No **Membership:** Yes
Non-Metal Spikes: No

The course has relatively small, elevated greens. One of the holes is located over a marsh, so check your tide schedule. Not available to public on weekends.

	1	2	3	4	5	6	7	8	9
PAR	4	5	4	4	4	3	4	4	3
YARDS	423	457	380	442	324	152	390	317	207
HDCP	3	15	9	1	11	17	5	13	7
	10	11	12	13	14	15	16	17	18
PAR	4	5	4	4	4	3	4	4	3
YARDS	423	457	380	442	324	152	390	317	207
HDCP	4	16	10	2	12	18	6	14	8

Directions: Take Route 1 toward Newbury. Course is a sand wedge shot from Governor Dummer Academy.

4✪ =Excellent 3✪ =Very Good 2✪ =Good   **Boston's North Shore & Central MA**

Pakachoag Golf Course 47

Upland St., Auburn, MA (508) 755-3291

Club Pro: Joe Keefe
Pro Shop: Limited inventory
Payment: Cash only
Tee Times: Weekends & holidays
Fee 9 Holes: Weekday: $8.00
Fee 18 Holes: Weekday: $16.00
Cart Rental: No
Lessons: Yes   **Schools:** N/A
Driving Range: No
Other: Snack Bar

Tees	Holes	Yards	Par	USGA	Slope
BACK	NA				
MIDDLE	9	6510	72	70.0	119
FRONT	NA				

Weekend: $10.00
Weekend: $20.00
Discounts: Senior & Junior
Junior Golf: No **Membership:** Yes
Non-Metal Spikes: Yes

Many improvements planned for 1999 season. Historical site of first liquid rocket launch by Robert Goddard. Walking course, long holes, open fairways. Good for long hitters and placement players.

	1	2	3	4	5	6	7	8	9
PAR	4	4	4	3	5	4	4	3	5
YARDS	376	329	395	143	563	372	377	189	511
HDCP	5	9	1	9	2	4	6	7	3
	10	11	12	13	14	15	16	17	18
PAR	4	4	4	3	5	4	4	3	5
YARDS	376	329	395	143	563	372	377	189	511
HDCP	6	8	2	9	1	4	7	5	3

Directions: From Route 20 to Greenwood St. to Upland St. From I-290 use Auburn St. Exit to Route 12 (Southbridge St.). Left at lights. 1/4 mile right, take Burnap St. up hill to Pakachoag St. and go left. 2 miles to Upland St.

Pine Ridge Country Club 48

Pleasant St., N. Oxford, MA (508) 892-9188

Club Pro: Mark Larrabee
Pro Shop: Full inventory
Payment: Visa, MC, Amex, cash
Tee Times: 5 days adv.
Fee 9 Holes: Weekday: $15.00
Fee 18 Holes: Weekday: $22.00
Cart Rental: $24.00/18 $15.00/9
Lessons: $50/hour   **Schools:** no
Driving Range: No
Other: Clubhouse / Lockers / Showers / Snack bar / Restaurant / Bar-lounge

Tees	Holes	Yards	Par	USGA	Slope
BACK	18	6002	71	69.7	120
MIDDLE	18	5763	71	68.3	117
FRONT	18	5307	72	69.6	117

Weekend: $17.00
Weekend: $28.00
Discounts: Senior & Junior
Junior Golf: No **Membership:** Yes
Non-Metal Spikes: Yes

Player friendly with a courteous staff. Playable at all handicap holes. Small greens, challenging short game. www.pineridgecc.com

	1	2	3	4	5	6	7	8	9
PAR	4	3	4	4	4	5	4	4	3
YARDS	295	144	437	161	382	390	330	358	148
HDCP	13	17	1	11	3	9	5	7	15
	10	11	12	13	14	15	16	17	18
PAR	4	3	5	4	5	3	4	4	5
YARDS	270	188	431	403	482	166	354	344	480
HDCP	18	14	8	2	6	16	12	10	4

Directions: East to access from MA Pike (Exit 10) or CT, Route 84. Call.

Quaboag Country Club   49

Monson, MA (413) 267-5294

Club Pro: Thomas Sullivan, PGA
Pro Shop: Full inventory
Payment: Cash only
Tee Times: 1 day advance
Fee 9 Holes: Weekday: $15(10am-2pm)
Fee 18 Holes: Weekday: $25(10am-2pm)
Cart Rental: $8.00/ person
Lessons: $30/30 min. **Schools:** no
Driving Range: No
Other: Bar/lounge, Snack bar, lockers and showers

Tees	Holes	Yards	Par	USGA	Slope
BACK	NA				
MIDDLE	9	5 760	68	67.2	116
FRONT	9	5220	70	72	113

Weekend: N/A
Weekend: N/A
Discounts: N/R
Junior Golf: No **Membership:** Yes
Non-Metal Spikes: No

NE/ CTRL MA

This is a relatively short course, but tight. Not too many hazards. Fairly large greens. Semi-private.

	1	2	3	4	5	6	7	8	9
PAR	4	3	4	4	4	4	4	3	4
YARDS	350	225	435	430	360	350	250	130	350
HDCP	5	11	1	3	9	13	15	17	7
	10	11	12	13	14	15	16	17	18
PAR	4	3	4	4	4	4	4	3	4
YARDS	350	225	435	430	360	350	250	130	350
HDCP	5	11	1	3	9	13	15	17	7

Directions: Take I-90 to Exit 6 in Palmer. Turn right. Go 2 lights, turn left. Go 3 miles to golf course on Route 32. Course in on the right.

Quail Hollow Golf & CC   50

Old Turnpike Rd., Oakham, MA (508) 882-5516

Club Pro: Alan Monacelli
Pro Shop: Full inventory
Payment: Visa, MC, cash
Tee Times: Preferred
Fee 9 Holes: Weekday: $10.00
Fee 18 Holes: Weekday: $20.00
Cart Rental: $6/person for 9 holes
Lessons: $35.00/30 min **Schools:** No
Driving Range: $2.50/ sm. $4.00/med.
Other: Clubhouse / Restaurant/ Bar-lounge / Snack Bar

Tees	Holes	Yards	Par	USGA	Slope
BACK	9	6000	70	68.6	121
MIDDLE	9	5800	70	67.6	116
FRONT	9	4600	70	68.6	112

Weekend: $13.00
Weekend: $22.00
Discounts: None
Junior Golf: Yes **Membership:** Yes-limited
Non-Metal Spikes: No

COUPON

Expanding to 18 holes. 1999 rates TBA. Open April 1 - November 1.

	1	2	3	4	5	6	7	8	9
PAR	4	3	4	4	4	4	5	3	4
YARDS	340	170	340	330	340	385	490	105	300
HDCP	3	1	9	11	15	13	7	17	5
	10	11	12	13	14	15	16	17	18
PAR	4	3	4	4	4	4	5	3	4
YARDS	340	170	340	330	340	385	490	105	300
HDCP	4	2	10	12	16	14	8	18	6

Directions: Route 290 to Worcester to Route 122 North to Oakham to Old Turnpike Road. Course is 3.5 miles off Route 122.

4✪ =Excellent 3✪ =Very Good 2✪ =Good   **Boston's North Shore & Central MA**

Rockport Golf Course

51

Rockport, MA (978) 546-3340

Club Pro: Stephen Clayton
Pro Shop: Full inventory
Payment: Visa, MC
Tee Times: 1 day in advance
Fee 9 Holes: Weekday: $17.00
Fee 18 Holes: Weekday: $26.00
Cart Rental: $26.00/18 $14.00/9
Lessons: $30.00/halfhour **Schools:** No
Driving Range: Practice Area
Other: No

Tees	Holes	Yards	Par	USGA	Slope
BACK	N/A				
MIDDLE	9	5938	72	68.8	120
FRONT	9	5434	74	71.2	115

Weekend: $17.00, after 3:30 pm
Weekend: $26.00, after 3:30 pm
Discounts: None
Junior Golf: No **Membership:** Waiting List
Non-Metal Spikes: Yes

Semi-private challenging 9 hole course. Traps and brooks thru course. Closed to the public on weekends until 3:30. Excellent for novice golfers with all holes visible from tees.

	1	2	3	4	5	6	7	8	9
PAR	3	4	4	5	5	4	3	4	4
YARDS	163	338	353	489	489	421	136	395	355
HDCP	15	11	1	5	7	5	17	3	7
	10	11	12	13	14	15	16	17	18
PAR	3	4	4	5	4	5	3	4	4
YARDS	163	338	353	489	409	455	136	395	355
HDCP	16	12	2	6	4	10	18	4	8

Directions: Route 128 North to end, follow signs to Route 127 (Rockport) 5 miles, at town center take right onto Country Club Road.

Rolling Green GC

52

911 Lowell St., Andover, MA (978)475-4066

Club Pro: Joe Russo
Pro Shop: Full inventory
Payment: Visa, MC
Tee Times: No
Fee 9 Holes: Weekday: $12.00
Fee 18 Holes: Weekday: $18.00
Cart Rental: Pull cart
Lessons: $25/30 min. **Schools:** No
Driving Range: Yes
Other: Snack bar / Restaurant / Bar-lounge

Tees	Holes	Yards	Par	USGA	Slope
BACK					
MIDDLE	9	1500	27	N/A	N/A
FRONT					

Weekend: $12.00
Weekend: $18.00
Discounts: Senior & Junior, $10.00 Wkdays
Junior Golf: No **Membership:** N/R
Non-Metal Spikes: No

The course is a short par 3 that offers a challenge to the average golfer.

	1	2	3	4	5	6	7	8	9
PAR	3	3	3	3	3	3	3	3	3
YARDS	180	195	105	170	240	120	175	170	145
HDCP	5	2	9	6	1	8	3	4	7
	10	11	12	13	14	15	16	17	18
PAR									
YARDS									
HDCP									

Directions: Take I-93 to Exit 43. Right onto Route 133 East.

Rowley Country Club   53

Rowley, MA (978) 948-2731

Club Pro: Dennis Nestle
Pro Shop: Limited inventory
Payment: Visa, MC
Tee Times: 1 week in adv.
Fee 9 Holes: Weekday: $15.00
Fee 18 Holes: Weekday: $28.00
Cart Rental: $24.00/18 $12.00/9
Lessons: $35/30 min. **Schools:** Yes
Driving Range: $8/lg. $5/med. $3/sm.
Other: Clubhouse / Restaurant / Bar-lounge

Tees	Holes	Yards	Par	USGA	Slope
BACK	N/A				
MIDDLE	9	6380	72	70.7	127
FRONT	9	4940	70	67.5	109

Weekend: $17.00
Weekend: $32.00
Discounts: Senior & Junior 1/2 price
Junior Golf: Yes **Membership:** Yes
Non-Metal Spikes: No

NE/ CTRL MA

A challenging course situated among towering pines in a picturesque country setting, with water hazards on three holes. Pleasant staff.

	1	2	3	4	5	6	7	8	9
PAR	4	3	4	5	4	4	3	5	4
YARDS	360	190	360	480	350	325	205	475	310
HDCP	7	11	1	3	15	17	13	5	9
	10	11	12	13	14	15	16	17	18
PAR	4	3	4	5	4	4	3	5	4
YARDS	390	210	435	480	360	360	225	500	365
HDCP	8	12	2	4	16	18	14	6	10

Directions: I-95 to Exit 54 (Rowley/Georgetown). Route 133 East. Take first left after 3/4 mile to Dodge Road. Take Dodge Road to the end. Take left and course is on the right.

Sagamore Spring GC   54

Lynnfield, MA (781) 334-3151

Club Pro: Kelli Kostick,PGA, LPGA
Pro Shop: Full inventory
Payment: Cash only
Tee Times: 4 Days advance
Fee 9 Holes: Weekday: $18.00 (Fri. $19.00)
Fee 18 Holes: Weekday: $30.00 (Fri. $32.00)
Cart Rental: $22.00/18 $11.00/9
Lessons: $34/30 min. **Schools:** No
Driving Range: $4.50/lg. bucket
Other: Clubhouse/Showers/Snack bar

Tees	Holes	Yards	Par	USGA	Slope
BACK	18	5936	70	68.6	119
MIDDLE	18	5505	70	66.5	114
FRONT	18	4784	70	66.5	112

Weekend: $20.00
Weekend: $36.00
Discounts: Senior.Spring or Fall
Junior Golf: Yes **Membership:** No
Non-Metal Spikes: Preferred

No tank tops. Well groomed, rolling terrain. Moderate challenge. Wildlife sanctuary. A classic since 1928. A pleasure to play at any skill level. Open March 15 - December 31.

	1	2	3	4	5	6	7	8	9
PAR	5	4	5	4	4	3	4	3	3
YARDS	465	344	473	364	276	146	336	179	198
HDCP	10	4	6	2	16	18	12	14	8
	10	11	12	13	14	15	16	17	18
PAR	4	5	5	4	3	4	4	3	3
YARDS	247	499	431	398	137	330	317	185	180
HDCP	13	5	7	1	17	3	9	15	11

Directions: Exit 41 off I-95 (Route 128). Turn right off exit ramp onto Main Street. Three miles.

4✪ =Excellent **3✪** =Very Good **2✪** =Good   **Boston's North Shore & Central MA**

Shaker Hills Golf Club

Harvard, MA (978) 772-2227

Club Pro: Pat O'Hara, Head Pro
Pro Shop: Full Inventory
Payment: MC, Visa, cash
Tee Times: Yes, call
Fee 9 Holes: Weekday: No
Fee 18 Holes: Weekday: $50.00/with cart
Cart Rental: Included
Lessons: $35.00/half hour **Schools:** No
Driving Range: $5.00/sm. bucket
Other: Clubhouse/Snack bar

Tees	Holes	Yards	Par	USGA	Slope
BACK	18	6394	71	69.5	128
MIDDLE	18	5914	71	67.3	121
FRONT	18	5001	71	67.9	116

Weekend: No
Weekend: $55.00/ with cart
Discounts: None
Junior Golf: Yes **Membership:** No
Non-Metal Spikes: Yes

Rated #4 public course in Massachusetts by *Golf Digest* in 1997. Private course conditions. Caddy service available by advance reservation. Walking is allowed. www.shakerhills.com

	1	2	3	4	5	6	7	8	9
PAR	4	5	3	4	5	3	4	4	4
YARDS	318	475	170	425	515	149	312	353	311
HDCP	13	7	15	5	1	17	9	3	11
	10	11	12	13	14	15	16	17	18
PAR	4	4	4	3	4	5	3	4	4
YARDS	363	352	351	138	280	518	184	285	415
HDCP	10	6	8	18	12	2	14	16	4

Directions: Route 495 to Exit 30 (Route 2A West). Four miles to Shaker Road on left. Course is 1/2 mile on left.

St. Mark's Golf Course

Southborough, MA (508) 460-0946

Club Pro: No
Pro Shop: Limited inventory
Payment: Cash, checks
Tee Times: No
Fee 9 Holes: Weekday: $13.00
Fee 18 Holes: Weekday: $21.00
Cart Rental: $22.00/18 $11.00/9
Lessons: Yes **Schools:** No
Driving Range: Practice area
Other: No

Tees	Holes	Yards	Par	USGA	Slope
BACK					
MIDDLE	9	5810	70	67.1	117
FRONT					

Weekend: $15.00
Weekend: $23.00
Discounts: None
Junior Golf: No **Membership:** Yes
Non-Metal Spikes: No

Open to public. Large landing areas where drivers can be used on most par 4's and 5's. Good for beginners. Challenging, small greens. Inquire about ongoing weekday specials.

	1	2	3	4	5	6	7	8	9
PAR	4	3	5	4	4	4	3	4	4
YARDS	325	155	445	345	375	335	195	320	410
HDCP	7	17	13	5	1	15	11	9	3
	10	11	12	13	14	15	16	17	18
PAR	4	3	5	4	4	4	3	4	4
YARDS	325	155	445	345	375	335	195	320	410
HDCP	8	18	14	6	2	16	12	10	4

Directions: Take Route 9 West, to Route 85 North. Course is 1 mile after intersection.

Stony Brook Golf Course   57

Southboro, MA (508) 485-3151

Club Pro: Jack Hester, PGA
Pro Shop: No
Payment: No
Tee Times: No
Fee 9 Holes: Weekday: $8.00
Fee 18 Holes: Weekday: $11.00
Cart Rental: Pull Carts, $1.00
Lessons: $25.00/hour **Schools:** No
Driving Range: No
Other: Snack bar, accessories.

Tees	Holes	Yards	Par	USGA	Slope
BACK					
MIDDLE	9	1190	27	N/A	N/A
FRONT					

Weekend: $9.00
Weekend: $12.00
Discounts: None
Junior Golf: No **Membership:** No
Non-Metal Spikes: Yes

NE/CTRL MA

A par 3 course, good for beginners and experienced golfers who want to practice their irons. Course opened in 1972. Designed by Ernest Callender

	1	2	3	4	5	6	7	8	9
PAR	3	3	3	3	3	3	3	3	3
YARDS	106	103	205	114	100	153	163	106	140
HDCP	N/A								
	10	11	12	13	14	15	16	17	18
PAR									
YARDS									
HDCP									

Directions: Accessible from routes I-90, I-495 and Route 9. Located in Southboro off of Route 30 on Valley Road.

Townsend Ridge Country Club ✪✪   58

40 Scales Lane, Townsend, MA (978)-597-8400

Club Pro: Matt Johnson, Head Pro
Pro Shop: Full inventory
Payment: Visa, MC, Amex
Tee Times: 7 days advance
Fee 9 Holes: Weekday: N/A
Fee 18 Holes: Weekday: $26.00
Cart Rental: $12.60
Lessons: $35/30 min. **Schools:** Jr.
Driving Range: Yes
Other: Clubhouse/ 19th hole lounge/ Full bar/ Outings encouraged!

Tees	Holes	Yards	Par	USGA	Slope
BACK	18	6188	70	70.2	125
MIDDLE	18	5814	70	68.5	123
FRONT	18	4709	71	68.3	115

Weekend: N/A
Weekend: $33.00
Discounts: Senior & Junior
Junior Golf: Yes **Membership:** Yes
Non-Metal Spikes: Yes

COUPON

"Holes range from easy to "terrifying". When matured the greens will be a pleasure. Very scenic. Many amenities and services." R.W.

	1	2	3	4	5	6	7	8	9
PAR	4	4	3	4	5	4	3	4	4
YARDS	312	375	126	383	457	308	156	349	351
HDCP	13	5	17	1	11	7	15	3	9
	10	11	12	13	14	15	16	17	18
PAR	4	4	5	4	4	3	4	3	4
YARDS	375	377	460	328	429	135	359	170	364
HDCP	6	2	10	4	8	18	12	16	14

Directions: Exit 31 off Route 495. Go West on Route 119 for 15 miles. Take first left after Townsend Ford on to Scales Lane.

4✪ =Excellent 3✪ =Very Good 2✪ =Good   **Boston's North Shore & Central MA 111**

Trull Brook Golf Course   59

N. Tewksbury, MA   (978) 851-6731

Club Pro: Al Santos
Pro Shop: Full inventory
Payment: Visa, MC
Tee Times: 1 week adv.

Tees	Holes	Yards	Par	USGA	Slope
BACK	18	6335	72	68.2	115
MIDDLE	18	6006	72	68.2	115
FRONT	18	5165	72	70.2	118

Fee 9 Holes: Weekday: $17.00 after 3pm   **Weekend:** $20.00 after 3pm
Fee 18 Holes: Weekday: $33.00M-Th.   **Weekend:** $37.00 F/S/S/H
Cart Rental: $26.00/18 $13.00/9   **Discounts:** Senior & Junior
Lessons: Yes **Schools:** No   **Junior Golf:** No **Membership:** No
Driving Range: No   **Non-Metal Spikes:** Yes
Other: Clubhouse / Lockers / Showers / Snack bar

New first tee. A Geoffrey Cornish design, this course incorporates the natural beauty of rolling hills, the Merrimac River and Trull Brook. Dress code. Open March - December.

	1	2	3	4	5	6	7	8	9
PAR	4	5	4	3	4	3	5	4	4
YARDS	338	498	383	123	368	138	470	353	323
HDCP	12	8	2	18	4	16	10	6	14

	10	11	12	13	14	15	16	17	18
PAR	4	3	5	4	4	3	4	5	4
YARDS	323	168	463	323	343	178	373	458	383
HDCP	11	15	9	5	1	17	7	13	3

Directions: From Route 495 or 93, take Route 133 exit, follow West toward Lowell. At Mobil station, sharp right onto River Road. Course is 1/3 mile on left.

Tyngsboro CC   60

Tyngsboro, MA   (978) 649-7334

Club Pro: Joe Russo
Pro Shop: Full inventory
Payment: Cash only
Tee Times: Weekends

Tees	Holes	Yards	Par	USGA	Slope
BACK	9	5120	70	63.2	104
MIDDLE	9	4794	70	65.2	104
FRONT	9	4046	70	62.6	97

Fee 9 Holes: Weekday: $12.00   **Weekend:** $14.00
Fee 18 Holes: Weekday: $20.00   **Weekend:** $24.00
Cart Rental: $20/18$12/9   **Discounts:** Senior
Lessons: Private and Group **Schools:** N/R   **Junior Golf:** No **Membership:** Yes
Driving Range: No   **Non-Metal Spikes:** Yes
Other: Snack bar / Bar-lounge

Major improvements in 1998. The course requires accurate shots and is easy to walk. Dress code.

	1	2	3	4	5	6	7	8	9
PAR	4	4	3	5	3	5	4	4	3
YARDS	320	314	216	430	160	463	282	249	140
HDCP	7	9	5	3	11	1	15	13	17

	10	11	12	13	14	15	16	17	18
PAR	4	4	3	5	3	5	4	4	3
YARDS	321	314	216	430	160	463	282	249	140
HDCP	8	10	6	4	12	2	16	14	18

Directions: Take Route 3 to Exit 35; onto Route 1B East; approximately 2.5 miles.

Wachusett CC

61

W. Boylston, MA (508) 835-4484

Club Pro: Dennis Selvitella, PGA
Pro Shop: Full inventory
Payment: Visa, MC, Amex
Tee Times: 5 days adv.
Fee 9 Holes: Weekday: $17.00, 7am-11-am **Weekend:** $25 after 2pm, $20 after 4pm
Fee 18 Holes: Weekday: $27.00 **Weekend:** $37.00
Cart Rental: $26.00/18 **Discounts:** None
Lessons: Yes **Schools:** No **Junior Golf:** Yes **Membership:** Yes, wait list
Driving Range: Yes **Non-Metal Spikes:** Yes
Other: Snack bar / Bar-lounge / Banquet facilities

Tees	Holes	Yards	Par	USGA	Slope
BACK	18	6608	72	71.4	124
MIDDLE	18	6206	72	71	123
FRONT	18	6216	73	70.0	120

NE/ CTRL MA

A Donald Ross gem Impressive with rolling terrain and superbly manicured, tree-lined fairways. The 8th hole is a 430 yard dogleg that narrows to a well protected green.

	1	2	3	4	5	6	7	8	9
PAR	4	5	4	3	5	3	4	4	4
YARDS	388	518	380	145	507	175	360	436	426
HDCP	9	1	11	17	3	15	13	7	5
	10	11	12	13	14	15	16	17	18
PAR	5	4	4	3	4	5	4	4	3
YARDS	494	430	426	203	330	508	316	374	192
HDCP	10	2	4	8	16	6	12	14	18

Directions: Take Mass Pike 290 to 190, Exit 4 onto Route 12 North. Approximately 2 miles to Franklin Street, turn left. At end of road turn left onto Prospect.

Wenham Country Club

62

Wenham, MA (978) 468-4714

Club Pro: John Thoren, Jr.
Pro Shop: Full inventory
Payment: Cash only
Tee Times: No
Fee 9 Holes: Weekday: $18.00 **Weekend:** $35.00
Fee 18 Holes: Weekday: $30.00 **Weekend:** $35.00
Cart Rental: $25.00/18 $13.00/9 **Discounts:** None
Lessons: $30/30 min **Schools:** N/R **Junior Golf:** No **Membership:** Yes, wait list
Driving Range: No **Non-Metal Spikes:** No
Other: Clubhouse / Snack bar

Tees	Holes	Yards	Par	USGA	Slope
BACK	N/A				
MIDDLE	18	4429	65	62.3	102
FRONT	18	4258	67	63.8	96

This tight course requires accuracy: hpilly terrain and small greens. Open April - November. Semi-private.

	1	2	3	4	5	6	7	8	9
PAR	4	3	3	4	3	4	3	4	3
YARDS	338	115	187	237	208	284	183	278	140
HDCP	4	18	12	16	8	6	10	2	14
	10	11	12	13	14	15	16	17	18
PAR	3	5	3	3	4	4	4	4	4
YARDS	216	413	186	132	236	382	270	266	358
HDCP	3	7	11	17	5	13	1	9	15

Directions: Take Route 128 to exit 20 North, Route 1A. Course is 3 miles on right.

Westboro CC 63

Westboro, MA (508) 366-9947

Club Pro: Jack A. Negoshian
Pro Shop: Yes
Payment: Visa, MC, cash
Tee Times: Wknds, 1 day
Fee 9 Holes: Weekday: $14.00
Fee 18 Holes: Weekday: $20.00
Cart Rental: $20.00/18 $12.00/9
Lessons: Weekdays before 8 am **Schools:** No
Driving Range: No
Other: Restaurant / Bar-lounge

Tees	Holes	Yards	Par	USGA	Slope
BACK	N/A				
MIDDLE	9	6210	71	69.2	118
FRONT	N/A				

Weekend: $15.00 after 4:00 pm
Weekend: $24.00
Discounts: Senior & Junior
Junior Golf: No **Membership:** Waiting list
Non-Metal Spikes: Yes

The course is hilly with small greens. The par five third hole is a pretty, uphill approach shot to a scenic green. Open April - November.

	1	2	3	4	5	6	7	8	9
PAR	5	4	5	4	3	4	3	4	4
YARDS	412	265	492	390	168	341	149	411	415
HDCP	12	14	2	4	16	10	18	8	6

	10	11	12	13	14	15	16	17	18
PAR	5	3	5	4	3	4	3	4	4
YARDS	429	236	531	407	190	346	163	430	433
HDCP	11	13	1	3	15	9	17	7	5

Directions: Route 9 to Route 30 toward Westboro. Take a right at the stop sign. Course is 1 mile past center of town on the right.

Westminster CC 64

Westminster, MA (978) 874-5938

Club Pro: Tom Richardson
Pro Shop: Full inventory
Payment: Cash, Visa, MC
Tee Times: Yes
Fee 9 Holes: Weekday: $11.00, after 5 pm
Fee 18 Holes: Weekday: $22.00
Cart Rental: $22.00
Lessons: Yes **Schools:** No
Driving Range: No
Other: Clubhouse / Lockers / Showers / Snack bar / Restaurant / Bar-lounge

Tees	Holes	Yards	Par	USGA	Slope
BACK	18	6491	71	70.9	133
MIDDLE	18	6223	71	69.5	123
FRONT	18	5453	71	70.0	115

Weekend: $15.00
Weekend: $28.00
Discounts: None
Junior Golf: N/R **Membership:** Yes
Non-Metal Spikes: Yes

The course is challenging. The front nine holes are flat and the back nine are very hilly. Open April 15 - October 31.

	1	2	3	4	5	6	7	8	9
PAR	4	4	4	4	4	4	4	4	3
YARDS	422	396	344	384	353	316	333	312	173
HDCP	1	3	7	5	9	17	11	15	13

	10	11	12	13	14	15	16	17	18
PAR	3	4	3	4	5	4	5	3	5
YARDS	131	381	224	452	532	314	548	157	451
HDCP	18	8	12	2	4	10	6	16	14

Directions: Take Route 2 to Route 140 East. Take an immediate right after bridge, through Westminster Center. Follow 2 miles. Left onto Nichols. Bear right at fork onto Ellis, Course is 1 mile on right.

Winchendon CC ▶ 65

Winchendon, MA   (978) 297-9897

Club Pro: Peter Dupuis, PGA
Pro Shop: Full Inventory
Payment: Cash only
Tee Times: Yes, 3 days adv.
Fee 9 Holes: Weekday: $11.00
Fee 18 Holes: Weekday: $18.00
Cart Rental: $22.00/18 $14.00/9
Lessons: Yes **Schools:** No
Driving Range: No
Other: Clubhouse / Bar-lounge / Snack bar / Banquets / Outings

Tees	Holes	Yards	Par	USGA	Slope
BACK	N/A				
MIDDLE	18	5317	70	65.7	114
FRONT	18	5107	72	68.5	116

Weekend: $13.00 after 1:00pm
Weekend: $22.00
Discounts: None
Junior Golf: Yes **Membership:** Yes
Non-Metal Spikes: Yes

COUPON

NE/ CTRL MA

Donald Ross gem built into the hills of northern Massachusetts: breathtaking views of Mt. Monadnock, with postage-stamp greens and narrow fairways, accuracy is at a premium.

	1	2	3	4	5	6	7	8	9
PAR	4	4	3	4	3	3	4	5	4
YARDS	233	272	237	223	204	170	309	467	377
HDCP	16	6	2	18	14	12	10	4	8
	10	11	12	13	14	15	16	17	18
PAR	4	4	4	4	3	5	3	4	5
YARDS	364	364	361	281	143	490	155	268	399
HDCP	5	13	1	11	17	3	9	15	7

Directions: Route 2 to Route 140 North to Route 12. Take left onto Route 12. Go 6 miles. Take first left at McDonalds. Take left on to Ash St. Course is at top of hill.

Woburn Country Club ▶ 66

Woburn, MA   (781) 933-9880

Club Pro: Paul Parajeckas, PGA
Pro Shop: Full inventory
Payment: Cash only
Tee Times: 2 days / weekends only
Fee 9 Holes: Weekday: $16.00
Fee 18 Holes: Weekday: $24.00
Cart Rental: $24.00/18 $14.00/9
Lessons: $35.00/half hour **Schools:** No
Driving Range: No
Other: Restaurant / Snack bar / Function Hall

Tees	Holes	Yards	Par	USGA	Slope
BACK	N/A				
MIDDLE	9	2977	68	68.9	121
FRONT	9	2565	70	68.0	104

Weekend: $17.00
Weekend: $27.00
Discounts: Senior & Junior (Wkdays only)
Junior Golf: Yes **Membership:** Yes
Non-Metal Spikes: Preferred

Small greens. Need a good short game to score well, every lie in the book. No tank tops.

	1	2	3	4	5	6	7	8	9
PAR	4	4	4	4	4	4	3	4	3
YARDS	373	363	359	371	410	326	190	389	215
HDCP	7	5	11	9	1	15	17	3	13
	10	11	12	13	14	15	16	17	18
PAR	4	4	4	4	4	3	4	4	3
YARDS	362	374	331	387	405	337	182	402	197
HDCP	8	6	12	10	4	14	18	2	16

Directions: I-93 to Route 128 South, Exit 33A (Winchester), straight through Woburn Four Corners, take left at first set of lights onto Country Club Road.

4✪ =Excellent 3✪ =Very Good 2✪ =Good   **Boston's North Shore & Central MA 115**

CHAPTER 3
Western Massachusetts

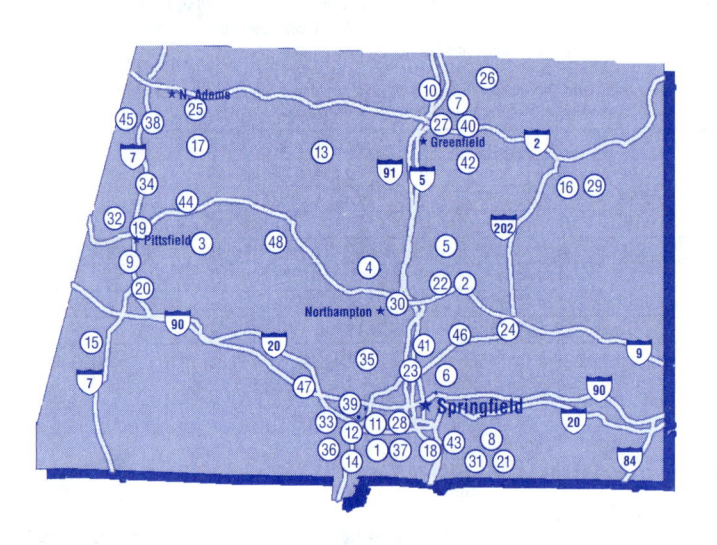

Course	#	Course	#	Course	#
Agawam Municipal CC	1	Forest Park CC	17	Shaker Farms CC	33
Amherst Golf Club	2	Franconia Muni. GC	18	Skyline Country Club	34
Bas Ridge Golf Course	3	GEAA Golf Club	19	Southampton CC	35
Beaver Brook CC	4	Greenock Country Club	20	Southwick CC	36
Cherry Hills GC	5	Hampden Country Club	21	St. Anne Country Club	37
Chicopee Municipal GC	6	Hickory Ridge CC	22	Taconic Golf Club	38
Country Club of Greenfield	7	Holyoke Country Club	23	Tekoa Country Club	39
Country Club of Wilbraham	8	Mill Valley CC	24	The Meadows Golf Club	40
Cranwell Resort	9	North Adams CC	25	The Orchards Golf Club	41
Crumpin-Fox Club	10	Northfield CC	26	Thomas Memorial CC	42
Dunroamin CC	11	Oak Ridge Golf Club	27	Veteran's Golf Club	43
East Mountain CC	12	Oak Ridge Golf Club	28	Wahconah CC	44
Edge Hill GC	13	Petersham CC	29	Waubeeka Golf Links	45
Edgewood Golf Club	14	Pine Grove Golf Club	30	Westover Golf Course	46
Egremont Country Club	15	Pine Knoll Par 3	31	Whippernon CC	47
Ellinwood CC	16	Pontoosuc Lake CC	32	Worthington GC	48

Agawam Municipal CC   1

Route 57, Feeding Hills, MA (413) 786-2194

Club Pro: Ron Dunn
Pro Shop: Yes
Payment: Cash only
Tee Times: 3 days adv.
Fee 9 Holes: Weekday: $8.00
Fee 18 Holes: Weekday: $13.00
Cart Rental: $9.00/18, $5.00/9
Lessons: Private & Group   **Schools:** No
Driving Range: No
Other: Snack bar / Bar-lounge

Tees	Holes	Yards	Par	USGA	Slope
BACK	N/A				
MIDDLE	18	6119	71	67.0	110
FRONT	18	5345	71	71.2	110

Weekend: $11.00
Weekend: $16.00
Discounts: Junior
Junior Golf: Yes   **Membership:** Limited
Non-Metal Spikes: Preferred

W MA

A friendly course. No water holes but 1 creek and 8 sand traps. Total irrigation. The 9th hole is referred to as "Cardiac Hill," and for good reason. Weekend specials before 8 am and after 1 pm.

	1	2	3	4	5	6	7	8	9
PAR	5	4	3	4	3	4	4	5	3
YARDS	480	375	144	465	121	360	385	560	175
HDCP	13	9	15	3	17	7	11	1	5
	10	11	12	13	14	15	16	17	18
PAR	5	4	4	3	4	3	5	5	3
YARDS	475	395	348	160	322	145	554	475	180
HDCP	8	4	14	16	12	18	2	10	6

Directions: Take I-90 (Mass Pike) to I-91 to Route 57 (Agawam). Go north on Route 57, club is in the town of Feeding Hills.

Amherst Golf Club   2

S. Pleasant, Amherst, MA (413) 256-6894

Club Pro: Dave Twohig
Pro Shop: Full inventory
Payment: Visa, MC
Tee Times: No
Fee 9 Holes: Weekday: $23.00
Fee 18 Holes: Weekday: $23.00
Cart Rental: $10.00/pp18 $6.00pp/9
Lessons: $30.00/half hour   **Schools:** No
Driving Range: No
Other: Clubhouse / Lockers / Showers / Snack bar

Tees	Holes	Yards	Par	USGA	Slope
BACK	N/A				
MIDDLE	9	6100	70	68.9	117
FRONT	9	5608	72	68.9	122

Weekend: $23.00
Weekend: $23.00
Discounts: None
Junior Golf: No   **Membership:** Yes
Non-Metal Spikes: Yes

Always in good shape. May be the best greens in Western Mass. The course is short in length with small greens. $16.00 when playing with a member.

	1	2	3	4	5	6	7	8	9
PAR	4	4	4	3	4	4	5	4	3
YARDS	390	375	405	160	350	340	525	310	200
HDCP	5	7	3	13	9	15	1	17	11
	10	11	12	13	14	15	16	17	18
PAR	4	4	4	3	4	4	5	4	3
YARDS	390	375	405	160	350	340	525	310	188
HDCP	6	8	4	14	10	16	2	18	12

Directions: Take Mass Pike to Route 181 to Route 9 into Amherst. Course is located by Amherst College.

4✪ =Excellent   3✪ =Very Good   2✪ =Good

Bas Ridge Golf Course

Plunkett St., Hinsdale, MA (413) 655-2605

Club Pro:
Pro Shop: No
Payment: Cash only
Tee Times: Yes
Fee 9 Holes: Weekday: TBA
Fee 18 Holes: Weekday: TBA
Cart Rental: $16.00/18, $10.00/9
Lessons: No **Schools:** N/R
Driving Range: No
Other: Clubhouse / Bar-lounge

Tees	Holes	Yards	Par	USGA	Slope
BACK					
MIDDLE	18	4933	70	N/A	N/A
FRONT					

Weekend: TBA
Weekend: TBA
Discounts: None
Junior Golf: No **Membership:** Yes
Non-Metal Spikes: No

COUPON

Nine additional holes opened in September '98. Call for new rates and new scorecard. Open April 1 - November 1.

	1	2	3	4	5	6	7	8	9
PAR	4	4	3	4	5	3	5	4	4
YARDS	280	332	166	307	425	100	550	230	300
HDCP									
	10	11	12	13	14	15	16	17	18
PAR	4	4	3	4	3	4	4	4	4
YARDS	325	265	185	240	160	250	240	318	260
HDCP									

Directions: Take Mass Pike to Lee exit, take left onto Route 8. Course is located off Route 8 south of Pittsfield.

Beaver Brook CC

Main St., Haydenville, MA (413) 268-7229

Club Pro: N/A
Pro Shop: Limited inventory
Payment: Cash only
Tee Times: Weekends, 2 days adv.
Fee 9 Holes: Weekday: $10.00
Fee 18 Holes: Weekday: $16.00
Cart Rental: $20.00/18, $10.00/9
Lessons: No **Schools:** No
Driving Range: No
Other: Clubhouse / Snack bar / Bar-lounge

Tees	Holes	Yards	Par	USGA	Slope
BACK	N/R				
MIDDLE	9	6092	72	68.1	110
FRONT	9	4960	72	67.7	107

Weekend: $13.00
Weekend: $19.00
Discounts: Senior & Junior
Junior Golf: No **Membership:** Yes
Non-Metal Spikes: Yes

COUPON

Beautifully laid out and maintained nine hole course. The course sports two brooks and four ponds.

	1	2	3	4	5	6	7	8	9
PAR	4	4	5	3	4	4	4	3	5
YARDS	403	323	496	146	361	370	290	167	490
HDCP	1	11	3	17	5	9	15	13	7
	10	11	12	13	14	15	16	17	18
PAR	4	4	5	3	4	4	4	3	5
YARDS	403	323	496	146	361	370	290	167	490
HDCP	2	12	4	18	6	10	16	14	8

Directions: Route 91 to exit 19 North. Continue to end; make right. Course is 2 miles on State Rd. (Route 9 West).

Cherry Hills GC　　　　　　　　　　▶ 5

323 Montague Rd., N. Amherst (413) 256-4071

Club Pro: No
Pro Shop: Limited inventory
Payment: Most major
Tee Times: No
Fee 9 Holes: Weekday: $10.00
Fee 18 Holes: Weekday: $13.00
Cart Rental: $20.00/18 $10.00/9
Lessons: No **Schools:** No
Driving Range: No
Other: Snack-bar

Tees	Holes	Yards	Par	USGA	Slope
BACK	9	5556	70	65.7	101
MIDDLE	9	5340	72	65.7	101
FRONT	9	4940	70	N/A	N/A

Weekend: $12.00
Weekend: $15.00
Discounts: Senior & Junior
Junior Golf: No **Membership:** Yes
Non-Metal Spikes: No

W MA

Good beginner course with easy walking. Upgraded in 1997.

	1	2	3	4	5	6	7	8	9
PAR	5	3	4	4	4	4	5	4	3
YARDS	555	159	298	341	406	291	415	296	183
HDCP	2	15	9	5	3	18	8	13	6
	10	11	12	13	14	15	16	17	18
PAR	5	4	4	3	4	4	5	4	3
YARDS	579	270	288	165	396	300	425	290	158
HDCP	1	17	10	14	4	16	7	12	11

Directions: Take I-91 to Hadley exit, right on Route 9 into Amherst. Go North on Route 16 for 3 miles, turn right at light onto Pine St and onto Route 63. Course is 1/2 mile on right.

Chicopee Municipal GC　　　✪✪　▶ 6

Bernett Rd., Chicopee, MA (413) 594-9295

Club Pro: Thomas DiRico, PGA
Pro Shop: Full inventory
Payment: Cash/Credit
Tee Times: Yes
Fee 9 Holes: Weekday: $10.50
Fee 18 Holes: Weekday: $17.00
Cart Rental: $20.00/18
Lessons: Yes **Schools:** No
Driving Range: No
Other: Clubhouse / Snack bar

Tees	Holes	Yards	Par	USGA	Slope
BACK	18	6742	71	73.0	126
MIDDLE	18	6109	71	70.4	120
FRONT	18	5123	71	72.45	115

Weekend: $18.00
Weekend: $18.00
Discounts: Senior Residents
Junior Golf: Yes **Membership:** Yes
Non-Metal Spikes: Yes

Ranked 7th in state by USA Today in "places to play in Massachusetts." Layout offers narrow fairways, blind shots, hazards, and good drainage.

	1	2	3	4	5	6	7	8	9
PAR	4	5	3	4	4	4	5	3	4
YARDS	382	481	173	316	433	354	535	193	285
HDCP	7	5	17	11	1	9	3	13	15
	10	11	12	13	14	15	16	17	18
PAR	4	3	3	4	4	5	3	5	4
YARDS	362	157	160	340	391	473	173	534	367
HDCP	10	18	16	14	6	4	12	2	8

Directions: Take Mass. Pike to Exit 6, turn right at light; course is 2 1/2 miles on left.

4✪ =Excellent 3✪ =Very Good 2✪ =Good

Country Club of Greenfield

7

244 Country Club Rd., Greenfield, MA (413)773-7530

Club Pro: Kevin Piecuch
Pro Shop: Yes
Payment: Cash and check
Tee Times: No

Tees	Holes	Yards	Par	USGA	Slope
BACK	18	6400	72	69.0	118
MIDDLE	18	6300	72	69.0	114
FRONT	18	6200	72	71.3	114

Fee 9 Holes: Weekday: $15.00 **Weekend:** $30.00
Fee 18 Holes: Weekday: $30.00 **Weekend:** $30.00
Cart Rental: $26.25/18, $13.13/9 **Discounts:** Senior & Junior- $25.00 fee
Lessons: $25.00/30 min. **Schools:** No **Junior Golf:** Yes **Membership:** Yes
Driving Range: $3.50/lge, $2.50sm **Non-Metal Spikes:** Preferred
Other: Full restaurant / Clubhouse / Bar-lounge / Snack Bar / Showers

COUPON

Rolling landscape that is wide open for the driver. Greens are generally flat. This is a fine moderately challenging course. Open April 1 - Nov. 15. James "Bucky" O'Brien, Director of Golf.

	1	2	3	4	5	6	7	8	9
PAR	4	3	4	4	3	5	4	5	4
YARDS	380	144	421	380	130	565	283	455	362
HDCP	11	15	1	7	17	3	13	9	5

	10	11	12	13	14	15	16	17	18
PAR	4	3	5	4	5	3	4	4	4
YARDS	357	185	470	280	570	145	315	387	320
HDCP	8	10	6	16	2	12	18	4	14

Directions: Route 91, take Exit 27. Turn right at Route 5 and 10. Take right at first set of lights onto Silver St. Country Club Rd. is fourth street on right.

Country Club of Wilbraham

8

Wilbraham, MA (413)596-8887

Club Pro: Daril Pacinella
Pro Shop: Full inventory
Payment: Cash
Tee Times: No

Tees	Holes	Yards	Par	USGA	Slope
BACK	9	6350	72	69.3	120
MIDDLE	9	6292	72	69.3	120
FRONT	9	5646	72	71.2	108

Fee 9 Holes: Weekday: $16.00 after 3 **Weekend:** $22.00 after 3
Fee 18 Holes: Weekday: $32.00 **Weekend:** $35.00
Cart Rental: $11.00, pull-no charge **Discounts:** None
Lessons: $40.00/half hour **Schools:** No **Junior Golf:** For Residents **Membership:** Yes
Driving Range: Yes **Non-Metal Spikes:** Preferred
Other:

Semi-private. Residents of Wilbraham after 3:00, or as a guest with a member.

	1	2	3	4	5	6	7	8	9
PAR	4	3	4	4	3	5	4	5	4
YARDS	380	162	364	416	137	484	258	528	373
HDCP	11	14	8	2	18	10	15	4	6

	10	11	12	13	14	15	16	17	18
PAR	4	3	4	4	3	5	4	5	4
YARDS	375	185	378	426	157	499	266	543	361
HDCP	12	13	7	1	17	9	16	3	5

Directions: Take I-90 (MA. Trpke) West to Exit 7, Belchertown/Ludlow. Turn left at end of ramp. Follow signs to Wilbraham. Call for details.

Cranwell Resort & Golf Club ✪✪✪ 9

Lee Road, Lenox, MA (413) 637-1364

Club Pro: David Strawn
Pro Shop: Full inventory
Payment: Visa, MC, Amex, Disc.
Tee Times: 1 week adv.
Fee 9 Holes: Weekday: N/A
Fee 18 Holes: Weekday: $65.00 cart incl.
Cart Rental: $14.00/person
Lessons: $35/30 min. **Schools:** Yes
Driving Range: $5.00/bucket
Other: Hotel / Lockers / Showers / Snack bar / Restaurant / Bar-lounge

Tees	Holes	Yards	Par	USGA	Slope
BACK	18	6346	70	70.0	125
MIDDLE	18	6169	70	70.0	125
FRONT	18	5602	72	72.4	129

Weekend: N/A
Weekend: $85.00 cart included
Discounts: None
Junior Golf: No **Membership:** Yes
Non-Metal Spikes: Yes

W MA

Scottish style course with heavy rough and panoramic mountain views. 9 hole play offered in spring and fall only. www.cranwell.com

	1	2	3	4	5	6	7	8	9
PAR	4	4	3	5	3	4	4	4	4
YARDS	410	461	154	504	233	393	375	363	418
HDCP	7	1	17	5	11	9	13	15	3
	10	11	12	13	14	15	16	17	18
PAR	4	4	3	4	4	5	3	4	4
YARDS	272	405	204	428	341	501	170	321	393
HDCP	16	4	10	2	12	8	18	14	6

Directions: Take Mass Pike to Exit 2, take Route 20 West. Course is 10 minutes up.

Crumpin-Fox Club ✪✪✪✪ 10

Bernardston, MA (413) 648-9101

Club Pro: Ron Beck
Pro Shop: Full inventory
Payment: Visa, MC, Amex
Tee Times: 3 days adv.
Fee 9 Holes: Weekday: $32.00
Fee 18 Holes: Weekday: $64.00
Cart Rental: $14.00/18 $9.00/9
Lessons: $60.00/hour **Schools:** Jr. & Sr.
Driving Range: $5.00/half hour
Other: Restaurant / Clubhouse / Hotel / Bar-lounge / Lockers / Snack Bar / Showers / Tennis

Tees	Holes	Yards	Par	USGA	Slope
BACK	18	7007	72	74.2	141
MIDDLE	18	6539	72	72.4	137
FRONT	18	6023	72	70.8	131

Weekend: $32.00
Weekend: $64.00
Discounts: Junior
Junior Golf: Yes **Membership:** Yes
Non-Metal Spikes: Yes

Award winning, magnificent course. Included in Golf Magazine's top 100 US courses. Ron Beck named Teacher of the Year by Ct.PGA. Four sets of tees. www.sandri.com

	1	2	3	4	5	6	7	8	9
PAR	4	4	3	4	5	4	4	5	3
YARDS	363	323	146	315	481	379	325	529	160
HDCP	5	13	15	11	7	3	9	1	17
	10	11	12	13	14	15	16	17	18
PAR	4	3	4	4	5	3	4	5	4
YARDS	368	131	359	346	487	138	376	491	378
HDCP	4	18	12	10	14	16	2	6	8

Directions: Take I-91 to Exit 28A (between Brattleboro, VT and Greenfield, MA). Follow Route 10 North for 1 mile, take left on Parmenter Road and follow signs to club.

4✪ =Excellent 3✪ =Very Good 2✪ = Good

Dunroamin CC

11

Gilbertville, MA (413) 477-8880

Club Pro: Warren Nelson
Pro Shop: Full inventory
Payment: Cash only
Tee Times: No
Fee 9 Holes: Weekday: $12.00
Fee 18 Holes: Weekday: $22.00
Cart Rental: $12.00/18; $6.00/9, per person
Lessons: Yes **Schools:** No
Driving Range: $2.50/bucket
Other: Clubhouse / Lockers / Showers / Snack bar / Bar-lounge

Tees	Holes	Yards	Par	USGA	Slope
BACK	N/A				
MIDDLE	9	5914	70	68.6	117
FRONT	9	4802	70	66.8	106

Weekend: $12.00
Weekend: $22.00
Discounts: None
Junior Golf: Yes **Membership:** No
Non-Metal Spikes: No

The course is closed to the public on Sundays 9:00 am - 2:00 pm.

	1	2	3	4	5	6	7	8	9
PAR	3	4	4	5	4	4	4	3	4
YARDS	204	331	393	493	322	310	367	166	277
HDCP	10	12	2	6	8	14	4	18	16

	10	11	12	13	14	15	16	17	18
PAR	3	4	4	5	4	4	4	3	4
YARDS	228	349	405	549	336	318	385	182	299
HDCP	9	11	1	5	7	13	3	17	15

Directions: Take Mass Pike to Exit 8, follow Route 32 for 15 miles into Gilbertville, course is on right.

East Mountain CC

12

Westfield, MA (413) 568-1539

Club Pro: Ted Perez Jr.
Pro Shop: Full inventory
Payment: Visa, MC, Amex, cash
Tee Times: 1 week adv.
Fee 9 Holes: Weekday: $11.00
Fee 18 Holes: Weekday: $18.00
Cart Rental: $21.00/18 $12.00/9
Lessons: Yes, by appointment **Schools:** No
Driving Range: $6.00, $4.00, $2.75
Other: Clubhouse / Snack bar / Lounge

Tees	Holes	Yards	Par	USGA	Slope
BACK	18	6118	71	67.5	107
MIDDLE	18	5819	71	66.4	105
FRONT	18	4564	71	61.7	96

Weekend: $12.50
Weekend: $21.00
Discounts: Senior & Junior Wkdays
Junior Golf: Yes **Membership:** Associate
Non-Metal Spikes: No

This flat course is well groomed and has generous fairways. Small greens.

	1	2	3	4	5	6	7	8	9
PAR	4	4	3	5	4	4	4	4	3
YARDS	305	361	149	495	372	426	319	352	175
HDCP	16	8	18	4	10	2	14	12	6

	10	11	12	13	14	15	16	17	18
PAR	3	5	5	3	4	5	4	3	4
YARDS	159	492	481	168	394	536	429	174	331
HDCP	15	5	9	13	7	3	1	17	11

Directions: Take Mass Pike to Exit 3, follow Route 202 N to East Mountain Road. Course is 1.5 miles down on right.

Edge Hill GC   13

Ashfield, MA (413)625-6018

Club Pro:
Pro Shop: Limited inventory
Payment: Personal checks, Cash
Tee Times: N/A
Fee 9 Holes: Weekday: $10.00
Fee 18 Holes: Weekday: $14.00
Cart Rental: $20.00/18 $10.00/9
Lessons: $30.00/45 min. **Schools:** No
Driving Range: $4.00/lg. $2.50/sm.
Other: Full restaurant/ Clubhouse/ Bar/ Lounge

Tees	Holes	Yards	Par	USGA	Slope
BACK	9	3250	36	69.2	123
MIDDLE	9	3110	36	67.6	119
FRONT	9	2990	36	66.0	115

Weekend: $12.00
Weekend: $16.00
Discounts: None
Junior Golf: No **Membership:** Yes
Non-Metal Spikes: N/R

COUPON

W MA

Mountain course designed by Mark Graves. Four years old. Very challenging course demands position. Open May- November.

	1	2	3	4	5	6	7	8	9
PAR	5	4	3	4	4	3	5	4	4
YARDS	520	300	150	320	370	160	520	370	400
HDCP	6	18	10	8	12	14	1	16	4
	10	11	12	13	14	15	16	17	18
PAR									
YARDS									
HDCP									

Directions: Take Route 116 from South Deerfield of I-91 to Conway-Ashfield. Turn right in Ashfield at Baptist Corner Rd. Follow signs.

Edgewood Golf Club   14

Southwick, MA (413) 569-6826

Club Pro: Mike Grigley, Steve Benoit
Pro Shop: Full inventory
Payment: Cash only
Tee Times: 4 days adv.
Fee 9 Holes: Weekday: $10.00
Fee 18 Holes: Weekday: $15.00
Cart Rental: $22.00/18 $11.00/9
Lessons: $30.00/half hour **Schools:** No
Driving Range: $4.00/lg. $2.00/sm.
Other: Clubhouse / Showers / Snack bar / Restaurant / Bar-lounge

Tees	Holes	Yards	Par	USGA	Slope
BACK	18	6510	71	67.6	113
MIDDLE	18	6050	71	67.6	113
FRONT	18	5580	71	71.8	109

Weekend: $13.00
Weekend: $19.00
Discounts: Senior & Junior
Junior Golf: Yes **Membership:** Yes
Non-Metal Spikes: No

A very challenging and scenic course.

	1	2	3	4	5	6	7	8	9
PAR	5	4	4	5	4	3	4	3	4
YARDS	450	415	315	523	385	170	390	205	340
HDCP	10	4	16	2	6	18	12	14	8
	10	11	12	13	14	15	16	17	18
PAR	4	3	4	3	5	5	4	3	4
YARDS	295	160	375	150	545	480	355	150	340
HDCP	11	15	5	17	1	3	9	13	7

Directions: Take Mass Pike to Springfield. From Springfield take Route 57 to Southwick. Route 57 goes through Routes 10 and 202. Go through center of town. Take a left on Depot. Right onto Sheep Pasture Road, follow it around to the right.

4✪ =Excellent 3✪ =Very Good 2✪ =Good

Egremont Country Club 15

Great Barrington, MA (413) 528-4222

Club Pro: Marc Levesque, PGA
Pro Shop: Full inventory
Payment: Visa, MC or cash
Tee Times: 1 day adv.

Tees	Holes	Yards	Par	USGA	Slope
BACK	18	6200	71	67.0	117
MIDDLE	18	5659	71	66.3	115
FRONT	18	4814	71	66.6	104

Fee 9 Holes: Weekday: N/A **Weekend:** N/A
Fee 18 Holes: Weekday: $20.00 **Weekend:** $30.00
Cart Rental: $24.00/18 **Discounts:** Senior, Thurs.
Lessons: $35/45 min. **Schools:** No **Junior Golf:** Yes **Membership:** Yes
Driving Range: $3.50/lg. **Non-Metal Spikes:** Yes
Other: Clubhouse / Lockers / Showers / Snack bar / Restaurant / Bar-lounge /Tennis Courts / Pool

COUPON

The course is set among the beautiful Berkshire Mountains. There are 11 water holes. Open April - October. www.bcn.net/~egremont

	1	2	3	4	5	6	7	8	9
PAR	4	4	3	4	5	3	4	4	3
YARDS	335	243	175	389	497	139	314	317	151
HDCP	7	15	5	3	1	17	11	9	13
	10	11	12	13	14	15	16	17	18
PAR	4	4	5	5	3	4	4	4	4
YARDS	338	275	397	538	152	330	323	385	361
HDCP	8	18	6	2	14	12	16	10	4

Directions: Take Taconic State Parkway or Route 7 to Route 23 to Great Barrington.

Ellinwood CC 16

Athol, MA (978) 249-7460

Club Pro: No
Pro Shop: Full inventory
Payment: Visa, MC
Tee Times: Yes

Tees	Holes	Yards	Par	USGA	Slope
BACK	18	6207	71	70.1	122
MIDDLE	18	5737	71	67.8	117
FRONT	18	5047	72	68.7	111

Fee 9 Holes: Weekday: $12.00 **Weekend:** $13.00
Fee 18 Holes: Weekday: $22.00 **Weekend:** $27.00
Cart Rental: $24.00/18 $12.00/9 **Discounts:** None
Lessons: No **Schools:** No **Junior Golf:** No **Membership:** Yes
Driving Range: No **Non-Metal Spikes:** Yes
Other: Clubhouse / Snack bar / Bar-lounge / Showers/ Banquet Hall

COUPON

No back and forth holes. Every hole offers a different challenge.

	1	2	3	4	5	6	7	8	9
PAR	4	4	3	5	5	3	4	3	4
YARDS	390	315	155	465	410	157	405	156	355
HDCP	3	11	15	5	9	13	1	17	7
	10	11	12	13	14	15	16	17	18
PAR	3	4	3	5	3	4	5	4	5
YARDS	210	282	133	445	118	356	470	425	490
HDCP	6	14	16	12	18	4	10	2	8

Directions: Take Route 2 to Athol exit. Take left on Pleasant. The course is 2 miles down.

Forest Park CC

17

Adams, MA (413) 743-3311

Club Pro: No
Pro Shop: Yes
Payment: Cash /check only
Tee Times: No
Fee 9 Holes: Weekday: $10.00
Fee 18 Holes: Weekday: $16.00
Cart Rental: $20.00/18 $10.00/9
Lessons: No **Schools:** No
Driving Range: No
Other: Clubhouse/Lockers/Showers/Snack bar / Bar-lounge/Banquet Hall

Tees	Holes	Yards	Par	USGA	Slope
BACK	N/A				
MIDDLE	9	5183	68	63.8	110
FRONT	9	4646	68	63.8	110

Weekend: $10.00
Weekend: $16.00
Discounts: None
Junior Golf: Yes **Membership:** Yes
Non-Metal Spikes: No

COUPON

W MA

Picturesque views of the Berkshire Hills from one of the oldest clubs in New England. Short, challenging and hilly with sand traps and no water holes.

	1	2	3	4	5	6	7	8	9
PAR	4	4	3	4	3	4	4	4	4
YARDS	270	341	157	327	147	333	314	389	277
HDCP	15	1	17	7	9	11	3	5	13
	10	11	12	13	14	15	16	17	18
PAR	4	4	3	4	3	4	4	4	4
YARDS	280	358	162	327	147	349	330	389	286
HDCP	16	2	18	8	10	12	4	6	14

Directions: Take Mass Pike to Lee exit. Take Route 8 to Adams. Take left at statue on Park Street to Maple Street. Take first left on to Forest Park Avenue.

Franconia Muni. GC

18

Springfield, MA (413) 734-9334

Club Pro: Daniel DiRico
Pro Shop: Full inventory
Payment: Cash only
Tee Times: Weekends
Fee 9 Holes: Weekday: $10.50 after 3:00
Fee 18 Holes: Weekday: $13.50 after 9:00
Cart Rental: $20.00/18, $10.50/9
Lessons: $22.00/1/2 hour **Schools:** No
Driving Range: No
Other: Clubhouse / Snack bar / Restaurant / Bar-lounge

Tees	Holes	Yards	Par	USGA	Slope
BACK	18	6153	71	68.7	118
MIDDLE	18	5825	71	67.1	115
FRONT	18	5348	71	67.1	115

Weekend: $12.00 after 3:00
Weekend: $15.50, $12 after 3
Discounts: Senior & Junior
Junior Golf: Yes **Membership:** Yes
Non-Metal Spikes: No

A nice combination of holes.

	1	2	3	4	5	6	7	8	9
PAR	4	4	4	5	3	4	4	3	4
YARDS	314	307	349	557	124	412	360	162	387
HDCP	15	11	9	1	17	3	5	13	7
	10	11	12	13	14	15	16	17	18
PAR	5	4	5	4	3	4	4	3	4
YARDS	491	307	468	368	132	350	282	173	282
HDCP	6	10	4	2	18	8	12	14	16

Directions: Take Mass Pike to Route 291 West to 91 South. Take Longmeadow Exit. At 2nd light take a left onto Converge Street. At end take left onto Dwight Road. Follow to course.

4✪ =Excellent 3✪ =Very Good 2✪ =Good

GEAA Golf Club

19

Pittsfield, MA (413) 443-5746

Club Pro: Ed Rossi
Pro Shop: Full inventory
Payment: Cash /checks only
Tee Times: Yes Weekends
Fee 9 Holes: Weekday: $9.00
Fee 18 Holes: Weekday: $15.00
Cart Rental: $16.00/18, $9.00/9
Lessons: No **Schools:** No
Driving Range: Yes. Bring own balls.
Other: Restaurant/Club House/Snack bar / Bar-lounge/Lockers/Showers

Tees	Holes	Yards	Par	USGA	Slope
BACK	9	6360	72	70.0	111
MIDDLE	9	6205	72	69.6	117
FRONT	9	5274	72	69.4	110

Weekend: $12.00
Weekend: $20.00
Discounts: None
Junior Golf: Yes **Membership:** Yes
Non-Metal Spikes: No

Gently rolling hills and windy all year round. Tree lined fairways with beautiful view of Mt. Greylock.

	1	2	3	4	5	6	7	8	9
PAR	4	3	4	3	4	4	4	5	5
YARDS	332	155	391	179	379	362	276	456	549
HDCP	15	17	1	11	5	7	13	9	3
	10	11	12	13	14	15	16	17	18
PAR	4	3	4	3	4	4	4	5	5
YARDS	332	155	391	179	379	362	276	456	549
HDCP	16	18	2	12	6	8	14	10	4

Directions: Take Mass Pike to Lee Exit, follow Route 7N through Lee, Lenox, 1/2 mile past Reed Middle School is Crane Street, take right to the course.

Greenock Country Club

★★★ 20

W. Park St., Lee, MA (413) 243-3323

Club Pro: Micheal Bechard
Pro Shop: Full inventory
Payment: Cash/ Check only
Tee Times: Sat. and Sun., Call
Fee 9 Holes: Weekday: $18.00
Fee 18 Holes: Weekday: $26.00
Cart Rental: $22.00/18 $11.00/9
Lessons: $25/lesson **Schools:** No
Driving Range: No
Other: Clubhouse / Lockers / Showers / Snack bar / Restaurant / Bar-lounge

Tees	Holes	Yards	Par	USGA	Slope
BACK	9	6140	74	68.9	120
MIDDLE	9	5898	74	68.9	120
FRONT	9	5686	74	72.2	123

Weekend: $22.00
Weekend: $40.00
Discounts: None
Junior Golf: Yes **Membership:** Yes
Non-Metal Spikes: Yes

Small postage stamp greens. Ratings are for 18 holes.

	1	2	3	4	5	6	7	8	9
PAR	4	3	5	4	5	5	3	4	4
YARDS	330	158	391	300	423	453	168	360	364
HDCP	12	16	2	14	4	10	18	6	8
	10	11	12	13	14	15	16	17	18
PAR	4	3	5	4	5	5	3	4	4
YARDS	345	168	408	307	441	465	184	372	390
HDCP	11	15	1	13	3	9	17	5	7

Directions: Exit 2 on Mass. Pike. Take right on Housatonic Street to the Center of Lee. Come to the stop sign next to town park. Take West Park Street up the hill over the RR tracks. Course on right.

Hampden Country Club   ★★ 21

Wilbraham Rd., Hampden, MA (413) 566-8010

Club Pro: Brian Doyle
Pro Shop: Full inventory
Payment: Visa, MC, Cash
Tee Times: 7 days adv.
Fee 9 Holes: Weekday: $13.00   **Weekend:** N/A
Fee 18 Holes: Weekday: $23, $16 after 3pm   **Weekend:** $32.00, $19 after 3pm
Cart Rental: $24/18   **Discounts:** Junior
Lessons: Yes   **Schools:** No   **Junior Golf:** Yes   **Membership:** No
Driving Range: Yes. $5.00 /large   **Non-Metal Spikes:** No
Other: Clubhouse / Bar-Lounge / Snack Bar / Lockers / Showers

COUPON

Tees	Holes	Yards	Par	USGA	Slope
BACK	18	6833	72	72.5	129
MIDDLE	18	6349	72	70.1	126
FRONT	18	5283	72	72.3	113

W MA

A Friel Golf Company. Moderately hilly; challenging; water comes into play on seven holes. Immaculate condition. Banquet hall seats 300.

	1	2	3	4	5	6	7	8	9
PAR	4	5	3	4	4	4	4	5	3
YARDS	323	533	201	359	364	374	368	517	150
HDCP	7	1	17	5	13	9	11	3	15

	10	11	12	13	14	15	16	17	18
PAR	4	5	3	4	5	3	4	4	4
YARDS	362	555	185	350	529	163	319	347	350
HDCP	16	2	14	6	4	18	12	10	8

Directions: I-91, Exit 1 (Longmeadow.) Second set of lights, left onto Converse Street. Follow to end, take right on Dwight Road, then immediate left at intersection onto Maple Street. 2 miles to 83 South, turn right, 1 mile. Left onto Hampden Road 5 miles to club on right.

Hickory Ridge CC   ★★★ 22

S. Amherst, MA (413) 253-9320

Club Pro: Rick Fleury
Pro Shop: Full inventory
Payment: Cash, Visa, Amex, MC
Tee Times: 1 day adv.
Fee 9 Holes: Weekday: $17.50   **Weekend:** $24.00
Fee 18 Holes: Weekday: $35.00   **Weekend:** $48.00
Cart Rental: $25.00/18 $13.00/9   **Discounts:** Junior
Lessons: $30.00/30 min.   **Schools:** No   **Junior Golf:** Yes   **Membership:** Yes
Driving Range: $4.00/lg. $3.00/sm.   **Non-Metal Spikes:** Yes
Other: Clubhouse / Lockers / Showers / Snack bar / Restaurant / Bar-lounge

Tees	Holes	Yards	Par	USGA	Slope
BACK	18	5794	72	72.5	129
MIDDLE	18	6427	72	71.1	128
FRONT	18	5340	74	70.4	117

The course plays long and relatively wide with last two holes rated among the top 10 in Massachusetts. Open April - October.

	1	2	3	4	5	6	7	8	9
PAR	5	4	4	4	3	5	4	3	4
YARDS	500	375	325	380	201	510	345	174	435
HDCP	5	11	13	7	15	15	3	17	1

	10	11	12	13	14	15	16	17	18
PAR	4	5	4	4	4	3	5	3	4
YARDS	365	451	410	340	352	144	481	183	444
HDCP	8	14	4	10	12	18	6	16	2

Directions: Take Route 9 East from I-91 in Northampton to Route 116 in Amherst.. Go south on Route 116 for 2.5 miles to West Pomeroy Lane. Right onto West Pomeroy for 1/2 mile.

4★ =Excellent 3★ =Very Good 2★ =Good

Holyoke Country Club 23

Holyoke, MA (413) 534-1933

Club Pro: Via Wightman
Pro Shop: Full inventory
Payment: Visa, MC
Tee Times: No
Fee 9 Holes: Weekday: $14.00
Fee 18 Holes: Weekday: $20.00
Cart Rental: $12.00/18 $6.00/9
Lessons: $20.00/30minutes **Schools:** Yes
Driving Range: No

Tees	Holes	Yards	Par	USGA	Slope
BACK	N/A				
MIDDLE	9	6299	72	71	118
FRONT	9	5446	75	N/A	N/A

Weekend: N/A
Weekend: $25.00 with member
Discounts: Junior
Junior Golf: Yes **Membership:** Yes
Non-Metal Spikes: No

Other: Clubhouse / Lockers / Showers / Snack bar / Restaurant / Bar-lounge

One of the most challenging and scenic nine hole golf courses in Western Massachusetts. Beautiful layout, with fast greens and narrow fairways.

	1	2	3	4	5	6	7	8	9
PAR	4	4	4	4	5	4	4	3	4
YARDS	343	356	409	292	472	407	323	121	347
HDCP	10	2	4	16	8	6	14	18	12
	10	11	12	13	14	15	16	17	18
PAR	4	4	4	4	5	4	4	3	4
YARDS	353	370	425	302	488	411	343	150	387
HDCP	9	1	3	15	7	5	13	17	11

Directions: From Springfield: I-91 North, Exit 17A to traffic light, turn left onto Route 5, approximately 2 1/2 miles. At the Delaney Restaurant go through entrance, past restaurant 50 yards, then turn left to country club.

Mill Valley CC 24

Belchertown, MA (413) 323-4079

Club Pro: TBA
Pro Shop: Limited inventory
Payment: Cash only
Tee Times: No
Fee 9 Holes: Weekday: $9.00
Fee 18 Holes: Weekday: $14.00
Cart Rental: $18.00/18 $12.00/9
Lessons: No **Schools:** No
Driving Range: No

Tees	Holes	Yards	Par	USGA	Slope
BACK	N/A				
MIDDLE	18	5879	72	67	110
FRONT	18	4556	72	67	110

Weekend: $12.00
Weekend: $18.00
Discounts: Senior & Junior
Junior Golf: Yes **Membership:** Yes
Non-Metal Spikes: No

Other: Restaurant / Bar-lounge/Snack Bar

This nine hole course has two sets of tees.

	1	2	3	4	5	6	7	8	9
PAR	5	5	4	4	3	4	4	3	4
YARDS	482	520	320	305	190	360	285	160	250
HDCP	6	2	15	13	11	8	4	18	17
	10	11	12	13	14	15	16	17	18
PAR	5	5	4	4	3	4	4	3	4
YARDS	512	525	330	315	190	370	295	212	258
HDCP	5	1	14	12	10	7	3	9	16

Directions: Take Mass Pike to Exit 7. Follow Route 21 (becomes Route 202) to Belchertown. Go right onto Route 181. Course is about 2 miles on right.

North Adams CC

Clarksburg, MA (413) 664-9011

Club Pro: No
Pro Shop: Limited inventory
Payment: Visa, MC
Tee Times: weekends & holidays
Fee 9 Holes: Weekday: $9.00
Fee 18 Holes: Weekday: $15.00
Cart Rental: $19.00/18 $9.50/9
Lessons: No **Schools:** No
Driving Range: No
Other: Snack bar / Bar-lounge

Tees	Holes	Yards	Par	USGA	Slope
BACK					
MIDDLE	9	3030	36	69.4	114
FRONT	9	2782	36	69.8	120

Weekend: $11.00
Weekend: $17.00
Discounts: None
Junior Golf: Yes **Membership:** Yes
Non-Metal Spikes: Yes

25

W MA

The course is challenging with narrow fairways.

	1	2	3	4	5	6	7	8	9
PAR	4	3	4	4	5	4	4	3	5
YARDS	350	165	355	310	505	410	285	165	485
HDCP	10	15	6	13	3	5	12	17	9
	10	11	12	13	14	15	16	17	18
PAR									
YARDS									
HDCP									

Directions: Take Route 2 to Route 8; go North 2 miles. Course is on left side.

Northfield CC

East Northfield, MA (413) 498-2432

Club Pro: Bill Tenney
Pro Shop: Full inventory
Payment: Visa, MC
Tee Times: No
Fee 9 Holes: Weekday: $10.00
Fee 18 Holes: Weekday: $20.00
Cart Rental: $21.00/18 $10.50/9
Lessons: No **Schools:** No
Driving Range: No
Other: Snack bar

Tees	Holes	Yards	Par	USGA	Slope
BACK	N/A				
MIDDLE	9	5520	71	66.2	121
FRONT	9	4810	72	68.0	121

Weekend: $12.00
Weekend: $24.00
Discounts: None
Junior Golf: Yes **Membership:** No
Non-Metal Spikes: Yes

26

A sporty nine holes constructed around the turn of the century. Very difficult to shoot the course rating. Extensive day camp program. Open April - November.

	1	2	3	4	5	6	7	8	9
PAR	4	4	4	4	5	3	3	4	4
YARDS	430	300	320	260	450	170	130	270	380
HDCP	5	11	3	15	1	9	17	13	7
	10	11	12	13	14	15	16	17	18
PAR	5	4	4	4	5	3	3	4	4
YARDS	430	300	320	260	450	170	130	270	380
HDCP	6	12	4	16	2	10	18	14	8

Directions: Course is on Routes 10 and 63, one mile north of the center of town. Take Holton Street, turn right into parking lot.

4✪ =Excellent 3✪ =Very Good 2✪ =Good

Oak Ridge Golf Club   27

W. Gill Rd, Gill, MA (413) 863-9693

Club Pro: No
Pro Shop: Limited inventory
Payment: Cash only
Tee Times: No
Fee 9 Holes: Weekday: $11.00
Fee 18 Holes: Weekday: $21.00
Cart Rental: $22.00/18 $12.00/9
Lessons: No **Schools:** No
Driving Range: No
Other: Snack bar / Clubhouse / Bar-lounge

Tees	Holes	Yards	Par	USGA	Slope
BACK	9	2952	36	68.7	117
MIDDLE	9	5813	72	68.7	117
FRONT	9	2595	36	70.0	117

Weekend: $13.00
Weekend: $25.00
Discounts: Senior & Junior
Junior Golf: No **Membership:** Yes
Non-Metal Spikes: Yes

COUPON

Scenic rolling hills, well groomed. Special rates for seniors (60+) and weekdays prior to 11:00. Open March - November.

	1	2	3	4	5	6	7	8	9
PAR	4	4	5	4	4	4	4	4	3
YARDS	290	319	481	364	300	329	410	240	128
HDCP	13	11	9	5	3	7	1	17	15
	10	11	12	13	14	15	16	17	18
PAR	4	4	5	4	4	4	4	4	3
YARDS	315	340	487	374	308	335	414	246	133
HDCP	14	12	10	6	4	8	2	18	16

Directions: From I-91 North, take Exit 27 East and follow signs to golf course. From I-91 South, take Exit 27 and follow signs to golf course.

Oak Ridge Golf Club   ✪✪   28

Feeding Hills, MA (413) 789-7307

Club Pro: Jim Modzelesky
Pro Shop: Full inventory
Payment: Cash only
Tee Times: 1 wk / wkdys: Wed/wkds
Fee 9 Holes: Weekday: $15.00
Fee 18 Holes: Weekday: $28.00
Cart Rental: $26.00/18 $15.00/9
Lessons: $36.00/half hour **Schools:** No
Driving Range: N/A
Other: Clubhouse / Lockers / Showers / Bar-lounge / Snack Bar

Tees	Holes	Yards	Par	USGA	Slope
BACK	18	6702	70	71.2	124
MIDDLE	18	6390	70	70.0	120
FRONT	18	5307	70	70.0	124

Weekend: $20.00 after 2 pm
Weekend: $33.00
Discounts: Senior wkdays
Junior Golf: Yes **Membership:** Yes
Non-Metal Spikes: Preferred

COUPON

Excellent condition, flowers throughout course are very beautiful. A New England beauty. Open March 1 - December 1.

	1	2	3	4	5	6	7	8	9
PAR	4	4	4	3	4	5	4	3	4
YARDS	379	379	395	191	378	570	385	151	387
HDCP	13	3	9	15	11	1	7	17	5
	10	11	12	13	14	15	16	17	18
PAR	4	3	5	3	4	4	5	3	4
YARDS	431	195	559	176	352	363	493	200	406
HDCP	8	16	2	18	12	10	4	14	6

Directions: Take exit 3 Agawam/Southwick off I-91. Take Route 57 West to end. Take left then first left at Oak Ridge sign. Course 1/4 mi. on right.

Petersham CC ▶ 29

Petersham, MA (978) 724-3388

Club Pro: Don Cross
Pro Shop: Full inventory
Payment: Cash only
Tee Times: Weekends, 2 days adv.
Fee 9 Holes: Weekday: $12.00
Fee 18 Holes: Weekday: $20.00
Cart Rental: $22.00/18, $12.00/9
Lessons: $35/lesson **Schools:** No
Driving Range: No
Other: Clubhouse / Lockers / Showers / Snack bar / Bar-lounge

Tees	Holes	Yards	Par	USGA	Slope
BACK	9	6007	70	68.9	116
MIDDLE	9	5486	70	66.4	114
FRONT	9	5032	72	69.1	114

Weekend: $13.00
Weekend: $22.00
Discounts: None
Junior Golf: Yes **Membership:** Yes
Non-Metal Spikes: Yes

W MA

"This course is a bargain," D.C. Donald Ross design from 1922. At an elevation of 1,380 feet, this course offers beautiful scenery and a well maintained golf course.

	1	2	3	4	5	6	7	8	9
PAR	4	3	4	4	5	4	4	3	4
YARDS	328	205	344	422	475	365	376	124	316
HDCP	15	7	5	3	6	11	1	17	13
	10	11	12	13	14	15	16	17	18
PAR	4	3	4	4	5	4	4	3	4
YARDS	343	220	368	432	489	380	385	131	343
HDCP	16	8	10	4	8	12	2	18	16

Directions: Take Route 2 to Petersham/Athol Exit 17, take right onto Route 32, follow 6 miles, course is on left.

Pine Grove Golf Club ▶ 30

Northampton, MA (413) 584-4570

Club Pro: Ray Millette
Pro Shop: Limited inventory
Payment: Cash only
Tee Times: Yes
Fee 9 Holes: Weekday: $8.00
Fee 18 Holes: Weekday: $15.00
Cart Rental: $20.00/18, $10.00/9
Lessons: Yes **Schools:** No
Driving Range: No
Other: Clubhouse / Snack bar / Bar-lounge

Tees	Holes	Yards	Par	USGA	Slope
BACK	N/A				
MIDDLE	18	6115	72	68.8	121
FRONT	18	4890	72	67.3	114

Weekend: $12.00
Weekend: $18.00
Discounts: Senior
Junior Golf: No **Membership:** N/A
Non-Metal Spikes: No

Open April 1 - December 1.

	1	2	3	4	5	6	7	8	9
PAR	4	5	5	3	4	3	4	4	4
YARDS	315	475	500	140	350	165	370	385	335
HDCP	16	8	10	14	3	7	4	2	13
	10	11	12	13	14	15	16	17	18
PAR	4	3	4	4	5	3	4	5	4
YARDS	375	125	370	330	470	140	360	600	310
HDCP	12	9	5	15	11	18	6	1	17

Directions: I-91 to Exit 18. Left off exit, Route 5N about 1.5 miles to light. Left onto Route 9W to next light. Straight through light, then bear left onto Route 66 for 3 miles, and bear left onto Wilson Road.

4✪ =Excellent 3✪ =Very Good 2✪ =Good

Western Massachusetts 131

Pine Knoll Par 3

East Longmeadow, MA (413)525-8320

Club Pro: No
Pro Shop: No
Payment: Cash only
Tee Times: No
Fee 9 Holes: Weekday: $6.00
Fee 18 Holes: Weekday: $6.00
Cart Rental: No
Lessons: Yes **Schools:** No
Driving Range: Adjacent
Other:

Tees	Holes	Yards	Par	USGA	Slope
BACK	N/A				
MIDDLE	18	1567	54	N/A	N/A
FRONT					

Weekend: $6.50
Weekend: $6.50
Discounts: Senior & Junior Wkdays
Junior Golf: N/R **Membership:** No
Non-Metal Spikes: No

Easy Walker. Open March-November.

	1	2	3	4	5	6	7	8	9
PAR	3	3	3	3	3	3	3	3	3
YARDS	86	64	80	92	78	60	72	60	102
HDCP	N/A								

	10	11	12	13	14	15	16	17	18
PAR	3	3	3	3	3	3	3	3	3
YARDS	74	96	48	130	114	124	115	85	87
HDCP									

Directions: I-91 to Exit 4. Go to end of Summer Ave., bear right by McDonald's. 1 1/2 mi. to Porter Road. Left turn onto Porter to course entrance on left.

Pontoosuc Lake CC

Pittsfield, MA (413) 445-4217

Club Pro: Bob Dastoli
Pro Shop: Limited inventory
Payment: Cash only
Tee Times: Weekends & Holidays
Fee 9 Holes: Weekday: No
Fee 18 Holes: Weekday: $15.00
Cart Rental: $18.00/18 $9.00/9
Lessons: Yes **Schools:** No
Driving Range: No
Other: Snack bar / Bar-lounge

Tees	Holes	Yards	Par	USGA	Slope
BACK	N/R				
MIDDLE	18	6207	70	69.7	116
FRONT	N/R				

Weekend: No
Weekend: $17.00
Discounts: Senior, Weekdays
Junior Golf: No **Membership:** Yes
Non-Metal Spikes: No

The course is a rolling Berkshires course with beautiful large trees and dense woods. Considered moderately difficult. Very walkable. No one under 14.

	1	2	3	4	5	6	7	8	9
PAR	4	4	5	3	4	4	4	3	4
YARDS	367	295	597	137	372	284	404	223	361
HDCP	11	14	1	18	3	13	5	12	8

	10	11	12	13	14	15	16	17	18
PAR	4	3	4	4	3	5	3	4	5
YARDS	411	152	386	355	173	593	196	360	541
HDCP	2	17	4	10	15	6	16	9	7

Directions: Take Route 7 onto Hancock West; approx. 1 mile on Ridge Ave; then .3 miles and turn left on Kirkwood Dr.

Shaker Farms CC   33

Shaker Rd, Westfield, MA (413) 562-2770

Club Pro: Tom Miron
Pro Shop: Full inventory
Payment: Visa, MC
Tee Times: Yes, preferably
Fee 9 Holes: Weekday: $10.00
Fee 18 Holes: Weekday: $18.00
Cart Rental: $11.55/18
Lessons: Yes **Schools:** No
Driving Range: Yes
Other:

Tees	Holes	Yards	Par	USGA	Slope
BACK	18	6804	72	71.9	125
MIDDLE	18	6669	72	71.9	125
FRONT	18	5212	72	71.9	125

Weekend: $15.00
Weekend: $24.00
Discounts: None
Junior Golf: Yes **Membership:** Yes
Non-Metal Spikes: Yes

W MA

Home of Ladies Michelob Futures Classic. Well-developed, some water, very scenic, semi-private. Members only weekends until noon. Dress code.

	1	2	3	4	5	6	7	8	9
PAR	5	4	4	5	4	5	3	4	3
YARDS	540	375	365	495	420	614	225	420	175
HDCP	11	9	15	13	5	1	7	3	17
	10	11	12	13	14	15	16	17	18
PAR	4	4	3	4	3	4	4	5	4
YARDS	325	368	165	380	167	390	405	470	370
HDCP	8	12	18	10	16	4	2	6	14

Directions: Take I-90 (MA Pike) to Exit 3 Westfield. Follow Routes 10 and 202 South to Route 20. Stay on Route 20 E passing Westfield shops, Turn right on Route 187 at blinking light. Follow to course.

Skyline Country Club   34

Rt. 7, Lanesborough, MA (413) 445-5584

Club Pro: Jim Mitus
Pro Shop: Yes
Payment: MC, Visa, cash
Tee Times: 1 week adv.
Fee 9 Holes: Weekday: $9.50
Fee 18 Holes: Weekday: $17.00
Cart Rental: $18.00/18 $9.00/9
Lessons: $30/45 Min. **Schools:** No
Driving Range: Yes
Other: Snack bar / Bar-lounge

Tees	Holes	Yards	Par	USGA	Slope
BACK	18	6250	72	71.2	123
MIDDLE	18	6100	72	70.4	123
FRONT	18	4900	72	70.9	113

Weekend: $11.00
Weekend: $19.00
Discounts: None
Junior Golf: Yes **Membership:** Yes
Non-Metal Spikes: No

COUPON

The course is somewhat hilly; considered moderately difficult.

	1	2	3	4	5	6	7	8	9
PAR	4	5	3	4	4	4	3	5	4
YARDS	369	487	127	331	363	390	196	540	379
HDCP	6	4	18	8	2	12	10	16	14
	10	11	12	13	14	15	16	17	18
PAR	4	3	5	4	4	3	5	4	4
YARDS	395	167	490	343	295	167	432	362	379
HDCP	3	13	1	5	17	11	9	15	7

Directions: Take Mass Pike to Exit 2 (Lee). Go north on Route 7. Course is approximately 20 miles on right.

4✪ =Excellent 3✪ =Very Good 2✪ = Good

Southampton CC

Southampton, MA (413) 527-9815

Club Pro: John Strycharz
Pro Shop: Limited inventory
Payment: Cash only
Tee Times: 1 week adv.
Fee 9 Holes: Weekday: $15.00, twilight $8
Fee 18 Holes: Weekday: $15.00
Cart Rental: $16.00/18 $8.00/9
Lessons: No **Schools:** No
Driving Range: No
Other: Snack bar / Restaurant / Bar-lounge
Weekend: $13.00, after 5 pm
Weekend: $22.00
Discounts: None
Junior Golf: No **Membership:** No
Non-Metal Spikes: No

Tees	Holes	Yards	Par	USGA	Slope
BACK	18	6585	72	69.0	114
MIDDLE	18	6135	72	69.0	114
FRONT	18	5125	71	67.0	113

This meticulously maintained course is moderately easy with large greens, rolling hills and panoramic views. This course gets busy on the weekends.

	1	2	3	4	5	6	7	8	9
PAR	4	3	4	3	4	5	4	4	5
YARDS	325	165	380	165	310	455	400	390	460
HDCP	13	17	8	16	14	11	1	3	5
	10	11	12	13	14	15	16	17	18
PAR	3	5	5	3	4	4	4	4	4
YARDS	140	485	460	200	340	365	405	325	365
HDCP	18	4	6	15	10	7	2	12	9

Directions: Take Mass Pike to Westfield Exit; go north on Route 10. Course is on right 8 miles.

Southwick CC

Southwick, MA (413) 569-0136

Club Pro: No
Pro Shop: Full inventory
Payment: Cash only
Tee Times: 1 day adv.
Fee 9 Holes: Weekday: $11.00
Fee 18 Holes: Weekday: $17.00
Cart Rental: $22.00/18, $12.00/9
Lessons: No **Schools:** N/R
Driving Range: No
Other: Snack bar / Restaurant / Lounge
Weekend: $13.00
Weekend: $21.00
Discounts: Senior
Junior Golf: Yes **Membership:** Yes
Non-Metal Spikes: Preferred

Tees	Holes	Yards	Par	USGA	Slope
BACK	N/A				
MIDDLE	18	6100	71	64.8	102
FRONT	18	5570	71	64.7	103

The course is flat and wide open; considered an easy walker. Putting green.

	1	2	3	4	5	6	7	8	9
PAR	4	5	3	4	4	3	4	4	4
YARDS	410	525	175	400	430	120	325	300	355
HDCP	2	5	8	6	3	16	13	15	10
	10	11	12	13	14	15	16	17	18
PAR	5	4	4	4	3	4	4	4	4
YARDS	490	290	320	315	125	450	415	310	345
HDCP	7	18	12	14	17	1	4	11	8

Directions: Take Mass Pike I-90 Exit 3, Westfield; turn right onto Route 202. Course is approximate 4 miles South of Westfield.

St. Anne Country Club

Feeding Hills, MA (413) 786-2088

Club Pro: Bob Mucha
Pro Shop: Limited inventory
Payment: Visa, MC
Tee Times: 1 week adv.
Fee 9 Holes: Weekday: $9.00
Fee 18 Holes: Weekday: $13.00
Cart Rental: $21.00/18 $10.50/9
Lessons: Yes **Schools:** No
Driving Range: No
Other: Snack bar / Bar-lounge

Weekend: $13.00 after 12 pm
Weekend: $18.00
Discounts: Senior
Junior Golf: No **Membership:** Yes
Non-Metal Spikes: Yes

Tees	Holes	Yards	Par	USGA	Slope
BACK	18	6608	72	70.8	116
MIDDLE	18	6500	72	69.5	115
FRONT	18	5566	72	70.0	115

The back nine is wide open. The front is a little tighter. Considered easy to moderate. 2 players for $42 with cart on weekdays.

	1	2	3	4	5	6	7	8	9
PAR	4	4	3	4	5	4	4	5	3
YARDS	411	362	153	364	540	388	390	500	151
HDCP	11	9	15	13	1	3	5	7	17
	10	11	12	13	14	15	16	17	18
PAR	4	3	4	4	4	3	5	4	5
YARDS	320	140	374	358	300	185	527	390	559
HDCP	12	18	10	14	16	6	2	8	4

Directions: Take Route 57 to Bradley Field Exit (Route 75 South). At first lights take right onto Silver Street, at end of road turn right onto Shoemaker. Country club is approximately 1/2 mile on left.

Taconic Golf Club ✪✪✪✪

Williamstown, MA (413) 458-3997

Club Pro: Rick Pohle
Pro Shop: Full inventory
Payment: Credit cards and checks
Tee Times: 7 days adv.
Fee 9 Holes: Weekday: No
Fee 18 Holes: Weekday: $125.00 (Incl. cart)
Cart Rental: Included in greens fee
Lessons: $35.00/3/4 hour **Schools:**
Driving Range: Yes
Other: Clubhouse / Lockers / Showers / Snack-bar / Bar-lounge

Weekend: No
Weekend: No
Discounts: None
Junior Golf: Yes **Membership:** No
Non-Metal Spikes: Yes

Tees	Holes	Yards	Par	USGA	Slope
BACK	18	6230	71	69.9	124
MIDDLE	18	6002	71	68.9	121
FRONT	18	5202	71	69.9	123

Built in 1896 and revamped in 1927, this scenic club is championship caliber, although the greens fees are higher than any Berkshire course. Holes have lush fairways with wide tree lines.

	1	2	3	4	5	6	7	8	9
PAR	5	4	4	4	3	4	4	4	3
YARDS	475	391	409	358	172	361	402	394	188
HDCP	18	10	2	12	16	8	4	6	14
	10	11	12	13	14	15	16	17	18
PAR	5	4	4	4	3	4	4	3	5
YARDS	506	470	363	391	173	426	430	221	510
HDCP	13	1	7	9	15	5	3	11	17

Directions: Route 2 West to Williamstown; left on Route 43 South; 3rd street on right.

4✪ =Excellent 3✪ =Very Good 2✪ = Good

Tekoa Country Club 39

Westfield, MA (413) 568-1064

Club Pro: Scott Coviello
Pro Shop: Full inventory
Payment: Cash only
Tee Times: 1 week adv.
Fee 9 Holes: Weekday: $12.50
Fee 18 Holes: Weekday: $20.00
Cart Rental: $23.00/18 $12.00/9
Lessons: $60.00/hour **Schools:** No
Driving Range:
Other: Clubhouse / Lockers / Showers / Snack bar / Restaurant / Bar-lounge / Banquet

Tees	Holes	Yards	Par	USGA	Slope
BACK	18	6002	70	69.6	118
MIDDLE	18	5673	70	68.2	116
FRONT	18	5128	74	71.0	116

Weekend: $15.50
Weekend: $25.00
Discounts: Senior
Junior Golf: Yes **Membership:** Yes
Non-Metal Spikes: Preferred

Easy walking, unique design. Tekoa Mountain in view, fairways sculptured, greens firm and flat. Dress code. Indoor hitting dome for winter practice.

	1	2	3	4	5	6	7	8	9
PAR	4	4	3	5	4	3	4	4	4
YARDS	345	385	135	475	345	210	417	365	340
HDCP	11	1	17	13	7	5	15	3	9
	10	11	12	13	14	15	16	17	18
PAR	4	3	5	4	5	4	3	4	3
YARDS	345	145	470	380	465	345	130	415	200
HDCP	6	16	12	4	14	10	18	2	8

Directions: Take Mass. Pike Exit 3. Bear right to center of Westfield. Take right onto Route 20, follow for 2 miles.

The Meadows Golf Club 40

Greenfield, MA (413)773-9047

Club Pro: No
Pro Shop: Limited inventory
Payment: Visa, MC
Tee Times: No
Fee 9 Holes: Weekday: $10.00
Fee 18 Holes: Weekday: $14.00
Cart Rental: $10.00/9, $2.00 pull
Lessons: No **Schools:** No
Driving Range: No
Other: Bar/Lounge

Tees	Holes	Yards	Par	USGA	Slope
BACK	9	5716	72	66.6	106
MIDDLE	9	5600	72	66.6	106
FRONT	9	5094	72	66.6	106

Weekend: $12.00
Weekend: $17.00
Discounts: Senior
Junior Golf: N/R **Membership:** Yes
Non-Metal Spikes: No

"Flat, straight- Easy walk. Good conditions." 'Player".

	1	2	3	4	5	6	7	8	9
PAR	5	3	4	4	4	3	5	4	4
YARDS	475	155	320	280	255	135	470	365	345
HDCP	11	7	5	13	17	15	9	1	3
	10	11	12	13	14	15	16	17	18
PAR	5	3	4	4	4	3	5	4	4
YARDS	475	163	320	280	255	135	470	365	345
HDCP	12	8	6	14	18	16	10	2	4

Directions: From Route 2- take Route 5 South, through Greenfield center. Course is 1.5- 2 miles on right after center.

The Orchards Golf Club ✪✪✪ 41

South Hadley, MA 413-534-3806

Club Pro: Ed Twohig
Pro Shop: Full inventory
Payment: Cash, Credit
Tee Times: 2-3 weeks in advance
Fee 9 Holes: Weekday: $75.00 M-Th
Fee 18 Holes: Weekday: $75.00 M-Th
Cart Rental: $26.00/18 $22.00/9
Lessons: Yes, **Schools:** No
Driving Range: $7.00/Bucket
Other:

Tees	Holes	Yards	Par	USGA	Slope
BACK	18	6527	71	71.1	125
MIDDLE	18	6232	71	69.9	123
FRONT	18	5583	72	72.7	133

Weekend: N/A
Weekend: N/A
Discounts: None
Junior Golf: Members **Membership:** Yes
Non-Metal Spikes: Yes

W MA

Restoration program on-going. Limited tee times are available for non-members. Designed by Donald Ross. Course has very scenic view of the valley and hilly terrain.

	1	2	3	4	5	6	7	8	9
PAR	4	4	5	4	3	4	3	4	5
YARDS	409	348	488	394	144	394	188	380	479
HDCP	4	14	10	2	18	16	6	8	12
	10	11	12	13	14	15	16	17	18
PAR	3	4	4	4	4	5	3	4	
YARDS	163	352	322	432	401	375	445	153	412
HDCP	15	7	9	3	13	11	1	17	5

Directions: Take I-91 to Route 202 North to Route 116 North to S. Hadley Center. The course is 1/2 mile beyond the center, on the right.

Thomas Memorial Golf & CC 42

Turner Falls, MA (413)863-8003

Club Pro:
Pro Shop: Limited inventory
Payment: Cash only
Tee Times: No
Fee 9 Holes: Weekday: $9.00
Fee 18 Holes: Weekday: $16.00
Cart Rental: $18.90/18 $10.50/9
Lessons: Schools: No
Driving Range: No
Other: Bar-Lounge/Snack Bar

Tees	Holes	Yards	Par	USGA	Slope
BACK	N/A				
MIDDLE	9	5103	70	66.0	N/A
FRONT	9	4634	70	68.0	N/A

Weekend: $12.00
Weekend: $20.00
Discounts: None
Junior Golf: No **Membership:** Yes
Non-Metal Spikes: No

COUPON

Interesting-hilly-several blind holes-narrow fairways, some water hazards. 2 holes have 2 separate greens. Many improvements.

	1	2	3	4	5	6	7	8	9
PAR	4	4	4	4	5	4	3	4	3
YARDS	360	323	235	280	460	352	128	256	145
HDCP	3	7	18	11	5	1	16	9	14
	10	11	12	13	14	15	16	17	18
PAR	4	4	4	4	5	4	3	4	3
YARDS	360	323	300	240	460	352	128	256	145
HDCP	4	8	12	13	6	2	17	10	15

Directions: From Route 2 West-turn left at lights for Turners Falls. Ask for directions when arriving in town.

4✪ =Excellent 3✪ =Very Good 2✪ =Good   **Western Massachusetts 137**

Veteran's Golf Club   43

Springfield, MA (413) 783-9611

Club Pro: Robert W. Downes
Pro Shop: Full inventory
Payment: Cash only
Tee Times: Sat., Sun.
Fee 9 Holes: Weekday: N/A
Fee 18 Holes: Weekday: $13.50, $10.50 aftr 3
Cart Rental: $20.00/18, $10.00/9
Lessons: $25/halfhour **Schools:**
Driving Range: No
Other: Snack bar

Tees	Holes	Yards	Par	USGA	Slope
BACK	18	6350	72	69.9	116
MIDDLE	18	6115	72	69.9	116
FRONT	18	5884	72	70.2	112

Weekend: N/A
Weekend: $15.50, $12 after 3
Discounts: Senior & Junior
Junior Golf: No **Membership:** Yes
Non-Metal Spikes: No

The course is moderately difficult. The front nine is fairly flat; the back nine are hilly.

	1	2	3	4	5	6	7	8	9
PAR	4	4	5	4	3	4	3	4	5
YARDS	290	381	496	350	200	332	143	292	498
HDCP	14	6	8	10	12	2	16	18	4
	10	11	12	13	14	15	16	17	18
PAR	4	4	5	4	5	3	4	4	3
YARDS	373	421	510	360	490	173	300	334	172
HDCP	3	1	7	9	5	17	15	11	13

Directions: Call course for directions.

Wahconah CC   44

Dalton, MA (413) 684-2864

Club Pro: Paul Daniels
Pro Shop: Full inventory
Payment: Cash, Check
Tee Times: 1 week adv.
Fee 9 Holes: Weekday: N/A
Fee 18 Holes: Weekday: $50.00
Cart Rental: $24.00/18
Lessons: $25-30.00/halfhour **Schools:** Jr
Driving Range: $4.00/bucket
Other: Clubhouse / Restaurant / Bar-lounge

Tees	Holes	Yards	Par	USGA	Slope
BACK	18	6567	71	71.9	126
MIDDLE	18	6223	71	69.9	123
FRONT	18	5835	71	68.6	119

Weekend: N/A
Weekend: $60.00
Discounts: None
Junior Golf: Yes **Membership:** 3 year wait list
Non-Metal Spikes: Yes

A beautiful semi-private course, considered to be moderately difficult. Open April 15 - Nov. 15.

	1	2	3	4	5	6	7	8	9
PAR	4	3	4	4	4	3	5	4	4
YARDS	382	206	398	300	360	147	476	390	388
HDCP	12	10	8	14	6	16	18	4	2
	10	11	12	13	14	15	16	17	18
PAR	4	4	4	3	5	4	4	3	5
YARDS	368	340	371	203	480	349	430	177	458
HDCP	13	15	7	5	3	9	1	11	17

Directions: Take Mass Pike to Exit 2. Follow Route 9 North from Amherst into Dalton. In Dalton, take left onto Orchard Road. Course is approximately 1/2 mile on left.

Waubeeka Golf Links   45

So. Williamstown, MA (413) 458-8355

Tees	Holes	Yards	Par	USGA	Slope
BACK	18	6394	72	70.9	127
MIDDLE	18	6024	72	69.5	124
FRONT	18	5023	72	71.2	111

Club Pro: Jeff Gazaille
Pro Shop: Full inventory
Payment: Visa, MC, Amex, Dis.
Tee Times: Yes
Fee 9 Holes: Weekday: $15.00   **Weekend:** $20.00
Fee 18 Holes: Weekday: $25.00   **Weekend:** $30.00
Cart Rental: $25.00/18 + tax   **Discounts:** Junior Wkdays
Lessons: $25.00/half hour   **Schools:** Jr.   **Junior Golf:** Yes   **Membership:** Yes
Driving Range: Irons only   **Non-Metal Spikes:** Yes
Other: Clubhouse / Lockers / Showers / Snack bar / Restaurant / Bar-lounge

COUPON

W MA

Well-groomed, scenic, Audubon Society member. Open April - November. Dress code.

	1	2	3	4	5	6	7	8	9
PAR	4	4	4	4	3	5	3	5	4
YARDS	351	370	330	286	132	482	161	473	318
HDCP	9	1	5	11	15	3	7	13	17
	10	11	12	13	14	15	16	17	18
PAR	4	4	3	5	4	4	3	5	4
YARDS	348	405	167	480	410	342	169	453	347
HDCP	2	6	12	8	4	10	14	18	16

Directions: Mass Pike, Exit 2 (Lee) to Route 20 North to Route 7 North. Course is on left going north about 45 minutes from exit.

Westover Golf Course   46

Granby, MA (413) 547-8610

Tees	Holes	Yards	Par	USGA	Slope
BACK	18	7025	72	74.0	131
MIDDLE	18	6610	72	71.9	129
FRONT	18	5580	72	71.9	115

Club Pro: James Casagrande
Pro Shop: Full inventory
Payment: Cash/Credit Card
Tee Times: 2 days adv.
Fee 9 Holes: Weekday: No   **Weekend:** No
Fee 18 Holes: Weekday: $16.00   **Weekend:** $18.00
Cart Rental: $17.00/18 $11.00/9   **Discounts:** Senior & Junior
Lessons: $35.00/45 minutes   **Schools:** Jr. & Sr.   **Junior Golf:** N/R   **Membership:** No
Driving Range: $5.50/lg. bucket   **Non-Metal Spikes:** Yes
Other: Clubhouse / Lockers / Showers / Snack bar / Restaurant / Bar-lounge

Fantastic layout, very challenging. Dress code: no cutoffs or tank tops. Schools for all ages and abilities. Open April 1 - December.

	1	2	3	4	5	6	7	8	9
PAR	4	4	4	3	4	4	5	3	5
YARDS	390	410	335	207	396	419	489	163	532
HDCP	9	7	13	15	11	1	3	17	5
	10	11	12	13	14	15	16	17	18
PAR	3	4	5	3	4	4	4	4	5
YARDS	160	422	490	160	364	405	373	354	541
HDCP	16	2	4	18	12	8	10	14	6

Directions: I-91 to I-90 to Exit 5. Go left on Route 33 North, follow for approximately 5 miles to New Ludlow Road. Take right and go 3 miles to South Street.

4✪ =Excellent   3✪ =Very Good   2✪ =Good

Western Massachusetts 139

Whippernon CC

Russell, MA (413) 862-3606

Club Pro: No
Pro Shop: Limited inventory
Payment: Cash only
Tee Times: 1 week adv.
Fee 9 Holes: Weekday: $9.00
Fee 18 Holes: Weekday: $13.00
Cart Rental: $18/8, $11/9
Lessons: No **Schools:** No
Driving Range: No
Other: Snack bar / Bar-lounge

Tees	Holes	Yards	Par	USGA	Slope
BACK	9	5678	68	N/A	113
MIDDLE	9	5186	68	N/A	113
FRONT	9	4012	68	N/A	113

Weekend: $11.00
Weekend: $15.00
Discounts: Senior & Junior
Junior Golf: No **Membership:** Yes
Non-Metal Spikes: No

COUPON

Many improvements. A challenging course.

	1	2	3	4	5	6	7	8	9
PAR	3	4	4	4	3	5	3	4	4
YARDS	185	305	310	305	170	448	160	360	350
HDCP	17	3	11	5	13	1	15	7	9

	10	11	12	13	14	15	16	17	18
PAR	3	4	4	4	3	5	3	4	4
YARDS	185	305	310	305	170	448	160	360	350
HDCP	18	4	12	6	14	2	16	8	10

Directions: Take Route 20; course is 6 miles west of Westfield.

Worthington GC

Worthington, MA (413) 238-4464

Club Pro: Erik E. Tiele
Pro Shop: Full inventory
Payment: Cash, Credit
Tee Times: Yes, 1 week adv.
Fee 9 Holes: Weekday: $10.00
Fee 18 Holes: Weekday: $18.00
Cart Rental: $18.00/18 $10.00/9
Lessons: $30.00/ 45 minutes **Schools:** No
Driving Range: $3.00/ bucket
Other: Clubhouse / Snack bar / Restaurant / Bar-lounge

Tees	Holes	Yards	Par	USGA	Slope
BACK	N/A				
MIDDLE	9	5579	70	66.8	116
FRONT	9	5229	73	66.8	116

Weekend: $12.00
Weekend: $22.00
Discounts: None
Junior Golf: Yes **Membership:** Yes
Non-Metal Spikes: No

COUPON

1904 clubhouse offers panoramic views from a 2000 ft. elevation. This hilly and challenging course sports a fifth green that is probably the smallest in New England. Open May 1 - October 31.

	1	2	3	4	5	6	7	8	9
PAR	4	4	4	4	3	3	5	5	3
YARDS	333	322	340	301	201	148	528	476	148
HDCP	7	11	5	13	9	17	1	3	15

	10	11	12	13	14	15	16	17	18
PAR	4	4	4	4	4	3	5	4	3
YARDS	351	347	340	301	240	152	464	406	181
HDCP	8	10	6	12	14	18	2	4	16

Directions: Take I-91 to Northampton. Then take Route 9 North to Route 143 and continue to Worthington Center; then take Buffinton Hill to Ridge Road.

CHAPTER 4
Southeastern Massachusetts & Rhode Island

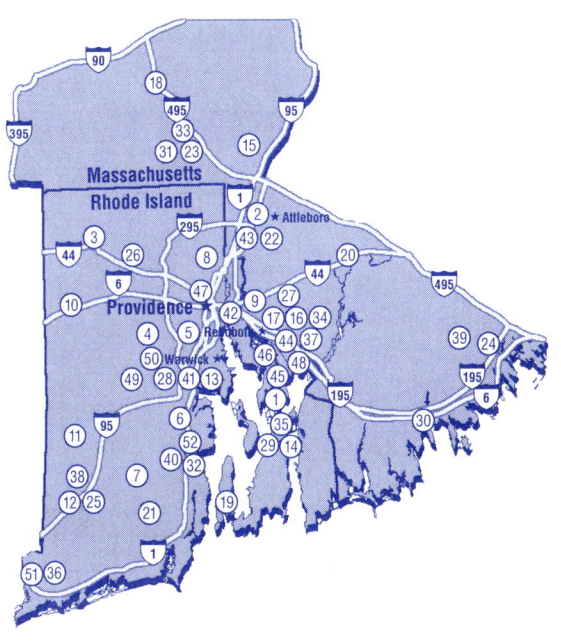

Bristol Golf Club	1	Hopedale CC	18	Pond View Golf Course	36
Chemawa Golf Course	2	Jamestown Golf & CC	19	Rehoboth Country Club	37
Country View Golf Club	3	John F. Parker GC	20	Richmond Country Club	38
Coventry Pines Golf Club	4	Laurel Lane GC	21	Rochester Golf Club	39
Cranston Country Club	5	Locust Valley Golf Course	22	Rolling Greens GC	40
East Greenwich CC	6	Maplegate Country Club	23	Seaview Country Club	41
Exeter Country Club	7	Marion Golf Course	24	Silver Spring Golf Club	42
Fairlawn Golf Course	8	Meadow Brook GC	25	Stone-E-Lea Golf Course	43
Fire Fly Country Club	9	Melody Hill Golf Course	26	Sun Valley CC	44
Foster Country Club	10	Middlebrook CC	27	Swansea Country Club	45
Foxwoods Executive GC at Lindhbrook	11	Midville Country Club	28	Touisset Country Club	46
Foxwoods Golf & CC At Boulder Hills	12	Montaup Country Club	29	Triggs Memorial GC	47
		New Bedford Muni. GC	30	Wampanoag Golf Club	48
Goddard Park GC	13	New England CC	31	Washington Village GC	49
Green Valley CC	14	North Kingstown Muni	32	West Warwick CC	50
Heather Hill CC	15	Pine Acres Executive GC	33	Winnapaug Golf Course	51
Hidden Hollow CC	16	Pine Valley Golf Club	34	Woodland Greens GC	52
Hillside CC	17	Pocasset Country Club	35		

NEW ENGLAND GOLFGUIDE

Bristol Golf Club 1

Tupelo St., Bristol, RI (401) 253-9844

Club Pro: To be announced
Pro Shop: No
Payment: Cash only
Tee Times: No
Fee 9 Holes: Weekday: $10.00
Fee 18 Holes: Weekday: $10.00
Cart Rental: $15.00/18
Lessons: No **School:** No
Driving Range: No
Other: Snack bar/ bar-lounge

Tees	Holes	Yards	Par	USGA	Slope
BACK					
MIDDLE	9	2273	33	69.9	118
FRONT					

Weekend: $12.00
Weekend: $12.00
Discounts: None
Junior Golf: No **Membership:** Yes
Non-Metal Spikes: Required

A good course for beginners.

	1	2	3	4	5	6	7	8	9
PAR	3	4	3	3	3	4	5	4	4
YARDS	137	254	148	130	167	337	480	320	300
HDCP	N/A								
	10	11	12	13	14	15	16	17	18
PAR									
YARDS									
HDCP									

Directions: Take Route 195 East to Exit 2, follow Route 136 to Tupelo Street, take right and course is on left.

Chemawa Golf Course 2

N. Attleboro, MA (508) 399-7330

Club Pro: No
Pro Shop: No
Payment: Cash only
Tee Times: No
Fee 9 Holes: Weekday: $14.00
Fee 18 Holes: Weekday: $19.00
Cart Rental: $22.00/18 $11.00/9
Lessons: No **School:** No
Driving Range: No
Other: Snack bar / Bar-lounge

Tees	Holes	Yards	Par	USGA	Slope
BACK	18	5267	68	N/A	113
MIDDLE	18	4884	68	N/A	110
FRONT	18	4351	69	N/A	109

Weekend: $17.00
Weekend: $25.00
Discounts: Senior
Junior Golf: No **Membership:** No
Non-Metal Spikes: Required

Nine additional holes opened in Spring '97. Gentle, rolling terrain with wide fairways. Water plays on holes 3, 5, 7 and 8.

	1	2	3	4	5	6	7	8	9
PAR	4	4	4	4	4	4	5	4	3
YARDS	334	286	324	321	312	236	427	265	136
HDCP	7	15	11	9	5	1	3	13	17
	10	11	12	13	14	15	16	17	18
PAR	4	3	4	3	3	4	3	4	4
YARDS	348	126	309	146	198	332	109	265	410
HDCP	2	14	10	12	16	6	18	8	4

Directions: I-95 South to I-295 toward Woonsocket, Route 1 South. Take right onto May Street, then take a right onto Cushman Road.

Country View Golf Club

Burrillville, RI (401) 568-7157

Club Pro: Rick Finlayson
Pro Shop: Full inventory
Payment: Visa, MC
Tee Times: 7 days adv.
Fee 9 Holes: Weekday: No
Fee 18 Holes: Weekday: $22.00
Cart Rental: $22.00/18 $12.00/9
Lessons: $35.00/half hour **School:** No
Driving Range: No
Other: Clubhouse / Lockers / Showers / Snack bar / Restaurant / Bar-lounge

Tees	Holes	Yards	Par	USGA	Slope
BACK	18	6067	70	69.2	119
MIDDLE	18	5721	70	67.7	116
FRONT	18	4932	70	67.0	105

Weekend: No
Weekend: $27.00
Discounts: Senior, wkdays only
Junior Golf: No **Membership:** Yes
Non-Metal Spikes: Required

A well maintained, mature course with plush fairways and greens. Open April - November.

	1	2	3	4	5	6	7	8	9
PAR	4	4	5	3	4	4	4	3	4
YARDS	379	281	485	178	332	392	386	184	367
HDCP	9	11	7	15	17	1	3	13	5
	10	11	12	13	14	15	16	17	18
PAR	4	3	4	4	4	5	3	4	4
YARDS	318	126	341	347	315	461	137	344	348
HDCP	10	18	4	6	12	14	16	2	8

SE MA /RI

Directions: From I-295 take Exit 8 (Route 7 North. After 12 miles, take a left onto Tarklin Road. Then a left onto Cowell Road.

Coventry Pines Golf Club

Coventry, RI (401) 397-9482

Club Pro:
Pro Shop: Limited inventory
Payment: Cash only
Tee Times: No
Fee 9 Holes: Weekday: $11.00
Fee 18 Holes: Weekday: $18.00
Cart Rental: $20/18 $10.00/9
Lessons: No **School:** No
Driving Range: No
Other: Snack Bar

Tees	Holes	Yards	Par	USGA	Slope
BACK	N/A				
MIDDLE	9	3170	36	68.0	113
FRONT	9	3120	36	70.0	113

Weekend: $13.00
Weekend: $20.00
Discounts: Senior
Junior Golf: No **Membership:** No
Non-Metal Spikes: Not Required

A very scenic course with rolling hills and tree-lined fairways. 3 water holes. Coventry is noted for their Par 5 sixth which has two different greens, men's and ladies. Open March- December.

	1	2	3	4	5	6	7	8	9
PAR	4	4	3	5	4	5	4	3	4
YARDS	375	308	169	484	408	520	357	187	362
HDCP	9	17	15	3	5	1	11	7	13
	10	11	12	13	14	15	16	17	18
PAR									
YARDS									
HDCP									

Directions: I-95 to RI Eexit 6 (Route 3). Continue north on Route 3 for one mile. Take a left on Harkney Hill Rd. The course is 2 mi. on the left.

4⊕ =Excellent 3⊕ =Very Good 2⊕ =Good   **Southeastern MA & Rhode Island**

Cranston Country Club ★★ 5

Cranston, RI (401) 826-1683

Club Pro: Edward Hanley
Pro Shop: Yes
Payment: Cash, Credit Card
Tee Times: Yes
Fee 9 Holes: Weekday: $20.00 Mon-Thurs **Weekend:** $22.00 Fri-Sun
Fee 18 Holes: Weekday: $29.00 Mon-Thurs **Weekend:** $32.00 Fri-Sun
Cart Rental: $23.00/18
Discounts: Senior
Lessons: Yes **School:** Yes
Junior Golf: N/R **Membership:** Yes
Driving Range: Yes
Non-Metal Spikes: Required
Other: Clubhouse / Lockers / Showers / Snack bar / Bar / Banquet Facilities

Tees	Holes	Yards	Par	USGA	Slope
BACK	18	6636	72.8	72.8	125
MIDDLE	18	6149	71	71.3	124
FRONT	18	5396	71.9	N/A	120

New Pro shop and banquet facilities. New natural grass driving range. 3 newly designed holes with water features.

	1	2	3	4	5	6	7	8	9
PAR	5	4	4	3	4	4	4	3	4
YARDS	529	348	375	180	338	346	344	173	410
HDCP	1	11	17	9	7	5	13	15	3
	10	11	12	13	14	15	16	17	18
PAR	4	4	3	5	4	3	4	5	4
YARDS	345	377	125	475	349	166	369	545	355
HDCP	8	4	18	12	14	16	10	2	6

Directions: I-95 to Route 37 West (Exit 14). Go to end of Route 37, turn left. Go 0.2 mile to intersection, turn right; 0.4 mile to stop sign, bear right. Proceed 0.2 mile to crossroads and turn left (Phoenix Avenue). 2 miles to golf course.

East Greenwich CC 6

E. Greenwich, RI (401) 884-5656

Club Pro: Larry Rittmann
Pro Shop: No
Payment: Cash only
Tee Times: No
Fee 9 Holes: Weekday: $12.00 **Weekend:** $15.00
Fee 18 Holes: Weekday: $20.00 **Weekend:** $23.00
Cart Rental: $18.00/18 $10.00/9
Discounts: Senior, $2.00 for 1st nine.
Lessons: Yes **School:** Jr. & Sr.
Junior Golf: No **Membership:** Yes
Driving Range: No
Non-Metal Spikes: Required
Other: Snack bar / Bar-lounge

Tees	Holes	Yards	Par	USGA	Slope
BACK	N/R				
MIDDLE	9	6042	70	68.6	N/A
FRONT	N/R				

Featuring a new layout opening in spring of 1999: 250 yards in additional length. Open Spring - December. Scorecard below is reprint of previous layout.

	1	2	3	4	5	6	7	8	9
PAR	4	4	4	4	5	3	4	4	3
YARDS	364	310	354	325	512	151	408	387	210
HDCP	9	13	11	7	3	17	5	1	15
	10	11	12	13	14	15	16	17	18
PAR	4	4	4	4	5	3	4	4	3
YARDS	364	310	354	325	512	151	408	387	210
HDCP	10	14	12	8	4	18	6	2	16

Directions: Take I 95 North or South to East Greenwich Exit (#8). Head South on Route 2 to next traffic light (Division Rd.). Take right. Course is 1/2 mile on left.

Exeter Country Club 7

Exeter, RI   (401) 295-8212

Club Pro: No
Pro Shop: Full inventory
Payment: Visa, MC $25 minimum
Tee Times: 1 day, call after 8AM
Fee 9 Holes: Weekday: $15.00 after 1:00
Fee 18 Holes: Weekday: $25.00
Cart Rental: $20.00/18 for 2 riders
Lessons: No   **School:** No
Driving Range: $8.00/lg. $5.00/med.
Other: Clubhouse / Snack bar / Lockers / Bar-lounge / Full Restaurant

Weekend: $18.00 after 4:00
Weekend: $30.00
Discounts: Junior
Junior Golf: No   **Membership:** Yes, waiting list
Non-Metal Spikes: Required

Tees	Holes	Yards	Par	USGA	Slope
BACK	18	6919	72	72.3	123
MIDDLE	18	6390	72	69.9	116
FRONT	18	5733	72	72.1	115

Scenic and long, featuring a covered bridge on the 13th hole. Course has a beautiful layout with strategically placed hazards. Open March - November.

	1	2	3	4	5	6	7	8	9
PAR	4	5	3	5	3	4	4	4	4
YARDS	350	530	190	510	180	360	420	370	400
HDCP	9	3	13	5	17	11	1	15	7
	10	11	12	13	14	15	16	17	18
PAR	4	3	4	4	5	4	4	3	5
YARDS	400	150	330	310	480	350	370	200	490
HDCP	8	16	18	10	4	12	2	14	6

SE MA /RI

Directions: Take I-95 to Route 4 (exit 9 south) into Exeter (approx. 4-5 mi.), take Route 102 North. Course is on left.

Fairlawn Golf Course 8

Lincoln, RI   (401) 334-3937

Club Pro: No
Pro Shop: No
Payment: Cash only
Tee Times: No
Fee 9 Holes: Weekday: $9.00
Fee 18 Holes: Weekday: $13.00
Cart Rental: Pull carts
Lessons: No   **School:** No
Driving Range: No
Other: Clubhouse / Beer and Wine

Weekend: $11.00
Weekend: $16.00
Discounts: Senior
Junior Golf: No   **Membership:** Yes
Non-Metal Spikes: Required

Tees	Holes	Yards	Par	USGA	Slope
BACK					
MIDDLE	9	2534	54	52.2	N/A
FRONT					

COUPON

The course is relatively easy to walk. Open April - November.

	1	2	3	4	5	6	7	8	9
PAR	3	3	3	3	3	3	3	3	3
YARDS	133	181	121	167	91	110	110	161	193
HDCP	14	1	11	3	17	5	15	9	7
	10	11	12	13	14	15	16	17	18
PAR	3	3	3	3	3	3	3	3	3
YARDS	133	181	121	167	91	110	110	161	193
HDCP	15	2	12	4	18	6	16	10	8

Directions: I-95 North to Route 146 North to Sherman Avenue exit. Course is on right. You can't miss it!

4🟦 =Excellent **3🟦** =Very Good **2🟦** =Good   **Southeastern MA & Rhode Island 145**

Fire Fly Country Club   9

Seekonk, MA (508) 336-6622

Club Pro: Phil Fecteau, PGA
Pro Shop: Full inventory
Payment: Visa, MC
Tee Times: Yes, for weekends
Fee 9 Holes: Weekday: $14.50
Fee 18 Holes: Weekday: $19.50
Cart Rental: $23.00/18 $11.50/9
Lessons: $30-35/30 min. **School:** No
Driving Range: $4.50 per bucket
Other: Snack bar / Restaurant / Bar-lounge

Tees	Holes	Yards	Par	USGA	Slope
BACK	18	3262	60	55.4	81
MIDDLE	18	3206	60	58.0	87
FRONT	18	2043	60	58.0	87

Weekend: N/A
Weekend: $22.00 Twilight rate
Discounts: Senior & Junior
Junior Golf: Yes **Membership:** Yes
Non-Metal Spikes: Not Required

This executive course is a local favorite. Great for beginners and seasoned golfers who would like to practice their short game. Junior clinics available at the Golf Learning Center.

	1	2	3	4	5	6	7	8	9
PAR	3	3	3	3	5	3	4	4	3
YARDS	145	150	148	147	441	122	286	251	123
HDCP	11	9	7	5	1	17	3	13	15
	10	11	12	13	14	15	16	17	18
PAR	4	3	3	3	3	3	3	4	3
YARDS	240	146	126	87	139	155	182	240	134
HDCP	10	6	12	18	8	4	2	14	16

Directions: Take I-95 to I-195 East, take Seekonk/Barrington Exit. Bear right toward Seekonk. At light take left then another left at the next light. At fork in the road, bear left. Take a right at Firefly.

Foster Country Club   10

Foster, RI (401) 397-7750

Club Pro: No
Pro Shop: Full inventory
Payment: Visa, MC
Tee Times: 7 days in advance
Fee 9 Holes: Weekday: $14.00
Fee 18 Holes: Weekday: $22.00
Cart Rental: $22.00/18 $12.00/9
Lessons: None **School:** No
Driving Range: Practice Nets
Other: Clubhouse / Snack bar / Restaurant / Bar-lounge / 180-seat Banquet hall

Tees	Holes	Yards	Par	USGA	Slope
BACK	18		72	71.5	117
MIDDLE	18	6187	72	71.5	117
FRONT	18	5499	72	70.0	112

Weekend: N/A
Weekend: $25.00
Discounts: Junior
Junior Golf: **Membership:** No
Non-Metal Spikes: Not Required

COUPON

A Friel Golf Company. Course condition best ever in 30 years. Dress code. Great Italian food. Weekday golf and meal specials. Open April - November. Twilight on weekends.

	1	2	3	4	5	6	7	8	9
PAR	4	4	3	5	4	4	3	5	4
YARDS	356	340	241	595	295	425	130	485	310
HDCP	5	11	9	3	13	1	17	7	15
	10	11	12	13	14	15	16	17	18
PAR	4	4	5	4	5	4	4	3	3
YARDS	405	310	495	375	450	295	315	170	195
HDCP	4	16	10	2	8	12	6	18	14

Directions: Take I-95 to Route 102 North to Route 14. Left on Route 14 to Moosup Valley Road (on right) to Johnson Road (on right.) Follow to course.

Foxwoods Executive GC at Lindhbrook 11

Hope Valley, RI (401) 539-8700

Club Pro: Brian Warnock
Pro Shop: Full inventory
Payment: Visa, MC
Tee Times: Yes
Fee 9 Holes: Weekday: $10.00 Twilight
Fee 18 Holes: Weekday: $15.00
Cart Rental: Yes
Lessons: $25/30 min. **School:** No
Driving Range: No
Other: Snack bar / Restaurant / Bar-lounge

Weekend: $10.00 Twilight
Weekend: $18.00 F/S/S/H
Discounts: Senior & Junior
Junior Golf: Yes **Membership:** Yes
Non-Metal Spikes: Required

Tees	Holes	Yards	Par	USGA	Slope
BACK					
MIDDLE	18	2869	54	N/A	N/A
FRONT					

COUPON

The course is a challenging par 3 with numerous water holes. Call ahead for availability tournament preempt play. Accept Wampum for food, beverage, and merchandise. www.foxwoods.golf

	1	2	3	4	5	6	7	8	9
PAR	3	3	3	3	3	3	3	3	3
YARDS	132	146	171	172	150	168	158	175	125
HDCP	16	14	4	10	12	6	8	2	12
	10	11	12	13	14	15	16	17	18
PAR	3	3	3	3	3	3	3	3	3
YARDS	139	143	127	180	181	192	143	183	184
HDCP	15	17	11	3	9	7	13	5	1

SE MA/RI

Directions: Take I-95 to Exit 2. If Northbound - bear right; if Southbound - turn left. Course 800 yards from I-95 on right.

Foxwoods Golf & CC at Boulder Hills ○○ 12

Route 138, Richmond, RI 02898 (401-539-4653)

Club Pro: Thomas Tally
Pro Shop: Full inventory
Payment: Visa, MC, Amex, Chacks
Tee Times: 5 days advance
Fee 9 Holes: Weekday: $25 w/ cart aftr 5 pm
Fee 18 Holes: Weekday: $40.00 w/ cart
Cart Rental: $12.00pp, mandatory
Lessons: $30.00/45 min. **School:** Jr.
Driving Range: Yes
Other: Full restaurant / Cub House / Bar / Lounge / Lockers / Snack Bar / Showers / Banquet Fac.

Weekend: $25.00 w/ cart
Weekend: $52.00 w/ cart
Discounts: Senior & Junior
Junior Golf: Yes **Membership:** Yes
Non-Metal Spikes: Required

Tees	Holes	Yards	Par	USGA	Slope
BACK	18	6004	70	70.9	129
MIDDLE	18	5627	70	70.9	125
FRONT	18	4881	70	70.9	123

COUPON

Golf club partnered with the Mashantucket Pequot Tribal Nation who own the Foxwoods Resort Casino. We accept Wampum for golf, food, beverage and merchandise. www.foxwoods.golf

	1	2	3	4	5	6	7	8	9
PAR	3	4	4	5	4	3	5	3	4
YARDS	120	290	410	465	380	107	448	137	333
HDCP	15	9	1	5	3	17	7	13	11
	10	11	12	13	14	15	16	17	18
PAR	4	4	3	4	4	5	4	4	3
YARDS	368	344	167	331	398	430	415	331	153
HDCP	2	6	18	10	4	14	8	12	16

Directions: From I-95, take RI Exit 3A. Golf course is 3/4 mile east of highway on Route 138 on the right.

4✪ = Excellent 3✪ = Very Good 2✪ = Good   **Southeastern MA & Rhode Island   147**

Goddard Park GC ▸ 13

Warwick, RI (401) 884-9834

Club Pro: No
Pro Shop: Limited inventory
Payment: Cash only
Tee Times: No
Fee 9 Holes: Weekday: $6.00
Fee 18 Holes: Weekday: $12.00
Cart Rental: $10/9
Lessons: No **School:** No
Driving Range: No
Other: Clubhouse / Snack bar / Park / Picnic Facilities / Shower

Tees	Holes	Yards	Par	USGA	Slope
BACK	NA				
MIDDLE	9	3024	36	N/A	N/A
FRONT	NA				

Weekend: $8.00
Weekend: $16.00
Discounts: Senior
Junior Golf: No **Membership:** No
Non-Metal Spikes: Not Required

The course is located inside Goddard State Park. There is a beach, horse paths and jogging trails. The course is open and easy to walk.

	1	2	3	4	5	6	7	8	9
PAR	5	4	3	4	5	4	3	4	4
YARDS	500	375	185	286	496	300	168	390	324
HDCP	N/A								
	10	11	12	13	14	15	16	17	18
PAR									
YARDS									
HDCP									

Directions: Take I-95 South to Route 4 cutoff, take first exit (East Greenwich). Take Route 401 and follow signs to course.

Green Valley CC ▸ 14

Portsmouth, RI (401) 847-9543

Club Pro: Gary P. Dorsi
Pro Shop: Full inventory
Payment: Visa, MC, Amex
Tee Times: 3 days advance
Fee 9 Holes: Weekday: No
Fee 18 Holes: Weekday: $30.00
Cart Rental: $24.00/18 $12.00/9
Lessons: $30/30 min. **School:** Yes
Driving Range: $3.00/bucket
Other: Snack bar

Tees	Holes	Yards	Par	USGA	Slope
BACK	18	6830	71	72.1	122
MIDDLE	18	6721	71	71.6	120
FRONT	18	5459	71	69.5	120

Weekend: No
Weekend: $30.00
Discounts: Junior
Junior Golf: Yes **Membership:** Yes, Junior
Non-Metal Spikes: Preferred

Located on Aquidneck Island, the course is made very challenging by long par 3s and windy conditions. Twilight rates.

	1	2	3	4	5	6	7	8	9
PAR	4	4	4	5	3	4	4	3	4
YARDS	361	454	386	541	175	392	354	201	424
HDCP	15	3	7	1	11	9	13	17	5
	10	11	12	13	14	15	16	17	18
PAR	5	3	3	4	4	4	4	5	4
YARDS	605	220	125	327	440	334	394	540	368
HDCP	2	12	18	6	10	8	16	4	14

Directions: Take Route 195 to Route 24 South, follow Route 114 South, Raytheon Corp is on right. Take left on Union St. (a few mi. past Raytheon Corp.), club is on left 1/2 mile.

Heather Hill CC ▶ 15

Plainville, MA (508) 695-0309

Club Pro: Mike Consetino
Pro Shop: Limited inventory
Payment: Cash only
Tee Times: Weekends, 1 week adv.
Fee 9 Holes: Weekday: $13.00
Fee 18 Holes: Weekday: $17.00
Cart Rental: $22.00/18 $11.00/9
Lessons: Yes **School:** No
Driving Range: Yes
Other: Clubhouse / Snack bar / Bar-lounge

Tees	Holes	Yards	Par	USGA	Slope
BACK	18	6005	72	67.8	117
MIDDLE	18	5724	72	66.5	115
FRONT	18	4736	70	67.1	111

Weekend: $16.00
Weekend: $24.00
Discounts: None
Junior Golf: No **Membership:** No
Non-Metal Spikes: Preferred

This 27 hole course is nicely conditioned, scenic and well laid out. The middle and south courses play for 18. North course is 9 holes, 3368 yards. A real bargain for the price. Open year round.

	1	2	3	4	5	6	7	8	9
PAR	3	4	4	5	4	4	5	3	4
YARDS	340	397	489	373	274	419	197	173	339
HDCP	7	3	11	5	13	1	15	17	9
	10	11	12	13	14	15	16	17	18
PAR	3	4	5	4	4	4	5	3	4
YARDS	388	169	518	334	317	367	183	413	315
HDCP	6	16	8	10	18	4	14	2	12

SE MA /RI

Directions: Take I-495 to Exit 15, follow Route 1A South to Route 106, take right on Route 106 (West Bacon St.) in Plainville Center. Course is on right.

Hidden Hollow C. C. ▶ 16

Rehoboth, MA (508) 252-9392

Club Pro: No
Pro Shop: No
Payment: Cash only
Tee Times: No
Fee 9 Holes: Weekday: No
Fee 18 Holes: Weekday: $14.00
Cart Rental: Yes
Lessons: No **School:** No
Driving Range: No
Other: Snack bar / Bar-lounge/ Clubhouse (1735)

Tees	Holes	Yards	Par	USGA	Slope
BACK					
MIDDLE	9	5810	70	N/A	N/A
FRONT					

Weekend: No
Weekend: $17.00
Discounts: None
Junior Golf: No **Membership:** No
Non-Metal Spikes: Not Required

The course is short and picturesque, quaint and old fashioned. Very popular with female golfers.

	1	2	3	4	5	6	7	8	9
PAR	4	4	3	4	4	5	4	3	4
YARDS	341	307	187	382	400	481	313	233	261
HDCP	7	11	17	5	3	1	9	15	13
	10	11	12	13	14	15	16	17	18
PAR	4	4	3	4	4	5	4	3	4
YARDS	341	307	187	382	400	481	313	233	261
HDCP	8	12	18	6	4	2	10	16	14

Directions: I-195 to MA exit 2. North off exit to Davis St. Right on Davis to Pleasant St. Left on Pleasant. Course is one mi. on left.

4✪ =Excellent 3✪ =Very Good 2✪ =Good

Hillside CC   17

Rehoboth, MA (508) 252-9761

Club Pro:
Pro Shop: Full inventory
Payment: Visa, MC, Discover
Tee Times: 7 days advance
Fee 9 Holes: Weekday: $14.00
Fee 18 Holes: Weekday: $17.00
Cart Rental: $24.00/18
Lessons: Yes **School:** No
Driving Range: Yes
Other: Full food and beverage / Functions / Swimming Pool

Weekend: $15.00
Weekend: $25.00
Discounts: Senior & Junior
Junior Golf: Yes **Membership:** Yes
Non-Metal Spikes: Not Required

Tees	Holes	Yards	Par	USGA	Slope
BACK	18	6245	71	69.8	123
MIDDLE	18	6075	71	69.2	123
FRONT					

COUPON

	1	2	3	4	5	6	7	8	9
PAR	5	3	4	3	4	4	5	4	4
YARDS	480	175	440	170	320	340	505	325	440
HDCP	5	15	1	17	13	7	9	11	3
	10	11	12	13	14	15	16	17	18
PAR	4	4	3	4	4	3	5	4	4
YARDS	330	310	145	380	390	350	170	465	340
HDCP	12	16	18	2	4	8	14	10	6

Directions: Take Route 24 S. Off at Route 44. 1 mile west of intersection of Routes 118 & 44, take River St to Hillside Ave.

Hopedale CC   ★★   18

Hill St., Hopedale, MA (508) 473-9876

Club Pro: No
Pro Shop: Full inventory
Payment: Cash/ check only.
Tee Times: No
Fee 9 Holes: Weekday: $15, w/member
Fee 18 Holes: Weekday: $25 w/ member
Cart Rental: $22.00/18
Lessons: No **School:** N/R
Driving Range: No
Other: Clubhouse/Bar-lounge/Snack Bar

Weekend: $15.00 with member
Weekend: $30.00 with member
Discounts: None
Junior Golf: Yes **Membership:** No
Non-Metal Spikes: Required

Tees	Holes	Yards	Par	USGA	Slope
BACK	9	6099	70	69	121
MIDDLE	9	6068	70	69	118
FRONT	9	5482	70	70.8	118

Semi-private, well manicured, tree lined on both sides of fairway. Water on first, third and sixth holes.

	1	2	3	4	5	6	7	8	9
PAR	4	5	3	4	4	4	4	4	3
YARDS	374	508	140	371	362	316	304	381	216
HDCP	2	6	18	10	12	14	16	4	8
	10	11	12	13	14	15	16	17	18
PAR	4	5	3	4	4	4	4	4	3
YARDS	383	508	172	400	393	334	312	396	229
HDCP	1	5	15	9	11	13	17	3	7

Directions: I-495 onto Route 85 Milford. Turn right onto Route 85 and right onto Route 16 thru center of Milford to Hopedale. At lights go left onto Hopedale St to end. Take right onto Green St to course.

Jamestown Golf & CC   19

Jamestown, RI (401) 423-9930

Club Pro: No
Pro Shop: Limited inventory
Payment: Cash only
Tee Times: No
Fee 9 Holes: Weekday: $13.00
Fee 18 Holes: Weekday: $20.00
Cart Rental: $18.00/18 $10.00/9
Lessons: No   **School:** No
Driving Range: No
Other: Clubhouse / Snack bar / Bar-lounge

Tees	Holes	Yards	Par	USGA	Slope
BACK	9	6337	72	69.7	110
MIDDLE	9	5978	72	69.7	110
FRONT	N/R				

Weekend: $14.00
Weekend: $21.00
Discounts: None
Junior Golf: Yes   **Membership:** No
Non-Metal Spikes: Required

New irrigation system installed spring of '97. For the first time ever the entire course is watered! Open March - Nov.

	1	2	3	4	5	6	7	8	9
PAR	4	5	4	4	3	5	3	4	4
YARDS	298	541	293	388	130	450	158	405	326
HDCP	13	1	9	7	17	5	15	3	11
	10	11	12	13	14	15	16	17	18
PAR	4	5	4	4	3	5	3	4	4
YARDS	298	541	293	388	130	450	158	405	326
HDCP	14	2	10	8	18	6	16	4	12

SE MA /RI

Directions: Take I-95 to Route 138 East. Go over Jamestown Bridge. Cross the island and follow signs to the Newport Bridge. When toll booths are in sight, stay to the right. Course is located just south of the Newport Bridge.

John F. Parker GC   20

Taunton, MA (508) 822-1797

Club Pro: No
Pro Shop: No
Payment: Cash only
Tee Times: No
Fee 9 Holes: Weekday: $10.00
Fee 18 Holes: Weekday: $13.00
Cart Rental: $20.00/18 $10.00/9
Lessons: No   **School:**
Driving Range: $3.00/lge bucket
Other: Snack bar / Bar-lounge

Tees	Holes	Yards	Par	USGA	Slope
BACK	N/R				
MIDDLE	9	3068	35	68.6	113
FRONT					

Weekend: $12.00
Weekend: $15.00
Discounts: Senior
Junior Golf: Yes   **Membership:** Yes
Non-Metal Spikes: Not Required

A good, overall challenge. Junior golf clinics available.

	1	2	3	4	5	6	7	8	9
PAR	4	4	4	5	4	3	4	4	3
YARDS	360	412	350	478	345	168	330	390	235
HDCP	9	1	13	11	7	17	15	5	3
	10	11	12	13	14	15	16	17	18
PAR									
YARDS									
HDCP									

Directions: Call course for directions from Providence or Boston.

4✪ =Excellent   3✪ =Very Good   2✪ =Good   **Southeastern MA & Rhode Island   151**

Laurel Lane GC

21

W. Kingston, RI (401) 783-3844

Club Pro: Ralph Lenihan
Pro Shop: Full inventory
Payment: Visa, MC
Tee Times: Yes
Fee 9 Holes: Weekday: $15.00
Fee 18 Holes: Weekday: $22.00
Cart Rental: $20.00/18 $12.00/9
Lessons: Yes **School:** No
Driving Range: Yes
Other: Clubhouse / Snack bar / Bar-lounge

Tees	Holes	Yards	Par	USGA	Slope
BACK	N/A				
MIDDLE	18	5806	71	68.1	114
FRONT	18	5381	70	70.8	115

Weekend: $15.00 after 4:00 pm
Weekend: $27.00
Discounts: Junior
Junior Golf: No **Membership:** Yes
Non-Metal Spikes: Not Required

Country setting, quiet, fun and challenging. Front nine fairly open, back nine tight. Proper attire required. Home course for URI and Narragansett. Open March - December.

	1	2	3	4	5	6	7	8	9
PAR	4	5	3	4	4	4	3	4	4
YARDS	389	480	147	363	315	245	206	320	303
HDCP	1	9	17	11	5	13	3	15	7
	10	11	12	13	14	15	16	17	18
PAR	3	5	3	5	4	4	4	4	4
YARDS	143	472	161	538	392	317	311	323	381
HDCP	18	10	14	2	4	12	16	6	8

Directions: From I-95 N: Exit 3A to Route 138 E. Approx. 7 mi. on right. From I-95 S: Exit 9, Exit 5B - Route 2 S to red light (Junction Route 138 W.) Turn right .1 mile on left.

Locust Valley Golf Course

22

Attleboro, MA (508) 222-1500

Club Pro: No
Pro Shop: Limited inventory
Payment: Visa, MC
Tee Times: No
Fee 9 Holes: Weekday: NA
Fee 18 Holes: Weekday: $15/$12 after 3
Cart Rental: $20.00/18 10.00/9
Lessons: No **School:** No
Driving Range: No
Other: Snack bar / Bar-lounge

Tees	Holes	Yards	Par	USGA	Slope
BACK	N/A				
MIDDLE	9	6130	71	69.3	121
FRONT	9	5230	72	NA	NA

Weekend: NA
Weekend: $19 /$13 after 3
Discounts: Senior & Junior Mon only
Junior Golf: No **Membership:** Yes
Non-Metal Spikes: Not Required

18 holes expected in 1999. Call for new rates. Wide open and an easy walker. Reduced fees after 3:00 pm. Ladies rate on Thurs. Call for new rates.

	1	2	3	4	5	6	7	8	9
PAR	5	5	4	4	4	3	4	3	4
YARDS	465	485	360	335	375	150	373	160	362
HDCP	5	15	7	1	3	17	9	13	11
	10	11	12	13	14	15	16	17	18
PAR	5	4	4	4	4	3	4	3	4
YARDS	475	440	370	342	380	180	350	174	372
HDCP	8	4	10	12	6	18	12	16	14

Directions: Take I-95 South, take Route 123A Exit, follow to end, take right, quick left onto Tylor Street, ends at course.

Maplegate Country Club　　23

Bellingham, MA (508) 966-4040

Club Pro: Mark Blades
Pro Shop: Limited Inventory
Payment: Cash , MC, Visa
Tee Times: 6 days adv.
Fee 9 Holes: Weekday: No
Fee 18 Holes: Weekday: $36.00
Cart Rental: $13.00/player
Lessons: Yes **School:** Jr. & Sr.
Driving Range: Yes
Other: Snack Bar

Tees	Holes	Yards	Par	USGA	Slope
BACK	18	6815	72	74.2	133
MIDDLE	18	5837	72	69.5	122
FRONT	18	4852	72	70.2	124

Weekend: No
Weekend: $43.00
Discounts: None
Junior Golf: Yes **Membership:** No
Non-Metal Spikes: Yes

COUPON

Site of Dave Pelz short game school. Set on rolling hills covered with pine, maple, oak, and beech trees. Landing areas designed to allow use of drivers for all par 4's and 5's. www.maplegate.com

	1	2	3	4	5	6	7	8	9
PAR	5	4	3	5	4	4	4	3	4
YARDS	515	335	173	522	431	435	417	145	434
HDCP	7	13	15	1	5	9	3	17	11
	10	11	12	13	14	15	16	17	18
PAR	4	4	3	4	5	3	5	4	4
YARDS	376	382	191	388	510	227	530	357	447
HDCP	14	10	18	8	4	16	2	12	6

SE MA/RI

Directions: I-495 to exit 18. Bear right off exit and take first right ot Maple St. Course will be 1 mile on left.

Marion Golf Course　　24

South Dr., Marion, MA (508) 748-0199

Club Pro:
Pro Shop: Limited inventory
Payment: Cash only
Tee Times: No
Fee 9 Holes: Weekday: $10.00
Fee 18 Holes: Weekday: $16.00
Cart Rental: No
Lessons: No **School:** No
Driving Range: No
Other: Club Rentals

Tees	Holes	Yards	Par	USGA	Slope
BACK	N/A				
MIDDLE	9	5390	68	67.0	116
FRONT	9	5040	74	67.2	106

Weekend: $10.00
Weekend: $16.00
Discounts: Senior & Junior
Junior Golf: No **Membership:** Yes
Non-Metal Spikes: Preferred

European Links. Signature hole # 9 is very challenging. Open year round.

	1	2	3	4	5	6	7	8	9
PAR	4	4	3	5	4	4	4	3	3
YARDS	315	290	175	460	365	430	365	180	115
HDCP	15	11	7	13	9	1	5	3	17
	10	11	12	13	14	15	16	17	18
PAR	4	4	3	5	4	4	4	3	3
YARDS	315	290	175	460	365	430	365	180	115
HDCP	16	12	8	14	10	2	6	4	18

Directions: Take I-495 South to I-95 South. Go to Exit 20. Turn on to Route 105. At second set of lights, turn right on to Pond Rd. Course in on right.

4 =Excellent **3** =Very Good **2** =Good　　**Southeastern MA & Rhode Island**

Meadow Brook GC   25

Richmond, RI (401) 539-8491

Club Pro: No
Pro Shop: Yes
Payment: Cash only
Tee Times: No
Fee 9 Holes: Weekday: No
Fee 18 Holes: Weekday: $12.00
Cart Rental: $15.00/18
Lessons: No **School:** N/A
Driving Range: No
Other: Clubhouse/Snack bar

Tees	Holes	Yards	Par	USGA	Slope
BACK	N/R				
MIDDLE	18	6075	71	70.1	118
FRONT	18	5605	73	N/A	N/A

Weekend: No
Weekend: $15.00, $6.00 after 5 pm
Discounts: None
Junior Golf: No **Membership:** No
Non-Metal Spikes: Not Required

The course is very level and well laid out. Open year round.

	1	2	3	4	5	6	7	8	9
PAR	4	3	4	4	3	5	4	4	5
YARDS	300	175	350	335	155	535	300	365	505
HDCP	13	15	7	9	17	1	11	5	3
	10	11	12	13	14	15	16	17	18
PAR	3	4	4	5	4	4	4	4	3
YARDS	180	385	350	485	395	385	340	395	140
HDCP	16	8	14	2	6	10	12	4	18

Directions: I-95 to exit 3A in RI. Continue on Route 138 East. Course is 1 mile East of I-95.

Melody Hill Golf Course   26

Harmony, RI (401) 949-9851

Club Pro: No
Pro Shop: Full inventory
Payment: Cash only
Tee Times: No
Fee 9 Holes: Weekday: $13.00
Fee 18 Holes: Weekday: $18.00
Cart Rental: $20.00/18 $10.00/9
Lessons: $25/45min **School:** No
Driving Range: No
Other: Clubhouse / Snack bar / Bar-lounge

Tees	Holes	Yards	Par	USGA	Slope
BACK					
MIDDLE	18	6185	71	69.0	113
FRONT					

Weekend: $14.00
Weekend: $21.00
Discounts: Seniors. M-F (except holidays)
Junior Golf: Yes **Membership:** No
Non-Metal Spikes: Required

Many new improvements. Lessons given by a certified teacher of golf. Open April - November.

	1	2	3	4	5	6	7	8	9
PAR	4	4	4	3	4	3	4	5	4
YARDS	360	315	385	95	465	145	425	500	235
HDCP	10	13	8	18	3	17	5	1	14
	10	11	12	13	14	15	16	17	18
PAR	5	4	5	3	4	3	4	4	4
YARDS	445	405	535	185	360	165	355	400	410
HDCP	2	6	4	15	11	16	12	7	9

Directions: Take Route 44 West toward CT, take first left after fire station in Harmony Center onto Saw Mill Road.

Middlebrook CC

> 27

Rehoboth, MA (508) 252-9395

Club Pro: No
Pro Shop: Limited inventory
Payment: Cash only
Tee Times: No
Fee 9 Holes: Weekday: $12.00
Fee 18 Holes: Weekday: $16.00
Cart Rental: $20.00/18 $12.00/9
Lessons: No **School:** No
Driving Range: No
Other: Snack bar / Bar-lounge / Clubhouse

Tees	Holes	Yards	Par	USGA	Slope
BACK	N/A				
MIDDLE	9	5592	70	65.5	108
FRONT	9	5018	70	N/A	108

Weekend: $15.00
Weekend: $20.00
Discounts: Senior
Junior Golf: No **Membership:** No
Non-Metal Spikes: Preferred

Full time starter. The course is a good course for beginners and veterans alike. Water comes into play three holes including the monstrous par-5 fifth. Open April 1-Nov. 30.

	1	2	3	4	5	6	7	8	9
PAR	4	4	4	4	5	3	3	4	4
YARDS	360	360	301	350	500	213	130	300	290
HDCP	9	5	15	3	1	7	17	13	11
	10	11	12	13	14	15	16	17	18
PAR	4	4	4	4	5	3	3	4	4
YARDS	373	340	320	340	510	180	145	280	300
HDCP	10	6	16	4	2	8	18	14	12

SE MA /RI

Directions: Take I-195 to MA Exit 2. North off exit to Davis St. Right on Davis to Pleasant St. Left on Pleasant. Course is one mi. on right.

Midville Country Club

> 28

W. Warwick, RI (401) 828-9215

Club Pro: No
Pro Shop: Limited inventory
Payment: Cash only
Tee Times: No
Fee 9 Holes: Weekday: $17.00
Fee 18 Holes: Weekday: $24.00
Cart Rental: $24.00/18 $12.00/9
Lessons: No **School:** No
Driving Range: No
Other: Clubhouse / Snack bar / Bar-lounge

Tees	Holes	Yards	Par	USGA	Slope
BACK	9	5940	70	68.3	115
MIDDLE	9	5558	70	68.2	114
FRONT	9	4680	70	N/A	N/A

Weekend: $18.00
Weekend: $28.00
Discounts: Senior, Mon.-Fri.
Junior Golf: No **Membership:** No
Non-Metal Spikes: Required

COUPON

The course is well maintained. Open April - December.

	1	2	3	4	5	6	7	8	9
PAR	4	4	4	4	3	5	3	4	4
YARDS	334	314	327	346	145	523	145	309	336
HDCP	7	5	3	9	17	1	15	13	11
	10	11	12	13	14	15	16	17	18
PAR	4	4	4	4	3	5	3	4	4
YARDS	334	314	327	346	145	523	145	309	336
HDCP	12	10	6	4	18	2	14	8	16

Directions: Take I-95 to Route 113 West Exit. Go straight through 3 sets of lights. Cross bridge, bear right and then straight through the fourth light. Course is 1 mi. on left.

4✪ =Excellent 3✪ =Very Good 2✪ =Good

Montaup Country Club

29

Portsmouth, RI (401) 683-9107

Club Pro: Stephen Diemoz
Pro Shop: Full inventory
Payment: Cash, Credit Card, Check
Tee Times: 1 day adv.
Fee 9 Holes: Weekday: N/A
Fee 18 Holes: Weekday: $35/11:30 -3:30pm
Cart Rental: $26.00/18
Lessons: $25.00/half hour **School:** No
Driving Range: No
Other: Clubhouse / Snack bar / Restaurant / Bar-lounge

Tees	Holes	Yards	Par	USGA	Slope
BACK	18	6481	71	71.4	123
MIDDLE	18	6120	71	70.5	121
FRONT	18	5458	73	72.3	120

Weekend: N/A
Weekend: $35/after 1:30pm
Discounts: None
Junior Golf: Yes **Membership:** Yes
Non-Metal Spikes: Required

Open April - December.

	1	2	3	4	5	6	7	8	9
PAR	4	4	3	4	5	4	5	3	4
YARDS	404	404	214	363	509	352	525	135	333
HDCP	3	1	7	5	11	9	17	13	15
	10	11	12	13	14	15	16	17	18
PAR	3	4	3	5	3	4	5	4	4
YARDS	148	405	175	504	138	395	445	404	295
HDCP	10	6	14	16	12	2	8	4	18

Directions: Take Route 24 to Anthony Rd. Exit. Right off ramp; course is visible from ramp.

New Bedford Muni. GC

30

New Bedford, MA (508) 996-9393

Club Pro: Jeffrey Lopes, Mgr.
Pro Shop: Yes
Payment: Cash only
Tee Times: No
Fee 9 Holes: Weekday: N/A
Fee 18 Holes: Weekday: $15.00
Cart Rental: $12.00 per person
Lessons: No **School:** No
Driving Range: Yes, $3.00/bucket
Other: Snack bar / Restaurant / Bar-lounge

Tees	Holes	Yards	Par	USGA	Slope
BACK	N/A				
MIDDLE	18	6490	72	70	120
FRONT	18	5908	74	NA	111

Weekend: N/A
Weekend: $20.00
Discounts: None
Junior Golf: No **Membership:** Yes
Non-Metal Spikes: Required

The course is moderately difficult and hilly. Twilight rates.

	1	2	3	4	5	6	7	8	9
PAR	4	4	4	4	3	4	5	3	5
YARDS	418	392	413	343	168	312	537	140	470
HDCP	9	4	2	12	16	18	5	17	14
	10	11	12	13	14	15	16	17	18
PAR	5	4	4	3	5	4	4	3	4
YARDS	559	386	442	166	489	335	359	181	300
HDCP	6	13	1	8	3	15	10	11	7

Directions: Take Route 140 in New Bedford to Exit 3. Bear right.

New England CC ◎◎ 31

Bellingham, MA (508) 883-2300

Club Pro: Mark Laviano
Pro Shop: Full Inventory
Payment: MC/Visa
Tee Times: 3 dys/Wknd, 5 dys/Wkday
Fee 9 Holes: Weekday: None
Fee 18 Holes: Weekday: $45.00 Includes cart
Cart Rental: Carts Included
Lessons: $30.00/half hour **School:** clinics
Driving Range: Yes
Other: Clubhouse / Snack bar / Bar-lounge

Tees	Holes	Yards	Par	USGA	Slope
BACK	18	6430	71	71.1	130
MIDDLE	18	5867	71	67.2	122
FRONT	18	4908	71	68.7	115

Weekend: None
Weekend: $60.00 Includes cart
Discounts: None
Junior Golf: Yes **Membership:** Yes
Non-Metal Spikes: Required

New computerized GPS yardage system on each golf cart. Bent grass tees, fairways, greens. Reduced rates for pm play and walkers. Designed by Hale Irwin.

	1	2	3	4	5	6	7	8	9
PAR	5	4	4	3	5	3	4	4	4
YARDS	497	357	314	145	490	122	386	320	352
HDCP	5	9	13	15	1	17	7	11	3
	10	11	12	13	14	15	16	17	18
PAR	4	5	3	4	4	4	3	4	4
YARDS	355	501	145	382	327	297	140	340	397
HDCP	6	2	16	8	10	18	14	12	4

SE MA /RI

Directions: Route 495 to Exit 16 (King St.) Continue West on King St. for 6 mi. At light make a left onto Wrentham St. Bear right at the fire station onto Paine St. Course is .25 mi. on left.

North Kingstown Muni. ◎◎ 32

N. Kingstown, RI (401) 294-4051

Club Pro: Mark O'Brien, Head Pro
Pro Shop: Full inventory
Payment: Cash
Tee Times: 2 days adv.
Fee 9 Holes: Weekday: $15 after 12:30
Fee 18 Holes: Weekday: $24.00
Cart Rental: $23.00/18 $22.00/9
Lessons: Yes **School:** Jr.
Driving Range: $5/lg. $3/sm.
Other: Restaurant / Lounge

Tees	Holes	Yards	Par	USGA	Slope
BACK	18	6161	70	70.0	122
MIDDLE	18	5848	70	68.6	120
FRONT	18	5227	70	69.5	115

Weekend: $17.00 after 4:00
Weekend: $29.00
Discounts: Junior $5 after 6 pm
Junior Golf: Yes **Membership:** Yes. Residents
Non-Metal Spikes: Required

New clubhouse facility which offers a full reataurant and lounge overlooking golf course. Superbly maintained links style course overlooking Narraganset Bay. Open late March-Decr.

	1	2	3	4	5	6	7	8	9
PAR	4	4	3	5	4	4	5	3	4
YARDS	369	411	185	499	375	353	545	197	283
HDCP	11	1	15	9	7	5	3	13	17
	10	11	12	13	14	15	16	17	18
PAR	3	5	4	4	3	4	4	4	3
YARDS	171	559	333	403	194	413	398	315	158
HDCP	16	6	10	8	14	2	4	12	18

Directions: Route 95 to Route 4 (Exit 9). Take Route 403 South Exit - Quonset Point/North Kingstown - 3 miles enter Davisville Military Base - take 1st right, Callahan Road. Course is 1.2 miles on right.

4◎ =Excellent 3◎ =Very Good 2◎ =Good   **Southeastern MA & Rhode Island 157**

Pine Acres Executive GC

33

Bellingham, MA (508)883-2443

Club Pro: No
Pro Shop: No
Payment: Cash only
Tee Times: Wkends/Hldays
Fee 9 Holes: Weekday: $12.00
Fee 18 Holes: Weekday: $18.00
Cart Rental: $3.00 Pull
Lessons: Yes **School:** No
Driving Range: $8/lg. $5/med. $4/sm.
Other: Clubhouse/ Bar/ Lounge/ Snack Bar/ Mini Golf

Tees	Holes	Yards	Par	USGA	Slope
BACK	N/A				
MIDDLE	9	1146	28	N/A	N/A
FRONT	N/A				

Weekend: $12.00
Weekend: $20.00
Discounts: Senior
Junior Golf: Yes **Membership:** N/A
Non-Metal Spikes: Required

Seniors citizens 65 and up, $10 for 9 holes (excludes weekends and holidays). Challenging layout with 2 ponds, 1 dog leg, 2 incline, 1 decline, and 1 valley. Schools or groups welcome.

	1	2	3	4	5	6	7	8	9
PAR	3	3	3	3	3	3	4	3	3
YARDS	101	143	91	88	106	133	275	118	91
HDCP	N/A								
	10	11	12	13	14	15	16	17	18
PAR									
YARDS									
HDCP									

Directions: I-495 to exit 16 (King St.) South to Bellingham/ Woonsocket. About 7 mi. to the only set of lights. Take a left. Bear left at fork. 100 yards onto Wrentham Rd. Course is 1/2 mi. on left.

Pine Valley Golf Club

34

Rehoboth, MA (508) 336-9815

Club Pro: Bob Pacheo
Pro Shop: Limited inventory
Payment: Visa, MC
Tee Times: No
Fee 9 Holes: Weekday: N/A
Fee 18 Holes: Weekday: $14.00
Cart Rental: $20.00/18, $12.00/9
Lessons: Yes **School:**
Driving Range: No
Other: Snack bar / Bar-lounge

Tees	Holes	Yards	Par	USGA	Slope
BACK	N/A				
MIDDLE	9	3015	35	N/A	N/A
FRONT	9	2375	35	NA	NA

Weekend: N/A
Weekend: $17.00
Discounts: Senior, wkdays $10
Junior Golf: No **Membership:**
Non-Metal Spikes: Required

The course is considered fairly easy, with hills on holes 1 and 9, and water on 6.

	1	2	3	4	5	6	7	8	9
PAR	4	3	4	5	4	3	4	4	4
YARDS	387	172	397	568	306	218	383	301	283
HDCP	3	9	2	1	5	8	4	7	6
	10	11	12	13	14	15	16	17	18
PAR									
YARDS									
HDCP									

Directions: I-95 to I-195 East, take Exit 2 Route 136 North, left onto Davis, turn right at end of road.

Pocasset Country Club   35

Portsmouth, RI (401) 683-7300

Club Pro:
Pro Shop: Full inventory
Payment: Visa, MC, Disc
Tee Times: Available
Fee 9 Holes: Weekday: $13.00
Fee 18 Holes: Weekday: $18.00
Cart Rental: $20.00/18 $11.00/9
Lessons: Yes **School:** No
Driving Range: No
Other: Restaurant/Bar-lounge/ Snack Bar / Clubhouse

Tees	Holes	Yards	Par	USGA	Slope
BACK	N/A				
MIDDLE	9	5590	68	67	110
FRONT	9	5230	70	69.2	109

Weekend: $15.00
Weekend: $22.00
Discounts: Senior & Junior
Junior Golf: No **Membership:** Yes
Non-Metal Spikes: Required

COUPON

Beautiful views of bay. Located under Mt. Hope Bridge. Under new ownership. Old English design. Many renovations to clubhouse, pro shop, and golf course.

	1	2	3	4	5	6	7	8	9	
PAR	4	4	3	4	4	3	4	4	4	SE
YARDS	305	395	210	275	385	195	275	330	425	MA
HDCP	13	5	9	17	3	7	15	11	1	/RI
	10	11	12	13	14	15	16	17	18	
PAR	4	4	3	4	4	3	4	4	4	
YARDS	305	395	210	275	385	195	275	330	425	
HDCP	14	6	10	18	4	8	16	12	2	

Directions: From Route 24S, take Bristol exit. Turn right off ramp. Go to traffic light (1/2 mile) and turn right onto Bristol Ferry Rd. Course is 200 yds on right.

Pond View Golf Course   36

Shore Rd., Westerly, RI (401) 322-7870

Club Pro: Chris and Susan Bond
Pro Shop: Limited inventory
Payment: Visa, MC, Disc
Tee Times: Yes, 1 day
Fee 9 Holes: Weekday: $15.00
Fee 18 Holes: Weekday: $22.00
Cart Rental: $24.00/18 $14.00/9
Lessons: $35/30 min. **School:** Yes
Driving Range: $6.00/lg. bucket
Other: Clubhouse / Restaurant / Bar-lounge

Tees	Holes	Yards	Par	USGA	Slope
BACK	9	6506	72	69.9	117
MIDDLE	9	6422	72	68.4	116
FRONT	9	5348	72	68.9	115

Weekend: $18.00
Weekend: $25.00
Discounts: None
Junior Golf: Yes **Membership:** Yes
Non-Metal Spikes: Required

Course borders salt water pond with two holes along shoreline. Depending on wind, course plays differently every day. Open year round.

	1	2	3	4	5	6	7	8	9
PAR	4	4	3	4	5	4	4	3	5
YARDS	412	334	185	343	470	418	378	110	512
HDCP	3	15	9	7	13	1	11	17	5
	10	11	12	13	14	15	16	17	18
PAR	4	4	3	4	5	4	4	3	5
YARDS	420	345	195	370	475	425	385	120	525
HDCP	4	16	10	8	14	2	12	18	6

Directions: Take Exit 1 off I-95. Bear right off ramp onto Route 3 for 3 or 4 miles to Route 78 East. Take to Route 1. Turn left on Route 1. Go 2 miles to lights. Turn right at intersection. Take right onto Route 1A (Shore Rd.) for 1/2 mile.

4✪ =Excellent **3**✪ =Very Good **2**✪ =Good

Rehoboth Country Club   37

Rehoboth, MA (508) 252-6259

Club Pro: No
Pro Shop: Full inventory
Payment: Visa, MC
Tee Times: 3 days adv. Call (508) 252-4408
Fee 9 Holes: Weekday: $17.00
Fee 18 Holes: Weekday: $22.00
Cart Rental: $20.00/18, $10.00/9
Lessons: No **School:** Yes
Driving Range: No
Other: Snack bar / Clubhouse / Restaurant / Bar-lounge

Tees	Holes	Yards	Par	USGA	Slope
BACK	18	6950	72	72.5	125
MIDDLE	18	6295	72	69.5	117
FRONT	18	5450	72	70.4	115

Weekend: $19.00 after 4 pm
Weekend: $27.00
Discounts: Senior & Junior
Junior Golf: No **Membership:** No
Non-Metal Spikes: Required

Long beautiful course with large greens. Water comes into play on 9 holes. Open March-Dec.

	1	2	3	4	5	6	7	8	9
PAR	4	5	3	5	4	4	4	3	4
YARDS	380	500	155	550	400	310	300	155	410
HDCP	7	9	17	1	3	13	11	15	5
	10	11	12	13	14	15	16	17	18
PAR	5	4	3	4	4	4	3	5	4
YARDS	500	335	200	380	320	270	170	540	420
HDCP	8	10	16	4	12	14	18	2	6

Directions: From Providence: East on Route 44 to Route 118, turn left and 1st left to course. From Taunton: West on Route 44 to Route 118. Turn right, 1st left to course. From Attleboro: East on Route 118, right on Fairview to Homestead. Right, then 1st left onto Perryville.

Richmond Country Club ✪✪✪ 38

Richmond, RI (401) 364-9200

Club Pro: No
Pro Shop: Full inventory
Payment: Cash only
Tee Times: 1 day adv.
Fee 9 Holes: Weekday: No
Fee 18 Holes: Weekday: $25.00
Cart Rental: $20.00/18
Lessons: No **School:** No
Driving Range: No
Other: Restaurant / Clubhouse / Bar-Lounge / Banquet Facilities

Tees	Holes	Yards	Par	USGA	Slope
BACK	18	6515	71	69.9	117
MIDDLE	18	5827	71	68.5	114
FRONT	18	4974	71	70.4	113

Weekend: No
Weekend: $30.00
Discounts: None
Junior Golf: No **Membership:** N/R
Non-Metal Spikes: Required

Sculpted course, fairways challenging and narrow; bent grass from tee to green. Feel of North Carolina. Private conditions available for public play. Open April - November. Lower rates after 3pm.

	1	2	3	4	5	6	7	8	9
PAR	4	4	3	5	3	4	5	4	4
YARDS	318	353	204	504	165	428	450	277	285
HDCP	9	5	13	1	17	3	7	15	11
	10	11	12	13	14	15	16	17	18
PAR	4	5	3	5	4	3	5	3	4
YARDS	320	431	184	408	368	176	474	154	328
HDCP	14	10	16	2	6	8	4	18	12

Directions: I-95, Exit 3B; follow 2 miles. Left at flashing light onto Mechanic Street. 2.5 miles, turn right onto Sandy Pond Road.

Rochester Golf Club 39

Rochester, MA (508) 763-5155

Club Pro: Herb Giffen
Pro Shop: Yes
Payment: Cash only
Tee Times: Sat, Sun, & holidays
Fee 9 Holes: Weekday: $10.00
Fee 18 Holes: Weekday: $20.00
Cart Rental: No
Lessons: Private   **School:** No
Driving Range: No
Other: Snack bar

Tees	Holes	Yards	Par	USGA	Slope
BACK	18	5250	69	N/A	115
MIDDLE	18	4830	69	N/A	107
FRONT	18	4032	69	N/A	100

Weekend: $10.00
Weekend: $20.00
Discounts: None
Junior Golf: N/R **Membership:** No
Non-Metal Spikes: Required

The course is challenging with beautiful scenery.

	1	2	3	4	5	6	7	8	9
PAR	3	4	4	4	3	5	4	4	3
YARDS	156	386	258	252	128	435	250	312	116
HDCP	14	2	9	15	16	11	18	6	13
	10	11	12	13	14	15	16	17	18
PAR	4	3	4	4	3	4	4	4	5
YARDS	280	110	272	290	180	260	280	373	492
HDCP	10	17	12	7	3	8	4	1	5

SE MA /RI

Directions: Take I-195 to Rochester Exit, follow Route 105 approximately 4 miles north on right.

Rolling Greens GC 40

N. Kingstown, RI (401) 294-9859

Club Pro: No
Pro Shop: Limited inventory
Payment: Cash only
Tee Times: No
Fee 9 Holes: Weekday: $12.00
Fee 18 Holes: Weekday: $17.00
Cart Rental: $20.00/18 $12.00/9
Lessons: No **School:** No
Driving Range: No
Other: Clubhouse / Snack bar / Restaurant / Bar-lounge

Tees	Holes	Yards	Par	USGA	Slope
BACK	N/R				
MIDDLE	9	6144	70	N/A	N/A
FRONT	N/R				

Weekend: $14.00
Weekend: $20.00
Discounts: None
Junior Golf: No **Membership:** Yes
Non-Metal Spikes: Preferred

The course is hilly and has just one water hole. The remodeled 7th hole has a new green.

	1	2	3	4	5	6	7	8	9
PAR	4	4	4	3	5	4	4	3	4
YARDS	339	353	383	147	550	325	315	220	440
HDCP	13	5	7	17	3	9	11	15	1
	10	11	12	13	14	15	16	17	18
PAR	4	4	4	3	5	4	4	3	4
YARDS	339	353	383	147	550	325	315	220	440
HDCP	14	6	8	18	4	10	12	16	2

Directions: Take I-95 South to Route 4, N. Kingston. Get onto Route 102 West toward Exeter, 1.25 miles, course is on right.

4✪ =Excellent 3✪ =Very Good 2✪ =Good   **Southeastern MA & Rhode Island**

Seaview Country Club   41

Warwick, RI (401) 739-6311

Club Pro: Bill D'Angelos
Pro Shop: Full inventory
Payment: Visa, MC, Amex
Tee Times: Weekends
Fee 9 Holes: Weekday: $13.00
Fee 18 Holes: Weekday: $20.00
Cart Rental: $20/.0018 $10.00/9
Lessons: $20/halfhour **School:** No
Driving Range: $4-$6 bucket
Other: Clubhouse / Lockers / Showers / Restaurant / Bar-lounge

Tees	Holes	Yards	Par	USGA	Slope
BACK	N/A				
MIDDLE	9	5646	72	64.8	110
FRONT	9	5054	72	66.8	117

Weekend: $15.00
Weekend: $24.00
Discounts: Senior
Junior Golf: Yes **Membership:** Yes
Non-Metal Spikes: Required

The course is short and very challenging with many water hazards and bunkers.

	1	2	3	4	5	6	7	8	9
PAR	4	4	4	5	3	3	4	4	5
YARDS	305	274	242	551	143	201	302	310	495
HDCP	7	13	15	1	17	3	9	5	11
	10	11	12	13	14	15	16	17	18
PAR	4	4	4	5	3	3	4	4	5
YARDS	305	274	242	551	143	201	302	310	495
HDCP	8	14	16	2	18	4	10	6	12

Directions: Take I-95 to Route 117 East, continue for 5 mi. Take right onto Warwick Neck Ave., right onto Meadow View Ave., Follow signs 1 mile to club.

Silver Spring Golf Club   42

E. Providence, RI (401) 434-9697

Club Pro: No
Pro Shop: No
Payment: Cash only
Tee Times: No
Fee 9 Holes: Weekday:
Fee 18 Holes: Weekday: $11.00
Cart Rental: No
Lessons: No **School:** No
Driving Range: No
Other: No

Tees	Holes	Yards	Par	USGA	Slope
BACK	N/A				
MIDDLE	6	1668	23	N/A	N/A
FRONT	N/A				

Weekend:
Weekend: $13.00
Discounts: None
Junior Golf: No **Membership:** Junior
Non-Metal Spikes: Not Required

This six hole course is fairly hilly with tree-lined fairways. A good practice course. Open May - December. You can play 6, 12 or 18 holes at various rates.

	1	2	3	4	5	6	7	8	9
PAR	4	5	3	3	5	3	0	0	0
YARDS	310	175	450	190	418	125	0	0	0
HDCP	7	1	13	10	4	16	0	0	0
	10	11	12	13	14	15	16	17	18
PAR									
YARDS									
HDCP									

Directions: Take I-195 to RI exit 4. Go south on Veterans Memorial Parkway. Course is 3 mi. on Route 103 South.

Stone-E-Lea Golf Course

Attleboro, MA (508) 222-9735

Club Pro: Edward C. Lapierre, PGA
Pro Shop: No
Payment: Cash only
Tee Times: No
Fee 9 Holes: Weekday: $11.00
Fee 18 Holes: Weekday: $17.00
Cart Rental: $20.00/18 $10.00/9
Lessons: $25.00/half hour **School:** No
Driving Range: No
Other: Snack bar / Bar /

Tees	Holes	Yards	Par	USGA	Slope
BACK	18	6251	69	69.5	116
MIDDLE	18	6030	69	67.8	112
FRONT	NA				

Weekend: $14.00
Weekend: $22.00
Discounts: Senior
Junior Golf: No **Membership:** No
Non-Metal Spikes: Not Required

Senior weekdays only - over 62. Open year round.

	1	2	3	4	5	6	7	8	9
PAR	4	4	4	3	4	4	3	4	4
YARDS	360	350	310	185	330	420	175	380	430
HDCP	9	5	11	13	17	1	15	3	7
	10	11	12	13	14	15	16	17	18
PAR	5	4	4	4	4	3	4	4	3
YARDS	490	390	410	390	265	190	390	325	240
HDCP	14	12	4	8	18	6	2	16	10

SE MA /RI

Directions: Take I-95 to Exit PA (Newport Avenue South). At first light take left onto Cottage Street. Course is 2 miles on left. From R.I. take I-95 N to Exit 2A, remaining directions same.

Sun Valley CC

Rehoboth, MA (508) 336-8686

Club Pro: No
Pro Shop: Limited inventory
Payment: Cash only
Tee Times: No
Fee 9 Holes: Weekday: $16.00
Fee 18 Holes: Weekday: $21.00
Cart Rental: $20.00/18, $11.00/9
Lessons: $35.00/half hour **School:** No
Driving Range: $5.00/lg. bucket
Other: Restaurant / Clubhouse / Bar-lounge / Lockers / Snack Bar / Showers

Tees	Holes	Yards	Par	USGA	Slope
BACK	18	6734	71	71.0	118
MIDDLE	18	6383	71	71.0	118
FRONT	18	5654	71	71.0	N/A

Weekend: N/A
Weekend: $26 / $18 after 2 pm
Discounts: Senior. Weekdays.
Junior Golf: No **Membership:** No
Non-Metal Spikes: Required

COUPON

Par 71 championship course, flat, willow tree lined, large fairways (wide), some brooks, greens excellent, shirts required. Open March - November.

	1	2	3	4	5	6	7	8	9
PAR	4	4	5	3	4	3	5	4	4
YARDS	345	336	475	180	380	155	510	415	400
HDCP	13	11	5	15	9	17	3	1	7
	10	11	12	13	14	15	16	17	18
PAR	4	5	4	3	4	4	3	4	4
YARDS	365	450	425	172	380	400	195	385	415
HDCP	14	4	2	18	10	8	16	12	6

Directions: Route I-195 West to Route 114A to Route 44 East for 3 miles. Take right on Lake Street, 1 mile to course.

4⊙ =Excellent 3⊙ =Very Good 2⊙ =Good

Swansea Country Club 45

Swansea, MA (508) 379-9886

Club Pro: Glenn Kornasky
Pro Shop: Limited inventory
Payment: Most major
Tee Times: Thurs noon for following wkdys

Tees	Holes	Yards	Par	USGA	Slope
BACK	18	6809	72	72.6	129
MIDDLE	18	6355	72	70.6	121
FRONT	18	5103	72	69.3	111

Fee 9 Holes: Weekday: $16.00 **Weekend:** $20.00
Fee 18 Holes: Weekday: $26.00 **Weekend:** $32.00, $22 after 2pm
Cart Rental: $23.00/18, $13.00/9 **Discounts:** Senior & Junior
Lessons: Private and Group **School:** No **Junior Golf:** Yes **Membership:** Yes
Driving Range: $4.00/lg., $2.50/sm. **Non-Metal Spikes:** Required
Other: Clubhouse / Snack bar / Restaurant / Bar-lounge / Outdoor patio & tent / Junior golf.

COUPON

Championship layout. Tree lined. Water hazards on seven holes. Nine and eighteen are difficult finishing holes. Open year round.

	1	2	3	4	5	6	7	8	9
PAR	4	5	4	3	4	3	4	5	4
YARDS	331	496	415	206	353	113	366	472	419
HDCP	15	7	3	9	13	17	5	11	1
	10	11	12	13	14	15	16	17	18
PAR	4	3	4	5	4	3	4	5	4
YARDS	300	170	366	615	251	203	365	478	436
HDCP	16	14	6	2	18	8	10	12	4

Directions: Mass. Exit 2 off I-195. Course is one mile south of freeway.

Touisset Country Club 46

Swansea, MA (508) 679-9577

Club Pro: Les Brigham
Pro Shop: Full inventory
Payment: Cash, Visa, MC
Tee Times: No

Tees	Holes	Yards	Par	USGA	Slope
BACK	N/A				
MIDDLE	9	6211	71	69.1	111
FRONT	9	5565	73	71.0	114

Fee 9 Holes: Weekday: $13.00 **Weekend:** $16.00
Fee 18 Holes: Weekday: $16.00 **Weekend:** $19.00
Cart Rental: $23.00/18 $13.00/9 **Discounts:** Senior & Junior
Lessons: $12.50/half hour **School:** No **Junior Golf:** Yes **Membership:** No
Driving Range: No **Non-Metal Spikes:** N/R
Other: Snack bar / Restaurant / Bar-lounge / Clubhouse / Lockers, Practice area and putting greens.

Nine hole course with four sets of tees. Fairly flat but challenging. Open year round if possible.

	1	2	3	4	5	6	7	8	9
PAR	4	4	4	4	3	4	3	5	4
YARDS	324	291	373	388	118	448	160	534	393
HDCP	11	13	9	3	17	1	15	5	7
	10	11	12	13	14	15	16	17	18
PAR	4	4	4	4	3	5	3	5	4
YARDS	324	305	383	405	140	514	164	547	400
HDCP	12	14	8	4	18	10	16	6	2

Directions: Exit 3 off I-95, Route 6 West. Left at first traffic light onto Maple Street. Straight 3/4 mile to 221 Pearse Road.

Triggs Memorial GC   47

Providence, RI (401) 521-8460

Club Pro: Mike Ryan
Pro Shop: Limited inventory
Payment: Visa, MC, Cash
Tee Times: 1 week adv.
Fee 9 Holes: Weekday: $16.00
Fee 18 Holes: Weekday: $26.00
Cart Rental: $24/18
Lessons: Yes **School:** No
Driving Range: No
Other: Clubhouse / Lockers / Showers / Snack bar / Restaurant / Bar-lounge

Tees	Holes	Yards	Par	USGA	Slope
BACK	18	6522	72	72.8	128
MIDDLE	18	6302	72	71.7	125
FRONT	18	5392	72	73.1	123

Weekend: $16.50
Weekend: $29.00
Discounts: Seniors, weekdays only
Junior Golf: Yes **Membership:** No
Non-Metal Spikes: Not Required

Host to several professional events. Classic Ross: subtle, tough, enjoyable, long open fairways, many green side bunkers and undulating greens. Proper dress required.

	1	2	3	4	5	6	7	8	9
PAR	4	4	4	3	4	5	3	4	4
YARDS	402	425	457	200	327	445	191	341	402
HDCP	9	3	1	17	11	7	15	13	5
	10	11	12	13	14	15	16	17	18
PAR	5	4	3	5	3	5	4	4	4
YARDS	513	350	200	462	158	508	319	412	410
HDCP	8	10	16	12	18	4	14	2	6

SE MA /RI

Directions: Route 95 to exit 22. Follow signs to Pleasant Valley Parkway. Take exit, go through 4 lights. Take a left onto Chalkstone. Course is 1.5 miles on right.

Wampanoag Golf Club   48

N. Swansea, MA (508) 379-9832

Club Pro: N/A
Pro Shop: Yes
Payment: Cash only
Tee Times: No
Fee 9 Holes: Weekday: $14.00
Fee 18 Holes: Weekday: $16.00
Cart Rental: $20.00/18 $15.00/9
Lessons: No **School:** No
Driving Range: No
Other: Snack bar / Bar-lounge

Tees	Holes	Yards	Par	USGA	Slope
BACK	N/R				
MIDDLE	9	5761	70	69.5	112
FRONT	9	5027	74	69.5	112

Weekend: $16.00
Weekend: $20.00
Discounts: Senior Wkdays
Junior Golf: No **Membership:** No
Non-Metal Spikes: Not Required

This course has a good mix of long par threes and short par fives. Long ball hitters have a definite advantage. Open year round.

	1	2	3	4	5	6	7	8	9
PAR	4	4	4	3	5	4	4	4	3
YARDS	355	400	400	150	450	301	355	300	120
HDCP	8	2	4	16	6	14	10	12	18
	10	11	12	13	14	15	16	17	18
PAR	4	4	4	3	5	4	4	3	4
YARDS	360	423	413	155	458	305	361	170	285
HDCP	7	1	3	15	5	13	11	9	17

Directions: Take I-95 to Exit 2 (Warren/Newport), turn right onto Route 6. Turn left at Mason Street. At stop sign turn right on Old Providence Road.

4 = Excellent 3 = Very Good 2 = Good   **Southeastern MA & Rhode Island**

Washington Village Golf Course   49

Coventry, RI (401) 823-0010

Club Pro: Bob DiPadua
Pro Shop: Limited inventory
Payment: Visa, MC
Tee Times: No
Fee 9 Holes: Weekday: $12.00
Fee 18 Holes: Weekday: $18.00
Cart Rental: $21.00/18 $10.50/9
Lessons: $25.00/30 min. **School:** No
Driving Range: No
Other: Bar-lounge/Snack Bar

Tees	Holes	Yards	Par	USGA	Slope
BACK	N/A				
MIDDLE	9	2525	33	N/A	N/A
FRONT	9	1993	33	N/A	N/A

Weekend: $13.00
Weekend: $19.00
Discounts: Senior
Junior Golf: Yes **Membership:** Yes
Non-Metal Spikes: Preferred

Course is well kept and is easy to walk.

	1	2	3	4	5	6	7	8	9
PAR	3	4	3	4	5	3	4	3	4
YARDS	175	360	150	310	470	200	360	200	300
HDCP	15	1	17	5	9	13	3	11	7
	10	11	12	13	14	15	16	17	18
PAR									
YARDS									
HDCP									

Directions: Take I-95 to Route 117 West, follow 5 miles into Coventry; follow signs.

West Warwick Country Club, The   50

West Warwick, RI (401) 821-9789

Club Pro: No
Pro Shop: Limited inventory
Payment: Most major
Tee Times: No
Fee 9 Holes: Weekday: $18.00
Fee 18 Holes: Weekday: $28.00
Cart Rental: $24.00/18, $12.00/9
Lessons: No **School:** No
Driving Range: No
Other: Bar-lounge/Snacks/ Restaurant /Banquet facilities

Tees	Holes	Yards	Par	USGA	Slope
BACK					
MIDDLE	9	6030	70	67.6	120
FRONT	N/A				

Weekend: $20.00
Weekend: $30.00
Discounts: None
Junior Golf: No **Membership:** Yes, also junior.
Non-Metal Spikes: Required

New owner-operator. Unique layout on both sides of road. First four holes are hilly. Back five across street are parallel and fairly flat. One set of tees.

	1	2	3	4	5	6	7	8	9
PAR	4	4	3	4	4	4	4	3	5
YARDS	419	338	140	390	360	363	333	162	510
HDCP	1	13	15	3	7	9	11	17	5
	10	11	12	13	14	15	16	17	18
PAR	4	4	3	4	4	4	4	3	5
YARDS	419	338	140	390	360	363	333	162	510
HDCP	2	14	16	4	8	10	12	18	6

Directions: From !-95, take Route 113 West for 1 mile. At intersection of Route 2. go straight through, onto East Ave. for 1/2 mile. Turn right onto River St. for 1/4 mile. River St. becomes Wakefield St. at light. Club is 1.5 miles at top of hill.

Winnapaug Golf Course ⭐⭐ 51

Westerly, RI (401) 596-1237

Tees	Holes	Yards	Par	USGA	Slope
BACK	18	6345	72	70.6	118
MIDDLE	18	5919	72	67.9	111
FRONT	18	5113	72	69.1	110

Club Pro: Kirk Strong
Pro Shop: Limited inventory
Payment: Visa, MC
Tee Times: 1 week adv.
Fee 9 Holes: Weekday: $17.00 **Weekend:** $17.00
Fee 18 Holes: Weekday: $30.00 **Weekend:** $30.00
Cart Rental: $24.00/18 $12.00/9 **Discounts:** None
Lessons: $25/halfhour **School:** No **Junior Golf:** Yes **Membership:** Yes
Driving Range: No **Non-Metal Spikes:** Not Required
Other: Clubhouse / Snack bar / Restaurant / Bar-lounge

The course was designed by Donald Ross in 1922. It has tight, short fairways with demanding greens. Open year round.

	1	2	3	4	5	6	7	8	9
PAR	4	5	3	4	4	3	4	4	5
YARDS	319	484	156	402	270	106	344	322	508
HDCP	13	6	8	2	15	18	10	12	4
	10	11	12	13	14	15	16	17	18
PAR	4	4	3	5	4	5	3	4	4
YARDS	395	348	141	472	383	451	140	376	302
HDCP	3	11	17	9	1	7	15	5	13

SE MA/RI

Directions: Take Route 95 North to Exit 92, take right onto Route 2, follow to Route 78, follow signs for beaches. Turn left onto Route 1A, course is 1 mile on left.

Woodland Greens GC 52

N. Kingstown, RI (401) 294-2872

Tees	Holes	Yards	Par	USGA	Slope
BACK	N/A				
MIDDLE	9	6046	70	N/R	N/R
FRONT	9	5744	70	67.1	110

Club Pro: No
Pro Shop: Full inventory
Payment: Cash only
Tee Times: No
Fee 9 Holes: Weekday: $15.00 **Weekend:** $17.00
Fee 18 Holes: Weekday: $22.00 **Weekend:** $25.00
Cart Rental: $24.0018,$13.00/9 **Discounts:** Senior
Lessons: No **School:** No **Junior Golf:** Yes **Membership:** Yes
Driving Range: No **Non-Metal Spikes:** Required
Other: Snack bar / Bar-lounge

The course has tight fairways and fast greens. Open March - December.

	1	2	3	4	5	6	7	8	9
PAR	4	5	3	5	3	4	4	3	4
YARDS	360	413	198	505	152	330	297	203	414
HDCP	7	5	11	3	15	9	17	13	1
	10	11	12	13	14	15	16	17	18
PAR	4	5	3	5	3	4	4	3	4
YARDS	360	413	198	505	152	330	297	203	414
HDCP	8	6	12	4	16	10	18	14	2

Directions: Take I-95 South to Route 4 South, take left at 2nd light onto Stony Lane; at 1st intersection take left onto Old Baptist Road, course is 1/8 mile on left.

4⭐ =Excellent 3⭐ =Very Good 2⭐ =Good

CHAPTER 5
New Hampshire

Course	#
Amherst Country Club	1
Androscoggin Valley CC	2
Angus Lea Golf Course	3
Applewood Golf Links	4
Atkinson Country Club	5
Balsams Panorama GC, The	6
Balsams-Coashaukee GC	7
Beaver Meadow GC	8
Bethlehem CC	9
Blackmount Country Club	10
Bramber Valley Golf Course	11
Bretwood Golf Course (North)	12
Bretwood Golf Course (South)	13
Buckmeadow Golf Club	14
Campbell's Scottish Highlands	15
Candia Woods	16
Carter Country Club	17
CC of New Hampshire	18
Claremont CC	19
Colebrook CC	20
Countryside Golf Club	21
Den Brae Golf Course	22
Derryfield CC	23
Duston Country Club	24
Eagle Mountain House	25
East Kingston GC	26
Eastman Golf Links	27
Exeter Country Club	28
Farmington CC	29
Fore-U-Golf Center	30
Franklin Greens Golf & CC	31
Green Meadow GC (North)	32
Green Meadow GC (South)	33
Hale's Location Country Club	34
Hanover Country Club	35
Hickory Pond Inn & GC	36
Hidden Valley R.V. and GP	37
Highlands Links GC	38
Hoodkroft CC	39
Hooper Golf Club	40
Indian Mound GC	41
Intervale Country Club	42
Jack O'Lantern Resort	43
John H. Cain GC	44
Keene Country Club	45
Kingston Fairways	46
Kingswood Golf Club	47
Kona Mansion Inn	48
Laconia Country Club	49
Lakeview Golf Club	50
Lisbon Village Country Club	51
Lochmere Golf & CC	52
Londonderry CC	53
Loudon Country Club	54
Maplewood Casino & CC	55
Monadnock CC	56
Mt. Washington Hotel	57
Nippo Lake Golf Club	58
North Conway CC	59
Oak Hill Golf	60
Overlook	61
Passaconaway CC	62
Pease Golf Course	63
Perry Hollow Golf & CC	64
Pheasant Ridge CC	65
Pine Grove Springs CC	66
Pine Valley CC	67
Plausawa Valley CC	68
Ponemah Green	69
Portsmouth CC	70
Rochester Country Club	71
Rockingham CC	72
Sagamore-Hampton GC	73
Shattuck GC, The	74
Souhegan Woods GC	75
Sunningdale GC	76
Sunset Hill Golf Course	77
Tory Pines Resort	78
Twin Lake Villa GC	79
Waterville Valley	80
Waukewan Golf Club	81
Waumbek CC, The	82
Wentworth Resort GC	83
Whip-Poor-Will GC	84
White Mountain CC	85
Windham Golf Club	86
Woodbound Inn GC	87

Amherst Country Club 1

Ponemah Rd., Amherst, NH (603) 673-9908

Club Pro: Joe Shea
Pro Shop: Full inventory
Payment: Visa, MC, Cash, Check
Tee Times: 5 day adv.
Fee 9 Holes: Weekday: $18.00
Fee 18 Holes: Weekday: $28.00
Cart Rental: $24.00/18 $15.00/9
Lessons: Yes **School:** No
Driving Range: Yes
Other: Clubhouse / Bar-lounge / Snack Bar
Weekend: $23.00 after 3:00 pm
Weekend: $38.00
Discounts: Senior Weekdays
Junior Golf: No **Membership:** Yes
Non-Metal Spikes: Required

Tees	Holes	Yards	Par	USGA	Slope
BACK	18	6520	72	70.7	123
MIDDLE	18	6000	72	68.7	118
FRONT	18	5575	74	74.2	126

Souhegan River meanders through course affecting six holes; the course sits in River Valley. Flat terrain; penncross greens with variety of contours.

	1	2	3	4	5	6	7	8	9
PAR	4	5	3	5	4	4	3	4	4
YARDS	300	475	188	460	370	338	183	412	373
HDCP	17	3	7	5	11	13	9	1	15
	10	11	12	13	14	15	16	17	18
PAR	4	4	4	3	5	4	4	5	3
YARDS	350	260	344	135	455	330	391	508	128
HDCP	10	18	2	16	8	12	4	6	14

Directions: Take I-93 to I-293 in Manchester, NH. Then take Route 101 West to Amherst and Route 122 South. The club is located on Route 122, 3 miles on left.

NH

Androscoggin Valley CC ✪✪ 2

Route. 2, Gorham, NH (603) 466-9468

Club Pro: Gifford Nutbrown
Pro Shop: Full inventory
Payment: Visa, MC
Tee Times: 1 day adv.
Fee 9 Holes: Weekday: $15.00
Fee 18 Holes: Weekday: $20.00
Cart Rental: $25.00/18 $15.00/9
Lessons: $25.00/half hour **School:** N/R
Driving Range: $5.00/lg. $2.50/sm.
Other: Clubhouse / Snack bar / Bar-lounge / Lockers / Showers
Weekend: $15.00
Weekend: $24.00
Discounts: Junior 14 & under, 1/2 price
Junior Golf: Yes **Membership:** N/R
Non-Metal Spikes: Not Required

Tees	Holes	Yards	Par	USGA	Slope
BACK	N/A				
MIDDLE	18	5499	70	68.9	116
FRONT	N/A				

Flat course with a scenery of the mountains. Some holes border the Androscoggin River. Open May 1 - October 31.

	1	2	3	4	5	6	7	8	9
PAR	5	4	3	5	4	3	3	4	3
YARDS	453	365	157	451	287	178	146	284	189
HDCP	4	2	16	6	12	8	18	10	14
	10	11	12	13	14	15	16	17	18
PAR	4	4	4	3	5	3	4	5	4
YARDS	359	347	230	206	524	134	336	507	346
HDCP	7	5	15	11	1	17	13	3	9

Directions: From I-93 take Route 3 through Twin Mountain to Route 115 East to Route 2. Take Route 2 to Gorham. At light, take a right through town. Cross bridge, club is on left.

4✪ =Excellent 3✪ =Very Good 2✪ =Good

Angus Lea Golf Course

West Main St., Hillsboro, NH (603) 464-5404

Club Pro: Russell Niven & Curtis Niven
Pro Shop: Full inventory
Payment: Visa, MC
Tee Times: Wkends/Holdys
Fee 9 Holes: Weekday: $12.50
Fee 18 Holes: Weekday: $21.00
Cart Rental: $22.00/18 $11.00/9
Lessons: $30.00/half hour **School:** No
Driving Range: No
Other: Snack bar / Bar-lounge / Tennis courts

Tees	Holes	Yards	Par	USGA	Slope
BACK	N/A				
MIDDLE	9	4638	66	60.0	94
FRONT	9	4194	66	65.6	101

Weekend: $12.50
Weekend: $21.00
Discounts: None
Junior Golf: Yes **Membership:** Yes
Non-Metal Spikes: Not Required

Bordered by the Contoocook River, the course is watered and wooded. Beautiful view from large screened porch.

	1	2	3	4	5	6	7	8	9
PAR	4	3	3	4	4	4	4	3	4
YARDS	283	150	160	300	310	435	245	161	275
HDCP	10	18	16	6	4	2	12	14	8
	10	11	12	13	14	15	16	17	18
PAR	4	3	3	4	4	4	4	3	4
YARDS	283	150	160	300	310	435	245	161	275
HDCP	9	17	15	5	3	1	11	13	7

Directions: Located on Main St. (Route 202/9) in Hillsboro. Exit #5 from Route I-89. 1/2 mile on left after traffic light in downtown.

Applewood Golf Links

Range Rd., Windham, NH (603) 898-6793

Club Pro: Jim Ellis
Pro Shop: Full inventory
Payment: Cash, MC, Visa
Tee Times: No
Fee 9 Holes: Weekday: $12.00
Fee 18 Holes: Weekday: $20.00
Cart Rental: $8.00/18 $8.00/9
Lessons: $30.00/half hour **School:** Jr. & Sr.
Driving Range: $6.00/lg. bucket
Other: Snack Bar

Tees	Holes	Yards	Par	USGA	Slope
BACK	9	1867	27	56.0	82
MIDDLE	9	1367	27	56.0	82
FRONT	N/R				

Weekend: $12.00
Weekend: $20.00
Discounts: Senior
Junior Golf: Yes **Membership:** Jr. & Sr.
Non-Metal Spikes: Required

COUPON

"An impeccably maintained par 3 that's pure fun to play." A.P. Attention given to junior golfers. Open April 1 - December 1.

	1	2	3	4	5	6	7	8	9
PAR	3	3	3	3	3	3	3	3	3
YARDS	179	150	136	170	123	129	158	147	175
HDCP	5	15	11	3	17	13	9	7	1
	10	11	12	13	14	15	16	17	18
PAR									
YARDS									
HDCP									

Directions: I-93 to Exit 3 in NH. Right at end of ramp onto Route 111. 500 yards to course and range.

Atkinson Country Club　　　　　5

Providence Hill Road, Atkinson, NH (603)-362-5681

Club Pro: Joe Healey, PGA
Pro Shop: Limited inventory
Payment: Visa, MC, Checks
Tee Times: 5 days adv.

Tees	Holes	Yards	Par	USGA	Slope
BACK	9	6534	72	72.7	140
MIDDLE	9	6077	72	70.8	138
FRONT	9	4847	72	67.6	115

Fee 9 Holes: Weekday: $16.00　　**Weekend:** $18.00
Fee 18 Holes: Weekday: $25.00　　**Weekend:** $30.00
Cart Rental: $11.00/18, $6.00/9 per player　　**Discounts:** Senior
Lessons: Yes　**School:** No　　**Junior Golf:** No　**Membership:** Yes, Inner Club
Driving Range: Yes　　**Non-Metal Spikes:** Required
Other: Snack bar

Well maintained. Rolling tree-lined fairways. A challenge for all abilities. **www.atkinsoncc.com**

	1	2	3	4	5	6	7	8	9
PAR	5	3	4	4	5	4	3	4	4
YARDS	485	180	350	400	481	366	185	380	300
HDCP	3	11	13	5	15	1	9	7	17
	10	11	12	13	14	15	16	17	18
PAR	4	3	5	4	3	4	5	4	4
YARDS	346	144	477	317	127	354	481	370	334
HDCP	16	12	2	8	18	10	4	6	14

Directions: From I-495, take exit 50 (Route 97). Go straight across Route 97, left at 4-way stop. Follow 3 miles to end, left on Sawyer Av. Course is 1 mile on left. Call for directions from I-93.

NH

Balsams Panorama GC, The　✪✪✪　6

Dixville Notch, NH (603) 255-4961

Club Pro: Bill Hamblen
Pro Shop: Full inventory
Payment: Visa, MC, Amex, Discover
Tee Times: 3 days adv.

Tees	Holes	Yards	Par	USGA	Slope
BACK	18	6804	72	73.9	136
MIDDLE	18	6097	72	70.5	130
FRONT	18	5069	72	67.8	115

Fee 9 Holes: Weekday: No　　**Weekend:** No
Fee 18 Holes: Weekday: $60.00　　**Weekend:** $60.00
Cart Rental: $34.00/18 $22.00/9　　**Discounts:** None
Lessons: $40.00/half hour　**School:** Sr.　　**Junior Golf:** No　**Membership:** Yes
Driving Range: $4.00/lg.　　**Non-Metal Spikes:** Not Required
Other: Clubhouse / Restaurant / Bar-lounge / Resort Hotel

COUPON

Open fairways, small, inverted bent grass greens, strategic bunkers. Nationally acclaimed resort by major publications. Appropriate golf attire required. Strictly enforced! **www.thebalsams.com**

	1	2	3	4	5	6	7	8	9
PAR	4	5	4	4	3	5	3	4	4
YARDS	366	457	376	363	175	463	157	346	316
HDCP	9	5	3	13	17	1	15	11	7
	10	11	12	13	14	15	16	17	18
PAR	4	4	4	4	3	5	3	4	5
YARDS	320	302	323	423	191	501	173	365	480
HDCP	12	10	6	2	8	18	16	14	4

Directions: 1) Take I-93 N to exit 35, Route 3 N to Colebrook, east on Route 26 for 10 miles, or 2) Take I-91 to exit at St. Johnsbury, Route 2. Go east on Route 2 to Lancaster, take Route 3 N to Colebrook, and east on Route 26 for 10 miles.

4✪ = Excellent　3✪ = Very Good　2✪ = Good

Balsams-Coashaukee Golf Course 7

Dixville Notch, NH (603) 255-4961

Club Pro: Bill Hamblen
Pro Shop: Full inventory
Payment: MC, Visa, Discover, Amex
Tee Times: None required

Tees	Holes	Yards	Par	USGA	Slope
BACK	N/A				
MIDDLE	9	1917	64	57.2	78
FRONT	N/A				

Fee 9 Holes: Weekday: **Weekend:**
Fee 18 Holes: Weekday: $25.00   **Weekend:** $25.00
Cart Rental: $25.00/18 $17.00/9   **Discounts:** None
Lessons: Yes **School:** Sr.   **Junior Golf:** No **Membership:** Yes
Driving Range: No   **Non-Metal Spikes:** Not Required
Other:

A 9 hole executive layout adjacent the Balsams resort hotel. www.thebalsams.com

	1	2	3	4	5	6	7	8	9
PAR	4	3	3	4	4	4	3	4	3
YARDS	304	147	174	223	265	236	145	313	110
HDCP	N/A								
	10	11	12	13	14	15	16	17	18
PAR	4	3	3	4	4	4	3	4	3
YARDS	304	147	174	223	265	236	145	313	110
HDCP	N/A								

Directions: 1) Take I-93 N to Exit 35, Route 3 N to Colebrook, east on Route 26 for 10 miles, or 2) Take I-91 to Exit at St. Johnbury, Route 2. Go east on Route 2 to Lancaster, take Route 3 N to Colebrook, and east on Route 26 for 10 miles.

Beaver Meadow GC ★★ 8

Concord, NH (603) 228-8954

Club Pro: Ed Deshaies
Pro Shop: Full inventory
Payment: Visa, MC
Tee Times: Weekends, 2 days adv.

Tees	Holes	Yards	Par	USGA	Slope
BACK	18	6356	72	70.8	127
MIDDLE	18	6034	72	69.2	121
FRONT	18	6519	72	71.8	123

Fee 9 Holes: Weekday: $15.00   **Weekend:** $14 after 3:00
Fee 18 Holes: Weekday: $24.00   **Weekend:** $27.00
Cart Rental: $23.00/18 $13.00/9   **Discounts:** Srs. on annual basis
Lessons: $35.00/half hour **School:** No   **Junior Golf:** Residents **Membership:** Yes
Driving Range: $3.00- $5.00   **Non-Metal Spikes:** Required
Other: Clubhouse / Snack bar / Bar-lounge

Over 100 years young. Oldest course in N.H. Site of State Amateur. Great public course. Easy to walk. Junior program for residents only. Open April 15 - November 11.

	1	2	3	4	5	6	7	8	9
PAR	4	5	3	5	4	3	4	4	4
YARDS	341	480	153	474	336	138	366	414	315
HDCP	9	5	15	1	13	17	7	3	11
	10	11	12	13	14	15	16	17	18
PAR	5	4	4	3	4	4	5	3	4
YARDS	527	320	301	130	347	400	560	156	276
HDCP	6	10	14	18	8	4	2	16	12

Directions: Take I-93 to exit 15 West (North Main St.). At second light take right onto Route 3 North. Course is 3.1 miles on right.

Bethlehem CC

9

Bethlehem, NH (603) 869-5745

Club Pro: Wayne Natti
Pro Shop: Full inventory
Payment: Visa, MC
Tee Times: Yes
Fee 9 Holes: Weekday: $15.00
Fee 18 Holes: Weekday: $22.00
Cart Rental: $12.00 pp/18
Lessons: $25.00/half hour **School:** No
Driving Range: No
Other: BCC Restaurant / Club repair service

Tees	Holes	Yards	Par	USGA	Slope
BACK	18	5808	70	68.2	114
MIDDLE	18	5619	70	68.5	113
FRONT	18	5008	70	63.0	98

Weekend: $18.00
Weekend: $24.00
Discounts: None
Junior Golf: Yes **Membership:** Yes
Non-Metal Spikes: Not Required

Open May - October. Some course renovation.

	1	2	3	4	5	6	7	8	9
PAR	4	4	3	4	4	4	3	4	4
YARDS	413	319	210	264	402	399	157	328	288
HDCP	3	11	7	17	5	1	15	9	13
	10	11	12	13	14	15	16	17	18
PAR	3	5	3	4	4	5	4	4	4
YARDS	95	487	153	417	260	501	270	296	360
HDCP	18	6	12	2	16	4	14	10	8

Directions: Exit 40 from I-93. 2.5 miles on Route 302.

NH

Blackmount Country Club

10

N Haverhill, NH (603) 787-6564

Club Pro: No
Pro Shop: Yes
Payment: Cash and checks
Tee Times: No
Fee 9 Holes: Weekday: $10.00
Fee 18 Holes: Weekday: $13.00
Cart Rental: $15.00/18, $10.00/9
Lessons: Yes **School:** No
Driving Range: Yes
Other: Snack bar / Gazebo

Tees	Holes	Yards	Par	USGA	Slope
BACK	9	2995	36	N/A	N/A
MIDDLE	9	2658	36	N/A	N/A
FRONT	9	2316	36	N/A	N/A

Weekend: $15.00
Weekend: $18.00
Discounts: Senior & Junior
Junior Golf: No **Membership:** Yes
Non-Metal Spikes: Not Required

COUPON

"Kiosks have been added to each hole. More substance to fairways." R.W.

	1	2	3	4	5	6	7	8	9
PAR	3	5	4	5	4	4	4	3	4
YARDS	150	400	333	383	217	317	350	142	366
HDCP	13	7	1	11	15	9	3	17	5
	10	11	12	13	14	15	16	17	18
PAR									
YARDS									
HDCP									

Directions: From I-91, take Bradford ,Vt. exit to NH Route 10 to village of North Haverhill,NH. Turn onto Briar Hill Rd., across from aldrich's General Store. Bear right for 1.5 miles.

4✿ =Excellent 3✿ =Very Good 2✿ =Good

New Hampshire 173

Bramber Valley Golf Course   11

Greenland, NH 03840 (603) 436-4288

Club Pro: John Stacy, PGA
Pro Shop: Limited inventory
Payment: Cash, Check
Tee Times: No
Fee 9 Holes: Weekday: $12.00
Fee 18 Holes: Weekday: $20.00
Cart Rental: $18.00/18 $10.00/9
Lessons: $25/30 min. **School:** Jr.
Driving Range: $3.00/sm, $6.00/lg
Other: Clubhouse / Bar-Lounge

Tees	Holes	Yards	Par	USGA	Slope
BACK	N/R				
MIDDLE	9	4228	64	61.4	103
FRONT	N/R				

Weekend: $12.00
Weekend: $20.00
Discounts: Senior
Junior Golf: Yes **Membership:** No
Non-Metal Spikes: Required

COUPON

Course built in 1994, James Petropolus, architect. Greens are excellent. Executive layout. Collared shirts required.

	1	2	3	4	5	6	7	8	9
PAR	3	4	3	4	3	4	4	3	4
YARDS	133	333	107	312	160	260	315	180	314
HDCP	13	1	17	7	15	9	5	11	3
	10	11	12	13	14	15	16	17	18
PAR	3	4	3	4	3	4	4	3	4
YARDS	133	333	107	312	160	260	315	180	314
HDCP	14	2	18	8	16	10	5	12	4

Directions: I-95 North or South, take exit 3A. Go west on Route 33 for about 3 miles. Blue sign for club is after Golf & Ski Warehouse.

Bretwood Golf Course (North)   12

Keene, NH (603) 352-7626

Club Pro: Matt Barrett
Pro Shop: Full inventory
Payment: Visa, MC, Disc.
Tee Times: Weekends, 3 days adv.
Fee 9 Holes: Weekday: $16.00
Fee 18 Holes: Weekday: $25.00
Cart Rental: $20.00/18 $12.00/9
Lessons: $30/30 min. **School:** No
Driving Range: $4.00/lg. bucket
Other: Clubhouse / Snack bar

Tees	Holes	Yards	Par	USGA	Slope
BACK	18	6434	72	73.7	136
MIDDLE	18	5822	72	71.8	131
FRONT	18	5140	72	68.9	125

Weekend: $18.00
Weekend: $32.00
Discounts: None
Junior Golf: No **Membership:** Yes
Non-Metal Spikes: Not Required

Many bunkers and water hazards provide challenges, and four sets of tees allow you to make the course as demanding as you wish.

	1	2	3	4	5	6	7	8	9
PAR	4	5	3	4	5	4	5	3	4
YARDS	406	530	170	297	458	353	465	130	360
HDCP	9	1	15	13	11	3	7	17	5
	10	11	12	13	14	15	16	17	18
PAR	4	4	4	3	4	4	3	5	4
YARDS	300	313	345	100	285	329	137	481	368
HDCP	2	12	10	16	4	6	18	8	14

Directions: Take I-91 North to Route 9 East to Keene. Follow hospital signs to Court St. East Surry Rd. is off Upper Court St. 1.5 mi. to course.

Bretwood Golf Course (South)   13

Keene, NH (603) 352-7626

Club Pro: Matt Barrett
Pro Shop: Full inventory
Payment: Visa, MC, Disc.
Tee Times: Weekends, 3 days adv.
Fee 9 Holes: Weekday: $16.00
Fee 18 Holes: Weekday: $25.00
Cart Rental: $20.00/18 $12.00/9
Lessons: $30/30 min. **School:** No
Driving Range: $4.00/lg. bucket
Other: Clubhouse / Snack bar

Tees	Holes	Yards	Par	USGA	Slope
BACK	18	6345	72	73.3	139
MIDDLE	18	5645	72	70.0	136
FRONT	18	4990	70	68.0	127

Weekend: $18.00
Weekend: $32.00
Discounts: None
Junior Golf: No **Membership:** Yes
Non-Metal Spikes: Not Required

The addition of 9 holes divides course into 2 independent 18 hole courses, with a single club house. Amenities, features and fees for North and South are the same. Challenging courses.

	1	2	3	4	5	6	7	8	9
PAR	5	5	3	4	4	4	3	4	4
YARDS	456	512	161	324	275	296	162	336	361
HDCP	15	3	13	7	17	11	9	1	5
	10	11	12	13	14	15	16	17	18
PAR	5	4	3	5	4	4	3	4	4
YARDS	426	338	121	475	300	312	125	330	335
HDCP	2	12	10	16	4	6	18	8	14

Directions: Take I-91 North to Route 9 East to Keene. Follow hospital signs to Court St. East Surry Rd. is off Upper Court St. 1.5 mi. to course.

NH

Buckmeadow Golf Club   14

Amherst, NH (603) 673-7077

Club Pro: Virginia Young
Pro Shop: Limited inventory
Payment: Cash, Check
Tee Times: Public/ Members
Fee 9 Holes: Weekday: $12.00
Fee 18 Holes: Weekday: $20.00
Cart Rental: $18.00/18 $10.00/9
Lessons: Yes **School:** No
Driving Range: No
Other: Bar-Lounge / Snack Bar

Tees	Holes	Yards	Par	USGA	Slope
BACK	9	4850	66	61.8	101
MIDDLE	9	4680	66	60.9	100
FRONT	9	4560	68	66.2	103

Weekend: $14.00
Weekend: $24.00
Discounts: Senior
Junior Golf: No **Membership:** Yes. 100 max.
Non-Metal Spikes: Not Required

Elevated greens and tees. Shot maker's course. Executive.

	1	2	3	4	5	6	7	8	9
PAR	4	3	4	4	4	3	4	3	4
YARDS	320	120	190	335	345	175	330	185	340
HDCP	1	17	15	9	5	13	7	11	3
	10	11	12	13	14	15	16	17	18
PAR	4	3	4	4	4	3	4	3	4
YARDS	320	120	190	335	345	175	330	185	340
HDCP	2	18	16	10	6	14	8	12	4

Directions: Course is 1.5 miles off Route 101 outside of Milford.

4✪ =Excellent 3✪ =Very Good 2✪ =Good

Campbell's Scottish Highlands 15

Brady Ave., Salem, NH (603) 894-4653

Club Pro: Tony Zdurko
Pro Shop: Yes
Payment: Visa, MC
Tee Times: 5 days adv.

Tees	Holes	Yards	Par	USGA	Slope
BACK	18	6249	71	68.9	124
MIDDLE	18	5746	71	66.4	114
FRONT	18	5056	71	68.4	114

Fee 9 Holes: Weekday: $15.00   **Weekend:** $18.00
Fee 18 Holes: Weekday: $28.00   **Weekend:** $35.00
Cart Rental: $24.00/18 $16.00/9   **Discounts:** Seniors, carts only
Lessons: $30.00/half hour **School:** N/A   **Junior Golf:** No **Membership:** No
Driving Range: Yes   **Non-Metal Spikes:** Required
Other: Clubhouse / Bar-Lounge / Lockers / Shower / Snack Bar

Course sculpted from 135 acres of picturesque uplands and meadows. Open, rolling fairways and "true rolling" velvet greens. Links style course with well-placed hazards, very challenging.

	1	2	3	4	5	6	7	8	9
PAR	4	5	3	4	5	4	3	4	4
YARDS	341	454	185	418	482	358	167	260	352
HDCP	13	5	15	3	1	7	17	9	11
	10	11	12	13	14	15	16	17	18
PAR	4	3	4	4	4	3	4	4	5
YARDS	295	162	330	322	395	125	303	305	492
HDCP	10	16	12	8	2	18	6	14	4

Directions: I-93 to Exit 2. Bear right off ramp. Right at first set of lights onto South Policy Road. Right onto Route 38 at next set of lights. 1.5 miles to left onto Brady Avenue. Course 1/2 mile on right.

Candia Woods 16

Candia, NH (603) 483-2307

Club Pro: Ted Bishop
Pro Shop: Full inventory
Payment: Cash, Visa, MC
Tee Times: 5 days adv.

Tees	Holes	Yards	Par	USGA	Slope
BACK	18	6558	71	70.9	121
MIDDLE	18	6307	71	69.4	118
FRONT	18	5582	73	71.7	127

Fee 9 Holes: Weekday: $17.00   **Weekend:** $20.00
Fee 18 Holes: Weekday: $27.00   **Weekend:** $37.00
Cart Rental: $24.00/18 $12.00/9   **Discounts:** Senior & Junior
Lessons: $34/30 min. **School:** No   **Junior Golf:** Yes **Membership:** Yes
Driving Range: $5.00/bucket   **Non-Metal Spikes:** Required
Other: Restaurant / Bar-lounge / Lockers / Showers / Snack bar / Pavilion

Course framed by gorgeous rustic views with large fairways and greens. We are noted for our service. Please - no jeans of any kind, wear collared shirts. Open April 1 - November 30.

	1	2	3	4	5	6	7	8	9
PAR	4	4	4	4	3	4	4	3	5
YARDS	409	349	355	389	183	357	382	195	521
HDCP	5	13	17	1	15	3	9	11	7
	10	11	12	13	14	15	16	17	18
PAR	5	4	4	4	4	3	5	3	4
YARDS	464	443	394	309	308	158	540	146	405
HDCP	14	2	4	10	12	16	6	18	8

Directions: Take I-93, Exit 7 to Route 101 East. Take Exit 3. Straight at stop sign, right at next stop sign. Club is 1/8 mile on left at top of hill.

Carter Country Club 17

Lebanon, NH (603) 448-4483

Club Pro: Harold Webb
Pro Shop: Full inventory
Payment: Most major
Tee Times: No
Fee 9 Holes: Weekday: $10.00
Fee 18 Holes: Weekday: $20.00
Cart Rental: $20.00/18 $10.00/9
Lessons: $20.00/half hour **School:** No
Driving Range: No
Other: Restaurant / Clubhouse / Bar-lounge

Tees	Holes	Yards	Par	USGA	Slope
BACK	9	5600	72	68.1	116
MIDDLE	9	5450	72	66.1	114
FRONT	9	5130	72	71.7	127

Weekend: $10.00
Weekend: $20.00
Discounts: Senior & Junior
Junior Golf: Yes **Membership:** Yes
Non-Metal Spikes: Not Required

COUPON

Established in 1920. Semi-hilly course, very scenic, especially nice in the fall, small greens, very sloped! Open April - November.

	1	2	3	4	5	6	7	8	9
PAR	4	3	5	4	4	5	4	4	3
YARDS	350	155	470	365	280	480	265	285	75
HDCP	2	3	5	1	7	4	6	8	9
	10	11	12	13	14	15	16	17	18
PAR	4	3	5	4	4	5	4	4	3
YARDS	350	155	470	365	280	480	265	285	75
HDCP	2	3	5	1	7	4	6	8	9

Directions: Just a short pitch off I-89, Exit 19.

CC of New Hampshire 18

N. Sutton, NH (603) 927-4246

Club Pro: Kevin Gibson
Pro Shop: Full inventory
Payment: Visa, MC, DIS
Tee Times: 1 week adv.
Fee 9 Holes: Weekday: $16.00
Fee 18 Holes: Weekday: $27.00
Cart Rental: $24.00/18, $14.00/9
Lessons: $30.00/half hour **School:** No
Driving Range: $8.00/lg., $4.00/sm. bucket
Other: Clubhouse / Showers / Snack bar / Restaurant / Bar-lounge / Hotel

Tees	Holes	Yards	Par	USGA	Slope
BACK	18	6743	72	71.6	125
MIDDLE	18	6256	72	69.6	122
FRONT	18	5416	72	71.7	127

Weekend: $25.00
Weekend: $34.00
Discounts: None
Junior Golf: No **Membership:** No
Non-Metal Spikes: Not Required

COUPON

The front nine is level, the back are hilly. Rated in the top 5 golf courses in New Hampshire by *Golf Digest*. Home of the N.E. Senior Open. A Friel Golf Company.

	1	2	3	4	5	6	7	8	9
PAR	4	3	5	4	4	3	4	5	4
YARDS	380	160	495	330	346	169	376	452	380
HDCP	8	18	6	12	14	16	10	2	4
	10	11	12	13	14	15	16	17	18
PAR	4	3	4	5	4	3	4	4	5
YARDS	410	124	351	471	366	169	412	400	465
HDCP	5	17	13	7	11	15	1	3	9

Directions: One mile off I-89 at Exit 10. Follow signs to Winslow State Park.

4❍ =Excellent 3❍ =Very Good 2❍ =Good

Claremont CC ▶ 19

Maple Ave., Claremont, NH (603) 542-9550

Club Pro: Chuck LaRoche, PGA
Pro Shop: Limited inventory
Payment: Cash, Check
Tee Times: No

Tees	Holes	Yards	Par	USGA	Slope
BACK	N/A				
MIDDLE	9	5418	68	64.7	104
FRONT	9	4830	72	N/R	113

Fee 9 Holes: Weekday: $12.00 **Weekend:** $14.00
Fee 18 Holes: Weekday: $20.00 **Weekend:** $24.00
Cart Rental: $24.00/18, $14.00/9 **Discounts:** None
Lessons: $25/30 min. **School:** N/R **Junior Golf:** Yes **Membership:** Yes
Driving Range: No **Non-Metal Spikes:** Required
Other: Clubhouse / Bar-Lounge / Snack Bar / Lockers / Showers

Old style course. Established 1914. Small greens, hilly with woods.

	1	2	3	4	5	6	7	8	9
PAR	4	4	4	4	4	3	4	3	4
YARDS	420	328	273	262	275	174	434	169	312
HDCP	4	12	14	10	16	6	2	18	8
	10	11	12	13	14	15	16	17	18
PAR	4	4	4	4	4	3	4	3	4
YARDS	428	336	286	277	284	215	446	177	322
HDCP	3	11	13	9	15	5	1	17	7

Directions: Claremont exit off I-91 to downtown. Follow Pleasant Street to Maple Avenue. Make right turn. About 1/2 mile on left.

Colebrook CC ▶ 20

Colebrook, NH (603) 237-5566

Club Pro: No
Pro Shop: Limited inventory
Payment: Visa, MC, Disc.
Tee Times: No

Tees	Holes	Yards	Par	USGA	Slope
BACK	N/A				
MIDDLE	9	5893	72	67.1	105
FRONT	9	4368	73	72.3	105

Fee 9 Holes: Weekday: $18.00 **Weekend:** $18.00
Fee 18 Holes: Weekday: $18.00 **Weekend:** $18.00
Cart Rental: $20.00/18 $15.00/9 **Discounts:** Mon: Sr $10, Jr $12
Lessons: No **School:** No **Junior Golf:** Yes **Membership:** Yes.
Driving Range: No **Non-Metal Spikes:** Not Required
Other: Restaurant / Bar-lounge / Motel

COUPON

Ladies: Wednesday $10.00 greens fee. Open May 1 - October (weather permitting). www.journeysnorth.com/ccc

	1	2	3	4	5	6	7	8	9
PAR	4	4	3	4	6	3	5	3	4
YARDS	345	328	191	289	612	186	518	122	300
HDCP	11	6	4	13	7	9	2	17	14
	10	11	12	13	14	15	16	17	18
PAR	4	4	3	4	6	3	5	3	4
YARDS	345	350	134	376	612	186	518	181	300
HDCP	12	5	16	1	8	10	3	18	15

Directions: From I-93 or I-91, take Route 3 North from Littleton, NH. When in Colebrook, take right onto Route 26 East about 1/2 mile. Club is on left.

Countryside Golf Club   21

Dunbarton, NH (603) 774-5031

Club Pro: Chuck Urwin, PGA
Pro Shop: Full inventory
Payment: Visa, MC, Amex
Tee Times: Weekends, 1 week adv.
Fee 9 Holes: Weekday: $12.00
Fee 18 Holes: Weekday: $20.00
Cart Rental: $22.00/18 $12.00/9
Lessons: $35/45 min. **School:** No
Driving Range: $3.50/lg., $2.00/sm bucket
Other: Clubhouse / Snack bar / Bar-lounge / Function Room

Tees	Holes	Yards	Par	USGA	Slope
BACK	N/R				
MIDDLE	9	6314	72	69.2	126
FRONT	9	6002	72	69.2	126

Weekend: $14.00
Weekend: $24.00
Discounts: None
Junior Golf: Yes **Membership:** No
Non-Metal Spikes: Preferred

Challenging nine hole course is a Bill Mitchell design with beautiful mountain views. Course demands accuracy and the playing of smart golf. Noted for velvet bent grass greens.

	1	2	3	4	5	6	7	8	9
PAR	4	4	3	5	4	4	4	3	5
YARDS	305	369	138	483	386	365	344	143	466
HDCP	17	11	13	1	9	3	7	15	5
	10	11	12	13	14	15	16	17	18
PAR	4	4	3	5	4	4	4	3	5
YARDS	305	369	138	483	386	365	344	143	466
HDCP	18	12	14	2	10	4	8	16	6

Directions: Take Route 101 to Route 114 toward Goffstown. Take Route 13 N at Sully's Superette. 4 miles. Club on left.

NH

Den Brae Golf Course   22

Sanbornton, NH 03269 (603) 934-9818

Club Pro: Tom Gilley
Pro Shop: Full inventory
Payment: Visa, MC
Tee Times: Weekends, Holidays
Fee 9 Holes: Weekday: $12.00
Fee 18 Holes: Weekday: $16.00
Cart Rental: $20.00/18 $10.00/9
Lessons: $23.00/half hour **School:** No
Driving Range: $3.00/lg. bucket
Other: Clubhouse / Snack bar / Bar-lounge

Tees	Holes	Yards	Par	USGA	Slope
BACK	9	5926	72	N/A	109
MIDDLE	9	5810	72	67.2	109
FRONT	9	5236	72	N/A	126

Weekend: $14.00
Weekend: $22.00
Discounts: None
Junior Golf: Yes **Membership:** Yes
Non-Metal Spikes: Not Required

COUPON

Shirts (no tank tops), greens excellent, Scotch type fairways. Open April - October.

	1	2	3	4	5	6	7	8	9
PAR	4	4	3	5	4	4	4	4	4
YARDS	361	237	166	451	267	356	278	350	380
HDCP	7	17	11	5	15	1	13	9	3
	10	11	12	13	14	15	16	17	18
PAR	4	4	3	5	4	4	4	4	4
YARDS	371	247	175	484	271	368	306	355	387
HDCP	7	17	11	5	15	1	13	9	3

Directions: Take I-93 to Exit 22, go south on Route 127 for 1.5 miles, right on Prescott Road, .3 mile on right.

4✪ =Excellent **3**✪ =Very Good **2**✪ =Good

Derryfield CC ▶ 23

Manchester, NH (603) 669-0235

Club Pro: Mike Ryan, Head Pro
Pro Shop: Full inventory
Payment: Cash only
Tee Times: No
Fee 9 Holes: Weekday: $15.00
Fee 18 Holes: Weekday: $24.00
Cart Rental: $22.00/18 $12.00/9
Lessons: $30.00/half hour **School:** No
Driving Range: No
Other: Snack bar / Restaurant / Bar-lounge

Tees	Holes	Yards	Par	USGA	Slope
BACK	18	6144	70	68.0	113
MIDDLE	18	5714	70	67.9	116
FRONT	18	5524	71	71.0	125

Weekend: $15.00
Weekend: $24.00
Discounts: None
Junior Golf: Yes **Membership:** Yes
Non-Metal Spikes: Not Required

Built in 1932, the second nine was added years later. The course is hilly with small greens so accurate approach shots are key. Wide open fairways let you open up.

	1	2	3	4	5	6	7	8	9
PAR	4	4	3	4	4	4	4	3	4
YARDS	302	386	176	349	361	363	349	159	313
HDCP	15	5	9	7	11	3	1	13	17
	10	11	12	13	14	15	16	17	18
PAR	4	4	3	4	4	4	4	5	4
YARDS	312	409	146	238	327	327	320	504	374
HDCP	14	2	18	16	10	6	12	8	4

Directions: Route I-93 North to Exit 8. Bear right at the bottom of the ramp. At second set of lights, take a left. Course is on the left.

Duston Country Club ▶ 24

Hopkinton, NH (603) 746-4234

Club Pro: Ken Hamel
Pro Shop: Full inventory
Payment: Visa, MC
Tee Times: Weekends & holidays
Fee 9 Holes: Weekday: $9.00
Fee 18 Holes: Weekday: $14.00
Cart Rental: $16.00/18, $10.00/9
Lessons: Yes **School:** No
Driving Range: No
Other: Clubhouse / Snack bar / Bar-lounge

Tees	Holes	Yards	Par	USGA	Slope
BACK					
MIDDLE	9	2109	32	59.2	99
FRONT					

Weekend: $11.00
Weekend: $16.00
Discounts: Senior & Junior Wkdays
Junior Golf: Yes **Membership:** Yes
Non-Metal Spikes: Not Required

A family run scenic nine hole course built in 1926. Scottish style bunkers and lush greens. Some hills. Greens are small to medium in size. Open April - Nov.

	1	2	3	4	5	6	7	8	9
PAR	4	3	4	3	4	4	3	4	3
YARDS	295	117	350	133	265	299	194	273	170
HDCP	7	17	3	15	13	9	1	11	5
	10	11	12	13	14	15	16	17	18
PAR									
YARDS									
HDCP									

Directions: Take I-89 north to Exit 5 onto Routes 202 & 9 for 3 1/2 miles. Exit Country Club Road.

Eagle Mountain House   25

Jackson, NH (603) 383-9090

Club Pro: Julie Rivers
Pro Shop: Yes
Payment: Visa, MC, Amex, Dis
Tee Times: 1 week adv.
Fee 9 Holes: Weekday: $12.00
Fee 18 Holes: Weekday: $16.00
Cart Rental: $20.00/18 $15.00/9
Lessons: $30/45 min. **School:** Junior
Driving Range: Yes
Other: Hotel / Lockers / Showers / Snack bar / Restaurant / Bar-lounge

Tees	Holes	Yards	Par	USGA	Slope
BACK					
MIDDLE	9	4308	64	61.0	96
FRONT					

Weekend: $18.00
Weekend: $24.00
Discounts: Junior
Junior Golf: Yes **Membership:** Yes
Non-Metal Spikes: Not Required

COUPON

Breathtaking views of mountains. New driving range. Full inventory. $12 twilight fee. Open late May - late October. www.journeysnorth.com/mwv/eagle.html

	1	2	3	4	5	6	7	8	9
PAR	4	3	4	5	3	3	3	3	4
YARDS	255	190	310	395	146	192	170	208	288
HDCP	7	13	5	1	17	11	15	9	3
	10	11	12	13	14	15	16	17	18
PAR	4	3	4	5	3	3	3	3	4
YARDS	255	190	310	395	146	192	170	208	288
HDCP	8	14	6	2	18	12	16	10	4

Directions: I-95 North to Spaulding Turnpike. Turns into Route 16 North. Continue into Jackson to Carter Notch Road.

East Kingston GC   26

E. Kingston, NH (603) 642-4414

Club Pro: Mike Andersen
Pro Shop: Yes
Payment: Cash only
Tee Times: No
Fee 9 Holes: Weekday: $14.00
Fee 18 Holes: Weekday: $24.00
Cart Rental: $22.00/18 $11.00/9
Lessons: Yes **School:** No
Driving Range: Yes
Other: Clubhouse / Snack bar / Bar-lounge

Tees	Holes	Yards	Par	USGA	Slope
BACK	18	6271	70	70.4	119
MIDDLE	18	5978	69	69.1	116
FRONT	18	5219	70	N/A	N/A

Weekend: $17.00
Weekend: $29.00
Discounts: Senior & Junior $2 Wkdays only
Junior Golf: No **Membership:** No
Non-Metal Spikes: Not Required

A well maintained course; very scenic. While course is mostly level, the first hole drops over 40 yards. Open April - November.

	1	2	3	4	5	6	7	8	9
PAR	4	3	4	3	5	4	4	4	4
YARDS	365	145	367	165	479	415	368	358	357
HDCP	10	18	2	11	12	7	4	15	5
	10	11	12	13	14	15	16	17	18
PAR	4	4	4	4	3	4	4	3	4
YARDS	441	374	363	414	150	294	356	136	410
HDCP	1	8	3	9	17	13	14	16	6

Directions: Take I-95 Exit 1 in New Hampshire (Route 107). The course is 6 miles on right. From Route 125 Kingston, take Route 107 East, 3 1/2 miles.

4⛳ =Excellent 3⛳ =Very Good 2⛳ =Good

Eastman Golf Links

27

Grantham, NH (603) 863-4500

Club Pro: Dick Tuxbury
Pro Shop: Full inventory
Payment: Visa, MC, Amex
Tee Times: 2 days adv.

Tees	Holes	Yards	Par	USGA	Slope
BACK	18	6731	71	73.5	137
MIDDLE	18	6338	71	71.7	133
FRONT	18	5499	73	71.9	128

Fee 9 Holes: Weekday: $25.00 **Weekend:** $25.00
Fee 18 Holes: Weekday: $38.00 **Weekend:** $38.00
Cart Rental: $31.00/18 $21.00/9 **Discounts:** None
Lessons: $25.00/half hour **School:** No **Junior Golf:** Yes **Membership:** Yes
Driving Range: $2.50/bucket **Non-Metal Spikes:** Required
Other: Clubhouse / Snack bar / Restaurant / Bar-lounge

This is a very challenging mountain course with tree-lined fairways and tight greens. Cart required on weekends.

	1	2	3	4	5	6	7	8	9
PAR	4	5	3	4	4	4	3	5	4
YARDS	354	544	167	353	389	409	189	493	395
HDCP	11	5	17	13	3	9	15	7	1
	10	11	12	13	14	15	16	17	18
PAR	4	4	4	3	4	3	5	4	4
YARDS	322	384	443	189	384	113	441	385	384
HDCP	12	6	4	16	2	18	14	8	10

Directions: Take I-89 to Exit 13; course is right off exit ramp.

Exeter Country Club

28

Exeter, NH (603) 772-4752

Club Pro: Donald R. Folsom
Pro Shop: Full inventory
Payment: Visa, MC
Tee Times: N/A

Tees	Holes	Yards	Par	USGA	Slope
BACK	N/A				
MIDDLE	9	5522	70	67.8	115
FRONT	9	5157	74	70.5	125

Fee 9 Holes: Weekday: $16.00 **Weekend:** $17.00
Fee 18 Holes: Weekday: $24.00 **Weekend:** $27.00
Cart Rental: $20.00/18 $10.00/9 **Discounts:** None
Lessons: $35.00/half hour **School:** Jr. **Junior Golf:** Yes **Membership:** Yes Waiting list
Driving Range: No **Non-Metal Spikes:** Not Required
Other: Restaurant / Clubhouse / Snack Bar / Showers / Bar-lounge

Rolling terrain with a variety of challenges. Not overly difficult. Open April 1 - December 1.

	1	2	3	4	5	6	7	8	9
PAR	4	3	5	4	4	4	4	3	4
YARDS	379	160	460	361	365	250	281	165	300
HDCP	5	17	9	3	1	15	11	7	13
	10	11	12	13	14	15	16	17	18
PAR	4	3	5	4	4	4	4	3	4
YARDS	381	170	473	366	370	260	286	180	315
HDCP	6	18	10	8	4	2	16	12	8	14

Directions: Take I 95 to Hampton, NH exit to Route 101 West, Exit to Route 108 to Stratham, Exeter. Bear left. Go right at 3rd light, take 1st left, then the next right. Go right at end of street. Course is on left.

Farmington CC

29

Farmington, NH (603) 755-2412

Club Pro: Bert Prenaveau, PGA
Pro Shop: Full inventory
Payment: Cash only
Tee Times: Weekends
Fee 9 Holes: Weekday: No
Fee 18 Holes: Weekday: $17.00
Cart Rental: $20.00/18 $12.00/9
Lessons: $25.00/half hour **School:** No
Driving Range: No
Other: Clubhouse / Snack bar / Bar-lounge

Tees	Holes	Yards	Par	USGA	Slope
BACK	N/A				
MIDDLE	9	6245	72	70.0	127
FRONT	9	5456	72	70.8	116

Weekend: No
Weekend: $22.00
Discounts: None
Junior Golf: Yes **Membership:** Yes
Non-Metal Spikes: Required

Challenging redesigned course.

	1	2	3	4	5	6	7	8	9
PAR	4	4	3	5	4	3	5	4	4
YARDS	350	350	140	491	375	135	516	406	345
HDCP	13	7	17	5	9	15	3	1	11
	10	11	12	13	14	15	16	17	18
PAR	4	4	3	5	4	3	5	4	4
YARDS	335	394	128	500	335	196	484	435	330
HDCP	14	8	18	6	10	16	4	2	12

Directions: From Route I-95 take Spaulding Turnpike to Exit 15. Then take Route 11 North to Route 153. About 1 mile.

NH

Fore-U-Golf Center

30

West Lebanon, NH, 603-298-9702

Club Pro: B. Botha, C. Mansfield, H. Webb
Pro Shop: No
Payment: Cash only
Tee Times: No
Fee 9 Holes: Weekday: $7.50. $5 for jrs.
Fee 18 Holes: Weekday: $7.50. $8 for jrs.
Cart Rental: None
Lessons: $30 for 30 minuted **School:** No
Driving Range: Yes
Other: Share parking lot with Golf and Ski Warehouse

Tees	Holes	Yards	Par	USGA	Slope
BACK					
MIDDLE	9	1031	27		
FRONT	9	907	27		

Weekend: $7.50. $5 for jrs.
Weekend: $7.50. $8 for jrs.
Discounts: Junior
Junior Golf: N/R **Membership:** No
Non-Metal Spikes: N/R

COUPON

Lighted for night play. Fun, challenging par 3 golf course. Open March-November.

	1	2	3	4	5	6	7	8	9
PAR	3	3	3	3	3	3	3	3	3
YARDS	130	78	96	65	193	138	124	111	96
HDCP	N/A								
	10	11	12	13	14	15	16	17	18
PAR									
YARDS									
HDCP									

Directions: I-89 exit 20 to Route 12A South. Approximately 1 mile on right.

4☻ = Excellent 3☻ = Very Good 2☻ = Good

New Hampshire 183

Franklin Greens Golf & Country Club   31

Franklin, NH (603) 934-3033

Club Pro: No
Pro Shop: Full inventory
Payment: Visa, MC, Amex, Disc.
Tee Times: Wknds/Hldys
Fee 9 Holes: Weekday: $14.00
Fee 18 Holes: Weekday: $20.00
Cart Rental: $20.00/18 $14.00/9
Lessons: No **School:** No
Driving Range: No
Other: Snack bar / Bar-lounge / Full Restaurant

Tees	Holes	Yards	Par	USGA	Slope
BACK	N/A				
MIDDLE	9	6045	70	69.4	121
FRONT	N/A				

Weekend: $16.00
Weekend: $24.00
Discounts: Senior Mon 1/2 off
Junior Golf: No **Membership:** Yes
Non-Metal Spikes: Required

COUPON

In 1998, the new ownership refurbished course and completely remodelled and redesigned clubhouse. Formerly Mojalaki CC. **www.golf-nh.com**

	1	2	3	4	5	6	7	8	9
PAR	4	4	3	4	4	4	5	3	4
YARDS	295	310	143	445	426	330	475	181	380
HDCP	17	12	16	1	10	13	7	14	3
	10	11	12	13	14	15	16	17	18
PAR	4	4	3	5	4	4	4	3	4
YARDS	280	335	110	510	410	370	400	235	410
HDCP	18	6	15	9	8	4	11	5	2

Directions: I-93 to Exit 20. South 4 miles on Route 3 to downtown Franklin, left onto Prospect Street. Clubhouse 1 mile up the hill on right .

Green Meadow GC #1, The Prairie   32

Steele Rd., Hudson, NH (603) 889-1555

Club Pro: Patrick O'Keefe
Pro Shop: Yes
Payment: Visa, MC, Disc, Cash
Tee Times: Weekends, 1 week adv.
Fee 9 Holes: Weekday: $16.00 after 4:00
Fee 18 Holes: Weekday: $27.00
Cart Rental: $24.00/18
Lessons: $30.00/30 min **School:** No
Driving Range: $5.00/lg.
Other: Snack bar / Bar-lounge / Showers

Tees	Holes	Yards	Par	USGA	Slope
BACK	18	6160	70	68.2	112
MIDDLE	18	5809	70	66.5	108
FRONT	18	4877	70		

Weekend: $1800 after 4:00
Weekend: $34.00
Discounts: Senior
Junior Golf: Yes **Membership:** No
Non-Metal Spikes: Not Required

A Friel Golf Company course set along the Merrimac River. Formerly the North Course, changed by designer Friel in 1998.

	1	2	3	4	5	6	7	8	9
PAR	4	4	3	4	4	3	5	4	4
YARDS	334	328	141	376	341	169	471	411	364
HDCP	12	14	18	6	10	16	2	4	8
	10	11	12	13	14	15	16	17	18
PAR	4	3	4	3	4	4	4	4	5
YARDS	353	157	324	153	329	410	313	329	506
HDCP	11	15	9	1	5	7	17	13	3

Directions: Take Route 3 to Exit 34. Take right off ramp. Left at first light. Bear left as you cross Tyngsboro Bridge. Follow Route 3A 2.5 miles. Take a left on Steele Rd . to course.

Green Meadow GC # 2, The Jungle　　33

Steele Rd., Hudson, NH (603) 889-1555

Club Pro: Patrick O'Keefe
Pro Shop: Yes
Payment: Cash, MC, Visa, Discover
Tee Times: Weekends, 1 week adv.
Fee 9 Holes: Weekday: $16.00 after 4:00
Fee 18 Holes: Weekday: $27.00
Cart Rental: $24.00/18
Lessons: $30.00/30 min   **School:** No
Driving Range: $5.00/lg.
Other: Snack bar / Bar-lounge / Showers

Tees	Holes	Yards	Par	USGA	Slope
BACK	18	6774	70	71.4	122
MIDDLE	18	6182	72	69.1	120
FRONT	18	5352	72		

Weekend: $18.00 after 4:00
Weekend: $34.00
Discounts: Senior
Junior Golf: Yes   **Membership:** No
Non-Metal Spikes: Not Required

A Friel Golf Company. Formerly the South Course.

	1	2	3	4	5	6	7	8	9
PAR	4	4	5	3	4	4	4	3	5
YARDS	368	341	513	164	351	405	366	185	479
HDCP	12	14	2	18	10	6	8	16	4
	10	11	12	13	14	15	16	17	18
PAR	4	3	4	5	4	4	3	4	5
YARDS	358	137	370	538	382	368	132	355	512
HDCP	11	15	9	1	5	7	17	13	3

Directions: Take Route 3 to Exit 34. Take right off ramp. Left at first light. Bear left as you cross Tyngsboro Bridge. Follow Route 3A 2.5 miles. Take a left on Steele Rd. to course.

NH

Hale's Location Country Club ⭐⭐ 34

North Conway, NH 603-356-2140

Club Pro: Jonathan Rivers
Pro Shop: Full inventory
Payment: All major cards,
Tee Times: May 1st for season
Fee 9 Holes: Weekday: Seasonal - call
Fee 18 Holes: Weekday:
Cart Rental: $12.00pp/18 $7.00pp/9
Lessons: $30.00/45 min.   **School:** No
Driving Range: No
Other: Club house / Hotel / Restaurant / Bar-lounge / Snack bar / Lockers / Showers

Tees	Holes	Yards	Par	USGA	Slope
BACK	9	6050	72	68.2	122
MIDDLE	9	5632	72	66.8	117
FRONT	9	5016	72	67.4	113

Weekend:
Weekend:
Discounts: None
Junior Golf: No   **Membership:** Yes
Non-Metal Spikes: Required

COUPON

Great 9 hole layout with breath taking views. Bent grass fairways and greens. Golf rates vary seasonally. No metal spikes. Open May-Nov.

	1	2	3	4	5	6	7	8	9
PAR	5	4	3	4	5	3	4	4	4
YARDS	458	312	148	256	468	130	334	368	342
HDCP	1	5	15	13	3	17	11	7	9
	10	11	12	13	14	15	16	17	18
PAR	5	4	3	4	5	3	4	4	4
YARDS	458	312	148	256	468	130	334	368	342
HDCP	2	6	16	14	4	18	12	8	10

Directions: Take route 16 to traffic light in Conway. Turn on to Washington St., then right on to West Side Road; 5 miles on left.

4⭐ =Excellent 3⭐ =Very Good 2⭐ =Good

Hanover Country Club

Hanover, NH (603) 646-2000

Club Pro: Bill Johnson, PGA
Pro Shop: Full inventory
Payment: Visa, MC
Tee Times: 5 days adv.
Fee 9 Holes: Weekday: No
Fee 18 Holes: Weekday: $31.00
Cart Rental: $14.00/18
Lessons: $30.00/half hour **School:** No
Driving Range: No
Other: Clubhouse / Lockers / Showers / Snack bar

Tees	Holes	Yards	Par	USGA	Slope
BACK	N/R				
MIDDLE	18	5876	69	68.7	118
FRONT	18	5468	73	74.9	134

Weekend: No
Weekend: $31.00
Discounts: None
Junior Golf: Yes **Membership:** Yes
Non-Metal Spikes: Not Required

Since 1896... A lush New England antique. Home of Dartmouth golf. Short course expanded to Par 73. Practice area has 4 holes, one par 3, 2 par 4 and 1 par 5. Junior clinics.

	1	2	3	4	5	6	7	8	9
PAR	4	4	4	3	3	4	3	5	4
YARDS	430	416	341	107	200	345	174	476	440
HDCP	3	5	13	17	11	7	15	9	1
	10	11	12	13	14	15	16	17	18
PAR	4	4	3	4	3	5	4	3	5
YARDS	408	330	171	350	155	515	385	155	478
HDCP	2	12	14	8	16	6	4	18	10

Directions: Hanover / Dartmouth Exit on both I-89 and I-91 to center of town. North on Main Street. Extension on north side of campus.

Hickory Pond Inn and Golf Course

Durham, NH (603) 659-7642

Club Pro: Ray Gillespie
Pro Shop: Limited inventory
Payment: Most major
Tee Times: No
Fee 9 Holes: Weekday: $7.00
Fee 18 Holes: Weekday: $11.00
Cart Rental: N/R
Lessons: Yes **School:** No
Driving Range: Yes
Other: Inn, Banquet Room, Snacks, Hotel

Tees	Holes	Yards	Par	USGA	Slope
BACK	18	1670	54		
MIDDLE	18	1238	54		
FRONT					

Weekend: $7.00
Weekend: $11.00
Discounts: Senior & Junior
Junior Golf: Yes **Membership:** Yes
Non-Metal Spikes: Not Required

Bed and breakfast, 20 luxurious rooms. Holes 1-9 are golf holes. Back nine are "quite a unique concept. The holes are chain baskets on poles perfect for Frisbee or disc golf. Great family fun." A.P.

	1	2	3	4	5	6	7	8	9
PAR	3	3	3	3	3	3	3	3	3
YARDS	80	68	69	89	70	88	85	82	78
HDCP	N/A								
	10	11	12	13	14	15	16	17	18
PAR	3	3	3	3	3	3	3	3	3
YARDS	59	57	57	45	59	69	55	64	64
HDCP									

Directions: Take I-95 to Route 16 (Spaulding Turnpike). Take Exit 6W (route 4). Continue on Route 4 to Route 108 South. Go 4 miles to intersection of Route 108 and Stagecoach Rd.

Hidden Valley R.V. and Golf Park

37

Derry, NH (603) 887-3767

Club Pro: No
Pro Shop: Limited inventory
Payment: Visa, MC, Checks
Tee Times: 5 days adv.
Fee 9 Holes: Weekday: $8.00
Fee 18 Holes: Weekday: $12.00
Cart Rental: $7.50/18 $5.00/9
Lessons: No **School:** No
Driving Range: No
Other:

Tees	Holes	Yards	Par	USGA	Slope
BACK					
MIDDLE	9	1185	27	N/A	N/A
FRONT	9	985	27	N/A	N/A

Weekend: $9.00
Weekend: $14.00
Discounts: Senior
Junior Golf: N/R **Membership:** Yes
Non-Metal Spikes: Not Required

COUPON

Bring your RV and enjoy Par 3 golf.! New 9 holes, Par 36 will be ready for 1999. Open April 15- Nov. 1.

	1	2	3	4	5	6	7	8	9
PAR	3	3	3	3	3	3	3	3	3
YARDS	180	170	85	115	100	150	115	105	165
HDCP	1	3	9	6	7	4	5	8	2
	10	11	12	13	14	15	16	17	18
PAR									
YARDS									
HDCP									

Directions: Route 93 to Exit 4 to rotary. Take E. Derry Rd. for 4 1/2 miles. Sign on left- 1 mile to park.

NH

Highlands Links GC

38

Plymouth, NH (603) 536-3452

Club Pro: Joe Clark, Sr.,PGA Master
Pro Shop: Full inventory
Payment: Cash, Credit
Tee Times: No
Fee 9 Holes: Weekday: $10.00
Fee 18 Holes: Weekday: $15.00
Cart Rental: $22.00/18 $12.00/9
Lessons: Yes, Inquire! **School:** Yes
Driving Range: No
Other: Clubhouse

Tees	Holes	Yards	Par	USGA	Slope
BACK	N/A				
MIDDLE	9	2970	54	59.0	97
FRONT	9	2710	64	NA	NA

Weekend: $10.00
Weekend: $15.00
Discounts: Senior & Junior
Junior Golf: Yes **Membership:** Yes
Non-Metal Spikes: N/R

COUPON

Golf lessons by Joe Clark, Sr. ,PGA Master teacher! Club fitting.

	1	2	3	4	5	6	7	8	9
PAR	3	3	3	3	3	3	3	3	3
YARDS	210	185	140	165	145	130	165	190	155
HDCP	3	9	11	15	13	17	5	1	7
	10	11	12	13	14	15	16	17	18
PAR	3	3	3	3	3	3	3	3	3
YARDS	210	185	140	165	145	130	165	190	155
HDCP	4	10	12	16	14	18	6	2	8

Directions: Take I-93 to Exit 25 from North or South. Take left onto Holderness Road which turns into Route 175 South. Go straight through stop sign, take first left onto Mt. Prospect Road. Course is 1.5 miles up hill.

4✪ =Excellent 3✪ =Very Good 2✪ =Good

New Hampshire 187

Hoodkroft CC

39

Derry, NH (603) 434-0651

Club Pro: Richard Berberian
Pro Shop: Full inventory
Payment: Visa, MC
Tee Times: Tues for weekend
Fee 9 Holes: Weekday: $16.00
Fee 18 Holes: Weekday: $24.00
Cart Rental: $24.00/18 $12.00/9
Lessons: $30/30 min. **School:** No
Driving Range: No
Other: Clubhouse / Bar-lounge / Snack bar / Showers

Tees	Holes	Yards	Par	USGA	Slope
BACK	9	6471	71	70.3	120
MIDDLE	9	6466	71	70.3	120
FRONT	9	4984	71	70.2	116

Weekend: $17.00
Weekend: $27.00
Discounts: Senior. Wkdays only.
Junior Golf: Yes **Membership:** Yes. Wait. list.
Non-Metal Spikes: Required

Mostly flat, open fairways, lots of water. Large open greens. Open April 1 - October 30.

	1	2	3	4	5	6	7	8	9
PAR	4	4	3	5	4	4	4	3	4
YARDS	335	430	187	555	355	400	340	175	426
HDCP	13	3	11	1	9	5	15	17	7
	10	11	12	13	14	15	16	17	18
PAR	4	4	3	5	4	4	4	3	5
YARDS	355	420	224	538	375	380	360	155	456
HDCP	14	10	16	2	4	12	6	18	8

Directions: Take Exit 4 in N.H. off I-293, head east on Route 102. Go about 2 miles. Golf course is on right hand side.

Hooper Golf Club

★★★ **40**

Walpole, NH (603)756-4020

Club Pro: Jay Clace
Pro Shop: Full inventory
Payment: Visa, MC- merchandise only
Tee Times: No
Fee 9 Holes: Weekday: $23.00
Fee 18 Holes: Weekday: $23.00
Cart Rental: $22.00/18 $13.00/9
Lessons: No **School:** No
Driving Range: No
Other: Full Restaurant/ Clubhouse/ Hotel

Tees	Holes	Yards	Par	USGA	Slope
BACK	N/A				
MIDDLE	18	6014	71	69.3	122
FRONT	18	5446	72	73.5	132

Weekend: $23.00
Weekend: $23.00
Discounts: None
Junior Golf: Yes **Membership:**
Non-Metal Spikes: Required

A private course feel. Stone walls line almost all fairways. Bed and breakfast $50.00 for two. This is a busy course, so call ahead. Open April- October.

	1	2	3	4	5	6	7	8	9
PAR	5	4	4	3	5	3	4	4	4
YARDS	456	427	285	155	474	194	311	381	336
HDCP	9	1	7	17	5	15	13	11	3
	10	11	12	13	14	15	16	17	18
PAR	4	4	4	3	5	3	4	4	4
YARDS	435	427	275	155	481	194	311	381	336
HDCP	2	4	10	18	8	16	14	12	6

Directions: I-91 to Exit 5- Route 5 South to Route 12 South. After 1/2 mile, take first left onto South Street. Go to the end of South Street to Prospect Hill.

Indian Mound GC

Center Ossipee, NH (603) 539-7733

Club Pro: Warner Tickle
Pro Shop: Full inventory
Payment: Cash or credit card.
Tee Times: Yes
Fee 9 Holes: Weekday: N/A
Fee 18 Holes: Weekday: $32.00
Cart Rental: $22.00/18 $12.00/9
Lessons: $25.00/half hour **School:** Jr. camp
Driving Range: No
Other: Clubhouse / Restaurant / Bar-lounge

Tees	Holes	Yards	Par	USGA	Slope
BACK	18	5675	70	67.1	118
MIDDLE	18	5360	70	67.1	118
FRONT	18	4713	70	67.5	117

Weekend: N/A
Weekend: $32.00
Discounts: Yes
Junior Golf: No **Membership:** Yes
Non-Metal Spikes: Required

COUPON

The course is relatively level with few water holes. Well groomed. $18.00 after 3 pm any day. Open April - October 31.

	1	2	3	4	5	6	7	8	9
PAR	4	5	4	3	4	4	4	3	4
YARDS	300	475	410	132	302	286	335	180	375
HDCP	10	6	2	14	16	18	8	12	4
	10	11	12	13	14	15	16	17	18
PAR	4	3	4	4	5	4	3	5	3
YARDS	345	123	325	400	470	382	114	505	195
HDCP	5	17	13	1	3	11	15	7	9

Directions: Take Route 16 to Center Ossipee Exit. Course is 1/2 mile from exit.

NH

Intervale Country Club

Manchester, NH (603) 647-6811

Club Pro: Matt Thibeault, PGA
Pro Shop: Full inventory
Payment: Cash or Personal check
Tee Times: No
Fee 9 Holes: Weekday: $15.00
Fee 18 Holes: Weekday: $24.00
Cart Rental: $20.00/18 $10.00/9
Lessons: $30.00/half hour **School:** No
Driving Range: No
Other: Restaurant / Bar-lounge

Tees	Holes	Yards	Par	USGA	Slope
BACK	N/A				
MIDDLE	9	6154	72	68.9	107
FRONT	9	5713	76	71.6	121

Weekend: $15.00
Weekend: $24.00
Discounts: None
Junior Golf: No **Membership:** Yes
Non-Metal Spikes: Required

Semi-private: Members only weekends and holidays until 3:00 pm and weekdays 4:00 - 6:00 pm. Open April - November.

	1	2	3	4	5	6	7	8	9
PAR	3	4	4	5	4	4	4	3	5
YARDS	222	338	334	463	441	342	284	137	516
HDCP	7	15	13	5	1	9	11	17	3
	10	11	12	13	14	15	16	17	18
PAR	3	4	4	5	4	4	4	3	5
YARDS	222	338	334	463	441	342	284	137	516
HDCP	8	16	14	6	2	10	12	18	4

Directions: Exit 7 off 293 North. Course is 1/2 mile on right. Exit 10 off 93, left and course is 2 mi. on left.

4 = Excellent   3 = Very Good   2 = Good

Jack O'Lantern Resort   43

Woodstock, NH (603) 745-3636

Club Pro: Fletcher Ivey
Pro Shop: Full inventory
Payment: Visa, MC, Amex, Disc.
Tee Times: 24 hrs. adv.
Fee 9 Holes: Weekday: $20.00
Fee 18 Holes: Weekday: $33.00
Cart Rental: $26.00/18 $16.00/9
Lessons: $25.00/half hour **School:** No
Driving Range: No
Other: Restaurant / Hotel / Bar-lounge / Snack bar

Tees	Holes	Yards	Par	USGA	Slope
BACK	N/A				
MIDDLE	18	6003	70	67.7	113
FRONT	18	4917	71	67.0	113

Weekend: $23.00
Weekend: $36.00
Discounts: None
Junior Golf: No **Membership:** No
Non-Metal Spikes: Required

A scenic resort course at the foothills of the White Mountains. Open May - October. Unlimited play after 3:00 pm for $18.00.

	1	2	3	4	5	6	7	8	9
PAR	4	4	4	4	3	4	4	3	4
YARDS	370	365	414	362	175	421	320	175	325
HDCP	10	12	4	6	17	2	16	14	8
	10	11	12	13	14	15	16	17	18
PAR	4	4	3	5	4	4	3	4	5
YARDS	335	395	160	519	292	305	140	410	520
HDCP	13	3	11	9	5	15	18	1	7

Directions: Exit 30 off I-93.

John H. Cain GC   44

Newport, NH (603) 863-7787

Club Pro: John W. Pawlak
Pro Shop: Full inventory
Payment: Visa, MC, Cash
Tee Times: 7 days adv.
Fee 9 Holes: Weekday: $20.00
Fee 18 Holes: Weekday: $27.00
Cart Rental: $22.00/18 $13.00/9
Lessons: $20.00/half hour **School:** No
Driving Range: $3.50/med. bucket
Other: Clubhouse / Snack bar / Bar-lounge / Lockers

Tees	Holes	Yards	Par	USGA	Slope
BACK	18	6415	71	71.4	133
MIDDLE	18	6005	71	68.3	127
FRONT	18	4738	71	63.8	112

Weekend: $22.00
Weekend: $31.00
Discounts: Junior
Junior Golf: Yes **Membership:** Yes
Non-Metal Spikes: Required

Flat layout, easy walking. Front nine has narrow greens. Back nine has seven ponds. The Sugar River runs through it.

	1	2	3	4	5	6	7	8	9
PAR	5	4	4	3	4	4	3	4	4
YARDS	511	321	315	179	373	375	145	269	369
HDCP	8	4	6	14	2	12	16	18	10
	10	11	12	13	14	15	16	17	18
PAR	5	3	4	4	4	4	3	4	5
YARDS	477	138	387	379	375	341	169	375	507
HDCP	15	17	3	1	13	9	11	5	7

Directions: I-89 North to Exit 9. Follow Route 103 to Newport. Take Unity Rd. (on left) 1 mile to golf course . Can be seen from Unity Road.

Keene Country Club

✪✪✪ 45

Keene, NH (603) 352-9722

Club Pro: Charlie Kamal
Pro Shop: Full inventory
Payment: Visa/MC
Tee Times: No
Fee 9 Holes: Weekday: $29.00
Fee 18 Holes: Weekday: $58.00
Cart Rental: Included in greens fee
Lessons: $35/30 min. **School:** No
Driving Range: $4.00/bucket
Other: Restaurant / Clubhouse / Bar-lounge / Lockers / Showers / Snack Bar / Pool / Tennis

Tees	Holes	Yards	Par	USGA	Slope
BACK	18	6131	72	69.4	124
MIDDLE	18	5912	72	69.4	124
FRONT	18	5352	75	72.2	130

Weekend: $29.00
Weekend: $58.00 after 1 pm
Discounts: None
Junior Golf: Yes **Membership:** Yes
Non-Metal Spikes: Required

Greens in excellent condition. Course gets hillier and tighter.

	1	2	3	4	5	6	7	8	9
PAR	5	4	3	4	4	4	5	3	4
YARDS	463	285	149	401	370	380	525	215	320
HDCP	11	15	17	3	9	1	5	7	13
	10	11	12	13	14	15	16	17	18
PAR	3	4	4	5	4	4	5	3	4
YARDS	162	302	390	484	400	327	505	165	288
HDCP	18	12	2	8	4	16	6	10	14

Directions: Take I-91 to Keene exit Route 9. From Keene at flashing light take left onto Base Hill Rd to course.

Kingston Fairways

46

E. Kingston, NH ((603)642-7722

Club Pro:
Pro Shop: Full inventory
Payment: Cash only
Tee Times: No
Fee 9 Holes: Weekday: $14.00
Fee 18 Holes: Weekday: $24.00
Cart Rental: $22.00/18 $11.00/9
Lessons: No **School:** No
Driving Range: No
Other: Club house and snack bar

Tees	Holes	Yards	Par	USGA	Slope
BACK	N/A				
MIDDLE	9	2864	35	33.2	113
FRONT	9	2669	36	N/A	N/A

Weekend: $17.00
Weekend: $29.00
Discounts: Senior & Junior Wkdays
Junior Golf: No **Membership:** No
Non-Metal Spikes: Not Required

#8 hole is par 6. Terrain is generally gentle and easy walking.

	1	2	3	4	5	6	7	8	9
PAR	3	4	4	4	4	3	4	6	3
YARDS	125	341	329	347	381	154	429	598	160
HDCP	9	3	6	5	4	8	2	1	7
	10	11	12	13	14	15	16	17	18
PAR									
YARDS									
HDCP									

Directions: From I-95, go 8 miles south on route 107.

4✪ =Excellent 3✪ =Very Good 2✪ =Good

Kingswood Golf Club

47

Wolfeboro, NH (603) 569-3569

Club Pro: David Pollini, PGA
Pro Shop: Full inventory
Payment: Visa, MC
Tee Times: 3 days adv.

Tees	Holes	Yards	Par	USGA	Slope
BACK	18	6360	72	71.1	125
MIDDLE	18	5860	72	68.8	122
FRONT	18	5300	72	73.1	130

Fee 9 Holes: Weekday: $20.00 after 4 pm **Weekend:** $20.00 after 4 pm
Fee 18 Holes: Weekday: $48.00 inc. cart **Weekend:** $48.00 inc. cart
Cart Rental: $26/18 $13.00/9 **Discounts:** None
Lessons: $45/hr. **School:** No **Junior Golf:** Yes **Membership:** Yes
Driving Range: $4.00/lg., $2.00/sm. **Non-Metal Spikes:** Required
Other: Snack bar / Bar-lounge

The course is hilly with five ponds. Has an excellent iron practice range with a green to hit with short irons (190 yard range). Open April - October 31. Reduced fees after 2 pm w/o cart.

	1	2	3	4	5	6	7	8	9
PAR	4	5	3	4	4	3	4	4	4
YARDS	405	455	175	380	335	150	375	315	375
HDCP	7	6	15	1	11	17	9	13	3
	10	11	12	13	14	15	16	17	18
PAR	4	5	4	3	4	4	5	4	4
YARDS	360	490	410	205	360	300	495	405	370
HDCP	12	16	2	14	8	18	6	4	10

Directions: Take Route 28 North 1/4 mile past Kingswood High School. Turn left onto Kingswood Road.

Kona Mansion Inn

48

Moultonboro, NH (603) 253-4900

Club Pro: Kevin Crowley
Pro Shop: No
Payment: Visa, MC
Tee Times: No

Tees	Holes	Yards	Par	USGA	Slope
BACK					
MIDDLE	9	1170	27	N/A	N/A
FRONT					

Fee 9 Holes: Weekday: $12.50 **Weekend:** $12.50
Fee 18 Holes: Weekday: $12.50 **Weekend:** $12.50
Cart Rental: Yes **Discounts:** None
Lessons: No **School:** No **Junior Golf:** No **Membership:** Yes-seasonal
Driving Range: No **Non-Metal Spikes:** Not Required
Other: Hotel / Full Service Restaurant

A resort on Lake Winnipesaukee. Twi-light rates $10 after 4:00. Par 3.

	1	2	3	4	5	6	7	8	9
PAR	3	3	3	3	3	3	3	3	3
YARDS	105	150	130	135	128	150	162	125	85
HDCP									
	10	11	12	13	14	15	16	17	18
PAR									
YARDS									
HDCP									

Directions: From I-93 take Exit 23 and follow to the end in Meredith 11 miles, left on Route 3 to lights, right on Route 25. 9 miles to Moultonboro Neck Road on right. Go right, 2.5 miles to Kona Road on right. Follow signs.

Laconia Country Club ✪✪✪ 49

Lakeport, NH (603) 524-1273

Club Pro: Mike Marquis, PGA
Pro Shop: Full inventory
Payment: Visa, MC, Amex
Tee Times: 1 week adv.

Tees	Holes	Yards	Par	USGA	Slope
BACK	18	6314	72	71.7	128
MIDDLE	18	6103	71	70.7	126
FRONT	18	5397	73	72.1	125

Fee 9 Holes: Weekday: N/A **Weekend:** N/A
Fee 18 Holes: Weekday: $85.00 inc. cart **Weekend:** N/A
Cart Rental: Included **Discounts:** For jr. memberships
Lessons: $25.00/half hour **School:** Jr **Junior Golf:** Yes **Membership:** Yes
Driving Range: $5.00/lg. $2.50/sm. **Non-Metal Spikes:** Preferred
Other: Clubhouse / Lockers / Showers / Snack bar / Restaurant / Bar-lounge / Tennis Courts

The course plays long; most golfers will use all of their clubs. Open April 15 - November 15. No weekends for public.

	1	2	3	4	5	6	7	8	9
PAR	4	4	5	4	4	4	3	4	4
YARDS	375	380	525	262	345	310	221	302	357
HDCP	7	9	1	15	3	17	13	11	5
	10	11	12	13	14	15	16	17	18
PAR	3	4	4	4	5	4	3	4	4
YARDS	135	417	382	305	480	340	202	418	394
HDCP	18	4	12	16	2	8	14	6	10

Directions: Take I-93N to Exit 20, left off ramp. Follow 6 or 7 miles; go past Canton Chevrolet and take left onto Elm Street. Course is on right.

NH

Lakeview Golf Club 50

Ladd Hill Road, Belmont, NH 03220 (603-524-2220)

Club Pro: No
Pro Shop: Full inventory
Payment: Cash only
Tee Times: No

Tees	Holes	Yards	Par	USGA	Slope
BACK	N/R				
MIDDLE	9	6220	70	69	N/A
FRONT	9	4540	74	72.0	N/A

Fee 9 Holes: Weekday: $14.00 **Weekend:** $14.00
Fee 18 Holes: Weekday: $20.00 **Weekend:** $20.00
Cart Rental: $20.00/18, $12.00/9 **Discounts:** None
Lessons: No **School:** No **Junior Golf:** No **Membership:** Yes
Driving Range: No **Non-Metal Spikes:** N/R
Other:

COUPON

A beautiful nine hole golf course overlooking a panorama of lakes and mountains. Good walking course in excellent condition. Dress code.

	1	2	3	4	5	6	7	8	9
PAR	5	4	4	4	3	4	3	5	3
YARDS	505	315	290	425	220	435	175	550	195
HDCP	3	13	15	5	9	11	17	1	7
	10	11	12	13	14	15	16	17	18
PAR	5	4	4	4	3	4	3	5	3
YARDS	505	315	290	425	220	435	175	550	195
HDCP	4	14	15	6	10	12	18	2	8

Directions: I-93 to to Exit 20, then east towards Laconia on Routes 3 & 11. Cross Winnisquam bridge and up 1 mile to set of lights. Take right-across from Belknap Mall.

4✪ = Excellent 3✪ = Very Good 2✪ = Good

New Hampshire

Lisbon Village Country Club   51

Bishop Road, Lisbon, NH (603)-838-6004

Club Pro: Phil Armstrong
Pro Shop: Limited inventory
Payment: Cash or Check
Tee Times: Suggested
Fee 9 Holes: Weekday: $12.00
Fee 18 Holes: Weekday: $24.00
Cart Rental: $20/18, $10/9
Lessons: Yes **School:** No
Driving Range: $3.50/Lge, $2.50/Sm
Other: Full restaurant / Club House / Hotel / Bar / Lounge / Snack bar

Tees	Holes	Yards	Par	USGA	Slope
BACK	N/A				
MIDDLE	9	5801	72	69.7	126
FRONT	9	4931	72	70.6	127

Weekend: $12.00
Weekend: $24.00
Discounts: None
Junior Golf: Yes **Membership:** Yes
Non-Metal Spikes: Required

COUPON

Scenic White Mt. course designed and built by Ralph Barten. Bent grass greens. The epitome of target golf. Requires a deft touch with irons and woods. Open May through October.

	1	2	3	4	5	6	7	8	9
PAR	4	5	4	4	3	4	5	4	3
YARDS	255	535	310	397	211	248	440	350	148
HDCP	15	1	11	5	7	13	3	9	17
	10	11	12	13	14	15	16	17	18
PAR	4	5	4	5	3	4	4	4	3
YARDS	265	518	369	435	172	272	366	352	158
HDCP	16	2	8	6	12	14	4	10	18

Directions: From I-93, exit 42, go west on Route 302 for 7 miles. Go right on Lyman Rd. for 3/4 mile, then left on Bishop Rd. for 3/4 mile to course.

Lochmere Golf & CC   52

Rt. 3, Tilton, NH (603) 528-4653

Club Pro: Vic Stanfield
Pro Shop: Full inventory
Payment: Visa, MC
Tee Times: 3 days adv.
Fee 9 Holes: Weekday: $14.00
Fee 18 Holes: Weekday: $28.00
Cart Rental: $22.00/18 $13.00/9
Lessons: $25.00/half hour **School:** No
Driving Range: $4.00/bucket
Other: Restaurant / Clubhouse / Bar-Lounge / Snack Bar / Function Room

Tees	Holes	Yards	Par	USGA	Slope
BACK	18	6675	72	71.8	127
MIDDLE	18	6267	72	69.9	122
FRONT	18	5267	72	68.9	120

Weekend: $18.00
Weekend: $35.00
Discounts: None
Junior Golf: N/R **Membership:** Yes
Non-Metal Spikes: Required

Phil Wogan and George Sargent design, August 1992. Bent fairways and greens. 18 holes opened August, 1997: 9 redesigned, 9 newly constructed! Greens fees subject to change.

	1	2	3	4	5	6	7	8	9
PAR	4	5	4	4	3	4	4	4	4
YARDS	350	500	347	373	160	401	377	323	390
HDCP	3	9	17	7	15	5	1	11	13
	10	11	12	13	14	15	16	17	18
PAR	4	4	3	4	4	4	5	3	5
YARDS	330	340	140	350	368	363	481	163	472
HDCP	12	17	18	4	10	6	2	14	8

Directions: I-93 Exit 20 (Laconia/Tilton). Go 1.5 miles east on Route 3. Course is on left.

Londonderry CC 53

Londonderry, NH (603) 432-9789

Club Pro: Mike Aldrich, PGA
Pro Shop: Yes
Payment: Cash only
Tee Times: Wed. AM for weekend
Fee 9 Holes: Weekday: $13.00
Fee 18 Holes: Weekday: $22.00
Cart Rental: $18.00/18 $10.00/9
Lessons: Yes **School:** No
Driving Range: Netted Area
Other: Bar-lounge

Tees	Holes	Yards	Par	USGA	Slope
BACK	N/A				
MIDDLE	18	3740	62	57.2	86
FRONT	18	3210	62	57.4	87

Weekend: $14.00
Weekend: $24.00
Discounts: Senior
Junior Golf: Yes **Membership:** Annual Passes
Non-Metal Spikes: Required

Picturesque course offers excellent greens and challenging fairways

	1	2	3	4	5	6	7	8	9
PAR	3	3	4	4	3	3	3	3	3
YARDS	200	160	235	215	130	130	140	95	165
HDCP	2	4	10	18	16	12	6	14	8
	10	11	12	13	14	15	16	17	18
PAR	3	3	4	4	4	4	4	4	3
YARDS	155	115	300	310	310	235	370	345	130
HDCP	11	15	7	3	13	9	1	5	7

Directions: Take I-93 to Exit 4, left onto Route 102, follow to Route 128, take right onto Route 128, follow 4 miles to Litchfield Road. Take left onto Kimball Road. Course is 1 1/2 miles down.

NH

Loudon Country Club 54

Loudon, NH 03301 (603)783-3372

Club Pro: Kim Healey
Pro Shop: Limited inventory
Payment: Visa, MC
Tee Times: Wknds/Hldys
Fee 9 Holes: Weekday: $14.00
Fee 18 Holes: Weekday: $20.00
Cart Rental: $20.00/18, $10.00/9
Lessons: Yes **School:** No
Driving Range: $5/Lg.,$3/Sm.
Other: Full restuarant, Bar/Lounge, Clubhouse

Tees	Holes	Yards	Par	USGA	Slope
BACK	18	6232	70	70.4	127
MIDDLE	18	5777	72	68.3	124
FRONT	18	4702	72	67.0	112

Weekend: $15.00
Weekend: $25.00
Discounts: Sr. & Jr., weekdays
Junior Golf: No **Membership:** Yes
Non-Metal Spikes: Required

COUPON

Expanded to 18 holes. Challenging for all abilities and all ages.

	1	2	3	4	5	6	7	8	9
PAR	4	5	4	3	4	5	4	3	4
YARDS	256	490	298	158	358	455	363	145	375
HDCP	13	3	11	15	5	1	9	17	7
	10	11	12	13	14	15	16	17	18
PAR	4	3	5	3	4	4	5	4	4
YARDS	326	191	471	133	238	336	460	363	361
HDCP	10	16	2	18	14	8	4	6	12

Directions: I-93 to I-393. Take Exit 3 from 393, left at lights to Route 106 North for 7.5 miles. Course is on left.

4✪ =Excellent 3✪ =Very Good 2✪ =Good

Maplewood Casino & CC

55

Bethlehem, NH (603) 869-3335

Club Pro: Trevor Howard
Pro Shop: Full inventory
Payment: Visa, MC, Disc, Cash
Tee Times: Yes
Fee 9 Holes: Weekday: $16.00
Fee 18 Holes: Weekday: $25.00
Cart Rental: $24.00/18 $16.00/9
Lessons: No **School:** No
Driving Range: $4.00/lg. bucket

Tees	Holes	Yards	Par	USGA	Slope
BACK	18	6200	72	68.0	115
MIDDLE	18	6001	72	67.4	113
FRONT	18	5013	71	68.8	113

Weekend: $20.00
Weekend: $30.00
Discounts: None
Junior Golf: No **Membership:** Yes
Non-Metal Spikes: Required

COUPON

Other: Clubhouse / Showers / Lockers / Bar-lounge/ Hotel, guest suites

Stay and Play packages. 20 new guest suites available in 1890, restored clubhouse. Cart required from 8 am - 2 pm on weekends. Packages include 2 players and cart for $56.

	1	2	3	4	5	6	7	8	9
PAR	5	4	4	4	4	4	4	3	4
YARDS	445	399	277	388	367	373	319	150	355
HDCP	3	1	15	7	9	5	13	17	11
	10	11	12	13	14	15	16	17	18
PAR	4	3	3	4	4	5	6	4	3
YARDS	355	163	201	321	279	527	651	287	144
HDCP	6	14	16	8	10	4	2	12	18

Directions: I-93 Exit 40 onto Route 302 East. Approx. 5 miles.

Monadnock CC

56

Peterborough, NH (603) 924-7769

Club Pro: Dana Hennessy
Pro Shop: Limited inventory
Payment: Cash or checks
Tee Times: No
Fee 9 Holes: Weekday: $12.00
Fee 18 Holes: Weekday: $16.00
Cart Rental: Pull carts $1.00
Lessons: Yes **School:** No
Driving Range: Cage, $2.50/bucket

Tees	Holes	Yards	Par	USGA	Slope
BACK					
MIDDLE	9	1576	29	54.0	76
FRONT			32		

Weekend: $14.00
Weekend: $18.00
Discounts: None
Junior Golf: Yes **Membership:** Yes
Non-Metal Spikes: Preferred

COUPON

Other: Clubhouse / Snack bar / Bar-lounge / 2 Tennis Courts / Banquet facility

While the men's Par is 29 and the women's 32, don't be fooled. This course can be challenging for both veterans and beginners. The scenic beauty alone is worth the trip!

	1	2	3	4	5	6	7	8	9
PAR	4	3	3	3	3	4	3	3	3
YARDS	241	108	205	150	166	257	134	162	153
HDCP	9	17	1	13	3	7	15	5	11
	10	11	12	13	14	15	16	17	18
PAR									
YARDS									
HDCP									

Directions: From East or West Route 101. From North or South Route 202. Located on High Street.

Mt. Washington Hotel 57

Bretton Woods, NH (603) 278-4653

Club Pro: Jon Wood
Pro Shop: Full inventory
Payment: Visa, MC, Amex, Disc.
Tee Times: 48 hours
Fee 9 Holes: Weekday: $18.00 **Weekend:** $21.00
Fee 18 Holes: Weekday: $30.00 **Weekend:** $35.00
Cart Rental: $22.00/18 $13.00/9 **Discounts:** None
Lessons: Private and Group **School:** No **Junior Golf:** No **Membership:** Yes
Driving Range: Yes **Non-Metal Spikes:** Required
Other: Resort hotel / Golf packages / Restaurant / Clubhouse / Bar-lounge / Lockers / Showers

Tees	Holes	Yards	Par	USGA	Slope
BACK	27	6638	71	71.2	123
MIDDLE	27	6156	71	70.1	123
FRONT	27	5336	71	70.0	118

Donald Ross designed course with new irrigation, located at the base of Mt. Washington. 18 hole putting green. Mt. Pleasant is the additional 9 hole Geoffrey Cornish designed course with 3215 yds.

	1	2	3	4	5	6	7	8	9
PAR	3	4	4	4	3	5	4	4	4
YARDS	194	360	420	385	132	510	305	410	380
HDCP	15	11	1	7	17	5	13	3	9
	10	11	12	13	14	15	16	17	18
PAR	5	5	4	4	3	4	3	4	4
YARDS	515	475	300	383	190	290	175	375	355
HDCP	2	8	18	4	14	12	16	6	10

Directions: Take I-93, Exit 35 to Route 302 to Bretton Woods.

Nippo Lake Golf Club 58

Barrington, NH (603) 664-7616

Club Pro: No
Pro Shop: Full inventory
Payment: Visa, MC
Tee Times: Recommended
Fee 9 Holes: Weekday: $13.00 **Weekend:** $15.00
Fee 18 Holes: Weekday: $20.00 **Weekend:** $2200
Cart Rental: $22.00/18 $12.00/9 **Discounts:** None
Lessons: $30/45 min. **School:** Jr. **Junior Golf:** Yes **Membership:** Yes
Driving Range: $4.00/bucket **Non-Metal Spikes:** Preferred
Other: Clubhouse / Snack bar / Restaurant / Bar-lounge / Video instruction

Tees	Holes	Yards	Par	USGA	Slope
BACK	N/A				
MIDDLE	9	5170	68	64.5	105
FRONT	9	4823	68	65.8	103

COUPON

An executive golf course nestled in beautiful mountain setting. New owners, new outlook. Senior clinics. Lessons available by Rick Rogers, Golf Associate. Additional 9 holes added next season.

	1	2	3	4	5	6	7	8	9
PAR	4	5	3	4	4	3	4	4	3
YARDS	298	500	191	347	303	152	319	324	152
HDCP	1	13	9	5	3	15	11	7	17
	10	11	12	13	14	15	16	17	18
PAR	4	5	3	4	4	3	4	4	3
YARDS	314	500	152	338	303	165	359	282	154
HDCP	2	14	12	6	4	16	10	8	18

Directions: Take Spalding Turnpike North. Take Exit 13 (Route 202 North). Take right onto Route 126. Go 1/4 mile, then take a left onto Province Road.

4✪ =Excellent 3✪ =Very Good 2✪ =Good **New Hampshire 197**

North Conway CC

59

N. Conway, NH (603) 356-9391

Club Pro: Larry Gallagher
Pro Shop: Full inventory
Payment: Visa, MC
Tee Times: 3 days adv.
Fee 9 Holes: Weekday: N/A
Fee 18 Holes: Weekday: $30.00, M-Th
Cart Rental: $24.00/18
Lessons: By appointment **School:** Junior
Driving Range: No
Other: Restaurant / Clubhouse / Hotel / Bar-Lounge / Snack Bar / Public Dining Room

Tees	Holes	Yards	Par	USGA	Slope
BACK	18	6659	71	71.9	126
MIDDLE	18	6281	71	70.3	123
FRONT	18	5530	71	71.4	120

Weekend: N/A
Weekend: $49.00, Inc. Cart
Discounts: Senior
Junior Golf: Yes **Membership:** Yes
Non-Metal Spikes: Required

Located at the base of the White Mountains, it is surprisingly level – except for the first tee. Water comes into play on five holes. Open April 20 - October 31. Twilight fees.

	1	2	3	4	5	6	7	8	9
PAR	4	4	4	3	4	4	3	5	4
YARDS	408	410	352	126	320	369	213	504	375
HDCP	1	5	11	17	7	13	9	15	3
	10	11	12	13	14	15	16	17	18
PAR	4	5	4	3	4	3	4	5	4
YARDS	347	475	400	165	428	149	367	533	340
HDCP	10	8	4	16	2	18	12	6	14

Directions: Take Route 16 to Main Street North Conway. Next to Rail Road Station.

Oak Hill Golf Course

60

Meredith, NH (603) 279-4438

Club Pro: No
Pro Shop: Full inventory
Payment: Cash, Visa, MC
Tee Times: No
Fee 9 Holes: Weekday: $12.00
Fee 18 Holes: Weekday: $19.00
Cart Rental: $20.00/18 $12.00/9
Lessons: No **School:** No
Driving Range: No
Other: Snack bar / Bar-lounge

Tees	Holes	Yards	Par	USGA	Slope
BACK	N/R				
MIDDLE	9	4468	68	60.6	90
FRONT	9	3890	68	64.6	111

Weekend: $12.00
Weekend: $19.00
Discounts: None
Junior Golf: No **Membership:** Yes
Non-Metal Spikes: Not Required

Short regulation New England course with five greens blind from tee. Good challenge for your irons. Wooded & scenic. No tank tops. Open late April to November.

	1	2	3	4	5	6	7	8	9
PAR	4	3	4	4	3	4	3	4	5
YARDS	252	136	257	281	169	239	135	300	465
HDCP	9	15	7	5	13	11	17	3	1
	10	11	12	13	14	15	16	17	18
PAR	4	3	4	4	3	4	3	4	5
YARDS	252	136	257	281	169	239	135	300	465
HDCP	10	16	8	6	14	12	18	4	2

Directions: Take I-93, Exit 23 Route 104 East, 8.5 miles to double blinking light. Turns right onto Pease Road 1.5 miles. Parking on left.

Overlook GC
61

Hollis, NH (603) 465-2909

Club Pro: Dick Dichard
Pro Shop: Full Inventory
Payment: MC, Visa, Dis.
Tee Times: 7 days adv.

Tees	Holes	Yards	Par	USGA	Slope
BACK	18	6539	71	70.2	127
MIDDLE	18	6051	71	68.2	124
FRONT	18	5230	72	68.2	124

Fee 9 Holes: Weekday: N/A   **Weekend:** N/A
Fee 18 Holes: Weekday: $30.00   **Weekend:** $40.00
Cart Rental: $24.00/18   **Discounts:** None
Lessons: Yes, **School:** Yes, group rates   **Junior Golf:** Yes **Membership:** No
Driving Range: No   **Non-Metal Spikes:** Not Required
Other: Clubhouse / Showers / Snack bar / Bar-lounge

A Friel Golf Company. The front nine are fairly hilly, while the back nine are somewhat flat. Bunkers come into play along the entire tract. Junior golf clinic in summer.

	1	2	3	4	5	6	7	8	9
PAR	5	4	4	4	3	4	4	3	4
YARDS	535	299	433	390	177	345	292	167	326
HDCP	3	11	1	5	9	13	17	15	9
	10	11	12	13	14	15	16	17	18
PAR	5	4	4	4	3	4	4	3	5
YARDS	522	350	346	390	164	341	320	138	516
HDCP	4	10	18	8	12	6	14	16	2

Directions: Take Route 3 to Exit 5W (Route 111 West). Continue 4 miles. Course is on the right.

Passaconaway CC
62

Litchfield, NH (603) 424-4653

Club Pro: Rick Thibeault, PGA
Pro Shop: Full Inventory
Payment: Cash, Visa, MC
Tee Times: 5 days adv.

Tees	Holes	Yards	Par	USGA	Slope
BACK	18	6855	71	72.2	126
MIDDLE	18	6462	71	70.7	123
FRONT	18	5369	72	70.3	118

Fee 9 Holes: Weekday: $17.00   **Weekend:** $25.00 after 3:00p.m.
Fee 18 Holes: Weekday: $28.00   **Weekend:** $38.00
Cart Rental: $24.00/18 $16.00/9   **Discounts:** Sr., Jr., & Ladies
Lessons: $40/30 min. **School:** Yes   **Junior Golf:** Yes **Membership:** Yes
Driving Range: No   **Non-Metal Spikes:** Required
Other: Restaurant / Showers

Bent grass tees - fairways - greens, open - more links style. Collared shirt required, shorts okay, no cutoffs. Open April 15 - November 30. Junior golf clinics.

	1	2	3	4	5	6	7	8	9
PAR	5	3	4	3	5	4	4	4	4
YARDS	532	150	424	172	556	454	443	379	307
HDCP	12	16	6	14	10	2	4	8	18
	10	11	12	13	14	15	16	17	18
PAR	4	4	4	3	5	4	4	3	4
YARDS	352	327	395	203	502	348	321	169	428
HDCP	11	13	1	5	7	17	15	9	3

Directions: I-293 (Manchester) to Exit 2 (Route 3A.) Go south approx. 6 miles. Golf course on right.

4✪=Excellent 3✪=Very Good 2✪=Good

Pease Golf Course

63

Portsmouth, NH (603) 433-1331

Club Pro: Scott D. Devito
Pro Shop: Full inventory
Payment: Visa, MC, Amex, Cash
Tee Times: 3 days adv.
Fee 9 Holes: Weekday: $15.00
Fee 18 Holes: Weekday: $30.00
Cart Rental: $22.00/18 $11.00/9
Lessons: $25-$35.00/half hour **School:** Jr.
Driving Range: $5.00/lg., $3.00/sm. bucket
Other: Clubhouse / Bar-Lounge / Snack Bar / Showers / Lockers

Tees	Holes	Yards	Par	USGA	Slope
BACK	18	6346	71	70.8	128
MIDDLE	18	5901	71	69.0	125
FRONT	18	5243	71	69.9	120

Weekend: $15.00
Weekend: $30.00
Discounts: None
Junior Golf: Yes **Membership:** Yes
Non-Metal Spikes: Required

While the course is not long, the par threes play long due to small greens. No cut offs or tank tops allowed. Open March - December.

	1	2	3	4	5	6	7	8	9
PAR	5	5	3	4	4	4	4	4	3
YARDS	465	471	160	315	343	310	370	364	150
HDCP	5	1	17	11	7	13	9	3	15
	10	11	12	13	14	15	16	17	18
PAR	4	3	4	5	3	5	3	4	4
YARDS	322	185	385	535	143	481	162	365	375
HDCP	12	16	6	2	14	4	18	10	8

Directions: I-95 to exit 3 in NH from the south, exit 3B from the north. Follow Route 101 East to Sherburne Road. Course is located on Country Club Road.

Perry Hollow Golf & CC

64

Middleton Rd., Wolfboro, NH (603) 569-3055

Club Pro: Gary Brown
Pro Shop: Full inventory
Payment: Visa, MC, Amex, Dis
Tee Times: Yes. 1 week adv
Fee 9 Holes: Weekday: $16.00
Fee 18 Holes: Weekday: $28.00
Cart Rental: $24.00/18 $14.00/9
Lessons: $35.00/halfhour **School:** Yes
Driving Range: Yes
Other: Restaurant/Bar-lounge/Snack Bar

Tees	Holes	Yards	Par	USGA	Slope
BACK	18	6338	71	71.0	134
MIDDLE	18	5797	71	68.3	126
FRONT	18	4788	71	67.0	113

Weekend: $20.00
Weekend: $32.00
Discounts: Junior
Junior Golf: Yes **Membership:** Yes
Non-Metal Spikes: Required

Very scenic. A challenging Cornish & Silva layout with holes cut through the woods. Every hole is memorable.

	1	2	3	4	5	6	7	8	9
PAR	4	3	4	5	4	3	4	4	4
YARDS	296	141	340	446	387	116	354	393	324
HDCP	10	16	14	4	8	18	6	2	12
	10	11	12	13	14	15	16	17	18
PAR	5	4	3	4	3	5	4	4	4
YARDS	516	322	192	341	154	504	373	312	286
HDCP	5	7	11	3	17	1	9	13	15

Directions: From Route 28 S in Wolfboro, 2.5 miles on Middleton Rd. Or from Route 153, 7.5 miles North on Kings Highway.

Pheasant Ridge CC

65

Gilford, NH (603) 524-7808

Club Pro: Jim Swarthout
Pro Shop: Full inventory
Payment: Visa, MC, Disc
Tee Times: 7 days adv.
Fee 9 Holes: Weekday: $15.00
Fee 18 Holes: Weekday: $22.00
Cart Rental: $22.00/18 $14.00/9
Lessons: $30.00/half hour **School:** No
Driving Range: Yes, grass tee
Other: Snack bar / Bar-lounge/ 400 seat function hall

Tees	Holes	Yards	Par	USGA	Slope
BACK	N/A				
MIDDLE	9	6142	70	67.1	103
FRONT	9	5144	70	70.1	116

Weekend: $17.00
Weekend: $24.00
Discounts: None
Junior Golf: No **Membership:** No
Non-Metal Spikes: Not Required

COUPON

The course is wide open and hilly with majestic mountain and lake views. Additional 9 holes under construction, scheduled to open summer '99. A Friel Golf Company.

	1	2	3	4	5	6	7	8	9
PAR	4	4	5	4	4	3	4	4	3
YARDS	353	373	473	410	369	207	253	440	183
HDCP	5	9	15	1	13	7	17	3	11
	10	11	12	13	14	15	16	17	18
PAR	4	4	5	4	4	3	4	4	3
YARDS	380	317	503	400	402	190	273	396	220
HDCP	2	18	14	10	8	12	16	6	4

Directions: Take I-93 to Exit 20 (3 North), follow 11 miles onto Routes 3/11. Take 2nd exit, right off ramp then next right onto Country Club Rd. Course is 1/2 mile up hill on left.

NH

Pine Grove Springs CC

66

Rt. 9A, Spofford, NH (603) 363-4433

Club Pro: Eric Sandstrum, Head Pro
Pro Shop: Yes
Payment: Visa, MC, Cash, Check
Tee Times: Weekends
Fee 9 Holes: Weekday: $20.00 All day
Fee 18 Holes: Weekday: $20.00 All day
Cart Rental: $24/18 $13/9 $20/all day
Lessons: $30/30 min. **School:** No
Driving Range: No - 2 practice holes
Other: Snack bar / Bar-lounge

Tees	Holes	Yards	Par	USGA	Slope
BACK	9	6276	72	70.2	132
MIDDLE	9	5848	72	70.2	132
FRONT	9	5694	72	71.0	129

Weekend: $25 All day
Weekend: $25 All day
Discounts: Senior
Junior Golf: Yes **Membership:** Yes
Non-Metal Spikes: Not Required

A very challenging course, with tight fairways and small greens. Very well kept. All day weekday, $20. All day weekend, $25.00. Open April - October.

	1	2	3	4	5	6	7	8	9
PAR	4	4	5	4	3	4	5	4	3
YARDS	277	378	578	357	166	374	436	330	183
HDCP	14	4	2	6	18	8	12	10	16
	10	11	12	13	14	15	16	17	18
PAR	4	4	5	4	3	4	5	4	3
YARDS	277	378	578	357	166	374	436	330	183
HDCP	13	3	1	5	17	7	11	9	15

Directions: Located on Route 9A near Spofford Lake.

4⊙ =Excellent 3⊙ =Very Good 2⊙ =Good

New Hampshire 201

Pine Valley CC   67

Rt. 38, Pelham, NH (603) 635-7979

Club Pro: Todd Madden
Pro Shop: Yes
Payment: Visa, MC
Tee Times: Weekends until noon
Fee 9 Holes: Weekday: $13.00
Fee 18 Holes: Weekday: $19.00
Cart Rental: $20.00/18 $12.00/9
Lessons: By appt. **School:** No
Driving Range: No
Other: Snack bar / Bar-lounge

Tees	Holes	Yards	Par	USGA	Slope
BACK	9	6030	70	90	128
MIDDLE	9	5820	70	67.0	119
FRONT	9	5410	72	70	125

Weekend: $15.00
Weekend: $25.00
Discounts: Junior
Junior Golf: Yes **Membership:** Yes
Non-Metal Spikes: Required

COUPON

New sprinklers throughout course has dramatically improved conditions. Beverage cart available. Robbie Hardy named head teaching professional. The course is challenging, yet easy to walk.

	1	2	3	4	5	6	7	8	9
PAR	4	3	5	4	4	4	4	4	3
YARDS	290	200	510	295	335	410	320	320	125
HDCP	16	6	4	12	8	2	10	14	18
	10	11	12	13	14	15	16	17	18
PAR	4	3	5	4	4	4	4	4	3
YARDS	310	230	530	315	360	450	350	330	140
HDCP	15	5	3	11	7	1	9	13	17

Directions: Take I-93 to Exit 1; follow Route 38 South; course is located 5 miles up on left.

Plausawa Valley CC   68

Pembroke, NH (603) 228-8861

Club Pro: Lionel R. Dupuis
Pro Shop: Full inventory
Payment: Credit card
Tee Times: Yes
Fee 9 Holes: Weekday: $16.00
Fee 18 Holes: Weekday: $25.00
Cart Rental: $26.00/18 $13.00/9
Lessons: $30/45 min. **School:** No
Driving Range: $4.50, $3.50, $2.50
Other: Clubhouse / Lockers / Showers / Snack bar / Restaurant / Bar-lounge / Pull Carts available

Tees	Holes	Yards	Par	USGA	Slope
BACK	18	6572	72	72.6	138
MIDDLE	18	6162	72	72.6	131
FRONT	18	5416	73	72.6	128

Weekend: $18.00 after 12:00
Weekend: $30.00
Discounts: Senior & Junior
Junior Golf: Yes **Membership:** Yes
Non-Metal Spikes: Required

COUPON

Front nine: open, flat. Back nine: woods, hilly, undulating greens. Semi-private. Free clinics for juniors, 6-15 years of age.

	1	2	3	4	5	6	7	8	9
PAR	5	4	4	3	4	3	4	4	5
YARDS	477	412	365	165	448	198	366	387	487
HDCP	10	4	12	16	2	15	11	6	9
	10	11	12	13	14	15	16	17	18
PAR	4	4	5	3	5	4	3	4	4
YARDS	404	430	568	184	551	327	144	365	266
HDCP	7	5	3	17	1	13	18	8	14

Directions: Take I-93 Exit 13 South to Route 3. Course is 4 miles on right.

Ponemah Green

69

Amherst, NH (603) 672-4732

Club Pro: Steve Poremba, Head Pro
Pro Shop: Limited inventory
Payment: Visa, MC
Tee Times: 3 days adv.
Fee 9 Holes: Weekday: $14.00
Fee 18 Holes: Weekday: $23.00
Cart Rental: $22.00/18 $11.00/9
Lessons: $60/hour $35/half hour **School:** No
Driving Range: Lighted - $5.00/lg.
Other: Clubhouse / Snack Bar

Tees	Holes	Yards	Par	USGA	Slope
BACK	9	4420	68	59.7	97
MIDDLE	9	4320	68	59.7	97
FRONT	9	3608	68	71.0	104

Weekend: $17.00
Weekend: $27.00
Discounts: Senior & Junior
Junior Golf: Yes **Membership:** Yes
Non-Metal Spikes: Required

COUPON

Links style executive course with undulating fairways and nice views. Great condition. Satelite site for Golf School affiliated with Mt. Snow. Open April-October.

	1	2	3	4	5	6	7	8	9
PAR	3	3	4	4	4	4	4	4	4
YARDS	111	129	252	238	394	251	292	229	314
HDCP	17	15	13	11	1	9	5	3	7
	10	11	12	13	14	15	16	17	18
PAR	3	3	4	4	4	4	4	4
YARDS	111	129	252	238	394	251	292	229	314
HDCP	18	16	14	12	2	10	6	4	8

Directions: From I-293, take Route 101 west to Amherst. Then take Route 122 to the course located 1/2 mile past Amherst Country Club.

NH

Portsmouth CC

✪✪✪ **70**

Greenland, NH (603) 436-9719

Club Pro: Joel St. Laurent
Pro Shop: Full inventory
Payment: Visa, MC, Disc, cash
Tee Times: 1 day adv.
Fee 9 Holes: Weekday: No
Fee 18 Holes: Weekday: $60.00
Cart Rental: $25.00/18
Lessons: $45/50 min. **School:** N/R
Driving Range: $5.00/lg. $3.00/sm.
Other: Snack bar / Bar-lounge

Tees	Holes	Yards	Par	USGA	Slope
BACK	18	7050	72	72.0	127
MIDDLE	18	6609	72	71.5	123
FRONT	18	5478	76	70.3	135

Weekend: No
Weekend: $60.00
Discounts: None
Junior Golf: No **Membership:** No
Non-Metal Spikes: Required

Set along the coastal marsh of Great Bay. Beautifully maintained, it is open with gently rolling hills and nice bunkers. A constant sea breeze creates a challenge. The large, fast greens.

	1	2	3	4	5	6	7	8	9
PAR	4	4	4	5	3	4	5	3	4
YARDS	386	425	365	494	157	412	504	219	371
HDCP	13	5	15	1	17	7	3	11	9
	10	11	12	13	14	15	16	17	18
PAR	4	5	4	3	5	4	3	4	4
YARDS	418	511	447	152	455	329	143	401	420
HDCP	10	8	2	18	4	14	16	12	6

Directions: I-95 to Route 33 West (Greenland Exit). Follow (tiny) signs. Course is approximately 2 miles from I-95.

4✪ =Excellent 3✪ =Very Good 2✪ =Good

New Hampshire 203

Rochester Country Club

71

Church St., Gonic, NH (603) 332-9892

Club Pro: Bill Cassell
Pro Shop: Full inventory
Payment: Visa, MC
Tee Times: No

Tees	Holes	Yards	Par	USGA	Slope
BACK	18	6596	72	72.2	125
MIDDLE	18	6309	72	70.5	123
FRONT	18	5414	73	70.4	123

Fee 9 Holes: Weekday: No   **Weekend:** No
Fee 18 Holes: Weekday: $50.00   **Weekend:** $50.00
Cart Rental: Included in fee   **Discounts:** None
Lessons: $35/30 min. **School:** No   **Junior Golf:** Yes **Membership:** Yes. Wait. list.
Driving Range: No   **Non-Metal Spikes:** Required
Other: Clubhouse / Lockers / Showers / Snack bar / Restaurant / Bar-lounge / Pool

The course is hilly with narrow fairways. A very good test of golfing skills, particularly the 13th hole.

	1	2	3	4	5	6	7	8	9
PAR	4	5	4	3	4	3	5	4	4
YARDS	322	481	447	205	306	132	490	407	324
HDCP	10	4	2	14	16	18	8	6	12
	10	11	12	13	14	15	16	17	18
PAR	4	5	3	4	4	5	3	4	4
YARDS	362	548	223	430	314	489	193	392	302
HDCP	9	3	15	1	11	5	17	7	13

Directions: Take Spaulding Turnpike to Exit 12, follow Route 125 South for 1.5 miles, course is on left.

Rockingham CC

72

Newmarket, NH (603) 659-9956

Club Pro: No
Pro Shop: Full inventory
Payment: Visa, MC, Disc., cash
Tee Times: 5 days adv. (non-members)

Tees	Holes	Yards	Par	USGA	Slope
BACK	9	2980	35		
MIDDLE	18	5855	70	65.3	104
FRONT	9	5244	74	65.3	104

Fee 9 Holes: Weekday: $13.00   **Weekend:** $14.00
Fee 18 Holes: Weekday: $21.00   **Weekend:** $22.00
Cart Rental: $22.00/18 $11.00/9   **Discounts:** Senior & Students
Lessons: Yes **School:**   **Junior Golf:** No **Membership:** Yes
Driving Range: No   **Non-Metal Spikes:** Preferred
Other: Clubhouse / Snack bar / Bar-lounge / Grill

The course is level and well kept with only 2 water holes.

	1	2	3	4	5	6	7	8	9
PAR	4	4	3	4	4	4	3	4	5
YARDS	386	315	175	393	315	380	125	306	480
HDCP	2	10	14	6	16	4	18	12	8
	10	11	12	13	14	15	16	17	18
PAR	4	4	3	4	4	4	3	4	5
YARDS	437	322	187	405	325	386	146	335	485
HDCP	1	9	13	5	15	3	17	11	7

Directions: Take I-95 to Hampton Exit (Route 101 West) to Route 108. North to course.

Sagamore-Hampton GC 73

N. Hampton, NH (603) 964-5341

Club Pro: No
Pro Shop: Limited inventory
Payment: Visa, MC, Amex
Tee Times: 7 dys/wknds & hldy; 2 others
Fee 9 Holes: Weekday: $14.00
Fee 18 Holes: Weekday: $25.00
Cart Rental: Limited number
Lessons: Teaching pro. **School:** No
Driving Range: No
Other: Clubhouse / Snack bar / Bar-lounge/ Group Outings/ USGA Handicap services

Tees	Holes	Yards	Par	USGA	Slope
BACK	18	6014	71	67.4	110
MIDDLE	18	5647	71	67.4	110
FRONT	18	5008	71	71.5	111

Weekend: $16.00
Weekend: $27.00
Discounts: Senior & Junior
Junior Golf: N/R **Membership:** Freq.Player Deal
Non-Metal Spikes: Preferred

COUPON

A beautiful 18-hole layout that conforms to and compliments its natural surroundings. An enjoyable challenge for all abilities. Open April - December.

	1	2	3	4	5	6	7	8	9
PAR	4	4	4	3	4	5	3	5	3
YARDS	291	325	352	135	300	463	192	424	166
HDCP	16	15	6	12	13	14	3	9	11
	10	11	12	13	14	15	16	17	18
PAR	5	3	4	5	3	4	5	3	4
YARDS	527	172	380	446	125	284	456	190	419
HDCP	2	4	5	8	17	18	7	10	1

Directions: Take I-95 to Exit 2. Take right onto Route 101 W, follow 1.2 miles. Take right onto Route 111, follow 2.5 miles. Take left onto Route 151 N, follow 1.1 miles. Course is on right.

NH

Shattuck GC, The ⚪⚪ 74

Jaffrey, NH (603) 532-4300

Club Pro: Lyman J. Doane
Pro Shop: Full Inventory
Payment: MC, Visa, Amex, Cash
Tee Times: 4 days adv.
Fee 9 Holes: Weekday: N/A July & August
Fee 18 Holes: Weekday: $45 with cart, M-Th
Cart Rental: $13.00
Lessons: $30/30 min. **School:** No
Driving Range: $4.00/lg
Other: Bar-Lounge / Snack bar

Tees	Holes	Yards	Par	USGA	Slope
BACK	18	6701	71	74.1	145
MIDDLE	18	6077	71	71.0	140
FRONT	18	4632	71	73.1	139

Weekend: N/A July & August
Weekend: $56.00 with cart F/S/S
Discounts: None
Junior Golf: Yes **Membership:** Yes
Non-Metal Spikes: Required

#1 course in N.H. in 1993 & 1994. Bent grass tee to green. Target golf at its best. Requires very conservative play. Great mountain vistas. $39 in September w/o cart. Open May - December 1.

	1	2	3	4	5	6	7	8	9
PAR	4	3	4	4	5	5	3	4	4
YARDS	357	146	343	312	551	508	183	373	356
HDCP	5	17	9	13	1	3	15	7	11
	10	11	12	13	14	15	16	17	18
PAR	4	4	3	4	3	5	4	4	4
YARDS	394	407	155	303	121	508	367	313	380
HDCP	6	4	16	14	18	2	10	12	8

Directions: Take Route 202 North to Route 124 (Jaffrey Center). Continue West on Route 124 for 2.3 miles. Course is on the right.

4⚪ =Excellent 3⚪ =Very Good 2⚪ =Good   **New Hampshire 205**

Souhegan Woods GC

Amherst, NH (603) 673-0200

Club Pro: Bill Meier
Pro Shop: Full inventory
Payment: MC, Visa, Dis
Tee Times: 7 days adv.
Fee 9 Holes: Weekday: $17.00
Fee 18 Holes: Weekday: $30.00
Cart Rental: $24.00/18 $15.00/9
Lessons: $50.00/ hour **School:** No
Driving Range: $5.00/lg. bucket
Other: Clubhouse / Bar-Lounge / Snack Bar / Showers

Tees	Holes	Yards	Par	USGA	Slope
BACK	18	6497	72	70.4	120
MIDDLE	18	6122	72	68.7	117
FRONT	18	5423	71/69	65.6	111

Weekend: No
Weekend: $38.00
Discounts: None
Junior Golf: Membership: No
Non-Metal Spikes: Not Required

Designed to challenge all golfers. In superb condition and well spread out. A challenge is to stay out of the 63 strategically placed sand traps. Open April - November. A Friel Golf Company

	1	2	3	4	5	6	7	8	9
PAR	4	4	3	5	4	5	4	3	4
YARDS	375	312	168	445	402	501	337	149	355
HDCP	8	14	16	6	4	2	12	18	10
	10	11	12	13	14	15	16	17	18
PAR	4	3	4	4	5	4	4	3	5
YARDS	312	153	343	368	510	349	406	166	469
HDCP	13	17	9	7	1	11	3	15	5

Directions: Route 3 (Everett Tpke.) to Exit 11. Left at exit, right at Burger King. Follow Amherst Rd. 4.3 miles.

Sunningdale GC

Somersworth, NH (603) 742-8056

Club Pro: Alan Richard
Pro Shop: Full inventory
Payment: Visa, MC, Cash, Check
Tee Times: Yes
Fee 9 Holes: Weekday: $14.00
Fee 18 Holes: Weekday: $23.00
Cart Rental: $22.00/18 $12.00/9
Lessons: $25.00/45 min **School:** No
Driving Range: $5.00/lg.
Other: Clubhouse / Bar-Lounge / Lockers

Tees	Holes	Yards	Par	USGA	Slope
BACK	9	3455	36	69.9	119
MIDDLE	9	3165	36	69.9	119
FRONT	9	3015	37	68.8	113

Weekend: $15.00
Weekend: $26.00
Discounts: Senior & Junior
Junior Golf: Yes **Membership:** Yes
Non-Metal Spikes: N/R

Hilly and fairly narrow. Scenic elevated Par three #5 hole. No tank tops. Open April - Nov.

	1	2	3	4	5	6	7	8	9
PAR	4	5	4	5	3	4	4	3	4
YARDS	385	500	325	470	185	350	420	200	330
HDCP	7	5	17	3	11	13	1	9	15
	10	11	12	13	14	15	16	17	18
PAR									
YARDS									
HDCP									

Directions: Exit 9 off Spaulding Turnpike. Straight through intersection on Route 9. Right on Stackpole Rd. just past Walmart. Right onto Green St. 1/3 mi. on right.

Sunset Hill Golf Course

Sugar Hill, NH (603) 823-7244

Club Pro: Dr. Richard Thomas
Pro Shop: Yes
Payment: Cash, Check
Tee Times: Yes
Fee 9 Holes: Weekday: $12.00   **Weekend:** $14.00
Fee 18 Holes: Weekday: $18.00   **Weekend:** $20.00
Cart Rental: $20.00/18 $14.00/9   **Discounts:** None
Lessons: Private, Group, Clinics   **School:** No   **Junior Golf:** No   **Membership:** Yes
Driving Range: No   **Non-Metal Spikes:** Not Required
Other: Snack bar / Restaurant / Country inn with golf and hotel packages.

Tees	Holes	Yards	Par	USGA	Slope
BACK	N/A				
MIDDLE	9	3954	66	58.2	81
FRONT	N/A				

COUPON

Sporty, challenging style. Stay 'n' play from $169 per couple. Panoramic views of both the White Mountains (NH) and the Green Mountains (VT). Open April - November.

	1	2	3	4	5	6	7	8	9
PAR	4	4	4	4	3	4	3	4	3
YARDS	257	286	231	229	169	210	157	260	178
HDCP	5	3	7	9	15	11	17	1	13
	10	11	12	13	14	15	16	17	18
PAR	4	4	4	4	3	4	3	4	3
YARDS	257	286	231	229	169	210	157	260	178
HDCP	6	4	8	10	16	12	18	2	4

Directions: Take I-93 to Exit 38; take right over Franconia Bridge, take Sugar Hill Road (Route 117), 2 miles, take left onto Sunset Road; course is 1/2 mile on right.

NH

Tory Pines Resort

Rt. 47, Francestown, NH (603) 588-2923

Club Pro: Bruce Nasa
Pro Shop: Full inventory
Payment: Visa, MC, Amex
Tee Times: 5 days adv.
Fee 9 Holes: Weekday: $14.00   **Weekend:** $16.00
Fee 18 Holes: Weekday: $25.00   **Weekend:** $32.00
Cart Rental: $13.00/18 $7.00/9   **Discounts:** Senior
Lessons: $30/30 min.   **School:** Yes   **Junior Golf:** Yes   **Membership:** Yes
Driving Range: $4.00/lg.   **Non-Metal Spikes:** Required
Other: Restaurant / Clubhouse / Hotel-Inn / Bar-Lounge / Snack bar

Tees	Holes	Yards	Par	USGA	Slope
BACK	18	6100	71	70.7	138
MIDDLE	18	5437	71	68.0	133
FRONT	18	4639	71	70.8	124

A newly designed Donald Ross golf course, narrow fairways and very small greens. Ranked in the top 3 in New England for scenic views. Golf school on premises.

	1	2	3	4	5	6	7	8	9
PAR	4	4	3	5	4	3	5	4	4
YARDS	306	325	144	486	328	181	410	311	346
HDCP	11	9	17	1	7	15	3	13	5
	10	11	12	13	14	15	16	17	18
PAR	4	4	4	5	4	4	3	4	3
YARDS	339	285	333	389	320	315	168	288	163
HDCP	6	14	4	2	8	12	16	10	18

Directions: Take Route 3 North to Route 101A West; follow into Milford; turn right onto Route 13 to New Boston. Take Route 136 to Francestown Center; take right onto Route 47. Course is 4 miles on right.

4✪ =Excellent   3✪ =Very Good   2✪ =Good

Twin Lake Villa Golf Course

New London, NH (603)526-6460

Club Pro: N/A
Pro Shop: Limited inventory
Payment: Personal checks
Tee Times: 7 days in adv.
Fee 9 Holes: Weekday: $12.00
Fee 18 Holes: Weekday: $16.00
Cart Rental: $2.00/9
Lessons: No **School:** No
Driving Range: No
Other: Hotel / Clay Tennis / Shuffle Board / Swimming / Boating / Fishing.

Tees	Holes	Yards	Par	USGA	Slope
BACK	9	1496	27		
MIDDLE	9	1328	27		
FRONT	9	1151	27		

Weekend: $12.00
Weekend: $16.00
Discounts: Senior, $2 off
Junior Golf: N/R **Membership:** Yes
Non-Metal Spikes: Not Required

100 yrs. old in 1997. Beautifully groomed. Proper attire required. Lodging, meals and golf packages available. Open May 15-Oct. 15.

	1	2	3	4	5	6	7	8	9
PAR	3	3	3	3	3	3	3	3	3
YARDS	135	107	116	116	200	182	173	172	127
HDCP									
	10	11	12	13	14	15	16	17	18
PAR									
YARDS									
HDCP									

Directions: I-89, New London exit. Straight through town, pass college(Colby-Sawyer). Straight up hill to Hotel and Golf Shop.

Waterville Valley

Waterville, NH (603) 236-4805

Club Pro: Bill Baker, PGA
Pro Shop: Full inventory
Payment: Visa, MC, Amex, Dis
Tee Times: 48 hours adv.
Fee 9 Holes: Weekday: $17.00
Fee 18 Holes: Weekday: $23.00
Cart Rental: Yes, Pull or Gas
Lessons: $30/30 min. **School:** No
Driving Range: No
Other: Clubhouse / Snack bar / Club storage

Tees	Holes	Yards	Par	USGA	Slope
BACK					
MIDDLE	9	4716	64	63	105
FRONT					

Weekend: $19.00
Weekend: $25.00
Discounts: None
Junior Golf: Yes **Membership:** Yes
Non-Metal Spikes: Required

COUPON

The course is short but sweet. Mountain resort. Open May 27 - October 15. Junior clinic Tues., Wed., and Thurs. morning.

	1	2	3	4	5	6	7	8	9
PAR	4	3	3	4	3	3	4	4	4
YARDS	371	124	150	410	220	150	251	377	351
HDCP	5	17	15	1	3	11	13	9	7
	10	11	12	13	14	15	16	17	18
PAR	4	3	3	4	3	3	4	4	4
YARDS	371	124	150	353	220	115	251	377	351
HDCP	6	18	16	2	4	12	14	10	8

Directions: Take I-93 to Exit 28; follow Route 49 for 12 miles.

Waukewan Golf Club

81

Meredith, NH (603) 279-6661

Club Pro: M. D.Hale Jr.,Golf Dir.
Pro Shop: Full inventory
Payment: Cash or credit card
Tee Times: Yes
Fee 9 Holes: Weekday: $18.00
Fee 18 Holes: Weekday: $28.00
Cart Rental: $24.00/18 $14.00/9
Lessons: $15.00/half hour **School:** No
Driving Range: $5.00/lg. bucket
Other: Clubhouse / Snack bar / Bar-lounge

Tees	Holes	Yards	Par	USGA	Slope
BACK	N/A				
MIDDLE	18	5735	71	67.1	120
FRONT	18	5020	73	68.7	112

Weekend: $18.00
Weekend: $28.00
Discounts: None
Junior Golf: Yes **Membership:** Yes
Non-Metal Spikes: Not Required

COUPON

Family owned and constructed. Scenic view of White Mountains of NH; natural setting in country environment. Premium on shot selection and positioning of ball. Open May - October.

	1	2	3	4	5	6	7	8	9
PAR	4	4	3	4	4	5	3	5	4
YARDS	390	330	140	275	255	550	170	470	395
HDCP	6	12	18	16	14	4	10	8	2
	10	11	12	13	14	15	16	17	18
PAR	4	3	4	4	4	4	3	5	4
YARDS	270	190	250	410	290	420	210	490	230
HDCP	9	11	17	3	15	1	7	5	13

Directions: Take Exit 23 from I-93 North, Route 104 to Meredith, Route 3 North toward Plymouth 3 miles from Meredith traffic junction, left turn onto Waukewan Road.

NH

Waumbek CC, The

82

Jefferson, NH (603) 586-7777

Club Pro: Larry Fellows
Pro Shop: Full inventory
Payment: Visa, MC, Cash
Tee Times: Wknds
Fee 9 Holes: Weekday: $12.00
Fee 18 Holes: Weekday: $20.00
Cart Rental: $20.00/18 $14.00/9
Lessons: Appointment only **School:**
Driving Range:
Other: Snack Bar

Tees	Holes	Yards	Par	USGA	Slope
BACK	18	6128	71	69.9	107
MIDDLE	18	5874	71	69.9	107
FRONT	18	4772	71	69.9	107

Weekend: $15.00
Weekend: $25.00
Discounts: Senior & Junior
Junior Golf: N/R **Membership:** No
Non-Metal Spikes: Not Required

COUPON

Challenging course. The oldest 18 hole course in New Hampshire. Ball magnetizes toward Cherry Mountain — don't aim for the hole, aim for the mountain. A Friel Golf Company.

	1	2	3	4	5	6	7	8	9
PAR	4	4	5	4	4	4	4	3	3
YARDS	333	370	500	310	320	390	290	200	195
HDCP	11	1	5	7	13	3	9	15	17
	10	11	12	13	14	15	16	17	18
PAR	4	5	4	4	3	4	4	5	3
YARDS	310	465	387	280	110	340	335	490	170
HDCP	12	10	2	16	18	8	6	4	14

Directions: I-93 to Exit 35 (Route 3 North). Follow Route 3 for 12 miles, then take a right onto 115 North. Follow 115 North for 6.7 miles. Take a left onto 115A. Golf course is 4 miles down on the right.

4✪ =Excellent 3✪ =Very Good 2✪ =Good

New Hampshire 209

Wentworth Resort GC ▶ 83

Rt. 16, Jackson, NH (603) 383-9641

Club Pro: Bob McGraw
Pro Shop: Full inventory
Payment: MC, Visa, Amex, Disc.
Tee Times: 5 days adv.

Tees	Holes	Yards	Par	USGA	Slope
BACK	N/A				
MIDDLE	18	5581	70	66.0	115
FRONT	18	5087	70	71.1	120

Fee 9 Holes: Weekday: $25 aftr 11am w/cart **Weekend:** No
Fee 18 Holes: Weekday: $35 (Includes Cart) **Weekend:** $49.00 (Includes Cart)
Cart Rental: $22.00/18 $14.00/9   **Discounts:** Junior
Lessons: $35.00/45 minutes **School:** No   **Junior Golf:** Yes **Membership:** Yes
Driving Range: No   **Non-Metal Spikes:** Not Required
Other: Snack bar / Restaurant / Bar-lounge / Tent

COUPON

A short, but challenging course situated in beautiful Jackson Village. Enjoy the rolling hills and the covered bridge crossing the Ellis River on the White Mountain's second oldest course.

	1	2	3	4	5	6	7	8	9
PAR	4	4	4	3	5	3	3	4	4
YARDS	359	336	365	185	454	180	144	295	305
HDCP	3	13	5	7	1	9	17	15	11
	10	11	12	13	14	15	16	17	18
PAR	4	4	4	3	4	4	4	5	4
YARDS	337	349	304	147	411	291	307	479	333
HDCP	8	6	12	16	2	18	14	4	10

Directions: I-95 to Spaulding Turnpike. Take Route 16 to Jackson Village.

Whip-Poor-Will GC ▶ 84

Hudson, NH 03051   603-889-9706

Club Pro: Jeff Wirsal
Pro Shop: Full inventory
Payment: Visa, MC, Disc
Tee Times: Yes, 7 days in advance

Tees	Holes	Yards	Par	USGA	Slope
BACK	9	6030	72	68.5	125
MIDDLE	9	5980	72	68.5	125
FRONT	9	5094	72	69.9	119

Fee 9 Holes: Weekday: $1500   **Weekend:** $18.00
Fee 18 Holes: Weekday: $22.00   **Weekend:** $28.00
Cart Rental: $24.00/18 $16.00/9   **Discounts:** Senior
Lessons: $30/hour **School:** No   **Junior Golf:** **Membership:** No
Driving Range: No   **Non-Metal Spikes:** Not Required
Other: Clubhouse / Snack Bar / Bar Lounge

COUPON

A Friel Golf Company

	1	2	3	4	5	6	7	8	9
PAR	4	3	4	4	5	4	4	5	3
YARDS	330	170	345	315	485	402	280	498	165
HDCP	11	17	5	9	7	3	13	1	15
	10	11	12	13	14	15	16	17	18
PAR	4	3	4	4	5	4	4	5	3
YARDS	330	170	345	315	485	402	280	498	165
HDCP	12	18	6	10	8	4	14	2	16

Directions: From I-93, take Exit 4 to Route 102 West approx 7 miles. Course in on left at Marsh Road just after Alverine High School.

White Mountain CC   85

N. Ashland Rd., Ashland, NH (603) 536-2227

Club Pro: Gregg Sufat
Pro Shop: Full inventory
Payment: Visa, MC
Tee Times: 1 week adv.

Tees	Holes	Yards	Par	USGA	Slope
BACK	18	6464	71	70.4	122
MIDDLE	18	5963	71	67.9	119
FRONT	18	5410	73	70.2	118

Fee 9 Holes: Weekday: $16.00   **Weekend:** $20.00 after 3pm
Fee 18 Holes: Weekday: $27.00   **Weekend:** $34.00
Cart Rental: $22/18 $14.00/9   **Discounts:** None
Lessons: $25.00/half hour **School:** No   **Junior Golf: Membership:** No
Driving Range: $4.00/lg. bucket   **Non-Metal Spikes:** Not Required
Other: Bar-lounge / Snack Bar / Townhouse Rentals

COUPON

Small airport between third and fifth holes, manicured fairways, soft velvet greens, challenging yet "golfer friendly." Open May - October. A Friel Golf Company

	1	2	3	4	5	6	7	8	9
PAR	4	4	4	3	5	4	3	5	4
YARDS	327	334	325	174	524	300	172	508	312
HDCP	9	13	15	17	1	7	11	5	3
	10	11	12	13	14	15	16	17	18
PAR	4	3	4	4	4	4	4	4	4
YARDS	356	154	356	385	321	301	359	410	356
HDCP	12	18	8	4	14	16	6	2	10

Directions: I-93 North, Exit 24, left off ramp for 1 mile. Right onto North Ashland Road, 2.5 miles on left.

NH

Windham Golf Club ✪✪ 86

1 Country Club Rd., Windham, NH, 603-434-2093

Club Pro: Joanne Flynn, PGA
Pro Shop: Full inventory
Payment: Visa, MC
Tee Times: 7 days a week, 5 days in adv.

Tees	Holes	Yards	Par	USGA	Slope
BACK	18	6442	72	71.3	137
MIDDLE	18	6033	72	69.1	133
FRONT	18	5584	72	69.1	123

Fee 9 Holes: Weekday: $17.00   **Weekend:** $20.00
Fee 18 Holes: Weekday: $32.00   **Weekend:** $37.00
Cart Rental: $12 pp/18, $6 pp/9   **Discounts:** Junior
Lessons: $40/30 min. **School:** No   **Junior Golf:** Yes **Membership:** No
Driving Range: $6.00/Lg, $4.00/Sm/   **Non-Metal Spikes:** Not Required
Other: Full Restaurant / Club house / Bar-Lounge / Snack Bar

Challenging layout carved out of rolling landscape. A full service public country club. Open Year round (when possible). Jay Carey, Ass't Pro. Junior clinics on Tues. in summer.

	1	2	3	4	5	6	7	8	9
PAR	5	4	3	4	5	3	4	4	3
YARDS	5	351	138	353	454	111	364	351	148
HDCP	5	7	13	11	3	17	9	1	15
	10	11	12	13	14	15	16	17	18
PAR	4	4	5	4	3	5	4	4	4
YARDS	255	340	435	207	157	424	370	317	287
HDCP	14	6	4	18	16	8	2	10	12

Directions: I-93 North to Exit 3. Take Route 111 west 1 1/2 miles. Then right on Church St. to fire station, then right on to N. Lowell for 1 mile. Left onto Londonderry Rd. 1/2 mile and left on Country Club Rd.

4✪ =Excellent 3✪ =Very Good 2✪ =Good

Woodbound Inn GC

87

Woodbound Rd., Jaffrey, NH (603) 532-8341

Club Pro: No
Pro Shop: No
Payment: Visa, MC, Amex, cash
Tee Times: No
Fee 9 Holes: Weekday: $12.00
Fee 18 Holes: Weekday: $12.00
Cart Rental: Pull carts
Lessons: No **School:** No
Driving Range: No
Other: Snack bar / Restaurant / Gift Shop / Bar-Lounge

Tees	Holes	Yards	Par	USGA	Slope
BACK					
MIDDLE	9	2104	54	N/A	N/A
FRONT					

Weekend: $12.00
Weekend: $12.00
Discounts: Senior
Junior Golf: No **Membership:** No
Non-Metal Spikes: Required

COUPON

A course that is good for families, seniors, beginners or corporate outings. 18 different tee boxes. www.NHWeb.com/woodbound/Index.HTML

	1	2	3	4	5	6	7	8	9
PAR	3	3	3	3	3	3	3	3	3
YARDS	114	138	94	128	109	79	142	117	131
HDCP									
	10	11	12	13	14	15	16	17	18
PAR	3	3	3	3	3	3	3	3	3
YARDS	114	138	94	128	109	79	142	117	131
HDCP									

Directions: Take I-495 to Route 119 West 10 miles from NH border. Follow signs to course.

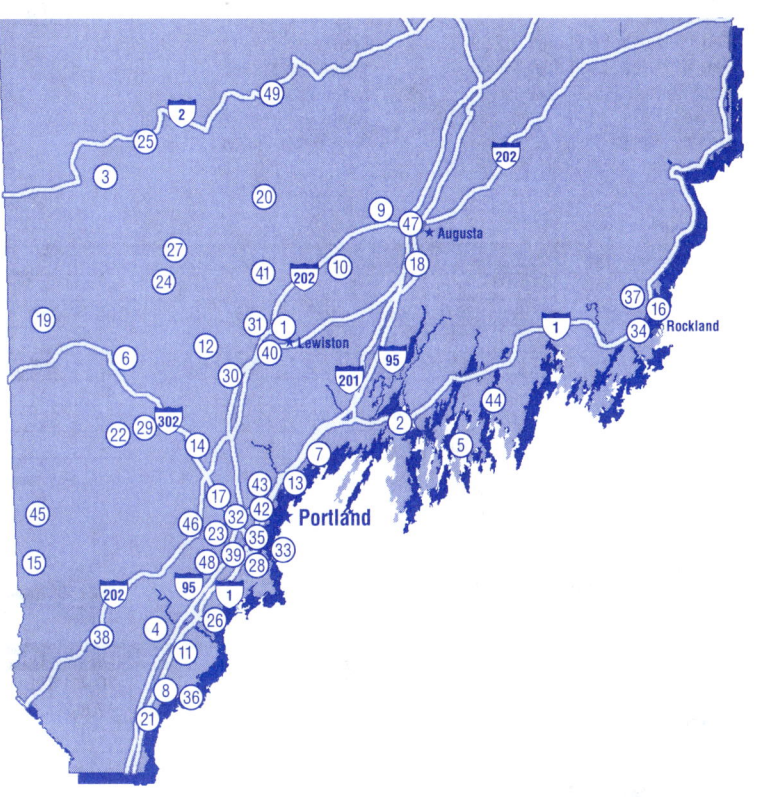

CHAPTER 6
Southern Maine

Apple Valley GC	1	Kennebec Heights CC	18	Sable Oaks Golf Club	35
Bath Country Club	2	Lake Kezar CC	19	Salmon Falls GC	36
Bethel Inn & CC	3	Maple Lane Inn & GC	20	Samoset Resort GC	37
Biddeford & Saco CC	4	Merriland Farm Par 3 GC	21	Sanford Country Club	38
Boothbay Region CC	5	Naples Golf and CC	22	South Portland Muni	39
Bridgton Highlands CC	6	Nonesuch River GC	23	Spring Brook GC	40
Brunswick Golf Club	7	Norway Country Club	24	Turner Highland GC	41
Cape Arundel Golf Club	8	Oakdale CC	25	Twin Falls Golf Course	42
Capitol City GC	9	Old Orchard Bch CC	26	Val Halla Golf Course	43
Cobbossee Colony GC	10	Paris Hill Country Club	27	Wawenock CC	44
Dutch Elm Golf Course	11	Pleasant Hill CC	28	West Newfield GC	45
Fairlawn Golf Club	12	Point Sebago Golf Club	29	Westerly Winds GC	46
Freeport Country Club	13	Poland Spring CC	30	Western View Golf Club	47
Frye Island Golf Course	14	Prospect Hill GC	31	Willowdale Golf Club	48
Golf at Province Lake	15	River Meadow GC	32	Wilson Lake CC	49
Goose River GC	16	Riverside Municipal GC	33		
Gorham Country Club	17	Rockland Golf Club	34		

NEW ENGLAND GOLFGUIDE   **Southern Maine 213**

Apple Valley GC

Pinewoods Rd., Lewiston, ME (207) 784-9773

Club Pro: Terry Russell
Pro Shop: Full inventory
Payment: Cash only
Tee Times: No
Fee 9 Holes: Weekday: $12.00
Fee 18 Holes: Weekday: $18.00
Cart Rental: $18.00/18 $9.00/9
Lessons: $20.00/half hour **School:** No
Driving Range: No
Other: Clubhouse / Snack bar

Tees	Holes	Yards	Par	USGA	Slope
BACK	N/A				
MIDDLE	9	5037	70	64.3	108
FRONT	9	4798	72	66.8	109

Weekend: $12.00
Weekend: $18.00
Discounts: None
Junior Golf: Yes **Membership:** Yes
Non-Metal Spikes: Preferred

Open April 15 - November 15.

	1	2	3	4	5	6	7	8	9
PAR	4	4	3	5	3	4	4	4	4
YARDS	239	258	147	445	108	333	312	300	350
HDCP	13	7	15	5	17	3	11	9	1
	10	11	12	13	14	15	16	17	18
PAR	4	4	3	5	3	4	4	4	4
YARDS	235	256	177	450	115	343	299	310	360
HDCP	14	8	16	6	18	4	12	10	2

Directions: Take ME Turnpike to Exit 13; take right onto Dyer Road. Take left onto Pinewoods Road, course is 2 miles on left.

Bath Country Club

Whiskeag Rd., Bath, ME (207) 442-8411

Club Pro: Shawn Arsenault, PGA,
Pro Shop: Full inventory
Payment: Cash and credit cards
Tee Times: Yes
Fee 9 Holes: Weekday: $15/$12 after 5 pm
Fee 18 Holes: Weekday: $25.00
Cart Rental: $24.00/18 $12.00/9
Lessons: $25/30 min. **School:** No
Driving Range: No
Other: Clubhouse / Restaurant / Lounge / Lockers

Tees	Holes	Yards	Par	USGA	Slope
BACK	18	6216	70	70.2	128
MIDDLE	18	5751	70	67.8	123
FRONT	18	4708	70	67.0	115

Weekend: $15.00/ $12 after 5 pm
Weekend: $25.00
Discounts: None
Junior Golf: No **Membership:** Yes, Jr. Discount
Non-Metal Spikes: Preferred

One of the finest nine hole courses in the state. Fairways are tight and tree-lined. The eighth hole is an outstanding par 4. Series of lessons offered. College scholarship offered for juniors.

	1	2	3	4	5	6	7	8	9
PAR	4	4	5	4	4	3	4	4	3
YARDS	356	375	504	393	354	173	417	432	203
HDCP	11	5	13	7	17	9	3	1	15
	10	11	12	13	14	15	16	17	18
PAR	4	4	4	3	4	4	3	5	4
YARDS	298	358	303	132	393	356	186	528	393
HDCP	14	8	16	18	2	4	10	6	4

Directions: From I-95, take Route 1N. From 1N take New Meadows Rd. Exit. Go right at stop sign. Go 1 1/4 miles to next stop sign. Go straight through on to Ridge Road for 1 1/4 miles to 18th tee. Go right.

Bethel Inn & CC

Broad St., Bethel, ME (207) 824-6276

Tees	Holes	Yards	Par	USGA	Slope
BACK	18	6330	72	70.6	130
MIDDLE	18	6029	72	69.1	127
FRONT	18	5280	72	71.4	129

Club Pro: Phil Grear
Pro Shop: Full inventory
Payment: MC, Visa, Amex, Cash
Tee Times: 2 days adv.
Fee 9 Holes: Weekday: N/A   **Weekend:** N/A
Fee 18 Holes: Weekday: $65.00 pp with cart   **Weekend:** $65.00
Cart Rental: Included   **Discounts:** Junior
Lessons: $35/30 min.   **School:** Jr. & Sr.   **Junior Golf:** Yes   **Membership:** Yes
Driving Range: $3.00/lg. bucket   **Non-Metal Spikes:** Preferred
Other: Clubhouse / Showers / Snack bar / Restaurant / Bar-lounge / Lodging

COUPON

Cornish designed golf course in Maine's White Mountains with spectacular views of western Maine. Long fairways play to true rolling bent grass greens. Open May - November. www.bethelinn.com

	1	2	3	4	5	6	7	8	9
PAR	4	4	3	4	5	3	4	5	4
YARDS	340	262	130	370	492	141	361	500	292
HDCP	11	13	17	1	7	15	3	5	9
	10	11	12	13	14	15	16	17	18
PAR	4	5	3	4	4	4	3	5	4
YARDS	325	546	179	294	397	400	151	506	343
HDCP	18	4	14	16	2	6	10	8	12

Directions: Maine Turnpike to Exit 11, Gray. Take Route 26 North to Bethel. Route 26 becomes Main Street in Bethel. Follow Main Street to the top. Course is on left behind Main Inn.

Biddeford & Saco CC

Old Orchard Rd., Saco, ME (207) 282-5883

Tees	Holes	Yards	Par	USGA	Slope
BACK	18	6196	71	69.6	123
MIDDLE	18	5744	71	68.6	114
FRONT	18	5433	72	71.4	117

Club Pro: Tim Angis
Pro Shop: Full inventory
Payment: All major
Tee Times: 3 days, June-Sept.
Fee 9 Holes: Weekday: No   **Weekend:** No
Fee 18 Holes: Weekday: $30.00   **Weekend:** $35.00
Cart Rental: $25.00/18   **Discounts:** None
Lessons: $25.00/half hour   **School:** No   **Junior Golf:** Yes   **Membership:** No
Driving Range: Yes   **Non-Metal Spikes:** Required
Other: Restaurant / Snack bar / Bar-lounge / Lockers / Showers

Originally designed by Donald Ross. A pleasure to walk, it is fun, superbly maintained, and has a very friendly staff. Rated by Golf Digest in top 500.

	1	2	3	4	5	6	7	8	9
PAR	4	3	5	4	4	4	4	3	4
YARDS	347	181	496	343	391	242	340	153	425
HDCP	9	17	3	7	5	11	13	15	1
	10	11	12	13	14	15	16	17	18
PAR	3	4	5	4	4	3	4	5	4
YARDS	145	438	467	317	316	129	317	412	285
HDCP	16	2	4	14	8	18	12	6	10

Directions: Take I-95 to Exit 5 Maine Turnpike. Straight to American Motorcycle on right. Take right on Old Orchard Road, course is 1/2 mile on left.

4✪ =Excellent   3✪ =Very Good   2✪ =Good

Boothbay Region CC

5

Boothbay, ME (207) 633-6085

Club Pro: Greg Sandell
Pro Shop: Full inventory
Payment: Visa, MC, Amex, Disc
Tee Times: Required
Fee 9 Holes: Weekday: $17.50
Fee 18 Holes: Weekday: $25.00
Cart Rental: $20.00/18 $12.00/9
Lessons: $30.00/half hour **School:** No
Driving Range: $5.00/sm $7.00/lg
Other: Restaurant / Clubhouse / Snack bar / Bar-lounge

Tees	Holes	Yards	Par	USGA	Slope
BACK	9	2714	35	66.1	118
MIDDLE	9	2668	35	66.1	118
FRONT	9	2458	35	67.2	115

Weekend: $17.50
Weekend: $25.00
Discounts: $12 Wkdys only after 5
Junior Golf: Yes **Membership:** Yes
Non-Metal Spikes: Required

COUPON

Good nine hole course in the heart of the Boothbay region. Excellent New England layout: a little on the short side but small tough greens. Open April - November.

	1	2	3	4	5	6	7	8	9
PAR	4	3	4	4	4	5	3	4	4
YARDS	346	176	323	295	353	448	121	311	295
HDCP	9	8	3	11	6	1	17	13	15
	10	11	12	13	14	15	16	17	18
PAR									
YARDS									
HDCP									

Directions: I-95 to Route 1, to Route 27. 10 miles, take left across from Texaco station onto Country Club Road. Course on right

Bridgton Highlands CC

6

Bridgton, ME (207) 647-3491

Club Pro: Wayne Hill
Pro Shop: Full inventory
Payment: Cash, Check, Credit
Tee Times: 3 days adv.
Fee 9 Holes: Weekday: $15.00
Fee 18 Holes: Weekday: $22.00
Cart Rental: Yes
Lessons: $25.00/half hour **School:** No
Driving Range: No
Other: Snack bar / Restaurant / Bar-lounge / Clubhouse

Tees	Holes	Yards	Par	USGA	Slope
BACK	18	6059	72	70.2	126
MIDDLE	18	5820	72	69.3	123
FRONT	18	5428	74	70.0	119

Weekend: $15.00
Weekend: $26.00
Discounts: $14 after 3 pm
Junior Golf: Yes **Membership:** Yes
Non-Metal Spikes: No

COUPON

Nine hole course built in the 1930s. Two holes were recently replaced. The course is fully irrigated. Expanded to 18 holes in 1996.

	1	2	3	4	5	6	7	8	9
PAR	4	3	4	5	4	4	5	3	4
YARDS	440	145	376	440	345	304	434	150	320
HDCP	1	17	3	9	13	5	7	11	15
	10	11	12	13	14	15	16	17	18
PAR	3	4	4	3	4	5	4	4	5
YARDS	156	320	379	150	350	444	275	297	495
HDCP	12	14	4	18	10	6	2	8	16

Directions: Take Route 302 in Bridgton to Highland Rd. Course is 1.9 miles on the right.

Brunswick Golf Club 7

River Rd., Brunswick, ME (207) 725-8224

Club Pro: Chris J. Doyle
Pro Shop: Full inventory
Payment: Visa, MC
Tee Times: Weekends

Tees	Holes	Yards	Par	USGA	Slope
BACK	18	6609	72	69.9	126
MIDDLE	18	6251	72	70	123
FRONT	18	5772	74	71.6	123

Fee 9 Holes: Weekday: $20.00 **Weekend:** $20.00
Fee 18 Holes: Weekday: $35.00 **Weekend:** $35.00
Cart Rental: No **Discounts:** None
Lessons: $30.00/half hour **School:** No **Junior Golf:** No **Membership:** Yes
Driving Range: Yes **Non-Metal Spikes:** Required
Other: Clubhouse / Snack bar / Bar-lounge / Lockers

Regulation 18 hole championship golf course. Hosted 1997 Maine Amateur. Well suited for players of all abilities. Prices vary in spring and fall.

	1	2	3	4	5	6	7	8	9
PAR	4	5	5	3	3	4	4	4	5
YARDS	355	547	485	179	110	440	332	364	494
HDCP	15	3	11	5	17	1	9	13	7
	10	11	12	13	14	15	16	17	18
PAR	4	3	4	4	4	3	5	4	4
YARDS	353	172	297	363	430	145	490	300	395
HDCP	6	12	16	8	2	18	10	14	4

Directions: Take I-295 to Brunswick; at 2nd light take left onto River Rd. Follow to course.

Cape Arundel Golf Club ✪✪ 8

Kennebunkport, ME (207) 967-3494

Club Pro: Ken Raynor
Pro Shop: Full inventory
Payment: Cash only
Tee Times: 1 day adv.

Tees	Holes	Yards	Par	USGA	Slope
BACK	N/A				
MIDDLE	18	5869	69	67	117
FRONT	18	5134	70	N/A	106

Fee 9 Holes: Weekday: $20 off season **Weekend:** $35.00
Fee 18 Holes: Weekday: $35, $20 after 5pm **Weekend:** $35.00
Cart Rental: $20.00/18 $12.00/9 **Discounts:** None
Lessons: $75.00/hour **School:** No **Junior Golf:** Yes **Membership:** No
Driving Range: No **Non-Metal Spikes:** Preferred
Other: Clubhouse / Lockers

A very challenging links course with small greens. Known as President Bush's home course. Members only 11:00 am - 2:00 pm daily.

	1	2	3	4	5	6	7	8	9
PAR	4	4	3	4	4	3	4	4	5
YARDS	375	311	154	398	350	118	381	370	480
HDCP	7	13	15	1	11	17	5	3	9
	10	11	12	13	14	15	16	17	18
PAR	4	4	4	3	4	4	3	4	4
YARDS	345	320	415	165	386	322	220	365	394
HDCP	8	16	2	14	4	18	12	10	6

Directions: Take I-95 to Biddeford Exit, take left off ramp. At 1st light take hairpin right turn at a 5-way intersection; follow 5 miles; at flashing yellow turn left onto Log Cabin Rd. Follow 4 miles; take 2nd right onto Old River Rd. to course.

4✪ =Excellent 3✪ =Very Good 2✪ =Good

Capitol City GC ▶ 9

Augusta, ME (207) 623-0504

Club Pro: No
Pro Shop: Limited inventory
Payment: No
Tee Times: No
Fee 9 Holes: Weekday: $10.00
Fee 18 Holes: Weekday: $15.00
Cart Rental: $9.00/9
Lessons: No **School:** No
Driving Range: No
Other: Snack bar, club house facilities.

Tees	Holes	Yards	Par	USGA	Slope
BACK	18	2790	36	N/A	N/A
MIDDLE	18	3881	63	N/A	N/A
FRONT	18	2297	36	N/A	N/A

Weekend: $8.00
Weekend: $12.00
Discounts: None
Junior Golf: N/R **Membership:** Yes
Non-Metal Spikes: Required

This has been a challenging par 3 golf course. The back 9 is presently being extended to Par 36. Fun course, good for families and beginners.

	1	2	3	4	5	6	7	8	9
PAR	3	3	3	3	3	3	3	3	3
YARDS	100	103	110	101	147	162	124	125	119
HDCP	N/A								
	10	11	12	13	14	15	16	17	18
PAR	3	4	4	5	5	4	3	4	4
YARDS	153	350	274	479	520	306	183	262	263
HDCP									

Directions: From I-95 take second exit in Augusta to Route 27. Take First right (at video store) onto Old Belgrade Road, then dog leg to right to course.

Cobbossee Colony GC ▶ 10

Monmouth, ME (207) 268-4182

Club Pro: Lon Wasser
Pro Shop: Yes
Payment: Visa, MC, Amex
Tee Times: Sunday
Fee 9 Holes: Weekday: $10.00
Fee 18 Holes: Weekday: $10.00
Cart Rental: $13.00/18 $7.00/9
Lessons: Yes **School:** Jr.
Driving Range: Yes
Other: Snack bar / Clubhouse

Tees	Holes	Yards	Par	USGA	Slope
BACK	N/A				
MIDDLE	9	2374	34	62	102
FRONT	N/A				

Weekend: $10.00
Weekend: $12.00
Discounts: None
Junior Golf: N/R **Membership:** Yes
Non-Metal Spikes: Not Required

Resort golf course built in the 1920's and 30's. Very short with small greens. Open April - November.

	1	2	3	4	5	6	7	8	9
PAR	5	4	4	3	4	3	4	3	4
YARDS	514	270	303	212	340	110	275	125	225
HDCP	3	6	5	2	4	9	1	7	8
	10	11	12	13	14	15	16	17	18
PAR									
YARDS									
HDCP									

Directions: Turn left off 295 Gardiner - Litchfield Exit. Go about 4 miles on Routes 126 and 9. Turn right on Hallowell - Litchfield Road. 1.5 miles to Hardscrabble Road. Follow for 1.5 miles.

Dutch Elm Golf Course

Arundel, ME (207) 282-9850

Club Pro: Norm Hevey
Pro Shop: Full inventory
Payment: Cash, Visa and MC
Tee Times: Yes
Fee 9 Holes: Weekday: $18.00
Fee 18 Holes: Weekday: $28.00
Cart Rental: $22.00/18 $12.00/9
Lessons: $20/30 min. **School:** No
Driving Range: Yes
Other: Bar-lounge / Snack bar

Tees	Holes	Yards	Par	USGA	Slope
BACK	18	6280	72	71.0	125
MIDDLE	18	5900	72	69.8	121
FRONT	18	5400	72	70.1	115

Weekend: On Availability
Weekend: $30.00
Discounts: Senior. Wkdays.
Junior Golf: Yes **Membership:** No
Non-Metal Spikes: Required

11

COUPON

Nine holes built in 1965, other nine opened in 1981. Course is scenic, challenging, and very well manicured. Total irrigation. No cutoffs, tank tops, or swimsuits. Seasonal rates; Inquire.

	1	2	3	4	5	6	7	8	9
PAR	4	4	4	4	4	5	3	3	4
YARDS	300	430	276	347	326	493	202	182	326
HDCP	15	1	7	5	9	3	13	17	11
	10	11	12	13	14	15	16	17	18
PAR	4	3	3	5	5	5	4	4	4
YARDS	356	156	181	440	486	431	300	342	357
HDCP	6	18	16	12	2	10	14	8	4

Directions: Off Maine Turnpike, take Exit 4. Turn right on Route 111, go 1 mile to Citgo station. Bear left, go 1 mile to stop sign. Turn right, course is on left.

Fairlawn Golf Club

Poland, ME (207) 998-4277

Club Pro: David Bartasius
Pro Shop: Limited inventory
Payment: Visa, MC
Tee Times: No
Fee 9 Holes: Weekday: No
Fee 18 Holes: Weekday: $16.00
Cart Rental: $12.00/18 $6.50/9
Lessons: $30.00/half hour **School:** No
Driving Range: $3 lg./ $2 sm. bucket
Other: Clubhouse / Lockers / Showers / Snack bar / Bar-lounge

Tees	Holes	Yards	Par	USGA	Slope
BACK	N/A				
MIDDLE	18	6300	72	68.6	118
FRONT	18	5379	72	70.7	112

Weekend: No
Weekend: $18.00
Discounts: None
Junior Golf: Yes **Membership:** No
Non-Metal Spikes: Not Required

12

S ME

Condominiums available for monthly rent overlooking 18th green. Twilight fees after 5:00 pm. Open May 1 - until it snows.

	1	2	3	4	5	6	7	8	9
PAR	4	3	5	4	4	4	5	3	4
YARDS	323	205	544	409	364	357	497	182	317
HDCP	13	9	7	1	5	3	11	15	17
	10	11	12	13	14	15	16	17	18
PAR	4	3	5	3	4	4	5	4	4
YARDS	394	133	491	154	358	363	535	341	333
HDCP	2	18	12	14	6	4	8	10	16

Directions: From Maine Turnpike, Exit 12, take right off exit; take first right (Kittyhawk). Go to end of road and take left (Lewiston Junction Road.) At first stop sign take right. Course on left. From West, take Route 26 South to Route 122. Take right onto Route 122 and follow signs.

4✪ =Excellent 3✪ =Very Good 2✪ =Good

Southern Maine 219

Freeport Country Club   13

Freeport, ME (207) 865-4922

Club Pro: No
Pro Shop: Yes
Payment: MC, Visa
Tee Times: Weekends
Fee 9 Holes: Weekday: $13.00
Fee 18 Holes: Weekday: $13.00
Cart Rental: $18.00/18 $9.00/9
Lessons: No **School:** No
Driving Range: No
Other: Clubhouse / Snack bar

Tees	Holes	Yards	Par	USGA	Slope
BACK					
MIDDLE	9	5900	72	69.0	116
FRONT	9	5088	72	69.1	108

Weekend: $16.00
Weekend: $16.00
Discounts: Junior
Junior Golf: No **Membership:** Yes
Non-Metal Spikes: Required

Located within 5 minutes of L.L. Bean, this course is an excellent alternative to shopping in Freeport. The course has a links-style layout with open fairways. A great value.

	1	2	3	4	5	6	7	8	9
PAR	4	4	4	4	5	3	4	3	5
YARDS	378	321	403	260	418	177	306	156	531
HDCP	3	15	1	17	13	5	7	9	11
	10	11	12	13	14	15	16	17	18
PAR	4	4	4	4	5	3	4	3	5
YARDS	388	390	353	250	453	197	316	148	460
HDCP	4	2	14	18	10	6	8	12	16

Directions: I-95 North to Exit 17, US Route 1. Look for a big wooden Indian on right. Continue 1 mile and turn left on Old County Road. Continue to course.

Frye Island Golf Course   14

Raymond, ME (207) 655-3551

Club Pro: No
Pro Shop: Yes
Payment: Cash, Credit Cards
Tee Times: Weekends
Fee 9 Holes: Weekday: $16.00
Fee 18 Holes: Weekday: $16.00
Cart Rental: $25.00/18 $15.00/9
Lessons: No **School:** No
Driving Range: No
Other: Snack bar

Tees	Holes	Yards	Par	USGA	Slope
BACK	9	6278	72	70.0	123
MIDDLE	9	6046	72	69.4	121
FRONT	9	5302	72	72.4	126

Weekend: $25.00
Weekend: $25.00
Discounts: None
Junior Golf: No **Membership:** Yes
Non-Metal Spikes: Required

This course is narrow with water holes and tree-lined fairways. Open May 1 - November 1. Off season rates. www.fryeisland.com.

	1	2	3	4	5	6	7	8	9
PAR	4	5	4	3	4	4	5	3	4
YARDS	378	481	391	160	358	293	456	155	351
HDCP	7	5	1	13	11	17	9	15	3
	10	11	12	13	14	15	16	17	18
PAR	4	5	4	3	4	4	5	3	4
YARDS	378	481	391	160	358	293	456	155	351
HDCP	8	6	2	14	12	18	10	16	4

Directions: Take Exit 8 (Westbrook) to Route 302 (2 mi.) to Raymond Cape Rd. (20 mi.) to Frye Island Ferry Landing (5 mi.).

Golf at Province Lake ▶ 15

Parsonsfield, ME Route 153 (207) 793-9577

Club Pro: Rob S. Berube
Pro Shop: Yes
Payment: Visa, MC
Tee Times: Yes

Tees	Holes	Yards	Par	USGA	Slope
BACK	18	6500	71	70.0	119
MIDDLE	18	5900	71	68.8	114
FRONT	18	5000	71	69	112

Fee 9 Holes: Weekday: $18.00   **Weekend:** $20.00
Fee 18 Holes: Weekday: $28.00   **Weekend:** $32.00
Cart Rental: $11 pp   **Discounts:** Junior
Lessons: $20.00/half hour **School:** No   **Junior Golf:** Yes **Membership:** Yes
Driving Range: Yes   **Non-Metal Spikes:** Required
Other: Clubhouse / Snack bar / Restaurant / Bar-lounge / Function Room

COUPON

Good back nine. Challenging course. Stay & Play affiliate is Purity Springs Resort in E. Madison, NH.

	1	2	3	4	5	6	7	8	9
PAR	4	5	3	4	3	5	4	4	4
YARDS	270	452	211	342	155	550	380	370	327
HDCP	15	3	17	9	17	1	7	9	11
	10	11	12	13	14	15	16	17	18
PAR	4	3	4	4	3	5	4	4	4
YARDS	335	150	304	333	118	480	387	366	284
HDCP	8	16	14	10	18	2	6	4	12

Directions: I-95 to Route 16 (Spaulding Tpk.) to Route 153. Go 12 miles north. OR access Route 153 from Route 25.

Goose River GC ▶ 16

Rockport, ME (207) 236-8488

Club Pro: Chris Christie
Pro Shop: Full inventory
Payment: Cash, MC, Visa
Tee Times: Yes

Tees	Holes	Yards	Par	USGA	Slope
BACK	N/A				
MIDDLE	9	6056	71	68.5	119
FRONT	9	5208	72	68.5	119

Fee 9 Holes: Weekday: $15.00   **Weekend:** $15.00
Fee 18 Holes: Weekday: $25.00   **Weekend:** $25.00
Cart Rental: $22.00/18 $12.00/9   **Discounts:** None
Lessons: $30.00/half hour **School:** No   **Junior Golf:** Yes **Membership:** Yes
Driving Range: No   **Non-Metal Spikes:** Required
Other: Snack bar

A challenging course, Goose River comes into play on four holes. There are only nine greens but eighteen different tees. Open May - October 31.

	1	2	3	4	5	6	7	8	9
PAR	5	4	4	4	5	3	4	3	3
YARDS	581	341	372	403	495	163	326	189	179
HDCP	1	11	7	5	3	17	9	13	15
	10	11	12	13	14	15	16	17	18
PAR	5	4	4	4	5	3	4	3	4
YARDS	540	338	295	336	422	190	349	231	306
HDCP	2	8	16	6	4	18	10	14	12

Directions: North on I-95, north on Route 1. Follow Route 1 into Camden and follow signs.

4✪ =Excellent 3✪ =Very Good 2✪ =Good

Gorham Country Club 17

McLellan Rd., Gorham, ME (207) 839-3490

Club Pro: Mark Fogg
Pro Shop: Yes
Payment: Cash or check
Tee Times: Wknds/ Hldys
Fee 9 Holes: Weekday: $14.00
Fee 18 Holes: Weekday: $24.00
Cart Rental: $22.00/18 $12.00/9
Lessons: Yes **School:** No
Driving Range: Yes
Other: Lockers / Showers / Snack bar

Tees	Holes	Yards	Par	USGA	Slope
BACK	18	6552	71	70.1	120
MIDDLE	18	6334	71	68.3	116
FRONT	18	5868	73	71.4	124

Weekend: $14.00
Weekend: $24.00
Discounts: None
Junior Golf: Yes **Membership:** Yes
Non-Metal Spikes: Not Required

A championship 18-hole layout located on a Game Preserve. A beautiful and challenging course for all abilities.

	1	2	3	4	5	6	7	8	9
PAR	4	4	4	3	4	3	4	4	5
YARDS	324	344	369	160	406	141	391	378	488
HDCP	14	6	4	16	2	18	8	10	12
	10	11	12	13	14	15	16	17	18
PAR	5	4	4	3	4	3	4	4	5
YARDS	561	427	365	155	424	168	358	375	500
HDCP	9	3	5	17	1	15	11	7	13

Directions: Take I-95 to Exit 7. Follow Route 114 to Gorham. Take right onto McLellan Road.

Kennebec Heights Country Club 18

Rt. 201, Farmingdale, ME (207) 582-2000

Club Pro: Yes
Pro Shop: Full inventory
Payment: Visa, MC
Tee Times: Required
Fee 9 Holes: Weekday: $15.00
Fee 18 Holes: Weekday: $25.00
Cart Rental: $20.00/18, $11.00/9
Lessons: Yes **School:** Jr. & Sr.
Driving Range: $3.50/lg., $2.50/sm. bucket
Other: Snack bar

Tees	Holes	Yards	Par	USGA	Slope
BACK	18	6003	70	69.0	129
MIDDLE	18	5525	70	67.1	123
FRONT	18	4800	70	67.7	119

Weekend: $15.00
Weekend: $25.00
Discounts: Senior & Junior
Junior Golf: Yes **Membership:** Yes
Non-Metal Spikes: Preferred

COUPON

Recent back nine laid out by Cornish & Silva. Very impressive and very attractive.

	1	2	3	4	5	6	7	8	9
PAR	4	4	3	5	4	3	4	3	4
YARDS	274	297	105	461	381	185	210	162	330
HDCP	16	10	14	2	8	18	6	12	4
	10	11	12	13	14	15	16	17	18
PAR	4	4	3	4	5	3	4	4	5
YARDS	241	300	136	279	502	145	336	392	489
HDCP	11	15	13	5	1	17	7	9	3

Directions: Take I-95 to Augusta Exit; follow Route 202. Take Route 201 South to course.

Lake Kezar CC

Lovell, ME (207) 925-2462

Tees	Holes	Yards	Par	USGA	Slope
BACK	18	5961	72	63.3	117
MIDDLE	18	5585	72	65.7	111
FRONT	18	5088	72	68.8	114

Club Pro:
Pro Shop: Limited inventory
Payment: Cash only
Tee Times: 7 days adv. members,
Fee 9 Holes: Weekday: $14.00 **Weekend:** $16.00
Fee 18 Holes: Weekday: $20.00 **Weekend:** $24.00
Cart Rental: $20.00/18 $11.00/9 **Discounts:** None
Lessons: $15/hlf hour, $20 couple **School:** No **Junior Golf:** Yes **Membership:** Yes
Driving Range: No **Non-Metal Spikes:** Required
Other: Snack bar / Bar-lounge

Very scenic, pine trees, mountains, meandering brook, quiet. Design by Ross. Club was one room school house. Nine more holes opened in 1998.

	1	2	3	4	5	6	7	8	9
PAR	4	4	4	4	3	4	3	5	4
YARDS	292	305	299	291	136	383	201	498	272
HDCP	7	9	11	15	17	1	3	5	13
	10	11	12	13	14	15	16	17	18
PAR	5	4	3	4	5	4	3	4	5
YARDS	450	278	123	334	481	326	153	282	526
HDCP	12	10	18	6	4	8	16	14	2

Directions: Take I-95 to Route 302. At the base of Pleasant Mountain, take right onto Knights Hill Rd., follow to Lovell Village. Go north on Route 5. Course is 2 miles up on Route 5.

Maple Lane Inn and Golf Club

Livermore, ME (207) 897-6666

Tees	Holes	Yards	Par	USGA	Slope
BACK	9	6038	70	65	118
MIDDLE	9	5594	70	62.8	114
FRONT	9	705330	70	65.8	118

Club Pro: Dennis Grasso
Pro Shop: Full inventory
Payment: Visa, MC
Tee Times: No
Fee 9 Holes: Weekday: $11.00 **Weekend:** $13.00
Fee 18 Holes: Weekday: $15.00 **Weekend:** $18.00
Cart Rental: $20.00 **Discounts:** Senior
Lessons: Yes **School:** Jr. & Sr. **Junior Golf:** Yes **Membership:** Yes
Driving Range: No **Non-Metal Spikes:** Not Required
Other: Snack bar/ Dining room and patio/ Hotel

Newly remodeled course. 5 Bedroom Inn (Affordable Golf), Stay and Play Packages.
www.Livfalls.com/mapleIn.HTML

	1	2	3	4	5	6	7	8	9
PAR	4	5	3	4	5	4	4	3	3
YARDS	356	347	555	370	155	170	348	540	168
HDCP	11	9	5	1	17	15	3	7	13
	10	11	12	13	14	15	16	17	18
PAR	4	4	5	4	3	3	4	5	3
YARDS	356	347	555	370	155	170	358	540	168
HDCP	12	10	6	2	18	16	4	8	14

Directions: Take I-95 to Auburn Exit. Take Route 4 to Livermore- Livermore Falls town line. Take a right before bridge onto River Rd. (From Augusta, take Route 17 S to 133 N.)

4✪ =Excellent 3✪ =Very Good 2✪ =Good

Merriland Farm Par 3 Golf　21

Wells, ME (207) 646-0508

Club Pro:
Pro Shop: No
Payment: Cash only
Tee Times: No
Fee 9 Holes: Weekday: $9.00
Fee 18 Holes: Weekday: $14.00
Cart Rental: No
Lessons: No **School:** No
Driving Range:
Other: Cafe specializing in raspberry & blueberry baked goods.

Weekend: $9.00
Weekend: $14.00
Discounts: None
Junior Golf: No **Membership:** Yes
Non-Metal Spikes: Required

Tees	Holes	Yards	Par	USGA	Slope
BACK					
MIDDLE	9	838	27		
FRONT					

A well maintained par 3 course that will challenge the short game of an experienced player, yet allow new golfers to enjoy the game.

	1	2	3	4	5	6	7	8	9
PAR	3	3	3	3	3	3	3	3	3
YARDS	83	96	119	111	67	86	63	109	104
HDCP									
	10	11	12	13	14	15	16	17	18
PAR									
YARDS									
HDCP									

Directions: I-95 to Exit 2(Wells). Left onto Route 109 to mile to Route 1. Left onto Route 1 about 1.5 miles to Coles Hill Road on left. !.5 Miles up Coles Hill Road to Course on right.

Naples Golf and Country Club　22

Route 114, Naples, ME. 207-693-6424

Club Pro: Harry W. Andrews, PGA
Pro Shop: Limited inventory
Payment: Visa, MC, DIS
Tee Times: No
Fee 9 Holes: Weekday: $18.00
Fee 18 Holes: Weekday: $24.00
Cart Rental: $24.00/18, $12.00/9
Lessons: $30/30 minutes **School:** No
Driving Range: No
Other: Full restaurant/ Clubhouse/ Bar/Lounge

Weekend: $18.00 after 1pm
Weekend: $24.00
Discounts: None
Junior Golf: No **Membership:** Yes
Non-Metal Spikes: Required

COUPON

Tees	Holes	Yards	Par	USGA	Slope
BACK	NA				
MIDDLE	9	6554	72	68.5	115
FRONT	9	5216	72	NA	113

Scenic on Lake.

	1	2	3	4	5	6	7	8	9
PAR	5	4	4	4	4	4	4	4	3
YARDS	480	350	365	425	375	347	405	365	165
HDCP	15	13	5	1	7	11	3	9	17
	10	11	12	13	14	15	16	17	18
PAR	5	4	4	4	4	4	4	4	3
YARDS	480	350	365	425	375	347	405	365	165
HDCP	16	14	6	2	8	12	4	10	18

Directions: Exit 8 from Maine Turnpike. Turn right on Riverside St.. 3 Miles to Route 302. Left on Route 302 for 30 miles to Naples. Take left on Route 114 in Naples Village. Course is 1 mile.

Nonesuch River Golf Club   23

Scarborough, ME (207) 883-0007

Club Pro: Anne McClure, PGA
Pro Shop: Yes
Payment: Visa, MC, Disc., Checks
Tee Times: 7 days adv.
Fee 9 Holes: Weekday: $15.00
Fee 18 Holes: Weekday: $27.00
Cart Rental: $24.00
Lessons: Yes **School:** Yes
Driving Range: $4.00/sm. $6.00/lg.
Other: Snack Bar/ Clubhouse/ Bar-Lounge

Tees	Holes	Yards	Par	USGA	Slope
BACK	18	6218	70	68.8	119
MIDDLE	18	6218	70	66.9	116
FRONT	18	5268	70	68.8	109

Weekend: $20.00
Weekend: $33.00
Discounts: None
Junior Golf: Yes **Membership:** Yes
Non-Metal Spikes: Required

COUPON

"True rolling greens its strong suit. A work in progress as fairways grow in." R.W. Bent grass tees, fairways and greens, excellent condition. Open April 25- Nov. 15. www.megolf.com

	1	2	3	4	5	6	7	8	9
PAR	4	3	5	3	4	3	4	4	4
YARDS	389	153	519	214	362	164	348	414	430
HDCP	13	17	1	11	15	7	9	5	3
	10	11	12	13	14	15	16	17	18
PAR	5	4	4	4	4	3	5	3	4
YARDS	492	373	333	397	381	160	489	174	426
HDCP	12	4	10	14	8	18	2	16	6

Directions: Maine Turnpike to Exit 6. Turn left out of toll. Turn left at Route 114. Course is .5 miles on left.

Norway Country Club   24

S ME

Norway, ME (207) 743-9840

Club Pro: Dave Mazzeo
Pro Shop: Full inventory
Payment: Cash, Checks
Tee Times: No
Fee 9 Holes: Weekday: $12.00
Fee 18 Holes: Weekday: $20.00 All Day
Cart Rental: $16.00/18 $8.00/9
Lessons: $35/30 min. **School:** Clinics
Driving Range: Open to public
Other: Restaurant / Clubhouse / Snack bar / Bar-lounge

Tees	Holes	Yards	Par	USGA	Slope
BACK	N/R				
MIDDLE	9	5808	70	66.6	107
FRONT					

Weekend: $12.00
Weekend: $20.00
Discounts: None
Junior Golf: Yes **Membership:** Yes
Non-Metal Spikes: N/R

COUPON

Recent upgrades to course and clubhouse. New driving range.

	1	2	3	4	5	6	7	8	9
PAR	4	3	4	4	4	3	5	4	4
YARDS	375	187	327	300	430	167	465	420	233
HDCP	9	7	11	13	1	15	5	3	17
	10	11	12	13	14	15	16	17	18
PAR	4	3	4	4	4	3	5	4	4
YARDS	375	187	327	300	430	167	465	420	233
HDCP	10	8	12	14	2	16	6	4	18

Directions: Take I-95 to Exit 11 (North Portland). Take Route 26 North to Norway, course is 1 mile past lake.

4 =Excellent 3 =Very Good 2 = Good   **Southern Maine   225**

Oakdale CC

25

River Road, Mexico, ME (207) 364-3951

Club Pro: Steve Hodgkins
Pro Shop:
Payment: Visa, MC, Dis
Tee Times: Weekends, am.
Fee 9 Holes: Weekday: $15.00
Fee 18 Holes: Weekday: $15.00
Cart Rental: $24.00/18, $12.00/9
Lessons: $20.00/ 30 min. **School:** No
Driving Range:
Other: Club house, snack bar, cocktails.

Tees	Holes	Yards	Par	USGA	Slope
BACK	N/A				
MIDDLE	9	6198	72	68.8	119
FRONT	9	5757	74	73.9	125

Weekend: $20.00
Weekend: $20.00
Discounts: None
Junior Golf: Yes **Membership:** Yes
Non-Metal Spikes: Required

Course built in 1923. Hilly fairways and challenging greens.

	1	2	3	4	5	6	7	8	9
PAR	4	5	4	3	4	4	4	4	4
YARDS	327	515	340	175	440	390	295	233	365
HDCP	11	15	13	6	1	3	9	17	7
PAR	10	11	12	13	14	15	16	17	18
YARDS	345	498	350	150	460	380	340	200	395
HDCP	12	18	14	4	16	6	10	8	2

Directions: I-95 to exit 12, the route 4 North to Route 108 towards Rumford. Then to Route 2 West to course.

Old Orchard Beach CC

26

Old Orchard Beach, ME (207) 934-4513

Club Pro: Gene McNabb
Pro Shop: Full inventory
Payment: Visa, MC, Amex
Tee Times: No
Fee 9 Holes: Weekday: $15.00
Fee 18 Holes: Weekday: $22.00
Cart Rental: $19.00/18, $11.00/9
Lessons: $18/30 min. **School:** No
Driving Range: Yes
Other: No

Tees	Holes	Yards	Par	USGA	Slope
BACK	9	2953	35	N/A	N/A
MIDDLE	9	2744	35	66.4	114
FRONT	9	2584	35	69.7	113

Weekend: $15.00
Weekend: $22.00
Discounts: None
Junior Golf: Yes **Membership:** Yes
Non-Metal Spikes: Required

COUPON

Well conditioned, sporty layout. Twi-light rate at 5 pm every day is $10.00. www.dunegrass.com

	1	2	3	4	5	6	7	8	9
PAR	4	4	4	3	4	4	4	3	5
YARDS	378	380	340	126	339	282	298	156	445
HDCP	5	3	9	17	7	15	13	11	1
	10	11	12	13	14	15	16	17	18
PAR									
YARDS									
HDCP									

Directions: Exit 5 off Route 95 to 2B (Route 1 North). In 1/10 mile take Ross Road off Route 1 (on right) for 2 miles to Wild Dunes Way on right. Follow signs.

Paris Hill Country Club 27

Paris Hill Rd., Paris, ME (207) 743-2371

Club Pro: Harvey LaMontagne
Pro Shop: Full inventory
Payment: Cash or check
Tee Times: No
Fee 9 Holes: Weekday: $15.00
Fee 18 Holes: Weekday: $15.00
Cart Rental: $16.00/18 $8.00/9
Lessons: $25-$45/half hour **School:** Yes
Driving Range: No
Other: Clubhouse / Snack bar / Bar-lounge

Tees	Holes	Yards	Par	USGA	Slope
BACK	N/A				
MIDDLE	9	4637	66	62.1	102
FRONT	N/A				

Weekend: $15.00
Weekend: $15.00 all day
Discounts: None
Junior Golf: N/R **Membership:** Yes
Non-Metal Spikes: Not Required

COUPON

Built in 1899 overlooking beautiful Oxford Hills and mountains. Home of world renowned Harvey LaMontagne Golf Improvement Center. Open May - October. Twilight rates.

	1	2	3	4	5	6	7	8	9
PAR	4	4	4	3	4	3	4	3	4
YARDS	350	260	231	194	352	125	309	129	355
HDCP	5	11	13	9	1	17	7	15	3
	10	11	12	13	14	15	16	17	18
PAR	4	4	4	3	4	3	4	3	4
YARDS	350	260	231	221	352	125	309	129	355
HDCP	6	12	14	10	2	18	8	16	4

Directions: Off Route 26 South Paris.

Pleasant Hill CC 28

S ME

Scarborough, ME (207) 883-4425

Club Pro: Gene McNabb
Pro Shop: Limited inventory
Payment: Cash only
Tee Times: No
Fee 9 Holes: Weekday: $12.00
Fee 18 Holes: Weekday: $12.00
Cart Rental: Pull Carts
Lessons: $18.00/half hour **School:** N/R
Driving Range: No
Other: Snack bar

Tees	Holes	Yards	Par	USGA	Slope
BACK	N/A				
MIDDLE	9	4786	34	62.3	87
FRONT					

Weekend: $14.00
Weekend: $14.00
Discounts: Senior
Junior Golf: No **Membership:** N/R
Non-Metal Spikes: N/R

The course is well conditioned, very level and considered an easy walker. Popular with senior citizens who do not use auto carts.

	1	2	3	4	5	6	7	8	9
PAR	4	4	4	4	3	3	4	4	4
YARDS	303	345	310	248	140	187	366	264	230
HDCP	N/A	N/A	N/A	N/A	N/A	N/A	N/A	N/A	N/A
	10	11	12	13	14	15	16	17	18
PAR									
YARDS									
HDCP									

Directions: Take I-95 to Route 1 South Portland Exit. Follow Route 1 South. Turn left at Pleasant Hill; right onto Chamberlain Road to course.

4✪ =Excellent 3✪ =Very Good 2✪ =Good

Point Sebago Golf Club   ★★★   29

Route 302, Casco, ME (207) 655-7948

Club Pro: Fran O'Keefe, PGA
Pro Shop: Full inventory
Payment: Visa, MC, Disc.
Tee Times: 7 days in adv.
Fee 9 Holes: Weekday: $25.00   **Weekend:** $29.00
Fee 18 Holes: Weekday: $45.00   **Weekend:** $55.00
Cart Rental: Included   **Discounts:** None
Lessons: $30/30 min. $50/hr. **School:** Jr.,Sr.   **Junior Golf:** No **Membership:** Yes
Driving Range: Yes   **Non-Metal Spikes:** Required
Other: Resort/ Restaurant/ Snack Bar. Walking allowed.

Tees	Holes	Yards	Par	USGA	Slope
BACK	18	7002	72	73.7	135
MIDDLE	18	6474	72	71.3	130
FRONT	18	5645	72	67.5	122

COUPON

A Golf and Beach Resort with an 18 hole championship course, 10 tennis courts and extensive beaches and boat slips. Resort entertainment. **www.pointsebago.com**

	1	2	3	4	5	6	7	8	9
PAR	5	3	4	4	4	4	5	3	4
YARDS	502	154	388	375	335	383	549	181	418
HDCP	7	17	5	11	9	15	1	13	3
	10	11	12	13	14	15	16	17	18
PAR	4	5	4	4	3	4	4	3	5
YARDS	390	533	380	370	163	302	361	183	507
HDCP	12	2	6	8	18	14	10	16	4

Directions: Turn off Maine Turnpike at Exit 8 and follow signs to Route 302 West for approximately 22.5. Look for Chute's Cafe in Casco. Take next left at church.

Poland Spring CC   30

Rt. 26, Poland Spring, ME (207) 998-6002

Club Pro:
Pro Shop: Full inventory
Payment: Cash or credit card
Tee Times: Yes
Fee 9 Holes: Weekday: N/A   **Weekend:** N/A
Fee 18 Holes: Weekday: $21.00   **Weekend:** $21.00
Cart Rental: $21.00/18   **Discounts:** None
Lessons: No **School:** No   **Junior Golf:** No **Membership:** Yes
Driving Range: No   **Non-Metal Spikes:** Required
Other: Clubhouse / Lockers / Showers / Snack bar / Restaurant / Bar-lounge / Hotel

Tees	Holes	Yards	Par	USGA	Slope
BACK	18	6200	71	68.2	119
MIDDLE	18	5854	71	67.2	117
FRONT	18	5097	74	68.6	110

Oldest eighteen hole resort course in U.S (1893) designed by Donald Ross. Played by sports legends as well as many U.S. Presidents. Open May 1-Nov. 1. **www.polandspringinns.com**

	1	2	3	4	5	6	7	8	9
PAR	4	4	4	4	4	3	4	3	4
YARDS	340	303	387	407	309	145	380	179	316
HDCP	9	11	1	5	13	17	3	15	7
	10	11	12	13	14	15	16	17	18
PAR	4	5	4	3	4	4	5	4	4
YARDS	294	410	287	159	401	410	531	265	331
HDCP	16	8	12	18	4	2	6	14	10

Directions: Take Maine Turnpike Exit 11 (Gray) to Route 26, approx. 10 miles to course.

Prospect Hill GC   31

So. Main St., Auburn, ME (207) 782-9220

Club Pro: Ron Vaillancourt
Pro Shop: Full inventory
Payment: Visa, MC, Disc
Tee Times: No
Fee 9 Holes: Weekday: $10.00
Fee 18 Holes: Weekday: $16.00
Cart Rental: $18.00/18 $10.00/9
Lessons: $25.00/half hour **School:** Yes
Driving Range: No
Other: Snack bar / Bar-lounge

Tees	Holes	Yards	Par	USGA	Slope
BACK	N/A				
MIDDLE	18	5846	71	69.9	110
FRONT	18	5227	71	69.9	111

Weekend: $12.00
Weekend: $18.00
Discounts: None
Junior Golf: Yes **Membership:** Yes
Non-Metal Spikes: Required

COUPON

The front nine are wide open with a few small creeks, while the back nine have four ponds and tree-lined fairways.

	1	2	3	4	5	6	7	8	9
PAR	5	4	3	4	3	4	4	4	4
YARDS	460	350	210	230	225	395	370	260	290
HDCP	5	9	17	16	14	8	4	12	13
	10	11	12	13	14	15	16	17	18
PAR	4	4	5	4	4	3	4	4	4
YARDS	412	290	510	276	357	138	366	311	396
HDCP	1	11	6	10	3	18	2	15	7

Directions: Take I-95 to Exit 12, left off ramp, look for signs.

River Meadow GC   32

Lincoln St., Westbrook, ME (207) 854-1625

Club Pro: Dick Dennison
Pro Shop: Full inventory
Payment: Cash only
Tee Times: No
Fee 9 Holes: Weekday: $12.00
Fee 18 Holes: Weekday: $12.00
Cart Rental: $16.00/18 $9.00/9
Lessons: $25/30 min. **School:** Yes
Driving Range: No
Other: Clubhouse / Snack bar

Tees	Holes	Yards	Par	USGA	Slope
BACK	9	5830	70	67.0	112
MIDDLE	9	5518	70	67.0	112
FRONT	9	5210	72	67.0	112

Weekend: $14.00
Weekend: $14.00
Discounts: Senior
Junior Golf: N/R **Membership:** Yes
Non-Metal Spikes: Required

S ME

Rolling terrain with plenty of brooks and streams running through it. Lots of trees, not much sand, ponds. Greens are excellent. Open April 1st - November 15th.

	1	2	3	4	5	6	7	8	9
PAR	4	4	4	3	4	4	4	3	5
YARDS	371	411	248	139	350	350	295	150	445
HDCP	7	1	11	15	3	9	13	17	5
	10	11	12	13	14	15	16	17	18
PAR	4	4	4	3	4	4	4	3	5
YARDS	371	411	248	139	350	350	295	150	445
HDCP	8	2	12	16	6	10	14	18	6

Directions: Maine Turnpike to Exit 8 to Route 25 into Westbrook. In town take a right onto Bridge St. at the lights. First left onto Lincoln St. to course.

4⊙ =Excellent 3⊙ =Very Good 2⊙ =Good   **Southern Maine 229**

Riverside Municipal Golf Course   33

Riverside St., Portland, ME (207) 797-3524

Club Pro: David Grygiel
Pro Shop: Full inventory
Payment: Visa, MC, Cash
Tee Times: Weekends

Tees	Holes	Yards	Par	USGA	Slope
BACK	18	6370	72	69.2	115
MIDDLE	18	6052	72	67.5	112
FRONT	18	5630	73	70.7	112

Fee 9 Holes: Weekday: $12.00   **Weekend:** $15.00
Fee 18 Holes: Weekday: $18.00   **Weekend:** $22.00
Cart Rental: $22.00/18 $11.00/9   **Discounts:** Senior & Junior. Weekdays
Lessons: $30.00/30 min **School:** No   **Junior Golf:** Yes **Membership:** Yes
Driving Range: $4.00/lg. bucket   **Non-Metal Spikes:** Required
Other: Clubhouse / Lockers / Showers / Snack bar / Restaurant / Bar-lounge

27 holes available. South course is an additional 9 hole regulation course with 3102 yards. Wide fairways, medium speed greens, only a little hilly. Open April 15 - November 10.

	1	2	3	4	5	6	7	8	9
PAR	5	4	3	5	4	3	4	4	4
YARDS	450	365	202	488	322	197	314	324	396
HDCP	5	7	15	3	9	17	11	13	1
	10	11	12	13	14	15	16	17	18
PAR	5	4	4	3	4	4	4	4	4
YARDS	540	384	414	167	346	338	334	374	382
HDCP	6	8	2	18	10	16	14	12	4

Directions: Maine Turnpike to Exit 8. Follow signs to course.

Rockland Golf Club   34

Old County Rd, Rockland, ME (207) 594-9322

Club Pro: Eenan Flanagan
Pro Shop: Full inventory
Payment: Visa, MC
Tee Times: 2 days adv.

Tees	Holes	Yards	Par	USGA	Slope
BACK	18	6121	70	69.3	118
MIDDLE	18	6010	70	67.2	109
FRONT	18	5583	73	71.8	119

Fee 9 Holes: Weekday: $20.00   **Weekend:** $20.00
Fee 18 Holes: Weekday: $35.00   **Weekend:** $35.00
Cart Rental: $24.00/18 $16.00/9 **Discounts:** None
Lessons: $25.00/half hour **School:** No   **Junior Golf:** Yes **Membership:** Yes
Driving Range: No   **Non-Metal Spikes:** Required
Other: Clubhouse / Bar-lounge / Snack Bar / Showers

The front nine are wooded, while the back nine are in the open overlooking a lake. The first hole has a nice ocean view. Considered to have the finest putting surfaces.

	1	2	3	4	5	6	7	8	9
PAR	5	4	4	4	3	4	5	4	3
YARDS	529	385	266	367	132	300	472	414	216
HDCP	6	14	18	10	16	12	8	2	4
	10	11	12	13	14	15	16	17	18
PAR	3	3	4	4	4	5	4	4	3
YARDS	195	223	290	446	394	595	345	251	190
HDCP	11	3	15	1	5	7	9	17	13

Directions: I-95 to Coastal Route 1 through Thomaston. Left onto old Country Road to course 3.5 miles on left.

Sable Oaks Golf Club ✪✪✪ 35

S. Portland, ME (207) 775-6257

Club Pro: Jim Furlong
Pro Shop: Full inventory
Payment: Visa, MC, Disc
Tee Times: Recommended/7 days
Fee 9 Holes: Weekday: $16.00
Fee 18 Holes: Weekday: $27.00
Cart Rental: $22.00/18 $14/9
Lessons: $25.00/45 min. **School:** No
Driving Range: No
Other: Hotel/Snack bar / Bar-lounge / Function Hall/ Showers / Locker room

Tees	Holes	Yards	Par	USGA	Slope
BACK	18	6359	70	71.8	138
MIDDLE	18	6056	70	70.4	134
FRONT	18	4786	72	69.4	116

Weekend: $20.00 after 3:00
Weekend: $34.00
Discounts: None
Junior Golf: Membership: No
Non-Metal Spikes: Not Required

COUPON

Championship course, rated #2 in Maine by *Golf Digest*. Requires accuracy. The par five 14th is a beautiful signature hole. Adjacent to South Portland Marriott. A Friel Golf Company

	1	2	3	4	5	6	7	8	9
PAR	4	5	4	4	5	3	4	3	4
YARDS	389	460	419	398	442	170	319	138	394
HDCP	8	16	2	4	12	14	10	18	6
	10	11	12	13	14	15	16	17	18
PAR	4	3	4	3	5	4	4	3	4
YARDS	378	159	437	171	443	384	383	164	408
HDCP	15	13	1	7	11	3	9	17	5

Directions: Take I-95 to Exit 7 (Maine Mall) Go right at light. At 4th light, go left on Running Hill Rd. Take the second right onto Country Club Drive.

Salmon Falls GC 36

S ME

Hollis, ME (207) 929-5233 or 1-800-734-1616

Club Pro: John Barber, PGA
Pro Shop: Full inventory
Payment: Visa, MC, Amex
Tee Times: 5 days adv.
Fee 9 Holes: Weekday: $13.00
Fee 18 Holes: Weekday: $20.00
Cart Rental: $20.00/18 $10.00/9
Lessons: $25/half hour $35/hour **School:** Jr.
Driving Range: $3.50/med bucket
Other: Clubhouse / Snack bar / Restaurant / Bar-lounge / Hotel

Tees	Holes	Yards	Par	USGA	Slope
BACK	N/A				
MIDDLE	18	5848	72	67.6	119
FRONT	18	5193	70	69.5	121

Weekend: $13.00
Weekend: $20.00
Discounts: Sr. 65 plus- $17.00/18
Junior Golf: Yes **Membership:** No
Non-Metal Spikes: Preferred

COUPON

The course is considered fairly open, with scenic views along the Saco River. Beginners are asked to come after 1 p.m. on weekends. Motel and restaurant on site. **www.milepost.org/co/sr**

	1	2	3	4	5	6	7	8	9
PAR	4	4	3	5	5	3	4	4	4
YARDS	365	250	190	500	455	165	303	251	404
HDCP	4	18	8	6	10	12	14	16	2
	10	11	12	13	14	15	16	17	18
PAR	4	4	3	5	5	3	4	4	4
YARDS	380	245	235	510	460	165	310	265	395
HDCP	5	17	1	7	9	11	13	15	3

Directions: I-95 to Exit 5 (Saco), follow Route 112 North. Follow signs.

4✪ =Excellent 3✪ =Very Good 2✪ =Good

Samoset Resort GC 37

220 Warrenton St., Rockport, ME (207) 594-1431

Club Pro: Bob O'Brian
Pro Shop: Full inventory
Payment: All major cards, checks
Tee Times: Yes

Tees	Holes	Yards	Par	USGA	Slope
BACK	18	6548	70	70.8	129
MIDDLE	18	6018	70	69.7	125
FRONT	18	5620	70	68.4	122

Fee 9 Holes: Weekday: $30.00-$60.00 **Weekend:** $30.00-$60.00
Fee 18 Holes: Weekday: $55.00-$100.00 **Weekend:** $55.00-$100.00
Cart Rental: $30.00/18 $18.00/9 **Discounts:** Senior & Junior
Lessons: $30.00/half hour **School:** Jr. & Sr. **Junior Golf:** Yes **Membership:** Yes
Driving Range: $4.50/bucket **Non-Metal Spikes:** Required
Other: Clubhouse / Snack bar / Restaurant / Bar-lounge / Resort Hotel / Golf Simulator

Golf Clubhouse opened in 1997; pro shop, indoor golf, locker rooms, and an 80-seat restaurant. Reduced rates for hotel guests. www.samoset.com

	1	2	3	4	5	6	7	8	9
PAR	4	4	3	5	4	4	3	4	4
YARDS	355	388	190	481	298	380	176	330	312
HDCP	4	8	14	12	18	2	6	10	16
	10	11	12	13	14	15	16	17	18
PAR	4	3	5	3	4	4	4	4	4
YARDS	338	120	494	208	375	355	435	400	383
HDCP	13	17	3	7	15	11	1	9	5

Directions: Maine Turnpike to Exit 9, Route 95 to Exit 22, Route 1 North through Rockland. Turn right onto Waldo Avenue.

Sanford Country Club 38

Rt. 4, Sanford, ME (207) 324-5462

Club Pro: Mark L'Heureux
Pro Shop: Full inventory
Payment: Cash, Visa, MC
Tee Times: Yes

Tees	Holes	Yards	Par	USGA	Slope
BACK	18	6726	72	73.2	128
MIDDLE	18	6217	72	70.5	122
FRONT	18	5320	74	66.5	114

Fee 9 Holes: Weekday: **Weekend:**
Fee 18 Holes: Weekday: $27.00 **Weekend:** $30.00
Cart Rental: $24.00/18 $12.00/9 **Discounts:** None
Lessons: $30.00/45 min **School:** Jr. **Junior Golf:** Yes **Membership:** Yes
Driving Range: $4.00 **Non-Metal Spikes:** Required
Other: Restaurant / Clubhouse / Bar-lounge / Lockers / Snack bar / Showers

Open April 15 - November 15. Twilight after 5 pm rate.

	1	2	3	4	5	6	7	8	9
PAR	4	4	5	4	4	4	4	3	4
YARDS	342	313	557	417	348	429	332	135	423
HDCP	11	15	7	5	9	1	13	17	3
	10	11	12	13	14	15	16	17	18
PAR	4	4	5	4	4	4	4	3	4
YARDS	349	325	565	425	356	435	340	145	430
HDCP	12	16	8	6	10	2	14	18	4

Directions: From I-95 Exit 2 head north on Route 109 for approx. 10 miles to Route 4 Intersection. Take left off 109 to Route 4 South for 2.5 miles. Located on left.

South Portland Muni.

39

Wescott Rd., S. Portland, ME (207) 775-0005

Club Pro:
Pro Shop: Limited inventory
Payment: Cash/Check only
Tee Times: No
Fee 9 Holes: Weekday: $9.00
Fee 18 Holes: Weekday: $9.00
Cart Rental: Pull carts
Lessons: Group lessons **School:** No
Driving Range: No
Other: Snack bar

Tees	Holes	Yards	Par	USGA	Slope
BACK					
MIDDLE	9	2071	33	59.0	92
FRONT					

Weekend: $10.00
Weekend: $10.00
Discounts: None
Junior Golf: No **Membership:** Yes, residents
Non-Metal Spikes: Not Required

Well maintained! Polite staff! Carts are not required.

	1	2	3	4	5	6	7	8	9
PAR	4	3	4	3	5	3	3	4	4
YARDS	340	140	238	132	372	167	122	285	275
HDCP	N/A								
	10	11	12	13	14	15	16	17	18
PAR									
YARDS									
HDCP									

Directions: Take I 95 to Exit 3 (Westbrook Street). Go East on Westbrook Street (about 3/10 of a mile). Take a left onto Wescott Street. The clubhouse is on the left under Bradts Memorial Library.

Spring Brook GC

40

S ME

Rt. 202, Leeds, ME (207) 946-5900

Club Pro: Dick Carroll
Pro Shop: Full inventory
Payment: Visa, MC
Tee Times: Weekends, Holidays
Fee 9 Holes: Weekday: $15.00 after 2 pm
Fee 18 Holes: Weekday: $20.00 all day
Cart Rental: $20.00/18
Lessons: $25.00/30 min **School:** No
Driving Range: $2.00 bucket
Other: Clubhouse / Lockers / Showers / Snack bar / Bar-lounge

Tees	Holes	Yards	Par	USGA	Slope
BACK	18	6408	71	70.4	127
MIDDLE	18	6163	71	69.2	125
FRONT	18	4989	74	70.8	123

Weekend: $15.00 after 2pm
Weekend: $20.00 all day
Discounts: Senior
Junior Golf: Yes **Membership:** Yes
Non-Metal Spikes: Not Required

A Scottish-style course with rolling hills and Scottish-style rough. The course has many blind shots. Challenging to the average player. Known to have some of the best greens in Maine.

	1	2	3	4	5	6	7	8	9
PAR	4	3	4	4	4	4	5	3	4
YARDS	415	160	410	350	335	385	520	168	340
HDCP	7	17	1	9	13	5	3	15	11
	10	11	12	13	14	15	16	17	18
PAR	4	4	5	3	4	3	5	4	4
YARDS	420	290	460	180	350	210	480	325	365
HDCP	4	18	12	16	14	2	6	10	8

Directions: Maine Turnpike to Lewiston Exit to Route 202 East. Course is 10 miles outside of Lewiston-Auburn.

4✪ =Excellent 3✪ =Very Good 2✪ =Good

Turner Highland Golf Course

41

Turner, ME (207) 224-7060

Club Pro: No
Pro Shop: Full inventory
Payment: Yes
Tee Times: Yes
Fee 9 Holes: Weekday: $14.00
Fee 18 Holes: Weekday: $20.00
Cart Rental: $20/18, $12/9
Lessons: Yes **School:** No
Driving Range: $2/bucket
Other: Lockers, showers, snack bar, restaurant.

Tees	Holes	Yards	Par	USGA	Slope
BACK	N/A				
MIDDLE	18	6008	71	N/A	N/A
FRONT	18	4726	71	N/A	N/A

Weekend: $14.00
Weekend: $20.00
Discounts: None
Junior Golf: No **Membership:** Yes
Non-Metal Spikes: Required

COUPON

Now 18 holes. Back 9 opened in August 1997. A scenic golf course situated high on a hill. "A well maintained local popular favorite." S.R.

	1	2	3	4	5	6	7	8	9
PAR	4	5	4	3	4	5	4	3	4
YARDS	280	442	282	149	365	452	372	204	376
HDCP	14	12	16	18	2	4	10	6	8
	10	11	12	13	14	15	16	17	18
PAR	3	4	4	4	5	3	5	4	3
YARDS	135	365	370	430	592	125	500	387	182
HDCP	17	7	13	1	3	15	11	5	9

Directions: Exit 12 from I-95 towards Auburn. Get onto Route 4 North. Turn right onto Route 117. Stay on Route 117 for 8.5 miles. Course is on the right.

Twin Falls Golf Course

42

364 Spring St., Westbrook, ME (207) 854-5397

Club Pro: No
Pro Shop: Limited inventory
Payment: Cash only
Tee Times: No
Fee 9 Holes: Weekday: $12.00
Fee 18 Holes: Weekday: $12.00
Cart Rental: $16.00/18 $8.00/9
Lessons: No **School:** No
Driving Range: No
Other: Clubhouse / Snack bar

Tees	Holes	Yards	Par	USGA	Slope
BACK	N/R				
MIDDLE	18	4880	66	61.3	90
FRONT	N/R				

Weekend: $14.00
Weekend: $14.00
Discounts: Senior Wkdays $11
Junior Golf: No **Membership:** Yes
Non-Metal Spikes: Not Required

"Fine public course for beginners. Course dates only to 1970, but has old time feel. Keep your drive on #1 to the left of center as the brook hidden from view will come into play." A.P.

	1	2	3	4	5	6	7	8	9
PAR	4	3	3	4	4	3	4	4	4
YARDS	364	165	137	374	408	185	248	301	258
HDCP	1	15	17	3	5	13	11	7	9
	10	11	12	13	14	15	16	17	18
PAR	4	3	3	4	4	3	4	4	4
YARDS	364	165	137	374	408	185	248	301	258
HDCP	2	16	18	4	6	14	12	8	10

Directions: Take I-95 to Exit 7, follow Maine Mall Rd. to Spring Street to course.

Val Halla Golf Course 43

Cumberland, ME (207) 829-2225

Club Pro: Kevin Roberts
Pro Shop: Full inventory
Payment: Visa, MC
Tee Times: Yes
Fee 9 Holes: Weekday: $17.00
Fee 18 Holes: Weekday: $22.00
Cart Rental: Must rent cart
Lessons: $30.00/half hour **School:** No
Driving Range: $4.00/ bucket
Other: Snack bar / Lounge
Weekend: $17.00 after 2 pm
Weekend: $30.00
Discounts: Senior & Junior
Junior Golf: Yes **Membership:** Yes
Non-Metal Spikes: Required

Tees	Holes	Yards	Par	USGA	Slope
BACK	18	6567	72	71.1	126
MIDDLE	18	6201	72	69.3	122
FRONT	18	5437	72	71.4	120

COUPON

Bent grass, good shape, wooded, hilly, scenic, brooks and streams, excellent layout. Open April 15 - November 1.

	1	2	3	4	5	6	7	8	9
PAR	4	3	5	4	4	4	4	3	5
YARDS	350	142	553	383	394	340	369	175	484
HDCP	16	18	2	4	6	12	10	14	8
	10	11	12	13	14	15	16	17	18
PAR	4	4	3	5	5	4	4	3	4
YARDS	376	347	148	465	440	388	294	155	398
HDCP	7	11	13	9	5	1	15	17	3

Directions: From Portland take 295 N to Exit 10. Follow Route 9 to Cumberland Center. The course is off Greely Road on Val Halla Road.

Wawenock CC 44

S ME

Rt. 129, Walpole, ME (207) 563-3938

Club Pro: Leon Oliver
Pro Shop: Yes
Payment: MC, Visa
Tee Times: July - August
Fee 9 Holes: Weekday: $16.00
Fee 18 Holes: Weekday: $22.00
Cart Rental: $22.00/18 $14.00/9
Lessons: Yes **School:** No
Driving Range: Yes
Other: Clubhouse / Bar-Lounge / Snack bar / Showers
Weekend: $16.00
Weekend: $22.00
Discounts: None
Junior Golf: Yes **Membership:** Yes
Non-Metal Spikes: Preferred

Tees	Holes	Yards	Par	USGA	Slope
BACK	N/R				
MIDDLE	9	6112	70	70.0	120
FRONT					

A fine nine hole tract in the Boothbay Region. The course is fairly open, but challenging with small greens and hills. Open May - October.

	1	2	3	4	5	6	7	8	9
PAR	4	4	3	5	4	4	4	3	4
YARDS	330	339	235	527	412	294	357	134	368
HDCP	13	3	5	7	1	15	11	17	9
	10	11	12	13	14	15	16	17	18
PAR	4	4	3	5	4	4	4	3	4
YARDS	330	399	235	527	412	294	357	134	368
HDCP	14	4	6	8	2	16	12	18	10

Directions: Take Route 1 to Route 129; follow for 7 miles.

4⊙ = Excellent 3⊙ = Very Good 2⊙ = Good

West Newfield Golf Course   45

West Newfield, ME (207-793-2478)

Club Pro: Ray Leavitt, PGA
Pro Shop: Full inventory
Payment: cash or check
Tee Times: Suggested
Fee 9 Holes: Weekday: $15.00
Fee 18 Holes: Weekday: $15.00
Cart Rental: $15.00/18 $9.00/9
Lessons: $25.00/halfhour **School:** No
Driving Range: No
Weekend: $15.00
Weekend: $15.00
Discounts: Junior
Junior Golf: N/R **Membership:** Yes
Non-Metal Spikes: Not Required
Other: 200 year old tavern serving lunch and dinner. Available for golf outings. Adult, Jr. clinics.

Tees	Holes	Yards	Par	USGA	Slope
BACK					
MIDDLE	9	4340	64	N/A	
FRONT	N/A				

Open May to Nov. Executive golf course. New renovated holes for '98. Undulating greens mounded on sides. Scottish style links. Owner/designer is Brian Schlinder. Twilight rates.

	1	2	3	4	5	6	7	8	9
PAR	3	3	4	5	3	4	3	4	3
YARDS	125	135	350	485	155	320	150	320	130
HDCP	17	9	13	5	15	3	1	11	7
	10	11	12	13	14	15	16	17	18
PAR	3	3	4	5	3	4	3	4	3
YARDS	125	135	350	485	155	320	150	320	130
HDCP	18	10	14	6	16	4	2	12	8

Directions: I-95 to route 16. Take route 153 to East Wakefield. Then take route 110E for 1.5 miles from center of town. Left at first intersection. Stay on paved road to the course.

Westerly Winds GC   46

Westbrook, ME (207) 854-9463

Club Pro: No
Pro Shop: Limited inventory
Payment: Visa, MC
Tee Times: No
Fee 9 Holes: Weekday: $7.00
Fee 18 Holes: Weekday: $7.00
Cart Rental: No
Lessons: $30.00/half hour **School:** Jr. & Sr.
Driving Range: $8.00/Jumbo bucket
Weekend: No
Weekend: $8.00
Discounts: None
Junior Golf: Yes **Membership:** Yes
Non-Metal Spikes: Not Required
Other: Clubhouse / Snack bar / Miniature Golf / Batting Cages / Golf Clinics

Tees	Holes	Yards	Par	USGA	Slope
BACK					
MIDDLE	9	806	27		
FRONT					

COUPON

A "family oriented" par 3 course. Great place to learn and practice. Variety of sports available. Open March - October.

	1	2	3	4	5	6	7	8	9
PAR	3	3	3	3	3	3	3	3	3
YARDS	86	160	128	104	62	60	81	63	62
HDCP	5	1	2	4	9	3	6	8	7
	10	11	12	13	14	15	16	17	18
PAR									
YARDS									
HDCP									

Directions: Take I-95 to Exit 8. Approximately 5 minutes from Exit 8. Follow signs to course.

Western View Golf Club   47

Augusta, ME (207) 622-5309

Club Pro: Roland Duquette
Pro Shop: Limited inventory
Payment: Visa, MC, Amex, Disc
Tee Times: No
Fee 9 Holes: Weekday: $9.00
Fee 18 Holes: Weekday: $12.00
Cart Rental: $14.00/18 $9.00/9
Lessons: $25/30 min. **School:** N/R
Driving Range: $3.00/bucket
Other: Snack bar / Clubhouse / Bar-lounge

Tees	Holes	Yards	Par	USGA	Slope
BACK	NA				
MIDDLE	9	5400	70	64.5	107
FRONT	9	5012	72	68.0	110

Weekend: $10.00
Weekend: $14.00
Discounts: Junior, if member.
Junior Golf: Yes **Membership:** Yes
Non-Metal Spikes: Not Required

Fairly challenging. Hilly and slopey.

	1	2	3	4	5	6	7	8	9
PAR	4	3	4	3	5	4	4	4	4
YARDS	305	180	260	150	445	315	285	385	375
HDCP	7	15	13	17	1	11	9	3	5
	10	11	12	13	14	15	16	17	18
PAR	4	3	4	3	5	4	4	4	4
YARDS	305	180	260	150	445	315	285	385	375
HDCP	8	16	14	18	2	12	10	4	6

Directions: Course is located 4 miles from Augusta on Route 3. From Route 95, take Exit 30 East. Go until rotary, follow signs to Route 3 East for about 3 to 4 miles. At the Bolton Hill Road sign, take a right and follow to course.

Willowdale Golf Club   48

S ME

Scarborough, ME (207)883-9351

Club Pro: Pam Lewis, Manager
Pro Shop: Limited inventory
Payment: Visa, MC, DIS, Personal checks
Tee Times: 3 days prior for wknds.
Fee 9 Holes: Weekday: $14.00
Fee 18 Holes: Weekday: $24.00
Cart Rental: $22.00/18, $12.00/9
Lessons: By Appt. **School:** No
Driving Range: No
Other: Clubhouse/ Snack Bar/ Showers

Tees	Holes	Yards	Par	USGA	Slope
BACK	NA				
MIDDLE	18	5980	70	67.9	110
FRONT	18	5344	70	67.9	112

Weekend: $14.00
Weekend: $24.00
Discounts: None
Junior Golf: No **Membership:** Yes
Non-Metal Spikes: Required

Beautiful corse situated on the Scarborough Marsh. Nice seabreezes. Mosquito controlled, watered fairways. Friendly people oriented course.

	1	2	3	4	5	6	7	8	9
PAR	4	5	4	4	3	4	3	4	4
YARDS	375	498	398	375	195	376	156	339	340
HDCP	11	3	5	9	4	10	16	12	13
	10	11	12	13	14	15	16	17	18
PAR	4	3	4	4	4	3	4	4	5
YARDS	405	145	356	391	321	154	375	276	505
HDCP	1	18	6	2	15	17	7	14	8

Directions: Exit 6 off Maine Turnpike. US 95 to Route1. Turn left onto Route. 1 North,. First light ,turn right. 1/4 mi.

4✪ =Excellent 3✪ =Very Good 2✪ =Good

Wilson Lake CC

★★★ 49

Weld Rd., Wilton, ME (207) 645-2016

Club Pro: Rick Carlton
Pro Shop: Limited inventory
Payment: Visa, MC
Tee Times: Weekends

Tees	Holes	Yards	Par	USGA	Slope
BACK	9	6159	70	68.8	117
MIDDLE	9	6044	70	68.8	117
FRONT	9	5614	74	71.9	119

Fee 9 Holes: Weekday: $12.00 **Weekend:** $12.00
Fee 18 Holes: Weekday: $20.00 **Weekend:** $20.00
Cart Rental: $20.00/18 $12.00/9 **Discounts:** Junior on membership.
Lessons: $15.00/45 minutes **School:** No **Junior Golf:** Yes **Membership:** Yes
Driving Range: No **Non-Metal Spikes:** Preferred
Other: Clubhouse / Bar-Lounge / Snack bar / Lockers / Showers

The second hole is an excellent par 3 Panoramic views of Lake Wilson. Junior clinics. Open May - October.

	1	2	3	4	5	6	7	8	9
PAR	4	3	5	4	4	4	3	4	4
YARDS	399	159	501	406	364	379	135	327	352
HDCP	10	16	4	1	8	6	18	14	12
	10	11	12	13	14	15	16	17	18
PAR	4	3	5	4	4	4	3	4	4
YARDS	399	159	501	406	364	379	135	327	352
HDCP	9	15	3	1	7	5	17	13	11

Directions: Take Route 4 to Route 2 to Route 156 into Wilton. Course is on Weld Rd. in Wilton.

CHAPTER 7

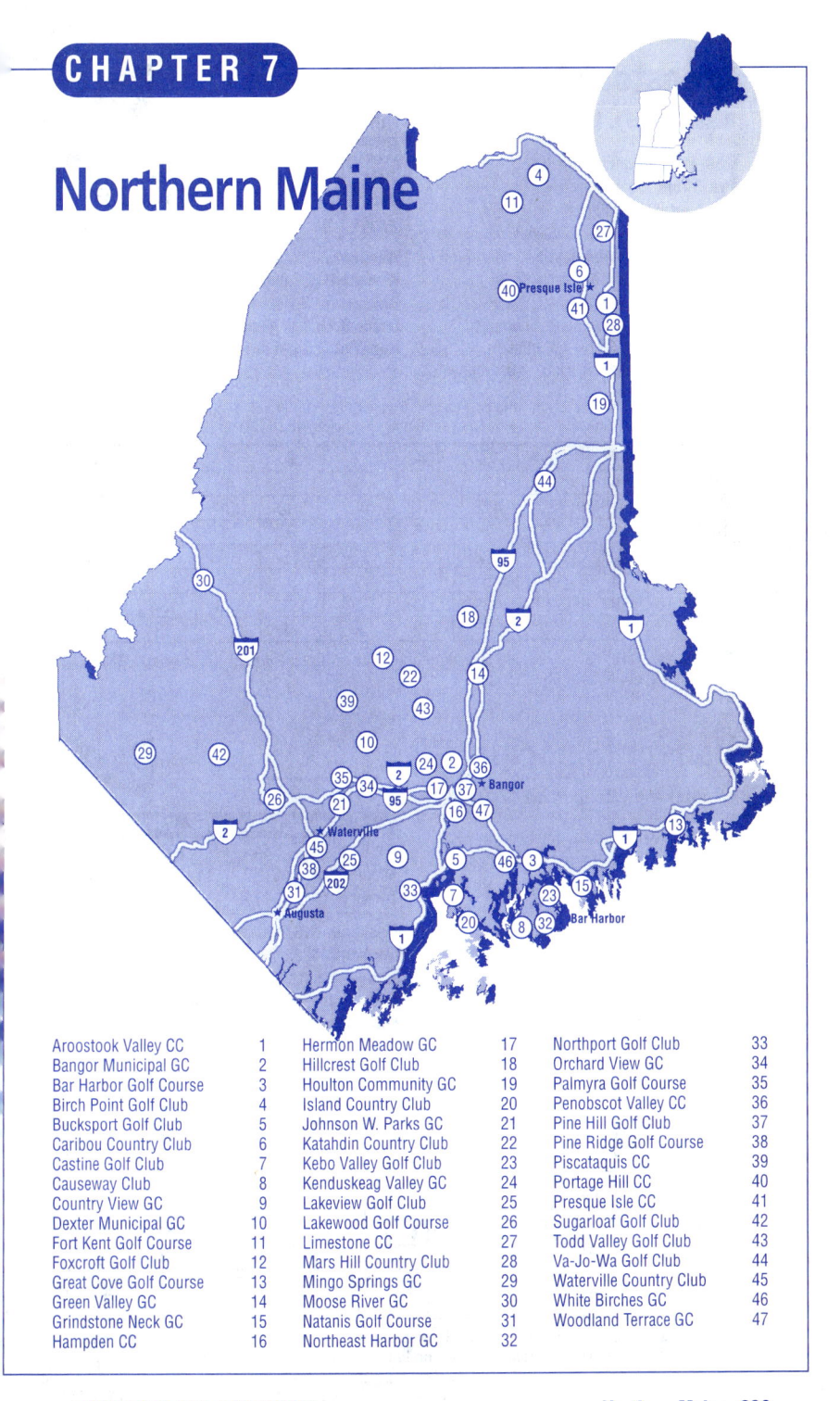

Northern Maine

Aroostook Valley CC	1	Hermon Meadow GC	17	Northport Golf Club	33
Bangor Municipal GC	2	Hillcrest Golf Club	18	Orchard View GC	34
Bar Harbor Golf Course	3	Houlton Community GC	19	Palmyra Golf Course	35
Birch Point Golf Club	4	Island Country Club	20	Penobscot Valley CC	36
Bucksport Golf Club	5	Johnson W. Parks GC	21	Pine Hill Golf Club	37
Caribou Country Club	6	Katahdin Country Club	22	Pine Ridge Golf Course	38
Castine Golf Club	7	Kebo Valley Golf Club	23	Piscataquis CC	39
Causeway Club	8	Kenduskeag Valley GC	24	Portage Hill CC	40
Country View GC	9	Lakeview Golf Club	25	Presque Isle CC	41
Dexter Municipal GC	10	Lakewood Golf Course	26	Sugarloaf Golf Club	42
Fort Kent Golf Course	11	Limestone CC	27	Todd Valley Golf Club	43
Foxcroft Golf Club	12	Mars Hill Country Club	28	Va-Jo-Wa Golf Club	44
Great Cove Golf Course	13	Mingo Springs GC	29	Waterville Country Club	45
Green Valley GC	14	Moose River GC	30	White Birches GC	46
Grindstone Neck GC	15	Natanis Golf Course	31	Woodland Terrace GC	47
Hampden CC	16	Northeast Harbor GC	32		

NEW ENGLAND GOLFGUIDE

Aroostook Valley CC

Russell Rd., Ft. Fairfield, ME (207) 476-8083

Club Pro: Steven Leitch
Pro Shop: Yes
Payment: Visa, MC
Tee Times: Weekends, 2 days adv.
Fee 9 Holes: Weekday: $12.00
Fee 18 Holes: Weekday: $22.00
Cart Rental: $22.00/18 $12.00/9
Lessons: $15.00/half hour **School:** No
Driving Range: $2.00/sm. bucket
Other: Clubhouse / Snack bar / Bar-lounge / Lockers / Showers

Tees	Holes	Yards	Par	USGA	Slope
BACK	18	6304	72	69.6	117
MIDDLE	18	5957	72	68.4	113
FRONT	18	5373	72	74.1	119

Weekend: $12.00
Weekend: $22.00
Discounts: None
Junior Golf: Yes **Membership:** Yes
Non-Metal Spikes: Required

The pro shop is in the U.S., but the course is in Canada. No need to clear customs. A very beautiful course; difficult inclines on back nine make it challenging.

	1	2	3	4	5	6	7	8	9
PAR	4	4	5	3	5	4	4	3	4
YARDS	375	327	478	132	440	308	334	139	365
HDCP	1	13	7	15	3	9	11	17	5
	10	11	12	13	14	15	16	17	18
PAR	4	4	5	3	5	3	4	3	5
YARDS	382	322	489	189	510	156	383	134	494
HDCP	6	16	4	12	8	14	2	18	10

Directions: Take I-95 to last exit; take right onto Route 1 to Ft. Fairfield, cross bridge. Take first right. Follow Russell Road to course.

Bangor Municipal GC

Webster Ave., Bangor, ME (207) 941-0232

Club Pro: Brian Enman
Pro Shop: Full inventory
Payment: Cash, Visa, MC
Tee Times: No
Fee 9 Holes: Weekday: $12.00
Fee 18 Holes: Weekday: $20.00
Cart Rental: $20.00/18 $10.00/9
Lessons: $30.00/45 minutes **School:** No
Driving Range: $3.00/lg. bucket
Other: Restaurant / Clubhouse / Bar-Lounge

Tees	Holes	Yards	Par	USGA	Slope
BACK	18	6345	71	69.2	115
MIDDLE	18	6150	71	67.9	112
FRONT	18	5172	71	69.1	111

Weekend: $13.00
Weekend: $22.00
Discounts: Yes
Junior Golf: Yes **Membership:** Residents
Non-Metal Spikes: Preferred

27 holes including a nine hole course with 3215 yards, par 36, USGA rating 69.6 and a slope of 128. Open April 15 - November 15.

	1	2	3	4	5	6	7	8	9
PAR	4	4	3	5	4	3	4	4	4
YARDS	335	395	165	530	330	200	400	410	415
HDCP	11	7	17	9	13	15	3	1	5
	10	11	12	13	14	15	16	17	18
PAR	4	3	4	4	4	5	3	4	5
YARDS	400	200	400	315	410	470	165	340	480
HDCP	6	16	2	10	4	14	18	8	12

Directions: Take I-95 North to Exit 46 (Hammond St.); sharp right onto Norway Road at stop sign. Take right at next stop sign. Course is on left.

Bar Harbor Golf Course

Rt. 204, Trenton, ME (207) 667-7505

Club Pro: Earl Choate
Pro Shop: Full inventory
Payment: Visa, MC
Tee Times: No
Fee 9 Holes: Weekday: $22.00
Fee 18 Holes: Weekday: $35.00
Cart Rental: $28.00/18 $15.00/9
Lessons: $20.00/half hour **School:** Yes
Driving Range: No
Other: Clubhouse / Snack bar / Bar-lounge

Tees	Holes	Yards	Par	USGA	Slope
BACK	18	6667	71	71.1	122
MIDDLE	18	6437	71	70.2	122
FRONT	18	5428	71	70.4	122

Weekend: $22.00
Weekend: $35.00
Discounts: None
Junior Golf: N/R **Membership:** Yes
Non-Metal Spikes: Preferred

One of the best kept secrets in the state. The course is a links-style tract designed by Phil Wogan. Located adjacent to the ocean, it is very challenging.

	1	2	3	4	5	6	7	8	9
PAR	4	4	5	3	4	4	4	3	4
YARDS	421	389	518	152	404	412	365	170	341
HDCP	4	6	8	17	2	10	12	16	14
	10	11	12	13	14	15	16	17	18
PAR	4	3	4	5	4	4	4	3	5
YARDS	423	153	297	593	374	323	405	156	541
HDCP	9	18	11	3	7	13	1	15	5

Directions: Take Route 3 to Bar Harbor. Course is located at intersection of Route 3 and Route 204 in Trenton.

Birch Point Golf Club

Madawaska, ME (207) 895-6957

Club Pro: Larry Plourde
Pro Shop: Full inventory
Payment: Credit card, check, cash
Tee Times: No
Fee 9 Holes: Weekday: $10.00
Fee 18 Holes: Weekday: $15.00
Cart Rental: $15.00/18 $10.00/9
Lessons: Yes **School:** N/R
Driving Range: $2.00/bucket
Other: Bar-lounge/Restaurant

Tees	Holes	Yards	Par	USGA	Slope
BACK	9	2955	35	N/A	N/A
MIDDLE	9	2760	35	N/A	N/A
FRONT	9	2565	36	N/A	N/A

Weekend: $10.00
Weekend: $15.00
Discounts: Junior
Junior Golf: N/R **Membership:** Yes
Non-Metal Spikes: No

Very pretty course located next to Long Lake.

	1	2	3	4	5	6	7	8	9
PAR	4	4	4	4	3	4	5	4	3
YARDS	265	345	395	290	160	385	475	290	155
HDCP	9	2	1	5	4	6	7	8	3
	10	11	12	13	14	15	16	17	18
PAR									
YARDS									
HDCP									

Directions: Take Route 1 North to Madawaska. Left on Beauliew Rd. Take Birch Point Rd. to course.

4✪ =Excellent 3✪ =Very Good 2✪ =Good

Bucksport Golf Club

Rt. 49, Bucksport, ME (207) 469-7612

Club Pro: Wayne Hand
Pro Shop: Full inventory
Payment: Visa, MC
Tee Times: No
Fee 9 Holes: Weekday: $14.00
Fee 18 Holes: Weekday: $20.00
Cart Rental: $22.00/18 $11.00/9
Lessons: Yes **School:** No
Driving Range: $4.00/lg. $3.00/sm.
Other: Bar-Lounge / Snack bar / Lockers / Showers

Tees	Holes	Yards	Par	USGA	Slope
BACK	N/A				
MIDDLE	9	6779	74	72.5	136
FRONT	9	5972	74	72.2	115

Weekend: $15.00
Weekend: $22.00
Discounts: Junior
Junior Golf: Yes **Membership:** Yes
Non-Metal Spikes: Required

Nine holes with two sets of tees. Large greens. Course designed by Phil Wogan in 1967. A very challenging course to play. Open April - October.

	1	2	3	4	5	6	7	8	9
PAR	4	5	3	4	5	3	4	4	5
YARDS	360	456	164	400	502	188	378	358	548
HDCP	7	3	17	11	5	15	9	13	1
	10	11	12	13	14	15	16	17	18
PAR	4	5	3	4	5	3	4	4	5
YARDS	380	440	175	375	515	205	400	335	600
HDCP	8	4	18	12	6	16	10	14	2

Directions: From Augusta: Route 3 to Belfast. Route 1 North to Bucksport. From Bangor: Take Route 46 to Route 1 or 1A. Course is 3 miles from Down town Bucksport.

Caribou Country Club

Caribou, ME (207) 493-3933

Club Pro: Bill McGary
Pro Shop: Full inventory
Payment: Visa, MC
Tee Times: No
Fee 9 Holes: Weekday: $12.00
Fee 18 Holes: Weekday: $18.00
Cart Rental: $15.00/18 $10.00/9
Lessons: Yes **School:** No
Driving Range: Yes
Other: Restaurant / Clubhouse / Bar-lounge / Snack Bar / Lockers / Showers

Tees	Holes	Yards	Par	USGA	Slope
BACK	N/A				
MIDDLE	9	6429	72	69.6	116
FRONT	9	5631	72	69.6	116

Weekend: $12.00
Weekend: $18.00
Discounts: None
Junior Golf: Yes **Membership:** Yes, Junior
Non-Metal Spikes: Required

The course has a beautiful log cabin clubhouse. 9 hole layout with two sets of tees. Open May 1 - October 15.

	1	2	3	4	5	6	7	8	9
PAR	4	5	3	4	4	4	3	5	4
YARDS	340	515	195	330	360	340	150	530	400
HDCP	14	4	16	12	9	10	18	2	6
	10	11	12	13	14	15	16	17	18
PAR	4	4	3	4	4	4	3	5	5
YARDS	360	408	215	345	411	330	170	550	480
HDCP	13	3	15	11	8	7	17	17	5

Directions: Take Route 161 North; follow 1 1/2 miles outside Caribou; course is on right side.

Castine Golf Club 7

Battle Ave., Castine, ME (207) 326-8844

Club Pro: Tom Roberts
Pro Shop: Full inventory
Payment: Cash only
Tee Times: No
Fee 9 Holes: Weekday: $25.00 ($14 after 4) **Weekend:** $25.00 ($12 after 4)
Fee 18 Holes: Weekday: $25.00 ($14 after 4) **Weekend:** $25.00 ($12 after 4)
Cart Rental: $25.00/18 $15.00/9
Lessons: $40/45 min. **School:** No
Driving Range: $3.00/ bucket
Other: Clubhouse, Members only
Discounts: None
Junior Golf: Yes **Membership:** Yes
Non-Metal Spikes: Preferred

Tees	Holes	Yards	Par	USGA	Slope
BACK	N/A				
MIDDLE	9	5954	70	68.1	116
FRONT	9	5458	72	71.4	122

Semi private. Opened in 1897; redesigned in 1921 by Scotsman Willie Park Jr. Small greens, hilly terrain and contour mowed rough challenge all levels of players.

	1	2	3	4	5	6	7	8	9
PAR	4	3	4	3	4	4	5	4	4
YARDS	400	175	397	146	376	344	465	316	358
HDCP	3	15	1	17	5	9	7	13	11
	10	11	12	13	14	15	16	17	18
PAR	4	3	4	3	4	4	5	4	4
YARDS	400	175	397	146	376	344	465	316	358
HDCP	4	16	2	18	6	10	8	14	12

Directions: Route 1 & 3 through Bucksport. Turn right onto Route 175 to Route 166. Course is on right.

Causeway Club 8

Fernald Rd., S.W. Harbor, ME (207) 244-3780

Club Pro: Jeff McIntrie
Pro Shop: Full inventory
Payment: Visa, MC
Tee Times: No
Fee 9 Holes: Weekday: $22.00 **Weekend:** $22.00
Fee 18 Holes: Weekday: $30.00 All day **Weekend:** $30.00 All Day
Cart Rental: $15.00/18 $10.00/9 **Discounts:** None
Lessons: $25/45 min. **School:** No **Junior Golf:** Yes **Membership:** Yes
Driving Range: No **Non-Metal Spikes:** Preferred
Other: Clubhouse / Lockers/ Snack Bar

Tees	Holes	Yards	Par	USGA	Slope
BACK	N/R				
MIDDLE	9	2302	65	60.9	95
FRONT	9	2085	32	63.9	102

N ME

Fairly hilly course. Located on S.W. Harbor with scenic views. Closed to public after 6:00 p.m.

	1	2	3	4	5	6	7	8	9
PAR	4	4	4	4	4	3	3	3	3
YARDS	390	270	298	278	390	140	228	175	133
HDCP	4	12	11	17	2	16	5	7	15
	10	11	12	13	14	15	16	17	18
PAR	4	4	4	4	4	3	4	3	3
YARDS	402	305	310	262	392	158	266	178	143
HDCP	3	9	10	18	1	13	8	6	14

Directions: Take I-95 to ALT Route 1 into Ellsworth Center. Follow Route 3 toward Ellsworth Island (Route 102), follow signs to South West Harbor.

4⊕ =Excellent 3⊕ =Very Good 2⊕ =Good

Country View GC

Rt. 7, Brooks, ME (207) 722-3161

Club Pro: No
Pro Shop: Yes
Payment: Cash, Check
Tee Times: No
Fee 9 Holes: Weekday: $12.00
Fee 18 Holes: Weekday: $17.00
Cart Rental: $10.00/9
Lessons: Yes **School:** No
Driving Range: Yes
Other: Snack bar

Tees	Holes	Yards	Par	USGA	Slope
BACK	N/A				
MIDDLE	9	5900	72	N/A	N/A
FRONT	9	4960	72	N/A	N/A

Weekend: $12.00
Weekend: $17.00
Discounts: None
Junior Golf: N/R **Membership:** Yes
Non-Metal Spikes: Required

Considered one of the more difficult nine hole courses in the area. Always well maintained.

	1	2	3	4	5	6	7	8	9
PAR	4	4	5	3	4	5	4	4	3
YARDS	330	335	450	125	345	480	340	335	145
HDCP	5	13	3	17	11	1	9	7	15
	10	11	12	13	14	15	16	17	18
PAR	4	4	5	3	4	5	4	4	3
YARDS	340	350	460	140	375	500	350	345	155
HDCP	6	14	4	18	12	2	10	8	16

Directions: Take Route 1 to Route 137 North, take right onto Route 7. Course is 1 mile north of Brooks.

Dexter Municipal GC

Sunrise Ave., Dexter, ME (207) 924-6477

Club Pro: Gary R. Rees, PGA
Pro Shop: Full inventory
Payment: Cash only
Tee Times: No
Fee 9 Holes: Weekday: $12.00 all day
Fee 18 Holes: Weekday: $12.00 all day
Cart Rental: $19.00/18 $11.00/9
Lessons: Yes **School:** Jr.Yes
Driving Range: Yes
Other: Clubhouse / Snack bar

Tees	Holes	Yards	Par	USGA	Slope
BACK	9	5281	70	65.7	115
MIDDLE	9	5241	70	65.7	115
FRONT					

Weekend: $15.00 all day
Weekend: $15.00 all day
Discounts: Junior
Junior Golf: Yes **Membership:** Yes
Non-Metal Spikes: No

Not too long, but full of challenges. Lots of hills and ponds- fun course to play. Open April 15 - October 15.

	1	2	3	4	5	6	7	8	9
PAR	4	4	4	4	3	4	4	3	5
YARDS	275	285	338	242	173	260	390	179	444
HDCP	17	9	11	7	13	5	1	3	5
	10	11	12	13	14	15	16	17	18
PAR	4	4	4	4	3	4	4	3	5
YARDS	305	290	340	248	180	265	395	184	448
HDCP	12	14	10	8	16	6	2	4	18

Directions: From I-95 Exit 39, take Route 7 to Dexter (14 miles.) Left at Liberty Street, follow to end. Go left, course is second driveway on right.

Fort Kent Golf Course

11

Fort Kent, ME (207) 834-3149

Club Pro: Kelly O'Leary
Pro Shop: Full inventory
Payment: Visa, MC
Tee Times: No
Fee 9 Holes: Weekday: $10.00
Fee 18 Holes: Weekday: $16.00
Cart Rental: $15.00/18 $10.00/9
Lessons: $20/lesson **School:** No
Driving Range: $2.00/bucket
Other: Restaurant / Clubhouse / Bar-lounge / Lockers / Showers

Tees	Holes	Yards	Par	USGA	Slope
BACK	NA				
MIDDLE	9	6367	71	69.0	111
FRONT	9	5361	72	69.0	111

Weekend: $10.00
Weekend: $16.00
Discounts: None
Junior Golf: Yes **Membership:** Yes
Non-Metal Spikes: Required

The course, located a chip shot from the Canadian border, sports many challenges: bunkers, water hazards, and hills.

	1	2	3	4	5	6	7	8	9
PAR	4	4	3	4	3	4	4	4	5
YARDS	406	302	160	322	151	390	412	437	542
HDCP	1	15	13	17	9	7	5	3	11
	10	11	12	13	14	15	16	17	18
PAR	4	4	3	4	3	4	5	4	5
YARDS	412	310	181	328	159	398	460	449	548
HDCP	2	16	8	18	10	6	14	4	12

Directions: Take Route 161 to Fort Kent; follow 3 miles to course.

Foxcroft Golf Club

12

Dover Foxcroft (207) 564-8887

Club Pro: Louis G. Thibeault, PGA
Pro Shop: Yes
Payment: Personal checks, Cash
Tee Times: No
Fee 9 Holes: Weekday: $10.00
Fee 18 Holes: Weekday: $18.00
Cart Rental: $18.00/18 $10.00/9
Lessons: Yes **School:** No
Driving Range: No
Other: Snack Bar/ Clubhouse

Tees	Holes	Yards	Par	USGA	Slope
BACK	N/A				
MIDDLE	9	6123	72	66.1	107
FRONT	9	5526	74	67.0	101

Weekend: $10.00
Weekend: $18.00
Discounts: None
Junior Golf: No **Membership:** N/A
Non-Metal Spikes: No

N ME

Challenging, beautiful course specializing in open play.

	1	2	3	4	5	6	7	8	9
PAR	5	4	4	3	4	4	3	4	5
YARDS	488	439	428	110	340	272	168	401	490
HDCP	7	1	5	17	11	13	15	9	3
	10	11	12	13	14	15	16	17	18
PAR	5	4	4	3	4	4	3	4	5
YARDS	470	430	390	92	327	268	148	381	481
HDCP	8	2	6	18	12	14	16	10	4

Directions: Take Exit 39 from I-95 (Newport Exit) and follow Route 7 into Dover-Foxcroft. Turn left. Go right at traffic light. Take second right at Route 16. Follow 1.3 miles to sign at corner of Foxcroft Center Road and Route 16.

4✪ =Excellent 3✪ =Very Good 2✪ =Good

Great Cove Golf Course 13

Jonesboro, ME (207) 434-7200

Club Pro: No
Pro Shop: No
Payment: Cash only
Tee Times: No
Fee 9 Holes: Weekday: $5.00
Fee 18 Holes: Weekday: $10.00
Cart Rental: $10.00/18 $5.00/9
Lessons: No **School:** No
Driving Range: $2.00/sm. bucket
Other: Clubhouse / Snack bar

Weekend: $5.00
Weekend: $10.00
Discounts: None
Junior Golf: Yes **Membership:** Yes
Non-Metal Spikes: Preferred

Tees	Holes	Yards	Par	USGA	Slope
BACK					
MIDDLE	9	1694	30	55.1	84
FRONT					

Built, owned, and operated by Leon Sinford. Three tricky par 3's with natural hazards.

	1	2	3	4	5	6	7	8	9
PAR	4	3	4	3	4	3	3	3	3
YARDS	306	177	247	193	230	101	137	182	121
HDCP	2	8	1	7	3	9	6	4	5
	10	11	12	13	14	15	16	17	18
PAR									
YARDS									
HDCP									

Directions: 3 miles off Route 1 from Jonesboro. Located on Rogue Bluffs Rd.

Green Valley GC 14

Rt. 2, Lincoln, ME (207) 732-3006

Club Pro: No
Pro Shop: Limited inventory
Payment: Visa, MC
Tee Times: No
Fee 9 Holes: Weekday: $8.00
Fee 18 Holes: Weekday: $12.00
Cart Rental: $15.00/18 $8.00/9
Lessons: $16/lesson **School:** N/R
Driving Range: $3.00/bucket
Other: Clubhouse / Snack Bar

Weekend: $8.00
Weekend: $12.00 All Day
Discounts: None
Junior Golf: Yes **Membership:** Yes
Non-Metal Spikes: Preferred

Tees	Holes	Yards	Par	USGA	Slope
BACK	N/A				
MIDDLE	9	5706	70	65.8	112
FRONT	N/A				

Small greens-#5, par 4 with dog leg. The course is relatively easy to walk and well maintained. Open May - November.

	1	2	3	4	5	6	7	8	9
PAR	5	3	4	4	4	4	3	4	4
YARDS	502	190	283	250	360	376	160	366	366
HDCP	N/R	9	11	15	N/R	N/R	13	3	5
	10	11	12	13	14	15	16	17	18
PAR	5	3	4	4	4	4	3	4	4
YARDS	502	190	283	250	360	376	160	366	366
HDCP	N/R	10	12	16	N/R	N/R	14	4	6

Directions: Take I-95 to Howland Exit; follow Route 2 into Lincoln town center. Course is located off of Route 2.

Grindstone Neck GC

Winter Harbor, ME (207) 963-7760

Club Pro: Oscar Young
Pro Shop: Full inventory
Payment: Cash only
Tee Times: No
Fee 9 Holes: Weekday: $18.00
Fee 18 Holes: Weekday: $22.00
Cart Rental: No
Lessons: $10/30 min. **School:** No
Driving Range: No
Other: No

Tees	Holes	Yards	Par	USGA	Slope
BACK	N/A				
MIDDLE	9	6190	72	N/A	N/A
FRONT	9	5100	72	N/A	N/A

Weekend: $22.00
Weekend: $30.00
Discounts: Local Students
Junior Golf: No **Membership:** Yes
Non-Metal Spikes: Not Required

Semi-private, members tee time from 9-10:30am. Picturesque course located on Frenchman's Bay. Enjoy cool sea breezes, spectacular ocean views, while challenging your golfing skills.

	1	2	3	4	5	6	7	8	9
PAR	4	4	4	3	4	4	5	4	4
YARDS	345	340	317	138	413	335	457	343	407
HDCP	5	14	9	18	7	16	1	10	6
	10	11	12	13	14	15	16	17	18
PAR	4	4	4	3	4	4	5	4	4
YARDS	345	340	317	138	413	335	457	343	407
HDCP	15	8	17	2	11	3	12	4	13

Directions: Take Route 1 North to Route 186. Follow 6 miles to the course.

Hampden CC

Hampden, ME (207) 862-9999

Club Pro: No
Pro Shop: Limited inventory
Payment: Cash, Checks
Tee Times: No
Fee 9 Holes: Weekday: $7.00
Fee 18 Holes: Weekday: $10.00
Cart Rental: $15.00/18 $10.00/9
Lessons: Yes **School:** No
Driving Range: No
Other: Snack bar

Tees	Holes	Yards	Par	USGA	Slope
BACK	9	2570	36	N/R	N/R
MIDDLE	9	2737	36	66.0	108
FRONT	9	2550	36	N/R	112

Weekend: $10.00
Weekend: $15.00
Discounts: Sr.(Thurs)&Ladies-$5
Junior Golf: No **Membership:** Yes
Non-Metal Spikes: Required

The Par 5, 7th hole is the signature hole. The course is fairly wide open, friendly for beginners and seniors. Considered an easy walker. Tues. is Ladies day. After 5pm, weekdays unlimited.

	1	2	3	4	5	6	7	8	9
PAR	4	3	4	4	4	3	5	4	5
YARDS	320	170	330	295	257	195	450	310	410
HDCP	N/A	N/A	N/A	N/A	N/A	N/A	N/A	N/A	N/A
	10	11	12	13	14	15	16	17	18
PAR									
YARDS									
HDCP									

Directions: Take I-95 to Exit 43, follow Route 69 East for 1 1/2 miles, take Route 9 East for 2 miles, course in on right

4 = Excellent 3 = Very Good 2 = Good

Hermon Meadow GC 17

Bangor, ME (207) 848-3741

Tees	Holes	Yards	Par	USGA	Slope
BACK	18	6329	72	69.4	117
MIDDLE	18	5895	72	67.7	113
FRONT	18	5395	72	70.9	120

Club Pro: Mark Hall, PGA
Pro Shop: Full inventory
Payment: Most major
Tee Times: Weekends
Fee 9 Holes: Weekday: $12.00 **Weekend:** $12.00
Fee 18 Holes: Weekday: $20.00 **Weekend:** $20.00
Cart Rental: $18.00/18 $10.00/9
Discounts: Senior & Junior
Lessons: $50.00/ hour,videotape **School:** Jr. **Junior Golf:** Yes **Membership:** Yes
Driving Range: Yes **Non-Metal Spikes:** Not Required
Other: Clubhouse / Snack bar / Bar-lounge

COUPON

The course is relatively short and hilly. The greens are small and fast; back nine are heavily wooded. 4 target greens, grass tees and mats.

	1	2	3	4	5	6	7	8	9
PAR	4	4	3	5	4	5	4	3	4
YARDS	350	385	130	460	270	545	350	165	350
HDCP	7	9	17	3	15	1	11	5	13
	10	11	12	13	14	15	16	17	18
PAR	4	4	3	5	4	5	3	4	4
YARDS	265	310	160	430	320	510	135	370	390
HDCP	16	14	10	6	8	4	18	12	2

Directions: Take Union Street 4 miles past airport in Bangor, take left on Billings Road, course is 2 miles on left.

Hillcrest Golf Club 18

Millinocket, ME (207) 723-8410

Tees	Holes	Yards	Par	USGA	Slope
BACK	N/A				
MIDDLE	9	4954	66	62.6	98
FRONT	N/A				

Club Pro: No
Pro Shop: Full inventory
Payment: Visa, MC
Tee Times: No
Fee 9 Holes: Weekday: $12.00 **Weekend:** $12.00
Fee 18 Holes: Weekday: $16.00 **Weekend:** $16.00
Cart Rental: $20.00/18 $10.00/9
Discounts: Senior
Lessons: No **School:** No **Junior Golf:** Yes **Membership:** Yes
Driving Range: No **Non-Metal Spikes:** Required
Other: Clubhouse / Snack bar / Bar-lounge

Sits on bottom of Mt. Katahdin. Very nice short course, very tight with narrow, tree-lined fairways. Open April - October.

	1	2	3	4	5	6	7	8	9
PAR	4	3	4	4	4	4	3	3	4
YARDS	359	152	364	287	265	401	221	153	275
HDCP	5	15	3	7	11	1	13	17	9
	10	11	12	13	14	15	16	17	18
PAR	4	3	4	4	4	4	3	3	4
YARDS	359	152	364	287	265	401	221	153	275
HDCP	6	16	4	8	12	2	14	18	10

Directions: Take I-95 to Medway Exit, take left off ramp onto Route 157. Follow 12 miles to Medway Center. Take right at first light, then left at 3rd stop sign, then another left at the next stop sign. Stay on Westwood Avenue; course is straight ahead.

Houlton Community GC

19

Houlton, ME (207) 532-2662

Club Pro: Bob Gray
Pro Shop: Limited inventory
Payment: Cash, Check
Tee Times: No
Fee 9 Holes: Weekday: $10.00
Fee 18 Holes: Weekday: $18.00
Cart Rental: $20.00/18 $10.00/9
Lessons: $20/30 min. **School:** No
Driving Range: Yes
Other: Clubhouse / Snack bar / Bar-lounge

Tees	Holes	Yards	Par	USGA	Slope
BACK	N/A				
MIDDLE	9	6103	72	68.9	117
FRONT	9	5410	76	73.6	109

Weekend: $12.00
Weekend: $20.00
Discounts: None
Junior Golf: Yes **Membership:** Yes
Non-Metal Spikes: Required

COUPON

The course is adjacent to beautiful Nickerson Lake. Hilly, but other than a scenic view of the lake, has few water hazards. 2 sets of tees. Open May - September.

	1	2	3	4	5	6	7	8	9
PAR	4	5	3	4	4	5	4	3	4
YARDS	325	475	150	260	425	455	345	175	383
HDCP	15	5	13	17	1	11	9	3	7
	10	11	12	13	14	15	16	17	18
PAR	4	4	3	4	4	5	4	4	4
YARDS	390	375	170	285	385	475	365	285	380
HDCP	2	4	14	16	12	8	10	18	6

Directions: Take I-95 to Houlton Exit (last US Exit on I-95 North), follow signs to course.

Island Country Club

20

Sunset, ME (207) 348-2379

Club Pro: Yes
Pro Shop: Limited inventory
Payment: Cash, Checks
Tee Times: No
Fee 9 Holes: Weekday: $15.00 All day
Fee 18 Holes: Weekday: No
Cart Rental: Pull cart
Lessons: Yes **School:** No
Driving Range: No
Other: Clubhouse / Snack bar

Tees	Holes	Yards	Par	USGA	Slope
BACK	N/A				
MIDDLE	9	3865	62	58.8	97
FRONT	N/A				

Weekend: $20.00 All day
Weekend: No
Discounts: None
Junior Golf: No **Membership:** No
Non-Metal Spikes: Not Required

N ME

Hilly, greens medium, no alcohol on course. Open May 28 - September 30.

	1	2	3	4	5	6	7	8	9
PAR	4	4	3	3	3	3	3	4	4
YARDS	309	251	116	145	155	114	199	318	323
HDCP	9	7	15	13	11	17	5	1	3
	10	11	12	13	14	15	16	17	18
PAR	4	4	3	3	3	3	3	4	4
YARDS	309	297	116	145	155	114	199	277	323
HDCP	8	2	16	14	12	18	6	10	4

Directions: Take Route 1 to Route 15, follow to Deer Isle (West Side)

4 = Excellent **3** = Very Good **2** = Good

Johnson W. Parks GC   21

Pittsfield, ME (207) 487-5545

Club Pro: Michael Dugas
Pro Shop: Full inventory
Payment: Most major
Tee Times: No
Fee 9 Holes: Weekday: $12.00
Fee 18 Holes: Weekday: $16.00
Cart Rental: $19.00/18 $9.50/9
Lessons: $25/30 min. **School:** TBA
Driving Range: No
Other: Clubhouse / Sports Bar

Tees	Holes	Yards	Par	USGA	Slope
BACK	N/R				
MIDDLE	9	5803	70	68.3	119
FRONT	9	5114	70	68.1	111

Weekend: $14.00
Weekend: $18.00
Discounts: Senior & Junior
Junior Golf: Yes **Membership:** Yes
Non-Metal Spikes: Required

COUPON

One of central Maine's most popular courses. The tall pines, narrow fairways and series of streams adds to the challenge. Open April 25 - October 31. Teaching center under construction.

	1	2	3	4	5	6	7	8	9
PAR	4	4	5	3	4	4	4	3	4
YARDS	375	405	492	227	308	268	322	160	331
HDCP	15	1	9	3	11	17	5	7	13
	10	11	12	13	14	15	16	17	18
PAR	5	4	4	3	4	4	4	3	4
YARDS	436	416	412	167	326	252	322	199	385
HDCP	18	4	2	10	14	16	8	12	6

Directions: Take I-95 to Pittsfield Exit 38, go east off ramp. Take a left on to Route 1 52. 1/2 mile on the left.

Katahdin Country Club   22

Milo, ME (207) 943-2686

Club Pro: No
Pro Shop: Limited nventory
Payment: Cash only
Tee Times: No
Fee 9 Holes: Weekday: $11.00
Fee 18 Holes: Weekday: $11.00
Cart Rental: $16.00/18
Lessons: No **School:** N/R
Driving Range: No
Other: Clubhouse / Snack bar

Tees	Holes	Yards	Par	USGA	Slope
BACK	N/R				
MIDDLE	9	6006	72	64.7	102
FRONT	N/R				

Weekend: $11.00
Weekend: $11.00
Discounts: None
Junior Golf: N/R **Membership:** N/R
Non-Metal Spikes: Not Required

Wide open fairways, short cut rough and no water hazards. Open April 15 - November

	1	2	3	4	5	6	7	8	9
PAR	4	3	4	4	3	5	5	4	4
YARDS	360	150	330	260	185	496	495	440	287
HDCP	11	5	13	17	3	9	7	1	15
	10	11	12	13	14	15	16	17	18
PAR	4	3	4	4	3	5	5	4	4
YARDS	360	150	330	260	185	496	495	440	287
HDCP	12	6	14	18	4	10	8	2	16

Directions: Take I-95 North to LaGrange-Milo Exit, follow signs to course.

Kebo Valley Golf Club 23

Bar Harbor, ME (207) 288-3000

Club Pro: Gregg E. Baker, PGA
Pro Shop: Full inventory
Payment: Visa, MC, Amex, Cash
Tee Times: 3 days adv.
Fee 9 Holes: Weekday: $26.00
Fee 18 Holes: Weekday: $50.00
Cart Rental: $30.00/18
Lessons: $25.00/half hour **School:** No
Driving Range: No
Other: Clubhouse / Snack bar / Restaurant / Bar-lounge/Showers / Lockers

Tees	Holes	Yards	Par	USGA	Slope
BACK	18	6131	70	69.0	130
MIDDLE	18	5933	70	69.0	130
FRONT	18	5440	72	72	121

Weekend: $36.00
Weekend: $60.00
Discounts: None
Junior Golf: Yes **Membership:** Yes
Non-Metal Spikes: Required

COUPON

Eighth hole is one of the toughest par 4s around. Course is over 100 years old. Rated in top 50 public courses in U.S. by *Golf Digest*. Site of 1998 Maine Amateur Championship.

	1	2	3	4	5	6	7	8	9
PAR	4	4	4	3	5	3	4	4	3
YARDS	388	438	336	143	500	165	322	413	194
HDCP	7	3	11	17	9	13	15	1	5
	10	11	12	13	14	15	16	17	18
PAR	4	4	4	4	5	3	4	4	4
YARDS	338	400	283	390	530	146	258	349	340
HDCP	10	8	12	2	4	16	18	6	14

Directions: Take I 95 to Bangor, 395 to Route1A, Route 1A to Route 3, Route 3 to Route 233. Look for signs to course.

Kenduskeag Valley GC 24

Kenduskeag, ME (207) 884-7330

Club Pro: No
Pro Shop: Limited inventory
Payment: Cash, Check
Tee Times: No
Fee 9 Holes: Weekday: $7.00
Fee 18 Holes: Weekday: 10.00
Cart Rental: $12.00/18 $8.00/9
Lessons: No **School:** No
Driving Range: No
Other: Clubhouse / Snack bar

Tees	Holes	Yards	Par	USGA	Slope
BACK	N/A				
MIDDLE	9	5124	68	63.9	108
FRONT	9	4850	70	67.4	N/A

Weekend: $7.00
Weekend: $10.00
Discounts: Senior
Junior Golf: Yes **Membership:** Yes
Non-Metal Spikes: Preferred

N ME

An easy but pretty course. Rolling, built 1978, wooded and stream scenery, small greens, appropriate dress, no alcohol on course. Open May 1 - October 31.

	1	2	3	4	5	6	7	8	9
PAR	4	4	5	3	4	3	4	3	4
YARDS	324	350	491	108	290	150	402	158	314
HDCP	9	5	3	17	11	15	1	13	7
	10	11	12	13	14	15	16	17	18
PAR	4	4	5	3	4	3	4	3	4
YARDS	324	350	491	108	290	150	402	158	314
HDCP	10	6	4	18	12	16	2	14	8

Directions: From I-95, take Bangor / Broadway exit North. 11 miles on Route 15 to Kenduskeag. First left after village.

4⬤ =Excellent 3⬤ =Very Good 2⬤ =Good

Lakeview Golf Club   25

Burnham, ME (207) 948-5414

Club Pro: No
Pro Shop: Limited inventory
Payment: Cash only
Tee Times: 1 day adv.
Fee 9 Holes: Weekday: $10.00
Fee 18 Holes: Weekday: $15.00 All day
Cart Rental: No
Lessons: No **School:** No
Driving Range: No
Other: Snack bar/ Clubhouse/ Lockers

Tees	Holes	Yards	Par	USGA	Slope
BACK	9	6032	72	68.0	116
MIDDLE	9	5396	72	69.9	114
FRONT	9	5090	72	65.9	114

Weekend: $15.00
Weekend: $15.00
Discounts: Junior
Junior Golf: No **Membership:** Yes
Non-Metal Spikes: Not Required

An excellent walking course with level fairways. Highly recommended for senior citizens.

	1	2	3	4	5	6	7	8	9
PAR	4	4	3	3	4	5	5	4	4
YARDS	387	305	124	169	339	514	491	354	333
HDCP	7	13	17	15	9	1	3	5	11
	10	11	12	13	14	15	16	17	18
PAR	4	4	3	3	4	5	5	4	4
YARDS	387	305	124	169	339	514	491	354	333
HDCP	8	14	18	16	10	2	4	6	12

Directions: Take Route 139 from Fairfield to Burnham West. Course is on the left.

Lakewood Golf Course   26

Madison, ME (207) 474-5955

Club Pro: Bert DuMais
Pro Shop: Limited inventory
Payment: Cash only
Tee Times: Wknds & Hldys Am only
Fee 9 Holes: Weekday: $14.00
Fee 18 Holes: Weekday: $20.00
Cart Rental: $20.00/18 $10.00/9
Lessons: Yes **School:**
Driving Range: No
Other: Snack bar, bar/Lounge

Tees	Holes	Yards	Par	USGA	Slope
BACK	18	6278	72	70.1	128
MIDDLE	18	5720	70	66.3	110
FRONT	18	5490	74	71.9	120

Weekend: $14.00
Weekend: $20.00
Discounts: Junior
Junior Golf: No **Membership:** Yes
Non-Metal Spikes: Not Required

This course has four additional holes. The last five of the front nine are repeated. Practice, chipping, and putting areas. Open May - November.

	1	2	3	4	5	6	7	8	9
PAR	4	4	3	5	4	3	4	4	5
YARDS	356	435	160	471	285	141	325	410	510
HDCP	5	1	14	7	13	16	11	3	9
	10	11	12	13	14	15	16	17	18
PAR	3	4	4	3	4	3	4	4	5
YARDS	130	350	354	122	285	141	325	410	510
HDCP	17	6	18	15	8	18	12	4	2

Directions: Take Route 201; 5 miles past Shawhegan toward Bingham.

Limestone CC

Limestone, ME (207) 328-7277

Club Pro: Pete Weatherhead, Craig Phair
Pro Shop: Limited inventory
Payment: Visa, MC, Amex, Personal checks
Tee Times: No
Fee 9 Holes: Weekday: $11.00
Fee 18 Holes: Weekday: $16.00
Cart Rental: $10.00/9 $15.00/18
Lessons: $15/30 min. **School:** No
Driving Range: Yes. Irons only
Other: Clubhouse/ Hotel/ Bar/ Lounge/ Snack Bar. Golf and snowmobile packages available.

Weekend: $11.00
Weekend: $16.00
Discounts: Senior
Junior Golf: No **Membership:** Yes
Non-Metal Spikes: Required

Tees	Holes	Yards	Par	USGA	Slope
BACK					
MIDDLE	9	3355	36	70.4	114
FRONT	9	2870	36	71.4	116

27

Former Air Force course. Sited to capture the wind. Fairways lined with evergreens and hardwoods. Elevated greens at different angles. Beginner lessons are free.

	1	2	3	4	5	6	7	8	9
PAR	4	5	3	4	4	3	4	5	4
YARDS	415	525	160	370	355	225	390	515	400
HDCP	1	3	17	15	11	9	13	5	7
	10	11	12	13	14	15	16	17	18
PAR									
YARDS									
HDCP									

Directions: I-95 North to Holton then Route 1 North to Caribou. From Caribou take Route 89 East to Loring- Limestone. Take a left on Sawyer Rd. for 2.5 miles and club is located on the right.

Mars Hill Country Club

Mars Hill, ME (207) 425-4802

Club Pro: No
Pro Shop: Limited inventory
Payment: Visa, MC
Tee Times: No
Fee 9 Holes: Weekday: $10.00
Fee 18 Holes: Weekday: $18.00
Cart Rental: $8.00/18, $6.00/9
Lessons: No **School:** No
Driving Range: $2.00/sm bucket
Other: Club house / Full restaurant / Beer.

Weekend: $10.00
Weekend: $18.00
Discounts: Junior
Junior Golf: Yes **Membership:** Yes
Non-Metal Spikes: Required

Tees	Holes	Yards	Par	USGA	Slope
BACK	9	6286	72	68.8	120
MIDDLE	9	6113	72	68.8	120
FRONT	9	5384	72	68.8	120

28

N ME

Excellently maintained premier 9 hole golf course. Hilly with almost no level lies. A very good "family" golf course

	1	2	3	4	5	6	7	8	9
PAR	4	4	5	3	4	3	4	5	4
YARDS	398	380	470	163	363	125	309	447	315
HDCP	17	1	7	5	13	15	3	9	11
	10	11	12	13	14	15	16	17	18
PAR	4	4	5	3	4	3	4	5	4
YARDS	420	391	498	196	374	133	334	467	330
HDCP	18	2	8	6	14	16	4	10	12

Directions: i-95 to route US1 to Mars Hill. Then north 2 miles on route 1A. Turn right onto East Ridge Road. See sign to golf course.

4✪ =Excellent 3✪ =Very Good 2✪ = Good

Mingo Springs GC

29

Rangeley, ME (207) 864-5021

Club Pro: Mike DeRaps
Pro Shop: Full inventory
Payment: Visa, MC, Cash
Tee Times: Yes
Fee 9 Holes: Weekday: $20.00
Fee 18 Holes: Weekday: $26.00 All day
Cart Rental: $13.00 pp/18
Lessons: Yes $30.00 **School:** N/R
Driving Range: Yes
Other: Snack bar / Bar-lounge

Tees	Holes	Yards	Par	USGA	Slope
BACK	N/R				
MIDDLE	18	5923	70	66.3	109
FRONT					

Weekend: $20.00
Weekend: $26.00
Discounts: None
Junior Golf: N/R **Membership:** N/R
Non-Metal Spikes: Not Required

The course is exceptionally scenic. Open May - October 15. Watering system.

	1	2	3	4	5	6	7	8	9
PAR	4	4	4	3	4	4	3	4	5
YARDS	350	375	378	150	315	388	170	318	410
HDCP	9	7	5	17	11	1	15	13	3
	10	11	12	13	14	15	16	17	18
PAR	3	5	3	4	4	4	4	4	4
YARDS	152	522	125	400	360	276	419	363	392
HDCP	16	2	18	8	12	14	4	10	6

Directions: Take I-95 to Exit 12 (Auburn), pick up Route 4, follow into Rangeley.

Moose River GC

30

Rt. 201, Moose River, ME (207) 668-4841

Club Pro: No
Pro Shop: No
Payment: Cash only
Tee Times: No
Fee 9 Holes: Weekday: $10.00
Fee 18 Holes: Weekday: $18.00
Cart Rental: $15.00/18 $10.00/9
Lessons: No **School:** Yes
Driving Range: No
Other:

Tees	Holes	Yards	Par	USGA	Slope
BACK	N/R				
MIDDLE	9	3952	62	TBA	TBA
FRONT					

Weekend: $10.00
Weekend: $18.00
Discounts: Junior
Junior Golf: No **Membership:** Yes
Non-Metal Spikes: Not Required

Open May 15 - October 15.

	1	2	3	4	5	6	7	8	9
PAR	3	3	4	4	4	3	3	3	4
YARDS	204	168	213	248	259	168	171	169	376
HDCP	1	15	17	9	11	5	7	13	3
	10	11	12	13	14	15	16	17	18
PAR	3	3	4	4	4	3	3	3	4
YARDS	204	168	213	248	259	168	171	169	376
HDCP	2	16	18	10	12	6	8	14	4

Directions: Take I-95 to Fairfield Exit, follow route 201 North about 85 miles to Moose River.

Natanis Golf Course ✪✪ 31

Vassalboro, ME (207) 622-3561

Club Pro: Richard Browne
Pro Shop: Full inventory
Payment: Visa, MC
Tee Times: 1 week adv.
Fee 9 Holes: Weekday: $13.00
Fee 18 Holes: Weekday: $25.00
Cart Rental: $20.00/18 $10.00/9
Lessons: $30.00/ 45 minutes **School:** No
Driving Range: $3.50/lg. $2.50/ sm.
Other: Clubhouse / Lockers / Showers / Snack bar /restaurant

Tees	Holes	Yards	Par	USGA	Slope
BACK	9	3300	36	34.2	57
MIDDLE	9	3148	36	34.2	57
FRONT	N/A				

Weekend: $13.00
Weekend: $25.00
Discounts: None
Junior Golf: Yes **Membership:** Yes
Non-Metal Spikes: Not Required

27 hole course located in Central Maine. Scorecard below is the Tomahawk course. Indian Territory course is 3036 yards and Arrowhead is 2811 yards from the regular tees.

	1	2	3	4	5	6	7	8	9
PAR	5	3	3	5	4	4	4	4	4
YARDS	490	155	165	600	360	335	300	365	378
HDCP	5	9	8	1	6	3	7	4	2
	10	11	12	13	14	15	16	17	18
PAR									
YARDS									
HDCP									

Directions: Route 295 to Augusta / Winthrop Exit onto Route 201 to Webber Pond Road. Follow signs.

Northeast Harbor GC ✪✪✪ 32

N.E. Harbor, ME (207) 276-5335

Club Pro: Rob Gardner, PGA
Pro Shop: Full inventory
Payment: Visa, MC
Tee Times: No
Fee 9 Holes: Weekday: $50.00
Fee 18 Holes: Weekday: $50.00
Cart Rental: $36.00/18
Lessons: Private, Group, Jr. Clinic. **School:** Yes **Junior Golf:** Yes **Membership:** Yes
Driving Range: Members
Other: Clubhouse/ Lockers

Tees	Holes	Yards	Par	USGA	Slope
BACK	18	5430	69	67.8	120
MIDDLE	18	5278	69	66.7	118
FRONT	18	4530	71	67.3	116

Weekend: $50.00
Weekend: $50.00
Discounts: None
Non-Metal Spikes: Required

N ME

Located on Mt. Desert Island. Spectacular views. Several difficult holes, some very hilly, some flat. Dense woods.

	1	2	3	4	5	6	7	8	9
PAR	4	4	3	4	4	3	4	3	5
YARDS	325	320	149	425	305	127	284	155	457
HDCP	9	13	11	1	5	17	7	15	3
	10	11	12	13	14	15	16	17	18
PAR	5	4	3	4	3	4	4	4	4
YARDS	495	310	175	337	187	415	259	338	215
HDCP	4	10	16	12	18	2	14	6	8

Directions: Take I-95 to Bangor Exit (Route 1A), follow to Ellsworth, take Route 3 to Mt. Desert Island Arcadia National Park onto Route 102. Get onto Route 198, take right onto Sargent Drive.

4✪ =Excellent 3✪ =Very Good 2✪ =Good

Northport Golf Club ▶ 33

Belfast, ME (207) 338-2270

Club Pro: Paul Dailey, PGA
Pro Shop: Full inventory
Payment: Visa, MC
Tee Times: No
Fee 9 Holes: Weekday: $14.00
Fee 18 Holes: Weekday: $20.00
Cart Rental: $20.00/18 $15.00/9
Lessons: $25/45 minutes **School:** No
Driving Range: Yes
Other: Clubhouse / Snack bar

Tees	Holes	Yards	Par	USGA	Slope
BACK	N/A				
MIDDLE	9	6094	72	34.2	112
FRONT	9	5494	74	35.7	113

Weekend: $14.00
Weekend: $20.00
Discounts: None
Junior Golf: Yes **Membership:** Yes
Non-Metal Spikes: Not Required

Although tee times are not used it is advisable to call ahead because of club activities. Links type layout is popular for walkers and recreational players, but challenging for advanced players as well.

	1	2	3	4	5	6	7	8	9
PAR	4	4	3	4	5	4	5	4	3
YARDS	290	377	157	310	483	412	530	338	150
HDCP	15	5	11	13	7	3	1	9	17
	10	11	12	13	14	15	16	17	18
PAR	4	4	3	4	5	4	5	4	3
YARDS	290	377	157	310	483	412	530	338	150
HDCP	16	6	12	14	8	4	2	10	18

Directions: Turn East off Route 1 at Bayside Store. 20 minutes North of Camden Rockport or 5 minutes South of Belfast.

Orchard View GC ▶ 34

Newport, ME (207) 368-5600

Club Pro: No
Pro Shop: No
Payment: Cash only
Tee Times: No
Fee 9 Holes: Weekday: $10.00
Fee 18 Holes: Weekday: $15.00
Cart Rental: $15..00/18 $8.00/9
Lessons: No **School:** No
Driving Range: No
Other: Clubhouse / Snack bar / Restaurant / Bar-lounge

Tees	Holes	Yards	Par	USGA	Slope
BACK	N/A				
MIDDLE	9	4480	60	N/A	N/A
FRONT	N/A				

Weekend: $10.00
Weekend: $15.00, $20 at night
Discounts: None
Junior Golf: **Membership:** Yes
Non-Metal Spikes: Not Required

Fully lit for night play. Overlooks lake, pretty view. This executive course has challenging holes.

	1	2	3	4	5	6	7	8	9
PAR	3	4	3	3	3	3	3	4	4
YARDS	225	320	215	200	195	152	136	432	365
HDCP	9	5	7	13	11	15	17	1	3
	10	11	12	13	14	15	16	17	18
PAR	3	4	3	3	3	3	3	4	4
YARDS	225	320	215	200	195	152	136	432	365
HDCP	10	6	8	14	12	16	18	2	4

Directions: Take I-95 to Exit 39 (Newport), follow toward Newport. Straight through set of lights onto Route 7. Take right at Noah's Animal Park onto Old Corinna Rd. Course is 3/4 mi. on left.

Palmyra Golf Course

Palmyra, ME (207)938-4947

Club Pro: Thea Davis
Pro Shop: Limited inventory
Payment: Visa, MC
Tee Times: Sat&Sun, until noon
Fee 9 Holes: Weekday: $9.00
Fee 18 Holes: Weekday: $18.00
Cart Rental: $18.00 /18,$9.00/9
Lessons: Available **School:** Yes
Driving Range: $4,00/$3.50/$3.00
Other: Snack Bar / RV facility on property

Tees	Holes	Yards	Par	USGA	Slope
BACK	18	6617	72	70.1	120
MIDDLE	18	6367	72	69.0	118
FRONT	18	5464	72	69.0	118

Weekend: $9.00
Weekend: $18.00
Discounts:
Junior Golf: Yes **Membership:** Yes
Non-Metal Spikes: Not Required

COUPON

Course sits atop foothills in Palmyra. Long holes equalized by hard sun baked fairways. Smallish greens. A challenging course exemplified by the par 5 third hole. RV Park.

	1	2	3	4	5	6	7	8	9
PAR	4	4	5	3	4	4	4	3	5
YARDS	430	281	575	153	400	407	400	129	476
HDCP	11	13	1	15	7	5	3	17	9
	10	11	12	13	14	15	16	17	18
PAR	4	3	4	4	5	4	4	3	5
YARDS	386	150	350	387	487	373	304	198	481
HDCP	4	18	12	2	16	10	14	6	8

Directions: From I-95, take Exit 39 (Newport),get onto Route 2 West. Course is 4 miles on the right off of Lang Hill Rd.

Penobscot Valley CC

Maine St., Orono, ME (207) 866-2423

Club Pro: Colin Gillies
Pro Shop: Full inventory
Payment: MC, Visa
Tee Times: No
Fee 9 Holes: Weekday: N/A
Fee 18 Holes: Weekday: $45.00
Cart Rental: $22.00/18
Lessons: $25.00/half hour **School:** Yes
Driving Range: $3.00/Lge.
Other: Clubhouse / Lockers / Showers / Snack bar / Restaurant / Bar-lounge

Tees	Holes	Yards	Par	USGA	Slope
BACK	18	6445	72	71.2	128
MIDDLE	18	6301	72	70.5	126
FRONT	18	5796	74	73.9	128

Weekend: N/A
Weekend: $45.00
Discounts: Junior
Junior Golf: Yes **Membership:** Yes
Non-Metal Spikes: Required

N ME

This Donald Ross course holds many amateur tournaments. A shot maker's course, it is in great shape. The course is very challenging and hilly with scenic views.

	1	2	3	4	5	6	7	8	9
PAR	4	4	5	3	4	3	5	4	4
YARDS	396	396	471	143	354	163	443	337	384
HDCP	11	3	5	17	9	15	7	13	1
	10	11	12	13	14	15	16	17	18
PAR	5	4	4	4	3	5	3	4	4
YARDS	490	390	371	424	143	455	193	323	425
HDCP	6	14	12	10	18	8	4	16	2

Directions: Take I-95 to Kelly Rd. Exit 50, take right to US Route 2. Turn right. Follow to course.

4✪ =Excellent 3✪ =Very Good 2✪ =Good

Northern Maine 257

Pine Hill Golf Club   37

Outer Mill St., Brewer, ME (207) 989-3824

Club Pro: Buck Gagnier
Pro Shop: Limited inventory
Payment: Cash only
Tee Times: No
Fee 9 Holes: Weekday: $10.00
Fee 18 Holes: Weekday: $14.00
Cart Rental: $16.00/18 $8.00/9
Lessons: $15/30 min. **School:** No
Driving Range: $3.00/med.
Other: Clubhouse / Snack bar

Tees	Holes	Yards	Par	USGA	Slope
BACK	9	2979	36	66	100
MIDDLE	9	2749	36	66	100
FRONT	9	2580	36	67	99

Weekend: $14.00
Weekend: $15.00
Discounts: None
Junior Golf: No **Membership:** Yes
Non-Metal Spikes: Preferred

Mostly level. Very scenic. Good course for beginners and intermediates. Open April - October.

	1	2	3	4	5	6	7	8	9
PAR	4	4	4	4	3	5	4	5	3
YARDS	292	333	326	339	166	498	320	495	210
HDCP	11	13	7	1	17	3	9	5	15
	10	11	12	13	14	15	16	17	18
PAR									
YARDS									
HDCP									

Directions: Take I-395 to South Main St./Brewer Exit, follow signs to course.

Pine Ridge Golf Course   38

W. River Rd., Waterville, ME (207) 873-0474

Club Pro: No
Pro Shop: Limited inventory
Payment: Cash only
Tee Times: No
Fee 9 Holes: Weekday: $6.00 All Day
Fee 18 Holes: Weekday: $6.00 All day
Cart Rental: Pull cart $3.00
Lessons: Yes **School:** No
Driving Range: No
Other: Restaurant / Bar-lounge

Tees	Holes	Yards	Par	USGA	Slope
BACK					
MIDDLE	9	5147	54	N/A	N/A
FRONT					

Weekend: $7.00 All Day
Weekend: $7.00 All day
Discounts: Members only
Junior Golf: No **Membership:** Yes
Non-Metal Spikes: Preferred

Well built and maintained par 3. Great for beginners, seniors and people with little time.

	1	2	3	4	5	6	7	8	9
PAR	3	3	3	3	3	3	3	3	3
YARDS	160	135	110	125	220	100	125	175	135
HDCP	5	9	15	13	1	17	11	3	7
	10	11	12	13	14	15	16	17	18
PAR	3	3	3	3	3	3	3	3	3
YARDS	160	135	110	125	220	100	125	175	135
HDCP	5	9	15	13	1	17	11	3	7

Directions: I-95 (Maine Turnpike) to Waterville Exit. Follow signs for Thomas College.

Piscataquis CC 39

Dover Rd., Guilford, ME (207) 876-3203

Club Pro: Robert L. Dugas
Pro Shop: Full inventory
Payment: Cash only
Tee Times: No
Fee 9 Holes: Weekday: $10.00
Fee 18 Holes: Weekday: $15.00
Cart Rental: $20.00/18 $10.00/9
Lessons: $20.00/half hour **School:** No
Driving Range: No
Other: Clubhouse / Snack bar / Showers

Tees	Holes	Yards	Par	USGA	Slope
BACK	N/A				
MIDDLE	9	5414	69	64.6	109
FRONT	N/A				

Weekend: $12.00
Weekend: $18.00
Discounts: Senior Mondays
Junior Golf: Yes **Membership:** No
Non-Metal Spikes: Required

Hilly, scenic, greens are excellent. Dress code: no tank tops. Lots of pine separating fairways. Open April 15 - October 15.

	1	2	3	4	5	6	7	8	9
PAR	4	4	4	4	4	3	4	4	4
YARDS	352	324	251	290	370	164	268	348	377
HDCP	5	13	15	17	1	9	11	3	7
	10	11	12	13	14	15	16	17	18
PAR	4	4	3	4	4	3	4	4	4
YARDS	352	344	209	270	320	170	298	348	359
HDCP	6	14	2	18	8	16	12	4	10

Directions: Newport Exit Route 7 to Route 23 North. 25 miles from Newport.

Portage Hill CC 40

Rt. 11, Portage, ME (207) 435-8221

Club Pro: No
Pro Shop: No
Payment: Cash only
Tee Times: No
Fee 9 Holes: Weekday: $12.00
Fee 18 Holes: Weekday: $18.00 All day
Cart Rental: $18.00/18 $12.00/9
Lessons: No **School:** N/R
Driving Range: No
Other: Clubhouse / Snack bar / Bar-lounge.

Tees	Holes	Yards	Par	USGA	Slope
BACK	N/A				
MIDDLE	9	6164	72	69.5	113
FRONT	N/A				

Weekend: $12.00
Weekend: $18.00 All day
Discounts: None
Junior Golf: No **Membership:** N/R
Non-Metal Spikes: Not Required

N ME

The course is well maintained, hilly and scenic. Open from mid May to mid Sept.

	1	2	3	4	5	6	7	8	9
PAR	4	4	4	4	5	3	4	5	3
YARDS	432	323	321	343	478	128	388	504	165
HDCP	1	13	16	6	11	18	4	8	15
	10	11	12	13	14	15	16	17	18
PAR	4	4	4	4	5	3	4	5	3
YARDS	432	323	321	343	478	174	388	504	211
HDCP	N/R								

Directions: Take I-95 to Sherman/Patton Exit (Route 11). Follow Route 11 North into Portage (60 mi.).

4✪ =Excellent 3✪ =Very Good 2✪ =Good

Presque Isle CC 41

Presque Isle, ME (207) 764-0430

Club Pro: Barry Madore
Pro Shop: Full inventory
Payment: Visa, MC, Cash
Tee Times: No
Fee 9 Holes: Weekday: $12.00
Fee 18 Holes: Weekday: $20.00
Cart Rental: $20.00/18 $12/9
Lessons: $20/35 min. **School:** No
Driving Range: $3.00 /bucket.
Other: Clubhouse / Lockers / Showers / Restaurant/Lounge
Weekend: $12.00
Weekend: $20.00
Discounts: None
Junior Golf: Yes **Membership:** Yes
Non-Metal Spikes: Required

Tees	Holes	Yards	Par	USGA	Slope
BACK	18	6730	72	71.4	122
MIDDLE	18	6326	72	69.1	117
FRONT	18	5600	72	72.5	119

A very picturesque golf course. Front 9 designed by Architect Ben Gray. More recent back 9 designed by Geoffrey Cornish and Rick Hobbs.

	1	2	3	4	5	6	7	8	9
PAR	4	4	4	3	4	4	5	3	5
YARDS	343	400	363	167	423	389	463	146	465
HDCP	13	5	9	15	1	3	11	17	7
	10	11	12	13	14	15	16	17	18
PAR	4	4	5	4	4	5	3	3	4
YARDS	381	387	525	359	396	473	103	202	341
HDCP	12	10	4	8	6	2	18	16	14

Directions: From Presque Isle, take Route 167 to Route 205. You can't miss it, but if you do, call course for directions.

Sugarloaf Golf Club ★★★ 42

Bigelow, ME (207) 237-2000

Club Pro: J. Scott Hoisington
Pro Shop: Full inventory
Payment: Cash or credit card
Tee Times: 14 days adv.
Fee 9 Holes: Weekday: $46.00
Fee 18 Holes: Weekday: $95.00
Cart Rental: $9.00/9 $16.00/18
Lessons: $30.00/half-hour **School:** Jr. & Sr.
Driving Range: $3.00-6.00/bag
Other: Snack bar / Restaurant / Bar-lounge / Health club / Hotel
Weekend: $46.00
Weekend: $95.00
Discounts: Junior 50%
Junior Golf: Yes **Membership:** Yes
Non-Metal Spikes: Preferred

Tees	Holes	Yards	Par	USGA	Slope
BACK	18	6910	72	74.4	151
MIDDLE	18	6425	72	72.3	146
FRONT	18	5376	72	73.7	136

Breathtaking course! Rated one of the best in Maine. Also rated among the best resort courses in U.S. by *Golf Digest*. Discounted rates for guests.

	1	2	3	4	5	6	7	8	9
PAR	4	5	3	5	4	4	4	3	4
YARDS	406	510	190	506	387	371	363	169	389
HDCP	13	11	9	7	1	5	15	17	3
	10	11	12	13	14	15	16	17	18
PAR	4	3	5	4	4	3	5	4	4
YARDS	278	190	514	364	370	170	513	354	381
HDCP	18	12	4	8	16	14	10	6	2

Directions: Located 36 miles north of Farmington on Route 27 at Sugarloaf Mountain Ski Resort.

Todd Valley Golf Club

Charleston, ME (207) 285-7725

Club Pro: Kenneth J. Young
Pro Shop: Limited inventory
Payment: Cash only
Tee Times: No
Fee 9 Holes: Weekday: $8.00
Fee 18 Holes: Weekday: $12.00
Cart Rental: $8.00/9 $14.00/18
Lessons: Yes **School:** No
Driving Range: $3.00/lg
Other: Snack Bar
Weekend: $8.00
Weekend: $12.00
Discounts: None
Junior Golf: No **Membership:** No
Non-Metal Spikes: Not Required

Tees	Holes	Yards	Par	USGA	Slope
BACK	N/A				
MIDDLE	9	4672	66	61.1	93
FRONT	9	4042	66	61.1	93

Compared to a Coney Island roller coaster. Open from snow melt to snow fall.

	1	2	3	4	5	6	7	8	9
PAR	3	4	4	5	3	3	4	4	3
YARDS	183	255	315	487	120	150	250	280	196
HDCP	11	17	3	1	13	15	7	9	5
	10	11	12	13	14	15	16	17	18
PAR	3	4	4	5	3	3	4	4	3
YARDS	183	255	315	487	120	150	250	280	196
HDCP	12	18	4	2	14	16	8	10	6

Directions: From 95 Bangor west on Route 15. 20 miles to Charleston (1 mile after E. Corinth). Turn left on to Bacon Rd. Course is 1 mile on left.

Va-Jo-Wa Golf Club

Walker Rd., Island Falls, ME (207) 463-2128

Club Pro: Warren Walker
Pro Shop: Full inventory
Payment: MC, Visa, Dis.
Tee Times: Suggested
Fee 9 Holes: Weekday: $14.00
Fee 18 Holes: Weekday: $21.00
Cart Rental: $12pp/18, $7pp/9
Lessons: $25/30 min. by appt. **School:** No
Driving Range: No
Other: Clubhouse / Snack bar / Restaurant / Bar-lounge / Condos / Bag Storage
Weekend: $16.00
Weekend: $24.00
Discounts: 12 yrs. and under
Junior Golf: July **Membership:** Yes
Non-Metal Spikes: Required

Tees	Holes	Yards	Par	USGA	Slope
BACK	18	6223	72	70.4	125
MIDDLE	18	5862	72	69.1	121
FRONT	18	5862	72	69.6	115

Only course in 80 mile radius with full 18 holes. Back nine are considered championship caliber. Hilly, scenic and 6 water holes. Open May 1 - Oct.31.

	1	2	3	4	5	6	7	8	9
PAR	4	4	4	3	4	3	5	4	5
YARDS	308	445	283	207	378	116	517	354	531
HDCP	9	1	3	13	7	17	3	11	5
	10	11	12	13	14	15	16	17	18
PAR	4	3	4	4	4	5	3	4	5
YARDS	315	138	381	458	387	478	161	371	524
HDCP	12	18	14	2	6	8	16	10	4

Directions: Take I-95 to Island Falls Exit (#59); follow Route 2 East 3 miles; look for signs to VA-JO-WA.

4❂ =Excellent 3❂ =Very Good 2❂ =Good

Waterville Country Club   45

Oakland, ME (207) 465-9861

Club Pro: Don Roberts, PGA
Pro Shop: Full inventory
Payment: Cash only
Tee Times: No
Fee 9 Holes: Weekday: No
Fee 18 Holes: Weekday: $40.00
Cart Rental: $22.00/18
Lessons: $35/30 min. **School:** No
Driving Range: $3.00/bucket
Other: Snack bar / Restaurant / Bar-lounge

Tees	Holes	Yards	Par	USGA	Slope
BACK	18	6427	70	69.6	124
MIDDLE	18	6108	70	68.2	121
FRONT	18	5381	70	71.3	119

Weekend: No
Weekend: $40.00
Discounts: None
Junior Golf: Yes **Membership:** No
Non-Metal Spikes: Required

Waterville has hosted three New England Ladies Amateur and five Maine Amateur tournaments. Ranked fourth in the state by *Golf Digest*. Excellent course for all golfers. Cut out of the woods.

	1	2	3	4	5	6	7	8	9
PAR	4	3	5	4	4	3	4	4	5
YARDS	350	140	455	378	430	170	300	385	505
HDCP	15	13	17	3	1	9	7	5	11
	10	11	12	13	14	15	16	17	18
PAR	4	4	4	3	4	4	3	4	4
YARDS	435	410	370	200	355	330	185	370	340
HDCP	2	4	6	8	14	16	10	12	18

Directions: I-95 North to Exit 33 to Oakland. Waterville Country Club is 1 1/2 miles on left.

White Birches GC   46

Ellsworth, ME (207) 667-3621

Club Pro: Duffy McCallister
Pro Shop: Full inventory
Payment: Visa, MC, Amex
Tee Times: No
Fee 9 Holes: Weekday: $15.00 all day
Fee 18 Holes: Weekday: $15.00 all day
Cart Rental: $18.00/18 $10.00/9
Lessons: $35/30 min. **School:** NR
Driving Range: No
Other: Clubhouse / Bar-lounge / Restaurant / Motel

Tees	Holes	Yards	Par	USGA	Slope
BACK	9	5010	68	63.5	109
MIDDLE	9	4800	68	63.5	109
FRONT	9	4200	68	N/A	N/A

Weekend: $15.00 all day
Weekend: $15.00 all day
Discounts: None
Junior Golf: No **Membership:** Yes
Non-Metal Spikes: Not Required

Although fairly flat, the course is very challenging with numerous elevated greens and tees, 3-4 pond holes, and a couple of 90° dog leg holes. Open April - October.

	1	2	3	4	5	6	7	8	9
PAR	3	4	3	4	4	4	4	4	4
YARDS	228	301	151	280	263	256	271	350	306
HDCP	1	15	17	7	7	3	13	1	11
	10	11	12	13	14	15	16	17	18
PAR	3	4	3	4	4	4	4	4	4
YARDS	228	301	151	296	288	380	286	365	316
HDCP	2	16	18	8	10	6	12	4	14

Directions: Take I-95 to Route 45A Exit, follow to Ellsworth on Route 1 East; course is 1 1/2 miles on left.

Woodland Terrace GC

East Holden, ME (207) 989-3750

Club Pro: No
Pro Shop: Limited inventory
Payment: Visa, MC
Tee Times: No
Fee 9 Holes: Weekday: $7.50
Fee 18 Holes: Weekday: $10.50
Cart Rental: Pull carts
Lessons: No **School:** N/A
Driving Range: No
Other: Snack bar / Hotel

Tees	Holes	Yards	Par	USGA	Slope
BACK					
MIDDLE	9	1050	30	53	N/A
FRONT					

Weekend: $7.50
Weekend: $10.50
Discounts: Senior
Junior Golf: **Membership:** N/A
Non-Metal Spikes: Not Required

The course has resort facilities, including a pool, shuffleboard court, horseshoes, etc. The greens are well maintained. Open April - October. Tuesday is ladies day. All day fee $18.00.

	1	2	3	4	5	6	7	8	9
PAR	3	3	3	4	3	4	3	4	3
YARDS	147	125	130	250	195	215	115	200	110
HDCP	9	17	13	1	5	7	11	3	15

	10	11	12	13	14	15	16	17	18
PAR									
YARDS									
HDCP									

Directions: Take Route 95 North to Route 395 (Bar Harbor) to Route 1A (East Holden). Follow 2.25 miles to course on right side.

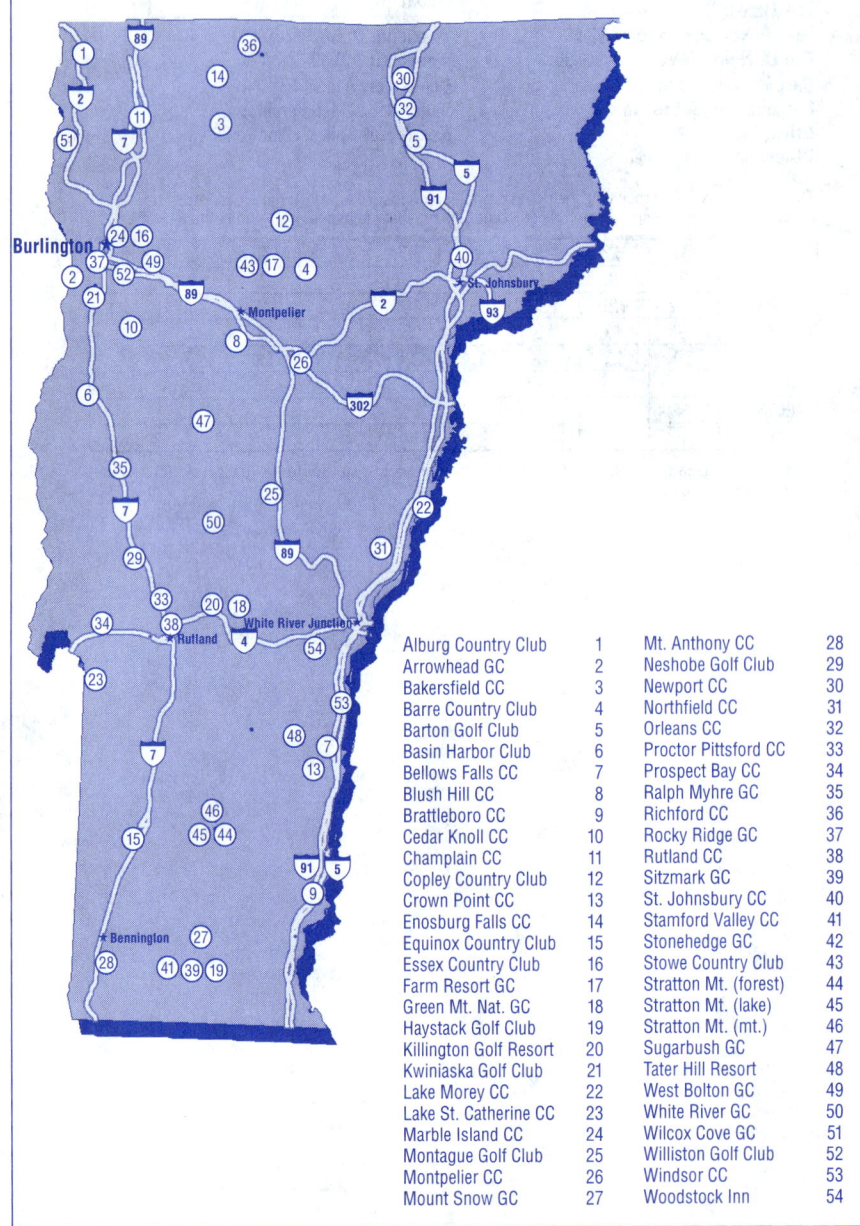

CHAPTER 8
Vermont

Club	#	Club	#
Alburg Country Club	1	Mt. Anthony CC	28
Arrowhead GC	2	Neshobe Golf Club	29
Bakersfield CC	3	Newport CC	30
Barre Country Club	4	Northfield CC	31
Barton Golf Club	5	Orleans CC	32
Basin Harbor Club	6	Proctor Pittsford CC	33
Bellows Falls CC	7	Prospect Bay CC	34
Blush Hill CC	8	Ralph Myhre GC	35
Brattleboro CC	9	Richford CC	36
Cedar Knoll CC	10	Rocky Ridge GC	37
Champlain CC	11	Rutland CC	38
Copley Country Club	12	Sitzmark GC	39
Crown Point CC	13	St. Johnsbury CC	40
Enosburg Falls CC	14	Stamford Valley CC	41
Equinox Country Club	15	Stonehedge GC	42
Essex Country Club	16	Stowe Country Club	43
Farm Resort GC	17	Stratton Mt. (forest)	44
Green Mt. Nat. GC	18	Stratton Mt. (lake)	45
Haystack Golf Club	19	Stratton Mt. (mt.)	46
Killington Golf Resort	20	Sugarbush GC	47
Kwiniaska Golf Club	21	Tater Hill Resort	48
Lake Morey CC	22	West Bolton GC	49
Lake St. Catherine CC	23	White River GC	50
Marble Island CC	24	Wilcox Cove GC	51
Montague Golf Club	25	Williston Golf Club	52
Montpelier CC	26	Windsor CC	53
Mount Snow GC	27	Woodstock Inn	54

264 Vermont   NEW ENGLAND GOLFGUIDE

Alburg Country Club 1

Rt. 79, Alburg, VT (802) 796-3586

Club Pro: No
Pro Shop: Limited inventory
Payment: Cash, Check
Tee Times: Call
Fee 9 Holes: Weekday: NA
Fee 18 Holes: Weekday: $20.00
Cart Rental: $25/18
Lessons: Yes **School:** No
Driving Range: $3.00/bucket
Other: Clubhouse / Snack bar / Bar-lounge

Tees	Holes	Yards	Par	USGA	Slope
BACK	18	6391	72	70.2	119
MIDDLE	18	N/A	72	70.2	119
FRONT	18	5536	75	71.2	120

Weekend: NA
Weekend: $25.00
Discounts: Junior
Junior Golf: Yes **Membership:** Yes
Non-Metal Spikes: Not Required

A good vacation course. A moderate challenge for a good time. Reduced rates after 2:00 pm. White tees added.

	1	2	3	4	5	6	7	8	9
PAR	5	3	4	5	4	4	3	5	4
YARDS	527	167	424	548	296	286	170	487	362
HDCP	6	16	2	5	12	11	17	7	10
	10	11	12	13	14	15	16	17	18
PAR	4	4	4	4	3	4	5	3	4
YARDS	307	367	447	360	180	432	469	143	419
HDCP	13	14	1	9	15	3	8	18	4

Directions: Take I-89 to Exit 17; take Route 2 to Champlain Islands North to Alburg; take Route 129 to course.

Arrowhead Golf Course 2

Milton, Vt., 802-893-0234

Club Pro: No
Pro Shop: Limited inventory
Payment: Cash, Check
Tee Times: No
Fee 9 Holes: Weekday: $11.00
Fee 18 Holes: Weekday: $11.00
Cart Rental: Yes
Lessons: $25.00/30 min. **School:** No
Driving Range: $5.00/lg. $3.00/sm.
Other: Club House

Tees	Holes	Yards	Par	USGA	Slope
BACK	9	1390	27	25.6	66
MIDDLE	9	1350	27	25.6	66
FRONT	9	1014	27	24.4	55

Weekend: $13.00
Weekend: $13.00
Discounts: Junior
Junior Golf: N/R **Membership:** Yes
Non-Metal Spikes: Not Required

VT

Par 3, 9 hole course uses Astroturf tees. Greens were designed by owner. 3rd hole is very challenging.

	1	2	3	4	5	6	7	8	9
PAR	3	3	3	3	3	3	3	3	3
YARDS	165	150	210	90	120	195	135	105	180
HDCP	3	5	1	9	7	2	6	8	4
	10	11	12	13	14	15	16	17	18
PAR									
YARDS									
HDCP									

Directions: Exit 18 from Route 89, go south on Route 7 approximately .5 mile. Turn right onto Gerogia Manor Road for .5 mile, take left on to old Stage for 1 mile, then right onto Murray Ave for 1.6 miles, Course is on left.

4✪ =Excellent 3✪ =Very Good 2✪ =Good

Bakersfield CC

Rt. 109, Bakersfield, VT (802) 933-5100

Club Pro: No
Pro Shop: Limited inventory
Payment: Visa, MC, Amex
Tee Times: No
Fee 9 Holes: Weekday: N/A
Fee 18 Holes: Weekday: $14.00 all day
Cart Rental: $18.00/18 $12.00/9
Lessons: No **School:** No
Driving Range: No
Other: Snack bar / Restaurant / Bar-lounge

Tees	Holes	Yards	Par	USGA	Slope
BACK	N/A				
MIDDLE	9	5940	70	69	115
FRONT	9	5220	70	68.7	108

Weekend: N/A
Weekend: $16.00 all day
Discounts: None
Junior Golf: Yes **Membership:** Jr membership
Non-Metal Spikes: Not Required

The course is very rustic and wildlife frequently comes onto the fairways. Formerly Wolf Run.

	1	2	3	4	5	6	7	8	9
PAR	4	4	3	4	5	4	4	3	4
YARDS	315	445	170	350	460	375	360	165	330
HDCP	N/A								
	10	11	12	13	14	15	16	17	18
PAR	4	4	3	4	5	4	4	3	4
YARDS	315	445	170	350	460	375	360	165	330
HDCP	N/A								

Directions: Take Route 108 through Bakersfield. Take right onto Boston Post Road. Follow signs.

Barre Country Club

Plainsfield Rd., Barre, VT (802) 476-7658

Club Pro: David Christy
Pro Shop: Full inventory
Payment: Visa, MC
Tee Times: 1 week adv.
Fee 9 Holes: Weekday: $20.00
Fee 18 Holes: Weekday: $35.00
Cart Rental: $15 pp/18 $9 pp/9
Lessons: $25-$30/30 min. **School:** No
Driving Range: $3.00/lg.
Other: Clubhouse / Lockers / Showers / Snack bar / Restaurant / Bar-lounge

Tees	Holes	Yards	Par	USGA	Slope
BACK	18	6237	71	70.2	123
MIDDLE	18	5986	71	69.2	119
FRONT	18	5410	71	71.7	124

Weekend: $20.00
Weekend: $35.00
Discounts: None
Junior Golf: Yes **Membership:** Yes
Non-Metal Spikes: Yes

"One of the hidden gems in Vermont." Reviewed by Vermont Golf Magazine.

	1	2	3	4	5	6	7	8	9
PAR	4	4	4	3	5	4	3	4	4
YARDS	368	393	302	190	455	339	142	370	393
HDCP	11	1	13	15	7	5	17	9	3
	10	11	12	13	14	15	16	17	18
PAR	5	4	4	3	4	5	3	4	4
YARDS	492	372	314	163	431	439	128	343	352
HDCP	4	6	12	16	2	10	18	14	8

Directions: Take I-89 to Exit 7 (to Barre), follow Route 14 3.9 miles. Follow signs.

Barton Golf Club 5

Rt. 1, Barton, VT (802) 525-1126

Club Pro: Brian King
Pro Shop: Limited inventory
Payment: Cash, Check
Tee Times: Yes
Fee 9 Holes: Weekday: $8.00
Fee 18 Holes: Weekday: $12.00
Cart Rental: $5.00 pp/9
Lessons: No **School:** No
Driving Range: No
Other: Snack Bar

Weekend: $8.00
Weekend: $12.00
Discounts: None
Junior Golf: No **Membership:** Yes
Non-Metal Spikes: Not Required

Tees	Holes	Yards	Par	USGA	Slope
BACK	N/A				
MIDDLE	9	5626	71	66	113
FRONT	N/A				

Relatively flat course with view of Jay Peak. Tree-defined fairways, small greens, sand traps. Grass remains green all season.

	1	2	3	4	5	6	7	8	9
PAR	4	4	5	4	4	3	5	3	4
YARDS	245	430	485	300	265	123	485	140	320
HDCP	11	3	1	13	15	17	5	7	9
	10	11	12	13	14	15	16	17	18
PAR	3	4	5	4	4	3	5	3	4
YARDS	211	420	470	320	272	140	520	150	330
HDCP	4	6	2	14	18	16	8	10	12

Directions: Exit 25 off I-91 N or Exit 26 off I-91 S. Follow signs to Barton. North on Route 5 to RR crossing. Cross and take immediate left. 1.5 miles to course.

Basin Harbor Club 6

Vergennes, VT (802) 475-2309

Club Pro: Leo Reynolds
Pro Shop: Full inventory
Payment: Visa, MC
Tee Times: 2 days adv.
Fee 9 Holes: Weekday: $25.00 after 4:30
Fee 18 Holes: Weekday: $42.00
Cart Rental: $26.00/18, $15.00/9
Lessons: $35/30 min **School:** No
Driving Range: $3.50sm $6.75/lg
Other: Clubhouse / Snack bar / Restaurant / Bar-lounge / Hotel

Weekend: $25.00 after 4:30
Weekend: $42.00
Discounts: None
Junior Golf: Yes **Membership:** Yes
Non-Metal Spikes: Required

Tees	Holes	Yards	Par	USGA	Slope
BACK	18	6513	72	71.5	122
MIDDLE	18	6232	72	70.4	120
FRONT	18	5745	72	68.1	116

VT

Fairly flat, located on Lake Champlain. Scenic view of lake and Adirondack Mountains. Collared shirt required. No cutoffs. Open May 1 - mid October.

	1	2	3	4	5	6	7	8	9
PAR	4	4	4	4	3	4	3	5	5
YARDS	360	361	398	328	103	323	150	458	475
HDCP	9	7	1	11	17	13	15	3	5
	10	11	12	13	14	15	16	17	18
PAR	4	4	5	3	4	4	3	5	4
YARDS	387	376	500	181	324	414	175	510	409
HDCP	16	10	6	18	8	2	14	4	12

Directions: Take Route 7 to Vergennes Exit. Straight through town on Route 22A. Cross over bridge, take right at sign to Basin Harbor. 1 mile to Basin Harbor Road, take right, 6 miles to course.

4 =Excellent **3** =Very Good **2** =Good

Bellows Falls CC 7

Rt. 103, Rockingham, VT (802) 463-9809

Club Pro: Jeremy Hyjek
Pro Shop: Full inventory
Payment: Visa, MC
Tee Times: No
Fee 9 Holes: Weekday: $15.00
Fee 18 Holes: Weekday: $24.00
Cart Rental: $22.00/18 $15.00/9
Lessons: Yes **School:** No
Driving Range: No
Other: Clubhouse / Restaurant / Bar

Tees	Holes	Yards	Par	USGA	Slope
BACK	N/A				
MIDDLE	9	5928	70	65.8	117
FRONT	9	5138	70	65.8	110

Weekend: $18.00
Weekend: $28.00
Discounts: None
Junior Golf: No **Membership:** Yes
Non-Metal Spikes: Required

COUPON

Course in operation since 1921. Very challenging. Owned by the membership. Open May 1 - November 1.

	1	2	3	4	5	6	7	8	9
PAR	4	5	3	3	4	4	4	3	5
YARDS	389	513	178	155	381	370	320	158	428
HDCP	4	8	10	16	6	2	12	18	14
	10	11	12	13	14	15	16	17	18
PAR	4	5	3	3	4	4	4	3	5
YARDS	402	529	194	177	391	380	355	170	438
HDCP	3	7	9	15	5	1	11	17	13

Directions: I-91 to Route 103 North. Appx. 3 miles, turn right onto Rockingham Road. Across from VT Country Store.

Blush Hill CC 8

Waterbury, VT (802) 244-8974

Club Pro: Jon Milne
Pro Shop: Full inventory
Payment: Visa, MC
Tee Times: Yes
Fee 9 Holes: Weekday: $16.00
Fee 18 Holes: Weekday: $18.00
Cart Rental: $21.00/18 $16.00/9
Lessons: $25/30 min. **School:** No
Driving Range: $3.00/lg. bucket
Other: Clubhouse / Lockers / Showers / Snack bar / Restaurant / Bar-lounge / Hotel

Tees	Holes	Yards	Par	USGA	Slope
BACK	N/A				
MIDDLE	9	4730	66	63.4	101
FRONT	9	4534	66	61.9	96

Weekend: $18.00
Weekend: $22.00
Discounts: None
Junior Golf: Yes **Membership:** Yes
Non-Metal Spikes: Preferred

COUPON

8 new tees in 1998, new scorecard yet to be printed. One of the most extraordinary scenic views in Vermont. Course kept in excellent shape. Open May 1 to October 15. **www.blushhill.com**

	1	2	3	4	5	6	7	8	9
PAR	4	4	4	3	4	3	3	4	4
YARDS	370	350	206	187	269	146	162	366	309
HDCP	3	1	13	15	7	17	11	5	9
	10	11	12	13	14	15	16	17	18
PAR	4	4	4	3	4	3	3	4	4
YARDS	370	350	206	187	269	146	162	366	309
HDCP	4	2	14	16	8	18	12	6	10

Directions: 1/2 mile off I-89 North on Route 100. 1000 feet left on Blush Hill Road, 1/2 mile behind Holiday Inn.

Brattleboro CC ▸ 9

Rt. 30, Brattleboro, VT (802) 257-7380

Club Pro: Micheal Zaranek
Pro Shop: Full inventory
Payment: Visa, MC
Tee Times: 2 days adv.
Fee 9 Holes: Weekday: $17.00
Fee 18 Holes: Weekday: $28.00
Cart Rental: $12.00/18, $8.00/9
Lessons: $25/30 min **School:** No
Driving Range: No
Other: Snack bar / Bar-lounge

Tees	Holes	Yards	Par	USGA	Slope
BACK	9	6265	71	69.8	117
MIDDLE	9	6320	71	69.8	117
FRONT	9	5440	71	71.0	115

Weekend: $17.00
Weekend: $28.00
Discounts: None
Junior Golf: Yes **Membership:** Yes
Non-Metal Spikes: Required

Built in 1914 with classical New England layout. Open May - October. Dress Code. Junior memberships.

	1	2	3	4	5	6	7	8	9
PAR	3	4	5	4	4	4	3	4	4
YARDS	205	370	505	380	385	325	155	345	395
HDCP	15	5	7	1	3	13	17	11	9
	10	11	12	13	14	15	16	17	18
PAR	3	4	5	5	4	4	3	4	4
YARDS	205	370	505	480	385	415	155	345	395
HDCP	16	6	8	12	4	2	18	14	10

Directions: Take I-91 S, Exit 3 or I-91 N, Exit 2. Follow to Brattleboro Center; follow Route 30 to course.

Cedar Knoll CC ▸ 10

Hinesburg, VT (802) 482-3186

Club Pro: No
Pro Shop: Limited inventory
Payment: Visa, MC, Amex
Tee Times: Weekends
Fee 9 Holes: Weekday: N/A
Fee 18 Holes: Weekday: $21, $13.65 aftr. 5pm
Cart Rental: $22.00/18
Lessons: Yes **School:** No
Driving Range: $2.00-$5.00/bucket
Other: Restaurant / Clubhouse / Bar-Lounge / Lockers / Showers / Snack Bar

Tees	Holes	Yards	Par	USGA	Slope
BACK	18	6541	72		
MIDDLE	18	6144	72	72.5	117
FRONT	18	5360	72	69.5	108

Weekend: N/A
Weekend: $21, $13.65 aftr 5pm
Discounts: Senior
Junior Golf: No **Membership:** Yes
Non-Metal Spikes: Not Required

VT

There are now an additional 9 holes with 2611 yards from the middle tees. Rolling hills. 250 acres allows for much spacing of holes. Beautiful scenery. Reduced rates after 5:00.

	1	2	3	4	5	6	7	8	9
PAR	5	3	4	4	5	3	4	4	4
YARDS	500	156	315	358	505	170	392	313	438
HDCP	3	17	5	11	7	15	9	13	1
	10	11	12	13	14	15	16	17	18
PAR	5	3	4	4	3	4	4	4	5
YARDS	494	169	298	333	156	291	341	315	536
HDCP	4	16	12	6	18	14	10	8	2

Directions: I-89, Exit 12; follow 5 miles to intersection of Routes 2A and 116. Take left and go 5 miles on 116. Course on right.

4✪ =Excellent 3✪ =Very Good 2✪ =Good

Champlain CC　　11

Swanton, VT (802) 527-1187

Club Pro: Michael Swim
Pro Shop: Full inventory
Payment: MC, Visa, Discover
Tee Times: Weekends, Holidays
Fee 9 Holes: Weekday: $14.00
Fee 18 Holes: Weekday: $23.00
Cart Rental: $22.00/18 $12.00/9
Lessons: $20.00/half hour **School:**
Driving Range: No
Other: Clubhouse / Lockers / Showers / Snack bar / Restaurant / Bar-lounge

Tees	Holes	Yards	Par	USGA	Slope
BACK	18	6237	70	69.9	123
MIDDLE	18	5959	70	68.8	121
FRONT	18	5266	70	70.4	117

Weekend: $16.00
Weekend: $26.00
Discounts: Junior
Junior Golf: Yes **Membership:** Yes
Non-Metal Spikes: Required

COUPON

The course is scenic with tree-lined fairways. Established in 1915.

	1	2	3	4	5	6	7	8	9
PAR	4	5	3	4	4	4	3	4	4
YARDS	359	472	157	377	355	360	135	350	342
HDCP	1	7	15	3	13	9	17	5	11
	10	11	12	13	14	15	16	17	18
PAR	4	4	3	4	3	5	4	4	4
YARDS	303	444	142	370	167	558	338	415	315
HDCP	16	2	18	8	14	4	10	6	12

Directions: Take I-89 to Exit 20; take Route 7 North 1/2 mile to course.

Copley Country Club　　12

Maple Rd., Morrisville, VT (802) 888-3013

Club Pro: No
Pro Shop: Full inventory
Payment: Visa, MC
Tee Times: No
Fee 9 Holes: Weekday: $15.00
Fee 18 Holes: Weekday: $22.00
Cart Rental: $26.00/18 $15.75/9
Lessons: Yes **School:** No
Driving Range: No
Other: Clubhouse / Lockers / Snack bar / Restaurant / Bar-lounge

Tees	Holes	Yards	Par	USGA	Slope
BACK	9	6000	70	67.4	112
MIDDLE	9	5549	70	67.4	112
FRONT	9	5020	70	68.0	104

Weekend: $15.00
Weekend: $22.00
Discounts: None
Junior Golf: Yes **Membership:** Yes
Non-Metal Spikes: Preferred

The course is level with a handful of tree-lined holes. Established 1932. Reduced 9 hole fee after 5 pm. Affiliated with Stowe/Copley Junior Golf School.

	1	2	3	4	5	6	7	8	9
PAR	4	3	4	4	3	5	4	4	4
YARDS	310	218	326	296	171	526	395	270	262
HDCP	7	15	5	13	17	1	3	11	9
	10	11	12	13	14	15	16	17	18
PAR	4	3	4	4	3	5	4	4	4
YARDS	310	218	326	296	171	526	396	270	262
HDCP	8	16	6	14	18	2	4	12	10

Directions: Take I-89 to Waterbury Exit, follow 18 miles to Morrisville.

Crown Point CC

Springfield, VT (802) 885-1010

Tees	Holes	Yards	Par	USGA	Slope
BACK	18	6602	72	71.2	123
MIDDLE	18	6120	72	69.1	119
FRONT	18	5542	72	71.3	117

Club Pro: Mark Bradley
Pro Shop: Full inventory
Payment: Visa, MC, cash
Tee Times: Required
Fee 9 Holes: Weekday: Call for rates **Weekend:** Call for rates
Fee 18 Holes: Weekday: Call for rates **Weekend:** Call for rates
Cart Rental: Yes **Discounts:** Senior & Junior
Lessons: Yes **School:** No **Junior Golf:** Yes **Membership:** Yes
Driving Range: Yes **Non-Metal Spikes:** Preferred
Other: Clubhouse / Showers / Restaurant / Bar-lounge

Dress code: collared shirts required, no jeans on weekends. No tank tops, t-shirts, gym shorts, or sweatpants. Open April 15 - November 1 (weather permitting.)

	1	2	3	4	5	6	7	8	9
PAR	4	5	4	4	3	4	5	4	3
YARDS	370	426	344	337	168	365	487	376	154
HDCP	13	7	11	9	15	3	1	5	17
	10	11	12	13	14	15	16	17	18
PAR	4	5	4	3	4	5	4	4	3
YARDS	344	463	390	158	344	459	381	371	183
HDCP	12	10	8	16	4	2	14	6	18

Directions: From I-91 North, Exit 7: turn right and follow to center of Springfield. Turn right onto Valley Street. Course 3 miles on left.

Enosburg Falls CC

Enosburg Falls, VT (802) 933-2296

Tees	Holes	Yards	Par	USGA	Slope
BACK	18	5580	72	67.4	116
MIDDLE	18	5418	72	66.8	115
FRONT	18	4633	72	63.4	108

Club Pro: Gary Shover, Instructor
Pro Shop: Full inventory
Payment: MC, Visa
Tee Times: Yes
Fee 9 Holes: Weekday: $13.00 + tax **Weekend:** $15.00 + tax
Fee 18 Holes: Weekday: $20.00 + tax **Weekend:** $23.00 + tax
Cart Rental: Yes **Discounts:** Junior
Lessons: Yes **School:** No **Junior Golf:** N/R **Membership:** Yes
Driving Range: No **Non-Metal Spikes:** Required
Other: Restaurant / Clubhouse / Lockers / Showers

A short course with a long par-three and par-five. Some great birdie opportunities. Special rates: jrs. & full-time students. Open May - October. www.homepages.together.net/~pmc1967/course.htm

	1	2	3	4	5	6	7	8	9
PAR	4	5	4	4	4	3	4	5	3
YARDS	249	498	337	251	350	115	331	552	119
HDCP	13	5	9	17	1	11	7	3	15
	10	11	12	13	14	15	16	17	18
PAR	4	3	4	5	5	3	4	4	4
YARDS	272	140	335	490	478	112	267	255	267
HDCP	12	14	10	4	2	18	6	8	16

Directions: Exit at St. Albans to Route 105 North; follow to Enosberg Falls. Take left at Jct. of Routes 108 and 105 to course.

4✪ = Excellent 3✪ = Very Good 2✪ = Good

Equinox Country Club   15

Rt. 7A, Manchester, VT (802) 362-3223

Club Pro: Richard Wood, PGA
Pro Shop: Full inventory
Payment: MC, Visa, Amex, Dis.
Tee Times: 7 days adv.
Fee 9 Holes: Weekday: N/A
Fee 18 Holes: Weekday: $80.00
Cart Rental: $19 pp/18
Lessons: $35.00/half hour   **School:** No
Driving Range: No
Other: Restaurant / Clubhouse / Snack bar / Bar-lounge / Hotel / Lockers / Showers

Tees	Holes	Yards	Par	USGA	Slope
BACK	18	6450	71	71.3	129
MIDDLE	18	6069	71	69.1	125
FRONT	18	5082	71	65.2	117

Weekend: N/A
Weekend: $90.00
Discounts: None
Junior Golf: No   **Membership:** N/R
Non-Metal Spikes: Required

Rebuilt in 1991. Many features restored. Brought to a standard of contemporary excellence. Greens are no longer small. Rates after 3 pm: $43 weekday, $50 weekend.

	1	2	3	4	5	6	7	8	9
PAR	4	4	4	3	4	4	5	4	4
YARDS	334	385	346	141	316	323	502	380	344
HDCP	15	3	11	17	13	5	7	1	9
	10	11	12	13	14	15	16	17	18
PAR	4	4	4	4	3	5	3	4	4
YARDS	336	361	347	401	112	462	181	403	395
HDCP	16	10	12	4	18	8	14	6	2

Directions: Located on Route 7A in Manchester.

Essex Country Club   16

Essex Junction, VT (802) 879-3232

Club Pro: No
Pro Shop: Limited inventory
Payment: Visa, MC
Tee Times: Yes
Fee 9 Holes: Weekday: N/A
Fee 18 Holes: Weekday: $22.00
Cart Rental: $24.00/18
Lessons: Yes   **School:** No
Driving Range: No
Other:

Tees	Holes	Yards	Par	USGA	Slope
BACK	N/A				
MIDDLE	18	6315	72	70.4	117
FRONT	18	5500	72	69.1	112

Weekend: N/A
Weekend: $24.00
Discounts: None
Junior Golf: Yes   **Membership:** No
Non-Metal Spikes: Not Required

COUPON

Eighteen holes with pastoral and mountain views. Seven holes carved from mature evergreen wood lot. Greens and fairways in excellent condition. Open mid April - November 15.

	1	2	3	4	5	6	7	8	9
PAR	4	3	4	4	5	4	5	4	3
YARDS	365	155	400	330	450	335	530	315	190
HDCP	7	17	1	11	15	5	9	4	3
	10	11	12	13	14	15	16	17	18
PAR	5	4	4	3	4	5	3	4	4
YARDS	580	320	355	130	360	530	170	350	450
HDCP	2	6	10	18	4	8	14	16	12

Directions: I-89 Exit - Williston Exit Route 2A to Essex 5 corner, then take Route 15 to Old Stage Road 3 miles north to course.

Farm Resort GC

17

Rt. 100, Morrisville, VT (802) 888-3525

Club Pro: Eileen Kask
Pro Shop: Full inventory
Payment: Visa, MC, Dis.
Tee Times: Yes
Fee 9 Holes: Weekday: $15.00, M-Th.
Fee 18 Holes: Weekday: $20.00, M-Th.
Cart Rental: $21.00/18 $14.00/9
Lessons: $45/50 min **School:** Junior
Driving Range: $3.25/med.,5.50/lg.
Other: Snack Bar / Beer / Wine / Motel

Tees	Holes	Yards	Par	USGA	Slope
BACK	9	6038	72	69.4	108
MIDDLE	9	5798	72	68.3	108
FRONT	9	5198	72	68.9	113

Weekend: $17.00, F,S,S
Weekend: $24.00, F, S, S,Hol.
Discounts: Junior
Junior Golf: Yes **Membership:** Yes
Non-Metal Spikes: Not Required

COUPON

Hilly, scenic and challenging course with three water holes. Great course for golfers of all abilities. Play & Stay at one location. Open May - October.

	1	2	3	4	5	6	7	8	9
PAR	4	4	5	3	3	5	4	3	5
YARDS	331	290	460	147	142	556	391	142	450
HDCP	9	11	3	15	17	1	7	13	5
	10	11	12	13	14	15	16	17	18
PAR	4	4	5	3	3	5	4	3	5
YARDS	331	290	460	147	142	556	391	142	450
HDCP	10	12	4	16	18	2	8	14	6

Directions: Take I-89 to Exit 10; follow Route 100 N for 15 miles to course.

Green Mountain National G. C. ✪✪✪

18

Barrows Town Rd., Sherburne, VT (802) 422-GOLF

Club Pro: Jeff Hadley, Head Pro
Pro Shop: Full inventory
Payment: Visa, MC, AMEX
Tee Times: 7 days in adv.
Fee 9 Holes: Weekday: $24.00
Fee 18 Holes: Weekday: $42.00
Cart Rental: $16.00/18 $10.00/9
Lessons: $60.00/hour **School:** Jr. & Adult
Driving Range: $6.00/lg. $3.00/sm.
Other: Bar/Lounge/Snack Bar

Tees	Holes	Yards	Par	USGA	Slope
BACK	18	6589	71	72.6	139
MIDDLE	18	6164	71	70.2	132
FRONT	18	4740	71	63.9	118

Weekend: $29.00
Weekend: $49.00
Discounts: Junior $26.00
Junior Golf: Yes **Membership:** Yes
Non-Metal Spikes: Required

COUPON

VT

Scenic, Green Mt. championship layout with many greens hidden from tees. Accuracy is a requirement. Opened August 1996. Bent grass. Designed by Gene Bates. www.gmngc.com

	1	2	3	4	5	6	7	8	9
PAR	5	4	4	4	3	5	3	4	4
YARDS	494	387	381	406	152	492	145	348	419
HDCP	7	9	11	1	15	5	17	13	3
	10	11	12	13	14	15	16	17	18
PAR	4	4	4	3	4	5	4	3	4
YARDS	396	350	375	157	326	437	359	169	371
HDCP	2	6	4	18	16	10	14	12	8

Directions: Exit 6 from I-91. Turn left onto Route 103 North for about 30 minutes. Take right on to Route 100 North. Go by Killington Mountain Road. Course is 2 miles on left. Travel time from I-91 is about 1 hour.

4✪ =Excellent 3✪ =Very Good 2✪ =Good

Haystack Golf Club

Mann Rd., Wilmington, VT (802) 464-8301

Club Pro: Dean Helm, PGA
Pro Shop: Full inventory
Payment: Visa, MC, Amex, Disc
Tee Times: 7 days adv.
Fee 9 Holes: Weekday:
Fee 18 Holes: Weekday: $40.00
Cart Rental: $15.00/person
Lessons: Yes **School:** Junior
Driving Range: $4.20/lg. Irons only
Other: Clubhouse / Lockers / Showers / Restaurant / Bar-lounge / Snack Bar / hotel

Weekend:
Weekend: $47, $24 after 4 w/cart
Discounts: Junior
Junior Golf: Yes **Membership:** Yes
Non-Metal Spikes: Preferred

Tees	Holes	Yards	Par	USGA	Slope
BACK	18	6549	72	71.7	128
MIDDLE	18	6164	72	69.3	125
FRONT	18	5396	74	71.4	122

Full championship course in dramatic mountain setting. Proper golf attire required. Call for discounts midweek! Group discounts. Open May 1 - November 1.

	1	2	3	4	5	6	7	8	9
PAR	4	4	5	3	4	4	3	5	4
YARDS	348	389	460	181	347	291	166	505	380
HDCP	9	1	7	13	11	15	17	3	5
	10	11	12	13	14	15	16	17	18
PAR	4	5	4	3	5	4	3	4	4
YARDS	328	509	352	160	516	343	165	301	423
HDCP	6	10	12	18	2	8	16	14	4

Directions: I-91 to Brattleboro, take Route 9 W to Wilmington. At light head north on Route 100 (3 miles.) Look for signs, turn left on Coldbrook Road (2 miles.) Take left on Mann Road (1.5 miles.) to gate.

Killington Golf Resort

Killington, VT (802) 422-6700

Club Pro: Dave Pfannenstein
Pro Shop: Full inventory
Payment: Visa, MC, Amex
Tee Times: Recommended
Fee 9 Holes: Weekday: Call
Fee 18 Holes: Weekday: Call
Cart Rental: Call
Lessons: $45.00/hour **School:** Jr. & Sr.
Driving Range: $4.50/lg, $3.50/sm. bucket
Other: Hotel / Clubhouse / Snack bar / Restaurant / Bar-lounge

Weekend: Call
Weekend: Call
Discounts: Junior
Junior Golf: Yes **Membership:** Yes
Non-Metal Spikes: Not Required

Tees	Holes	Yards	Par	USGA	Slope
BACK	18	6326	72	70.6	126
MIDDLE	18	5876	72	69.6	123
FRONT	18	5108	72	71.2	123

Carved out of the woods at Killington, this tight course requires tremendous shot-making accuracy. The expertly maintained layout makes great use of the natural slope. www.killington.com

	1	2	3	4	5	6	7	8	9
PAR	4	5	3	4	5	3	5	4	4
YARDS	354	485	163	395	452	138	480	321	270
HDCP	9	7	11	3	1	17	5	13	15
	10	11	12	13	14	15	16	17	18
PAR	4	5	4	4	3	4	4	3	4
YARDS	334	485	300	355	174	370	360	150	290
HDCP	14	4	12	8	16	2	6	18	10

Directions: From I-89 take Exit 1 onto Route 4 West to the Killington Road. Turn left onto Killington Road. Go 3.5 miles and look for signs.

Kwiniaska Golf Club

21

Shelburne, VT (802) 985-3672

Club Pro: Michael Bailey
Pro Shop: Full inventory
Payment: MC, Visa, Cash
Tee Times: Weekends & Holidays
Fee 9 Holes: Weekday: No
Fee 18 Holes: Weekday: $27.00
Cart Rental: $22.00
Lessons: Yes **School:** No
Driving Range: No
Other: Clubhouse / Locker room facilities/ Showers / Snack bar

Tees	Holes	Yards	Par	USGA	Slope
BACK	18	7037	72	72.5	128
MIDDLE	18	6777	72	71.2	125
FRONT	18	5632	72	72.6	119

Weekend: No
Weekend: $27.00
Discounts: None
Junior Golf: Yes **Membership:** No
Non-Metal Spikes: Not Required

Front nine are open and level. The back are rolling, with a stream crossing four fairways. View of the Green Mountains, the Adirondacks and Lake Champlain! Open April 15- Nov. 11.

	1	2	3	4	5	6	7	8	9
PAR	4	3	5	3	4	4	4	4	5
YARDS	424	182	480	174	465	381	432	383	552
HDCP	5	15	11	17	1	9	7	13	3
	10	11	12	13	14	15	16	17	18
PAR	4	4	3	5	4	3	5	4	4
YARDS	376	363	171	534	410	193	507	327	423
HDCP	18	6	16	8	10	12	2	14	4

Directions: Exit 14W from I-89. Follow signs to Spear Street then 5 miles south.

Lake Morey CC

22

Fairlee, VT (802) 333-4800

Club Pro: Bill Ross, Jr.
Pro Shop: Full inventory
Payment: Visa, MC
Tee Times: 4 days adv.
Fee 9 Holes: Weekday: $18.00
Fee 18 Holes: Weekday: $27.00
Cart Rental: $26.50/18
Lessons: $30.00/45 minutes **School:** No
Driving Range: $3.00/bucket
Other: Clubhouse / Showers / Snack bar / Restaurant / Bar-lounge / Hotel

Tees	Holes	Yards	Par	USGA	Slope
BACK	18	6024	70	69.4	120
MIDDLE	18	5807	70	68.4	118
FRONT	18	4942	70	68.0	116

Weekend: $18.00
Weekend: $34.00
Discounts: Senior, M-Tu.
Junior Golf: Yes **Membership:** Yes
Non-Metal Spikes: Required

COUPON

VT

The course has a level front nine and a hilly back nine. No lockers. Open May 1 - October 30.

	1	2	3	4	5	6	7	8	9
PAR	3	5	4	4	4	3	3	4	4
YARDS	213	460	356	337	334	158	114	395	321
HDCP	4	16	6	12	14	8	18	2	10
	10	11	12	13	14	15	16	17	18
PAR	4	4	5	5	4	3	4	3	4
YARDS	324	369	504	517	373	188	371	160	313
HDCP	15	5	1	7	3	9	11	17	13

Directions: Take I-91 North to Exit 15, take left off ramp and follow signs. 25 minutes north of White River Junction.

4 = Excellent 3 = Very Good 2 = Good

Lake St. Catherine CC   23

Poultney, VT (802) 287-9341

Club Pro: Bret Toon, PGA
Pro Shop: Full inventory
Payment: Visa, MC
Tee Times: Weekends and Holidays
Fee 9 Holes: Weekday: $11.55
Fee 18 Holes: Weekday: $21.00
Cart Rental: $15.75/9 $26.25/18
Lessons: $30/30 min. **School:** No
Driving Range: No
Other: Snack bar / Bar-lounge

Tees	Holes	Yards	Par	USGA	Slope
BACK	18	6293	72	70.9	127
MIDDLE	18	5971	72	69.1	123
FRONT	18	4940	72	68.2	116

Weekend: Twilight rate
Weekend: $28.35
Discounts: None
Junior Golf: Yes **Membership:** Yes
Non-Metal Spikes: N/R

Great views. Second oldest white oak in Vermont. Twilight rates. Open April-October.

	1	2	3	4	5	6	7	8	9
PAR	4	4	3	4	4	4	5	3	5
YARDS	402	308	147	425	360	333	488	185	414
HDCP	5	15	11	3	13	9	7	17	2
	10	11	12	13	14	15	16	17	18
PAR	5	4	4	4	3	4	3	4	5
YARDS	508	359	317	301	102	355	147	351	469
HDCP	4	14	10	1	12	8	6	16	18

Directions: Take Route 149 to Route 4 North, take Route 30 North to course. Between Rutland and Manchester, Vermont and Lake George, New York.

Marble Island CC   24

Malletts Bay, VT (802) 864-6800

Club Pro: No
Pro Shop: Limited inventory
Payment: Visa, MC
Tee Times: No
Fee 9 Holes: Weekday: $13.50
Fee 18 Holes: Weekday: $13.50
Cart Rental: $21.00/18 $12.00/9
Lessons: Private **School:** No
Driving Range: No
Other: Clubhouse / Snack bar / Restaurant / Bar-lounge / Lodging / Hotel

Tees	Holes	Yards	Par	USGA	Slope
BACK	9	4888	66	66.2	111
MIDDLE	9	4686	66	65.6	110
FRONT	9	4061	66	62.6	103

Weekend: $17, $15 after 5 pm   COUPON
Weekend: $17
Discounts: Senior. M-F.
Junior Golf: No **Membership:** Reg., Jr., Sr.
Non-Metal Spikes: Required

A resort course with a full conference center, pool, fitness center, tennis and a full marina. Spectacular views of Lake Champlain. Open May 1 - October 15.

	1	2	3	4	5	6	7	8	9
PAR	4	3	3	3	5	3	4	4	4
YARDS	225	143	157	142	440	174	272	390	400
HDCP	6	9	7	8	1	5	4	2	3
	10	11	12	13	14	15	16	17	18
PAR	4	3	3	3	5	3	4	4	4
YARDS	230	156	163	153	445	181	277	400	413
HDCP	6	9	7	8	1	5	4	2	3

Directions: Take I-89 to Colchester Exit, take a right onto Route 7. Left on Blakely Road (Route 127.) Follow 2.7 miles, take right onto Marble Island Road. Resort is at the end of the road.

Montague Golf Club

25

Randolph, VT (802) 728-3806

Club Pro: Matthew Gidney-Engberg
Pro Shop: Full inventory
Payment: Visa, MC, Cash, Check
Tee Times: Yes
Fee 9 Holes: Weekday: $15.75
Fee 18 Holes: Weekday: $22.00
Cart Rental: $24.00/18 $13.75/9
Lessons: Yes, PGA **School:** No
Driving Range: Yes
Other: Clubhouse / Snack bar / Bar-lounge

Tees	Holes	Yards	Par	USGA	Slope
BACK	18	5916	70	67.6	115
MIDDLE	18	5573	70	66.1	112
FRONT	18	5039	71	68.7	111

Weekend: $18.75
Weekend: $28.00
Discounts: Sr (Mon), Jr (w/ adult)
Junior Golf: Yes **Membership:** Yes
Non-Metal Spikes: Required

COUPON

Beautiful Vermont views with a rolling terrain. Challenging course with small 1920 style greens. Always in good condition. Don't let the yardage fool you, you'll need your A game to score here.

	1	2	3	4	5	6	7	8	9
PAR	4	4	4	3	4	5	3	4	3
YARDS	312	365	332	196	415	522	140	317	97
HDCP	7	5	11	13	3	1	15	9	17
	10	11	12	13	14	15	16	17	18
PAR	3	5	4	4	4	4	4	4	4
YARDS	159	486	298	300	340	276	335	376	307
HDCP	10	2	14	16	12	18	8	4	6

Directions: Take I-89 North to Exit 4. Follow Route 66 into downtown Randolph on Route 12 South. Take left on Merchant Rd. Go straight onto Randolph Avenue - end of road take left.

Montpelier CC

26

Montpelier, VT (802) 223-7457

Club Pro: Brian M. Haley
Pro Shop: Full inventory
Payment: Cash, Credit
Tee Times: Weekends, 1 day adv.
Fee 9 Holes: Weekday: $17.00
Fee 18 Holes: Weekday: $22.00
Cart Rental: $25.00/18 $14.00/9
Lessons: Private and Group **School:** N/R
Driving Range: No
Other: Clubhouse / Lockers / Showers / Snack bar / Restaurant / Bar-lounge

Tees	Holes	Yards	Par	USGA	Slope
BACK	9	2564	35	67.0	117
MIDDLE	9	2739	35	66.6	114
FRONT	9	2383	35	67.9	112

Weekend: $19.00
Weekend: $25.00
Discounts: None
Junior Golf: Yes **Membership:** Yes
Non-Metal Spikes: Required

VT

The course is relatively short but made challenging by the hilly terrain. Tuesday and Wednesday: twilight league after 3:30. Open April 1 - October 31.

	1	2	3	4	5	6	7	8	9
PAR	4	3	5	5	4	3	4	3	4
YARDS	358	155	422	459	226	149	325	191	279
HDCP	5	15	1	3	11	17	7	13	9
	10	11	12	13	14	15	16	17	18
PAR									
YARDS									
HDCP									

Directions: Take I-89 to Route 2 Exit, follow signs for Montpelier.

4⊙ = Excellent 3⊙ = Very Good 2⊙ = Good

Vermont 277

Mount Snow Golf Club 27

Crosstown Rd, Mt. Snow, VT (802) 464-3333x4654

Club Pro: Jay Morelli, PGA
Pro Shop: Limited inventory
Payment: Visa, MC, Amex
Tee Times: Yes
Fee 9 Holes: Weekday: $37.00
Fee 18 Holes: Weekday: $49.00 M-Th
Cart Rental: $20 pp/18 $15 pp/9
Lessons: $33/30 min. **School:** Yes
Driving Range: Yes. 3:00pm-5:30pm
Other: Clubhouse / Snack bar / Restaurant / Bar-lounge / Hotel

Tees	Holes	Yards	Par	USGA	Slope
BACK	18	6894	72	72.35	130
MIDDLE	18	6443	72	70.3	127
FRONT	18	5436	72	72.46	118

Weekend: $32.00 after 5:00
Weekend: $45, $63 w/ cart
Discounts: Junior
Junior Golf: Yes **Membership:** Yes
Non-Metal Spikes: Preferred

Monday-Thursday 18 hole fee includes cart and lunch. Weekend 18 hole fee does not include lunch. Beautiful scenic course overlooking hills of Vermont. Variety of instruction at golf school.

	1	2	3	4	5	6	7	8	9
PAR	4	4	3	4	5	3	5	4	4
YARDS	394	364	143	344	479	187	532	318	363
HDCP	11	3	17	15	7	9	1	13	5
	10	11	12	13	14	15	16	17	18
PAR	4	5	3	4	4	3	5	4	4
YARDS	372	577	147	403	420	142	474	388	396
HDCP	14	2	16	6	10	18	12	4	8

Directions: Take Exit 2 off I-91 in Brattleboro to Route 9 W. 20 miles to Wilmington, VT. Turn right at the stop light onto Route 100 N. About 6 miles, take a left on Crosstown Road. At top of hill on left.

Mt. Anthony CC 28

Bennington, VT (802) 447-7079

Club Pro: David Soucy, PGA
Pro Shop: Full inventory
Payment: Visa, MC, Amex
Tee Times: Yes
Fee 9 Holes: Weekday: $16.00
Fee 18 Holes: Weekday: $30.00
Cart Rental: $22 pp/18 $8 pp/9
Lessons: $35.00/half hour **School:** Junior
Driving Range: $4.00/lg., $2.00/lg. bucket
Other: Snack bar / Restaurant / Bar-lounge / Lockers / Showers

Tees	Holes	Yards	Par	USGA	Slope
BACK	18	6200	71	N/A	125
MIDDLE	18	6000	71	69.2	125
FRONT	18	5200	71	N/A	106

Weekend: $20.00
Weekend: $35.00
Discounts: Junior, beginner
Junior Golf: Yes **Membership:** No
Non-Metal Spikes: Preferred

A fun, challenging course with a couple of tough holes. Beautiful views with a friendly relaxed atmosphere. Open May - October.

	1	2	3	4	5	6	7	8	9
PAR	4	3	5	3	5	4	4	4	4
YARDS	366	182	474	104	538	369	338	331	304
HDCP	11	7	13	17	1	3	9	5	15
	10	11	12	13	14	15	16	17	18
PAR	4	4	4	3	3	4	5	4	4
YARDS	344	368	348	156	182	304	435	406	351
HDCP	6	4	8	18	10	14	16	2	12

Directions: Take Route 7 to Bennington Center, take right onto West Main St., 1/2 mile after Paradise Motel take first right onto Convent Ave., follow to end; take left, course is down on the right.

Neshobe Golf Club 29

Brandon, VT (802) 247-3611

Club Pro: Paul Politano, Head Pro
Pro Shop: Full inventory
Payment: MC, Visa
Tee Times: Yes
Fee 9 Holes: Weekday: $19.00
Fee 18 Holes: Weekday: $34.00
Cart Rental: $26.00/18 $14.00/9
Lessons: $25.00/half hour **School:** No
Driving Range: $6.00/lg., $2.50/sm.
Other: Clubhouse / Lockers / Showers / Snack bar / Restaurant / Bar-lounge / Horseshoes

Tees	Holes	Yards	Par	USGA	Slope
BACK	18	6362	72	71.6	125
MIDDLE	18	5865	72	68.7	122
FRONT	18	5046	71	64.9	115

Weekend: N/A
Weekend: $36.00
Discounts: None
Junior Golf: Yes **Membership:** Yes
Non-Metal Spikes: Required

COUPON

The course has a beautiful trout brook which runs along the fairways. Most tees overlook the Green Mountains. Course redesigned in 1995 by Steve Durkee. www.neshobe.com

	1	2	3	4	5	6	7	8	9
PAR	4	4	4	4	5	3	4	5	4
YARDS	309	317	339	389	508	132	384	458	272
HDCP	11	17	5	1	7	15	3	9	13
	10	11	12	13	14	15	16	17	18
PAR	3	5	3	4	5	4	4	3	4
YARDS	192	491	148	343	522	357	243	117	344
HDCP	14	8	16	4	2	6	12	18	10

Directions: From Route 7, take Route 73 East. Follow for 1 1/2 miles east of Brandon Center.

Newport CC 30

Newport, VT (802) 334-1634

Club Pro: Peter Matthews
Pro Shop: Full inventory
Payment: MC, Visa
Tee Times: 1 day adv.
Fee 9 Holes: Weekday: $15.00
Fee 18 Holes: Weekday: $22.00
Cart Rental: $22.00/18 $11.00/9
Lessons: $25.00/half hour **School:** N/A
Driving Range: $5.00/lg., $3.00/sm. bucket
Other: Restaurant / Clubhouse / Bar-Lounge / Lockers / Showers / Snack Bar

Tees	Holes	Yards	Par	USGA	Slope
BACK	18	6453	72	69.4	119
MIDDLE	18	6117	72	67.4	106
FRONT	18	5312	72	69.3	111

Weekend: $15.00
Weekend: $22.00
Discounts: None
Junior Golf: Yes **Membership:** Yes
Non-Metal Spikes: Required

COUPON

VT

Scenic lake and mountain view. Contoured fairways. Very friendly!!

	1	2	3	4	5	6	7	8	9
PAR	4	3	4	5	4	3	4	4	5
YARDS	354	172	356	484	326	150	397	335	469
HDCP	9	15	3	7	11	17	1	5	13
	10	11	12	13	14	15	16	17	18
PAR	5	4	4	3	4	4	4	3	5
YARDS	479	374	387	144	375	395	314	142	464
HDCP	12	6	8	18	4	2	10	16	14

Directions: Exit 27 off I-91. Head toward Newport about 1/2 mile. Take left and follow signs.

4✪ =Excellent 3✪ =Very Good 2✪ =Good

Northfield CC

31

Northfield, VT (802) 485-4515

Club Pro: No
Pro Shop: Limited inventory
Payment: Visa, MC, cash, checks
Tee Times: Yes
Fee 9 Holes: Weekday: $14.00
Fee 18 Holes: Weekday: $20.00
Cart Rental: $24.00/18 $12.00/9
Lessons: Private and Group **School:** N/R
Driving Range: No
Other: Snack bar / Restaurant / Bar-lounge / Clubhouse / Lockers / Showers

Tees	Holes	Yards	Par	USGA	Slope
BACK	9	5962	70	69.1	121
MIDDLE	9	5768	70	68.8	115
FRONT	9	4960	70	64.5	111

Weekend: $18.00
Weekend: $24.00
Discounts: None
Junior Golf: Yes **Membership:** Yes
Non-Metal Spikes: Required

The course is very hilly with numerous water holes. Men's and women's course each has 3 sets of tees.

	1	2	3	4	5	6	7	8	9
PAR	4	4	4	3	4	5	4	3	4
YARDS	348	314	276	148	377	532	336	183	367
HDCP	9	12	17	6	5	1	11	13	3
	10	11	12	13	14	15	16	17	18
PAR	4	4	3	3	5	5	4	3	4
YARDS	340	352	175	148	465	532	325	183	367
HDCP	10	8	18	15	7	18	15	16	4

Directions: Take I-89 to Exit 5, follow Route 12 to Route 12A. Course is 4 miles north of Norwich Center.

Orleans Country Club

32

Rt. 58, Orleans, VT (802) 754-2333

Club Pro: Robert Silvester
Pro Shop: Full inventory
Payment: MC, Visa
Tee Times: 1 day, after 9am
Fee 9 Holes: Weekday: $24.00
Fee 18 Holes: Weekday: $24.00
Cart Rental: $22.00/18 $11.00/9
Lessons: $20-$25/half hour **School:** No
Driving Range: $4.00/lg., $2.00 /sm.
Other: Clubhouse / Lockers / Showers / Snack bar / Restaurant / Bar-lounge

Tees	Holes	Yards	Par	USGA	Slope
BACK	18	6123	72	69.3	121
MIDDLE	18	5934	72	68.5	119
FRONT	18	5545	73	71.8	124

Weekend: $24.00
Weekend: $24.00
Discounts: None
Junior Golf: Yes **Membership:** Yes
Non-Metal Spikes: Preferred

The course has scenic mountain views on most holes. Considered challenging.

	1	2	3	4	5	6	7	8	9
PAR	5	4	3	5	4	4	4	3	4
YARDS	442	319	148	439	368	356	290	170	340
HDCP	11	9	17	13	3	1	7	15	5
	10	11	12	13	14	15	16	17	18
PAR	3	5	4	3	4	4	5	4	4
YARDS	202	479	359	134	426	290	495	285	392
HDCP	8	10	16	8	2	12	6	14	4

Directions: Take I-91 to Exit 26. Follow Route 58 1 1/2 miles east, turn right onto Country Club Road.

Proctor Pittsford CC   ▶ 33

Pittsford, VT (802) 483-9379

Club Pro: Merle Schoenfeld
Pro Shop: Full inventory
Payment: MC, Visa
Tee Times: 2 days adv.
Fee 9 Holes: Weekday: $15.00
Fee 18 Holes: Weekday: $27.00
Cart Rental: $24.00/18 $12.00/9
Lessons: $15.00/half hour **School:** No
Driving Range: $3.00/lg. bucket
Other: Restaurant / Clubhouse / Bar-lounge / Snack Bar / Showers

Weekend: $15.00
Weekend: $27.00
Discounts: None
Junior Golf: Yes **Membership:** No
Non-Metal Spikes: Required

Tees	Holes	Yards	Par	USGA	Slope
BACK	18	6052	70	69.4	121
MIDDLE	18	5728	70	67.7	118
FRONT	18	5446	72	66.1	115

COUPON

Beautiful views, excellent greens and fairways, good test of golf. Open April 15 to October 31.

	1	2	3	4	5	6	7	8	9
PAR	4	4	4	5	4	4	3	4	3
YARDS	325	386	308	489	370	326	133	281	219
HDCP	14	4	10	2	8	12	16	18	6
	10	11	12	13	14	15	16	17	18
PAR	4	3	5	4	4	4	4	3	4
YARDS	409	144	468	377	332	301	388	163	309
HDCP	5	13	7	1	9	17	3	11	15

Directions: Located 1 mile off Route 7. Take Route 7 for 4 miles north, take left after Nissan dealer. Go 1/2 mile, take right at "T" 3 miles on Corn Hill Road.

Prospect Bay CC   ▶ 34

Rt. 30, Bomoseen, VT (802) 468-5581

Club Pro: No
Pro Shop: Limited inventory
Payment: MC, Visa
Tee Times: No
Fee 9 Holes: Weekday: $12.00
Fee 18 Holes: Weekday: $17.00
Cart Rental: $24.00/18 $1200/9
Lessons: Yes **School:** N/R
Driving Range: No
Other: Clubhouse / Snack bar / Restaurant / Bar-lounge

Weekend: $15.00 after 1pm
Weekend: $22.00
Discounts: None
Junior Golf: No **Membership:** N/R
Non-Metal Spikes: Preferred

Tees	Holes	Yards	Par	USGA	Slope
BACK	N/R				
MIDDLE	9	2557	70	65.2	115
FRONT	N/R				

VT

The course is hilly and scenic. Open April - October.

	1	2	3	4	5	6	7	8	9
PAR	5	3	4	4	4	4	4	4	3
YARDS	405	155	315	295	270	310	245	380	130
HDCP	1	11	7	5	15	9	13	3	17
	10	11	12	13	14	15	16	17	18
PAR	5	3	4	4	4	4	4	4	3
YARDS	415	165	340	305	275	340	300	385	155
HDCP	2	12	8	6	16	10	14	4	18

Directions: Take US Route 4 to Exit 4; follow Route 30 North for 2 miles to course entrance.

4✪ =Excellent **3**✪ =Very Good **2**✪ =Good   **Vermont 281**

Ralph Myhre GC

Middlebury, VT (802) 443-5125

Club Pro: Jim Dayton
Pro Shop: Limited inventory
Payment: Cash, Visa
Tee Times: All week
Fee 9 Holes: Weekday: $29 all day
Fee 18 Holes: Weekday: $29 all day
Cart Rental: $28.00/18, $17.50/9
Lessons: Yes **School:** No
Driving Range: Yes
Other: Clubhouse / Snack bar / Showers
Weekend: $29 all day
Weekend: $29 all day
Discounts: Student
Junior Golf: Yes **Membership:** Yes
Non-Metal Spikes: Preferred

Tees	Holes	Yards	Par	USGA	Slope
BACK	18	6379	71	71.3	129
MIDDLE	18	6014	71	69.6	126
FRONT	18	5337	71	66.9	120

Open fairways with moderate hills. Owned by Middlebury College. Any student (any school) pays $14.00.

	1	2	3	4	5	6	7	8	9
PAR	5	4	4	3	4	4	3	4	4
YARDS	479	341	311	166	356	370	141	353	365
HDCP	18	3	16	12	6	13	15	8	7
	10	11	12	13	14	15	16	17	18
PAR	4	5	3	4	3	4	5	4	4
YARDS	404	522	152	325	126	363	512	351	377
HDCP	2	1	17	10	14	4	5	11	9

Directions: Route 7 to Route 30 South. Course is just beyond Middlebury College field house.

Richford Country Club

Rt. 106, Richford, VT (802) 848-3527

Club Pro: John Sheridan
Pro Shop: Limited inventory
Payment: Visa, MC
Tee Times: No
Fee 9 Holes: Weekday: $12.60, After 5 pm
Fee 18 Holes: Weekday: $18.90
Cart Rental: $18, $12 after 5 pm
Lessons: No **School:** No
Driving Range: No
Other: Clubhouse / Snack bar / Bar-lounge.
Weekend: $12.60, After 5PM
Weekend: $18.90
Discounts: Senior Thursdays
Junior Golf: Yes **Membership:** Yes
Non-Metal Spikes: Not Required

Tees	Holes	Yards	Par	USGA	Slope
BACK	N/R				
MIDDLE	9	2908	36	68.2	116
FRONT	9	2326	36	72	117

The course has excellent views of the Green Mountains. Many trees and hills make it challenging. Automatic sprinkling system for the fairways and greens. Open April to October.

	1	2	3	4	5	6	7	8	9
PAR	4	5	3	4	5	3	4	4	4
YARDS	283	453	170	400	453	175	309	376	289
HDCP	7	9	8	1	3	5	2	6	4
	10	11	12	13	14	15	16	17	18
PAR									
YARDS									
HDCP									

Directions: Take I-89 to St. Albans Exit. Follow Route 105 North to Richford (28 miles).

Rocky Ridge Golf Club   37

Rt. 116, St. George, VT (802) 482-2191

Club Pro: Ed Coleman
Pro Shop: Full inventory
Payment: Visa, MC, Cash
Tee Times: 7 days/week
Fee 9 Holes: Weekday: No
Fee 18 Holes: Weekday: $24.00
Cart Rental: $23.00
Lessons: No **School:** N/A
Driving Range: No
Other: Clubhouse / Lockers / Showers / Restaurant / Bar-lounge

Tees	Holes	Yards	Par	USGA	Slope
BACK	18	6282	72	70.3	126
MIDDLE	18	6000	72	69.1	124
FRONT	18	5230	72	65.6	117

Weekend: $22.00
Weekend: $22.00
Discounts: Senior, Mondays
Junior Golf: N/R **Membership:** Yes
Non-Metal Spikes: Preferred

Greens excellent, collared shirts. Open April 1 - November 1.

	1	2	3	4	5	6	7	8	9
PAR	4	5	3	5	4	4	4	3	4
YARDS	270	542	195	576	314	251	339	191	345
HDCP	17	1	11	7	5	13	9	15	3
	10	11	12	13	14	15	16	17	18
PAR	4	4	4	4	3	4	5	3	5
YARDS	395	289	312	367	156	315	460	163	513
HDCP	10	14	12	2	16	8	6	18	4

Directions: Take I-89 to Exit 12; follow Route 2A for 7 miles south to intersection of Route 116 and course.

Rutland Country Club   38

Grove St., Rutland, VT (802) 773-3254

Club Pro: Greg Nelson
Pro Shop: Full inventory
Payment: Visa, MC
Tee Times: 48 hrs. in adv.
Fee 9 Holes: Weekday: $35,cart included
Fee 18 Holes: Weekday: $70, cart included
Cart Rental: Included
Lessons: Yes **School:** No
Driving Range: No
Other: Clubhouse / Lockers / Showers / Snack bar / Restaurant / Bar-lounge

Tees	Holes	Yards	Par	USGA	Slope
BACK	18	6135	70	69.7	125
MIDDLE	18	5758	70	67.9	122
FRONT	18	5368	71	71.6	125

Weekend: After Noon
Weekend: After Noon
Discounts: None
Junior Golf: Yes **Membership:** Yes
Non-Metal Spikes: Required

The course has challenging greens as a result of management's effort to vary the terrain. A short distance, but accuracy is key. Open May - October.

	1	2	3	4	5	6	7	8	9
PAR	4	4	3	5	3	4	4	4	4
YARDS	379	381	125	463	215	366	322	368	300
HDCP	5	7	17	1	11	9	13	3	15
	10	11	12	13	14	15	16	17	18
PAR	4	4	3	5	4	3	4	4	4
YARDS	296	316	193	513	347	121	351	326	376
HDCP	16	10	14	2	6	18	4	12	8

Directions: From I 89 exit 1 take Route 4 West to Rutland. Take right onto Grove St. and follow signs to course.

4✪ =Excellent 3✪ =Very Good 2✪ =Good

Sitzmark Golf Course

Rt. 100, Wilmington, VT (802) 464-3384

Club Pro: No
Pro Shop: Yes
Payment: Visa, MC
Tee Times: No
Fee 9 Holes: Weekday: N/A
Fee 18 Holes: Weekday: $13.00
Cart Rental: $16.00
Lessons: Yes **School:** Yes
Driving Range: No
Other: Snack bar / Bar-lounge

Tees	Holes	Yards	Par	USGA	Slope
BACK	N/A				
MIDDLE	18	2300	54	N/A	N/A
FRONT	N/A				

Weekend: N/A
Weekend: $13.00
Discounts: None
Junior Golf: No **Membership:** Yes
Non-Metal Spikes: Not Required

An 18 hole par 3. Generally considered an "Iron Course," it provides a challenge for the experienced golfer and an excellent introduction for the beginner.

	1	2	3	4	5	6	7	8	9
PAR	3	3	3	3	3	3	3	3	3
YARDS	105	95	105	125	155	90	115	127	115
HDCP	13	15	11	5	1	17	9	3	7
	10	11	12	13	14	15	16	17	18
PAR	3	3	3	3	3	3	3	3	3
YARDS	90	110	105	126	120	90	105	90	115
HDCP	14	8	10	2	4	18	12	16	6

Directions: Take I-91 to Brattleboro, get on Route 9 to Wilmington, take Route 100 to course (5 miles).

St. Johnsbury CC

St. Johnsbury, VT (802) 748-9894

Club Pro: Larry Kelley
Pro Shop: Full inventory
Payment: Cash, credit card
Tee Times: 3 days adv.
Fee 9 Holes: Weekday: $14.00
Fee 18 Holes: Weekday: $30.00
Cart Rental: $26.00/18
Lessons: $35.00/45 minutes **School:** No
Driving Range: $3.00/bucket
Other: Clubhouse / Snack bar / Restaurant / Bar-lounge

Tees	Holes	Yards	Par	USGA	Slope
BACK	18	6373	70	70.4	129
MIDDLE	18	5860	70	68.6	125
FRONT	18	5480	70	71.3	120

Weekend: N/A
Weekend: $35.00
Discounts: Junior
Junior Golf: Yes **Membership:** Yes
Non-Metal Spikes: Required

COUPON

Rated the #1 course in VT to play for under $50 by *Golf Digest* and *USA Today*!
www.caladoniarecord.com

	1	2	3	4	5	6	7	8	9
PAR	4	4	3	4	3	5	3	5	4
YARDS	314	363	168	434	232	578	188	473	434
HDCP	11	9	17	3	13	1	15	5	7
	10	11	12	13	14	15	16	17	18
PAR	5	4	3	4	4	3	5	3	4
YARDS	496	385	176	398	395	195	575	203	366
HDCP	6	10	16	8	4	14	2	18	12

Directions: From I-91 North to Exit 23 (US Route 5); follow 3 miles. From I-91 South to Exit 22 to Route 5; follow 4 miles.

Stamford Valley CC   41

Rt. 9, Stamford, VT (802) 694-9144

Club Pro: No
Pro Shop: No
Payment: Cash only
Tee Times: No
Fee 9 Holes: Weekday: $7.00
Fee 18 Holes: Weekday: $12.00
Cart Rental: $16.00/18 $10.00/9
Lessons: No **School:** No
Driving Range: No
Other: Snack Bar

Tees	Holes	Yards	Par	USGA	Slope
BACK	N/R				
MIDDLE	9	2709	36	66.6	104
FRONT	N/R				

Weekend: $7.00
Weekend: $12.00
Discounts: None
Junior Golf: No **Membership:** Yes
Non-Metal Spikes: Not Required

The course is level and considered an easy walker.

	1	2	3	4	5	6	7	8	9
PAR	4	4	4	5	4	4	3	4	4
YARDS	232	288	342	392	330	320	215	355	235
HDCP	N/A								
	10	11	12	13	14	15	16	17	18
PAR									
YARDS									
HDCP									

Directions: Take Route 8 North (out of North Adams) about 5 miles over Stamford line.

Stonehedge GC   42

North Clarendon, VT (802) 773-2666

Club Pro:
Pro Shop: Yes
Payment: Cash, Checks
Tee Times: Yes
Fee 9 Holes: Weekday: $9.00
Fee 18 Holes: Weekday: $13.00
Cart Rental: N/A
Lessons: No **School:** No
Driving Range: No
Other: Snacks and Soft drinks

Tees	Holes	Yards	Par	USGA	Slope
BACK					
MIDDLE	9	1107	27		
FRONT					

Weekend: $10.00
Weekend: $15.00
Discounts: Yes
Junior Golf: No **Membership:** No
Non-Metal Spikes: Required

VT

Challenging Par 3 with pretty views- excellent greens, water and sand traps- easy course to walk.

	1	2	3	4	5	6	7	8	9
PAR	3	3	3	3	3	3	3	3	3
YARDS	153	84	181	152	86	77	180	93	101
HDCP	N/A	N/A	N/A	N/A	N/A	N/A	N/A	N/A	N/A
	10	11	12	13	14	15	16	17	18
PAR									
YARDS									
HDCP									

Directions: Located 3 miles South of Rutland, VT (No interstate nearby) at the junction of Routes 7 and 103.

4✪ =Excellent 3✪ =Very Good 2✪ =Good

Stowe Country Club

Stowe, VT (802) 253-4893

Club Pro: Lou Ruzzi, Head Pro
Pro Shop: Full inventory
Payment: Visa, MC, Amex
Tee Times: Anytime
Fee 9 Holes: Weekday: N/A
Fee 18 Holes: Weekday: $55.00
Cart Rental: $16pp/18 $9pp after 4
Lessons: Yes **School:** Golf School
Driving Range: $3.00/sm. $5.00/lg.
Other: Clubhouse / Lockers / Showers / Restaurant / Bar/ Hotel /Beverage Cart

Tees	Holes	Yards	Par	USGA	Slope
BACK	18	6185	72	69.3	117
MIDDLE	18	5772	72	67.5	114
FRONT	18	5346	74	68.5	112

Weekend: $29.00 after 4 pm
Weekend: $65.00
Discounts: None
Junior Golf: Yes **Membership:** Yes
Non-Metal Spikes: Required

Excellent stay & play golf package. Appears short in yardage, but the hills and elevated greens make it play longer. Open May - mid Oct.. Off season, off hour rates.

	1	2	3	4	5	6	7	8	9
PAR	5	3	5	3	4	5	4	3	4
YARDS	471	150	427	151	361	471	357	136	363
HDCP	9	15	5	13	3	11	1	17	7
	10	11	12	13	14	15	16	17	18
PAR	3	5	4	4	5	3	4	4	4
YARDS	173	447	368	324	443	158	355	339	278
HDCP	12	8	4	10	14	16	2	6	18

Directions: Exit 10 off I-89. Follow Route 100 for 10 miles to blinking light in center of Stowe village, turn left onto Route 108. Turn right directly past Whiskers Restaurant onto Cape Cod Road. Course straight ahead.

Stratton Mt. (forest)

Stratton, VT (802) 297-4114

Club Pro: David Rihm
Pro Shop: Full inventory
Payment: Visa, MC, Amex
Tee Times: Yes 14 days adv.
Fee 9 Holes: Weekday: $37.00
Fee 18 Holes: Weekday: $56.00
Cart Rental: $16.00/18 $9.00/9
Lessons: $35.00/half hour **School:** Yes
Driving Range: $4.00/med
Other: Clubhouse / Lockers / Showers / Snack bar / Restaurant / Bar-lounge

Tees	Holes	Yards	Par	USGA	Slope
BACK	9	6526	72	71.2	125
MIDDLE	9	6044	72	69.4	122
FRONT	9	5155	74	69.8	123

Weekend: $40.00
Weekend: $69.00
Discounts: None
Junior Golf: No **Membership:** Yes
Non-Metal Spikes: Not Required

The back 9 is the front 9 of "lake". Each tract incorporates many familiar Cornish design features while retaining individual identities.

	1	2	3	4	5	6	7	8	9
PAR	4	4	4	3	5	4	3	5	4
YARDS	372	387	305	129	467	295	140	504	379
HDCP	5	2	6	9	1	8	7	4	3
	10	11	12	13	14	15	16	17	18
PAR	4	4	4	3	4	5	3	4	5
YARDS	353	395	328	164	269	466	193	390	508
HDCP	6	1	8	7	9	4	5	3	2

Directions: Take I-91 to Brattleboro Exit, follow Route 30 East 30 miles to Bondville; look for signs to Stratton Mountain.

Stratton Mt. (lake) ✪✪✪ ▶ 45

Stratton, VT (802) 297-4114

Club Pro: David Rihm, PGA
Pro Shop: Full inventory
Payment: Visa, MC, Amex, Disc, Cash, Checks
Tee Times: Yes 14 days adv.

Tees	Holes	Yards	Par	USGA	Slope
BACK	9	6602	72	72.0	125
MIDDLE	9	6107	72	70.3	123
FRONT	9	5410	74	71.1	124

Fee 9 Holes: Weekday: $37.00 **Weekend:** $40.00
Fee 18 Holes: Weekday: $56.00 **Weekend:** $69.00
Cart Rental: $32.00 **Discounts:** None
Lessons: $35.00/half hour **School:** Golf School **Junior Golf:** No **Membership:** Yes
Driving Range: $4.00/med **Non-Metal Spikes:** Not Required
Other: Clubhouse / Lockers/ Snack bar / Restaurant / Bar/Lounge/Hotel

COUPON

Interesting and scenic challenge. Requires good shot management both off the tee and to the green. Sports center, tennis courts, horseback riding and mountain biking are available.

	1	2	3	4	5	6	7	8	9
PAR	4	4	4	3	4	5	3	4	5
YARDS	353	395	328	164	269	466	193	390	508
HDCP	6	1	8	7	9	4	5	3	2
	10	11	12	13	14	15	16	17	18
PAR	4	3	4	4	5	4	4	3	5
YARDS	323	186	372	355	545	304	358	150	448
HDCP	5	4	2	6	1	8	3	9	7

Directions: Exit 1 off I-91 in Vermont. Take Route 30 North to town off Bondville (about 40 miles from Brattleboro). Turn left on Sratton Access Rd. Go straight 2 miles.

Stratton Mt. (mountain) ✪✪✪ ▶ 46

Stratton, VT (802) 297-4114

Club Pro: David Rihm
Pro Shop: Full inventory
Payment: Visa, MC, Amex
Tee Times: Yes 14 days adv.

Tees	Holes	Yards	Par	USGA	Slope
BACK	9	6478	72	71.2	126
MIDDLE	9	6019	72	69.3	123
FRONT	9	5163	74	69.9	123

Fee 9 Holes: Weekday: $37.00 **Weekend:** $40.00
Fee 18 Holes: Weekday: $56.00 **Weekend:** $69.00
Cart Rental: $16.00/18 $9.00/9 **Discounts:** None
Lessons: $35.00/half hour **School:** Golf School **Junior Golf:** No **Membership:** Yes
Driving Range: $4.00/med. **Non-Metal Spikes:** Not Required
Other: Clubhouse / Lockers / Showers / Snack bar / Restaurant / Bar-lounge

COUPON

Site of the Stratton Mountain LPGA Classic. This outstanding course consists of three separate nine hole courses. Cornish design. Great vacation course.

	1	2	3	4	5	6	7	8	9
PAR	4	3	4	4	5	4	4	3	5
YARDS	323	186	372	355	545	304	358	150	448
HDCP	5	4	2	6	1	8	3	9	7
	10	11	12	13	14	15	16	17	18
PAR	4	4	4	3	5	4	3	5	4
YARDS	372	387	305	129	467	295	140	504	379
HDCP	5	2	6	9	1	8	7	4	3

Directions: Take I-91 to Brattleboro Exit, follow Route 30 East 30 miles to Bondville; look for signs to Stratton Mountain.

VT

4✪ =Excellent 3✪ =Very Good 2✪ =Good

Vermont 287

Sugarbush Golf Course

47

Warren, VT (802) 583-6725

Club Pro: Danny Caverly, Ray Davis
Pro Shop: Full inventory
Payment: Visa, MC, Amex, Disc
Tee Times: Yes

Tees	Holes	Yards	Par	USGA	Slope
BACK	18	6524	72	71.7	128
MIDDLE	18	5886	70	69.0	122
FRONT	18	5187	72	70.4	119

Fee 9 Holes: Weekday: No **Weekend:** No
Fee 18 Holes: Weekday: $42.00 **Weekend:** $49.00 (F/S/S)
Cart Rental: $16.00 pp/18 **Discounts:** Junior 50% off
Lessons: $50/ hour **School:** Yes **Junior Golf:** Yes **Membership:** Yes
Driving Range: $3/ sm $5/ lg **Non-Metal Spikes:** Not Required
Other: Restaurant/Clubhouse/Hotel/Bar-lounge/Lockers/Snack bar/ Showers/Schools

Breathtaking views. 2 and 3 day golf schools for seniors and juniors. Dress code. Open May - October. www.sugarbush.com

	1	2	3	4	5	6	7	8	9
PAR	4	4	4	4	3	4	4	3	4
YARDS	322	372	396	355	164	374	433	166	353
HDCP	13	1	5	9	15	3	7	17	11
	10	11	12	13	14	15	16	17	18
PAR	5	3	4	4	5	4	3	4	4
YARDS	504	118	395	325	449	352	157	329	322
HDCP	6	18	2	14	4	8	12	16	10

Directions: From I-89 S: Exit 10 to Route 100 S to Sugarbush Access Road. From I-89 N, take Exit 9 to Route 100B S to Route 100 S.

Tater Hill Resort

48

Chester, VT (802) 875-2517

Club Pro: Steve Gonsalves
Pro Shop: Full inventory
Payment: Visa, MC, Amex
Tee Times: 1 wk adv.

Tees	Holes	Yards	Par	USGA	Slope
BACK	18	6600	72	72.3	129
MIDDLE	18	6015	72	69.4	123
FRONT	18	4979	72	64.7	113

Fee 9 Holes: Weekday: Call for daily rates **Weekend:** Call for daily rates
Fee 18 Holes: Weekday: Call for daily rates **Weekend:** Call for daily rates
Cart Rental: Included in fee **Discounts:** Junior
Lessons: $35.00/half hour **School:** No **Junior Golf:** Yes **Membership:** Yes
Driving Range: $6/lg. $4/sm. **Non-Metal Spikes:** Required
Other: Clubhouse / Bar-lounge / Restaurant

COUPON

18-hole championship course offers over 6800 yards of play and was designed to optimize your golf experience by blending the natural beauty of VT with the dynamic layout. www.taterhill.com

	1	2	3	4	5	6	7	8	9
PAR	5	3	4	4	3	5	4	4	4
YARDS	475	133	370	352	130	407	397	305	362
HDCP	11	15	9	3	17	5	1	13	7
	10	11	12	13	14	15	16	17	18
PAR	3	4	4	4	4	3	5	4	5
YARDS	168	388	414	373	324	148	462	295	512
HDCP	16	6	4	12	14	18	2	10	8

Directions: Take I-91 to Exit 6; take left onto Route 103, turns into 11 West; 7 miles outside Chester look for signs to course.

West Bolton Golf Club   49

West Bolton, Jericho, VT (802) 434-4321

Club Pro: Jeffrey Brown
Pro Shop: Full inventory
Payment: Visa, MC, Disc.
Tee Times: 1 week adv.
Fee 9 Holes: Weekday: No
Fee 18 Holes: Weekday: $20.00
Cart Rental: $22.00/18 $11.00/9
Lessons: no **School:** Junior
Driving Range: No
Other: Clubhouse / Snack bar

Tees	Holes	Yards	Par	USGA	Slope
BACK	N/A				
MIDDLE	18	5661	72	64.1	115
FRONT	18	5165	72	72.5	111

Weekend: No
Weekend: $20.00
Discounts: Senior & Junior
Junior Golf: Yes **Membership:** Yes
Non-Metal Spikes: Required

While the course is not long, small greens make it challenging. The fairway trees are small, but the mountains surrounding the course are grand. Jr. day camps, M-Th, 8:30-12:00 in the summer.

	1	2	3	4	5	6	7	8	9
PAR	4	5	3	4	4	3	4	4	4
YARDS	303	481	149	248	353	191	329	359	295
HDCP	9	3	17	13	1	5	15	7	11
	10	11	12	13	14	15	16	17	18
PAR	3	5	4	5	3	5	4	4	4
YARDS	128	430	392	451	180	458	273	323	318
HDCP	18	8	2	4	16	6	14	10	12

Directions: I-89 to Exit 11 toward Richmond. Left at light (Four Corners). Go about 7 mi. and take a right at the West Bolton Golf Course sign. Continue for 4 miles.

White River Golf Club   50

Rt. 100, Rochester, VT (802) 767-4653

Club Pro: No
Pro Shop: Limited inventory
Payment: Cash, MC, Visa
Tee Times: Yes
Fee 9 Holes: Weekday: $15.00
Fee 18 Holes: Weekday: $20.00
Cart Rental: $20.00/18 $15.00/9
Lessons: Yes **School:** No
Driving Range: Yes
Other: Clubhouse / Bar-lounge / Snack Bar

Tees	Holes	Yards	Par	USGA	Slope
BACK	18	5314	68	65.6	115
MIDDLE	18	5038	68	62.6	112
FRONT	18	4068	68	64.6	104

Weekend: $15.00
Weekend: $20.00
Discounts: None
Junior Golf: **Membership:** Yes
Non-Metal Spikes: N/R

COUPON

A challenging walking course with sand and water. Open May - October.

	1	2	3	4	5	6	7	8	9
PAR	4	4	3	5	4	3	3	4	4
YARDS	285	315	185	525	250	150	140	415	263
HDCP	13	11	7	3	17	9	5	1	15
	10	11	12	13	14	15	16	17	18
PAR	4	4	3	5	4	3	3	4	4
YARDS	285	315	185	525	250	150	140	415	263
HDCP	14	12	8	4	17	10	6	2	16

Directions: I-89 to Route 107 West to Route 100 North. Course is 10 miles north on Route 100. Approx. halfway between Killington and Sugarbush.

VT

4✪ =Excellent 3✪ =Very Good 2✪ =Good

Wilcox Cove GC 51

Hgwy. 314, Grand Isle, VT (802) 372-8343

Club Pro: No
Pro Shop: No
Payment: Cash, Check
Tee Times: No
Fee 9 Holes: Weekday: $9.00
Fee 18 Holes: Weekday: $9.00
Cart Rental: Handcarts
Lessons: No **School:** No
Driving Range: No
Other: No

Tees	Holes	Yards	Par	USGA	Slope
BACK	N/A				
MIDDLE	9	1732	32	N/A	N/A
FRONT	N/A				

Weekend: $10.45, $6 after 6PM
Weekend: $10.45, $6 after 6PM
Discounts: None
Junior Golf: N/R **Membership:** Yes
Non-Metal Spikes: Not Required

COUPON

An executive type course on the West shore of Grand Isle, looking over Lake Champlain to the Adirondack Mountains of New York. A fairly level course.

	1	2	3	4	5	6	7	8	9
PAR	4	4	4	3	4	3	4	3	3
YARDS	240	210	254	120	245	190	185	193	95
HDCP	N/A	N/A	N/A	N/A	N/A	N/A	N/A	N/A	N/A
	10	11	12	13	14	15	16	17	18
PAR									
YARDS									
HDCP									

Directions: Take I-89 to Exit 17 (Route 2 North.) Take Route 314 past Grand Isle Ferry.

Williston Golf Club ✪✪✪ 52

Williston, VT (802) 878-3747

Club Pro: TBA
Pro Shop: Full inventory
Payment: Cash only
Tee Times: No
Fee 9 Holes: Weekday: No
Fee 18 Holes: Weekday: $20.00
Cart Rental: $21.00/18 $10.50/9
Lessons: $25.00/half hour **School:** No
Driving Range: No
Other: Clubhouse / Snack bar / Restaurant / Bar-lounge

Tees	Holes	Yards	Par	USGA	Slope
BACK	18	6621	69	N/R	N/R
MIDDLE	18	5651	70	66.6	113
FRONT	N/A				

Weekend: No
Weekend: $20.00
Discounts: None
Junior Golf: Yes **Membership:** Yes
Non-Metal Spikes: Not Required

Excellent maintenance. Automatic watering throughout course. Open May 1 - November 12.

	1	2	3	4	5	6	7	8	9
PAR	4	4	4	4	4	3	4	4	5
YARDS	382	395	315	287	280	230	298	385	458
HDCP	13	1	5	9	17	7	15	3	11
	10	11	12	13	14	15	16	17	18
PAR	4	3	4	4	4	3	3	4	5
YARDS	335	170	219	260	450	162	110	380	535
HDCP	10	12	4	16	2	14	18	6	8

Directions: I-89 to Exit 11 or 12; Route 2 East to North Williston Rd. Course is 1/2 mile on right. 7 miles east of Burlington, Vermont.

Windsor Country Club

53

Rt. 5, Windsor, VT (802) 674-6491

Club Pro: No
Pro Shop: Limited inventory
Payment: Visa, MC
Tee Times: Wknds/Mon/Tue
Fee 9 Holes: Weekday: $14.70
Fee 18 Holes: Weekday: $21.00
Cart Rental: $23.10/18 $13.65/9
Lessons: No **School:** No
Driving Range: No
Other: Restaurant / Clubhouse / Snack bar / Bar-lounge / Lockers / Showers

Tees	Holes	Yards	Par	USGA	Slope
BACK	N/R				
MIDDLE	9	5382	68	65.1	105
FRONT	9	4924	72	68.2	109

Weekend: $17.85
Weekend: $26.25,$14.50 after 4
Discounts: None
Junior Golf: Yes **Membership:** Yes
Non-Metal Spikes: Required

Short, with small greens. In excellent condition. Views of Mt. Ascutney and Connecticut River. New Hampshire is out of bounds. Junior Tournament.

	1	2	3	4	5	6	7	8	9
PAR	4	3	4	4	4	3	3	5	4
YARDS	332	215	333	309	383	176	140	442	340
HDCP	13	1	3	15	5	9	17	11	7
	10	11	12	13	14	15	16	17	18
PAR	4	3	4	4	4	3	3	5	4
YARDS	338	188	342	318	386	185	145	453	357
HDCP	14	2	4	16	6	10	18	12	8

Directions: Take I-91 to Exit 9, left on Route 5, course is 3.5 miles down.

Woodstock Inn & Resort

✪✪ **54**

Woodstock, VT (802) 457-6674

Club Pro: Jim Gunnare
Pro Shop: Full inventory
Payment: Cash, MC,Visa,Amex
Tee Times: Yes
Fee 9 Holes: Weekday: N/A
Fee 18 Holes: Weekday: $60.00
Cart Rental: $36.00
Lessons: $30.00/half hour **School:** Jr. & Sr.
Driving Range: $3.00/lg. bucket
Other: Clubhouse / Lockers / Showers / Restaurant / Bar-lounge/ Hotel / Snack Bar

Tees	Holes	Yards	Par	USGA	Slope
BACK	18	6001	69	69.0	121
MIDDLE	18	5555	69	67	117
FRONT	18	4924	71	67.0	113

Weekend: N/A
Weekend: $80.00
Discounts: None
Junior Golf: N/R **Membership:** Yes
Non-Metal Spikes: Required

COUPON

Course is over 100 years old. Lots of water, very well manicured. Open May 1 - October 30.

	1	2	3	4	5	6	7	8	9
PAR	5	3	4	4	3	5	3	4	4
YARDS	465	162	346	382	134	503	162	356	386
HDCP	9	13	5	1	15	3	17	11	7
	10	11	12	13	14	15	16	17	18
PAR	4	3	4	3	4	3	5	4	4
YARDS	350	131	381	150	272	144	520	315	396
HDCP	4	16	2	10	14	18	6	12	8

Directions: Take Route 4 West off I-89 to Woodstock.

VT

4✪ =Excellent 3✪ =Very Good 2✪ =Good

CHAPTER 9
Northern/Eastern Connecticut

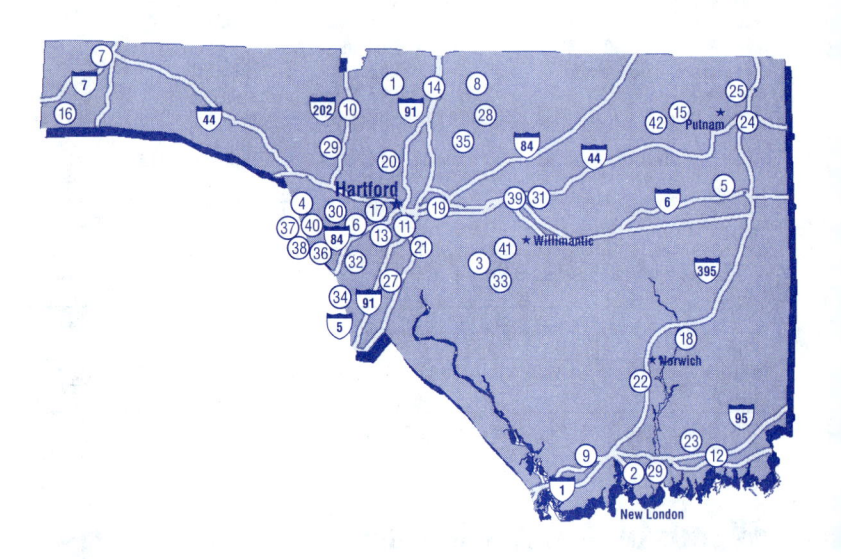

Airways Golf Course	1	Harrisville GC	15	Shennecosset GC	29
Birch Plain Golf Course	2	Hotchkiss School GC	16	Simsbury Farms GC	30
Blackledge CC	3	Keney Park Golf Club	17	Skungamaug River GC	31
Blue Fox Run	4	Lisbon Country Club	18	Stanley Golf Club	32
Brooklyn Hill GC	5	Manchester CC	19	Tallwood Country Club	33
Buena Vista GC	6	Millbrook Golf Course	20	Timberlin Golf Club	34
Canaan Country Club	7	Minnechaug GC	21	Topstone Golf Course	35
Cedar Knob GC	8	Norwich Golf Course	22	Tunxis Plantation CC (G)	36
Cedar Ridge GC	9	Pequot Golf Club	23	Tunxis Plantation CC (W)	37
Copper Hill CC	10	Putnam Country Club	24	Tunxis Plantation GC (R)	38
East Hartford GC	11	Raceway Golf Club	25	Twin Hills CC	39
Elmridge Golf Course	12	Rockledge CC	26	Willimantic CC	40
Goodwin Golf Course	13	Rolling Greens GC	27	Westwoods GC	41
Grassmere CC	14	Rolling Meadows CC	28	Woodstock GC	42

292 Northern/Eastern CT NEW ENGLAND GOLFGUIDE

Airways Golf Course

1070 S. Grand, Suffield, CT (860) 668-4973

Club Pro: Wayne Leal
Pro Shop: Limited inventory
Payment: Visa, MC, cash
Tee Times: 1 week adv.
Fee 9 Holes: Weekday: $10.00
Fee 18 Holes: Weekday: $19.50
Cart Rental: $20.00/18 $10.00/9
Lessons: No **School:** No
Driving Range: No
Other: Clubhouse / Snack bar

Weekend: $11.00
Weekend: $21.00
Discounts: Senior
Junior Golf: No **Membership:** Yes
Non-Metal Spikes: Not Required

Tees	Holes	Yards	Par	USGA	Slope
BACK	18	5845	71	66	106
MIDDLE	18	5493	71	65.0	103
FRONT	18	5154	71	65	103

COUPON

Beautiful, challenging course. Relatively flat and easy to walk. Open March - November.

	1	2	3	4	5	6	7	8	9
PAR	4	4	4	5	4	4	3	4	4
YARDS	336	351	351	487	301	282	147	320	273
HDCP	9	5	1	3	11	15	17	7	13
	10	11	12	13	14	15	16	17	18
PAR	3	5	4	3	4	3	5	4	4
YARDS	140	451	341	133	331	147	451	388	263
HDCP	18	8	10	16	6	14	4	2	12

Directions: Take I-91 to Exit 40 (Route 20) to East Granby. Turn right at fourth light (East Street). Course is 1.5 miles on right.

Birch Plain Golf Course

High Rock Rd., Groton, CT (860) 445-9918

Club Pro: No
Pro Shop: Limited inventory
Payment: Cash only
Tee Times: No
Fee 9 Holes: Weekday: No
Fee 18 Holes: Weekday: $15.00
Cart Rental: $18.00/18
Lessons: No **School:** N/R
Driving Range: $5.00/med $4.00/sm
Other: Snacks

Weekend: No
Weekend: $17.00
Discounts: Senior, Junior, Military
Junior Golf: N/R **Membership:** Yes
Non-Metal Spikes: Not Required

Tees	Holes	Yards	Par	USGA	Slope
BACK	N/R				
MIDDLE	18	2670	54	N/A	N/A
FRONT	N/R				

Course is under new management. On going renovations. Formerly Trumbull Golf Course.

	1	2	3	4	5	6	7	8	9
PAR	3	3	3	3	3	3	3	3	3
YARDS	107	170	148	228	206	124	113	137	129
HDCP	17	5	7	1	3	14	15	6	13
	10	11	12	13	14	15	16	17	18
PAR	3	3	3	3	3	3	3	3	3
YARDS	105	187	108	147	136	164	150	155	156
HDCP	18	2	16	9	12	4	8	10	11

Directions: I-95 S, take Route 349 (Clarence Sharp Highway.) At second light, go left. At next light, go right. Follow signs for Groton/New London Airport. Course on right.

4✪ = Excellent 3✪ = Very Good 2✪ = Good

Blackledge CC ✪✪ 3

190 West St., Hebron, CT (860)228-0250

Club Pro: Kevin J. Higgins
Pro Shop: Full inventory
Payment: Visa, MC
Tee Times: 1 week adv.
Fee 9 Holes: Weekday: $14.00
Fee 18 Holes: Weekday: $27.00
Cart Rental: $24.00/18 $12.00/9
Lessons: $30.00/half hour **School:** No
Driving Range: No
Other: Clubhouse / Snack bar / Restaurant / Bar-lounge

Tees	Holes	Yards	Par	USGA	Slope
BACK	18	6787	72	72.0	128
MIDDLE	18	6137	72	68.9	122
FRONT	18	5458	72	71.7	123

Weekend: $16.00
Weekend: $30.00
Discounts: Senior & Junior
Junior Golf: N/R **Membership:** Yes
Non-Metal Spikes: Not Required

COUPON

27 hole scenic championship course designed by Geoffrey Cornish. A new nine holes opened in 1995. Open March - December. The scorecard is for the Anderson and Gilead combination.

	1	2	3	4	5	6	7	8	9
PAR	4	4	4	5	4	3	4	3	5
YARDS	375	365	389	480	350	153	318	170	485
HDCP	11	13	1	3	7	17	9	15	5
	10	11	12	13	14	15	16	17	18
PAR	4	4	5	3	4	4	3	5	4
YARDS	316	408	465	142	383	369	179	425	365
HDCP	16	2	4	18	8	10	14	6	12

Directions: Take Route 2 East to Exit 8. Left off ramp, go 9 miles. Take a right onto West Street. Course is on the right.

Blue Fox Run 4

Nod Rd., Avon, CT (860)678-1679

Club Pro: Joe Cordani Jr., Hope Kelley
Pro Shop: Full inventory
Payment: Visa, MC, Amex
Tee Times: 7 days a week
Fee 9 Holes: Weekday: $17.00
Fee 18 Holes: Weekday: $27.00
Cart Rental: $28.00/18 $16.00/9
Lessons: $35/half hour $60/hr. **School:** Jr.
Driving Range: $3.00 token
Other: Restaurant / Bar-lounge/ Banquet facilities

Tees	Holes	Yards	Par	USGA	Slope
BACK	18	6116	71	69.4	116
MIDDLE	18	5782	71	67.9	113
FRONT	18	5171	71	69.5	116

Weekend: $17.00
Weekend: $31.00
Discounts: Senior & Junior
Junior Golf: Yes **Membership:** No
Non-Metal Spikes: Required

COUPON

Tournaments welcome, access to all levels of players. Outings encouraged. Open March 15 - December 1. www.bluefoxrun.com

	1	2	3	4	5	6	7	8	9
PAR	4	4	3	4	5	4	3	5	3
YARDS	326	291	134	319	470	361	189	486	150
HDCP	13	15	17	7	3	1	9	5	11
	10	11	12	13	14	15	16	17	18
PAR	4	4	5	4	5	3	4	3	4
YARDS	357	372	494	389	483	125	340	138	358
HDCP	10	12	14	2	4	16	6	18	8

Directions: I-84 Exit 39. to Route 4, Farmington Center, turn right onto Waterville Rd. ,(Route 10 North). Go 5 miles., cross over Route 44 intersection to Nod Road. Club 1/2 mile on left.

Brooklyn Hill GC   5

South St., Brooklyn, CT (860) 779-2400

Club Pro: R. Carignan
Pro Shop: Limited inventory
Payment: Cash, Check
Tee Times: Wkends 7 days adv.
Fee 9 Holes: Weekday: $10.00
Fee 18 Holes: Weekday: $17.00
Cart Rental: $20.00/18 $10.00/9
Lessons: $20.00/half hour **School:** No
Driving Range: $4.75/lg., $2.75/sm.
Other: Clubhouse / Snack bar / Bar-lounge

Tees	Holes	Yards	Par	USGA	Slope
BACK	N/R				
MIDDLE	9	5760	70	N/A	N/A
FRONT					

Weekend: $12.00
Weekend: $19.00
Discounts: None
Junior Golf: No **Membership:** Yes
Non-Metal Spikes: Preferred

The course is picturesque at the expense of being very hilly. Beware of the large pond.

	1	2	3	4	5	6	7	8	9
PAR	4	4	4	4	5	3	4	3	4
YARDS	385	350	340	410	460	130	420	135	250
HDCP	9	7	11	3	5	15	1	17	13
	10	11	12	13	14	15	16	17	18
PAR	4	4	4	4	5	3	4	3	4
YARDS	385	350	340	410	460	130	420	135	250
HDCP	10	8	12	4	6	16	2	18	14

Directions: Take I-395 to Route 6 West Exit; take left onto Allen Hill Rd. Take first left onto South St.; course is 1/2 mile on left.

Buena Vista GC   6

W. Hartford, CT (860)521-7359

Club Pro: Richard Crow
Pro Shop: Limited inventory
Payment: Cash only
Tee Times: No
Fee 9 Holes: Weekday: $8.75
Fee 18 Holes: Weekday: $17.50
Cart Rental: $10.00/9
Lessons: No **School:** No
Driving Range: No
Other: No

Tees	Holes	Yards	Par	USGA	Slope
BACK	N/A				
MIDDLE	9	1977	31	N/A	N/A
FRONT	9	1653	30	N/A	N/A

Weekend: $9.75
Weekend: $19.50
Discounts: Sr & Jr. Only W. Hartford residents.
Junior Golf: N/R **Membership:** W. Hartford res.
Non-Metal Spikes: Required

Tee renovations have enhanced this tough executive style course. A good challenge for all levels of golfers. $1.00 surcharge for metal spikes. Open April - December.

	1	2	3	4	5	6	7	8	9
PAR	4	4	4	3	3	3	3	3	4
YARDS	263	344	295	171	130	98	223	214	239
HDCP	4	1	3	7	8	9	5	2	6
	10	11	12	13	14	15	16	17	18
PAR									
YARDS									
HDCP									

Directions: Take I-84 to Exit 43 (Park Rd.); left off ramp; go through 3 lights, take left onto Buena Vista Road. Course on left. Parking lot shared with Cornerstone Pool.

4✪ =Excellent **3✪** =Very Good **2✪** =Good

Canaan Country Club

7

S. Canaan Rd., Canaan, CT (860) 824-7683

Club Pro: Paul Julian
Pro Shop: Full inventory
Payment: Cash only
Tee Times: No
Fee 9 Holes: Weekday: $13.00
Fee 18 Holes: Weekday: $25.00
Cart Rental: $25.00/18 $13.00/9
Lessons: Private Call **School:** No
Driving Range: Yes
Other: Snack bar / Restaurant / Function rooms

Tees	Holes	Yards	Par	USGA	Slope
BACK	N/R				
MIDDLE	9	3007	35	68.2	108
FRONT	N/R				

Weekend: $13.00
Weekend: $25.00
Discounts: None
Junior Golf: No **Membership:** Yes
Non-Metal Spikes: Not Required

The course is mostly flat with a few rolling hills. Considered a good walking course.

	1	2	3	4	5	6	7	8	9
PAR	4	5	3	5	4	4	3	3	4
YARDS	320	520	180	545	402	382	125	210	323
HDCP	11	1	15	3	5	7	17	13	9
	10	11	12	13	14	15	16	17	18
PAR									
YARDS									
HDCP									

Directions: Take Route 7 to Canaan. The course is on South Canaan Road across from Greet Memorial Hospital.

Cedar Knob GC

8

Billings Rd., Somers, CT (860) 749-3550

Club Pro: Jeffrey Swanson
Pro Shop: Full inventory
Payment: Cash or check
Tee Times: Wkends 3 days adv.
Fee 9 Holes: Weekday: $13.00
Fee 18 Holes: Weekday: $23.00
Cart Rental: $22.00/18 $11.00/9
Lessons: $25/30 min. **School:** No
Driving Range: Yes - must use own balls
Other: Clubhouse / Snack bar / Restaurant / Bar-lounge

Tees	Holes	Yards	Par	USGA	Slope
BACK	18	6734	72	72.3	119
MIDDLE	18	6298	72	70.3	116
FRONT	18	5784	74	73.8	126

Weekend: $15.00
Weekend: $25.00
Discounts: Senior & Junior
Junior Golf: Yes **Membership:** No
Non-Metal Spikes: Probable

Dress code, large greens. You will use every club in your bag. Open year round (weather permitting.)

	1	2	3	4	5	6	7	8	9
PAR	4	3	5	4	3	4	5	4	4
YARDS	384	154	482	397	209	319	478	327	328
HDCP	5	15	11	1	7	17	3	9	13
	10	11	12	13	14	15	16	17	18
PAR	5	4	4	4	3	4	3	5	4
YARDS	490	370	410	350	170	350	210	470	400
HDCP	6	10	2	14	18	12	8	16	4

Directions: Take Route 91 to Exit 47 (East toward Somers). Right onto Route 83; right on Billings Rd. Course is 1/2 mi. on left.

Cedar Ridge GC

9

E. Lyme, CT (860) 691-4568

Club Pro: No
Pro Shop: Full inventory
Payment: Cash only
Tee Times: 7 days adv.
Fee 9 Holes: Weekday: $12.00
Fee 18 Holes: Weekday: $15.50
Cart Rental: No
Lessons: No **School:** No
Driving Range: No
Other: Snacks only

Tees	Holes	Yards	Par	USGA	Slope
BACK	N/R				
MIDDLE	18	3025	54	N/A	N/A
FRONT	N/R				

Weekend: $14.00
Weekend: $20.50
Discounts: Senior
Junior Golf: No **Membership:**
Non-Metal Spikes: Required

Rolling hills, water hazards, course in excellent condition. Very challenging for the serious and pleasant for the amateur. Takes around two hours. Dress is casual. Open April - November.

	1	2	3	4	5	6	7	8	9
PAR	3	3	3	3	3	3	3	3	3
YARDS	157	110	172	103	200	160	122	145	160
HDCP	3	9	2	8	1	4	7	6	5
	10	11	12	13	14	15	16	17	18
PAR	3	3	3	3	3	3	3	3	3
YARDS	147	135	230	145	196	225	215	203	133
HDCP	6	8	1	7	3	2	5	4	9

Directions: I-95 Exit 74, left on Route 161 North. 1 mile to Drabik Road on left.

Copper Hill CC

10

E. Granby, CT (860) 653-6191

Club Pro: Vic Svenberg
Pro Shop: Full inventory
Payment: Cash only
Tee Times: 1 week adv.
Fee 9 Holes: Weekday: $10.50
Fee 18 Holes: Weekday: $19.50
Cart Rental: $20.00/18 $10.00/9
Lessons: Yes **School:** Jr.Yes
Driving Range: Yes
Other: Clubhouse / Snack bar / Restaurant / Bar-lounge

Tees	Holes	Yards	Par	USGA	Slope
BACK	N/R				
MIDDLE	18	5897	72	69	116
FRONT	18	5281	72	73.0	116

Weekend: $11.50
Weekend: $23.00
Discounts: Senior & Junior
Junior Golf: Yes **Membership:** Yes
Non-Metal Spikes: Required

The Golf Academy has various instruction programs. Country setting and gentle terrain. Open April - snowfall. **www.copperhillgolf.com.**

	1	2	3	4	5	6	7	8	9
PAR	4	4	3	5	4	3	4	5	4
YARDS	335	325	181	465	255	175	325	440	385
HDCP	13	5	7	11	3	9	17	5	1
	10	11	12	13	14	15	16	17	18
PAR	4	4	3	5	4	3	4	5	4
YARDS	335	370	133	478	270	184	360	465	416
HDCP	16	2	18	14	10	12	6	4	8

NE CT

Directions: Take Exit 40 off I-91 (Bradley Field Exit). Follow Route 20 west to Newgate Road (6 lights). Turn right on Newgate Road. Go past old Newgate prison to stop sign. Turn Right to course.

4✪=Excellent **3**✪=Very Good **2**✪=Good

Northern/Eastern CT 297

East Hartford GC 11

Long Hill St., E. Hartford, CT (860) 528-5082

Club Pro: Richard Thivia, PGA
Pro Shop: Full inventory
Payment: Cash only
Tee Times: Weekends, 1 week adv.
Fee 9 Holes: Weekday: $14.00
Fee 18 Holes: Weekday: $23.00
Cart Rental: $20.00/18 $11.00/9
Lessons: $25.00/half hour **School:** No
Driving Range: No
Other: Restaurant / Clubhouse / Bar-lounge / Lockers / Showers

Tees	Holes	Yards	Par	USGA	Slope
BACK	NA				
MIDDLE	18	6076	71	68.6	114
FRONT	18	5072	72	68.9	113

Weekend: $15.00
Weekend: $25.00
Discounts: Senior & Junior
Junior Golf: Yes **Membership:** No
Non-Metal Spikes: Not Required

Relatively short but challenging course which will require a player to use all the clubs in his or her bag. Large putting green. Dress code: no tank tops or cutoffs. Open April 1 - December 1.

	1	2	3	4	5	6	7	8	9
PAR	4	4	4	3	5	4	4	3	4
YARDS	305	397	322	123	508	415	308	127	385
HDCP	9	7	11	17	1	5	13	15	3
	10	11	12	13	14	15	16	17	18
PAR	5	3	4	4	4	3	4	4	5
YARDS	512	188	309	330	356	150	457	384	500
HDCP	2	16	12	14	8	18	4	6	10

Directions: I-84 to Exit 60, onto Burnside Avenue towards East Hartford. Enter East Hartford, take a right a second traffic light onto Long Hill Street. Proceed through three stop signs, course on right.

Elmridge Golf Course 12

Elmridge Rd., Pawcatuck, CT (860)599-2248

Club Pro: Thomas Jones
Pro Shop: Full inventory
Payment: Visa, MC, Amex
Tee Times: Yes
Fee 9 Holes: Weekday: $17.00
Fee 18 Holes: Weekday: $29.00
Cart Rental: $24.00/18 $12.00/9
Lessons: $30/30 min. **School:** No
Driving Range: Yes
Other: Clubhouse / Snack bar / Restaurant / Bar-lounge/ Outings

Tees	Holes	Yards	Par	USGA	Slope
BACK	18	6407	71	70.8	115
MIDDLE	18	6014	71	69.3	112
FRONT	18	5430	71	69.0	109

Weekend: $17.00 after 3 pm
Weekend: $31.00,$24 after 2pm
Discounts: None
Junior Golf: No **Membership:** Yes
Non-Metal Spikes: Required

27 holes allow variety of play : Red South, White West, and Blue North courses. Located seven miles from Foxwoods Casino. www.elmridgegolf.com

	1	2	3	4	5	6	7	8	9
PAR	4	4	4	5	4	3	4	3	4
YARDS	366	335	360	462	149	324	167	385	268
HDCP	3	8	2	4	5	6	7	1	9
	10	11	12	13	14	15	16	17	18
PAR	4	5	4	3	5	3	5	3	4
YARDS	365	485	342	149	576	340	365	206	370
HDCP	9	4	5	8	1	2	6	7	3

Directions: I-95 North, Exit 92 in CT. From north, go left. From south go right. Take first right on to Elmridge Road . Course is 1 mile on left.

Goodwin Golf Course   13

Maple Ave., Hartford, CT (860) 956-3601

Club Pro: Kevin Tierney
Pro Shop: Full inventory
Payment: Visa, MC, Amex
Tee Times: 5 days adv.
Fee 9 Holes: Weekday: $12.00
Fee 18 Holes: Weekday: $20.00
Cart Rental: $22.25/18 $13.25/9
Lessons: $30.00/half hour **School:** Yes
Driving Range: Yes
Other: Snack Bar

Tees	Holes	Yards	Par	USGA	Slope
BACK	18	6100	70	N/A	110
MIDDLE	18	6050	70	66.7	108
FRONT	18	5908	70	N/A	109

Weekend: $13.50
Weekend: $23.00
Discounts: Senior & Junior
Junior Golf: Yes **Membership:** Yes
Non-Metal Spikes: Not Required

COUPON

Eighteen hole regulation good contrast between open and tight holes. Fairway tree lined and narrow. Nine hole a good beginner course, flat, open. Open year round (weather permitting.)

	1	2	3	4	5	6	7	8	9
PAR	5	4	4	4	4	4	3	3	4
YARDS	486	315	367	322	370	286	127	155	332
HDCP	5	10	3	11	12	13	18	16	8
	10	11	12	13	14	15	16	17	18
PAR	4	3	5	4	4	3	4	4	4
YARDS	334	213	471	361	312	138	336	352	361
HDCP	15	2	1	9	14	17	7	4	6

Directions: I-91 to Exit 28. Take Routes 15, 5 South to Exit 85 (Route 99), follow ramp to first light. Right on Joran to right on Maple.

Grassmere CC   14

Enfield, CT (860) 749-7740

Club Pro: No
Pro Shop: Limited inventory
Payment: Cash, Checks
Tee Times: 2 weeks adv.
Fee 9 Holes: Weekday: $12.00
Fee 18 Holes: Weekday: $22.00
Cart Rental: $20.00/18 $10.00/9
Lessons: No **School:** No
Driving Range: No
Other: Clubhouse / Snack bar / Banquet facility

Tees	Holes	Yards	Par	USGA	Slope
BACK	N/A				
MIDDLE	9	6130	70	69.1	111
FRONT	9	5346	70	N/A	N/A

Weekend: $13.00
Weekend: $24.00
Discounts: Senior & Junior
Junior Golf: No **Membership:** No
Non-Metal Spikes: Not Required

Considered easy walking terrain. A friendly course in layout and staff. Open March 15 - December 31. Junior golfers encouraged.

	1	2	3	4	5	6	7	8	9
PAR	4	4	4	4	3	5	4	4	3
YARDS	360	390	405	415	160	475	320	360	180
HDCP	7	4	2	1	6	9	5	8	3
	10	11	12	13	14	15	16	17	18
PAR	4	4	4	4	3	5	4	4	3
YARDS	360	390	405	415	160	475	320	360	180
HDCP	7	4	2	1	6	9	5	8	3

Directions: From I-91 S: Exit 46; take right at end of ramp; right at 3rd light. Course is on right 5.5 miles. From I-91 N: Exit 45 to Route 140 E to Route 191 N. Left on Town Farms Road. Course on left.

4✪ =Excellent **3**✪ =Very Good **2**✪ =Good

Harrisville GC   15

Woodstock, CT (860) 928-6098

Club Pro: No
Pro Shop: Limited inventory
Payment: Cash, Check
Tee Times: Weekends
Fee 9 Holes: Weekday: $11.00
Fee 18 Holes: Weekday: $16.00
Cart Rental: $22.00/18 $11.00/9
Lessons: No **School:** No
Driving Range: No
Other: Snack bar

Tees	Holes	Yards	Par	USGA	Slope
BACK	N/R				
MIDDLE	9	2814	35	N/A	N/A
FRONT	9	2435	35	N/A	N/A

Weekend: $15.00
Weekend: $22.00
Discounts: None
Junior Golf: No **Membership:** No
Non-Metal Spikes: Not Required

Gentle hills, exceptional greens, nice overview of Woodstock Hill. Open April 1 - December 15.

	1	2	3	4	5	6	7	8	9
PAR	4	3	5	4	4	5	4	3	3
YARDS	267	165	500	267	427	460	295	233	200
HDCP	N/A								
	10	11	12	13	14	15	16	17	18
PAR									
YARDS									
HDCP									

Directions: Route 395 Exit 95 (Kennedy Drive.) Take right off exit to red light, take left onto Route 44 W. Go past auto dealer on right and take right onto Sabin Street. Go straight through Four Corners. Course 1/2 mile on left.

Hotchkiss School GC   16

Lakeville, CT (860) 435-9033

Club Pro: James Kennedy
Pro Shop: Limited inventory
Payment: Cash only
Tee Times: No
Fee 9 Holes: Weekday: $12.00
Fee 18 Holes: Weekday: $17.00
Cart Rental: $22.00/18 $11.00/9
Lessons: Yes **School:** N/R
Driving Range: No
Other: Snack Bar

Tees	Holes	Yards	Par	USGA	Slope
BACK	N/R				
MIDDLE	9	6072	70	68.8	117
FRONT	N/R				

Weekend: $15.00
Weekend: $25.00
Discounts: None
Junior Golf: No **Membership:** Yes
Non-Metal Spikes: Not Required

Hilly and heavily wooded. While the course is long, it is still suitable for beginners. Not available for public play until 11 am on weekends. Designed by Seth Raynor and Charles Banks.

	1	2	3	4	5	6	7	8	9
PAR	4	3	4	4	3	4	5	3	5
YARDS	420	192	401	370	128	347	500	165	520
HDCP	1	11	5	9	17	15	7	13	3
	10	11	12	13	14	15	16	17	18
PAR	4	4	4	4	3	4	4	3	5
YARDS	405	256	385	355	136	358	440	189	505
HDCP	2	16	8	10	18	14	4	12	6

Directions: Take Route 7 to 112 West to course or Route 44 to Route 112 East

Keney Park Golf Club

17

Hartford, CT (860)525-3656

Club Pro:
Pro Shop: Limited inventory
Payment: Visa, MC, Check
Tee Times: 1 wk. adv S/S/Hol.
Fee 9 Holes: Weekday: $12.00
Fee 18 Holes: Weekday: $20.00
Cart Rental: $21.00/18 $12.50/9
Lessons: Yes **School:** Yes
Driving Range: No
Other: Clubhouse / Lockers / Showers / Snack bar / Restaurant / Function

Tees	Holes	Yards	Par	USGA	Slope
BACK	18	6096	70	68.2	118
MIDDLE	18	5678	70	67.0	115
FRONT	18	5005	70	67.2	107

Weekend: $13.50
Weekend: $23.00
Discounts: Senior & Junior
Junior Golf: Membership: Yes
Non-Metal Spikes: Preferred

COUPON

Nestled among acres of natural forest, the course boasts a true links-style layout. The clubhouse is reminiscent of the grand architectural style of the late 20's. Open year round.

	1	2	3	4	5	6	7	8	9
PAR	4	5	3	4	4	3	4	4	4
YARDS	306	456	128	328	388	136	365	375	382
HDCP	13	7	17	11	1	15	9	3	5
	10	11	12	13	14	15	16	17	18
PAR	5	3	4	3	5	4	4	4	3
YARDS	518	178	287	161	438	363	366	349	154
HDCP	2	12	16	10	8	4	14	6	18

Directions: Course is 5 minutes north of downtown Hartford. Call course for directions.

Lisbon Country Club

18

Lisbon, CT (860) 376-4325

Club Pro: Cathy Williams Molocko
Pro Shop: Full inventory
Payment: Cash only
Tee Times: No
Fee 9 Holes: Weekday: $10.00
Fee 18 Holes: Weekday: $16.00
Cart Rental: $18.00/18 $10.00/9
Lessons: $15.00/half hour **School:** N/R
Driving Range: No
Other: Snack bar

Tees	Holes	Yards	Par	USGA	Slope
BACK	N/A				
MIDDLE	9	4685	66	65.5	102
FRONT					

Weekend: $12.00
Weekend: $18.00
Discounts: Senior
Junior Golf: N/R **Membership:** N/R
Non-Metal Spikes: N/R

Presents a challenge. Rolling hills and 6 water holes. Open March - November.

	1	2	3	4	5	6	7	8	9
PAR	3	4	4	3	5	3	4	4	3
YARDS	185	245	227	175	460	210	343	390	100
HDCP	N/A								
	10	11	12	13	14	15	16	17	18
PAR	3	4	4	3	5	3	4	4	3
YARDS	185	260	227	175	460	210	343	390	100
HDCP	N/A								

NE CT

Directions: From South take I-395 to Exit 83A. Left up 3/4 mile at railroad overpass, take left just before it onto Kendall Road. Course is on Kendall.

4◎=Excellent 3◎=Very Good 2◎=Good

Manchester CC   ★★ 19

Manchester, CT (860) 646-0226

Club Pro: Ralph DeNicolo
Pro Shop: Full inventory
Payment: MC, Visa
Tee Times: 2 days adv.

Tees	Holes	Yards	Par	USGA	Slope
BACK	N/R				
MIDDLE	18	6137	72	69.7	123
FRONT	18	5602	73	72.0	120

Fee 9 Holes: Weekday: $18.00 non-resident **Weekend:** $18.00 non-resident
Fee 18 Holes: Weekday: $35.00 **Weekend:** $35.00
Cart Rental: $22.00/18 $12.00/9 **Discounts:** Senior & Junior
Lessons: $30.00/half hour **School:** No **Junior Golf:** Yes **Membership:** Yes
Driving Range: Yes **Non-Metal Spikes:** Required
Other: Clubhouse / Lockers / Showers / Snack bar / Restaurant / Bar-lounge

Old style golf course. Variety of elevation changes. Built in 1917. Second nine built in 1923. Reduced fees available for residents. Open April - December. **www.mancc.com**

	1	2	3	4	5	6	7	8	9
PAR	4	4	5	5	3	4	4	3	4
YARDS	316	338	507	501	141	404	344	149	353
HDCP	13	11	3	9	17	1	5	15	7
	10	11	12	13	14	15	16	17	18
PAR	4	4	3	4	5	5	4	4	3
YARDS	293	337	135	334	522	506	397	372	188
HDCP	12	14	18	6	10	4	2	8	16

Directions: Take I-84 to Route 384 East (Exit 3). Take left 1000 yards up onto South Main Street. Course is on the left.

Millbrook Golf Course   20

Windsor, CT (860) 688-2575

Club Pro: Greg Steele, PGA
Pro Shop: Full inventory
Payment: Visa, MC, Amex
Tee Times: Yes

Tees	Holes	Yards	Par	USGA	Slope
BACK	18	6050	70	69.8	119
MIDDLE	18	5650	71	67.9	116
FRONT	18	5184	72	71.5	125

Fee 9 Holes: Weekday: $15.00 **Weekend:** $16.00
Fee 18 Holes: Weekday: $23.00 **Weekend:** $27.00
Cart Rental: $22.00/18 $11.00/9 **Discounts:** Senior
Lessons: Yes **School:** Yes **Junior Golf:** Yes **Membership:** Yes
Driving Range: Nearby **Non-Metal Spikes:** Required
Other: Clubhouse / Snack bar / Restaurant / Patio dining

Expanded golf shop and restaurant. The patio has an awning to provide shade. Overlooks challenging golf course. Proper attire required. Open April 1 - October 31. **www.ctgolfer.com/millbrook**

	1	2	3	4	5	6	7	8	9
PAR	4	4	4	4	5	3	3	4	4
YARDS	447	318	349	335	469	147	188	381	279
HDCP	1	11	13	7	5	17	9	3	15
	10	11	12	13	14	15	16	17	18
PAR	4	4	4	4	5	4	3	3	5
YARDS	391	279	315	282	445	337	140	200	465
HDCP	2	14	8	16	6	12	18	10	4

Directions: Exit 38 off I-91. Left onto Route 75, 1 mile to Pigeon Hill Road. Turn right, course 1/4 mile on left.

Minnechaug GC

Glastonbury, CT (860) 643-9914

Tees	Holes	Yards	Par	USGA	Slope
BACK	9	2654	35	67.4	112
MIDDLE	9	2527	35	66.5	110
FRONT	9	2186	35	62.7	102

Club Pro: No
Pro Shop: Soft goods only
Payment: Cash only
Tee Times: 1 week adv.
Fee 9 Holes: Weekday: $12.00   **Weekend:** $13.00
Fee 18 Holes: Weekday: N/A   **Weekend:** N/A
Cart Rental: $12.00/9   **Discounts:** Senior & Junior
Lessons: No **School:** No   **Junior Golf:** No **Membership:** No
Driving Range: No   **Non-Metal Spikes:** Required
Other: Menu/ Beer/ Snacks

9 holes only. Limited 18 hole play. Open April - November.

	1	2	3	4	5	6	7	8	9
PAR	4	4	5	4	5	3	4	3	3
YARDS	328	317	472	341	453	181	278	126	158
HDCP	5	1	3	2	6	4	9	8	7
	10	11	12	13	14	15	16	17	18
PAR									
YARDS									
HDCP									

Directions: 84 East to Route 384 East, Exit 3. Left off exit on Route 83. Follow for 3 miles. Course on right.

Norwich Golf Course

Norwich, CT (860) 889-6973

Tees	Holes	Yards	Par	USGA	Slope
BACK	18	6183	71	69.6	123
MIDDLE	18	5877	72	68.2	120
FRONT	18	5104	71	70.2	118

Club Pro: John Paesani
Pro Shop: Full inventory
Payment: Visa, MC
Tee Times: Weekends, 3 days adv.
Fee 9 Holes: Weekday: No   **Weekend:** No
Fee 18 Holes: Weekday: $26.00   **Weekend:** $29.00
Cart Rental: $10.50pp/wknd $9pp/wkdy   **Discounts:** After 5 pm
Lessons: $30.00/half hour **School:**   **Junior Golf:** Yes **Membership:** Yes
Driving Range: No   **Non-Metal Spikes:** Required
Other: Clubhouse / Lockers / Showers / Restaurant / Bar-lounge

The course is short but tricky. Overly aggressive play could lead to disaster. Designed by Donald Ross. Open April - November. $5.00 off for residents.

	1	2	3	4	5	6	7	8	9
PAR	4	4	4	4	5	4	4	4	3
YARDS	303	276	366	410	487	330	370	300	170
HDCP	15	11	5	1	7	13	3	9	17
	10	11	12	13	14	15	16	17	18
PAR	4	4	5	3	5	4	4	4	3
YARDS	355	388	503	105	545	170	330	303	166
HDCP	6	2	8	18	4	14	10	12	16

NE CT

Directions: Take I-95 to I-395 North to Exit 80E. Take right off ramp (West Main Street), follow to fifth light. Take right onto New London Turnpike. Course is 1/2 mile down on right.

4✪ =Excellent 3✪ =Very Good 2✪ =Good

Pequot Golf Club   23

Wheeler Rd., Stonington, CT (860) 535-1898

Club Pro: Jon Terenzi
Pro Shop: Full inventory
Payment: Visa, MC, Cash
Tee Times: 7 days adv.
Fee 9 Holes: Weekday: $15.00
Fee 18 Holes: Weekday: $22.00
Cart Rental: $24.00/18 $14.00/9
Lessons: $30.00/45 min. **School:** No
Driving Range: No
Other: Restaurant / Bar-lounge

Tees	Holes	Yards	Par	USGA	Slope
BACK	N/R				
MIDDLE	18	5903	70	67.2	108
FRONT	18	5246	71	69.4	112

Weekend: $17.00 after 12:00 pm
Weekend: $27, $23 after noon
Discounts: Senior & Junior
Junior Golf: No **Membership:** Yes
Non-Metal Spikes: Required

Short course with narrow fairways and small greens. Best public golf greens in the area. Open February 15 - December 2.

	1	2	3	4	5	6	7	8	9
PAR	4	4	4	4	4	3	4	4	3
YARDS	353	329	358	287	328	179	379	376	209
HDCP	9	13	5	15	7	17	1	3	11
	10	11	12	13	14	15	16	17	18
PAR	4	4	3	5	4	4	4	3	5
YARDS	276	361	149	469	417	336	339	193	565
HDCP	16	8	18	10	2	12	4	14	16

Directions: I-95 to Exit 91. Left off 95(S), right off 95(N). Go 1 mi. Take right onto Wheeler Rd.

Putnam Country Club   24

Putnam, CT (860)928-7748

Club Pro:
Pro Shop: Full inventory
Payment: Visa, MC, Disc
Tee Times: 3 days adv.
Fee 9 Holes: Weekday: $12.00
Fee 18 Holes: Weekday: $20.00
Cart Rental: $22.00/18 $12.00/9
Lessons: No **School:** Jr.
Driving Range: $6/lg. $5/md. $4/sm.
Other: Clubhouse/ Snack Bar/ Beer & Wine

Tees	Holes	Yards	Par	USGA	Slope
BACK	18	6131	71	68.6	114
MIDDLE	18	5819	71	67.7	109
FRONT	18	4910	71	68.8	114

Weekend: $15.00
Weekend: $24.00
Discounts: Senior & Junior Wkdays
Junior Golf: No **Membership:** Yes
Non-Metal Spikes: Required

COUPON

Well manicured bent grass greens. Quiet country setting. Tight tree lined fairways, very challenging. In late fall of 1996 opened new 9 holes, now an 18-hole facility. Open April 1 - November 30.

	1	2	3	4	5	6	7	8	9
PAR	5	4	4	3	4	5	3	4	3
YARDS	436	333	380	192	304	552	160	257	111
HDCP	12	9	1	7	13	2	15	14	17
	10	11	12	13	14	15	16	17	18
PAR	4	3	5	4	4	3	4	4	5
YARDS	373	151	479	315	385	134	395	360	502
HDCP	6	18	10	12	2	16	4	8	14

Directions: Route 395 exit 97 East on Route 44. 3 1/2 mile to public course, sign on right. Right onto East Putnam Rd. At 2nd stop sign take a right (Chase Rd.) Course is 1 mile on right.

Raceway Golf Club

25

Thompson, CT (860) 923-9591

Club Pro: Brian Morrow
Pro Shop: Full inventory
Payment: Cash only
Tee Times: 3 days adv.

Tees	Holes	Yards	Par	USGA	Slope
BACK	18	6412	71	70.0	111
MIDDLE	18	5916	71	67.7	106
FRONT	18	5437	71	71.3	117

Fee 9 Holes: Weekday: No **Weekend:** No
Fee 18 Holes: Weekday: $20.00 **Weekend:** $24.00
Cart Rental: $22.00/18 **Discounts:** None
Lessons: Call for info **School:** **Junior Golf:** Yes **Membership:**
Driving Range: $4.00/lg. bucket **Non-Metal Spikes:** Not Required
Other: Clubhouse / Lockers / Showers / Snack bar / Restaurant / Bar-lounge

A championship course; fairly flat with water on 6 holes.

	1	2	3	4	5	6	7	8	9
PAR	4	4	4	3	5	4	4	4	3
YARDS	277	387	304	152	536	392	350	402	174
HDCP	17	4	14	15	1	6	9	3	12
	10	11	12	13	14	15	16	17	18
PAR	5	4	4	5	3	4	4	3	4
YARDS	492	382	342	425	146	353	347	166	289
HDCP	2	7	11	5	16	8	10	13	18

Directions: Take I-395 to Exit 99; go into Thompson Center, left at blinking light onto Route 193. Follow signs to Thompson Speedway which will lead to the course.

Rockledge CC

✪✪ **26**

W. Hartford, CT (860) 521-3156

Club Pro: Richard F. Crowe
Pro Shop: Full inventory
Payment: Cash only
Tee Times: Yes

Tees	Holes	Yards	Par	USGA	Slope
BACK	18	6436	72	71.1	129
MIDDLE	18	6069	72	69.3	125
FRONT	18	5436	72	72.7	128

Fee 9 Holes: Weekday: $14.00 **Weekend:** $16.00
Fee 18 Holes: Weekday: $25.00 **Weekend:** $29.00
Cart Rental: $22.00/18 $13.00/9 **Discounts:** Senior
Lessons: $30/30 min. **School:** No **Junior Golf:** No **Membership:** Yes
Driving Range: $4.00/lg. bucket **Non-Metal Spikes:** Required
Other: Clubhouse / Lockers / Showers / Snack bar / Restaurant / Bar-lounge

Open April - December (weather permitting.) Resident fees and tee times. Lottery for weekends.

	1	2	3	4	5	6	7	8	9
PAR	4	4	4	4	3	5	4	3	5
YARDS	334	286	394	395	177	450	299	181	448
HDCP	13	17	1	3	9	15	11	7	5
	10	11	12	13	14	15	16	17	18
PAR	4	4	5	3	5	4	3	4	4
YARDS	404	302	465	136	515	357	152	381	393
HDCP	2	16	10	18	8	6	14	12	4

Directions: From I-84 West or East, take Exit 41. From West take a right off the exit, from East take a left off the exit. Course is 1/4 mile on left.

4✪ =Excellent **3✪** =Very Good **2✪** =Good

Rolling Greens GC   27

Rocky Hill, CT (860) 257-9775

Club Pro: Joe DeCandia
Pro Shop: Full inventory
Payment: Visa, MC
Tee Times: No
Fee 9 Holes: Weekday: $13.00
Fee 18 Holes: Weekday: $20.00
Cart Rental: $12 pp/18 $6 pp/9
Lessons: $30.00 **School:** No
Driving Range: No
Other: Clubhouse / Lockers / Showers / Restaurant / Bar-lounge

Tees	Holes	Yards	Par	USGA	Slope
BACK	N/A				
MIDDLE	9	6212	70	72.0	131
FRONT	9	5270	72	72.0	125

Weekend: $15.00
Weekend: $26.00
Discounts: Senior & Junior
Junior Golf: No **Membership:** Yes
Non-Metal Spikes: Required

COUPON

Rolling hills. Dress code (no tank tops or cut-off jeans.) Shot maker's course. Open March - November.

	1	2	3	4	5	6	7	8	9
PAR	4	5	3	4	4	4	4	3	4
YARDS	360	553	191	315	379	440	373	180	340
HDCP	9	1	15	13	5	3	7	17	11
	10	11	12	13	14	15	16	17	18
PAR	4	5	3	4	4	4	4	3	4
YARDS	374	533	160	322	363	458	354	165	352
HDCP	6	2	18	14	8	4	10	16	12

Directions: Exit 23 off I-91. Signs to Rolling Greens. Approx. 1 mile from exit.

Rolling Meadows Country Club   28

Ellington, CT (860) 870-5328

Club Pro: Dan Malarney, PGA, Jeff Swanson
Pro Shop: Full inventory
Payment: Cash only
Tee Times: 3 days adv.
Fee 9 Holes: Weekday: $13.00
Fee 18 Holes: Weekday: $23.00
Cart Rental: $11.00/9 $22.00/18
Lessons: N/R **School:** N/R
Driving Range: Yes
Other: Restaurant / Bar / Snacks

Tees	Holes	Yards	Par	USGA	Slope
BACK	18	6818	72	72.5	128
MIDDLE	18	6269	72	70	123
FRONT	18	5331	72	70.4	122

Weekend: $15.00
Weekend: $25.00
Discounts: Senior & Junior $10 wkdays
Junior Golf: Yes **Membership:** Yes
Non-Metal Spikes: Required

"Challenging layout. Every hole exhibits a different character. Down hill #8, a par 3 with water behind the green." R.W.

	1	2	3	4	5	6	7	8	9
PAR	5	4	3	5	4	4	4	3	4
YARDS	488	316	166	491	390	366	335	186	346
HDCP	5	15	11	1	7	17	3	9	13
	10	11	12	13	14	15	16	17	18
PAR	4	5	4	3	5	4	4	3	4
YARDS	383	473	366	163	490	433	345	190	342
HDCP	2	10	6	12	18	14	16	4	8

Directions: Route 91 to Route 140 or Route 84 to 83 to Route 140 (across from Brookside Park, Ellington).

Shennecosset GC

29

Plant St., Groton, CT (860) 445-0262

Club Pro: Todd Goodhue
Pro Shop: Full inventory
Payment: Visa, MC
Tee Times: 3 days adv.

Tees	Holes	Yards	Par	USGA	Slope
BACK	18	6491	72	71.1	122
MIDDLE	18	6142	72	69.5	118
FRONT	18	5796	76	73.2	121

Fee 9 Holes: Weekday: N/A **Weekend:** N/A
Fee 18 Holes: Weekday: $25.00 **Weekend:** $30.00
Cart Rental: $22.00/18 **Discounts:** Junior
Lessons: $25.00/half hour **School:** No **Junior Golf:** Yes **Membership:** Yes
Driving Range: No **Non-Metal Spikes:** Required
Other: Clubhouse / Snack bar / Restaurant / Bar-loung

Designed by Donald Ross with the old links-style architecture. Wide fairways, numerous traps and is generally windy. Open year round. Resident fees.

	1	2	3	4	5	6	7	8	9
PAR	4	4	4	3	5	3	5	4	4
YARDS	350	368	361	195	488	145	433	367	418
HDCP	13	5	3	15	9	17	11	7	1
	10	11	12	13	14	15	16	17	18
PAR	4	3	5	5	4	3	4	4	4
YARDS	400	160	460	542	323	116	343	362	311
HDCP	2	16	10	4	8	18	12	6	14

Directions: Take I-95 to Exit 87 (Clarence Sharp Highway); take right at second light. Take left at next light, proceed past Pfizer; course is on left side.

Simsbury Farms GC

30

Old Farms Rd., Simsbury, CT (860) 658-6246

Club Pro: John Verrengia
Pro Shop: Full inventory
Payment: Cash, Check, MC, Visa
Tee Times: 2 days adv.

Tees	Holes	Yards	Par	USGA	Slope
BACK	18	6421	72	69.8	120
MIDDLE	18	6104	72	68.3	118
FRONT	18	5439	72	70.1	117

Fee 9 Holes: Weekday: $13.00 **Weekend:** $15.00
Fee 18 Holes: Weekday: $24.00 **Weekend:** $28.00
Cart Rental: $24.00/18 $12.00/9 **Discounts:** Senior
Lessons: $34.50/half hour **School:** No **Junior Golf:** Yes **Membership:** Residents
Driving Range: $3.25-$4.50/bucket **Non-Metal Spikes:** Required
Other: Restaurants / Clubhouse / Showers

A nice hilly course. Good challenge, with a decent mix of holes. Open April - November.

	1	2	3	4	5	6	7	8	9
PAR	4	4	4	3	5	4	5	4	3
YARDS	341	375	361	135	487	361	528	286	178
HDCP	13	9	11	17	5	3	1	15	7
	10	11	12	13	14	15	16	17	18
PAR	4	4	5	3	5	4	3	4	4
YARDS	346	341	524	169	465	321	212	295	379
HDCP	14	12	2	16	4	10	6	18	8

NE CT

Directions: Take I-84 to 44 West toward Avon. Turn right onto Route 10; 3 mi. down turn left on Stratton Brook Rd. Road becomes Old Farms at church. Course 1 mile on right.

4✪ =Excellent 3✪ =Very Good 2✪ =Good

Skungamaug River GC   31

Folly Ln., Coventry, CT (860) 742-9348

Club Pro: Rick Nelson
Pro Shop: Full inventory
Payment: Visa, MC
Tee Times: 5 days adv.
Fee 9 Holes: Weekday: $12.50
Fee 18 Holes: Weekday: $24.00
Cart Rental: $10.50/18
Lessons: $25.00/half hour **School:** No
Driving Range: $3.00/med. bucket
Other: Clubhouse / Snack bar / Bar-lounge

Tees	Holes	Yards	Par	USGA	Slope
BACK	18	5785	70	69.4	120
MIDDLE	18	5624	70	68.6	118
FRONT	18	4838	71	69.3	123

Weekend: $14.00
Weekend: $26.50
Discounts: Senior
Junior Golf: Yes **Membership:** Yes
Non-Metal Spikes: Not Required

Rolling, tight — no back and forth here. Smallish, undulating greens always in super shape. No cutoffs or tank tops. Open April - December.

	1	2	3	4	5	6	7	8	9
PAR	4	3	4	5	3	4	5	3	4
YARDS	339	154	291	438	139	332	461	158	351
HDCP	8	18	10	6	16	2	4	12	14
	10	11	12	13	14	15	16	17	18
PAR	4	3	4	4	4	4	4	3	5
YARDS	376	171	363	371	395	290	323	189	483
HDCP	9	17	11	3	5	15	1	13	7

Directions: From I-84, Exit 68. South on Route 195, 1/4 mile to light. Turn right onto Goose Lane, follow yellow, triangular arrows on telephone poles. 3 miles to club.

Stanley Golf Club   32

Hartford Rd., New Britain, CT (860)827-8144

Club Pro: Ted Pisk
Pro Shop: Full inventory
Payment: Cash only
Tee Times: Weekends, 3 days adv.
Fee 9 Holes: Weekday: $13.00
Fee 18 Holes: Weekday: $21.00
Cart Rental: $20.50/18 $11.75/9
Lessons: $26.00/45 minutes **School:** N/R
Driving Range: No
Other: Clubhouse / Lockers / Showers / Restaurant / Bar-lounge

Tees	Holes	Yards	Par	USGA	Slope
BACK	27	6453	72	71.1	115
MIDDLE	27	6067	72	69.4	111
FRONT	27	5681	73	72.0	122

Weekend: $15.00
Weekend: $25.00
Discounts: Residents only.
Junior Golf: Yes **Membership:** Seasonal Pass
Non-Metal Spikes: Required

Voted by Hartford Courant as best hole (#7) in area. Many holes have excellent tee boxes for women. Each nine plays completely different. Open April - December.

	1	2	3	4	5	6	7	8	9
PAR	5	4	4	4	3	4	4	3	5
YARDS	492	347	370	387	165	296	415	136	508
HDCP	11	3	7	9	13	17	1	15	5
	10	11	12	13	14	15	16	17	18
PAR	4	3	5	4	4	4	3	4	5
YARDS	323	195	461	321	325	376	160	345	445
HDCP	8	10	14	2	12	6	18	4	16

Directions: Take I-84 to exit 39A, then right onto route 9S to Exit 30. Take right at end of ramp. Course is 4 miles on left.

Tallwood Country Club

33

Rt. 85, Hebron, CT (860) 646-1151

Club Pro: John Nowobilski
Pro Shop: Full inventory
Payment: Cash only
Tee Times: Yes
Fee 9 Holes: Weekday: $13.50
Fee 18 Holes: Weekday: $27.00
Cart Rental: $20.00/18 $10.00/9
Lessons: $25.00/half hour **School:** Jr.
Driving Range: $6.00/lg., $2.75/sm.
Other: Restaurant / Clubhouse / Snack bar

Tees	Holes	Yards	Par	USGA	Slope
BACK	18	6366	72	70.2	119
MIDDLE	18	6126	72	69.0	117
FRONT	18	5430	72	70.8	114

Weekend: $15.00
Weekend: $29.00
Discounts: Senior & Junior
Junior Golf: Yes **Membership:** Yes
Non-Metal Spikes: Not Required

Gently rolling fairways. No coolers. Collared shirts preferred. Open March - December.
www.ctgolfer.com/tallwoodcc

	1	2	3	4	5	6	7	8	9
PAR	5	4	3	5	4	3	4	4	3
YARDS	528	287	176	483	400	158	341	359	167
HDCP	4	16	14	12	2	18	8	6	10
	10	11	12	13	14	15	16	17	18
PAR	4	5	4	4	3	4	5	4	4
YARDS	296	500	361	346	157	364	460	377	366
HDCP	15	9	5	7	17	3	13	1	11

Directions: I-84 East to I-384. Exit 5 off I-384, right off exit puts you on Route 85 South. Course is on right.

Timberlin Golf Club

34

Kensington, CT (860) 828-3228

Club Pro: Lindsey Hansen
Pro Shop: Full inventory
Payment: Cash or check
Tee Times: 2 days adv.
Fee 9 Holes: Weekday: $16.00
Fee 18 Holes: Weekday: $23.00
Cart Rental: $23.00/18 $13.00/9
Lessons: $25.00/half hour **School:** No
Driving Range: Yes
Other: Clubhouse / Showers / Snack bar

Tees	Holes	Yards	Par	USGA	Slope
BACK	18	6733	72	72.2	129
MIDDLE	18	6342	72	70.4	126
FRONT	18	5477	72	72.0	125

Weekend: $17.00
Weekend: $27.00
Discounts: None
Junior Golf: Yes **Membership:** No
Non-Metal Spikes: Not Required

Long, beautiful, rolling terrain. Open April - November.

	1	2	3	4	5	6	7	8	9
PAR	5	4	4	3	4	5	3	4	4
YARDS	550	340	360	170	360	526	150	342	377
HDCP	3	5	11	17	9	1	15	13	7
	10	11	12	13	14	15	16	17	18
PAR	5	4	3	5	4	4	3	4	4
YARDS	492	361	160	477	362	400	163	359	393
HDCP	10	14	16	2	4	6	18	12	8

Directions: Located off Route 71 which runs between I-691 and Route 372. Course is on Route 364, .6 mile from Route 71.

4 = Excellent 3 = Very Good 2 = Good

Topstone Golf Course   35

South Windsor, CT (860) 648-4653

Club Pro: James McMillan
Pro Shop: Full inventory
Payment: Visa, MC
Tee Times: 14 /wkdys; 7/wknds
Fee 9 Holes: Weekday: $14.00
Fee 18 Holes: Weekday: $27.00
Cart Rental: $10.00 pp/18 $5.50 pp/9
Lessons: $30/30 min. **School:** No
Driving Range: No
Other: Bar/Restaurant

Tees	Holes	Yards	Par	USGA	Slope
BACK	18	6331	72	70.1	120
MIDDLE	18	6014	72	68.7	117
FRONT	18	4987	72	68.4	113

Weekend: $15.00
Weekend: $29.00
Discounts: Senior & Junior
Junior Golf: N/R **Membership:** No
Non-Metal Spikes: Not Required

Well designed and maintained course. Variety of tees for all abilities. Greens protected with bunkers. Front 9 open, back 9 cut into woods. #14 could be one of the toughest par 4's in the state." -R.W.

	1	2	3	4	5	6	7	8	9
PAR	4	5	4	3	5	4	4	3	4
YARDS	365	472	304	175	480	385	397	138	254
HDCP	10	12	8	4	14	6	2	18	16
	10	11	12	13	14	15	16	17	18
PAR	5	4	3	4	4	3	5	4	4
YARDS	482	389	167	340	399	140	471	320	336
HDCP	17	3	11	13	1	15	7	9	5

Directions: Take I-291 from either Routes 84 or 91. Take Exit 4 (Route 5). Go north on Route 5 for 4 miles, turn right onto Route 1 94 for .5 mile. Left on to Rye St. for 1.5 miles, Turn right on to Griffin St. for 1.25 miles.

Tunxis Plantation CC (Green)   36

Farmington, CT (860) 677-1367

Club Pro: Lou Pandolfi
Pro Shop: Full inventory
Payment: Visa, MC, Amex
Tee Times: Yes, call in advance
Fee 9 Holes: Weekday: $14.50
Fee 18 Holes: Weekday: $26.00
Cart Rental: $24.00/18 $13.00/9
Lessons: $27.00/half hour **School:** No
Driving Range: $3.25/bucket
Other: Restaurant / Clubhouse / Bar-lounge / Lockers / Snack Bar / Showers

Tees	Holes	Yards	Par	USGA	Slope
BACK	18	6354	70	70.0	120
MIDDLE	18	5958	70	68.1	117
FRONT	18	4883	70	71.0	115

Weekend: $16.50
Weekend: $30.00
Discounts: Senior & Junior. Wkdays only.
Junior Golf: Yes **Membership:** No
Non-Metal Spikes: Required

Course is located in Farmington Valley, next to Farmington River. Course in excellent condition. Open April 1 - November 20.

	1	2	3	4	5	6	7	8	9
PAR	4	5	4	4	3	4	4	3	4
YARDS	363	501	354	357	188	434	333	166	335
HDCP	5	9	1	7	11	3	15	17	13
	10	11	12	13	14	15	16	17	18
PAR	4	4	3	4	4	4	4	5	3
YARDS	348	345	165	373	342	291	397	481	185
HDCP	10	2	16	12	6	14	8	4	18

Directions: I-84 to Exit 39 (Route 4); first right over Farmington River.

Tunxis Plantation CC (White) 37

Farmington, CT (860)677-1367

Club Pro: Lou Pandolfi
Pro Shop: Full inventory
Payment: Visa, MC, Amex
Tee Times: Yes, Call in advance
Fee 9 Holes: Weekday: $14.50
Fee 18 Holes: Weekday: $26.00
Cart Rental: $24.00/18 $13.00/9
Lessons: $25.00/half hour **School:** No
Driving Range: $3.25/bucket
Other: Restaurant / Clubhouse / Bar-lounge / Lockers / Snack Bar / Showers

Weekend: $16.50
Weekend: $30.00
Discounts: Senior & Junior. Wkdays only.
Junior Golf: Yes **Membership:** No
Non-Metal Spikes: Required

Tees	Holes	Yards	Par	USGA	Slope
BACK	18	6638	72	71.0	121
MIDDLE	18	6241	72	71.5	125
FRONT	18	5744	72	71.5	116

Course is located in Farmington Valley, next to Farmington River. Course in excellent condition. Open April 1 - November 20.

	1	2	3	4	5	6	7	8	9
PAR	5	4	4	3	5	4	4	3	4
YARDS	526	407	343	153	476	366	358	147	332
HDCP	1	3	11	17	5	7	9	15	13
	10	11	12	13	14	15	16	17	18
PAR	4	5	4	5	3	4	3	4	4
YARDS	334	508	358	515	176	413	154	357	318
HDCP	16	2	6	4	14	8	18	10	12

Directions: I-84 to Exit 39 (Route 4); first right over Farmington River.

Tunxis Plantation GC (Red) 38

Farmington, CT (860) 677-1367

Club Pro: Lou Pandolfi
Pro Shop: Full inventory
Payment: Visa, MC, Amex
Tee Times: Yes, Call in advance
Fee 9 Holes: Weekday: $14.50
Fee 18 Holes: Weekday: $26.00
Cart Rental: $24.00/18 $13.00/9
Lessons: No **School:** No
Driving Range: No
Other: Restaurant / Clubhouse / Bar-lounge / Lockers / Snack Bar / Showers

Weekend: $16.50
Weekend: $30.00
Discounts: Senior & Junior. Wkdays only.
Junior Golf: Yes **Membership:** No
Non-Metal Spikes: Required

Tees	Holes	Yards	Par	USGA	Slope
BACK	9	3219	35	35.4	123
MIDDLE	9	2999	35	34.4	119
FRONT	9	2725	35	35.8	117

9 hole course in excellent condition located in Farmington Valley, next to Farmington River. Open April 1 - November 20.

	1	2	3	4	5	6	7	8	9
PAR	4	4	3	4	5	4	4	3	4
YARDS	348	395	141	322	483	396	366	177	371
HDCP	13	3	17	11	1	9	5	15	7
	10	11	12	13	14	15	16	17	18
PAR									
YARDS									
HDCP									

Directions: I-84 to Exit 39 (Route 4); first right over Farmington River.

4✪ =Excellent 3✪ =Very Good 2✪ =Good

Twin Hills CC

39

Rt. 31, Coventry, CT (860) 742-9705

Club Pro: John Nowobiliski & Eric Destefano
Pro Shop: Limited inventory
Payment: Cash only
Tee Times: 6 days Wkends
Fee 9 Holes: Weekday: $13.50
Fee 18 Holes: Weekday: $26.00
Cart Rental: $20.00/18 $10.00/9
Lessons: No **School:** No
Driving Range: No
Other: Clubhouse / Snack bar / Bar-lounge / Beer & Soda

Tees	Holes	Yards	Par	USGA	Slope
BACK	18	6262	71	69.7	118
MIDDLE	18	5954	71	68.6	116
FRONT	18	5249	71	69.5	116

Weekend: $15.00
Weekend: $28.00
Discounts: Senior & Junior
Junior Golf: N/R **Membership:** No
Non-Metal Spikes: Not Required

The course is excellent for beginners with few hazards. Open March-December.

	1	2	3	4	5	6	7	8	9
PAR	4	4	5	3	5	4	4	3	4
YARDS	380	284	530	144	502	348	446	152	357
HDCP	9	17	2	16	6	7	1	14	11
	10	11	12	13	14	15	16	17	18
PAR	4	4	4	3	4	5	3	4	4
YARDS	320	336	311	204	374	494	144	361	267
HDCP	13	15	10	4	5	3	12	8	18

Directions: Take I-84 to Route 31 South; follow 4 miles. Course is on the right.

Westwoods Golf Course

★★ **40**

Rt.177, Farmington, CT (860) 677-9192

Club Pro: Jim Tennant
Pro Shop: Full inventory
Payment: Cash only
Tee Times: Weekends, 7 days adv.
Fee 9 Holes: Weekday: $10.75
Fee 18 Holes: Weekday: $17.75
Cart Rental: $20.00/18 $12.00/9
Lessons: $30/30 min. **School:** No
Driving Range: Yes
Other: Snack bar / Bar-lounge / Clubhouse

Tees	Holes	Yards	Par	USGA	Slope
BACK	N/R				
MIDDLE	18	4407	61	58.6	85
FRONT	18	3547	61	59.5	85

Weekend: $13.25
Weekend: $21.25
Discounts: Senior & Junior
Junior Golf: Yes **Membership:** Yes
Non-Metal Spikes: Not Required

Numerous par 3s make it an easy walker. Has some challenging water holes. Reduced rates for residents.

	1	2	3	4	5	6	7	8	9
PAR	5	3	3	3	4	3	3	4	3
YARDS	494	164	135	187	315	204	159	344	235
HDCP	1	13	17	11	5	7	15	9	3
	10	11	12	13	14	15	16	17	18
PAR	4	3	3	4	3	4	3	3	3
YARDS	420	236	121	376	211	348	163	163	132
HDCP	2	6	18	4	8	10	14	12	16

Directions: Take I-84 to Bristol (Exit 39) Route 6; take Route 177 North. Course is 200 yards down on left.

Willimantic C. C.   ✪✪✪ 41

Willimantic, CT. 860-456-1971

Club Pro: John Boucher
Pro Shop: Full inventory
Payment: Visa, MC, Amex, Dis, Pers. checks
Tee Times: M-Th. 7am-3pm

Tees	Holes	Yards	Par	USGA	Slope
BACK	18	6271	71	70.5	121
MIDDLE	18	6003	71	69.2	119
FRONT	18	5106	71	68.5	113

Fee 9 Holes: Weekday: N/A   **Weekend:** N/A
Fee 18 Holes: Weekday: $40.00   **Weekend:** N/A
Cart Rental: $24.00   **Discounts:** Junior, $10.00 fee
Lessons: $25.00/half hour   **School:** No   **Junior Golf:** Yes   **Membership:**
Driving Range: No   **Non-Metal Spikes:** Required
Other: Full Restaurant/ Clubhouse/ Bar/Lounge/ Lockers/ Showers

Open to public on weekdays. Well worth the play. Play moves swiftly on this well maintained course. Long holes are compensated for by a number of short par 4's. Open April- November.

	1	2	3	4	5	6	7	8	9
PAR	4	4	4	4	4	5	3	4	4
YARDS	370	281	400	384	295	475	167	330	358
HDCP	11	15	1	3	17	13	9	7	5
	10	11	12	13	14	15	16	17	18
PAR	3	4	4	5	4	5	3	4	3
YARDS	110	388	286	485	414	483	154	417	206
HDCP	18	4	14	8	2	12	16	6	10

Directions: From Hartford, take Route 6 East for about 28 miles.

Woodstock Golf Course   ✪✪ 42

S. Woodstock, CT (860) 928-4130

Club Pro: Roland Allard
Pro Shop: Limited inventory
Payment: Cash only
Tee Times: Wknd, Hol., 1 day adv.

Tees	Holes	Yards	Par	USGA	Slope
BACK	N/A				
MIDDLE		9	2255	33	62.4	103
FRONT		9	1822	34	66.8	103

Fee 9 Holes: Weekday: $9.00   **Weekend:** $11.00
Fee 18 Holes: Weekday: $15.00   **Weekend:** $19.00
Cart Rental: $19.00/18 $10.00/9   **Discounts:** Sr & Jr Wkdays only
Lessons: $25.00/45 minutes   **School:** No   **Junior Golf:** Yes   **Membership:** No
Driving Range: Yes   **Non-Metal Spikes:** Required
Other: Clubhouse / Snack Bar / Lockers / Showers

COUPON

Established 1896. Over one hundred years old! Challenging, hilly course with small sloping greens. Target golf. Open April - November.

	1	2	3	4	5	6	7	8	9
PAR	3	4	4	3	4	4	3	4	4
YARDS	170	265	260	202	240	275	231	385	227
HDCP	6	8	3	4	7	2	5	1	9
	10	11	12	13	14	15	16	17	18
PAR									
YARDS									
HDCP									

NE CT

Directions: I-395 to Route 44 (Exit 97.) West on Route 44. Take Route 171 in Putnam, continue west. Follow 4.5 miles to Roseland Park Road, take right. Course 3/4 mile on left.

4✪ =Excellent 3✪ =Very Good 2✪ =Good

CHAPTER 10

Southern/Western Connecticut

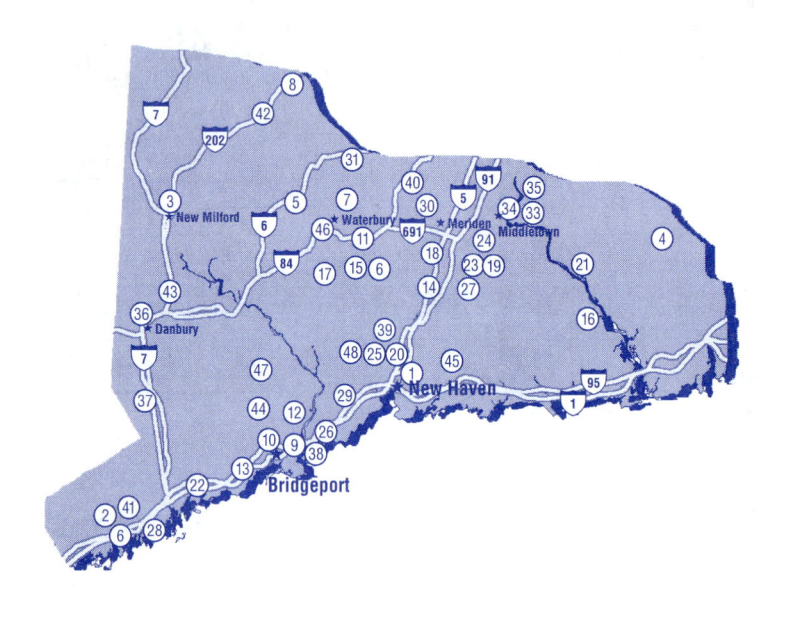

Alling Memorial GC	1	Hop Brook CC	17	Portland Golf Club	33
Bruce Memorial GC	2	Hunter Golf Club	18	Portland Golf Club West	34
Candlewood Valley CC	3	Indian Springs GC	19	Quarry Ridge GC	35
Chanticlair Golf Course	4	Laurel View CC	20	Richter Park GC	36
Crestbrook Park GC	5	Leisure Resort	21	Ridgefield Golf Club	37
E. Gaynor Brennan GC	6	Longshore Park	22	Short Beach Par 3 GC	38
East Mountain GC	7	Lyman Orch. GC (Jones)	23	Sleeping Giant GC	39
Eastwood CC	8	Lyman Orch. GC (Player)	24	Southington CC	40
Fairchild Wheeler GC (Blk)	9	Meadowbrook CC	25	Sterling Farms GC	41
Fairchild Wheeler GC (Rd)	10	Mill Stone CC	26	Stonybrook GC	43
Farmingbury Hill CC	11	Miner Hills GC	27	Sunset Hill GC	44
Grassy Hill Country Club	12	Oak Hills Park	28	Tashua Knolls CC	45
H. Smith Richardson GC	13	Orange Hills CC	29	Twin Lakes GC	46
Harbor Ridge Golf Club	14	Pattonbrook CC	30	Western Hills GC	47
Highland Greens GC	15	Pequabuck Golf Course	31	Whitney Farms	48
Hillside Links LLC	16	Pine Valley Golf Course	32	Woodhaven CC	

Alling Memorial GC

Eastern St., New Haven, CT (203) 946-8014

Club Pro: John Korolyshun
Pro Shop: Full inventory
Payment: Cash, Check
Tee Times: Weekends, 3 day adv.
Fee 9 Holes: Weekday: $15.00
Fee 18 Holes: Weekday: $23.00
Cart Rental: $22.00/18 $15.00/9
Lessons: Yes **School:** No
Driving Range: No
Other: Lockers / Showers / Restaurant / Bar-lounge

Tees	Holes	Yards	Par	USGA	Slope
BACK	18	6241	72	69.5	123
MIDDLE	18	5884	72	68.0	119
FRONT	18	5071	72	71.9	117

Weekend: $13.00
Weekend: $25.00
Discounts: Senior & Junior
Junior Golf: Yes **Membership:** No
Non-Metal Spikes: Required

The course has a mixed terrain with 2 water holes. Opened in late 1920's, has subsequently undergone major renovations. Open year round.

	1	2	3	4	5	6	7	8	9
PAR	4	4	3	5	4	4	4	4	4
YARDS	380	313	168	474	231	344	366	274	305
HDCP	3	13	11	1	17	5	9	15	7
	10	11	12	13	14	15	16	17	18
PAR	3	5	3	4	4	5	4	3	5
YARDS	148	464	174	337	408	493	331	203	471
HDCP	18	8	16	6	2	12	10	14	4

Directions: From I-91 Northbound, Exit 8, bear right to second light (Eastern Street), right 3/4 mile. Course on left.

Bruce Memorial Golf Course

Greenwich, CT, (203)531-7200

Club Pro: Joe Felder
Pro Shop: Full inventory
Payment: Cash or check
Tee Times: Weekdays, 1 day adv.
Fee 9 Holes: Weekday: $11.00
Fee 18 Holes: Weekday: $14.00
Cart Rental: $14.00/9, $21.00/18
Lessons: $30.00/half hour **School:** Yes
Driving Range: $6.00/lg. $3.00/sm.
Other: Full Restaurant/ Clubhouse/ Bar/ Lockers/ Showers

Tees	Holes	Yards	Par	USGA	Slope
BACK	18	6512	71	70.5	120
MIDDLE	18	6093	72	68.6	115
FRONT	18	5710	73	73.6	128

Weekend: $11.00
Weekend: $15.00
Discounts: Senior & Junior
Junior Golf: Yes **Membership:**
Non-Metal Spikes: Required

Open to residents of town and guests only. Front side fairly open and flat. Back side narrow and hilly. Open April 1 - Dec.1. $35.00 non-resident fee.

	1	2	3	4	5	6	7	8	9
PAR	4	4	5	4	3	4	3	5	4
YARDS	407	365	503	378	169	437	138	519	323
HDCP	5	7	13	3	15	1	17	9	11
	10	11	12	13	14	15	16	17	18
PAR	4	4	5	4	3	4	3	5	4
YARDS	407	365	503	378	169	437	138	519	323
HDCP	5	7	13	3	15	1	17	9	11

Directions: Merritt Parkway South to King St. Right turn approx. 3 miles to golf course on right. Any questions call (203) 531-7200.

SW CT

4✪ =Excellent 3✪ =Very Good 2✪ =Good

Candlewood Valley CC ▶ 3

Danbury Rd., New Milford, CT (860) 354-9359

Club Pro: John Farrell
Pro Shop: Full inventory
Payment: Visa, MC, Cash
Tee Times: 4-7 days adv.

Tees	Holes	Yards	Par	USGA	Slope
BACK	N/A				
MIDDLE	18	6404	72	70.3	120
FRONT	18	5362	72	70.9	126

Fee 9 Holes: Weekday: No **Weekend:** No
Fee 18 Holes: Weekday: $25.00 **Weekend:** $30.00
Cart Rental: $24.00/18 **Discounts:** Senior
Lessons: $25.00/half hour **School:** No **Junior Golf:** No **Membership:** No
Driving Range: $5.00/lg., $2.50/sm. **Non-Metal Spikes:** Required
Other: Clubhouse / Lockers / Showers / Snack bar / Restaurant / Bar-lounge / Banquet facilities

Changes to be made to holes # 4 & 5. Waiting to be re-rated. Demanding back nine. Open April1- December 1.

	1	2	3	4	5	6	7	8	9
PAR	4	4	5	4	3	3	4	4	4
YARDS	301	315	448	370	152	160	350	447	402
HDCP	18	14	8	16	10	12	4	2	6
	10	11	12	13	14	15	16	17	18
PAR	3	4	4	4	5	5	4	4	4
YARDS	210	413	390	418	530	459	366	386	316
HDCP	13	1	5	3	7	15	11	9	17

Directions: From Route 84, take Exit 7 (Brookfield/ New Milford). Follow to end. Turn right at light onto Route 7 North. Follow 4.1 miles to CVCC on the right.

Chanticlair Golf Course ▶ 4

Colchester, CT (860) 537-3223

Club Pro: No
Pro Shop: Full inventory
Payment: MC, Visa
Tee Times: 1 week adv.

Tees	Holes	Yards	Par	USGA	Slope
BACK	N/A				
MIDDLE	9	5983	70	69.8	117
FRONT	9	5001	70	69.1	112

Fee 9 Holes: Weekday: $13.00 **Weekend:** $14.00
Fee 18 Holes: Weekday: $20.00 **Weekend:** $21.00
Cart Rental: $20.00/18 $10.00/9 **Discounts:** Senior
Lessons: No **School:** No **Junior Golf:** No **Membership:** No
Driving Range: No **Non-Metal Spikes:** Required
Other: Clubhouse / Snack bar

The 4th hole has an elevated island green. Fairly flat; a good walking course.

	1	2	3	4	5	6	7	8	9
PAR	3	4	4	3	4	4	4	4	5
YARDS	192	385	345	138	364	362	345	350	441
HDCP	4	12	14	10	6	8	16	2	18
	10	11	12	13	14	15	16	17	18
PAR	3	4	4	3	4	4	4	4	5
YARDS	205	390	375	138	387	385	350	380	451
HDCP	7	11	9	13	3	5	15	1	17

Directions: Take Route 2 to State Police Barracks Exit; take left off ramp and go up hill. Make left onto Old Hebron Rd. at firehouse. Course 1/4 mile on right

Crestbrook Park GC 5

Watertown, CT (860) 945-5249

Club Pro: Kenneth Gemmell
Pro Shop: Full inventory
Payment: Cash only
Tee Times: Weekends, 2 days adv.
Fee 9 Holes: Weekday: $13.00
Fee 18 Holes: Weekday: $24.00
Cart Rental: $24.00/18 $12.00/9
Lessons: $25.00/half hour **School:** N/R
Driving Range: $5.50/lg., $4/med., $2/sm.
Other: Clubhouse / Snack bar / Restaurant / Bar-lounge / Pool / Tennis / Picnic

Tees	Holes	Yards	Par	USGA	Slope
BACK	18	6915	71	73.6	128
MIDDLE	18	6098	71	69.9	121
FRONT	18	5696	75	73.8	128

Weekend: $14.00
Weekend: $26.00
Discounts: Senior & Junior
Junior Golf: Yes **Membership:** N/R
Non-Metal Spikes: Required

The championship layout provides rolling hills and tree lined fairways. Greens are well kept and fast.

	1	2	3	4	5	6	7	8	9
PAR	4	4	4	5	3	4	4	3	5
YARDS	370	447	411	515	152	384	405	194	536
HDCP	13	1	5	9	17	7	11	15	3
	10	11	12	13	14	15	16	17	18
PAR	4	4	3	4	4	5	3	4	4
YARDS	357	401	160	337	333	463	210	308	393
HDCP	6	4	18	12	14	8	10	16	2

Directions: Route 8 to Echo Lake Rd. (turn left). Take right at 2nd light (Buckingham); another right at stop sign (Northfield). Course is 1/4 mi. on right on Northfield Rd.

E. Gaynor Brennan GC 6

Stillwater Rd., Stamford, CT (203) 324-4185

Club Pro: Robert Fraioli & William Fraioli
Pro Shop: Full inventory
Payment: Cash only
Tee Times: Residents only
Fee 9 Holes: Weekday: $18.00
Fee 18 Holes: Weekday: $25.00
Cart Rental: $22.00/18 $14.00/9
Lessons: Call 324-6507 **School:** No
Driving Range: No
Other: Snack bar / Restaurant / Bar-lounge / Showers

Tees	Holes	Yards	Par	USGA	Slope
BACK	N/A				
MIDDLE	18	5868	71	67.5	122
FRONT	18	5591	73	72.3	124

Weekend: N/A
Weekend: $33.00
Discounts: Senior & Junior
Junior Golf: Yes **Membership:** Yes
Non-Metal Spikes: Required

The greens are usually in excellent condition. Course is a bit hilly. Open year round. Resident discounts. Twi-light rates.

	1	2	3	4	5	6	7	8	9
PAR	4	4	3	5	4	5	4	4	3
YARDS	361	389	147	433	372	492	378	346	105
HDCP	7	5	13	9	3	15	1	11	17
	10	11	12	13	14	15	16	17	18
PAR	4	4	4	3	4	3	4	5	4
YARDS	354	321	341	225	397	177	279	428	323
HDCP	10	14	2	6	4	8	18	16	12

Directions: Take I-95 to Exit 6. Go north on West Ave. to end; take left onto West Broad St.; course is 1/4 mile down.

SW CT

4✪ =Excellent 3✪ =Very Good 2✪ =Good

East Mountain GC   7

Waterbury, CT (203) 753-1425

Club Pro: None
Pro Shop: Limited inventory
Payment: Cash only
Tee Times: Weekends, 3 days adv.
Fee 9 Holes: Weekday: $13.00
Fee 18 Holes: Weekday: $21.00
Cart Rental: $20.00/18 $12.00/9
Lessons: No **School:** N/R
Driving Range: yes
Other: Bar-Lounge

Tees	Holes	Yards	Par	USGA	Slope
BACK	18	5817	67	68.0	114
MIDDLE	18	5591	68	66.9	112
FRONT	18	5221	67	N/A	N/A

Weekend: $15.00
Weekend: $22.00
Discounts: Junior
Junior Golf: Yes **Membership:** N/R
Non-Metal Spikes: Required

Golfers must keep tee-shots in play. Don't be fooled by the short yardage and level terrain.

	1	2	3	4	5	6	7	8	9
PAR	4	4	4	3	4	5	4	3	4
YARDS	387	387	394	184	292	503	320	136	353
HDCP	7	3	5	15	11	1	13	17	9
	10	11	12	13	14	15	16	17	18
PAR	4	3	4	4	3	4	4	3	4
YARDS	348	221	398	355	163	356	375	183	346
HDCP	12	14	2	8	18	6	4	16	10

Directions: From Hartford: I-84 to Hamilton Avenue (Exit 23). Follow Route 69 West. Right onto East Mountain at Church.

Eastwood CC   8

Torrington, CT (860) 489-2630

Club Pro: No
Pro Shop: Limited inventory
Payment: Cash, Visa. MC, Disc
Tee Times: No
Fee 9 Holes: Weekday: $13.00
Fee 18 Holes: Weekday: $23.00
Cart Rental: $13.00 pp/18, $6.50 pp/9
Lessons: No **School:** No
Driving Range: No
Other: Restaurant / Clubhouse / Bar-lounge / Lockers / Snack Bar / Showers

Tees	Holes	Yards	Par	USGA	Slope
BACK	9	5866	72	67.8	113
MIDDLE	9	5582	72	66.5	111
FRONT	9	4718	72	N/A	N/A

Weekend: $16.00
Weekend: $26.00
Discounts: Seniors, weekdays
Junior Golf: No **Membership:** N/R
Non-Metal Spikes: possible

Some hills. Pretty views. Slightly challenging. Tight greens, narrow fairways, and rough make this course challenging but enjoyable. Open April - January.

	1	2	3	4	5	6	7	8	9
PAR	4	4	4	5	4	3	4	3	5
YARDS	363	309	348	411	275	131	286	137	531
HDCP	3	9	7	5	13	17	11	15	1
	10	11	12	13	14	15	16	17	18
PAR	4	4	4	5	4	3	4	3	5
YARDS	363	309	348	411	275	131	286	137	531
HDCP	4	10	8	6	14	18	12	16	2

Directions: Take Route 8 to Exit 45. Right on Winsted Road to light. Take right onto Kennedy Drive, up hill to four-way intersection. Left onto Torringford West Street. Straight until sharp corner. Course on left side.

Fairchild Wheeler GC (Black) 9

Bridgeport, CT (203) 373-5911

Club Pro: Sammy Samson
Pro Shop: Full inventory
Payment: Visa, MC, Cash
Tee Times: Yes.
Fee 9 Holes: Weekday: $16.00
Fee 18 Holes: Weekday: $23.00
Cart Rental: $26.00/18 for 2 player
Lessons: $35.00/half hour **School:** Jr. & Sr.
Driving Range: Yes
Other: Clubhouse / Snack bar / Restaurant / Bar-lounge / Lockers / Showers

Tees	Holes	Yards	Par	USGA	Slope
BACK	18	6559	71	71.0	124
MIDDLE	18	6402	71	70	124
FRONT	18	5947	72	70.0	119

Weekend: $20.00
Weekend: $30.00
Discounts: Senior & Junior
Junior Golf: Yes **Membership:** Yes
Non-Metal Spikes: Required

COUPON

Good, challenging course that offers some of the toughest par-fours around. Reduced rates for residents. Twilight specials. Reservation fees for non-residents. Open year round.

	1	2	3	4	5	6	7	8	9
PAR	4	4	3	4	4	4	3	5	5
YARDS	405	377	128	367	321	432	212	431	500
HDCP	4	8	18	6	16	2	14	12	10
	10	11	12	13	14	15	16	17	18
PAR	4	3	4	4	4	4	5	3	4
YARDS	417	153	407	421	314	418	512	191	396
HDCP	11	17	7	1	15	5	9	13	3

Directions: Take Merritt Parkway (Route 15) Exit 46 to Route 59 South (Easton Turnpike.) 1/2 mile on left.

Fairchild Wheeler GC (Red) 10

Bridgeport, CT (203) 373-5911

Club Pro: Sammy Samson, PGA
Pro Shop: Full inventory
Payment: Visa, MC, Cash
Tee Times: Yes
Fee 9 Holes: Weekday: $16.00
Fee 18 Holes: Weekday: $23.00
Cart Rental: $26.00/18 for 2 player
Lessons: $35.00/half hour **School:** Jr. & Sr.
Driving Range: Yes
Other: Clubhouse / Snack bar / Restaurant / Bar-lounge / Lockers / Showers

Tees	Holes	Yards	Par	USGA	Slope
BACK	18	6568	72	71.3	124
MIDDLE	18	6382	72	69.7	122
FRONT	18	5330	72	68.7	117

Weekend: $20.00
Weekend: $30.00
Discounts: Senior & Junior
Junior Golf: Yes **Membership:** Yes
Non-Metal Spikes: Required

COUPON

Flat, open course. Good for beginners and seniors. Reduced rates for residents. Twilight specials. Reservation fees for non-residents. Open year round.

	1	2	3	4	5	6	7	8	9
PAR	4	4	5	3	4	4	4	3	4
YARDS	440	402	480	127	308	412	337	190	387
HDCP	1	7	11	17	15	5	13	9	3
	10	11	12	13	14	15	16	17	18
PAR	5	4	3	4	4	3	4	5	5
YARDS	504	419	105	422	334	202	340	501	472
HDCP	2	8	18	10	12	16	14	4	6

Directions: Take Merritt Parkway (Route 15) Exit 46 to Route 59 South (Easton Turnpike.) 1/2 mile on left.

SW CT

4✪ =Excellent **3**✪ =Very Good **2**✪ =Good

Southern/Western CT 319

Farmingbury Hill CC   11

141 East St., Wolcott, CT (203) 879-8038

Club Pro: Craig Kealey
Pro Shop: Full inventory
Payment: Cash only
Tee Times: Weekends, 7 days adv.
Fee 9 Holes: Weekday: $12.00
Fee 18 Holes: Weekday: $21.00
Cart Rental: $22.00/18 $11.00/9
Lessons: $25.00 30 min **School:** No
Driving Range: Yes
Other: Snack bar / Bar-lounge

Tees	Holes	Yards	Par	USGA	Slope
BACK	N/R				
MIDDLE	9	6005	71	68.7	117
FRONT	9	5355	72	71.0	120

Weekend: $12.00
Weekend: $21.00
Discounts: Senior & Junior
Junior Golf: Yes **Membership:** No
Non-Metal Spikes: N/R

A hillside course with nice views. Easy to play. Open April 1 - Dec. 1.

	1	2	3	4	5	6	7	8	9
PAR	4	4	4	4	4	3	4	3	5
YARDS	340	419	310	373	321	102	401	190	510
HDCP	11	1	13	9	7	17	3	15	5
	10	11	12	13	14	15	16	17	18
PAR	4	4	4	4	4	3	4	4	5
YARDS	362	402	288	378	280	128	355	315	531
HDCP	10	2	14	4	12	18	8	16	6

Directions: I-84 to Cheshire Exit 28. Route 322 West, left up Southington Mountain. Right at top of hill, blinking light (East St.). Course is 1 mile on right.

Grassy Hill Country Club   12

Orange, CT (203)795-1422

Club Pro: Mark P. Mayette
Pro Shop: Limited inventory
Payment: Visa, MC
Tee Times: 3 days in adv.
Fee 9 Holes: Weekday: $19.00
Fee 18 Holes: Weekday: $28.00
Cart Rental: $6.00/9 $12.00/18
Lessons: $30.00/half hour **School:** N/A
Driving Range: $5.00/lg. $3.00/sm.
Other: Full restaurant/ Clubhouse/ Bar/Lounge/ Lockers/ Showers

Tees	Holes	Yards	Par	USGA	Slope
BACK	18	6118	70	70.5	122
MIDDLE	18	5849	70	69.4	119
FRONT	18	5209	71	71.1	118

Weekend: $28.00
Weekend: $45.00
Discounts:
Junior Golf: Yes **Membership:** N/A
Non-Metal Spikes: Required

Built in early '30's. A true championship course in hilly terrain. Excellent course working to regain past exquisite conditions of fairways and greens. Many memorable holes.

	1	2	3	4	5	6	7	8	9
PAR	4	4	3	4	5	3	4	4	5
YARDS	385	410	158	301	563	145	363	360	432
HDCP	7	1	17	15	3	9	11	5	13
	10	11	12	13	14	15	16	17	18
PAR	3	4	4	3	4	4	5	3	4
YARDS	169	384	277	175	319	421	496	165	326
HDCP	12	4	16	10	14	2	8	18	6

Directions: From I-95: Take Exit 39 a. Turn right, pass Howard Johnson's. At second dual traffic light, turn right. 2-1/2 miles to ClarkLane. turn right to Grassy Hill.

H. Smith Richardson GC   13

Fairfield, CT (203) 255-7300

Club Pro: Sean Garrity
Pro Shop: Full inventory
Payment: Cash only
Tee Times: No
Fee 9 Holes: Weekday: $17.00
Fee 18 Holes: Weekday: $22.50
Cart Rental: $21.00/18 $13.00/9
Lessons: $30/30 min. **School:** No
Driving Range: Yes
Other: Lockers / Showers / Restaurant / Bar-lounge

Tees	Holes	Yards	Par	USGA	Slope
BACK	N/R				
MIDDLE	18	6323	72	70.2	124
FRONT	N/R				

Weekend: $15.00 after 5pm
Weekend: $27.00
Discounts: Senior & Junior
Junior Golf: Yes **Membership:** Yes
Non-Metal Spikes: Required

This scenic hilly course ha a majestic view of Long Island Sound. Closed March.

	1	2	3	4	5	6	7	8	9
PAR	4	4	3	4	4	5	4	3	5
YARDS	375	310	160	339	397	503	383	180	486
HDCP	6	14	18	12	2	4	8	16	10
	10	11	12	13	14	15	16	17	18
PAR	4	4	3	5	4	4	3	4	5
YARDS	373	351	176	502	405	350	140	373	520
HDCP	3	13	15	7	1	11	17	5	9

Directions: Take Merritt Parkway to Black Rock Turnpike Exit 44/45 (Route 58). At rotary take left (Morehouse Highway).

Harbor Ridge Golf Club   14

Harrison Rd., Wallingford, CT (203) 269-6023

Club Pro: Al Pascale
Pro Shop: Full inventory
Payment: Cash only
Tee Times: Weekends, 3 days adv.
Fee 9 Holes: Weekday: $12.00
Fee 18 Holes: Weekday: $22.00
Cart Rental: $25.00/18 $13.00/9
Lessons: Yes **School:** No
Driving Range: No
Other: Bar-Lounge / Snack Bar

Tees	Holes	Yards	Par	USGA	Slope
BACK	9	6684	72	72.6	127
MIDDLE	9	6052	72	72.6	127
FRONT	9	5126	72	72.6	127

Weekend: $18.00
Weekend: $29.00
Discounts: Senior- Wkdays before 12:00
Junior Golf: Yes **Membership:** Yes
Non-Metal Spikes: Required

To expand to 18 holes in 1999. Rates TBA. The course has always been considered one of the most challenging in Connecticut: fast greens; hilly terrain.

	1	2	3	4	5	6	7	8	9
PAR	4	4	3	4	4	5	4	4	4
YARDS	371	324	102	381	373	511	287	315	362
HDCP	9	3	17	1	7	11	13	15	5
	10	11	12	13	14	15	16	17	18
PAR	4	4	3	4	4	5	4	4	4
YARDS	371	324	102	381	373	511	287	315	362
HDCP	10	4	18	2	6	12	14	16	6

Directions: Take I-91 to Exit 14. Take right onto Route 150 towards Wallingford. Take right onto Harrison Road.

SW CT

4⊙ =Excellent 3⊙ =Very Good 2⊙ =Good   Southern/Western CT

Highland Greens GC ▸ 15

Prospect, CT (203) 758-4022

Club Pro: No
Pro Shop: Limited inventory
Payment: Cash only
Tee Times: Same Day
Fee 9 Holes: Weekday: $10.00
Fee 18 Holes: Weekday: $19.00
Cart Rental: No
Lessons: Yes **School:** No
Driving Range: No
Other: Snack bar

Tees	Holes	Yards	Par	USGA	Slope
BACK	N/A				
MIDDLE	9	1398	27	N/A	N/A
FRONT	9	1322	27	N/A	N/A

Weekend: $11.00
Weekend: $21.00
Discounts: Senior
Junior Golf: No **Membership:** N/R
Non-Metal Spikes: Not Required

The course is an executive par 3. Completely lighted for night play. Slightly hilly. Open April - First Frost. **www.golfatnight.com**

	1	2	3	4	5	6	7	8	9
PAR	3	3	3	3	3	3	3	3	3
YARDS	132	192	115	135	188	185	157	128	166
HDCP	N/A								
	10	11	12	13	14	15	16	17	18
PAR									
YARDS									
HDCP									

Directions: Take I-84 to Exit 26 to Route 70 East to Route 68 West. At top of hill, left onto Cooke Road. Course is 1.6 miles on right.

Hillside Links LLC ▸ 16

Deep River, CT (860)526-9986

Club Pro: Mark Erwin
Pro Shop: Yes
Payment: Cash only
Tee Times: Wkends/Holdys
Fee 9 Holes: Weekday: $7.00
Fee 18 Holes: Weekday: $12.00
Cart Rental: Pull Carts $1.00
Lessons: Group & Private **School:** No
Driving Range: Warm up cages $2 / basket
Other: Golf balls / Hats / Candy / Soda

Tees	Holes	Yards	Par	USGA	Slope
BACK	N/A				
MIDDLE	9	932	27	N/A	N/A
FRONT	N/A				

Weekend: $8.00
Weekend: $14.00
Discounts: Senior 9-11 Wkdays $6.50
Junior Golf: N/R **Membership:** Multi-Play Pass
Non-Metal Spikes: Required

COUPON

A challenging Par 3 walking course with sand and water. The feel of a full size course on a small scale. Good for family fun. Spectators not allowed.

	1	2	3	4	5	6	7	8	9
PAR	3	3	3	3	3	3	3	3	3
YARDS	73	82	97	115	96	131	164	71	103
HDCP									
	10	11	12	13	14	15	16	17	18
PAR									
YARDS									
HDCP									

Directions: From Route 9 N or S take Route 80 East and turn onto Hillside Terrace. Follow road to end.

Hop Brook CC   17

Naugatuck, CT (203) 729-8013

Club Pro: Zane Chappy
Pro Shop: Yes
Payment: Cash, Check
Tee Times: Weekends, 2 days adv.
Fee 9 Holes: Weekday: $15.00
Fee 18 Holes: Weekday: $23.00
Cart Rental: $23.00/18 $13.00/9
Lessons: No **School:** No
Driving Range: No
Other: Clubhouse / Restaurant

Tees	Holes	Yards	Par	USGA	Slope
BACK	N/A				
MIDDLE	9	5934	72	67.8	109
FRONT	9	4898	72	67.8	109

Weekend: $19.00
Weekend: $26.00
Discounts: Senior & Junior
Junior Golf: Yes **Membership:** Yes
Non-Metal Spikes: Required

COUPON

The course is short and turns hilly near the end. Substantial discounts for residents. Open Mar - Dec. New greenskeeper has made a difference. Junior tournaments.

	1	2	3	4	5	6	7	8	9
PAR	5	3	4	4	5	4	4	4	3
YARDS	479	160	376	303	459	330	322	307	151
HDCP	7	9	3	15	5	11	13	1	17
	10	11	12	13	14	15	16	17	18
PAR	5	3	4	4	5	4	4	4	3
YARDS	491	171	390	333	478	350	340	326	168
HDCP	8	10	4	16	6	12	14	2	18

Directions: Take I-84 to Exit 17 to Route 63. Course is 3 miles down on left.

Hunter Golf Club   ✪✪   18

Meriden, CT (203) 634-3366

Club Pro: Dave Cook
Pro Shop: Full inventory
Payment: Visa, MC, Amex
Tee Times: Yes, Wknds
Fee 9 Holes: Weekday: $13.00
Fee 18 Holes: Weekday: $23.00
Cart Rental: $20.00/18 $12.00/9
Lessons: $35.00/half hour **School:** No
Driving Range: $5.00/lg. $3.00/sm.
Other: Clubhouse / Lockers / Showers / Snack bar / Restaurant / Bar-lounge

Tees	Holes	Yards	Par	USGA	Slope
BACK	18	6604	71	71.9	124
MIDDLE	18	6198	71	70.2	121
FRONT	18	5569	72	72.7	131

Weekend: $14.00
Weekend: $25.00
Discounts: None
Junior Golf: Yes **Membership:** Yes
Non-Metal Spikes: Required

Very scenic view, narrow fairways, hilly 610 yard Par 5, rewards patient players. Open year round, weather permitting. Ranked top 10 public by Connecticut Magazine.

	1	2	3	4	5	6	7	8	9
PAR	4	3	4	4	5	3	4	4	4
YARDS	368	196	408	354	525	162	431	416	364
HDCP	9	11	7	13	1	17	3	5	15
	10	11	12	13	14	15	16	17	18
PAR	5	3	4	4	4	4	4	3	5
YARDS	610	180	373	367	386	390	376	185	513
HDCP	2	16	6	14	4	8	12	18	10

Directions: From I-91 South: Exit 19. Right off ramp to first stop sign. Right on Bee Street, course 1/2 mile on left. From I-91 North or Merit Parkway North: Take East Main Street exit. Go straight through light onto Bee Street. Course 2 miles on left.

SW CT

4✪ =Excellent 3✪ =Very Good 2✪ =Good   **Southern/Western CT 323**

Indian Springs GC   19

Middlefield, CT (860) 349-8109

Club Pro: Paul Brown
Pro Shop: Yes
Payment: Cash only
Tee Times: Weekends for foursomes
Fee 9 Holes: Weekday: $12.00
Fee 18 Holes: Weekday: $22.00
Cart Rental: $26.00/18 $13.00/9
Lessons: $30.00/45 min. **School:** N/R
Driving Range: $4.25
Other: Snack bar / Bar-lounge

Tees	Holes	Yards	Par	USGA	Slope
BACK	N/R				
MIDDLE	9	6000	72	68.9	116
FRONT	N/R				

Weekend: $14.00
Weekend: $26.00
Discounts: None
Junior Golf: No **Membership:** N/R
Non-Metal Spikes: possible

The course is picturesque and hilly. Fairways allow for the liberal use of the driver. A moderately difficult course good for intermediates and beginners.

	1	2	3	4	5	6	7	8	9
PAR	4	5	3	4	5	4	3	4	4
YARDS	345	455	130	370	560	300	170	355	315
HDCP	7	5	17	13	3	9	15	1	11
	10	11	12	13	14	15	16	17	18
PAR	4	5	3	4	5	4	3	4	4
YARDS	345	455	130	370	560	300	170	355	315
HDCP	8	6	18	14	4	10	16	2	6

Directions: Take I-91 to East Main Street, take left off ramp. Follow 3 miles then take right onto Route 147. Take first left onto Chestnut Hill and follow signs.

Laurel View CC   20

Hamden, CT (203) 287-2656

Club Pro: Matt Menchetti
Pro Shop: Full inventory
Payment: Cash, Check
Tee Times: Weekends, 3 days adv.
Fee 9 Holes: Weekday: $14.00
Fee 18 Holes: Weekday: $20.00
Cart Rental: $20.00/18 $14.00/9
Lessons: $40.00/half hour **School:** N/R
Driving Range: $5.00/lg
Other: Clubhouse / Lockers / Showers / Snack bar / Restaurant / Bar-lounge

Tees	Holes	Yards	Par	USGA	Slope
BACK	18	6899	72	72.7	130
MIDDLE	18	6372	72	70.8	124
FRONT	18	5558	73	71.8	130

Weekend: $17.00
Weekend: $25.00
Discounts: Senior & Junior
Junior Golf: Yes **Membership:** N/R
Non-Metal Spikes: Preferred

The course terrain is hilly. Great layout provides for an interesting challenge. The course is a good value. Open April 1 - December 1.

	1	2	3	4	5	6	7	8	9
PAR	4	3	4	5	4	4	3	5	4
YARDS	330	132	390	505	435	310	230	510	420
HDCP	15	17	3	5	1	13	11	7	9
	10	11	12	13	14	15	16	17	18
PAR	4	5	3	4	5	4	4	3	4
YARDS	320	560	155	280	470	380	390	160	395
HDCP	12	2	16	14	8	4	6	18	10

Directions: Take I-91 to Exit 10, take left at the end of the ramp. At first light take left, right at next light (Dixwell Avenue). Through center of town, pass Town Hall on the right. 3/4 mile, take right (Shephard Avenue) Through 5 lights, take left (W. Shephard.) Course 3/4 on left.

Leisure Resort At Banner Lodge   21

10 Banner Rd., Moodus, CT (860) 873-9075

Club Pro: Dan Malarney
Pro Shop: Full inventory
Payment: Cash, Check
Tee Times: Wknds/Hldys, 3 days
Fee 9 Holes: Weekday: $13.00
Fee 18 Holes: Weekday: $24.00
Cart Rental: $22.00/18 $11.00/9
Lessons: $30.00/30 minutes **School:** Yes
Driving Range: $4.50/lg., $2.50/sm.
Other: Clubhouse / Snack Bar

Tees	Holes	Yards	Par	USGA	Slope
BACK	N/A				
MIDDLE	18	6022	72	68.9	118
FRONT	18	5776	74	73.7	123

Weekend: $15.00
Weekend: $26.00
Discounts: Senior & Junior
Junior Golf: No **Membership:** Yes
Non-Metal Spikes: Not Required

New ownership. Formerly Banner Lodge CC.

	1	2	3	4	5	6	7	8	9
PAR	4	4	4	4	3	5	5	3	4
YARDS	375	320	406	324	125	477	485	154	347
HDCP	9	13	3	11	17	5	1	15	7
	10	11	12	13	14	15	16	17	18
PAR	5	4	4	4	4	3	5	3	4
YARDS	475	318	366	288	422	144	501	154	341
HDCP	6	12	8	14	4	16	2	18	10

Directions: Take CT Route 9 to Exit 7; follow Route 82 East to Route 149 North. Continue to center of Moodus. Follow signs to course.

Longshore Park   22

Westport, CT (203) 341-1833

Club Pro: John Cooper
Pro Shop: Full inventory
Payment: Cash, Check
Tee Times: 3 days adv.
Fee 9 Holes: Weekday: $20.00
Fee 18 Holes: Weekday: $24.00
Cart Rental: $24.00/18 $18.00/9
Lessons: Yes **School:** No
Driving Range: Yes
Other: Snack bar / Restaurant / Bar-lounge

Tees	Holes	Yards	Par	USGA	Slope
BACK	18	5845	69	67.4	115
MIDDLE	18	5676	69	66.7	113
FRONT	18	5227	73	69.9	119

Weekend: $24.00
Weekend: $28.00
Discounts: Senior & Junior
Junior Golf: N/R **Membership:** No
Non-Metal Spikes: Not Required

Must be guest of resident to play this level executive course. Good course for beginners. Open April - December. Reduced rates for residents.

	1	2	3	4	5	6	7	8	9
PAR	4	3	4	4	4	4	5	3	4
YARDS	341	146	390	287	296	413	520	127	346
HDCP	9	13	5	15	11	1	3	17	7
	10	11	12	13	14	15	16	17	18
PAR	5	3	4	3	4	3	4	4	4
YARDS	459	192	289	189	401	166	383	344	397
HDCP	8	14	18	12	4	16	6	10	2

Directions: Take I-95 to Exit 18 to U.S. Route 1, left at 2nd light, Green Farms Road. Follow to next light, take left onto Campo. Course is on right.

SW CT

4✪ =Excellent 3✪ =Very Good 2✪ =Good

Lyman Orchards GC (Jones)   23

Middlefield, CT (860) 349-8055

Club Pro: Dick Bierkan
Pro Shop: Full inventory
Payment: Visa, MC, Amex
Tee Times: 7 days adv.
Fee 9 Holes: Weekday: $18.00
Fee 18 Holes: Weekday: $35.00
Cart Rental: $24.00/18 $12.00/9
Lessons: $75.00/ hour **School:** Yes
Driving Range: Yes
Other: Clubhouse / Lockers / Showers / Snack bar / Restaurant / Bar-lounge

Tees	Holes	Yards	Par	USGA	Slope
BACK	18	7011	72	73.2	129
MIDDLE	18	6614	72	71.2	127
FRONT	18	6200	72	69.3	123

Weekend: $25.00
Weekend: $47.00
Discounts: None
Junior Golf: Yes **Membership:** Yes
Non-Metal Spikes: Not Required

Each hole designed by Jones to be a demanding par or a comfortable bogey. Bent grass fairways and Penn Cross tees and greens. Open Mar- Nov. www.lymanorchards.com

	1	2	3	4	5	6	7	8	9
PAR	4	3	4	5	4	4	3	4	5
YARDS	416	175	374	552	390	350	175	373	548
HDCP	3	17	1	9	5	13	15	11	7
	10	11	12	13	14	15	16	17	18
PAR	4	3	5	4	4	4	4	3	5
YARDS	399	152	490	370	388	382	403	162	515
HDCP	8	18	14	10	4	6	2	16	12

Directions: Take I-91 to Exit 15 (Route 68 East). Left onto Route 157. Course is 1 mile on the right.

Lyman Orchards GC (Player)   24

Middlefield, CT (860) 349-8055

Club Pro: Dick Bierkan
Pro Shop: Full inventory
Payment: Visa, MC, Amex
Tee Times: 7 days adv.
Fee 9 Holes: Weekday: $18.00
Fee 18 Holes: Weekday: $35.00
Cart Rental: $24.00/18 $12.00/9
Lessons: $75.00/ hour **School:** Yes
Driving Range: Yes
Other: Clubhouse / Lockers / Showers / Snack bar / Restaurant / Bar-lounge

Tees	Holes	Yards	Par	USGA	Slope
BACK	18	6725	71	73	131
MIDDLE	18	6325	71	71.2	131
FRONT	18	5763	71	69.6	128

Weekend: $25.00
Weekend: $47.00
Discounts: None
Junior Golf: Yes **Membership:** Adult & Junior
Non-Metal Spikes: Not Required

In July 1994, Gary Player designed course which provides a challenge to the greens. Greens are fair and flat. Mon-Th Early Bird before 8 am. Open March - November. www.lymanorchards.com

	1	2	3	4	5	6	7	8	9
PAR	4	4	4	3	4	4	3	5	4
YARDS	400	367	374	173	386	342	191	578	381
HDCP	9	11	3	17	7	5	15	1	13
	10	11	12	13	14	15	16	17	18
PAR	4	3	4	3	5	4	3	5	5
YARDS	348	211	427	181	473	306	165	520	502
HDCP	2	14	4	16	12	10	18	8	6

Directions: Take I-91 to Exit 15 (Route 68 East). Left onto Route 157. Course is 1 mile on the right.

Meadowbrook CC

25

Hamden, CT (203) 281-4847

Club Pro: Sonny Chandler
Pro Shop: Limited inventory
Payment: Cash only
Tee Times: No
Fee 9 Holes: Weekday: $8.00
Fee 18 Holes: Weekday: $12.00
Cart Rental: $20.00/18 $10.00/9
Lessons: Yes **School:** No
Driving Range: $3.50/lg.
Other: Clubhouse / Snack bar

Tees	Holes	Yards	Par	USGA	Slope
BACK	N/A				
MIDDLE	9	5516	70	N/A	N/A
FRONT	9	4242	70		

Weekend: $9.00
Weekend: $14.00
Discounts: Senior & Junior
Junior Golf: N/R **Membership:** Yes
Non-Metal Spikes: Not Required

Open year round. Good practice course.

	1	2	3	4	5	6	7	8	9
PAR	4	3	5	4	4	4	4	4	3
YARDS	315	103	448	390	303	333	365	324	177
HDCP	7	17	1	3	11	5	9	13	15
	10	11	12	13	14	15	16	17	18
PAR	4	3	5	4	4	4	4	4	3
YARDS	315	103	448	390	303	333	365	324	177
HDCP	8	18	2	4	12	6	10	14	16

Directions: Take Wilbur Cross Parkway (Route 15) to Exit 60 toward center of Hamden. Course is right on Dixwell. Next to Miller Memorial Library.

Mill Stone CC

26

Milford, CT (203) 874-5900

Club Pro: No
Pro Shop: No
Payment: Cash only
Tee Times: No
Fee 9 Holes: Weekday: $12.00
Fee 18 Holes: Weekday: $12.00
Cart Rental: $17.00/18 Wkends
Lessons: No **School:** No
Driving Range: No
Other: Snack Bar

Tees	Holes	Yards	Par	USGA	Slope
BACK					
MIDDLE	9	2910	36	N/A	N/A
FRONT					

Weekend: $14.00
Weekend: $14.00
Discounts: Senior
Junior Golf: No **Membership:** N/R
Non-Metal Spikes: Not Required

The course is relatively level with fair greens. Excellent for the "August golfer" or the new player.

	1	2	3	4	5	6	7	8	9
PAR	4	5	3	4	4	5	3	4	4
YARDS	380	495	136	285	310	503	141	355	305
HDCP	N/A								
	10	11	12	13	14	15	16	17	18
PAR									
YARDS									
HDCP									

Directions: Take I-95 to Wheeler Farm Road Exit. Take left onto Herbert Street to course.

SW CT

4❂ =Excellent 3❂ =Very Good 2❂ =Good

Southern/Western CT 327

Miner Hills GC
27

Middletown, CT (860)635-0051

Club Pro: Yes
Pro Shop: Limited inventory
Payment: N/A
Tee Times: N/A
Fee 9 Holes: Weekday: $8.00
Fee 18 Holes: Weekday: N/A
Cart Rental: $10.00/9
Lessons: Yes **School:** No
Driving Range: Yes
Other: Club house /Snack bar/ Showers

Tees	Holes	Yards	Par	USGA	Slope
BACK	9	1790	30	N/A	N/A
MIDDLE	9	1695	30	N/A	N/A
FRONT	9	1435	30	N/A	N/A

Weekend: $10.00
Weekend: N/A
Discounts: Senior & Junior
Junior Golf: N/R **Membership:** N/A
Non-Metal Spikes: Not Required

COUPON

Designed, built, and financed by John S. Ott. Nestled in New England countryside. Challenging and beautiful executive course. Open March 25- Nov. 15.

	1	2	3	4	5	6	7	8	9
PAR	3	3	4	4	3	3	4	3	3
YARDS	150	155	300	220	145	175	300	110	140
HDCP	7	8	4	9	6	5	3	2	1
	10	11	12	13	14	15	16	17	18
PAR									
YARDS									
HDCP									

Directions: Exit 20 off I-91. Westfield district of Middletown, CT.

Oak Hills Park
28

Fillow St., Norwalk, CT (203) 838-1015

Club Pro: Vincent Grillo
Pro Shop: Full inventory
Payment: Cash, Check
Tee Times: 1 week adv., Residents
Fee 9 Holes: Weekday: No
Fee 18 Holes: Weekday: $29.00
Cart Rental: $23.00/18
Lessons: Call 853-8400 **School:** No
Driving Range: No
Other: Snack bar

Tees	Holes	Yards	Par	USGA	Slope
BACK	18	6407	71	70.5	125
MIDDLE	18	5920	71	68.0	120
FRONT	18	5221	72	69.2	119

Weekend: No
Weekend: $34.00
Discounts: Senior & Junior
Junior Golf: No **Membership:** Mens, womens
Non-Metal Spikes: Required

Front nine hilly, woods and a lot of water. Back nine flatter and more open. Twilight rates.

	1	2	3	4	5	6	7	8	9
PAR	4	4	3	4	3	4	4	5	4
YARDS	374	295	109	307	174	284	336	484	440
HDCP	7	11	17	9	15	13	3	5	1
	10	11	12	13	14	15	16	17	18
PAR	5	4	5	3	4	3	4	4	4
YARDS	528	365	501	154	386	205	342	336	300
HDCP	4	14	8	18	2	12	10	6	16

Directions: I-95, Exit 13. Right turn onto Route 1. Left onto Richards Avenue; right turn onto Fillow to Oak Hills Park.

Orange Hills CC

29

Racebrook Rd., Orange, CT (203) 795-4161

Club Pro: Walter E. Smith 779-5581
Pro Shop: Full inventory
Payment: Visa, MC
Tee Times: M-F 6 days S/S 2 days
Fee 9 Holes: Weekday: $16.00
Fee 18 Holes: Weekday: $26.00
Cart Rental: $25.00/18 $13.00/9
Lessons: No **School:** No
Driving Range: No
Other: Clubhouse / Snack bar / Bar-lounge

Tees	Holes	Yards	Par	USGA	Slope
BACK	18	6451	71	71.2	114
MIDDLE	18	6080	71	69.8	111
FRONT	18	5606	74	71.5	120

Weekend: $19.00
Weekend: $36.00
Discounts: None
Junior Golf: N/R **Membership:** No
Non-Metal Spikes: Required

This much improved course is hilly with a tight back nine. The par-four twelfth requires shot accuracy. Collared shirts required.

	1	2	3	4	5	6	7	8	9
PAR	4	5	3	4	4	4	4	4	3
YARDS	390	482	148	429	349	371	406	279	139
HDCP	9	5	17	3	11	7	1	13	15
	10	11	12	13	14	15	16	17	18
PAR	3	5	4	3	4	4	4	4	5
YARDS	207	462	368	153	384	339	306	413	459
HDCP	16	10	2	18	12	4	8	6	14

Directions: Take I-95 to Exit 41 to Route 1 to 2nd light. Take right. At next light take left after Racebrook Road (Route 114.) Course is 1.5 miles on right.

Pattonbrook CC

30

Southington, CT (860) 793-6000

Club Pro: No
Pro Shop: Full inventory
Payment: Visa, MC, Check
Tee Times: Weekends, 4 days adv.
Fee 9 Holes: Weekday: $10.50
Fee 18 Holes: Weekday: $17.00
Cart Rental: $20.00/18 $12.00/9
Lessons: No **School:** No
Driving Range: No
Other: Clubhouse / Lockers / Showers / Bar-lounge

Tees	Holes	Yards	Par	USGA	Slope
BACK	18	4335	60	60.6	97
MIDDLE	18	4059	60	58.5	93
FRONT	18	3640	60	59.1	92

Weekend: $13.00
Weekend: $21.00
Discounts: Seniors
Junior Golf: No **Membership:** Yes
Non-Metal Spikes: Required

COUPON

Tight fairways, rolling hills, pine trees and water holes. Small fast greens make this a challenging test of golf. Open March - October.

	1	2	3	4	5	6	7	8	9
PAR	4	3	4	3	3	3	3	4	3
YARDS	285	163	390	140	150	120	185	300	155
HDCP	13	9	1	15	11	13	5	3	7
	10	11	12	13	14	15	16	17	18
PAR	4	3	3	3	3	4	3	4	3
YARDS	380	175	160	215	205	315	140	426	155
HDCP	2	12	16	6	8	10	18	4	14

Directions: Take Exit 32 from I-84. Turn South onto Queen Street (Route 10), quick left onto Laning. Left onto Flanders and first left onto Pattonwood Drive.

SW CT

4✪ =Excellent 3✪ =Very Good 2✪ =Good

Pequabuck Golf Course

31

School St., Pequabuck, CT (860) 583-7307

Club Pro: Richard Toner
Pro Shop: Full inventory
Payment: Cash, Check
Tee Times: No

Tees	Holes	Yards	Par	USGA	Slope
BACK	18	6015	69	70.2	118
MIDDLE	18	5692	69	68.7	115
FRONT	18	5388	72	70.3	118

Fee 9 Holes: Weekday: $18 M-Th before 2 **Weekend:** $18.00 F/S/S/H after 2
Fee 18 Holes: Weekday: $34 M-Th before 2 **Weekend:** $34.00 F/S/S/H after 2
Cart Rental: $28.00/18 $15.00/9   **Discounts:** None
Lessons: $30.00/half hour **School:** No   **Junior Golf:** Yes **Membership:** Yes
Driving Range: Yes   **Non-Metal Spikes:** Required
Other: Restaurant / Clubhouse / Bar-Lounge / Snack Bar

Known for perfect fairways and greens. Great corporate guest opportunities for up to 16 guests. Front nine open, back nine tree-lined with difficult greens. Dress code.

	1	2	3	4	5	6	7	8	9
PAR	4	4	5	3	4	3	5	3	4
YARDS	286	424	470	169	322	155	465	174	371
HDCP	14	2	6	18	12	16	4	10	8
	10	11	12	13	14	15	16	17	18
PAR	3	4	4	4	4	4	3	4	4
YARDS	190	406	377	329	401	337	155	328	333
HDCP	9	1	5	13	3	11	17	7	15

Directions: I-84 to Route Exit 72. Follow Route 72 into Terryville. Go under railroad bridge. Take right onto School Street. Follow to club.

Pine Valley Golf Course

32

Welch St., Southington, CT (860) 628-0879

Club Pro: Jack McConachie
Pro Shop: Full inventory
Payment: Cash only
Tee Times: M-F 6 days S/S 3 days

Tees	Holes	Yards	Par	USGA	Slope
BACK	18	6325	71	70.6	123
MIDDLE	18	6043	71	70.1	117
FRONT	18	5482	73	72.0	122

Fee 9 Holes: Weekday: $14.00   **Weekend:** $18.00
Fee 18 Holes: Weekday: $26.00   **Weekend:** $30.00
Cart Rental: $26.00/18 $13.50/9   **Discounts:** None
Lessons: $30.00/half hour **School:** No   **Junior Golf:** Yes **Membership:** No
Driving Range: No   **Non-Metal Spikes:** Required
Other: Clubhouse / Lockers / Showers / Snack bar / Restaurant / Bar-lounge / Practice sand trap

The course's front nine are hilly, while the back nine are more level with water holes and very tight greens. Accuracy is essential. All players must have a collared shirt.

	1	2	3	4	5	6	7	8	9
PAR	5	4	3	4	4	4	5	3	4
YARDS	497	404	125	345	345	291	505	141	405
HDCP	8	4	16	12	14	10	6	18	2
	10	11	12	13	14	15	16	17	18
PAR	3	4	5	4	4	3	5	4	3
YARDS	170	366	510	426	353	160	476	340	180
HDCP	17	5	7	1	3	9	11	15	13

Directions: Take I-84 to Exit 31 North on Route 229. Course is 1 1/2 miles on left.

Portland Golf Club ✪✪ 33

Bartlett St., Portland, CT (860) 342-6107

Club Pro: Mark Sloan, PGA
Pro Shop: Full inventory
Payment: Cash only
Tee Times: 5 days adv.
Fee 9 Holes: Weekday: $14.00
Fee 18 Holes: Weekday: $27.00
Cart Rental: $24.00/18 $12.00/9
Lessons: $30/30 min. **School:** No
Driving Range: No
Other: Clubhouse / Lockers / Showers / Snack bar / Restaurant / Bar-lounge

Tees	Holes	Yards	Par	USGA	Slope
BACK	18	6213	71	70.8	124
MIDDLE	18	5802	71	68.9	121
FRONT	18	5039	71	68.6	118

Weekend: $17.00
Weekend: $32.00
Discounts: Senior & Junior
Junior Golf: Yes **Membership:** No
Non-Metal Spikes: Required

Rolling terrain, always in excellent condition. March 15 - January 1. Resident discount.

	1	2	3	4	5	6	7	8	9
PAR	4	5	4	3	4	4	4	3	4
YARDS	365	485	350	166	270	287	351	140	301
HDCP	5	3	9	7	15	11	1	17	13
	10	11	12	13	14	15	16	17	18
PAR	4	4	5	4	3	4	5	3	4
YARDS	303	373	489	377	177	360	471	165	372
HDCP	16	2	6	4	14	10	12	18	8

Directions: Take Route 2 to 17 South (left at exit); 9.5 miles down take left on Bartlett; course is less than 1 mile.

Portland Golf Club West ✪✪✪ 34

Gospel Lane, Portland, CT (860) 342-6111

Club Pro: Gerald J. D'Amora, PGA
Pro Shop: Full inventory
Payment: Cash only
Tee Times: Fri, Sat, Sun, 1 day adv.
Fee 9 Holes: Weekday: $11.50
Fee 18 Holes: Weekday: $22.00
Cart Rental: $20.00/18 $11.00/9
Lessons: $30/half hour **School:** No
Driving Range: Yes
Other: Restaurant / Bar-lounge / Snack Bar, Driving Range

Tees	Holes	Yards	Par	USGA	Slope
BACK	18	4012	60	60.4	84
MIDDLE	18	3620	60	60.4	84
FRONT	18	3154	60	60	79

Weekend: $13.50
Weekend: $25.00
Discounts: Senior Wkdays
Junior Golf: N/R **Membership:** No
Non-Metal Spikes: Required

A challenging executive par 60 course. The tract sports hills and water; greens are in great shape. The 18th hole proves to be a difficult home stretch. Open Apr. 1- Dec. 1.

	1	2	3	4	5	6	7	8	9
PAR	3	3	3	4	3	4	3	3	4
YARDS	148	130	145	264	140	339	113	137	351
HDCP	5	9	7	15	11	1	17	13	3
	10	11	12	13	14	15	16	17	18
PAR	4	3	3	3	3	3	4	4	3
YARDS	341	135	161	114	185	122	319	293	183
HDCP	2	18	6	10	8	14	16	12	4

Directions: Take I-91 to Route 9 to Route 66; left onto Route 17 (Gospel Lane); course is 1/2 mile on right.

4✪ =Excellent 3✪ =Very Good 2✪ =Good

Quarry Ridge GC

35

Rose Hill Rd., Portland, CT (860) 342-6113

Club Pro: John Lucas, Jr.
Pro Shop: Yes
Payment: Cash, Check, Visa, MC
Tee Times: 1 week adv.
Fee 9 Holes: Weekday: $19.50
Fee 18 Holes: Weekday: $35.00
Cart Rental: Included
Lessons: $35.00/half hour **School:** No
Driving Range: No
Other: Restaurant / Clubhouse / Bar-Lounge

Tees	Holes	Yards	Par	USGA	Slope
BACK	9	6266	72	70.4	124
MIDDLE	9	5784	70	68.2	120
FRONT	9	4876	72	67.1	118

Weekend: $21.50
Weekend: $39.00
Discounts: Senior
Junior Golf: No **Membership:** No
Non-Metal Spikes: Not Required

Very scenic, challenging layout with spectacular views of Connecticut River Valley. Open April - November.

	1	2	3	4	5	6	7	8	9
PAR	4	5	4	4	3	4	4	4	3
YARDS	304	435	388	286	145	370	329	361	173
HDCP	16	12	2	18	14	10	6	4	8
	10	11	12	13	14	15	16	17	18
PAR	4	5	4	4	3	4	4	4	3
YARDS	304	435	388	286	145	370	329	361	173
HDCP	16	12	2	18	14	10	6	4	8

Directions: From Hartford: Route 2 to Route 17 (left Exit 7.) Go 9 miles; take left onto Bartlett Street, go to end. Cross road to driveway of golf course.

Richter Park GC

✪✪✪✪ **36**

Danbury, CT (203) 792-2550

Club Pro: Ralph Salito Jr.
Pro Shop: Full inventory
Payment: MC, Visa, Cash
Tee Times: Yes, Weekends
Fee 9 Holes: Weekday: No
Fee 18 Holes: Weekday: $44.00
Cart Rental: $23.00
Lessons: $35.00/half hour **School:** No
Driving Range: No
Other: Clubhouse / Lockers / Showers / Snack bar / Restaurant / Bar-lounge

Tees	Holes	Yards	Par	USGA	Slope
BACK	18	6740	72	73	130
MIDDLE	18	6325	72	71.1	126
FRONT	18	5208	72	73.1	117

Weekend: No
Weekend: $44.00
Discounts: None
Junior Golf: N/R **Membership:** Yes
Non-Metal Spikes: Required

Challenging and pretty course retains a reputation for making even the most skillful golfers work hard: narrow fairways, approach shots require precision, www.ctgolfer.com/richterparkgc

	1	2	3	4	5	6	7	8	9
PAR	4	5	3	4	3	4	5	4	4
YARDS	372	491	150	389	170	388	507	335	314
HDCP	11	9	17	3	15	1	7	5	13
	10	11	12	13	14	15	16	17	18
PAR	4	4	5	3	4	4	5	3	4
YARDS	345	360	495	142	395	324	570	152	426
HDCP	10	12	6	16	8	14	2	18	4

Directions: I-84 West to Exit 2 or I-84 East to Exit 2B. Take right off ramp (Mill Plain Rd.); take second left onto Aunt Hack Rd. to course.

Ridgefield Golf Club   37

Ridgefield, CT (203) 748-7008

Club Pro: Vincent Adams
Pro Shop: Full inventory
Payment: Cash, Check
Tee Times: Yes, weekends
Fee 9 Holes: Weekday: N/A
Fee 18 Holes: Weekday: $40.00
Cart Rental: $24.00/18 $12.00/9
Lessons: $38.00/half hour **School:** N/R
Driving Range: $6.00
Other: Snack bar / Bar-Lounge

Tees	Holes	Yards	Par	USGA	Slope
BACK	18	6445	71	70.9	123
MIDDLE	18	6005	71	68.9	120
FRONT	18	5124	74	70.6	119

Weekend: N/A
Weekend: $40.00
Discounts: Senior & Junior
Junior Golf: Yes **Membership:** N/R
Non-Metal Spikes: Required

New Par 5 at #6- New tee at #14. Resident permit card necessary for reduced rates.

	1	2	3	4	5	6	7	8	9
PAR	4	4	3	4	3	5	4	4	4
YARDS	408	411	163	344	147	542	412	411	378
HDCP	12	8	16	14	18	2	10	4	6
	10	11	12	13	14	15	16	17	18
PAR	5	4	3	4	5	4	4	3	4
YARDS	564	311	147	351	469	395	311	127	386
HDCP	3	11	15	9	7	1	13	17	5

Directions: Take Exit 1 off I-84; Saw Mill Rd. to Old Ridgebury Rd. Course is on Old Ridgebury.

Short Beach Par 3 Golf Course   38

Stratford, CT (203)381-2070

Club Pro: Herb Wry
Pro Shop: Limited inventory
Payment: Personal checks, cash
Tee Times: 2 days adv. wknds
Fee 9 Holes: Weekday: $7.50
Fee 18 Holes: Weekday: $15.00
Cart Rental: $1.75/9
Lessons: Yes **School:** No
Driving Range: No
Other: Snack Bar/ Mini. Golf course

Tees	Holes	Yards	Par	USGA	Slope
BACK	9	1469	27		
MIDDLE	9	1270	27	N/A	N/A
FRONT	N/A				

Weekend: $9.50
Weekend: $19.00
Discounts: Senior & Junior
Junior Golf: Yes **Membership:** N/A
Non-Metal Spikes: Required

Par 3 nine holes on beachfront. Architect- Geoffrey Cornish. Proper attire required. Open March-January. Resident discounts.

	1	2	3	4	5	6	7	8	9
PAR	3	3	3	3	3	3	3	3	3
YARDS	125	154	98	170	88	130	218	162	125
HDCP									
	10	11	12	13	14	15	16	17	18
PAR									
YARDS									
HDCP									

Directions: Call for directions.

4✪ =Excellent **3**✪ =Very Good **2**✪ =Good

Sleeping Giant GC 39

Hamden, CT (203) 281-9456

Club Pro: Carl Swanson
Pro Shop: Full inventory
Payment: Cash only
Tee Times: Wknds & holidays
Fee 9 Holes: Weekday: $11.00
Fee 18 Holes: Weekday: $18.00
Cart Rental: $18.00/18, $10.00/9
Lessons: $25/half hour, $40 hour **School:** No
Driving Range: Yes
Other: Restaurant nearby

Tees	Holes	Yards	Par	USGA	Slope
BACK	9	2671	36	65.4	99
MIDDLE	9	2457	35	63.4	96
FRONT	9	2216	37	N/A	N/A

Weekend: $13.00
Weekend: $21.00
Discounts: Senior & Junior
Junior Golf: N/R **Membership:** No
Non-Metal Spikes: Not Required

Two new holes in '97. Extensive improvements, including new trees, tees, and watering system. Open March - November.

	1	2	3	4	5	6	7	8	9
PAR	4	4	3	5	3	4	4	4	4
YARDS	385	380	144	463	184	350	235	245	435
HDCP	4	3	9	1	8	5	7	6	2
	10	11	12	13	14	15	16	17	18
PAR									
YARDS									
HDCP									

Directions: Take I-91 to Exit 10. Right onto Whitney Avenue. Course is 3 miles on the right.

Southington CC 40

Savage St., Southington, CT (860) 628-7032

Club Pro: No
Pro Shop: Limited inventory
Payment: Cash only
Tee Times: Weekends, 5 days adv.
Fee 9 Holes: Weekday: $14.00
Fee 18 Holes: Weekday: $24.00
Cart Rental: $25.00/18 $13.00/9
Lessons: No **School:** No
Driving Range: No
Other: Snack bar / Bar-lounge

Tees	Holes	Yards	Par	USGA	Slope
BACK					
MIDDLE	18	5675	71	67.0	113
FRONT	18	5103	73	69.8	119

Weekend: $17.00
Weekend: $28.00
Discounts: Senior & Junior
Junior Golf: No **Membership:** Yes
Non-Metal Spikes: Required

The course is level and considered an easy walker. Front nine is a bit more hilly. Open March - November.

	1	2	3	4	5	6	7	8	9
PAR	4	4	3	5	4	5	3	4	4
YARDS	377	306	144	481	387	508	192	338	324
HDCP	5	14	17	3	7	1	15	9	10
	10	11	12	13	14	15	16	17	18
PAR	4	4	3	4	5	3	4	3	5
YARDS	300	316	96	323	453	202	323	160	445
HDCP	12	13	18	6	2	11	8	16	4

Directions: Take I-84 to Exit 27 (Route 691), take Exit 3; turn left, at 2nd light bear right; next light take right; next light turn left; take 1st left onto Savage Street.

Sterling Farms GC　　　　　　　　　　　　▶ 41

Newfield Ave., Stamford, CT (203) 461-9090

Club Pro: Angela Aulenti
Pro Shop: Full inventory
Payment: Cash only
Tee Times: 1 week adv.
Fee 9 Holes: Weekday: No
Fee 18 Holes: Weekday: $35.00
Cart Rental: $20.00/18
Lessons: Call 203-329-7888 **School:** Yes
Driving Range: Yes
Other: Restaurant

Tees	Holes	Yards	Par	USGA	Slope
BACK	18	6310	72	70.7	127
MIDDLE	18	6082	72	69.7	123
FRONT	18	5500	73	71.7	125

Weekend: No
Weekend: $33.00
Discounts: None
Junior Golf: Yes **Membership:** No
Non-Metal Spikes: Required

Head Professional was named 1998 PGA merchandiser of the year. Best golf shop in Connecticut. Course has hilly front nine; more level back nine; five lakes and two come into play on the 14th hole.

	1	2	3	4	5	6	7	8	9
PAR	4	5	4	4	3	5	4	3	4
YARDS	331	489	316	350	191	465	382	179	326
HDCP	17	9	15	5	3	7	1	13	11
	10	11	12	13	14	15	16	17	18
PAR	4	4	4	5	4	3	4	3	5
YARDS	397	307	341	477	393	147	301	215	475
HDCP	6	14	4	10	2	18	12	8	16

Directions: Merritt Pkwy S to Exit 35. Right onto High Ridge Rd. Left onto Vine (5 lights). Left at end to Newfield Ave. Club is 1/4 mi. on right.

Stonybrook GC　　　　　　　　　　　　▶ 42

Milton Rd., Litchfield, CT (860) 567-9977

Club Pro: Rich Bredice
Pro Shop: Full inventory
Payment: Visa, MC
Tee Times: Weekends
Fee 9 Holes: Weekday: $14.00
Fee 18 Holes: Weekday: $26.00
Cart Rental: $24.00/18 $12.00/9
Lessons: $26.00/half hour **School:** No
Driving Range: No
Other: Clubhouse / Snack bar / Bar-lounge / Lockers

Tees	Holes	Yards	Par	USGA	Slope
BACK	9	2990	35	69.2	124
MIDDLE	9	2875	35	68.6	122
FRONT	9	2658	36	68.0	121

Weekend: $17.00
Weekend: $32.00
Discounts: None
Junior Golf: No **Membership:** Yes
Non-Metal Spikes: Not Required

The course is known for its excellent conditions and constant upgrades. Terrain is rolling; greens contoured (medium/fast). Open March 15 - December 15.

	1	2	3	4	5	6	7	8	9
PAR	5	4	3	4	4	4	4	4	3
YARDS	530	374	150	369	335	300	359	295	163
HDCP	1	7	17	9	5	13	3	11	15
	10	11	12	13	14	15	16	17	18
PAR									
YARDS									
HDCP									

Directions: I-84 to Route 8 N. Take Litchfield Exit 42; follow signs to Litchfield Green (8 miles). Take Route 202 W at stop sign by green. At fourth light, take right onto Milton Road. Course 2 miles on left.

4✪ =Excellent 3✪ =Very Good 2✪ =Good

Sunset Hill GC

Brookfield, CT (203) 740-7800

Club Pro: No
Pro Shop: Limited inventory
Payment: Cash, Check
Tee Times: No
Fee 9 Holes: Weekday: $17.00
Fee 18 Holes: Weekday: $17.00
Cart Rental: $24.00/18 $12.00/9
Lessons: No **School:** No
Driving Range: No
Other: Clubhouse / Snack bar / Bar-lounge

Tees	Holes	Yards	Par	USGA	Slope
BACK	N/R				
MIDDLE	9	4692	69	62.6	100
FRONT	9	4692	70	66.3	100

Weekend: $23.00
Weekend: $23.00
Discounts: Senior & Junior
Junior Golf: N/R **Membership:** Yes
Non-Metal Spikes: Required

COUPON

The course is challenging and hilly. Open April - November.

	1	2	3	4	5	6	7	8	9
PAR	5	3	3	4	4	4	5	4	3
YARDS	452	145	116	278	304	270	426	278	125
HDCP	3	12	17	9	5	11	1	7	15
	10	11	12	13	14	15	16	17	18
PAR	5	3	3	4	4	4	4	4	3
YARDS	452	145	116	278	304	250	350	278	125
HDCP	4	14	18	10	6	12	2	8	16

Directions: Take I-84 to Exit 9; follow Route 25 North 3 miles; take left onto Sunset Hill Rd. to course.

Tashua Knolls CC

Trumbull, CT (203) 261-5989

Club Pro: Walter Bogues
Pro Shop: Full inventory
Payment: Cash or check
Tee Times: M-F 1 day S/S 3 day adv
Fee 9 Holes: Weekday: $18.00
Fee 18 Holes: Weekday: $26.00
Cart Rental: $23.00/18 $16.00/9
Lessons: $28.00/half hour **School:** No
Driving Range: $2.50 sm/$4.50 lg.
Other: Snack bar / Restaurant / Bar-lounge / Lockers / Showers

Tees	Holes	Yards	Par	USGA	Slope
BACK	18	6540	72	70.9	118
MIDDLE	18	6119	72	69.0	115
FRONT	18	5454	72	72.0	112

Weekend: $22.00
Weekend: $30.00
Discounts: Senior & Junior
Junior Golf: Yes **Membership:** Men's Club
Non-Metal Spikes: Required

Very challenging with an assortment of dog legs, water holes and tree-lined fairways. Host of the Ernie Kaulbach Pro-am Golf Classic. Resident rates.

	1	2	3	4	5	6	7	8	9
PAR	5	4	3	4	4	3	5	4	4
YARDS	532	317	151	342	353	192	480	354	356
HDCP	3	7	17	1	11	15	5	13	9
	10	11	12	13	14	15	16	17	18
PAR	4	4	3	4	5	4	5	3	4
YARDS	349	367	154	262	495	373	506	145	391
HDCP	10	12	18	14	2	8	4	16	6

Directions: Take Merritt Parkway (Route 15) to Exit 49 (Route 25); go straight, take left onto Tashua Knolls Lane.

Twin Lakes GC

▶ 45

North Branford, CT (203) 488-8778

Club Pro:
Pro Shop: Limited inventory
Payment: Cash only
Tee Times: N/A
Fee 9 Holes: Weekday: $5.00
Fee 18 Holes: Weekday: $10.00
Cart Rental: Pull carts $2.00
Lessons: No **School:** No
Driving Range: No
Other:

Tees	Holes	Yards	Par	USGA	Slope
BACK	N/A				
MIDDLE	9	851	27	N/A	N/A
FRONT	N/A				

Weekend: $6.00
Weekend: $12.00
Discounts: Senior
Junior Golf: Yes **Membership:** No
Non-Metal Spikes: Preferred

Open March 15- Oct. 15. This is a very short, 9 hole pare 3 course good for family fun.

	1	2	3	4	5	6	7	8	9
PAR	3	3	3	3	3	3	3	3	3
YARDS	118	98	86	84	85	88	134	80	78
HDCP	N/A								
	10	11	12	13	14	15	16	17	18
PAR									
YARDS									
HDCP									

Directions: From I-95, exit 55 on left. Take a left at first light. 2 miles, Twin Lakes Rd. on left.

Western Hills GC

▶ 46

Waterbury, CT (203) 756-1211

Club Pro: Tom Bracken
Pro Shop: Full inventory
Payment: Cash only
Tee Times: Weekends, 3 days adv.
Fee 9 Holes: Weekday: $13.00
Fee 18 Holes: Weekday: $21.00
Cart Rental: $18.00/18 $11.00/9
Lessons: Call 596-7424 **School:** No
Driving Range: No
Other: Clubhouse / Snack bar / Restaurant / Bar-lounge

Tees	Holes	Yards	Par	USGA	Slope
BACK	18	6427	72	71.1	125
MIDDLE	18	6246	72	69.4	122
FRONT	18	5393	72	70.4	121

Weekend: $15.00
Weekend: $22.00
Discounts: Junior
Junior Golf: No **Membership:** Yes
Non-Metal Spikes: Not Required

The course is a combination of hills, flat terrain, and one water hole. Fairly challenging.

	1	2	3	4	5	6	7	8	9
PAR	4	5	4	4	3	4	5	4	3
YARDS	346	471	375	353	167	378	530	397	145
HDCP	7	9	5	4	17	8	11	2	16
	10	11	12	13	14	15	16	17	18
PAR	4	3	4	5	4	5	3	4	4
YARDS	366	138	316	506	395	485	151	397	330
HDCP	6	18	10	12	1	13	15	3	14

Directions: Take I-84 to Exit 18. Bear left. Right at W. Union Street, left on Park Street. Course is 1 mile on the right.

SW CT

4✪ =Excellent 3✪ =Very Good 2✪ =Good

Southern/Western CT 337

Whitney Farms 47

Monroe, CT (203) 268-0707

Club Pro: Paul McGuire
Pro Shop: Full inventory
Payment: Visa, MC, Amex
Tee Times: Yes
Fee 9 Holes: Weekday: $22.00
Fee 18 Holes: Weekday: $40.00
Cart Rental: Included
Lessons: $35.00/half hour **School:** No
Driving Range: $5.00
Other: Clubhouse / Lockers / Showers / Snack bar / Restaurant / Bar-lounge

Tees	Holes	Yards	Par	USGA	Slope
BACK	18	6628	72	72.4	130
MIDDLE	18	6262	72	70.9	127
FRONT	18	5832	73	72.9	124

Weekend: $25.00 with cart
Weekend: $45.00 with cart
Discounts: None
Junior Golf: N/R **Membership:** No
Non-Metal Spikes: Required

Difficult layout with undulating greens. Residential neighborhood with many homes along front nine. Open April - December.

	1	2	3	4	5	6	7	8	9
PAR	4	4	5	3	4	5	3	5	3
YARDS	399	381	508	161	324	533	210	469	168
HDCP	11	5	1	15	13	3	7	9	17
	10	11	12	13	14	15	16	17	18
PAR	4	5	3	4	4	3	5	4	4
YARDS	341	522	132	329	324	164	547	335	415
HDCP	14	2	18	16	8	10	6	12	4

Directions: Merritt Pkwy. to Route 25. Take right on 111 and follow for 4 miles. Take right at intersection of Route 110. Course 1 mile on left.

Woodhaven CC 48

Bethany, CT (203) 393-3230

Club Pro: Dale Humphrey
Pro Shop: Full inventory
Payment: Cash, Check
Tee Times: 1 week adv.
Fee 9 Holes: Weekday: $15.00
Fee 18 Holes: Weekday: $25.00
Cart Rental: $26.00/18 $13.00/9
Lessons: Yes **School:** No
Driving Range: Yes
Other: Snack bar / Restaurant

Tees	Holes	Yards	Par	USGA	Slope
BACK	9	6774	72	72.7	128
MIDDLE	9	6294	72	70.6	123
FRONT	9	5718	74	73.0	125

Weekend: $18.00
Weekend: $32.00
Discounts: Senior
Junior Golf: No **Membership:** No
Non-Metal Spikes: Required

A family owned "Labor of Love," the course is scenic, challenging and easy walking.

	1	2	3	4	5	6	7	8	9
PAR	5	3	4	4	4	5	4	3	4
YARDS	517	156	331	375	342	542	350	152	382
HDCP	6	18	14	8	12	5	10	16	4
	10	11	12	13	14	15	16	17	18
PAR	5	3	4	4	4	5	4	3	4
YARDS	517	156	331	375	342	542	350	152	382
HDCP	7	17	9	2	11	3	15	13	1

Directions: Route 15 to Route 63 toward Hamden. Left on to Route 67. Go 2 1/2 miles, then right on Bearhill Rd. Follow Bearhill to Miller Rd. Course is on the left. From Route 8, take Exit 22 East on Route 67 1.5 miles to Bear Hill Rd. to Miller Rd.

Index to Golf Courses
Alphabetically by State

State		Page
Connecticut		
Airways Golf Course	Suffield	293
Alling Memorial GC	New Haven	315
Birch Plain Golf Course	Groton	293
Blackledge CC	Hebron	294
Blue Fox Run	Avon	294
Brooklyn Hill GC	Danielson	295
Bruce Memorial GC	Greenwich	315
Buena Vista GC	West Hartford	295
Canaan Country Club	Canaan	296
Candlewood Valley CC	New Milford	316
Cedar Knob GC	Somers	296
Cedar Ridge GC	East Lyme	297
Chanticlair Golf Course	Colchester	316
Copper Hill CC	East Granby	297
Crestbrook Park GC	Watertown	317
E. Gaynor Brennan GC	Stamford	317
East Hartford GC	East Hartford	298
East Mountain GC	Waterbury	318
Eastwood CC	Torrington	318
Elmridge Golf Course	Pawcatuck	298
Fairchild Wheeler GC (Blk)	Bridgeport	319
Fairchild Wheeler GC (Red)	Bridgeport	319
Farmingbury Hill CC	Wolcott	320
Gainfield Farms GC	Southbury	38
Goodwin Golf Course	Hartford	299
Grassmere CC	Enfield	299
Grassy Hill Country Club	Orange	320
H. Smith Richardson GC	Fairfield	321
Harbor Ridge Golf Club	Wallingford	321
Harrisville GC	Woodstock	300
Highland Greens GC	Prospect	322
Hillside Links LLC	Deep River,	322
Hop Brook CC	Naugatuck	323
Hotchkiss School GC	Lakeville	300
Hunter Golf Club	Meriden	323
Indian Springs GC	Middlefield	324
Keney Park Golf Club	Hartford	301
Laurel View CC	Hamden	324
Leisure Resort at Banner	Moodus	325
Lisbon Country Club	Lisbon	301
Longshore Park	Westport	325
Lyman Orchards GC (Jones)	Middlefield	326
Lyman Orchards GC (Player)	Middlefield	326
Manchester CC	Manchester	302
Meadowbrook CC	Hamden	327
Mill Stone CC	Milford	327
Millbrook Golf Course	Windsor	302
Miner Hills GC	Middletown	328

State		Page
Connecticut		
Minnechaug GC	Glastonbury	303
Norwich Golf Course	Norwich	303
Oak Hills Park	Norwalk	328
Orange Hills CC	Orange	329
Pattonbrook CC	Southington	329
Pequabuck Golf Course	Pequabuck	330
Pequot Golf Club	Stonington	304
Pine Valley Golf Course	Southington	330
Portland Golf Club	Portland	331
Portland Golf Club West	Portland	331
Putnam Country Club	Putnam	304
Quarry Ridge GC	Portland	332
Raceway Golf Club	Thompson	305
Richter Park GC	Danbury	332
Ridgefield Golf Club	Ridgefield	333
Rockledge CC	West Hartford	305
Rolling Greens GC	Rocky Hill	306
Rolling Meadows CC	Ellington	306
Shennecosset GC	Groton	307
Short Beach Par 3 GC	Stratford	333
Simsbury Farms GC	Simsbury	307
Skungamaug River GC	Coventry	308
Sleeping Giant GC	Hamden	334
South Pine Creek Par 3 GC	Fairfield	38
Southington CC	Southington	334
Stanley Golf Club	New Britain	308
Sterling Farms GC	Stamford	335
Stonybrook GC	Litchfield	335
Sunset Hill GC	Brookfield	336
Tallwood Country Club	Hebron	309
Tashua Knolls CC	Trumbull	336
The Orchards Golf Course	Milford	36
Timberlin Golf Club	Kensington	309
Topstone Golf Course	South Windsor	310
Tunxis Plantation CC (Green)	Farmington	310
Tunxis Plantation CC (White)	Farmington	311
Tunxis Plantation GC (Red)	Farmington	311
Twin Hills CC	Coventry	312
Twin Lakes GC	North Branford	337
Villa Hills Golf Course	Storrs	38
Western Hills GC	Waterbury	337
Westwoods Golf Course	Farmington	312
Whitney Farms	Monroe	338
Willimantic C. C.	Willimantic	313
Woodhaven CC	Bethany	338
Woodstock GC	S. Woodstock	313

NEW ENGLAND GOLFGUIDE

Massachusetts

State		Page
Acushnet River Valley GC	Acushnet	26
Agawam Municipal CC	Feedng Hills	117
Allendale Country Club	No. Dartmouth	26
Amesbury Golf & CC	Amesbury	83
Amherst Golf Club	Amherst	117
Atlantic Country Club	Plymouth	40
Ballymeade CC	North Falmouth	40
Bas Ridge Golf Course	Hinsdale	118
Bass River Golf Course	South Yarmouth	41
Bay Path Golf Course	East Brookfield	83
Bay Pointe CC	Onset	41
Bayberry Hills GC	Yarmouth	42
Beaver Brook CC	Haydenville	118
Bedrock Golf Club	Rutland	84
Berlin Country Club	Berlin	84
Beverly Golf & Tennis	Beverly	85
Blackstone National GC	Sutton	27
Blissful Meadows GC	Uxbridge	85
Blue Rock Golf Club	South Yarmouth	42
Bradford Country Club	Bradford	86
Braintree Muni. GC	Braintree	43
Brookmeadow CC	Canton	43
Butternut Farm GC	Stow	44
Candlewood Golf Club	Ipswich	86
Cape Ann Golf Club	Essex	87
Cape Cod CC	North Falmouth	44
Captains GC, The	Brewster	45
CC of Billerica	Billerica	87
Cedar Glen Golf Club	Saugus	88
Cedar Hill Golf Club	Stoughton	45
Chatham Seaside Links	Chatham	46
Chelmsford Country Club	Chelmsford	88
Chemawa Golf Course	N Attleboro	142
Chequessett Yacht & CC	Wellfleet	46
Cherry Hills GC	North Amherst	119
Chicopee Municipal GC	Chicopee	119
Clearview Golf Course	Millbury	89
Colonial Golf Club	Wakefield	89
Cotuit-Highground GC	Cotuit	47
Country Club of Greenfield	Greenfield	120
Country Club of Wilbraham	Wilbraham	120
Cranberry Valley GC	Harwich	47
Cranwell Resort & GC	Lenox	121
Crumpin-Fox Club	Bernardston	121
Crystal Springs CC	Haverhill	90
Cyprian Keyes	Boylston	37
Cyprian Keyes GC, Par 3	Boylston	37
D.W. Fields Golf Course	Brockton	48
Dennis Highlands	South Dennis	48
Dennis Pines GC	South Dennis	49
Dunroamin CC	Gilbertville	122
East Mountain CC	Westfield	122

Massachusetts

State		Page
Easton Country Club	South Easton	49
Edge Hill GC	Ashfield	123
Edgewood Golf Club	Southwick	123
Egremont Country Club	Great Barrington	124
Ellinwood CC	Athol	124
Falmouth Country Club	Falmouth	50
Far Corner Golf Course	West Boxford	91
Farm Neck Golf Club	Oak Bluffs	50
Fire Fly Country Club	Seekonk	146
Forest Park CC	Adams	125
Franconia Muni. GC	Springfield	125
Fresh Pond Golf Club	Cambridge	51
Gannon Muni. GC	Lynn	91
Gardner Municipal GC	Gardner	92
GEAA Golf Club	Pittsfield	126
George Wright GC	Hyde Park	51
Glen Ellen CC	Millis	52
Grand View Country Club	Leominster	92
Green Harbor Golf Club	Marshfield	52
Green Hill Municipal GC	Worcester	93
Green Valley GC	Newburyport	93
Greenock Country Club	Lee	126
Groton Country Club	Groton	94
Hampden Country Club	Hampden	127
Harwich Port Golf Club	Harwich Port	53
Heather Hill CC	Plainville	149
Hemlock Ridge GC	Fiskdale	94
Heritage Country Club	Charlton	95
Heritage Hill CC	Lakeville	53
Hickory Hill GC	Methuen	95
Hickory Ridge CC	S. Amherst	127
Hidden Hollow C. C.	Rehoboth	149
Highland Links	North Truro	54
Hillcrest Country Club	Leicester	96
Hillside CC	Rehoboth	150
Hillview Golf Course	North Reading	96
Holden Hills CC	Holden	97
Holly Ridge Golf Club	South Sandwich	54
Holyoke Country Club	Holyoke	128
Hopedale CC	Hopedale	150
Hyannis Golf Club	Hyannis	55
Indian Meadows Golf Club	Westboro	97
John F. Parker GC	Taunton	151
Juniper Hill GC (Lakeside)	Northboro	98
Juniper Hill GC (Riverside)	Northboro	98
Kelley Greens By The Sea	Nahant	99
Kings Way Golf Course	Yarmouthport	55
Lakeview Golf Club	Wenham	99
Lakeville Country Club	Lakeville	56
Leicester Country Club	Leicester	100
Leo J. Martin GC	Weston	56
Little Harbor CC	Wareham	57

340 Golf Course Index   NEW ENGLAND GOLFGUIDE

State		Page	State		Page
Massachusetts			**Massachusetts**		
Locust Valley Golf Course	Attleboro	152	Ponkapoag GC #1	Canton	68
Lost Brook Golf Club	Norwood	57	Ponkapoag GC #2	Canton	68
Lynnfield Center GC	Lynnfield	100	Pontoosuc Lake CC	Pittsfield	132
Maplegate Country Club	Bellingham	153	Poquoy Brook GC	Lakeville	69
Maplewood Golf Course	Lunenburg	101	Presidents Golf Course	Quincy	69
Marion Golf Course	E. Wareham	153	Putterham Meadows	Brookline	70
Maynard Country Club	Maynard	58	Quaboag Country Club	Monson	107
Merrimack Valley GC	Methuen	101	Quail Hollow Golf & CC	Oakham	107
Miacomet Golf Club	Nantucket	58	Quashnet Valley CC	Mashpee	70
Middlebrook CC	Rehoboth	155	Rehoboth Country Club	Rehoboth	160
Middleton Golf Course	Middleton	102	Ridder Golf Club	Whitman	71
Mill Valley CC	Belchertown	128	Rochester Golf Club	Rochester	161
Millwood Farm GC	Framingham	59	Rockland CC	Rockland	71
Mink Meadows GC	Vinyrd Haven	59	Rockport Golf Course	Rockport	108
Monoosnock CC	Leominster	102	Rolling Green GC	Andover	108
Mt. Hood Golf Course	Melrose	60	Round Hill CC	East Sandwich	72
Murphy's Garrison GC	Haverhill	103	Rowley Country Club	Rowley	109
Nabnasset Lake CC	Westford	103	Saddle Hill CC	Hopkinton	72
New Bedford Muni. GC	New Bedford	156	Sagamore Spring GC	Lynnfield	109
New England CC	Bellingham	157	Sandy Burr CC	Wayland	73
New Meadows GC	Topsfield	104	Scituate Country Club	Scituate	73
New Seabury CC (blue)	Mashpee	60	Shaker Farms CC	Westfield	133
New Seabury GC (green)	Mashpee	61	Shaker Hills Golf Club	Harvard	110
Newton Commonwealth GC	Newton	61	Skyline Country Club	Lanesborough	133
Nichols College GC	Dudley	104	South Shore CC	Hingham	74
North Adams CC	N. Adams	129	Southampton CC	Southampton	134
North Hill CC	Duxbury	62	Southwick CC	Southwick	134
Northampton CC	Leeds	27	Squirrel Run CC	Plymouth	74
Northfield CC	E Northfield	129	St. Anne Country Club	Feedng Hills	135
Norton Country Club	Norton	62	St. Mark's Golf Course	Southborough	110
Norwood Country Club	Norwood	63	Stone-E-Lea Golf Course	Attleboro	163
Oak Ridge Golf Club	Gill	130	Stoneham Oaks	Stoneham	75
Oak Ridge Golf Club	Feeding Hills	130	Stony Brook Golf Course	Southboro	111
Ocean Edge GC	Brewster	63	Stow Acres CC (north)	Stow	75
Olde Barnstable Fair. GC	Marstons Mills	64	Stow Acres CC (south)	Stow	76
Olde Salem Greens	Salem	105	Strawberry Valley GC	Abington	76
Olde Scotland Links	Bridgwater	64	Sun Valley CC	Rehoboth	163
Ould Newbury GC	Newbury	105	Swansea Country Club	Swansea	164
Pakachoag Golf Course	Auburn	106	Taconic Golf Club	Williamstown	135
Paul Harney GC	E. Falmouth	65	Tekoa Country Club	Westfield	136
Pembroke Country Club	Pembroke	65	The Brookside Club	Bourne	28
Petersham CC	Petersham	131	The Meadows Golf Club	Greenfield	136
Pine Acres Executive GC	Bellingham	158	The Orchards Golf Club	South Hadley	137
Pine Grove Golf Club	Northampton	131	The Woods of Westminster CC	Westminster	28
Pine Knoll Par 3	E. Longmeadow	132	Thomas Memorial Golf & CC	Turner Falls	137
Pine Meadows GC	Lexington	66	Touisset Country Club	Swansea	164
Pine Oaks GC	South Easton	66	Townsend Ridge CC	Townsend	111
Pine Ridge Country Club	N. Oxford	106	Trull Brook Golf Course	Tewksbury	112
Pine Valley Golf Club	Rehoboth	158	Twin Brooks GC At Sheraton	Hyannis	77
Pinecrest Golf Club	Holliston	67	Twin Springs Golf Club	Bolton	77
Plymouth Country Club	Plymouth	67	Tyngsboro CC	Tyngsboro	112

NEW ENGLAND GOLFGUIDE   **Golf Course Index 341**

State		Page	State		Page
Massachusetts			**Maine**		
Unicorn Golf Course	Stoneham	78	Goose River GC	Rockport	221
Veteran's Golf Club	Springfield	138	Gorham Country Club	Gorham	222
Wachusett CC	W. Boylston	113	Great Cove Golf Course	Jonesboro	246
Wading River GC	Norton	78	Green Valley GC	Lincoln	246
Wahconah CC	Dalton	138	Grindstone Neck GC	Winter Harbor	247
Wampanoag Golf Club	N. Swansea	165	Hampden CC	Hampden	247
Waubeeka Golf Links	S. Williamstown	139	Hermon Meadow GC	Bangor	248
Waverly Oaks Golf Club	Plymouth	29	Hillcrest Golf Club	Millinocket	248
Wayland Country Club	Wayland	79	Houlton Community GC	Houlton	249
Wedgewood Pines CC	Stow	79	Island Country Club	Sunset	249
Wenham Country Club	Wenham	113	Johnson W. Parks GC	Pittsfield	250
Westboro CC	Westborough	114	Katahdin Country Club	Milo	250
Westminster CC	Westminster	114	Kebo Valley Golf Club	Bar Harbor	251
Westover Golf Course	Ludlow	139	Kenduskeag Valley GC	Kenduskeag	251
Whippernon CC	Russell	140	Kennebec Heights CC	Farmingdale	222
Widow's Walk Golf Course	Scituate	80	Lake Kezar CC	Lovell	223
William J. Devine GC	Dorchester	80	Lakeview Golf Club	Burnham	99
Willowdale Golf Course	Mansfield	81	Lakewood Golf Course	Madison	252
Winchendon CC	Winchendon	115	Limestone CC	Limestone	253
Woburn Country Club	Woburn	115	Loons Cove Golf Course	Skowhegan	37
Woodbriar CC	Falmouth	81	Maple Lane Inn & GC	Livermore	223
Worthington GC	Worthington	140	Mars Hill Country Club	Mars Hill	253
			Merriland Farm Par 3 Golf	Wells	224
Maine			Mingo Springs GC	Rangeley	254
Apple Valley GC	Lewiston	214	Moose River GC	Moose River	254
Aroostook Valley CC	Ft.Fairfield	240	Naples Golf & CC	Naples	224
Bangor Municipal GC	Bangor	240	Natanis Golf Course	Vassalboro	255
Bar Harbor Golf Course	Trenton	241	Nonesuch River Golf Club	Scarborough	225
Bath Country Club	Bath	214	Northeast Harbor GC	N.E. Harbor	255
Belgrade Lakes CC	Belgrade	29	Northport Golf Club	Belfast	256
Bethel Inn & CC	Bethel	215	Norway Country Club	Norway	225
Biddeford & Saco CC	Saco	215	Oakdale CC	Rumford	226
Birch Point Golf Club	St. David	241	Old Orchard Beach CC	O. Orchard Beach	226
Boothbay Region CC	Boothbay	216	Orchard View GC	Newport	256
Bridgton Highlands CC	Bridgton	216	Palmyra Golf Course	Palmyra	257
Brunswick Golf Club	Brunswick	217	Paris Hill Country Club	Paris	227
Bucksport Golf Club	Bucksport	242	Penobscot Valley CC	Orono	257
Cape Arundel Golf Club	Kennebunkport	217	Pine Hill Golf Club	Brewer	258
Capitol City GC	Augusta	218	Pine Ridge Golf Course	Waterville	258
Caribou Country Club	Caribou	242	Piscataquis CC	Guilford	259
Castine Golf Club	Castine	243	Pleasant Hill CC	Scarborough	227
Causeway Club	S.W. Harbor	243	Point Sebago Golf Club	Casco	228
Cobbossee Colony GC	Monmouth	218	Poland Spring CC	Poland Sprng	228
Country View GC	Brooks	244	Portage Hill CC	Portgage	259
Dexter Municipal GC	Dexter	244	Presque Isle CC	Presque Isle	260
Dunegrass Golf Club	Old Orchard Beach	30	Prospect Hill GC	Auburn	229
Dutch Elm Golf Course	Arundel	219	River Meadow GC	Westbrook	229
Fairlawn Golf Club	Poland	219	Riverside Municipal GC	Portland	230
Fort Kent Golf Course	Fort Kent	245	Rockland Golf Club	Rockland	230
Foxcroft Golf Club	Dover Foxcroft	245	Sable Oaks Golf Club	South Portland	231
Freeport Country Club	Freeport	220	Salmon Falls GC	Hollis	231
Frye Island Golf Course	Raymond	220	Samoset Resort GC	Rockport	232
Golf at Province Lake	Parsonsfield	221			

State		Page
Maine		
Sanford Country Club	Sanford	232
Sebasco Harbor Resort GC	Sebasco Estates	30
South Portland Muni.	S. Portland	233
Spring Brook GC	Leeds	233
Squaw Mt. Village CC	Greenville Junction	31
St. Croix Country Club	Calais	31
Sugarloaf Golf Club	Carrabasset	260
The Ledges Golf Club	York	32
Todd Valley Golf Club	Charleston	261
Turner Highland GC	Turner	234
Twin Falls Golf Course	Westbrook	234
Va-Jo-Wa Golf Club	Island Falls	261
Val Halla Golf Course	Cumberland	235
Waterville Country Club	Waterville	262
Wawenock CC	Walpole	235
West Newfield Golf Course	West Newfield	236
Westerly Winds GC	Westbrook	236
Western View Golf Club	Augusta	237
White Birches GC	Ellsworth	262
Willowdale Golf Club	Scarborough	237
Wilson Lake CC	Wilton	238
Woodland Terrace GC	E Holden	263
New Hampshire		
Amherst Country Club	Amherst	169
Androscoggin Valley CC	Gorham	169
Angus Lea Golf Course	Hillsboro	170
Applewood Golf Links	Windham	170
Atkinson Country Club	Atkinson	171
Atkinson Country Club	Atkinson	171
Balsams Panorama GC, The	Dixville Notch	171
Balsams-Coashaukee GC	Dixville Notch	172
Beaver Meadow GC	Concord	172
Bethlehem CC	Behlehem	173
Blackmount Country Club	N. Haverhill	173
Bramber Valley Golf Course	Greenland	174
Bretwood GC (North)	Keene	174
Bretwood GC (South)	Keene	175
Buckmeadow Golf Club	Amherst	175
Campbell's Scottish Highlands	Salem	176
Candia Woods	Candia	176
Carter Country Club	Lebanon	177
CC of New Hampshire	North Sutton	177
Claremont CC	Claremont	178
Colebrook CC	Colebrook	178
Countryside Golf Club	Dunbarton	179
Den Brae Golf Course	Sanborton,	179
Derryfield CC	Manchester	180
Duston Country Club	Hopkinton	180
Eagle Mountain House	Jackson	181
East Kingston GC	East Kingston	181
Eastman Golf Links	Grantham	182

State		Page
New Hampshire		
Exeter Country Club	Exeter	182
Farmington CC	Farmington	183
Fore-U-Golf Center	West Lebanon	183
Franklin Greens Golf & CC	Franklin	184
Golf at Province Lake	Parsonfield	221
Green Meadow GC #1, Prairie	Hudson	184
Green Meadow GC # 2, Jungle	Hudson	185
Hale's Location CC	Intervale	185
Hanover Country Club	Hanover	186
Hickory Pond Inn & GC	Durham	186
Hidden Valley R.V. & GP	Derry	187
Highlands Links GC	Plymouth	187
Hoodkroft CC	Derry	188
Hooper Golf Club	Walpole	188
Indian Mound GC	Center Ossipee	189
Intervale Country Club	Manchester	189
Jack O'Lantern Resort	Woodstock	190
John H. Cain GC	Newport	190
Keene Country Club	Keene	191
Kingston Fairways	E. Kingston	191
Kingswood Golf Club	Wolfeboro	192
Kona Mansion Inn	Center Harbor	192
Laconia Country Club	Lakeport	193
Lakeview Golf Club	Winnisquam	193
Lisbon Village CC	Lisbon	194
Lochmere Golf & CC	Lochmere	194
Londonderry CC	Londonderry	195
Loudon Country Club	Loudon	195
Maplewood Casino & CC	Bethlehem	196
Monadnock CC	Peterborough	196
Mt. Washington Hotel	Bretton Woods	197
Nippo Lake Golf Club	Barrington	197
North Conway CC	N. Conway	198
Oak Hill Golf Course	Meredith	198
Overlook GC	Hollis	199
Owl's Nest Golf Club	Campton	32
Passaconaway CC	Litchfield	199
Pease Golf Course	Portsmouth	200
Perry Hollow Golf & CC	Wolfeboro	200
Pheasant Ridge CC	Gilford	201
Pine Grove Springs CC	Spofford	201
Pine Valley CC	Pelham	202
Plausawa Valley CC	Pembroke	202
Ponemah Green	Amherst	203
Portsmouth CC	Greenland	203
Ragged Mountain	Danbury	33
Rochester Country Club	Gonic	204
Rockingham CC	Newmarket	204
Sagamore-Hampton GC	North Hampton	205
Shattuck GC, The	Jaffrey	205
Souhegan Woods GC	Amherst	206

NEW ENGLAND GOLFGUIDE   Golf Course Index 343

State		Page	State		Page
New Hamphire			**Vermont**		
Stonebridge Country Club	Goffstown	33	Basin Harbor Club	Vergennes	267
Sunningdale GC	Somersworth	206	Bellows Falls CC	Rockingham	268
Sunset Hill Golf Course	Sugar Hill	207	Blush Hill CC	Waterbury	268
Tory Pines Resort	Francestown	207	Bradford Golf Course	Bradford	34
Twin Lake Villa Golf Course	New London	208	Brattleboro CC	Brattleboro	269
Waterville Valley	Waterville	208	Cedar Knoll CC	Hinesburg	269
Waukewan Golf Club	Meredith	209	Champlain CC	St. Albans	270
Waumbek CC, The	Jefferson	209	Copley Country Club	Morrisville	270
Wentworth Resort GC	Jackson	210	Crown Point CC	Springfield	271
Whip-Poor-Will GC	Hudson	210	Enosburg Falls CC	Ensburg Falls	271
White Mountain CC	Ashland	211	Equinox Country Club	Manchester	272
Windham Golf Club	Windham	211	Essex Country Club	Essex Junction	272
Woodbound Inn GC	Jaffrey	212	Farm Resort GC	Stowe	273
			Green Mountain Nat.GC	Sherburne	273
Rhode Island			Haystack Golf Club	Wilmington	274
Bristol Golf Club	Bristol	142	Killington Golf Resort	Killington	274
Country View Golf Club	Harrisville	143	Kwiniaska Golf Club	Shelburne	275
Coventry Pines Golf Club	Coventry	143	Lake Morey CC	Fairlee	275
Cranston Country Club	Cranston	144	Lake St. Catherine CC	Poultney	276
East Greenwich CC	E Greenwich	144	Marble Island CC	Colchester	276
Exeter Country Club	Exeter	182	Montague Golf Club	Randolph	277
Fairlawn Golf Course	Lincoln	145	Montpelier CC	Montpelier	277
Foster Country Club	Foster	146	Mount Snow Golf Club	Mt. Snow	278
Foxwoods/Lindhbrook	Hope Valley	147	Mt. Anthony CC	Bennington	278
Foxwoods/Boulder Hills	Richmond	147	Neshobe Golf Club	Brandon	279
Goddard Park GC	Warwick	148	Newport CC	Newport	279
Green Valley CC	Portsmouth	148	Northfield CC	Northfield	280
Jamestown Golf & CC	Jamestown	151	Okemo Valley Golf Club	Ludlow	35
Laurel Lane GC	West Kingston	152	Orleans Country Club	Orleans	280
Meadow Brook GC	Richmond	154	Proctor Pittsford CC	Pittsford	281
Melody Hill Golf Course	Harmony	154	Prospect Bay CC	Bomoseen	281
Midville Country Club	West Warwick	155	Ralph Myhre GC	Middlebury	282
Montaup Country Club	Portsmouth	156	Richford Country Club	Richford	282
North Kingstown Muni.	Davisville	157	Rocky Ridge Golf Club	Burlington	283
Pocasset Country Club	Portsmouth	159	Rutland Country Club	Rutland	283
Pond View Golf Course	Westerly	159	Sitzmark Golf Course	Wilmington	284
Richmond Country Club	Hope Valley	160	St. Johnsbury CC	St. Johnsbury	284
Rolling Greens GC	N. Kingston	161	Stamford Valley CC	Stamford	285
Seaview Country Club	Warwick	162	Stonehedge GC	North Clarendon	285
Silver Spring Golf Club	E Providence	162	Stowe Country Club	Stowe	286
Triggs Memorial GC	Providence	165	Stratton Mt. (forest)	Stratton	286
Washington Village GC	Coventry	166	Stratton Mt. (lake)	Stratton	287
Weekapaug Golf Club	Westerly	34	Stratton Mt. (mountain)	Stratton	287
West Warwick Country Club	West Warwick	166	Sugarbush Golf Course	Warren	288
Winnapaug Golf Course	Westerly	167	Tater Hill Resort	Chester	288
Woodland Greens GC	N. Kingstown	167	Vermont National CC	S. Burlington	35
			West Bolton Golf Club	Jericho	289
Vermont			White River Golf Club	Rochester	289
Alburg Country Clubl	Alburg	265	Wilcox Cove GC	Grand Isle	290
Arrowhead Golf Course	Milton	265	Williston Golf Club	Williston	290
Bakersfield CC	Bakersfield	266	Windsor Country Club	Windsor	291
Barcomb Hill Resort	South Hero	37	Woodstock Inn & Resort	Woodstock	291
Barre Country Club	Barre	266			
Barton Golf Club	Barton	267			

NEW ENGLAND GOLFGUIDE

FYI

COURSE CATEGORIES
- *Open Year Round*
- *Walkable*
- *Architect Designed*
- *Websites*
- *Day Camps*
- *Par 27 to 33 / Executive*

Open Year Round Courses

The courses listed below are open "year round". This, of course means "weather permitting". Be sure to call ahead.

Course Name	Location/phone
Ballymeade CC	N. Falmouth, MA (508) 540-4005
Bay Pointe CC	Onset, MA (508) 759-8802, 1-800-24T-TIME
D.W. Fields Golf Course	Brockton, MA (508) 580-7855
Dennis Highlands	Dennis, MA (508) 385-8347
Falmouth Country Club	Falmouth, MA (508) 548-3211
Far Corner Golf Course	W. Boxford, MA (978) 352-8300
Glen Ellen CC	Rt.115, Millis, MA (508) 376-2775
Heather Hill CC	Plainville, MA (508) 695-0309
Heritage Hill CC	Lakeville, MA (508) 947-7743
Holly Ridge Golf Club	S. Sandwich, MA (508) 428-5577
Lakeville Country Club	Lakeville, MA (508) 947-6630
Little Harbor CC	Wareham, MA (508) 295-2617
Marion Golf Course	South Dr., Marion, MA (508) 748-0199
Middleton Golf Course	Middleton, MA (978) 774-4075
Newton Commonwealth GC	Chestnut Hill, MA (617) 630-1971
Northampton CC	Leeds, MA (413) 586-1898
Poquoy Brook GC	Lakeville, MA (508) 947-5261
Round Hill CC	E. Sandwich, MA (508) 888-3384
Saddle Hill CC	Hopkinton, MA (508) 435-4630
Stone-E-Lea Golf Course	Attleboro, MA (508) 222-9735
Strawberry Valley GC	Abington, MA (781) 871-5566
Swansea Country Club	Swansea, MA (508) 379-9886
The Woods of Westminster CC	Westminster, MA 978-874-0500
Touisset Country Club	Swansea, MA (508) 679-9577
Twin Brooks GC At Sheraton	Hyannis, MA (508) 775-7775
Wading River GC	Rt. 123, Norton, MA (508) 226-1788
Wampanoag Golf Club	N. Swansea, MA (508) 379-9832
Wayland Country Club	Wayland, MA (508) 358-4775
Woodbriar CC	Falmouth, MA (508) 495-5500
Windham Golf Club	1 Country Club Rd., Windham, NH, 603-434-2093
Meadow Brook GC	Richmond, RI (401) 539-8491
Pond View Golf Course	Shore Rd., Westerly, RI (401) 322-7870
Weekapaug Golf Club	Westerly, RI 401-322-7870
Winnapaug Golf Course	Westerly, RI (401) 596-1237
Alling Memorial GC	Eastern St., New Haven, CT (203) 946-8014
Cedar Knob GC	Billings Rd., Somers, CT (860) 749-3550
E. Gaynor Brennan GC	Stillwater Rd., Stamford, CT (203) 324-4185
Fairchild Wheeler GC	Bridgeport, CT (203) 373-5911
Goodwin Golf Course	Maple Ave., Hartford, CT (860) 956-3601
Hunter Golf Club	Meriden, CT (203) 634-3366
Keney Park Golf Club	Hartford, CT (860)525-3656
Meadowbrook CC	Hamden, CT (203) 281-4847
Shennecosset GC	Plant St., Groton, CT (860) 445-0262

Walkable Courses

These courses are comfortable and enjoyable for those of us who want the exercise. THE NEW ENGLAND GOLFGUIDE® supports the USGA Walking Program, initiated in 1998.

Course Name	Slope	Location/phone
MASSACHUSETTS		
Allendale Country Club	124	No. Dartmouth, MA 508-992-8682
Bay Path Golf Course	113	East Brookfield, MA (508) 867-8161
Brookmeadow CC	118	Canton, MA (781) 828-4444
Candlewood Golf Club	N/A	Rt. 133, Ipswich, MA (978) 356-5377
Cherry Hills GC	101	323 Montague Rd., N. Amherst (413) 256-4071
D.W. Fields Golf Course	116	Brockton, MA (508) 580-7855
Green Valley GC	110	Newburyport, MA (978) 463-8600
Harwich Port Golf Club	N/A	Harwich Port, MA (508) 432-0250
Heritage Country Club	113	Charlton, MA (508) 248-51111
Kelley Greens By The Sea	87	Nahant, MA (781) 581-0840
Lakeview Golf Club	91	Main St., Rt. 1A, Wenham, MA (978) 468-6676
Leicester Country Club	118	Leicester, MA (508) 892-1390
Leo J. Martin GC	120	Weston, MA (781) 894-4903
Locust Valley Golf Course	121	Attleboro, MA (508) 222-1500
New England CC	122	Bellingham, MA (508) 883-2300
Pakachoag Golf Course	119	Upland St., Auburn, MA (508) 755-3291
Pine Knoll Par 3	N/A	East Longmeadow, MA (413)525-8320
Pinecrest Golf Club	103	Holliston, MA (508) 429-9871
Pontoosuc Lake CC	116	Pittsfield, MA (413) 445-4217
Shaker Hills Golf Club	121	Harvard, MA (978) 772-2227
Southwick CC	102	Southwick, MA (413) 569-0136
Tekoa Country Club	116	Westfield, MA (413) 568-1064
The Meadows Golf Club	106	Greenfield, MA (413)773-9047
Tyngsboro CC	104	Tyngsboro, MA (978) 649-7334
Willowdale Golf Course	N/A	Mansfield, MA (508) 339-3197
MAINE		
Belgrade Lakes CC	123	Belgrade Lakes, ME. 207-495-GOLF
Biddeford & Saco CC	114	Old Orchard Rd., Saco, ME (207) 282-5883
Green Valley GC	112	Rt. 2, Lincoln, ME (207) 732-3006
Hampden CC	108	Hampden, ME (207) 862-9999
Lakeview Golf Club	114	Burnham, ME (207) 948-5414
Northport Golf Club	112	Belfast, ME (207) 338-2270
Pleasant Hill CC	87	Scarborough, ME (207) 883-4425
NEW HAMPSHIRE		
Beaver Meadow GC	121	Concord, NH (603) 228-8954
John H. Cain GC	127	Newport, NH (603) 863-7787
Kingston Fairways	113	E. Kingston, NH ((603)642-7722
Lakeview Golf Club	N/A	Ladd Hill Road, Belmont, NH 03220 (603-524-2220)
Pine Valley CC	119	Rt. 38, Pelham, NH (603) 635-7979
RHODE ISLAND		
Fairlawn Golf Course	N/A	Lincoln, RI (401) 334-3937
Goddard Park GC	N/A	Warwick, RI (401) 884-9834
Washington Village GC	N/A	Coventry, RI (401) 823-0010
VERMONT		
Stamford Valley CC	104	Rt. 9, Stamford, VT (802) 694-9144
Stonehedge GC	N/A	North Clarendon, VT (802) 773-2666
White River Golf Club	112	Rt. 100, Rochester, VT (802) 767-4653
CONNECTICUT		
Airways Golf Course	103	1070 S. Grand, Suffield, CT (860) 668-4973
Canaan Country Club	108	S. Canaan Rd., Canaan, CT (860) 824-7683
Chanticlair Golf Course	117	Colchester, CT (860) 537-3223
Grassmere CC	111	Enfield, CT (860) 749-7740
Hillside Links LLC	N/A	Deep River, CT (860)526-9986
Southington CC	113	Savage St., Southington, CT (860) 628-7032

Architect Designed Public Courses

The "designer courses" listed below are the most recent of the Mungeam, Silva and Cornish team. Also listed are the 30 courses classically designed by Donald Ross.

Course Name	Location/phone
Designer: Silva with Cornish and/or Mungeam	
Acushnet River Valley GC	Acushnet,MA (508)-998-7777
Atlantic Country Club	Plymouth, MA (508) 759-6644
Blissful Meadows GC	Uxbridge, MA (508) 278-6113
Captains GC, The	Brewster, MA (508) 896-5100
Cyprian Keyes (Mungeam)	Boylston, MA (508) 869-9900
Kings Way Golf Course	Yarmouthport, MA (508) 362-8820
Norton Country Club	Norton, MA (508) 285-2400
Ocean Edge GC	Brewster, MA (508) 896-5911
Olde Scotland Links	Bridgewater, MA (508) 279-3344
Owl's Nest (Cornish & Mungeam)	Campton, NH (603) 726-3076
Shaker Hills Golf Club	Harvard, MA (978) 772-2227
Waverly Oaks Golf Club	Plymouth,MA. 508-224-6016
Sable Oaks Golf Club	S. Portland, ME (207) 775-6257
Golf at Province Lake	Parsonfield,ME Route 153 (207) 793-9577
Passaconaway CC	Litchfield, NH (603) 424-4653
Perry Hollow Golf & CC	MiddletonRd., Wolfboro, NH (603) 569-3055
Plausawa Valley CC	Pembroke, NH (603) 228-8861
Shattuck GC, The	Jaffrey, NH (603) 532-4300
White Mountain CC	N. Ashland Rd., Ashland, NH (603) 536-2227
Richmond Country Club	Richmond, RI (401) 364-9200
Designer: Donald Ross	
Bass River Golf Course	So. Yarmouth, MA (508) 398-9079
Cape Cod CC	N. Falmouth, MA (508) 563-9842
Ellinwood CC	Athol, MA (978) 249-7460
George Wright GC	Hyde Park, MA (617) 361-8313
Greenock Country Club	W. Park St., Lee, MA (413) 243-3323
Merrimack Valley GC	Methuen, MA (978) 685-9717
Newton Commonwealth GC	Chestnut Hill, MA (617) 630-1971
Petersham CC	Petersham, MA (978) 724-3388
Plymouth Country Club	Plymouth, MA 508) 746-0476
Ponkapoag GC #1	Canton, MA (781) 575-1001
Ponkapoag GC #2	Canton, MA (781) 575-1001
Sandy Burr CC	Wayland, MA (508) 358-7211
The Orchards Golf Club	South Hadley, MA 413-534-3806
Wachusett CC	W. Boylston, MA (508) 835-2264
Winchendon CC	Winchendon, MA (978) 297-9897
Biddeford & Saco CC	Old Orchard Rd., Saco, ME (207) 282-5883
Lake Kezar CC	Lovell, ME (207) 925-2462
Penobscot Valley CC	Maine St., Orono, ME (207) 866-2423
Poland Spring CC	Rt. 26, Poland Spring, ME (207) 998-6002
Balsams Panorama GC, The	Dixville Notch, NH (603) 255-4961
Bethlehem CC	Bethlehem, NH (603) 869-5745
Carter Country Club	Lebanon, NH (603) 448-4483
Franklin Greens Golf & CC	Franklin, NH (603) 934-3033
Maplewood Casino & CC	Bethlehem, NH (603) 869-3335
Mt. Washington Hotel	Bretton Woods, NH (603) 278-4653
Tory Pines Resort	Rt. 47, Francestown, NH (603) 588-2923
Triggs Memorial GC	Providence, RI (401) 521-8460
Winnapaug Golf Course	Westerly, RI (401) 596-1237
Norwich Golf Course	Norwich, CT (860) 889-6973
Pequot Golf Club	Wheeler Rd., Stonington, CT (860) 535-1898
Shennecosset GC	Plant St., Groton, CT (860) 445-0262

Courses with Websites

Golf is on the "information highway". Below is a list of courses with websites. These websites give a lot of information about what you can expect before you arrive. The golf course URL addresses are highlighted in the appropriate golf course chapter.

MASSACHUSETTS
Atlantic Country Club
Ballymeade CC
Bass River Golf Course
Bayberry Hills GC
Blackstone National Golf Club
Blue Rock Golf Club
Chelmsford Country Club
Cranwell Resort and Golf Club
Crumpin-Fox Club
Egremont Country Club
Holly Ridge Golf Club
Hyannis Golf Club
Maplegate Country Club
Middleton Golf Course
Nabnasset Lake CC
Newton Commonwealth GC
Ocean Edge GC
Pine Ridge Country Club
Poquoy Brook GC
Shaker Hills Golf Club
South Shore CC
The Brookside Club
Widow's Walk Golf Course

MAINE
Bethel Inn & CC
Dunegrass Golf Club
Frye Island Golf Course
Maple Lane Inn and Golf Club
Nonesuch River Golf Club
Old Orchard Bch CC
Point Sebago Golf Club
Poland Spring CC
Salmon Falls GC
Samoset Resort GC
Sebasco Harbor Resort GC

NEW HAMPSHIRE
Atkinson Country Club
Balsams Panorama GC, The
Colebrook CC
Eagle Mountain House
Franklin Greens Golf & CC
Owl's Nest Golf Club
Woodbound Inn GC

RHODE ISLAND
Foxwoods Executive GC
 at Lindhbrook
Foxwoods Golf & CC At Boulder Hills

VERMONT
Blush Hill CC
Green Mountain National G. C.
Killington Golf Resort
Neshobe Golf Club
St. Johnsbury CC
Sugarbush Golf Course
Tater Hill Resort

CONNECTICUT
Blue Fox Run
Copper Hill CC
Elmridge Golf Course
Highland Greens GC
Lyman Orchards GC
Manchester CC
Millbrook Golf Course
Richter Park GC
Tallwood Country Club

Courses With Day Camps

The 62 courses listed below have day camps with extensive learning programs for various junior age groups. Some offer full day or half day instruction. Some have a week long program. Others, only 2 or 3 days.

Course Name	Location/phone
MASSACHUSETTS	
Beverly Golf & Tennis	Beverly, MA (978) 922-9072
Blue Rock Golf Club	S. Yarmouth, MA (508) 398-9295
Captains GC, The	Brewster, MA (508) 896-5100
Chelmsford Country Club	66 Park Rd., Chelmsford, MA (978) 256-1818
Crumpin-Fox Club	Bernardston, MA (413) 648-9101
D.W. Fields Golf Course	Brockton, MA (508) 580-7855
Dennis Highlands	Dennis, MA (508) 385-8347
Dennis Pines GC	Rt. 134, S. Dennis, MA (508) 385-8347
Egremont Country Club	Great Barrington, MA (413) 528-4222
Fresh Pond Golf Club	Cambridge, MA (617) 349-6282
Groton Country Club	Groton, MA (978) 448-2564
Indian Meadows Golf Club	Westboro, MA (508) 836-5460
Juniper Hill GC	Northboro, MA (508) 393-2444
Leo J. Martin GC	Weston, MA (781) 894-4903
Middleton Golf Course	Middleton, MA (978) 774-4075
Northampton CC	Leeds, MA 413-586-1898
Northfield CC	East Northfield, MA (413) 498-2432
Pine Oaks GC	S. Easton, MA (508) 238-2320
Ponkapoag GC	Canton, MA (781) 575-1001
Presidents Golf Course	Quincy, MA (617) 328-3444
Rockland CC	Rockland, MA (781) 878-5836
Rowley Country Club	Rowley, MA (978) 948-2731
Saddle Hill CC	Hopkinton, MA (508) 435-4630
South Shore CC	Hingham, MA (781) 749-8479
Stow Acres CC	Randall Rd., Stow, MA (978) 568-1100
Tekoa Country Club	Westfield, MA (413) 568-1064
The Woods of Westminster CC	Westminster, MA (978) 874-0500
Townsend Ridge CC	Townsend,MA. (978) 597-8400
Wayland Country Club	Wayland, MA (508) 358-4775
MAINE	
Bethel Inn & CC	Broad St., Bethel, ME (207) 824-6276
Fairlawn Golf Club	Poland , ME (207) 998-4277
Naples Golf and CC	Route 114, Naples, ME. (207) 693-6424
Penobscot Valley CC	Maine St., Orono, ME (207) 866-2423
Samoset Resort GC	Rockport, ME (207) 594-1431
Sugarloaf Golf Club	Bigelow, ME (207) 237-2000
Westerly Winds GC	Westbrook, ME (207) 854-9463

NEW HAMPSHIRE
Applewood Golf Links   Range Rd., Windham, NH (603) 898-6793
Candia Woods   Candia, NH (603) 483-2307
Golf at Province Lake   Parsonfield,ME Route 153 (207) 793-9577
John H. Cain GC   Newport, NH (603) 863-7787
Nippo Lake Golf Club   Barrington, NH (603) 664-7616
Owl's Nest Golf Club   Campton,NH (603) 726-3076
Stonebridge Country Club   Goffstown,NH (603) 497-T-OFF (8633)
Sunningdale GC   Somersworth, NH (603) 742-8056
Windham Golf Club   Windham, NH, (603) 434-2093

VERMONT
Blush Hill CC   Waterbury, VT (802) 244-8974
Ralph Myhre GC   Middlebury, VT (802) 443-5125
West Bolton Golf Club   West Bolton, Jericho, VT (802) 434-4321

CONNECTICUT
Blue Fox Run   Nod Rd., Avon, CT (860)678-1679
Copper Hill CC   E. Granby, CT (860) 653-6191
Fairchild Wheeler GC   Bridgeport, CT (203) 373-5911
Lyman Orchards GC   Middlefield, CT (860) 349-8055
Millbrook Golf Course   Windsor, CT (860) 688-2575
Shennecosset GC   Plant St., Groton, CT (860) 445-0262
Sterling Farms GC   Newfield Ave., Stamford, CT (203) 461-9090
Tallwood Country Club   Rt. 85, Hebron, CT (860) 646-1151
Woodstock Golf Course   S. Woodstock, CT (860) 928-4130

Par 27 to 33 / Executive Courses

Course Name	Yards	Location/phone
Par 27 to 33		
Berlin Country Club	2233	25 Carr Rd., Berlin, MA (978) 838-2733
Candlewood Golf Club	2108	Rt. 133, Ipswich, MA (978) 356-5377
Cotuit-Highground GC	1360	Cotuit, MA (508) 428-9863
Cyprian Keyes GC, Par 3	1260	Boylston, MA (508) 869-9900
Murphy's Garrison GC	1005	Haverhill, MA (978) 374-9380
Pine Acres Executive GC	1146	Bellingham, MA (508) 883-2443
Rolling Green GC	1500	911 Lowell St., Andover, MA (978) 475-4066
Stoneham Oaks	1125	Stoneham, MA (781) 438-7888
Stony Brook Golf Course	1190	Southboro, MA (508) 485-3151
Woodbriar CC	1410	Falmouth, MA (508) 495-5500
Great Cove Golf Course	1694	Jonesboro, ME (207) 434-7200
Loons Cove Golf Course	1115	Skowhegan, ME (207) 474-9550
Merriland Farm Par 3 Golf	838	Wells, ME (207) 646-0508
South Portland Muni.	2071	Wescott Rd., S. Portland, ME (207) 775-0005
Westerly Winds GC	806	Westbrook, ME (207) 854-9463
Woodland Terrace GC	1050	East Holden, ME (207) 989-3750
Applewood Golf Links	1367	Range Rd., Windham, NH (603) 898-6793
Duston Country Club	2109	Hopkinton, NH (603) 746-4234
Fore-U-Golf Center	1031	West Lebanon,NH (603) 98-9702
Hidden Valley R.V.& GP	1185	Derry, NH (603) 887-3767
Kona Mansion Inn	1170	Moultonboro, NH (603) 253-4900
Monadnock CC	1576	Peterborough, NH (603) 924-7769
Twin Lake Villa GC	1328	New London, NH (603) 526-6460
Bristol Golf Club	2273	Tupelo St., Bristol, RI (401) 253-9844
Washington Village GC	2525	Coventry, RI (401) 823-0010
Arrowhead Golf Course	1350	Milton,Vt. (802) 893-0234
Barcomb Hill Resort	1108	South Hero, VT (802) 372-4135 Winter: 372-5398
Bradford Golf Course	2052	Bradford, VT (802) 222-5207
Stonehedge GC	1107	North Clarendon, VT (802) 773-2666
Wilcox Cove GC	1732	Hgwy. 314, Grand Isle, VT (802) 372-8343
Buena Vista GC	1977	W. Hartford, CT (860) 521-7359
Gainfield Farms GC	1384	Southbury, CT (203) 262-1100
Highland Greens GC	1398	Prospect, CT (203) 758-4022
Hillside Links LLC	932	Deep River, CT (860) 526-9986
Miner Hills GC	1695	Middletown, CT (860) 635-0051
Short Beach Par 3 GC	1270	Stratford, CT (203) 381-2070
South Pine Creek Par 3 GC	1240	Fairfield, CT (203) 256-3173
The Orchards GC	1625	Milford,CT. (203) 877-8200
Twin Lakes GC	851	North Branford, CT (203) 488-8778
Villa Hills Golf Course	1158	Storrs,CT. (860) 429-6344
Woodstock Golf Course	2255	S. Woodstock, CT (860) 928-4130
Executive Courses (Par 54)		
Blue Rock Golf Club	2563	S. Yarmouth, MA (508) 398-9295
Heritage Hill CC	2575	Lakeville, MA (508) 947-7743
Holly Ridge Golf Club	2715	S. Sandwich, MA (508) 428-5577
Lost Brook Golf Club	3002	Norwood, MA (781) 769-2550
Middleton Golf Course	3000	Middleton, MA (978) 774-4075
Pine Knoll Par 3	1567	East Longmeadow, MA (413) 525-8320
Rockland CC	3014	Rockland, MA (781) 878-5836
Twin Brooks GC At Sheraton	2621	Hyannis, MA (508) 775-7775
Wading River GC	2421	Rt. 123, Norton, MA (508) 226-1788
Pine Ridge Golf Course	5147	W. River Rd., Waterville, ME (207) 873-0474
Hickory Pond Golf Course.	1238	Durham, NH (603) 659-7642
Highlands Links GC	2970	Plymouth, NH (603) 536-3452
Woodbound Inn GC	2104	Woodbound Rd., Jaffrey, NH (603) 532-8341
Fairlawn Golf Course	2534	Lincoln, RI (401) 334-3937
Foxwoods Executive GC	2869	Hope Valley, RI (401) 539-8700
Sitzmark Golf Course	2300	Rt. 100, Wilmington, VT (802) 464-3384
Birch Plain Golf Course	2670	High Rock Rd., Groton, CT (860) 445-9918
Cedar Ridge GC	3025	E. Lyme, CT (860) 691-4568

NEW ENGLAND GOLFGUIDE

Merchants/Service

DIRECTORY & COUPONS

NEW ENGLAND GOLFGUIDE   Merchants Coupons & Directory 353

Merchants/Service Directory

Boston Links Golf
　　150 Federal Street, Boston, MA, (617) 261-0824
　　116 Huntington Ave., Boston, MA, (617) 859-1800

CT Pro Golf Discount
　　437 Westport Ave., Norwalk, CT, (203) 846-4864

Dick's Sporting Goods
　　179 Pavillion Dr., Manchester, CT, (860) 648-2700
　　2985 Berlin Turnpike, Newington, CT, (860) 666-3877
　　1081 Riverdale St.,W. Springfield, MA, (413) 781-6155

Dr. Golf
　　199 N. Main St., Andover, MA, (978) 470-4999

Edwin Watts Golf
　　200 Webster Street, Hanover, MA, (781) 871-6961

Golf Crafters
　　15 Cambridge Street, Burlington, MA, (781) 221-0011

Golf Day
　CT　561 Post Road, Fairfield, CT, (203) 254-1448
　　　3135 Berlin Turnpike, Newington, CT, (860) 667-8434
　　　45 Salem Turnpike, Norwich, CT, (860) 887-8004
　　　550 Boston Post Road, Orange, CT, (203) 891-8899
　　　775 Main Street South, Southbury, CT, (203) 267-7900
　　　Tri-City Plaza, Vernon, CT, (860) 870-8388
　　　Westbrook Factory Stores, Westbrook, CT, (860) 399-8800
　　　2537 Albany Ave., West Hartford, CT (860) 236-7888
　MA　4 Johnson Street, Auburn, MA, (508) 721-0081.
　　　Merchants Park, 1 Harrison, Blvd., Avon, MA, (508) 586-6522
　　　106 Milk Street, Boston, MA, (617) 695-1971
　　　29 Andover Street, Route 114, Danvers, MA, (978) 750-4410
　　　56 Davis Straits, Route 28, Falmouth, MA, (508) 540-9200
　　　60 Worcester Road, Framingham, MA (508) 872-3364
　　　1513 Iyanough Road, Hyannis, MA (508) 362-9700
　　　439 Pittsfield Road, Lenox, MA (413) 496-9815
　　　193 Boston Post Road West, Marlborough, MA, (508) 460-1414
　　　337 State Road, North Dartmouth, MA, (508) 994-0600
　　　Shaw's Plaza, Route 44, Raynham, MA, (508) 828-1400
　　　135 American Legion Parkway, Revere, MA, (781) 284-4653
　　　35 Commerce Way, Seekonk, MA, (508) 336-3961
　　　The Range, 2250 Providence Hwy., Walpole, MA, (508) 668-4979
　　　1458 Riverdale Street, West Springfield, MA, (413) 737-1666
　　　1 Oak Street, Westboro, MA, (508) 870-0520
　　　87 Providence Highway, Westwood, MA, (781) 461-0750
　　　60 Winter Street, Weymouth, MA, (781) 331-2600
　　　425 Washington Street, Woburn, MA, (781) 932-3900
　ME　Crossroads Plaza, Bangor, ME, (207) 941-9889
　　　200 Lower Main Street, Freeport, ME, (207) 865-2202
　　　Dansk Square, Route 1, Kittery, ME, (207) 439-5546
　　　198 Maine Mall, South Portland, ME, (207) 871-9344

Golf Day cont'd.
- NH 100 Cahill Road, Manchester, NH, (603) 623-0009
  Somerset Plaza, Route IOIA, Nashua, NH, (603) 595-8711
  375 Amherst Street, Nashua, NH, (603) 888-7333
  1857 White Mt. Highway, North Conway, NH, (603) 474-5858
  125 South Broadway, Salem, NH, (603) 893-3383
  1 Batchelder Road, Seabrook, NH, (603) 474-5858
- RI 1000 Bald Hill Road, Warwick, RI, (401) 828-1402

Golf Express
219 Lexington Street, Waltham, MA, (781) 893 4177

Golf Masters
452 Great Road, Acton, MA, (978) 264-0090
@Airport Driving Range Route 1, N. Attleboro, MA, (508) 643-2229
184 Broadway, Saugus, MA, (781) 231-1600

Golf & Ski Warehouse
Route 33, Greenland, NH, (603) 433-8585
Route 12A, West Lebanon, NH, (603) 298-8282

Golf Unlimited
15 West Union St., Ashland, MA, (508) 881-4653

Golf USA
470 Franklin Village Drive, Franklin, MA (508) 520-0192

Golfers Warehouse
65 Albany Turnpike, Canton, CT, (860) 693-6286
216 Murphy Rd., Hartford, CT, (860) 522-4829
196 Boston Post Road, Orange, CT (203) 799-3606
60 Freeway Drive, Cranston, RI, (401) 467-8740

Grip & Rip-It Golfworks
20 Diamond Hill Ave., Boylston, MA, (508) 869-6855

Jonathan's Pro Shop
Indian Head, North Conway, NH, (603) 356-2217

Kaufman Discount Golf
140 Park Street, Palmer, MA, (413) 283-2422

Mulligan's
210 Commercial St.. Provincetown, MA, (508) 4874-653

MVP Sports
- MA Cross Roads Plaza at Rtes 126 & I-95, Bellingham, MA, (508) 966-0030
  Granite Street, Braintree, MA, (781) 356-7600
  Westgate Mall, Brockton, MA, (508) 583-1100
  43A Middlesex Turnpike, Burlington, MA, (781) 270-9200
  281 Chelmsford Street, Route 110, Chelmsford, MA, (978) 250-0500
  110 High Street, exit 23N off Rte. 128, Danvers, MA, (973) 774-7512
  1207 Washington Street, Hanover, MA, (781) 826-7500
  291 Mystic Avenue, Medford, MA, (781) 391-2900
  336 Worcester Road, Sherwood Plaza, Natick, MA, (508) 650-1400
  230 Needham Street, Exit 19A off Rte. 128, Newton, MA, (617) 965-2480
  333 Providence Highway, Rte. 1 South. Norwood, MA, (781) 255-0400
  Rte.1, Saugus Plaza, Saugus, MA, (781) 231-5100

MVP Sports cont'd.
- **ME** Shops at Clarks Pond, South Portland, ME, (207) 773-0700
- **NH** Bedford Mall, off Route 3, Bedford, NH, (603) 668-3500
  Westside Plaza, Exit 7W, off Rte. 3, Nashua, NH, (603) 831-7740
  The Crossings at Fox Run, Nashua NH, (603) 422-6400

Nevada Bob's WS
1050 Riverdale Street, W. Springfield, MA (413) 734 4444

N.E. Golf Supply
21 Tolland Turnpike, Manchester, CT, (860) 646-7454
3243 Berlin Turnpike, Newington, CT, (860) 666-8014
406 Queen Street, Rte. 10, Southington, CT, (860) 628-8544
587 Southbridge Street, Rte. 12, Auburn, MA, (508) 832-6686

On The Green Golf Shop
549 Bedford Street, Rte. 18, Whitman, MA, (781) 447-3649

On The Greene
200 Great Road, #8B, Bedford, MA, (781) 275-4747

Rick's Golf USA
Route 16 North Conway, NH, (603) 356-6680

SporTech
One Lynwood Lane, Westford, MA, (978) 692-6123

Stow Acres CC
58 Randall Rd. Stow, MA, (978) 568-1100

Sun n' Air Range
210 Conant Street, Danvers, MA, (978)774-8180

Tee Time Magazine
P.O.Box 225, Whitman, MA, (781) 447-2299

The Club Clinic
186 South Main Street, East Windsor, CT, (860) 627-0427

The Golf Club Factory
351 Turnpike, Rte. 138, Canton, MA, (781) 828-1688

The Golf Market
1019 Building, Route 132, Hyannis, MA, (508) 7714653

The Golf Store of Hadley
Route 9, Hadley, MA, (413) 584-0032

Wayland Golf
890 Commonwealth Avenue, Boston, MA, (617) 277-3999
54 Middlesex Turnpike, Burlington, MA, (781) 221-0030
Solomon Pond Mall, Marlborough, MA, (508) 303-8394
28 Highland Avenue, Needham, MA (781) 444-6686
North Shore Mall, Rtes 114 and 128. Peabody, MA, (978) 531-5155
121 Old Sudbury Rd, Wayland, MA, (508) 358-4775

Whirlaway Golf
500 Merrimack Street, Methuen, MA, (978) 688-8356

Yankee Golfworks
38R Merrimac St, Unit 101, Newburyport, MA, (978) 465-6416

PRO GOLF DISCOUNT

437 Wesport Avenue
Norwalk, CT
(860) 846-4864

NEW ENGLAND GOLFGUIDE

$5 OFF
any purchase of $25 or more
(Excluding golf balls and gloves)

Coupon valid through 1999. One coupon per customer. Not valid on prior sales. Not combinable with any other coupon or promotion.

DR. GOLF Custom Fit Clubs

199 N. Main Street,
Shawsheen Plaza
Andover, MA
(978) 470-4999

NEW ENGLAND GOLFGUIDE

10% off purchase of custom fit, custom made clubs
15% off any other purchase (except shoes)

Valid through 1999. One coupon per customer. Not valid on prior sales. Excludes sale items. Store sales only. Not combinable with any other coupon or promotion.

Edwin Watts GOLF SHOPS
PRO-LINE GOLF EQUIPMENT

200 Webster Street
Hanover, MA
(781) 871-0000

NEW ENGLAND GOLFGUIDE

$5 OFF
any purchase of $25 or more

Valid through 1999. One Coupon per customer. Not valid on prior sales. Excludes sale items. Store sales only. Not combinable with any other coupon or promotion.

GOLF DAY
Only The Best Names...

Call (888) 234-GOLF
for the store nearest you.

See complete store list in the Directory.

NEW ENGLAND GOLFGUIDE

$5 OFF Any Purchase $25 or more*

90027029

WITH THIS COMPLETED COUPON
COUPON NOT VALID ON PURCHASE OF GOLF OR TENNIS BALLS

Name _____
Address: _____
City: _____ State _____ Zip: _____

*Excludes Tax. Coupon valid through 12/31/99. One coupon per person per promotion. Sorry, no phone or mail sales. Originals only. Coupon cannot be combined with any other coupon or promotion. No discounts on purchase of gift certificates. No cash value.

Merchandise Coupons

Golf Express

219 Lexington Street
Waltham, MA 02154
(781) 893-4177

NEW ENGLAND GOLFGUIDE

10% OFF
any purchase

Valid through 1999. One coupon per customer. Not valid on proior sales. Not combinable with any other coupon or promotion.

Golf Masters Pro Shops

452 Great Rd.
Acton, MA
(978) 264-0090

N. Attleboro, MA
(508) 643-2229

Saugus, MA
(781) 231-1600

NEW ENGLAND GOLFGUIDE

10% off any purchase of $50 or more,
$50 off any set custom irons,
$25 off any custom wood
(Excludes Golf Balls)

Valid through 1999. One coupon per customer. Not valid on prior sales. Not combinable with any other coupon or promotion.

GOLF & SKI WAREHOUSE

Route 12A
West Lebanon, NH
(603) 298-8282

Route 33
Greenland, NH
(603) 433-8585

NEW ENGLAND GOLFGUIDE

$20 OFF
any purchase of $100 or more

Valid through 1999. One coupn per customer. Not valid on prior sales. Excludes sale items. Not combinable with any other coupon or promotion.

Golf Unlimited

15 West Union Street
Ashland, MA 01721
(508) 881-4653

NEW ENGLAND GOLFGUIDE

$10 OFF
any purchase of $50 or more
(Excludes golf balls)

Valid through 1999. One Coupon per customer. Not valid on prior sales. Excludes sale items. Store sales only. Not combinable with any other coupon or promotion.

Merchandise Coupons

GOLFERS WAREHOUSE

Call for nearest store
(860) 522-6829

NEW ENGLAND GOLFGUIDE

$5 off
any purchase of $25 or more
(Excludes Golf Balls)

Valid through 1999. One Coupon per customer. Not valid on prior sales. Excludes sale items. Store sales only. Not combinable with any other coupon or promotion.

Grip & Rip-It Golfworks

20 Diamond Hill Avenue
Boylston, MA
(508) 869-6855

NEW ENGLAND GOLFGUIDE

Purchase of any iron set #3 through Pitching Wedge and receive a sand or lob wedge free.

Valid through 1999. One Coupon per customer. Not valid on prior sales. Not combinable with any other coupon or promotion.

Jonathan's PRO GOLF

Indian Head
North Conway, NH
(603) 356-2217
www.whitemountainhotel.com

NEW ENGLAND GOLFGUIDE

$5 OFF
any pair of shoes or golf bag.

Valid through 1999. One coupon per customer. Not valid on prior sales. Exclude sales items. Store sales only. Not combinable with any other coupon or promotion.

Mulligan's By the Sea

210 Commercial Street
Provincetown, MA
(508) 487-4653
www.golfshoppe.com

NEW ENGLAND GOLFGUIDE

$20 OFF
any purchase of $100
or more

Valid through 1999. One Coupon per customer. Not combinable with any other coupon or promotion.

Merchandise Coupons

NEW ENGLAND GOLFGUIDE   Merchandise & Service Coupons

Nevada Bob's
Discount Golf and Tennis

1050 Riverdale Street
West Springfield, MA
(413) 734-4444

NEW ENGLAND GOLFGUIDE

$10 OFF
any purchase of $50 or more

Valid through 1999. One Coupon per customer. Not valid on prior sales. Excludes sales item. Store sales only. Not combinable with any other coupon or promotion.

---

on the greene
BEDFORD'S GOLF SHOP

200 Great Road #8B
Bedford, MA., 01730
(781) 275-4747

NEW ENGLAND GOLFGUIDE

10% OFF
any set of woods

Valid through 1999. Not combinable with any other coupon or promotion.

Ricks's GOLF USA

Rte. 16
North Conway, NH
603-356-6680
www.rick'sgolfusa.com

NEW ENGLAND GOLFGUIDE

$10 OFF
any purchase of
$50 or more

Valid through 1999. One Coupon per customer. Not valid on prior sales. Excludes sales item. Not combinable with any other coupon or promotion.

Stow Acres Country Club

58 Randall Road
Stow, MA 01775
978-568-1100

NEW ENGLAND GOLFGUIDE

$10 OFF
any purchase of $50 or more
Sale items and golf balls not included

Valid through 1999. One Coupon per customer. Not valid on prior sales. Store sales only. Not combinable with any other coupon or promotion.

SUN 'N AIR DRIVING RANGE

210 Conant Street
Danvers, MA
(978) 774-8180

NEW ENGLAND GOLFGUIDE

Free Club Fitting
By appointment only

Valid through 1999. One Coupon per customer. Not combinable with any other coupon or promotion.

TEE TIME
New England Women's Golf Magazine

P.O. Box 225
Whitman, MA.
www.teetime-mag.com

NEW ENGLAND GOLFGUIDE

Tee Time Magazine $9.95
5 issues for the price of 4

Valid through 1999. Not combinable with any other coupon or promotion.

Merchandise Coupons

The Golf Market

1019 Building, Route 132
Hyannis, MA
(508) 771-4653

NEW ENGLAND GOLFGUIDE

$5 OFF
any purchase of $25 or more

Valid through 1999. One coupon per customer. Not valid on prior sales. Not combinable with any other coupon or promotion

---

Whirlaway Golf

500 Merrimack Street
Methuen, MA
(978) 688-8356

NEW ENGLAND GOLFGUIDE

$10 OFF
any purchase of $50 or more
(Excludes All Golf Balls)

Valid through 1999. One coupon per customer. Not valid on prior sales. Excludes sale items. Not combinable with any other coupon or promotion. Golf merchandise only.

Yankee Golfworks
38 R Merrimac Street
Newburyport, MA
(978) 465-6416

NEW ENGLAND GOLFGUIDE

20% OFF
on set or irons or woods

Valid through 1999. One Coupon per customer. Not valid on prior sales. Not combinable with any other coupon or promotion.

GIFT OFFER

20% OFF

1999 Edition
NEW ENGLAND GOLFGUIDE®

Offer includes a gift card.

Valid by mail only from the publisher.

I would like___copies x $14.35 $_____
MA residents add 72 cents per/book for MA tax
$_____
Add $1.85 per book for postage: $ _____
Amount enclosed $ _____

Make check payable and mail to:
NEW ENGLAND GOLFGUIDE®,
366 River Rd., Carlisle, MA, 01741

Be sure to include your name, and the names and addresses to which the books are to be sent.

Not a store coupon, redeemable from publisher only. Not combinable with any other promotion.

Merchandise Coupons

NEW ENGLAND GOLFGUIDE   Merchandise & Service Coupons 367

NEW ENGLAND GOLFGUIDE

Driving Range Coupons

& DIRECTORY

Driving Range Directory

Range	Grass tee / Mat tee	Fees	
Airport Driving Range North Attleboro, MA 508-643-2229 Dean Goodman **Jr. Golf Program:** Yes **Open:** Year round	10 40	small med. $3.00	large $5 x large $10
Bill Pappas Golf School N. Chelmsford, MA 978-251-3933 Bill Pappas **Jr. Golf Program:** Yes **Open:** Nov.1 - Apr. 1	0 11	small med.	large x large
Country Club of Billerica Billerica, MA 978-667-8061 Barrie Bruce, PGA **Jr. Golf Program:** Yes **Open:** Seasonal	30 0	small med. $4.00	large $6.00 x large
East Coast Golf Academy & Practice Ctr. Northboro, Ma (508) 842-3311 Gary Day, PGA **Jr. Golf Program:** Yes **Open:** Year round	120 15	small med. $5.50	large x large $10.00
Fairway, The Marlboro, MA 508-624-9999 Jack Graham **Jr. Golf Program:** **Open:** April1-Oct.15	8 31	small $3.00 med. $5.00	large $7.00 x large
Family Golf Centers of Easton South Easton, MA (508) 238-6007 Jim Adams **Jr. Golf Program:** Yes **Open:** Year round	30 60	small $3.50 med. $6.00	large $8.00 x large
Glen Ellen CC Golf Range Millis, MA (508)376-2775 Harry E. Parker, III **Jr. Golf Program:** yes **Open:** Seasonal	20 No	small med.	large $4.00 x large
Golf Country Middleton, MA (978)774-4476 Dean Peters, Rick Collins **Jr. Golf Program:** Yes **Open:** Year round	25 50	small $3.00 med. $4.50	large $6.00 x large $9.00
Golf Town Driving Range Saugus, MA 781-233-4455 John Brennan **Jr. Golf Program:** Yes **Open:** Year round	0 52	small $4.00 med. $7.00	large $9.00 x large
Hackers Paradise Golf Range E. Bridgewater, MA (508) 378-3441 Dave Nash, PGA **Jr. Golf Program:** **Open:**	44 20	small $4.00 med.	large $7.00 x large
Kimball Farm Driving Range Westford, MA (978)486-4944 Jim Callahan , Larry Finnegan **Jr. Golf Program:** Yes **Open:** Seasonal	30 58	small $4.00 med.	large $6.00 x large
Lakeview Driving Range & Mini Golf Lunenburg, MA 978-345-7070 No **Jr. Golf Program:** Yes **Open:** Seasonal	12 18	small $2.50 med. $4.00	large $6.00 x large
Lancaster Golf Super Center Lancaster, MA (978)537-8922 James Carey, PGA **Jr. Golf Program:** Yes **Open:** Year round	80 80	small $4.25 med.	large $5.50 x large $10.00
River's Edge Hudson, MA 978-562-7079 To be announced **Jr. Golf Program:** No **Open:**	15 25	small $3.00 med. $4.00	large $5.00 x large
Sarkisian Farms Driving Range Andover, MA (978)688-5522 Billy Max,PGA **Jr. Golf Program:** **Open:** Seasonal	No 33	small $4.00 med.	large $6.00 x large $9.00
Sportech Indoor Golf Westford, MA 978-692-6123 Jim Callahan,PGA **Jr. Golf Program:** Yes **Open:** Year Round	9 2	small med. $5.00	large $10.00 x large

Range	Grass tee / Mat tee	Fees	
Star* Land Hanover, MA (781)826-3083 Charles Estes, PGA Jr. Golf Program: No Open: Year round	5 42	small $5.00 med.	large $8.00 x large
Sun 'n Air Driving Range Danvers, MA (978)774-8180 PGA Jr. Golf Program: Yes Open: Seasonal	No 40	small $3.75 med.	large $6.00 x large 9.00
Swingaway Danvers, MA 978-777-4774 John Theo, PGA Jr. Golf Program: Open: Year round	0 60	small $4.500 med. $6.00	large $9.00 x large
T-Time Family Sports Center, Inc. Eastham, MA 508-255-5697 Dave Cusack Jr. Golf Program: Open: Seasonal	10 35	small $4.00 med. $5.00	large $7.00 x large $8.00
The Golf Gym at Ironwood Woburn, MA (781)933-6657 TBA Jr. Golf Program: Yes Open: Year round	5	small med.	large $4.75 x large
The Range Walpole, MA 508-668-6674 Joe Catalano, PGA Jr. Golf Program: Yes Open: Year round	40	small $3.00 med.	large $6.00 x large $13.00
Whirlaway Golf Center & DR Methuen, MA (978)688-8356 Billy Lodge, PGA Jr. Golf Program: Yes Open: Year round	25 37	small $5.00 large $7.00 xlarge $9.00 $4.00 $600 $8.00	
College Street Driving Range Lewiston, ME (207)786-7818 Terry Russell Jr. Golf Program: Open: April-Oct.	20 25	small $3.00 med. $4.00	large $5.00 x large $7.00
Sonny's Driving Range & Training Winterport, ME (207)223-5242 Sonny Reynolds Jr. Golf Program: Open: Year round	18 18	small $3.50 med.	large $5.00 x large $11.00
Tee Shots Golf Center Wells, ME 207-646-2727 Tim Kilcone Jr. Golf Program: Yes Open: Seasonal	0 20	small $3.00 med.	large $5.00 x large $7.00
Candia Woods Golf Links Candia, NH 603-483-2307 Geoff Williams, PGA Jr. Golf Program: Yes Open: Seasonal	25 0	small med.	large $5.00 x large
FORE-U-GOLF West Lebanon, NH 603-298-9702 Brian Botha,USGTF,Cory Mansfield, LPGA, Jr. Golf Program: Yes Open: Seasonal	10 45	small $4.00 med. $5.00	large $7.00 x large
Legends Golf & Family Recreation Hooksett, NH (603) 627-0099 Jozef Maston, PGA Jr. Golf Program: Yes Open: Seasonal	35 42	small med. $5.50	large $7.00 x large
Mammoth Green Driving Range Amherst, NH 603-882-7583 Glenn Keating Jr. Golf Program: No Open: Seasonal	5 22	small $3.50 med.	large $5.00 x large
The Golfers' Club and Learning Center Litchfield, NH (603)424-3200 Ray Kelm Jr. Golf Program: Yes Open: Seasonal	12 22	small $4.00 med. $5.50	large $7.00 x large
Belmont's Ridgefield Golf Range Ridgefield, CT (203)431-8989 Peter Belmont, PGA Jr. Golf Program: Yes Open: Year round	4 24	small $4.00 med.	large $7.00 x large

NEW ENGLAND GOLFGUIDE   **Driving Range Directory 371**

Range	Grass tee / Mat tee	fees	
Caddy Shack Oxford, CT 203-888-4531 John L. Radovich **Jr. Golf Program:** Yes **Open:** Seasonal	4 / 24	small $4.00 med. $5.00	large $7.00 x large
East Lyme Driving Range East Lyme, CT (203)739-1183 Matt Boland, Golf Professional **Jr. Golf Program:** yes **Open:** Seasonal	40 / N/A	small $3.75 med. $4.75	large $5.75 x large
Glastonbury Golf Practice Center Glastonbury, CT (860) 659-0334 Hal Carlson, USGTF **Jr. Golf Program:** Yes **Open:** Seasonal	0 / 28	small $3.50 med. $5.00	large $7.50 x large
Golf Quest Family Sports Centers Brookfield, CT 203-775-3556 Zane Chappy, PGA **Jr. Golf Program:** Yes **Open:** Year round	0 / 72	small $4.00 med. $8	large $10.00 x large
Golf Quest Family Sports Centers Southington, CT 860-621-3663 Zane Chappy, PGA **Jr. Golf Program:** Yes **Open:** Year round	0 / 72	small $4.00 med. $8.00	large $10.00 x large
Great Golf Learning Center Farmington, CT 860-676-0151 Peter Hart **Jr. Golf Program:** Yes **Open:** Year round	0 / 9	small med.	large $5.00 x large
Highland Ridge Golf Range LLC Mansfield, CT 860-423-9494 **Jr. Golf Program:** Yes **Open:** Seasonal	20 / 20	small $3.00 med. $5.00	large $7.5 x large $10.00
Iron City Golf Center East Windsor,, CT 860-654-1561 Joe McGlocklin, Chris Chartrand, Sean Rahilly, PGA **Jr. Golf Program:** Yes **Open:** Year round	20 / 25	small $4.00 med. $5.00	large $6.00 x large $8.00
Pleasant View Golf Center Somers, CT 860-749-5868 Joe McLaughlan, PGA **Jr. Golf Program:** Yes **Open:** Year round	20 / 10	small $3.00 med. 5	large $6.00 x large $10.00
Pleasant View Golf Park Enfield, CT 860-763-4202 Geoffrey Lyons, PGA **Jr. Golf Program:** Yes **Open:** Seasonal	40 / 10	small $3.00 med. $5.00	large $6.00 x large $10.00
Prospect Golf Driving Range Prospect, CT (203)758-4121 Jeffrey DelRosso, PGA **Jr. Golf Program:** **Open:** Year round	10 / 35	small $4.00 med. $5.00	large $7.00 x large
The Only Game In Town North Haven, CT 203-239-GOLF Lawrence D. North **Jr. Golf Program:** Yes **Open:** Seasonal	5 / 35	small 2 med. 4	large $6.00 x large 10.75
Toll Gate Golf Range Litchfield, CT 860-567-2110 John Callahan, PGA **Jr. Golf Program:** **Open:** Year round	10 / 21	small $4.00 med. $7.00	large $10.00 x large
Torza's Golf Center So. Windsor, CT (860)289-5646 John Shea **Jr. Golf Program:** **Open:** Year round	60 / 13	small $3.5 med. $4.75	large $6.25 x large $12.00
Tricon Golf Complex Middletown, CT 860-346-4653 No **Jr. Golf Program:** Yes **Open:** Seasonal	20 plannned / 18	small med. $4.00	large x large $6.00
Wedge Wood Golf Driving Range Windsor, CT 860-683-1821	30 / 8	small $3.00 med. $5.00	large $6.00 x large

NEW ENGLAND GOLFGUIDE

Airport Driving Range
582 Kelley Boulevard
North Attleboro, MA (508) 643-2229

- TYPE OF DISCOUNT
  Get 2 buckets of ball for the price of 1
- DAYS OF THE WEEK
  7 days a week
- HOURS OF THE DAY
  All day

Coupon expires 12/99 Can not be combined with any other offer.

NEW ENGLAND GOLFGUIDE

Bill Pappas Golf School
55 Middlesex Street
N. Chelmsford, MA (978) 251-3933

- TYPE OF DISCOUNT
  One half hour for free. (A $6 value)
- DAYS OF THE WEEK
  Weekdays only (except Holidays)
- HOURS OF THE DAY
  All Day

Coupon expires 12/99 Can not be combined with any other offer.

NEW ENGLAND GOLFGUIDE

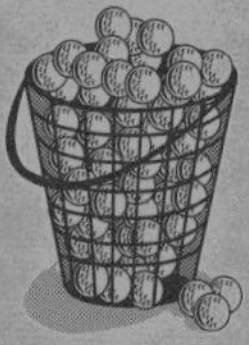

Country Club of Billerica
52 Baldwin Road
Billerica, MA (978) 667-8061

- TYPE OF DISCOUNT
  Get 2 buckets of ball for the price of 1
- DAYS OF THE WEEK
  7 days a week
- HOURS OF THE DAY
  All day

Coupon expires 12/99 Can not be combined with any other offer.

NEW ENGLAND GOLFGUIDE

East Coast Golf Academy & Practice Center
333 Southwest Cutoff
Northboro, Ma (508) 842-3311

- TYPE OF DISCOUNT
  Get 2 buckets of ball for the price of 1
- DAYS OF THE WEEK
  7 days a week
- HOURS OF THE DAY
  All Day

Coupon expires 12/99 Can not be combined with any other offer.

NEW ENGLAND GOLFGUIDE

Fairway, The
400 Hudson Street
Marlboro, MA (508) 624-9999

- TYPE OF DISCOUNT
  Buy one medium or large bucket. Get one bucket of same size free.
- DAYS OF THE WEEK
  7 days a week
- HOURS OF THE DAY
  10 am to 10 pm

Coupon expires 12/99 Can not be combined with any other offer.

NEW ENGLAND GOLFGUIDE

Glen Ellen CC Golf Range
84 Orchard Street
Millis, MA (508) 376-2775

- TYPE OF DISCOUNT
  3 buckets for the price of 2.
- DAYS OF THE WEEK
  Monday -Friday.
- HOURS OF THE DAY
  All day

Coupon expires 12/99 Can not be combined with any other offer.

NEW ENGLAND GOLFGUIDE

Golf Country
Route 114
Middleton, MA (978) 774-4476

- TYPE OF DISCOUNT
  2 large buckets for the price of 1.
- DAYS OF THE WEEK
  7 days a week
- HOURS OF THE DAY
  All Day

Coupon expires 12/99 Can not be combined with any other offer.

NEW ENGLAND GOLFGUIDE

Golf Town Driving Range
Route 1 North
Saugus, MA (781) 233-4455

- TYPE OF DISCOUNT
  Buy 1 large, get 1 small bucket of balls free
- DAYS OF THE WEEK
  7 days a week
- HOURS OF THE DAY
  All day

Coupon expires 12/99 Can not be combined with any other offer.

Driving Range Coupons

NEW ENGLAND GOLFGUIDE

Hackers Paradise Golf Range
798 N. Bedford St.
E. Bridgewater, MA (508) 378-3441

- TYPE OF DISCOUNT
  $1.00 off large bucket of balls.
- DAYS OF THE WEEK
  7 days a week
- HOURS OF THE DAY
  All Day

Coupon expires 12/99 Can not be combined with any other offer.

NEW ENGLAND GOLFGUIDE

Kimball Farm Driving Range
400 Littleton Road
Westford, MA (978) 486-4944

- TYPE OF DISCOUNT
  Get 2 buckets of ball for the price of 1
- DAYS OF THE WEEK
  7 days a week
- HOURS OF THE DAY

Coupon expires 12/99 Can not be combined with any other offer.

NEW ENGLAND GOLFGUIDE

Lakeview Driving Range & Mini Golf
Whalom Road
Lunenburg, MA (978) 345-7070

- TYPE OF DISCOUNT
  $1.00 off any medium or large bucket
- DAYS OF THE WEEK
  Weekdays only (except Holidays)
- HOURS OF THE DAY
  All day

Coupon expires 12/99 Can not be combined with any other offer.

NEW ENGLAND GOLFGUIDE

Lancaster Golf Super Center
Exit 34 on Route 2
Lancaster, MA (978) 537-8922

- TYPE OF DISCOUNT
  Two for one on "stick golf" pitching course (9 holes)
- DAYS OF THE WEEK
  Weekdays only (except Holidays)
- HOURS OF THE DAY
  All day

Coupon expires 12/99 Can not be combined with any other offer.

NEW ENGLAND GOLFGUIDE

River's Edge
18 Wellington Drive
Hudson, MA (978) 562-7079

- TYPE OF DISCOUNT
  Buy one small bucket, get one small bucket of balls free
- DAYS OF THE WEEK
  7 days a week
- HOURS OF THE DAY
  All day

Coupon expires 12/99 Can not be combined with any other offer.

NEW ENGLAND GOLFGUIDE

Sarkisian Farms Driving Range
159 Chandler Rd.
Andover, MA (978) 688-5522

- TYPE OF DISCOUNT
  $1.00 off any size bucket
- DAYS OF THE WEEK
  7 days a week
- HOURS OF THE DAY
  All day

Coupon expires 12/99 Can not be combined with any other offer.

NEW ENGLAND GOLFGUIDE

Sportech Indoor Golf
One Lynwood Lane
Westford, MA (978) 692-6123

- TYPE OF DISCOUNT
  $10.00 off one hour lesson
- DAYS OF THE WEEK
  7 days a week
- HOURS OF THE DAY
  All Day

Coupon expires 12/99 Can not be combined with any other offer.

NEW ENGLAND GOLFGUIDE

Star* Land
Route 53
Hanover, MA (781) 826-3083

- TYPE OF DISCOUNT
  Get 2 Regular buckets of balls for the price of 1
- DAYS OF THE WEEK
  7 days a week
- HOURS OF THE DAY
  All day

Coupon expires 12/99 Can not be combined with any other offer.

Driving Range Coupons

NEW ENGLAND GOLFGUIDE

Sun 'n Air Driving Range
210 Conant Street
Danvers, MA (978)774-8180

- TYPE OF DISCOUNT
  Buy 1 bucket and receive the same size bucket free.
- DAYS OF THE WEEK
  7 days a week
- HOURS OF THE DAY
  Call ahead for times

Coupon expires 12/99 Can not be combined with any other offer.

NEW ENGLAND GOLFGUIDE

Swingaway
180 Newbery Turnpike
Danvers, MA (978) 777-4774

- TYPE OF DISCOUNT
  Buy one bucket of balls and receive the same size bucket free
- DAYS OF THE WEEK
  7 days a week
- HOURS OF THE DAY
  All day

Coupon expires 12/99 Can not be combined with any other offer.

NEW ENGLAND GOLFGUIDE

T-Time Family Sports Center, Inc.
Route 6, North Eastham
Eastham, MA (508) 255-5697

- TYPE OF DISCOUNT
  Get 2 buckets of ball for the price of 1
- DAYS OF THE WEEK
  7 days a week
- HOURS OF THE DAY
  All day

Coupon expires 12/99 Can not be combined with any other offer.

NEW ENGLAND GOLFGUIDE

The Golf Gym at Ironwood
115 Cummings Park
Woburn, MA (781) 933-6657

- TYPE OF DISCOUNT
  $3.00 off for 18 holes of golf. $1.00 for 9 holes.
- DAYS OF THE WEEK
  Weekdays only (except Holidays)
- HOURS OF THE DAY
  9 am to 5 pm- 1 coupon per person, per group.

Coupon expires 12/99 Can not be combined with any other offer.

Driving Range Coupons

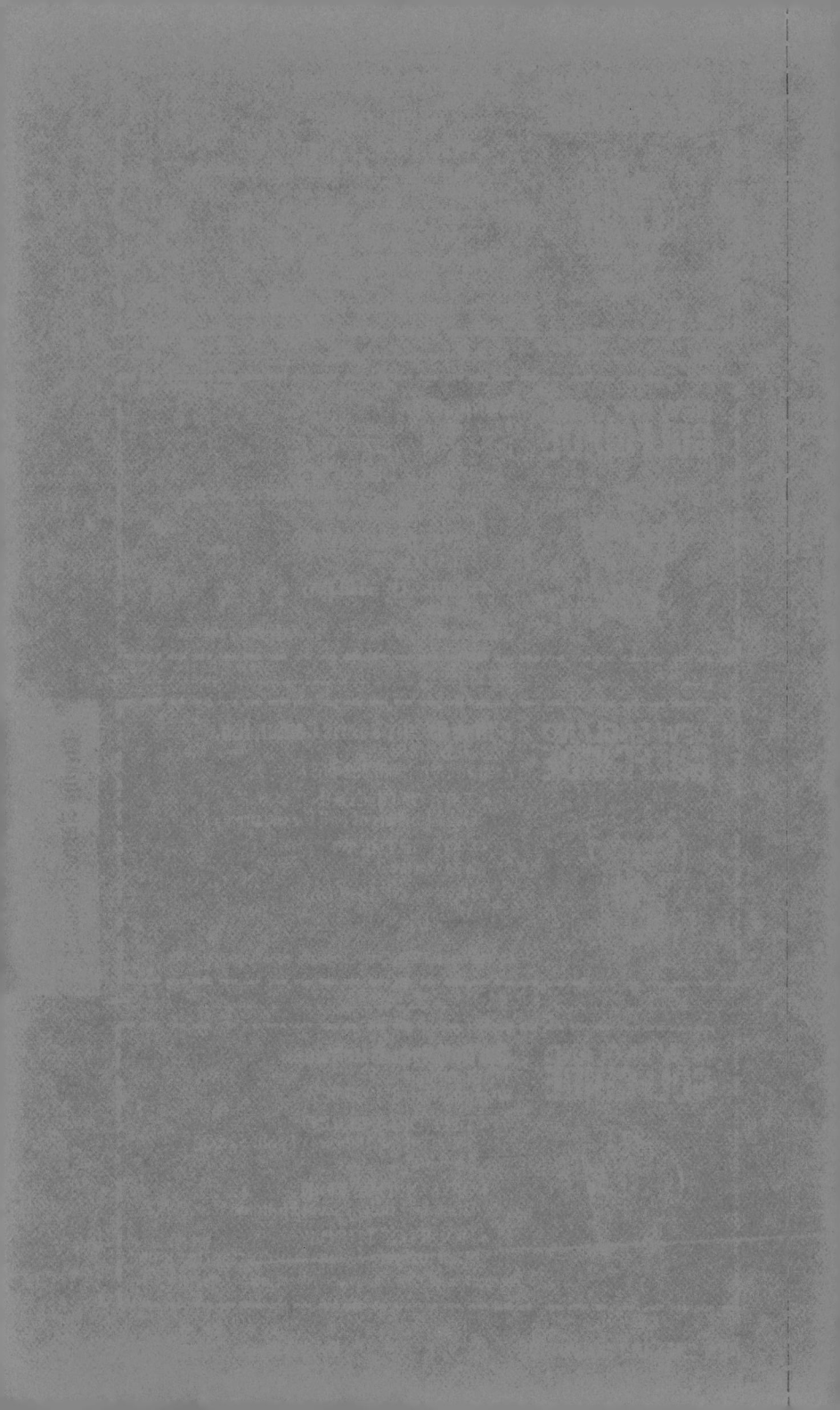

NEW ENGLAND GOLFGUIDE

The Range
2250 Providence Highway
Walpole, MA 508-668-6674

- TYPE OF DISCOUNT
  1 small bucket of balls free
- DAYS OF THE WEEK
  7 days a week
- HOURS OF THE DAY
  6 am-3 pm

Coupon expires 12/99 Can not be combined with any other offer.

NEW ENGLAND GOLFGUIDE

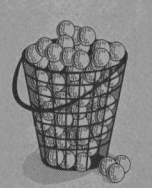

Whirlaway Golf Center & DR
500 Merrimack Street
Metheun, MA (978) 688-8356

- TYPE OF DISCOUNT
  Buy 1 large bucket, get 1 small bucket free
- DAYS OF THE WEEK
  Weekdays only (except Holidays),
  Mats only.
- HOURS OF THE DAY
  All day, outdoor driving range open all year

Coupon expires 12/99 Can not be combined with any other offer.

NEW ENGLAND GOLFGUIDE

Whirlaway Golf Center & DR
500 Merrimack Street
Methuen, MA (978) 688-8356

- TYPE OF DISCOUNT
  Buy 1/2 hour of indoor golf, get second 1/2 free.
- DAYS OF THE WEEK
  7 days a week
- HOURS OF THE DAY
  All day, indoor driving range open all year.

Coupon expires 12/99 Can not be combined with any other offer.

NEW ENGLAND GOLFGUIDE

College Street Driving Range
601 College Street
Lewiston, ME (207) 786-7818

- TYPE OF DISCOUNT
  $1.00 off any size bucket
- DAYS OF THE WEEK
  7 days a week
- HOURS OF THE DAY
  9 am to 9 pm

Coupon expires 12/99 Can not be combined with any other offer.

Driving Range Coupons

NEW ENGLAND GOLFGUIDE

Sonny's Driving Range & Training
108 Cove Road
Winterport, ME (207) 223-5242

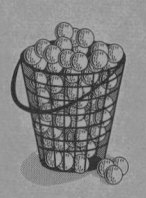

- TYPE OF DISCOUNT
  2 large buckets of balls for the price of 1
- DAYS OF THE WEEK
  Tues-Fri. noon -10 pm, Sat. -Sun. 10 am -10 pm
- HOURS OF THE DAY
  Tu thru Fri, noon -10 pm, Sa-Sun, 10-10 pm

Coupon expires 12/99 Can not be combined with any other offer.

NEW ENGLAND GOLFGUIDE

Tee Shots Golf Center
1126 North Berwick Road
Wells, ME 207-646-2727

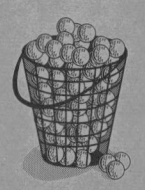

- TYPE OF DISCOUNT
  1 small bucket of balls free
- DAYS OF THE WEEK
  7 days a week
- HOURS OF THE DAY
  All Day

Coupon expires 12/99 Can not be combined with any other offer.

NEW ENGLAND GOLFGUIDE

Candia Woods Golf Links
313 South Road
Candia, NH 603-483-2307

- TYPE OF DISCOUNT
  Get 2 buckets of ball for the price of 1
- DAYS OF THE WEEK
  Weekdays only (except Holidays)
- HOURS OF THE DAY
  All day

Coupon expires 12/99 Can not be combined with any other offer.

NEW ENGLAND GOLFGUIDE

FORE-U-GOLF
298 Plainfield Rd.
West Lebanon, NH (603) 298-9702

- TYPE OF DISCOUNT
  Two medium buckets for the price of one.
- DAYS OF THE WEEK
  7 days a week
- HOURS OF THE DAY
  All day

Coupon expires 12/99 Can not be combined with any other offer.

Driving Range Coupons

NEW ENGLAND GOLFGUIDE

Legends Golf & Family Recreation
18 Legends Drive
Hooksett, NH (603) 627-0099

- TYPE OF DISCOUNT
  Get 2 buckets of ball for the price of 1
- DAYS OF THE WEEK
  7 days a week
- HOURS OF THE DAY
  All day

Coupon expires 12/99 Can not be combined with any other offer.

NEW ENGLAND GOLFGUIDE

Mammoth Green Driving Range
Route 101A
Amherst, NH (603) 882-7583

- TYPE OF DISCOUNT
  $1.00 off Lg. bucket or mini golf.
- DAYS OF THE WEEK
  7 days a week
- HOURS OF THE DAY
  All day

Coupon expires 12/99 Can not be combined with any other offer.

NEW ENGLAND GOLFGUIDE

The Golfers' Club and Learning Center
454 Charles Bancroft Hwy.
Litchfield, NH (603) 424-3200

- TYPE OF DISCOUNT
  Get 2 buckets of ball for the price of 1
- DAYS OF THE WEEK
  7 days a week
- HOURS OF THE DAY
  All day

Coupon expires 12/99 Can not be combined with any other offer.

NEW ENGLAND GOLFGUIDE

Belmont's Ridgefield Golf Range
824 Ethan Allen Highway
Ridgefield, CT (203) 431-8989

- TYPE OF DISCOUNT
  One small bucket of balls free.
- DAYS OF THE WEEK
  7 days a week
- HOURS OF THE DAY
  All Day

Coupon expires 12/99 Can not be combined with any other offer.

NEW ENGLAND GOLFGUIDE

Caddy Shack
2 West Street
Oxford, CT 203-888-4531

- TYPE OF DISCOUNT
  10% Off for Seniors and Juniors
- DAYS OF THE WEEK
  Weekdays only (except Holidays)
- HOURS OF THE DAY
  All day

Coupon expires 12/99 Can not be combined with any other offer.

NEW ENGLAND GOLFGUIDE

East Lyme Driving Range
298 Flanders Road
East Lyme, CT (203)739-1183

- TYPE OF DISCOUNT
  Get 2 buckets of ball for the price of 1
- DAYS OF THE WEEK
  7 days a week
- HOURS OF THE DAY
  All day

Coupon expires 12/99 Can not be combined with any other offer.

NEW ENGLAND GOLFGUIDE

Glastonbury Golf Practice Center
1029 Hebron Avenue
Glastonbury, CT (860) 659-0334

- TYPE OF DISCOUNT
  $1.00 off large bucket
- DAYS OF THE WEEK
  7 days a week
- HOURS OF THE DAY

Coupon expires 12/99 Can not be combined with any other offer.

NEW ENGLAND GOLFGUIDE

Golf Quest Family Sports Centers
1 Sand Cut Road
Brookfield, CT 203-775-3556

- TYPE OF DISCOUNT
  Get 2 buckets of ball for the price of 1
- DAYS OF THE WEEK
  7 days a week
- HOURS OF THE DAY
  All day, May to October

Coupon expires 12/99 Can not be combined with any other offer.

NEW ENGLAND GOLFGUIDE

Golf Quest Family Sports Centers
125 Jude Road
Southington, CT (860) 621-3663

- TYPE OF DISCOUNT
  Get 2 buckets of ball for the price of 1
- DAYS OF THE WEEK
  7 days a week
- HOURS OF THE DAY
  All day

Coupon expires 12/99 Can not be combined with any other offer.

NEW ENGLAND GOLFGUIDE

Great Golf Learning Center
10 Eastview Drive
Farmington, CT (860) 676-0151

- TYPE OF DISCOUNT
  1 small bucket of balls free
- DAYS OF THE WEEK
  Weekdays only (except Holidays)
- HOURS OF THE DAY
  10am -5pm

Coupon expires 12/99 Can not be combined with any other offer.

NEW ENGLAND GOLFGUIDE

Highland Ridge Golf Range LLC
164 Stafford Road
Mansfield, CT (860) 423-9494

- TYPE OF DISCOUNT
  $1.00 off any size
- DAYS OF THE WEEK
  7 days a week
- HOURS OF THE DAY
  All day

Coupon expires 12/99 Can not be combined with any other offer.

NEW ENGLAND GOLFGUIDE

Iron City Golf Center
20 North Road
East Windsor, CT (860) 654-1561

- TYPE OF DISCOUNT
  Buy one medium bucket, get one free.
- DAYS OF THE WEEK
  7 days a week
- HOURS OF THE DAY
  All Day

Coupon expires 12/99 Can not be combined with any other offer.

Driving Range Coupons

NEW ENGLAND GOLFGUIDE

Pleasant View Golf Center
Route 83 and South Road
Somers, CT (860) 749-5868

- TYPE OF DISCOUNT
  1 small bucket of balls free
- DAYS OF THE WEEK
  7 days a week
- HOURS OF THE DAY
  All day

Coupon expires 12/99 Can not be combined with any other offer.

NEW ENGLAND GOLFGUIDE

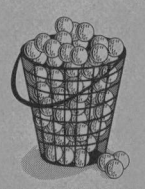

Pleasant View Golf Park
110 North Street
Enfield, CT (860) 763-4202

- TYPE OF DISCOUNT
  1 small bucket of balls free
- DAYS OF THE WEEK
  7 days a week
- HOURS OF THE DAY
  All day

Coupon expires 12/99 Can not be combined with any other offer.

NEW ENGLAND GOLFGUIDE

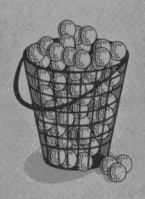

Prospect Golf Driving Range
144 Waterbury Prospect Road
Prospect, CT (203) 758-4121

- TYPE OF DISCOUNT
  20% off any lesson package
- DAYS OF THE WEEK
  7 days a week
- HOURS OF THE DAY
  9 am to 10 pm

Coupon expires 12/99 Can not be combined with any other offer.

NEW ENGLAND GOLFGUIDE

The Only Game In Town
275 Valley Service Road - North Haven, CT
(203) 239-GOLF

- TYPE OF DISCOUNT
  Buy one round of 9 or 18 holes min golf, get one round free.
- DAYS OF THE WEEK
  7 days a week, valid until mid- October, 1999
- HOURS OF THE DAY
  All day, one coupon per person.

Coupon expires 12/99 Can not be combined with any other offer.

Driving Range Coupons

NEW ENGLAND GOLFGUIDE

Toll Gate Golf Range
500 Torrington Road
Litchfield, CT 860-567-2110

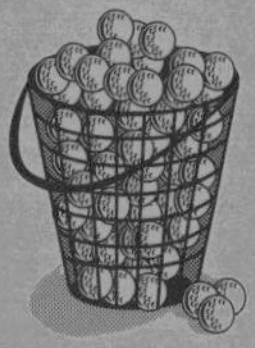

- TYPE OF DISCOUNT
  1 small bucket of balls free
- DAYS OF THE WEEK
  7 days a week
- HOURS OF THE DAY
  All day

Coupon expires 12/99 Can not be combined with any other offer.

NEW ENGLAND GOLFGUIDE

Torza's Golf Center
211 Sullivan Ave.
So. Windsor, CT (860)289-5646

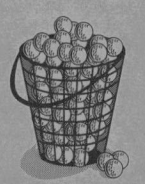

- TYPE OF DISCOUNT
  Get 2 buckets of ball for the price of 1
- DAYS OF THE WEEK
  7 days a week
- HOURS OF THE DAY
  All day

Coupon expires 12/99 Can not be combined with any other offer.

NEW ENGLAND GOLFGUIDE

Tricon Golf Complex
2015 South Main Street
Middletown, CT (860) 346-4653

- TYPE OF DISCOUNT
  New customers-buy one token, get one free
- DAYS OF THE WEEK
  7 days a week
- HOURS OF THE DAY
  All day

Coupon expires 12/99 Can not be combined with any other offer.

NEW ENGLAND GOLFGUIDE

Wedge Wood Golf Driving Range
79 Lamberton Road
Windsor, CT (860) 683-1821

- TYPE OF DISCOUNT
  1 small bucket of balls free
- DAYS OF THE WEEK
  7 days a week
- HOURS OF THE DAY
  All day

Coupon expires 12/99 Can not be combined with any other offer.

NEW ENGLAND GOLFGUIDE

Golf Course Coupons

& DIRECTORY

Golf Course Coupon Directory

Massachusetts

Atlantic Country Club	Plymouth	401
Ballymeade CC	North Falmouth	401
Bas Ridge Golf Course	Hinsdale	401
Bay Pointe CC	Onset	401
Beaver Brook CC	Haydenville	403
Bedrock Golf Club	Rutland	403
Blissful Meadows GC	Uxbridge	403
Bradford Country Club	Bradford	403
Cape Cod CC	North Falmouth	405
CC of Billerica	Billerica	405
Chatham Seaside Links	Chatham	405
Chelmsford Country Club	Chelmsford	405
Clearview Golf Course	Millbury	407
Colonial Golf Club	Wakefield	407
Country Club of Greenfield	Greenfield	407
Cranwell Resort & GC	Lenox	407
Crumpin-Fox Club	Bernardston	409
Cyprian Keyes GC & Par 3	Boylston	409
Edge Hill GC	Ashfield	409
Egremont Country Club	Great Barrington	409
Ellinwood CC	Athol	411
Far Corner Golf Course	West Boxford	411
Forest Park CC	Adams	411
Glen Ellen CC	Millis	411
Green Valley GC	Newburyport	413
Groton Country Club	Groton	413
Hampden Country Club	Hampden	413
Heritage Country Club	Charlton	413
Hillcrest Country Club	Leicester	415
Hillside CC	Rehoboth	415
Hillview Golf Course	North Reading	415
Hyannis Golf Club	Hyannis	415
Kelley Greens By The Sea	Nahant	417
Lakeview Golf Club	Wenham	417
Little Harbor CC	Wareham	417
Maplegate Country Club	Bellingham	417
Newton Commonwealth GC	Newton	419
North Hill CC	Duxbury	419
Northampton CC	Leeds	419
Norwood Country Club	Norwood	419
Oak Ridge Golf Club	Gill	421
Oak Ridge Golf Club	Feeding Hills	421
Ocean Edge GC	Brewster	421
Olde Scotland Links	Bridgwater	421
Pine Knoll Par 3	E. Longmeadow	423
Pontoosuc Lake CC	Pittsfield	423
Poquoy Brook GC	Lakeville	423
Quail Hollow Golf & CC	Oakham	423
Quashnet Valley CC	Mashpee	425
Round Hill CC	East Sandwich	425
Skyline Country Club	Lanesborough	425
Stoneham Oaks	Stoneham	425
Sun Valley CC	Rehoboth	427
Swansea Country Club	Swansea	427
The Woods of Westminster CC	Westminster	427
Thomas Memorial Golf & CC	Turner Falls	427
Townsend Ridge CC	Townsend	429
Whippernon CC	Russell	429
Winchendon CC	Winchendon	429
Woodbriar CC	Falmouth	429
Worthington GC	Worthington	431

Maine

Bar Harbor Golf Course	Trenton	431
Bath Country Club	Bath	431
Bethel Inn & CC	Bethel	431
Birch Point Golf Club	St. David	433
Boothbay Region CC	Boothbay	433
Bridgton Highlands CC	Bridgton	433
Country View GC	Brooks	433
Dexter Municipal GC	Dexter	435
Dunegrass Golf Club	Old Orchard Beach	435
Dutch Elm Golf Course	Arundel	435
Golf at Province Lake	Parsonsfield	453
Hermon Meadow GC	Bangor	435
Houlton Community GC	Houlton	437
Johnson W. Parks GC	Pittsfield	437
Kebo Valley Golf Club	Bar Harbor	437
Kennebec Heights CC	Farmingdale	437
Limestone CC	Limestone	439
Maple Lane Inn and GC	Livermore	439
Naples Golf and CC	Naples	439
Nonesuch River Golf Club	Scarborough	439
Norway Country Club	Norway	441
Old Orchard Bch CC	Old Orchard Beach	441
Palmyra Golf Course	Palmyra	441
Paris Hill Country Club	Paris	441
Point Sebago Golf Club	Casco	443
Presque Isle CC	Presque Isle	443
Prospect Hill GC	Auburn	443
Sable Oaks Golf Club	South Portland	443
Salmon Falls GC	Hollis	445
Turner Highland Golf Course	Turner	445
Va-Jo-Wa Golf Club	Island Falls	445
Val Halla Golf Course	Cumberland	445
Westerly Winds GC	Westbrook	447

New Hampshire

Applewood Golf Links	Windham	447
Balsams Panorama GC, The	Dixville Notch	447
Blackmount Country Club	N. Haverhill	447
Bramber Valley Golf Course	Greenland	449
Carter Country Club	Lebanon	449
CC of New Hampshire	North Sutton	449

Golf Course Coupon Directory

Den Brae Golf Course	Sanborton	451
Eagle Mountain House	Jackson	451
Fore-U-Golf Center	West Lebanon	451
Franklin Greens Golf & CC	Franklin	451
Golf at Province Lake	S. Effingham	453
Hale's Location CC	Intervale	453
Hidden Valley R.V. & GP	Derry	453
Highlands Links GC	Plymouth	453
Indian Mound GC	Center Ossipee	455
Lakeview Golf Club	Winnisquam	455
Lisbon Village Country Club	Lisbon	455
Loudon Country Club	Loudon	455
Maplewood Casino & CC	Bethlehem	457
Monadnock CC	Peterborough	457
Nippo Lake Golf Club	Barrington	457
Owl's Nest Golf Club	Campton	457
Pheasant Ridge CC	Gilford	459
Pine Valley CC	Pelham	459
Plausawa Valley CC	Pembroke	459
Ponemah Green	Amherst	459
Ragged Mountain	Danbury	461
Sagamore-Hampton GC	North Hampton	461
Souhegan Woods GC	Amherst	461
Stonebridge Country Club	Goffstown	461
Sunningdale GC	Somersworth	463
Sunset Hill Golf Course	Sugar Hill	463
Waterville Valley	Waterville	463
Waukewan Golf Club	Meredith	463
Waumbek CC, The	Jefferson	465
Wentworth Resort GC	Jackson	465
Whip-Poor-Will GC	Hudson	465
White Mountain CC	Ashland	465
Woodbound Inn GC	Jaffrey	467

Rhode Island

Country View Golf Club	Harrisville	467
Fairlawn Golf Course	Lincoln	467
Foster Country Club	Foster	467
Foxwoods Executive GC	Hope Valley	469
Foxwoods Golf & CC	Richmond	469
Midville Country Club	West Warwick	469
Pocasset Country Club	Portsmouth	469
Weekapaug Golf Club	Westerly	471

Vermont

Bellows Falls CC	Rockingham	471
Blush Hill CC	Waterbury	471
Champlain CC	St. Albans	471
Enosburg Falls CC	Ensburg Falls	473
Essex Country Club	Essex Junction	473
Farm Resort GC	Stowe	473
Green Mt. National G. C.	Sherburne	473
Killington Golf Resort	Killington	475
Lake Morey CC	Fairlee	475
Marble Island CC	Colchester	475
Montague Golf Club	Randolph	475
Neshobe Golf Club	Brandon	477
Newport CC	Newport	477
Proctor Pittsford CC	Pittsford	477
St. Johnsbury CC	St. Johnsbury	477
Stowe Country Club	Stowe	479
Stratton Mt.	Stratton	479
Tater Hill Resort	Chester	479
White River Golf Club	Rochester	479
Wilcox Cove GC	Grand Isle	481
Woodstock Inn & Resort	Woodstock	481

Connecticut

Airways Golf Course	Suffield	481
Blackledge CC	Hebron	481
Blue Fox Run	Avon	483
Fairchild Wheeler GC	Bridgeport	483
Goodwin Golf Course	Hartford	483
Hillside Links LLC	Deep River	483
Hop Brook CC	Naugatuck	485
Keney Park Golf Club	Hartford	485
Miner Hills GC	Middletown	485
Pattonbrook CC	Southington	485
Putnam Country Club	Putnam	487
Rolling Greens GC	Rocky Hill	487
Sunset Hill GC	Brookfield	487
Woodstock Golf Course	S. Woodstock	487

Atlantic Country Club
Plymouth, MA (508) 759-6644

- TYPE OF DISCOUNT
  $5.00 off greens fee
- DAYS OF THE WEEK
  Mon. thru Thurs.
- HOURS OF THE DAY
  All day (Excluding Twilight)

Coupon expires 12/99. Can not be combined with any other offer.

Ballymeade CC
N. Falmouth, MA (508) 540-4005

- TYPE OF DISCOUNT
  $5.00 off greens fee
- DAYS OF THE WEEK
  Weekdays only (except holidays)
- HOURS OF THE DAY
  Not valid July and August

Coupon expires 12/99. Can not be combined with any other offer.

Bas Ridge Golf Course
Plunkett St., Hinsdale, MA (413) 655-2605

- TYPE OF DISCOUNT
  Two players for the price of one
- DAYS OF THE WEEK
  Weekdays only (except holidays)
- HOURS OF THE DAY
  12 pm-4 pm

Coupon expires 12/99. Can not be combined with any other offer.

Bay Pointe CC
Onset, MA (508) 759-8802, 1-800-24T-TIME

- TYPE OF DISCOUNT
  18 holes and riding cart- $39 per person
- DAYS OF THE WEEK
  M-Th, June 1 - Sept. 30
- HOURS OF THE DAY
  After 11:30 am

Coupon expires 12/99. Can not be combined with any other offer.

Beaver Brook CC
Main St., Haydenville, MA (413) 268-7229

- TYPE OF DISCOUNT
  Two players for the price of one. Cart rental required.
- DAYS OF THE WEEK
  7 days a week
- HOURS OF THE DAY
  All day.

Coupon expires 12/99. Can not be combined with any other offer.

Bedrock Golf Club
Rutland, MA (508) 886-0202

- TYPE OF DISCOUNT
  $5.00 off greens fee.
- DAYS OF THE WEEK
  Weekdays only (except holidays)
- HOURS OF THE DAY
  Before 9:00 am

Coupon expires 12/99. Can not be combined with any other offer.

Blissful Meadows GC
Uxbridge, MA (508) 278-6113

- TYPE OF DISCOUNT
  4 players for the price of 3
- DAYS OF THE WEEK
  Mon -Thurs only (except holidays)
- HOURS OF THE DAY
  7 am - 11 am

Coupon expires 12/99. Can not be combined with any other offer.

Bradford Country Club
Bradford, MA (978) 372-8587

- TYPE OF DISCOUNT
  4 players for the price of 3
- DAYS OF THE WEEK
  Weekdays only (except holidays)
- HOURS OF THE DAY
  Before 1 pm. Advance tee times required. Gas carts not included.

Coupon expires 12/99. Can not be combined with any other offer.

Cape Cod CC
N. Falmouth, MA (508) 563-9842

- TYPE OF DISCOUNT
  $5.00 off greens fee
- DAYS OF THE WEEK
  M-Thurs (excluding 6/15- 9/16 and holidays)
- HOURS OF THE DAY
  All day. Power cart rental required.

Coupon expires 12/99. Can not be combined with any other offer.

CC of Billerica
Billerica, MA (978) 667-8061

- TYPE OF DISCOUNT
  4 to Play, 3 to Pay
- DAYS OF THE WEEK
  Weekdays only (except holidays)
- HOURS OF THE DAY
  9 am to 2 pm. Riding carts not included

Coupon expires 12/99. Can not be combined with any other offer.

Chatham Seaside Links
Chatham, MA, (508) 945-4774

- TYPE OF DISCOUNT
  $5.00 off greens fee
- DAYS OF THE WEEK
  Weekdays only (except holidays) before 6/15 and after Labor Day.
- HOURS OF THE DAY
  Afternoon.

Coupon expires 12/99. Can not be combined with any other offer.

Chelmsford Country Club
66 Park Rd., Chelmsford, MA (978) 256-1818

- TYPE OF DISCOUNT
  Two players for the price of one
- DAYS OF THE WEEK
  Weekdays only (except holidays)
- HOURS OF THE DAY
  Expires at 2:00 pm. With cart rental only.

Coupon expires 12/99. Can not be combined with any other offer.

NEW ENGLAND GOLFGUIDE

NEW ENGLAND GOLFGUIDE

Clearview Golf Course
Millbury, MA (508) 753-9201

- TYPE OF DISCOUNT
  18 holes with cart for $20.00
- DAYS OF THE WEEK
  Weekdays only (except holidays)
- HOURS OF THE DAY
  Before 10 am

Coupon expires 12/99. Can not be combined with any other offer.

NEW ENGLAND GOLFGUIDE

Colonial Golf Club
Wakefield, MA   (781) 245-0335

- TYPE OF DISCOUNT
  $5.00 off greens fee for 18 holes
- DAYS OF THE WEEK
  Weekdays only (except holidays)
- HOURS OF THE DAY
  7 am -9 am

Coupon expires 12/99. Can not be combined with any other offer.

NEW ENGLAND GOLFGUIDE

Country Club of Greenfield
244 Country Club Rd., Greenfield, MA
(413) 773 -7530

- TYPE OF DISCOUNT
  $5.00 off greens fee
- DAYS OF THE WEEK
  Weekdays only (except holidays)
- HOURS OF THE DAY
  All day

Coupon expires 12/99. Can not be combined with any other offer.

NEW ENGLAND GOLFGUIDE

Cranwell Resort and Golf Club
Lee Road, Lenox, MA (413) 637-1364

- TYPE OF DISCOUNT
  25% discount for 2-4 players
- DAYS OF THE WEEK
  Weekdays only (except holidays)
- HOURS OF THE DAY
  All day. Based on space availability.

Coupon expires 12/99. Can not be combined with any other offer.

Crumpin-Fox Club
Bernardston, MA (413) 648-9101

- TYPE OF DISCOUNT
  Call in advance to reserve our discounted golf and dinner package. (Discount has already been applied).
- DAYS OF THE WEEK
  7 days a week
- HOURS OF THE DAY
  All day

Coupon expires 12/99. Can not be combined with any other offer.

Cyprian Keyes GC and Par 3
Boylston, MA (508) 869-9900

- TYPE OF DISCOUNT
  $10.00 off a purchase of $50.00 or more
- DAYS OF THE WEEK
  7 days a week
- HOURS OF THE DAY
  All day. Does not include sales items, greens fees, golf carts, or lessons. Valid until 10/31/99.

Coupon expires 12/99. Can not be combined with any other offer.

Edge Hill GC
Ashfield, MA (413)625-6018

- TYPE OF DISCOUNT
  Two players for the price of one
- DAYS OF THE WEEK
  Weekdays only (except holidays)
- HOURS OF THE DAY
  All day

Coupon expires 12/99. Can not be combined with any other offer.

Egremont Country Club
Great Barrington, MA (413) 528-4222

- TYPE OF DISCOUNT
  25% discount for 2-4 players
- DAYS OF THE WEEK
  Weekdays only (except holidays)
- HOURS OF THE DAY
  Tee off by 1 pm. Call in advance for tee times.

Coupon expires 12/99. Can not be combined with any other offer.

Ellinwood CC
Athol, MA (978) 249-7460

- TYPE OF DISCOUNT
  25% discount for 2-4 players
- DAYS OF THE WEEK
  Weekdays only (except holidays)
- HOURS OF THE DAY
  All day

Coupon expires 12/99. Can not be combined with any other offer.

Far Corner Golf Course
W. Boxford, MA (978) 352-8300

- TYPE OF DISCOUNT
  6 lessons for the price of 5 with John O'Connor
- DAYS OF THE WEEK
  7 days a week
- HOURS OF THE DAY
  All day

Coupon expires 12/99. Can not be combined with any other offer.

Forest Park CC
Adams, MA (413) 743-3311

- TYPE OF DISCOUNT
  Two players for the price of one
- DAYS OF THE WEEK
  7 days a week
- HOURS OF THE DAY
  Please call ahead on weekends for availability

Coupon expires 12/99. Can not be combined with any other offer.

Glen Ellen CC
Rt.115, Millis, MA (508) 376-2775

- TYPE OF DISCOUNT
  $5.00 off greens fee for 18 holes.
- DAYS OF THE WEEK
  Mon.-Thurs.
- HOURS OF THE DAY
  Call ahead for tee times.

Coupon expires 12/99. Can not be combined with any other offer.

Green Valley GC
Newburyport, MA (978) 463-8600

- TYPE OF DISCOUNT
  Two players for the price of one for 9 holes only. Cart required.
- DAYS OF THE WEEK
  Weekdays only (except holidays)
- HOURS OF THE DAY
  5am-7pm

Coupon expires 12/99. Can not be combined with any other offer.

Groton Country Club
Groton, MA (978) 448-2564

- TYPE OF DISCOUNT
  Two players for the price of one
- DAYS OF THE WEEK
  Weekdays only (except holidays)
- HOURS OF THE DAY
  Call ahead for tee times

Coupon expires 12/99. Can not be combined with any other offer.

Hampden Country Club
Wilbraham Rd., Hampden, MA (413) 566-8010

- TYPE OF DISCOUNT
  $5.00 off 18 hole greens fee.
- DAYS OF THE WEEK
  Mon-Thurs, except holidays
- HOURS OF THE DAY
  All day. Power cart required.

Coupon expires 12/99. Can not be combined with any other offer.

Heritage Country Club
Charlton, MA (508) 248-51111

- TYPE OF DISCOUNT
  20% off Greens Fees for 1 or 2 players
- DAYS OF THE WEEK
  Mon- Thurs
- HOURS OF THE DAY
  10 am - 2 pm. No holidays. No tournaments

Coupon expires 12/99. Can not be combined with any other offer.

Hillcrest Country Club
Leicester, MA (508) 892-1855

- TYPE OF DISCOUNT
  Two players for the price of one
- DAYS OF THE WEEK
  Weekdays only (except Tuesdays)
- HOURS OF THE DAY
  All day

Coupon expires 12/99. Can not be combined with any other offer.

Hillside CC
Rehoboth, MA (508) 252-9761

- TYPE OF DISCOUNT
  Free golf cart with 2 paid greens fees.
- DAYS OF THE WEEK
  Mon- Thurs.(No Fri.) 7am to 1pm. - Weekends and holidays after 1pm.

Coupon expires 12/99. Can not be combined with any other offer.

Hillview Golf Course
No. Reading, MA (978) 664-4435

- TYPE OF DISCOUNT
  Four players for the price of three
- DAYS OF THE WEEK
  Weekdays only (except holidays)
- HOURS OF THE DAY
  Good only for April, October, November & December

Coupon expires 12/99. Can not be combined with any other offer.

Hyannis Golf Club
Hyannis, MA (508) 362-2606

- TYPE OF DISCOUNT
  $1.00 Off Bucket of Balls
- DAYS OF THE WEEK
  7 days a week
- HOURS OF THE DAY
  All day

Coupon expires 12/99. Can not be combined with any other offer.

NEW ENGLAND GOLFGUIDE

Kelley Greens By The Sea
Nahant, MA (781) 581-0840

- TYPE OF DISCOUNT
  Two players for the price of one
- DAYS OF THE WEEK
  Weekdays only (except holidays)
- HOURS OF THE DAY
  Before 4 pm

Coupon expires 12/99. Can not be combined with any other offer.

Lakeview Golf Club
Main St., Rt. 1A, Wenham, MA (978) 468-6676

- TYPE OF DISCOUNT
  Two players for the price of one
- DAYS OF THE WEEK
  Weekdays only (except holidays)
- HOURS OF THE DAY
  Before noon

Coupon expires 12/99. Can not be combined with any other offer.

Little Harbor CC
Wareham, MA (508) 295-2617

- TYPE OF DISCOUNT
  $4.00 off regular greens fee
- DAYS OF THE WEEK
  Weekdays only (except holidays and Weds.)
- HOURS OF THE DAY
  All day

Coupon expires 12/99. Can not be combined with any other offer.

Maplegate Country Club
Bellingham, MA (508) 966-4040

- TYPE OF DISCOUNT
  One free round of golf with three paying guests.
- DAYS OF THE WEEK
  Before noon Mon, Tues, Wed & Thurs (excuding holidays)
- HOURS OF THE DAY
  Valid April - October 29, 1999

Coupon expires 12/99. Can not be combined with any other offer.

NEW ENGLAND GOLFGUIDE

Newton Commonwealth GC
Chestnut Hill, MA (617) 630-1971

- TYPE OF DISCOUNT
  $5.00 off regular 18 hole greens fee (cart rental required)
- DAYS OF THE WEEK
  Monday - Thursday only
- HOURS OF THE DAY
  Before 5:00 pm

Coupon expires 12/99. Can not be combined with any other offer.

NEW ENGLAND GOLFGUIDE

North Hill CC
Duxbury, MA (781) 934-3249

- TYPE OF DISCOUNT
  Free Golf Cart with 2 paid Greens Fees
- DAYS OF THE WEEK
  7 days a week
- HOURS OF THE DAY
  All day

Coupon expires 12/99. Can not be combined with any other offer.

NEW ENGLAND GOLFGUIDE

Northampton CC
Leeds, MA 413-586-1898

- TYPE OF DISCOUNT
  2 for 1 with cart rental for 18 holes.
- DAYS OF THE WEEK
  Weekdays only (except holidays)
- HOURS OF THE DAY
  Weekdays before 12:00

Coupon expires 12/99. Can not be combined with any other offer.

NEW ENGLAND GOLFGUIDE

Norwood Country Club
Norwood, MA (781) 769-5880

- TYPE OF DISCOUNT
  Two players for the price of one
- DAYS OF THE WEEK
  Weekdays only (except holidays)
- HOURS OF THE DAY
  Before Noon. 18 hole power cart rental at regular weekday prices is required.

Coupon expires 12/99. Can not be combined with any other offer.

Golf Course Coupons

Oak Ridge Golf Club
W. Gill Rd, Gill, MA (413) 863-9693

- TYPE OF DISCOUNT
  Two players for the price of one
- DAYS OF THE WEEK
  Weekdays only (except holidays)
- HOURS OF THE DAY
  Prior to 1 pm

Coupon expires 12/99. Can not be combined with any other offer.

Oak Ridge Golf Club
Feeding Hills, MA (413) 789-7307

- TYPE OF DISCOUNT
  Two players for the price of one for 18 holes
- DAYS OF THE WEEK
  Weekdays only (except holidays)
- HOURS OF THE DAY
  Prior to 1:00 pm

Coupon expires 12/99. Can not be combined with any other offer.

Ocean Edge GC
Brewster, MA (508) 896-5911

- TYPE OF DISCOUNT
  4 players for the price of 3 for 18 holes
- DAYS OF THE WEEK
  Mon - Thurs. (except holidays)
- HOURS OF THE DAY
  All day. Valid April 1 to June 25 and after Labor Day. Advance tee times and power cart required.

Coupon expires 12/99. Can not be combined with any other offer.

Olde Scotland Links
Bridgewater, MA (508) 279-3344

- TYPE OF DISCOUNT
  1 riding cart with purchase of 2 green fees.
- DAYS OF THE WEEK
  M-Th (Except holidays)
- HOURS OF THE DAY
  All day. Not to be used during league, group or tournament play

Coupon expires 12/99. Can not be combined with any other offer.

Pine Knoll Par 3
East Longmeadow, MA (413) 525-8320

- TYPE OF DISCOUNT
  Two players for the price of one
- DAYS OF THE WEEK
  7 days a week
- HOURS OF THE DAY
  All day

Coupon expires 12/99. Can not be combined with any other offer.

Pontoosuc Lake CC
Pittsfield, MA (413) 445-4217

- TYPE OF DISCOUNT
  Two players for the price of one
- DAYS OF THE WEEK
  7 days a week
- HOURS OF THE DAY
  All day

Coupon expires 12/99. Can not be combined with any other offer.

Poquoy Brook GC
Lakeville, MA (508) 947-5261

- TYPE OF DISCOUNT
  20% off non sale golf apparel
- DAYS OF THE WEEK
  7 days a week
- HOURS OF THE DAY
  All day

Coupon expires 12/99. Can not be combined with any other offer.

Quail Hollow Golf & CC
Old Turnpike Rd., Oakham, MA (508) 882-5516

- TYPE OF DISCOUNT
  Two players for the price of one.
  Must take cart
- DAYS OF THE WEEK
  Mon-Fri
- HOURS OF THE DAY
  Before noon

Coupon expires 12/99. Can not be combined with any other offer.

NEW ENGLAND GOLFGUIDE

Quashnet Valley CC
Mashpee, MA (508) 477-4412

- TYPE OF DISCOUNT
  $4.00 off greens fee
- DAYS OF THE WEEK
  M - Th (except holidays)
- HOURS OF THE DAY
  All day

Coupon expires 12/99. Can not be combined with any other offer.

NEW ENGLAND GOLFGUIDE

Round Hill CC
E. Sandwich, MA (508) 888-3384

- TYPE OF DISCOUNT
  $5.00 off greens fee for up to 2 players
- DAYS OF THE WEEK
  Weekdays only (except holidays)
- HOURS OF THE DAY
  M-F. Excluding special offers
  & twilight rates

Coupon expires 12/99. Can not be combined with any other offer.

NEW ENGLAND GOLFGUIDE

Skyline Country Club
Rt. 7, Lanesborough, MA (413) 445-5584

- TYPE OF DISCOUNT
  Two players for the price of one. Cart rental required.
- DAYS OF THE WEEK
  Weekdays only (except holidays)
- HOURS OF THE DAY
  All day

Coupon expires 12/99. Can not be combined with any other offer.

NEW ENGLAND GOLFGUIDE

Stoneham Oaks
Stoneham, MA (781)-438-7888

- TYPE OF DISCOUNT
  9 hole special, $6.00 for Stoneham residents
  $7.00 for non-residents
- DAYS OF THE WEEK
  Weekdays only (except holidays)
- HOURS OF THE DAY
  7:00 am - 2:00 pm

Coupon expires 12/99. Can not be combined with any other offer.

Sun Valley CC
Rehoboth, MA (508) 336-8686

- TYPE OF DISCOUNT
  $2 off 1 round of golf ($1 seniors)
- DAYS OF THE WEEK
  Weekdays only (except holidays)
- HOURS OF THE DAY
  7 am to 1 pm

Coupon expires 12/99. Can not be combined with any other offer.

Swansea Country Club
Swansea, MA (508) 379-9886

- TYPE OF DISCOUNT
  18 holes, cart, 2 hot dogs, chips and soda: $33.50 per player. ($42.00 value per player)
- DAYS OF THE WEEK
  Weekdays only (except holidays)
- HOURS OF THE DAY
  11:00 am-1:00 pm. Must have 2 or 4 players.

Coupon expires 12/99. Can not be combined with any other offer.

The Woods of Westminster CC
Westminster, MA (978) 874-0500

- TYPE OF DISCOUNT
  2nd player at 50%
- DAYS OF THE WEEK
  7 days a week
- HOURS OF THE DAY
  All day

Coupon expires 12/99. Can not be combined with any other offer.

Thomas Memorial Golf & CC
Turner Falls, MA (413) 863-8003

- TYPE OF DISCOUNT
  Two players for the price of one
- DAYS OF THE WEEK
  Weekdays only (except holidays)
- HOURS OF THE DAY
  All day. Cart Rental for 2 Required.

Coupon expires 12/99. Can not be combined with any other offer.

Townsend Ridge Country Club
40 Scales Lane, Townsend, MA. (978) 597-8400

- TYPE OF DISCOUNT
  $5.00 off greens fee
- DAYS OF THE WEEK
  Mon.-Thurs. except holidays
- HOURS OF THE DAY
  All day. No jeans allowed. Must have collared shirt.

Coupon expires 12/99. Can not be combined with any other offer.

Whippernon CC
Russell, MA (413) 862-3606

- TYPE OF DISCOUNT
  $5.00 off greens fee for up to 2 players
- DAYS OF THE WEEK
  7 days a week
- HOURS OF THE DAY
  All day. Cart required

Coupon expires 12/99. Can not be combined with any other offer.

Winchendon CC
Winchendon, MA (978) 297-9897

- TYPE OF DISCOUNT
  $5.00 off greens fee
- DAYS OF THE WEEK
  Weekdays only (except holidays)
- HOURS OF THE DAY
  Call for tee times.

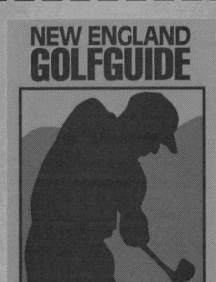

Coupon expires 12/99. Can not be combined with any other offer.

Woodbriar CC
Falmouth, MA (508) 495-5500

- TYPE OF DISCOUNT
  Only pay $15.00
- DAYS OF THE WEEK
  7 days a week
- HOURS OF THE DAY
  After 4:30 p.m

Coupon expires 12/99. Can not be combined with any other offer.

NEW ENGLAND GOLFGUIDE

Worthington GC
Worthington, MA (413) 238-4464

- TYPE OF DISCOUNT
  Two players for the price of one
- DAYS OF THE WEEK
  Weekdays only (except holidays)
- HOURS OF THE DAY
  Before noon

Coupon expires 12/99. Can not be combined with any other offer.

Bar Harbor Golf Course
Rt. 204, Trenton, ME (207) 667-7505

- TYPE OF DISCOUNT
  Two players for the price of one. Power cart required.
- DAYS OF THE WEEK
  Weekdays only (except holidays)
- HOURS OF THE DAY
  All day.

Coupon expires 12/99. Can not be combined with any other offer.

Bath Country Club
Whiskeag Rd., Bath, ME (207) 442-8411

- TYPE OF DISCOUNT
  Free golf cart with two 18 hole greens fees.
- DAYS OF THE WEEK
  7 days a week
- HOURS OF THE DAY
  All day.

Coupon expires 12/99. Can not be combined with any other offer.

Bethel Inn & CC
Broad St., Bethel, ME (207) 824-6276

- TYPE OF DISCOUNT
  2nd greens fee at 50% off
- DAYS OF THE WEEK
  Weekdays only (except holidays)
- HOURS OF THE DAY
  All day. Must make tee time no more than 48 hrs. in adv.

Coupon expires 12/99. Can not be combined with any other offer.

Birch Point Golf Club
Madawaska, ME (207) 895-6957

- TYPE OF DISCOUNT
  Power cart 1/2 price with 2 paid green fees
- DAYS OF THE WEEK
  7 days a week
- HOURS OF THE DAY
  All day

Coupon expires 12/99. Can not be combined with any other offer.

Boothbay Region CC
Boothbay, ME (207) 633-6085

- TYPE OF DISCOUNT
  Two players for the price of one
- DAYS OF THE WEEK
  Weekdays only (except holidays)
- HOURS OF THE DAY
  After 1 pm. Not valid in July and August.

Coupon expires 12/99. Can not be combined with any other offer.

Bridgton Highlands CC
Bridgton, ME (207) 647-3491

- TYPE OF DISCOUNT
  4 players for the price of 3.
- DAYS OF THE WEEK
  7 days a week, except weekdays only during July and August.
- HOURS OF THE DAY
  All day.

Coupon expires 12/99. Can not be combined with any other offer.

Country View GC
Rt. 7, Brooks, ME (207) 722-3161

- TYPE OF DISCOUNT
  Two players for the price of one
- DAYS OF THE WEEK
  Weekdays only (except holidays)
- HOURS OF THE DAY
  All day. With golf cart.

Coupon expires 12/99. Can not be combined with any other offer.

NEW ENGLAND GOLFGUIDE

Dexter Municipal GC
Sunrise Ave., Dexter, ME (207) 924-6477

- TYPE OF DISCOUNT
  Two players for the price of one
- DAYS OF THE WEEK
  Weekdays only (except holidays)
- HOURS OF THE DAY
  Best before 4:00

Coupon expires 12/99. Can not be combined with any other offer.

NEW ENGLAND GOLFGUIDE

Dunegrass Golf Club
Old Orchard Beach, Me 207-934-4513

- TYPE OF DISCOUNT
  $5.00 off 18 hole greens fee
- DAYS OF THE WEEK
  Weekdays only (except holidays)
- HOURS OF THE DAY
  All day

Coupon expires 12/99. Can not be combined with any other offer.

NEW ENGLAND GOLFGUIDE

Dutch Elm Golf Course
Arundel, ME (207) 282-9850

- TYPE OF DISCOUNT
  $5.00 off greens fee
- DAYS OF THE WEEK
  Weekdays only (except holidays)
- HOURS OF THE DAY
  PM only. Coupon to be used before
  Memorial Day or after Labor Day

Coupon expires 12/99. Can not be combined with any other offer.

NEW ENGLAND GOLFGUIDE

Hermon Meadow GC
Bangor, ME (207) 848-3741

- TYPE OF DISCOUNT
  1 player at 1/2 price
- DAYS OF THE WEEK
  7 days a week
- HOURS OF THE DAY
  All day

Coupon expires 12/99. Can not be combined with any other offer.

NEW ENGLAND GOLFGUIDE

Houlton Community GC
Houlton, ME (207) 532-2662

- TYPE OF DISCOUNT
  4 players for the price of 3.
- DAYS OF THE WEEK
  7 days a week
- HOURS OF THE DAY
  All day. Call for tee times.

Coupon expires 12/99. Can not be combined with any other offer.

NEW ENGLAND GOLFGUIDE

Johnson W. Parks GC
Pittsfield, ME (207) 487-5545

- TYPE OF DISCOUNT
  Two players for the price of one with cart
- DAYS OF THE WEEK
  7 days a week
- HOURS OF THE DAY
  Weekends and holidays after noon

Coupon expires 12/99. Can not be combined with any other offer.

NEW ENGLAND GOLFGUIDE

Kebo Valley Golf Club
Bar Harbor, ME (207) 288-3000

- TYPE OF DISCOUNT
  $5.00 off greens fee
- DAYS OF THE WEEK
  Weekdays only (except holidays)
- HOURS OF THE DAY
  All day Good April, May & after Labor day. Not combinable with other offers.

Coupon expires 12/99. Can not be combined with any other offer.

NEW ENGLAND GOLFGUIDE

Kennebec Heights Country Club
Rt. 201, Farmingdale, ME (207) 582-2000

- TYPE OF DISCOUNT
  Free Golf Cart with 2 paid Greens Fees
- DAYS OF THE WEEK
  Weekdays only (except holidays)
- HOURS OF THE DAY
  All day

Coupon expires 12/99. Can not be combined with any other offer.

Limestone CC
Limestone, ME (207) 328-7277

- TYPE OF DISCOUNT
  $5.00 off greens fee . Cart rental required.
- DAYS OF THE WEEK
  Weekdays only (except holidays)
- HOURS OF THE DAY
  All day

Coupon expires 12/99. Can not be combined with any other offer.

Maple Lane Inn and Golf Club
Livermore, ME (207) 897-6666

- TYPE OF DISCOUNT
  Two players for the price of one with cart
- DAYS OF THE WEEK
  7 days a week
- HOURS OF THE DAY
  Before 9 am

Coupon expires 12/99. Can not be combined with any other offer.

Naples Golf and Country Club
Route 114, Naples, ME. 207-693-6424

- TYPE OF DISCOUNT
  25% discount for 2-4 players
- DAYS OF THE WEEK
  Weekdays only (except holidays)
- HOURS OF THE DAY
  After 1 pm

Coupon expires 12/99. Can not be combined with any other offer.

Nonesuch River Golf Club
Scarborough, ME (207) 883-0007

- TYPE OF DISCOUNT
  Free small bucket of range balls with every 18 holes of golf paid for.
- DAYS OF THE WEEK
  7 days a week
- HOURS OF THE DAY
  All day

Coupon expires 12/99. Can not be combined with any other offer.

NEW ENGLAND GOLFGUIDE

Norway Country Club
Norway, ME (207) 743-9840

- TYPE OF DISCOUNT
  Greens fee- $15.00 for 18 holes
- DAYS OF THE WEEK
  7 days a week
- HOURS OF THE DAY
  After 4 pm

Coupon expires 12/99. Can not be combined with any other offer.

NEW ENGLAND GOLFGUIDE

Old Orchard Bch CC
Old Orchard Beach, ME (207) 934-4513

- TYPE OF DISCOUNT
  $5.00 off greens fee
- DAYS OF THE WEEK
  Weekdays only (except holidays)
- HOURS OF THE DAY
  All day

Coupon expires 12/99. Can not be combined with any other offer.

NEW ENGLAND GOLFGUIDE

Palmyra Golf Course
Palmyra, ME (207)938-4947

- TYPE OF DISCOUNT
  2 players and a cart is $40.00 for 18 holes.
- DAYS OF THE WEEK
  7 days a week
- HOURS OF THE DAY
  All day

Coupon expires 12/99. Can not be combined with any other offer.

NEW ENGLAND GOLFGUIDE

Paris Hill Country Club
Paris Hill Rd., Paris, ME (207) 743-2371

- TYPE OF DISCOUNT
  Two players for the price of one
- DAYS OF THE WEEK
  7 days a week
- HOURS OF THE DAY
  All day

Coupon expires 12/99. Can not be combined with any other offer.

NEW ENGLAND GOLFGUIDE

Point Sebago Golf Club
Route 302, Casco, ME (207)655-7948

- TYPE OF DISCOUNT
  $5.00 off greens fee
- DAYS OF THE WEEK
  7 days a week
- HOURS OF THE DAY
  After 1 pm

Coupon expires 12/99. Can not be combined with any other offer.

NEW ENGLAND GOLFGUIDE

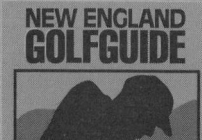

Presque Isle CC
Presque Isle, ME (207) 764-0430

- TYPE OF DISCOUNT
  Two players, 18 holes for the price of 9 holes each.
- DAYS OF THE WEEK
  M,W,Th,&F only (except holidays)
- HOURS OF THE DAY
  All day Power cart required at regular rate.

Coupon expires 12/99. Can not be combined with any other offer.

NEW ENGLAND GOLFGUIDE

Prospect Hill GC
So. Main St., Auburn, ME (207) 782-9220

- TYPE OF DISCOUNT
  4 green fees for the price of 3.
- DAYS OF THE WEEK
  7 days a week
- HOURS OF THE DAY
  All day.

Coupon expires 12/99. Can not be combined with any other offer.

NEW ENGLAND GOLFGUIDE

Sable Oaks Golf Club
S. Portland, ME (207) 775-6257

- TYPE OF DISCOUNT
  $5.00 off 18-hole greens fee
- DAYS OF THE WEEK
  Monday-Thursday, except holidays
- HOURS OF THE DAY
  All day. Power cart required.

Coupon expires 12/99. Can not be combined with any other offer.

Salmon Falls GC
Hollis, ME (207) 929-5233 or 1-800-734-1616

- TYPE OF DISCOUNT
  2 players and golfcart for 18 holes- $50.00
- DAYS OF THE WEEK
  Weekdays only
- HOURS OF THE DAY
  All day

Coupon expires 12/99. Can not be combined with any other offer.

Turner Highland Golf Course
Turner, ME (207) 224-7060

- TYPE OF DISCOUNT
  Two players for the price of one
- DAYS OF THE WEEK
  Weekdays only (except holidays)
- HOURS OF THE DAY
  After 10 am.

Coupon expires 12/99. Can not be combined with any other offer.

Va-Jo-Wa Golf Club
Walker Rd., Island Falls, ME (207) 463-2128

- TYPE OF DISCOUNT
  2 players at half price.
- DAYS OF THE WEEK
  7 days a week
- HOURS OF THE DAY
  All day. Power cart required.

Coupon expires 12/99. Can not be combined with any other offer.

Val Halla Golf Course
Cumberland, ME (207) 829-2225

- TYPE OF DISCOUNT
  Two players with cart for $60
- DAYS OF THE WEEK
  Weekdays only (except holidays)
- HOURS OF THE DAY
  Before 1 pm. Must call for tee time.

Coupon expires 12/99. Can not be combined with any other offer.

Westerly Winds GC
Westbrook, ME (207) 854-9463

- TYPE OF DISCOUNT
  25% discount for 2-4 players
- DAYS OF THE WEEK
  7 days a week
- HOURS OF THE DAY
  All day

Coupon expires 12/99. Can not be combined with any other offer.

Applewood Golf Links
Range Rd., Windham, NH (603) 898-6793

- TYPE OF DISCOUNT
  Two players for the price of one
- DAYS OF THE WEEK
  Weekdays only (except holidays)
- HOURS OF THE DAY
  Before 4:00 pm

Coupon expires 12/99. Can not be combined with any other offer.

Balsams Panorama GC, The
Dixville Notch, NH (603) 255-4961

- TYPE OF DISCOUNT
  Two players for the price of one
- DAYS OF THE WEEK
  Weekdays only (except holidays)
- HOURS OF THE DAY
  All day. Not valid 6/30 to 9/15.

Coupon expires 12/99. Can not be combined with any other offer.

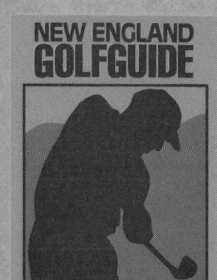

Blackmount Country Club
N Haverhill, NH (603) 787-6564

- TYPE OF DISCOUNT
  $3.00 off power cart rental with paid greens fee.
- DAYS OF THE WEEK
  Weekdays only (except holidays)
- HOURS OF THE DAY
  All day

Coupon expires 12/99. Can not be combined with any other offer.

Bramber Valley Golf Course
Greenland, NH 03840 (603) 436-4288

- TYPE OF DISCOUNT
  $2.00 off 18 holes
- DAYS OF THE WEEK
  7 days a week
- HOURS OF THE DAY
  All day

Coupon expires 12/99. Can not be combined with any other offer.

Carter Country Club
Lebanon, NH (603) 448-4483

- TYPE OF DISCOUNT
  Two players for the price of one
- DAYS OF THE WEEK
  Weekdays only (except holidays)
- HOURS OF THE DAY
  All day

Coupon expires 12/99. Can not be combined with any other offer.

CC of New Hampshire
N. Sutton, NH (603) 927-4246

- TYPE OF DISCOUNT
  $5.00 off 18 hole greens fee
- DAYS OF THE WEEK
  Monday-Thursday (except holidays)
- HOURS OF THE DAY
  All day. Power cart required.

Coupon expires 12/99. Can not be combined with any other offer.

Colebrook CC
Colebrook, NH (603) 237-5566

- TYPE OF DISCOUNT
  Two players for the price of one
- DAYS OF THE WEEK
  Weekdays only (except holidays)
- HOURS OF THE DAY
  All day. Power Cart Required.

Coupon expires 12/99. Can not be combined with any other offer.

Den Brae Golf Course
Sanbornton, NH 03269 (603) 934-9818

- TYPE OF DISCOUNT
  25% discount for 2-4 players
- DAYS OF THE WEEK
  Weekdays only (except holidays)
- HOURS OF THE DAY
  All day

Coupon expires 12/99. Can not be combined with any other offer.

Eagle Mountain House
Jackson, NH (603) 383-9090

- TYPE OF DISCOUNT
  Lunch special includes: golf, lunch and cart for 9 holes. Inquire
- DAYS OF THE WEEK
  Weekdays only (except holidays)
- HOURS OF THE DAY
  All day.

Coupon expires 12/99. Can not be combined with any other offer.

Fore-U-Golf Center
West Lebanon, NH (603) 298-9702

- TYPE OF DISCOUNT
  Two players for the price of one
- DAYS OF THE WEEK
  7 days a week
- HOURS OF THE DAY
  All day

Coupon expires 12/99. Can not be combined with any other offer.

Franklin Greens Golf & Country Club
Franklin, NH (603) 934-3033

- TYPE OF DISCOUNT
  $5.00 off each Greens Fee for up to 4 players
- DAYS OF THE WEEK
  Weekdays only (except holidays)
- HOURS OF THE DAY
  All day

Coupon expires 12/99. Can not be combined with any other offer.

Golf at Province Lake
Parsonfield, ME Route 153 (207) 793-9577

- TYPE OF DISCOUNT
  $5.00 off greens fee for up to 2 players
- DAYS OF THE WEEK
  Weekdays only (except holidays)
- HOURS OF THE DAY
  All day

Coupon expires 12/99. Can not be combined with any other offer.

Hale's Location Country Club
North Conway, NH (603) 356-2140

- TYPE OF DISCOUNT
  $5.00 off with purchase of two 18 hole greens fees and carts.
- DAYS OF THE WEEK
  Mon-Thurs, Except Holidays
- HOURS OF THE DAY
  All day

Coupon expires 12/99. Can not be combined with any other offer.

Hidden Valley R.V. and Golf Park
Derry, NH (603) 887-3767

- TYPE OF DISCOUNT
  Two players for the price of one
- DAYS OF THE WEEK
  Weekdays only (except holidays)
- HOURS OF THE DAY
  All day

Coupon expires 12/99. Can not be combined with any other offer.

Highlands Links GC
Plymouth, NH (603) 536-3452

- TYPE OF DISCOUNT
  Two players for the price of one (at regular adult fee)
- DAYS OF THE WEEK
  Weekdays only (except holidays)
- HOURS OF THE DAY
  All day

Coupon expires 12/99. Can not be combined with any other offer.

NEW ENGLAND GOLFGUIDE

Indian Mound GC
Center Ossipee, NH (603) 539-7733

- TYPE OF DISCOUNT
  $58.00 for two players and cart for 18 holes
- DAYS OF THE WEEK
  M-F
- HOURS OF THE DAY
  1 pm- 3 pm

Coupon expires 12/99. Can not be combined with any other offer.

Lakeview Golf Club
Ladd Hill Road, Belmont, NH 03220 (603) 524-2220

- TYPE OF DISCOUNT
  $5.00 off greens fee for up to 2 players
- DAYS OF THE WEEK
  Weekdays only (except holidays)
- HOURS OF THE DAY
  7:00 am- 5:00 pm

Coupon expires 12/99. Can not be combined with any other offer.

Lisbon Village Country Club
Bishop Road, Lisbon, NH (603)-838-6004

- TYPE OF DISCOUNT
  Free Golf Cart with 2 paid Greens Fees
- DAYS OF THE WEEK
  Weekdays only (except holidays)
- HOURS OF THE DAY
  All day

Coupon expires 12/99. Can not be combined with any other offer.

Loudon Country Club
Loudon, NH 03301 (603)783-3372

- TYPE OF DISCOUNT
  $5.00 off greens fee
- DAYS OF THE WEEK
  Weekdays only (except holidays)
- HOURS OF THE DAY
  All day

Coupon expires 12/99. Can not be combined with any other offer.

Maplewood Casino & CC
Bethlehem, NH (603) 869-3335

- TYPE OF DISCOUNT
  $5.00 off greens fee
- DAYS OF THE WEEK
  Weekdays only (except holidays)
- HOURS OF THE DAY
  7:00-6:00. Cart required for 18 holes only

Coupon expires 12/99. Can not be combined with any other offer.

Monadnock CC
Peterborough, NH (603) 924-7769

- TYPE OF DISCOUNT
  $2.00 off greens fee
- DAYS OF THE WEEK
  7 days a week(except holidays)
- HOURS OF THE DAY
  After noon

Coupon expires 12/99. Can not be combined with any other offer.

Nippo Lake Golf Club
Barrington, NH (603) 664-7616

- TYPE OF DISCOUNT
  Two players for the price of one
- DAYS OF THE WEEK
  Weekdays only (except holidays)
- HOURS OF THE DAY
  All day. Not Valid July or August.

Coupon expires 12/99. Can not be combined with any other offer.

Owl's Nest Golf Club
Campton, NH 603-726-3076

- TYPE OF DISCOUNT
  $5.00 off each greens fee up to 2 players
- DAYS OF THE WEEK
  Monday thru Thursday excluding holidays
- HOURS OF THE DAY
  After 1:00 pm

Coupon expires 12/99. Can not be combined with any other offer.

Pheasant Ridge CC
Gilford, NH (603) 524-7808

- TYPE OF DISCOUNT
  $5.00 off 18-hole greens fee
- DAYS OF THE WEEK
  Monday-Thursday (except holidays)
- HOURS OF THE DAY
  All day. Power cart required.

Coupon expires 12/99. Can not be combined with any other offer.

Pine Valley CC
Rt. 38, Pelham, NH (603) 635-7979

- TYPE OF DISCOUNT
  Discount golf cart rentals $2 off for 9 holes, $3 off for 18 holes
- DAYS OF THE WEEK
  Weekdays only (except holidays)
- HOURS OF THE DAY
  11:00 am-2:00 pm

Coupon expires 12/99. Can not be combined with any other offer.

Plausawa Valley CC
Pembroke, NH (603) 228-8861

- TYPE OF DISCOUNT
  25% discount for 2-4 players
- DAYS OF THE WEEK
  7 days a week (except holidays)
- HOURS OF THE DAY
  Only after 2 pm on weekends

Coupon expires 12/99. Can not be combined with any other offer.

Ponemah Green
Amherst, NH (603) 672-4732

- TYPE OF DISCOUNT
  Two players for the price of one
- DAYS OF THE WEEK
  Weekdays only (except holidays)
- HOURS OF THE DAY
  All day. Offer valid Sept. 8, 1998 through end of season

Coupon expires 12/99. Can not be combined with any other offer.

Ragged Mountain
Danbury, NH, (603) 768-3600

- TYPE OF DISCOUNT
  25% discount for 2-4 players
- DAYS OF THE WEEK
  Mon-Thurs. (except holidays)
- HOURS OF THE DAY
  All day

Coupon expires 12/99. Can not be combined with any other offer.

Sagamore-Hampton GC
N. Hampton, NH (603) 964-5341

- TYPE OF DISCOUNT
  4 players for the price of 3
- DAYS OF THE WEEK
  Weekdays only (except holidays)
- HOURS OF THE DAY
  All day

Coupon expires 12/99. Can not be combined with any other offer.

Souhegan Woods GC
Amherst, NH (603) 673-0200

- TYPE OF DISCOUNT
  $5.00 off 18-hole greens fee
- DAYS OF THE WEEK
  Monday-Thursday only (except holidays)
- HOURS OF THE DAY
  All day. Power cart required.

Coupon expires 12/99. Can not be combined with any other offer.

Stonebridge Country Club
Goffstown, NH 603-497-T-OFF (8633)

- TYPE OF DISCOUNT
  Two players for the price of one
- DAYS OF THE WEEK
  M-Th
- HOURS OF THE DAY
  All day

Coupon expires 12/99. Can not be combined with any other offer.

Sunningdale GC
Somersworth, NH (603) 742-8056

- TYPE OF DISCOUNT
  $2.00 off 9 holes. $4.00 off 18 holes.
- DAYS OF THE WEEK
  Weekdays only (except holidays)
- HOURS OF THE DAY
  All day.

Coupon expires 12/99. Can not be combined with any other offer.

Sunset Hill Golf Course
Sugar Hill, NH (603) 823-7244

- TYPE OF DISCOUNT
  Two players for the price of one for 18 holes. Power cart required. Tuesdays only.
- DAYS OF THE WEEK
  Mid-week special: Two 18 holes green fees, gas cart and lunch for $49.00 per twosome. Tee times required. Non-holidays.

Coupon expires 12/99. Can not be combined with any other offer.

Waterville Valley
Waterville, NH (603) 236-4805

- TYPE OF DISCOUNT
  1 player at half price.
- DAYS OF THE WEEK
  Weekdays only (except holidays)
- HOURS OF THE DAY
  All day. Tee times required.

Coupon expires 12/99. Can not be combined with any other offer.

Waukewan Golf Club
Meredith, NH (603) 279-6661

- TYPE OF DISCOUNT
  4 players for the price of 3.
- DAYS OF THE WEEK
  7 days a week
- HOURS OF THE DAY
  All day.

Coupon expires 12/99. Can not be combined with any other offer.

NEW ENGLAND GOLFGUIDE

Waumbek CC, The
Jefferson, NH (603) 586-7777

- TYPE OF DISCOUNT
  $5.00 off 18 hole greens fee.
- DAYS OF THE WEEK
  Monday-Thursday (except holidays)
- HOURS OF THE DAY
  All day. Power cart rental required.

Coupon expires 12/99. Can not be combined with any other offer.

Wentworth Resort GC
Rt. 16, Jackson, NH (603) 383-9641

- TYPE OF DISCOUNT
  Free cart rental
- DAYS OF THE WEEK
  Weekdays only (except holidays)
- HOURS OF THE DAY
  After 11:00 am

Coupon expires 12/99. Can not be combined with any other offer.

Whip-Poor-Will GC
Hudson, NH 03051   603-889-9706

- TYPE OF DISCOUNT
  $5.00 off 18-hole greens fee
- DAYS OF THE WEEK
  Monday-Thursday (except holidays)
- HOURS OF THE DAY
  All day. Power cart required

Coupon expires 12/99. Can not be combined with any other offer.

White Mountain CC
N. Ashland Rd., Ashland, NH (603) 536-2227

- TYPE OF DISCOUNT
  $5.00 off 18-hole greens fee
- DAYS OF THE WEEK
  Monday-Thursday (except holidays)
- HOURS OF THE DAY
  All day. Power cart required

Coupon expires 12/99. Can not be combined with any other offer.

Woodbound Inn GC
Woodbound Rd., Jaffrey, NH (603) 532-8341

- TYPE OF DISCOUNT
  Two players for the price of one
- DAYS OF THE WEEK
  7 days a week
- HOURS OF THE DAY
  All day

Coupon expires 12/99. Can not be combined with any other offer.

Country View Golf Club
Burrillville, RI (401) 568-7157

- TYPE OF DISCOUNT
  Two players for the price of one with use of cart
- DAYS OF THE WEEK
  Weekdays only (except holidays)
- HOURS OF THE DAY
  AM only

Coupon expires 12/99. Can not be combined with any other offer.

Fairlawn Golf Course
Lincoln, RI (401) 334-3937

- TYPE OF DISCOUNT
  $2.00 off greens fee
- DAYS OF THE WEEK
  Weekdays only (except holidays)
- HOURS OF THE DAY
  Before noon

Coupon expires 12/99. Can not be combined with any other offer.

Foster Country Club
Foster, RI (401) 397-7750

- TYPE OF DISCOUNT
  $5.00 off 18 hole greens fee.
- DAYS OF THE WEEK
  Monday-Thursday, except holidays.
- HOURS OF THE DAY
  All day. Power cart rental required.

Coupon expires 12/99. Can not be combined with any other offer.

Foxwoods Executive GC at Lindhbrook
Hope Valley, RI (401) 539-8700

- TYPE OF DISCOUNT
  Two players for the price of one
- DAYS OF THE WEEK
  7 days a week
- HOURS OF THE DAY
  7:00 - 9:00 am and after 5:00 pm. Call for tee times.

Coupon expires 12/99. Can not be combined with any other offer.

Foxwoods Golf & CC At Boulder Hills
Route 138, Richmond, RI 02898 (401-539-4653)

- TYPE OF DISCOUNT
  Free golf cart with 2 paid greens fees
- DAYS OF THE WEEK
  Mon-Thurs
- HOURS OF THE DAY
  After 1:30 pm

Coupon expires 12/99. Can not be combined with any other offer.

Midville Country Club
W. Warwick, RI (401) 828-9215

- TYPE OF DISCOUNT
  $8.00 off 2 players with cart per 9 holes. Starts 09/21/99.
- DAYS OF THE WEEK
  Weekdays only (except holidays)
- HOURS OF THE DAY
  All day

Coupon expires 12/99. Can not be combined with any other offer.

Pocasset Country Club
Portsmouth, RI (401) 683-7300

- TYPE OF DISCOUNT
  Two players for the price of one for 18 only
- DAYS OF THE WEEK
  Weekdays only (except holidays)
- HOURS OF THE DAY
  Before 4:00 pm

Coupon expires 12/99. Can not be combined with any other offer.

NEW ENGLAND GOLFGUIDE

Weekapaug Golf Club
Westerly, RI 401-322-7870

- TYPE OF DISCOUNT
  $3.00 off any greens fee
- DAYS OF THE WEEK
  Weekdays only (except holidays)
- HOURS OF THE DAY
  All day

Coupon expires 12/99. Can not be combined with any other offer.

NEW ENGLAND GOLFGUIDE

Bellows Falls CC
Rt. 103, Rockingham, VT (802) 463-9809

- TYPE OF DISCOUNT
  25% discount for 2-4 players
- DAYS OF THE WEEK
  Weekdays only (except holidays)
- HOURS OF THE DAY
  All day

Coupon expires 12/99. Can not be combined with any other offer.

NEW ENGLAND GOLFGUIDE

Blush Hill CC
Waterbury, VT (802) 244-8974

- TYPE OF DISCOUNT
  Two players for the price of one
- DAYS OF THE WEEK
  Weekdays only (except holidays)
- HOURS OF THE DAY
  Before 2 pm

Coupon expires 12/99. Can not be combined with any other offer.

NEW ENGLAND GOLFGUIDE

Champlain CC
Swanton, VT (802) 527-1187

- TYPE OF DISCOUNT
  Two players for the price of one
- DAYS OF THE WEEK
  Weekdays only (except holidays)
- HOURS OF THE DAY
  All day

Coupon expires 12/99. Can not be combined with any other offer.

Enosburg Falls CC
Enosburg Falls, VT (802) 933-2296

- **TYPE OF DISCOUNT**
  $5.00 off each greens fee for up tp 2 players
- **DAYS OF THE WEEK**
  7 days a week
- **HOURS OF THE DAY**
  All day

Coupon expires 12/99. Can not be combined with any other offer.

Essex Country Club
Essex Junction, VT (802) 879-3232

- **TYPE OF DISCOUNT**
  Two players for the price of one
- **DAYS OF THE WEEK**
  7 days a week
- **HOURS OF THE DAY**
  All Day. Golf cart required

Coupon expires 12/99. Can not be combined with any other offer.

Farm Resort GC
Rt. 100, Morrisville, VT (802) 888-3525

- **TYPE OF DISCOUNT**
  25% discount for 2-4 players
- **DAYS OF THE WEEK**
  7 days a week
- **HOURS OF THE DAY**
  After 1 pm. Call for tee times. Cart rental required.

Coupon expires 12/99. Can not be combined with any other offer.

Green Mountain National G. C.
Barrows Town Rd., Sherburne, VT (802) 422-GOLF

- **TYPE OF DISCOUNT**
  $5.00 off each greens fee for up to 2 players.
- **DAYS OF THE WEEK**
  Monday through Thursday (Non-Holidays)
- **HOURS OF THE DAY**

Coupon expires 12/99. Can not be combined with any other offer.

Killington Golf Resort
Killington, VT (802) 422-6700

- TYPE OF DISCOUNT
  Two greens fees for the price of one. Cart rental rquired.
- DAYS OF THE WEEK
  Weekdays (except July and August) and holidays.
- HOURS OF THE DAY
  All day

Coupon expires 12/99. Can not be combined with any other offer.

Lake Morey CC
Fairlee, VT (802) 333-4800

- TYPE OF DISCOUNT
  $5.00 off greens fee for up to 2 players
- DAYS OF THE WEEK
  7 days a week
- HOURS OF THE DAY
  All day Valid April 1 to June, Sept 15 to Oct 31

Coupon expires 12/99. Can not be combined with any other offer.

Marble Island CC
Malletts Bay, VT (802) 864-6800

- TYPE OF DISCOUNT
  Two players for the price of one
- DAYS OF THE WEEK
  Weekdays only (except holidays)
- HOURS OF THE DAY
  All day

Coupon expires 12/99. Can not be combined with any other offer.

Montague Golf Club
Randolph, VT (802) 728-3806

- TYPE OF DISCOUNT
  Two players for the price of one
- DAYS OF THE WEEK
  Weekdays only (except holidays)
- HOURS OF THE DAY
  All day

Coupon expires 12/99. Can not be combined with any other offer.

NEW ENGLAND GOLFGUIDE

Neshobe Golf Club
Brandon, VT (802) 247-3611

- TYPE OF DISCOUNT
  $5.00 off greens fee
- DAYS OF THE WEEK
  Weekdays only (except holidays)
- HOURS OF THE DAY
  After 8 am, call for tee time. Course may be closed for special events.

Coupon expires 12/99. Can not be combined with any other offer.

NEW ENGLAND GOLFGUIDE

Newport CC
Newport, VT (802) 334-1634

- TYPE OF DISCOUNT
  Free Golf Cart with 2 paid Greens Fees
- DAYS OF THE WEEK
  Weekdays only (except holidays)
- HOURS OF THE DAY
  After Noon

Coupon expires 12/99. Can not be combined with any other offer.

NEW ENGLAND GOLFGUIDE

Proctor Pittsford CC
Pittsford, VT (802) 483-9379

- TYPE OF DISCOUNT
  $5.00 off full price greens fee
- DAYS OF THE WEEK
  Weekdays only (except holidays)
- HOURS OF THE DAY
  All day

Coupon expires 12/99. Can not be combined with any other offer.

NEW ENGLAND GOLFGUIDE

St. Johnsbury CC
St. Johnsbury, VT (802) 748-9894

- TYPE OF DISCOUNT
  $5.00 off greens fee
- DAYS OF THE WEEK
  Weekdays only (except holidays)
- HOURS OF THE DAY
  After 12 Noon - call for times

Coupon expires 12/99. Can not be combined with any other offer.

Stowe Country Club
Stowe, VT (802) 253-4893

- TYPE OF DISCOUNT
  Only $39.00 after 1:00
- DAYS OF THE WEEK
  Weekdays only (except holidays)
- HOURS OF THE DAY
  After 1:00 p.m.

Coupon expires 12/99. Can not be combined with any other offer.

Stratton Mt.
Stratton, VT (802) 297-4114

- TYPE OF DISCOUNT
  Free Golf Cart with 2 paid Greens Fees
- DAYS OF THE WEEK
  Weekdays only (except holidays)
- HOURS OF THE DAY
  All day. Power cart rental required.

Coupon expires 12/99. Can not be combined with any other offer.

Tater Hill Resort
Chester, VT (802) 875-2517

- TYPE OF DISCOUNT
  20% discount for 2-4 players
- DAYS OF THE WEEK
  Weekdays only (except holidays)
- HOURS OF THE DAY
  After 12 noon

Coupon expires 12/99. Can not be combined with any other offer.

White River Golf Club
Rt. 100, Rochester, VT (802) 767-4653

- TYPE OF DISCOUNT
  Two players for the price of one
- DAYS OF THE WEEK
  7 days a week
- HOURS OF THE DAY
  All day. Tee time recommended.

Coupon expires 12/99. Can not be combined with any other offer.

Wilcox Cove GC
Hgwy. 314, Grand Isle, VT (802) 372-8343

- TYPE OF DISCOUNT
  Two players for the price of one
- DAYS OF THE WEEK
  Weekdays only (except holidays)
- HOURS OF THE DAY
  All day. N/A July 1 thru Labor Day

Coupon expires 12/99. Can not be combined with any other offer.

Woodstock Inn & Resort
Woodstock, VT (802) 457-6674

- TYPE OF DISCOUNT
  $5.00 off greens fee
- DAYS OF THE WEEK
  Weekdays only (except holidays)
- HOURS OF THE DAY

Coupon expires 12/99. Can not be combined with any other offer.

Airways Golf Course
1070 S. Grand, Suffield, CT (860) 668-4973

- TYPE OF DISCOUNT
  Two players for the price of one for 18 holes
- DAYS OF THE WEEK
  Weekdays only (except holidays)
- HOURS OF THE DAY
  Before 1 pm. Cart rental required

Coupon expires 12/99. Can not be combined with any other offer.

Blackledge CC
190 West St., Hebron, CT (860) 228-0250

- TYPE OF DISCOUNT
  Free Golf Cart with 2 paid greens fees
- DAYS OF THE WEEK
  M - Th (except holidays)
- HOURS OF THE DAY
  All day. Not valid from 5/15/99 to 9/15/99, expires 12/1/99

Coupon expires 12/99. Can not be combined with any other offer.

Blue Fox Run
Nod Rd., Avon, CT (860) 678-1679

- TYPE OF DISCOUNT
  Free Golf Cart with 2 paid greens fees
- DAYS OF THE WEEK
  M-Th
- HOURS OF THE DAY
  7 AM - 10 AM

Coupon expires 12/99. Can not be combined with any other offer.

Fairchild Wheeler GC
Bridgeport, CT (203) 373-5911

- TYPE OF DISCOUNT
  25% discount for 2-4 players
- DAYS OF THE WEEK
  7 days a week
- HOURS OF THE DAY
  Afternoon

Coupon expires 12/99. Can not be combined with any other offer.

Goodwin Golf Course
Maple Ave., Hartford, CT (860) 956-3601

- TYPE OF DISCOUNT
  Two players for the price of one
- DAYS OF THE WEEK
  Weekdays only (except holidays)
- HOURS OF THE DAY
  All day. Not valid 6/15 to 9/24

Coupon expires 12/99. Can not be combined with any other offer.

Hillside Links LLC
Deep River, CT (860) 526-9986

- TYPE OF DISCOUNT
  Two players for the price of one
- DAYS OF THE WEEK
  7 days a week
- HOURS OF THE DAY
  All day. Not to be combined with any other offers.

Coupon expires 12/99. Can not be combined with any other offer.

Hop Brook CC
Naugatuck, CT (203) 729-8013

- TYPE OF DISCOUNT
  Two players for the price of one
- DAYS OF THE WEEK
  Weekdays only (except holidays)
- HOURS OF THE DAY
  Before 3 pm. Motor cart required.

Coupon expires 12/99. Can not be combined with any other offer.

Keney Park Golf Club
Hartford, CT (860)525-3656

- TYPE OF DISCOUNT
  4 players pay 1/2 on greens fee.
- DAYS OF THE WEEK
  Wednesdays.
- HOURS OF THE DAY
  All day. Cart required.

Coupon expires 12/99. Can not be combined with any other offer.

Miner Hills GC
Middletown, CT (860)635-0051

- TYPE OF DISCOUNT
  Two with motor cart $11 each for 9 holes
- DAYS OF THE WEEK
  Weekdays only
- HOURS OF THE DAY
  Before 2 pm

Coupon expires 12/99. Can not be combined with any other offer.

Pattonbrook CC
Southington, CT (860) 793-6000

- TYPE OF DISCOUNT
  25% discount for 2-4 players
- DAYS OF THE WEEK
  Weekdays only (except holidays)
- HOURS OF THE DAY
  Opening to 1 pm

Coupon expires 12/99. Can not be combined with any other offer.

Putnam Country Club
Putnam, CT (860)928-7748

- TYPE OF DISCOUNT
  Two players for the price of one
- DAYS OF THE WEEK
  Weekdays only (except holidays)
- HOURS OF THE DAY
  7 am - 2 pm

Coupon expires 12/99. Can not be combined with any other offer.

Rolling Greens GC
Rocky Hill, CT (860) 257-9775

- TYPE OF DISCOUNT
  4 players for the price of 3
- DAYS OF THE WEEK
  Weekdays only (except holidays) from 7am to 2pm
- HOURS OF THE DAY
  Must call the day before. Power cart required.

Coupon expires 12/99. Can not be combined with any other offer.

Sunset Hill GC
Brookfield, CT (203) 740-7800

- TYPE OF DISCOUNT
  Two players for the price of one (cart rental required)
- DAYS OF THE WEEK
  Weekdays only (except holidays)
- HOURS OF THE DAY
  All day

Coupon expires 12/99. Can not be combined with any other offer.

Woodstock Golf Course
S. Woodstock, CT (860) 928-4130

- TYPE OF DISCOUNT
  25% discount for 4 players
- DAYS OF THE WEEK
  Weekdays only (except holidays)
- HOURS OF THE DAY
  11:00 am - 3:00 pm

Coupon expires 12/99. Can not be combined with any other offer.

NEW ENGLAND GOLFGUIDE®

THE PERFECT GIFT

for your boss, your employees, your husband, your wife, your kids, your best friend, your father, mother, father-in-law, mother-in-law, your brother, brother-in-law, sister, sister-in law, your significant other, and for
ANY GOLFER ON YOUR GIFT LIST!

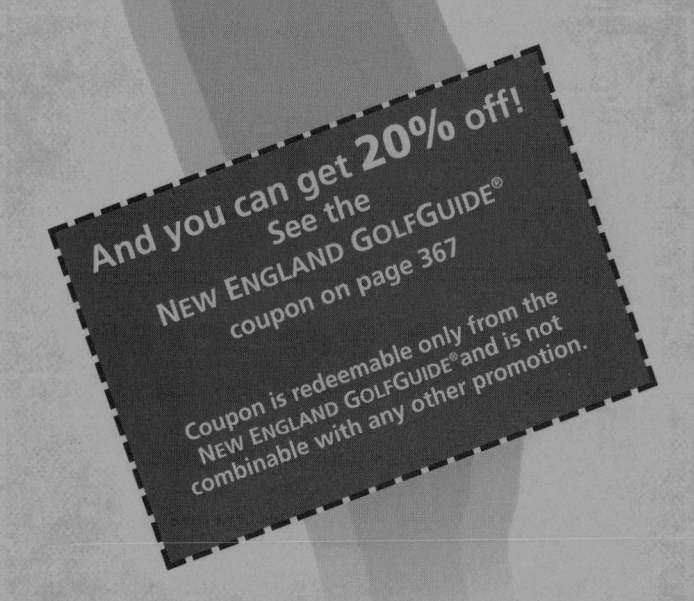

And you can get 20% off!
See the
NEW ENGLAND GOLFGUIDE®
coupon on page 367

Coupon is redeemable only from the NEW ENGLAND GOLFGUIDE® and is not combinable with any other promotion.